T0340090

PROBLEMS OF MARKET LIBERALISM

PROBLEMS OF
MARKET LIBERALISM

Edited by

**Ellen Frankel Paul, Fred D. Miller, Jr.,
and Jeffrey Paul**

CAMBRIDGE
UNIVERSITY PRESS

Published by the Press Syndicate of the University of Cambridge
The Pitt Building, Trumpington Street, Cambridge CB2 1RP, England
40 West 20th Street, New York, NY 10011, USA
10 Stamford Road, Oakleigh, Melbourne, Victoria 3166, Australia

First published 1998

Library of Congress Cataloging-in-Publication Data

Problems of Market Liberalism / edited by Ellen Frankel Paul,
Fred D. Miller, Jr., and Jeffrey Paul.   p.   cm.
Includes bibliographical references and index.
ISBN 0-521-64991-9
1. Free enterprise.   2. Liberalism.
3. Capitalism.
I. Paul, Ellen Frankel.   II. Miller,
Fred Dycus, 1944–   III. Paul, Jeffrey.
HB95.P666   1998
330.12'2–dc21   98-3392
CIP
ISBN 0-521-64991-9 paperback

Transferred to digital printing 2003

The essays in this book have also been published,
without introduction and index, in the semiannual journal
Social Philosophy & Policy, Volume 15, Number 2,
which is available by subscription.

CONTENTS

CONTENTS

INTRODUCTION

In recent years, Western societies have begun to reconsider and reeval-
uate the experiments in social-welfare provision that had seemed to hold
such promise in the postwar era. This process was accelerated by the
collapse of Communism in Eastern Europe and the former Soviet Union,
a development which discredited socialism generally and left Western
liberalism and free-market economic institutions as the most prominent
remaining paradigm for the organization of modern societies. Today, trends
toward freedom in international trade and toward the privatization of
some of the functions previously performed by government may be taken
as evidence of the increasing influence of market-oriented liberalism.

The essays in this volume assess the strength and impact of market
liberal or libertarian political theory, which, broadly conceived, advocates
a more carefully circumscribed role for the state and a greater reliance on
the ability of individuals and voluntary, private-sector institutions to confront social problems. Some of the essays deal with crucial theoretical
issues, asking whether the promotion of citizens' welfare can serve as the
justification for the establishment of government, or inquiring into the
nature of the constraints on individual behavior that exist in a liberal
social order. Some essays explore market liberal or libertarian positions
on specific public policy issues, such as affirmative action, ownership of
the airwaves, the provision of healthcare, or the regulation of food and
drugs. Other essays look at the nature and limits of property rights, the
morality of profit-making, or the provision of public goods. Still others
address the success or failure of libertarianism as a political movement,
suggesting ways in which libertarians can reach out to those who do not
share their views.

In the opening essay, "Why All Welfare States (Including Laissez-Faire
Ones) Are Unreasonable," Gerald F. Gaus challenges the idea that the
proper role of the state is to actively promote the well-being of its citizens.
Gaus argues that governments are not typically in a position to reasonably advance policy goals—and, in particular, that it is unreasonable for
governments to seek to advance social welfare. He contends that, because
of radical uncertainties about the causes of social processes, the consequences of government policies, and the complexity of the concept of
welfare, governments have very little idea of how to advance people's
well-being. In contrast, legislators have much more reliable access to
principles and rules, and Gaus maintains that, given a choice between
pursuing a public policy goal such as welfare (on the one hand) and
remaining faithful to classical-liberal principles (on the other), legislators
should choose the latter. His argument thus undermines the justification

of the interventionist welfare state, but it also casts doubt on defenses of laissez-faire political institutions that are based on claims about how these institutions promote individuals' welfare. As an alternative to popular welfarist conceptions of the state, Gaus defends the reasonableness of a government which upholds what the economist F. A. Hayek calls "end-independent abstract rules of conduct."

Gaus's essay touches upon the difficulties associated with understanding and measuring the welfare of individuals, and these difficulties are the focus of Robert Sugden's contribution to this volume, "Measuring Opportunity: Toward a Contractarian Measure of Individual Interest." Sugden observes that contractarian political theories seek to justify the constraints necessary for a liberal social order by showing that those constraints work in the interests of each individual, and he notes that this requires some unit of account in which to measure an individual's interests or well-being. A typical strategy for providing such a unit of account is to take each person's preferences as the measure of his well-being, but this approach runs into problems if individuals' preferences are unstable or fail to satisfy the conditions of "coherence" that are assumed in the theory of rational choice. Sugden maintains that there are no adequate *a priori* grounds for assuming that preferences are stable and coherent, and much evidence to suggest that, in fact, they often are not. He discusses the resulting difficulties for those who attempt to justify a liberal political system on contractarian grounds, and suggests that a solution might be found by using the range of opportunities open to a person as a measure of his well-being.

Like Sugden, Eric Mack is concerned with the justification of constraints on individual behavior in a liberal society. In "Deontic Restrictions Are Not Agent-Relative Restrictions," Mack analyzes a theory in moral and political philosophy which is commonly used to justify deontic constraints—that is, constraints on certain types of actions (such as killing the innocent) which have force in spite of any potentially valuable consequences of those actions. The theory Mack analyzes is one that explains deontic restrictions in terms of an agent's "agent-relative" reasons for acting in accordance with those restrictions, where agent-relative reasons are reasons based on the value of the action for the agent himself. As Mack observes, the emphasis on agent-relative reasons in contemporary moral philosophy has developed in response to the perceived flaws of utilitarianism and related consequentialist doctrines which rely on an abstract and impersonal concept of value. Mack maintains that moral theorists are justified in rejecting consequentialism's impersonal conception of the good and in embracing an agent-relative conception. He also believes that we should affirm the legitimacy of deontic restrictions on certain kinds of behavior, rather than accepting the consequentialist doctrine that the optimal promotion of the good is always right. But he questions whether deontic restrictions can be defended on the basis of an agent-relative conception of the good. Mack argues that this method of defending deontic restrictions ultimately fails; nevertheless, he concludes by suggesting a couple of ways in which the agent-relativity of value might lend some indirect support to the idea that such restrictions can be legitimate.

While Gaus, Sugden, and Mack explore the proper role of the state and the restrictions it can reasonably place on its citizens, the authors of the next four essays turn their attention to specific public policy issues. In "Why Even Egalitarians Should Favor Market Health Insurance," Daniel Shapiro defends a system of private medical insurance as a superior alternative to state-run health insurance. In the market health insurance system Shapiro describes, insurers would offer diverse health-care plans, often charging on the basis of expected risk, and the government's role would be limited to subsidizing the premiums of the indigent and those with uninsurable risks. Under national health insurance, in contrast, the government mandates comprehensive health insurance with a limited choice of plans; premiums or taxes are unrelated to health-care risks; and the government rations the supply of health-care services. Shapiro argues that most health-care risks and decisions are matters which are open to the agent's voluntary choice, and thus that even egalitarian critics of the market should favor risk rating and a wide selection of health-care plans — features that are found in market health insurance but not in national health insurance. He also maintains that government rationing in a national health insurance system is less fair than market distribution, because the former is less open to scrutiny than the latter, and because the long waiting periods which result from government rationing tend to have a more detrimental impact on the poor than on motivated, knowledgeable, and well-connected members of the middle and upper classes.

N. Scott Arnold addresses the legitimacy of preferential treatment programs in his contribution to this volume, "Affirmative Action and the Demands of Justice." Arnold argues that affirmative action programs in the United States that involve preferential treatment (in hiring, college admissions, and the awarding of contracts) are morally and politically unjustified, and that this is true even if such programs are in fact demanded by distributive or compensatory justice. He proposes two requirements that should be met when the state seeks to impose the demands of justice (as state officials see it) on civil society. The Public Justification requirement states that proponents of government action must engage in serious public debate over the legitimacy of their proposed reform, and must get an on-the-record vote of the legislature in order to pass it into law. The Anti-Hijacking requirement states that a reform should be instituted only after legislators have offered an intellectually honest accounting of the reform's intended and unintended beneficiaries and victims, in order to help ensure that the legislative process is not "hijacked" for the benefit of special interest groups. Arnold sketches a historical and legal account of preferential treatment programs in the United States, and maintains that these programs have not satisfied the two requirements. He concludes with a preemptive response to the likely objection that the Public Justification and Anti-Hijacking requirements would favor the status quo.

The role of government in exercising jurisdiction over the airwaves is the subject of Thomas W. Hazlett's essay "The Dual Role of Property Rights in Protecting Broadcast Speech." Hazlett begins by noting that much of the current law governing telecommunications in the United States paints private property rights as a threat to free speech. As an example, he cites a recent Supreme Court decision which permitted Congress to abridge the editorial discretion of private cable-system operators by forcing them to carry local (federally licensed) broadcast television stations. Critics of free-market institutions have extended this logic, characterizing private ownership of media outlets as a central threat to freedom of speech, one which can be remedied by "public interest" regulation or government ownership. Hazlett thinks that this logic is fundamentally flawed. He sketches an account of the early development of federal control over the radio spectrum in the 1920s, contending that when property rights to the spectrum are restricted, the resulting system favors incumbent broadcast station owners at the expense of greater media diversity. Hazlett concludes that there are at least two strong arguments in favor of establishing and protecting property rights in the airwaves: the traditional argument that private markets tend to offer better service to consumers than centrally planned alternatives; and the argument that property rights reduce the ability of industry incumbents to exclude new entrants, including those who cater to marginal, unpopular, out-of-the-mainstream tastes.

Daniel D. Polsby's essay explores the state's role in ensuring the safety of food and in controlling the use of potentially harmful drugs. In "Regulation of Foods and Drugs and Libertarian Ideals: Perspectives of a Fellow-Traveler," Polsby argues that, while some regulation in these areas is justifiable, the regulatory systems in place in the United States and in other modern welfare states are open to criticism on a number of fronts. He acknowledges that there are serious third-party effects or "externalities" that would be likely to arise in a completely unregulated food and drug market, including the criminogenic effects of cocaine, amphetamines, and certain other drugs, and the possibility that antibiotics could become less effective as a result of overuse. In these cases, Polsby notes, some form of government regulation is defensible as a public good, even if it is not the only option (or even the best option) available for dealing with these problems. Nevertheless, he argues that most current food and drug regulation is not justified in terms of controlling the imposition of external costs on people who have not agreed to bear them. Rather, most regulation is paternalistic; it rests on implied, and seldom defended, propositions concerning the supposed inability of individuals to act as agents for their own well-being. Polsby illustrates his discussion with examples from the U.S. regulatory system, showing how the Food and Drug Administration delays the approval of valuable new drugs and seems reluctant to allow individuals to make their own judgments when even the most moderate risks are involved. He concludes that, while libertarian arguments offer strong insights about how public policies fail, libertarians could offer a more formidable challenge to the anti-individualist orthodoxy of the welfare state if they would recognize the distinction between regulations based on paternalism and those based on considerations of the public good.

The next three essays analyze foundational issues about how economic and social relationships ought to be structured. The nature of profit is the subject of James W. Child's contribution to this volume, "Profit: The Concept and Its Moral Features." Child begins by noting the negative connotations attached to business and profit-making and suggests that these are the result of a "zero-sum" view of exchange, according to which one party to a trade can gain only at the expense of the other. He traces the origins and development of this zero-sum view in the works of Aristotle, Aquinas, and Adam Smith, and shows its culmination in Marx's theory of exploitation. In examining the zero-sum view, Child attempts to gain a better understanding of the moral status of profit-making: Is it a disreputable activity or a commendable one? Does it involve wrongdoing, or is it morally neutral (or perhaps even morally commendable) if it is done in accordance with some sort of commercial ethic? Child analyzes the concept of profit by using the example of a simple, two-person commercial transaction; as modern economists recognize, each party to such a transaction can gain without inflicting a loss on the other. On this view, profit is measured in terms of one's gain over one's own previous position, and this enables us to better understand why individuals wish to engage in trade in the first place. Indeed, as Child observes, in a free-market system the only way to motivate a potential trading partner to take part in a transaction is to offer him the prospect of some benefit.

The concept of natural property rights often lies at the center of libertarian arguments for strictly limiting the power of the state, and Robert Ehman raises questions about the application of such rights in his essay "Natural Property Rights: Where They Fail." Natural rights to property are thought to be held by individuals prior to (and independent of) the establishment of states and collective institutions, and are thought to serve as limits on the legitimacy of collective action. Ehman argues that such rights cannot be used to resolve disputes in cases where the legitimate exercise of one person's property rights has a negative impact on the exercise of another's rights. He also contends that such rights are inconsistent with certain forms of collective action that are necessary for the provision of public goods. In the course of his discussion, Ehman examines theories of natural property rights set out in the works of John Locke, Robert Nozick, and David Gauthier, but he finds that these theories are unable to provide a mechanism for settling rights conflicts or disputes over the financing of public goods. In light of this, Ehman suggests that we should appeal to a unanimously acceptable decision procedure for adjudicating these disagreements. He maintains that, in order for such a procedure to be unanimously acceptable, it must offer more or less equal prospects of favorable decisions for each party. From this perspective, Ehman concludes, the key to respecting the rights of each individual is to construct and maintain a consensual, impartial procedure for resolving disputes that natural rights alone cannot resolve.

The issue of class analysis in libertarian political theory is the subject of "Toward a Libertarian Theory of Class," Roderick T. Long's contribution to this volume. Long identifies the libertarian movement expansively, as embracing all those who seek a large-scale redistribution of power from the state to individuals and their freely formed associations. Long's libertarian movement comprises a range of groups not normally thought of as libertarian, including some socialists and populists in addition to advocates of capitalism. These groups are united in their opposition to the state, even though they offer differing accounts of the nature and source of the power of the ruling class. As Long observes, libertarians of the capitalist variety hold that a ruling class gains its strength from a powerful state and could not survive in a competitive marketplace. Libertarians of the socialist and populist varieties, by contrast, regard the marketplace itself as the source of the ruling class's power, and they seek, above all, to constrain the market. The libertarian capitalist view is thus a "statocratic" one, while the socialist-populist view can be characterized as "plutocratic." Long sketches the origins of the statocratic view in the writings of Adam Smith, and traces the origins of the plutocratic view in the works of Rousseau and Marx. He argues that neither view should be accepted uncritically, but that a composite view may be closer to the truth: he theorizes that powerful business interests collude with politicians to exercise the power of a ruling class. However, Long believes that the state plays the dominant role in this partnership; thus, a strict limitation of the powers of the state would be likely to lessen the serious imbalance of power between the rich and the poor that exists in modern societies. At the same time, he emphasizes that libertarian capitalists need to pay more attention to the dangers posed by the power of plutocrats.

The final three essays in this volume explore the viability and influence of libertarianism as a political theory and a movement. In "Libertarianism as if (the Other 99 Percent of) People Mattered," Loren E. Lomasky begins with a pair of suppositions: that libertarianism is the correct framework for political morality, and that most people reject libertarianism. Given these two suppositions, Lomasky asks, how should advocates of libertarianism relate to their fellow citizens? He contends that the same concern for civility that underlies libertarians' theory of respect for rights and peaceful accommodation (rather than aggression) will oblige them to respond to non-libertarians in a spirit of tolerance and cooperation. Lomasky distinguishes the kind of "cooperative libertarianism" that he endorses from "rejectionist libertarianism," which denies the legitimacy of social institutions that are not compatible with strict libertarianism and which tends to encourage its adherents to withdraw from the society of which they are a part. He argues that even those who believe that libertarianism is the correct political theory can acknowledge that nonlibertarians are not unreasonable when they express concerns about the justice of current property holdings, the provision of public goods in a laissez-faire system, the need for some minimal form of welfare provision, and similar issues. Even if these concerns are mistaken, Lomasky maintains, they are matters over which intelligent people may respectfully disagree. Thus, the proper strategy for advocates of libertarianism is to recognize that nonlibertarian social structures, while less than optimal, may nonetheless deserve some degree of allegiance—at least until one can persuade one's fellow citizens that these structures need to be changed. Lomasky concludes with a discussion of the limits of toleration, arguing that even "cooperative libertarians" should actively oppose practices and institutions—such as censorship or prohibitions against victimless crimes—that seek to forcibly impose a certain vision of the good life on individuals who are engaging in peaceful, rights-respecting activities.

In "On the Failure of Libertarianism to Capture the Popular Imagination," Jonathan R. Macey begins by noting that the libertarian concept of organizing society in order to have the smallest amount of government consistent with the rule of law has never been as successful as Communism and other ideologies in gaining popular support. Macey argues that libertarianism is unpopular because libertarians have not understood the political implications of risk aversion, which causes people to place a high value on insurance to provide for health care, disability benefits, old-age pensions, and similar services. If libertarians wish to be successful, Macey contends, they must show that government does a poorer job than free markets at providing these insurance services, and that, when government provides these services, it crowds out the private institutions and individuals who are potentially the best providers of insurance against misfortune. Moreover, Macey argues, libertarians must convince people that government undermines the quality of civic life by quashing non-governmental institutions that not only provide for people's welfare, but also provide outlets for civic virtue and civic expression that are superior to the outlets provided by the state.

The collection's final essay, Richard A. Epstein's "Imitations of Libertarian Thought," examines the ways in which rival political theories adopt and modify classical-liberal or libertarian ideas to serve their own ends. Epstein focuses on a pair of terms—"security" and "coercion"—and shows how the original, narrow meanings of these terms have been broadened by advocates of activist government. He notes that the narrow definition of "security" stresses the security of one's person, possessions, and right to engage in exchange, against the aggressive acts of others; and that, on the narrow definition, "coercion" involves chiefly the threat or use of force. In contrast, defenders of interventionist government offer a broad account of "security" which includes protection against fluctuations in economic well-being brought about by market activities, and they conceive of market effects as "coercive" when they worsen the condition of the poor. Epstein argues that the broad accounts of these concepts foster counterproductive policies—policies which may increase security or limit coercion for certain protected parties, but which undermine security and increase coercion (in the narrow sense) for everyone else. By way of illustration, Epstein discusses the "Economic Bill of Rights" proposed by Franklin D. Roosevelt near the end of World War II, and he contrasts Roosevelt's account of security with the account developed by F. A. Hayek. Epstein concludes by observing that the overuse of terms like "security" and "coercion" in describing cases of economic hardship or misfortune tends to weaken or diffuse public disapproval of genuine acts of coercion and threats to security.

Market liberal or libertarian political theory offers an alternative to interventionist policies that are increasingly being questioned by citizens around the world. The essays in this volume—written by leading philosophers, economists, and legal theorists—provide insights into the limits of government, develop market-oriented solutions to pressing social problems, and explore some defects in traditional libertarian theory and practice.

ACKNOWLEDGMENTS

The editors wish to acknowledge several individuals at the Social Philosophy and Policy Center, Bowling Green State University, who provided invaluable assistance in the preparation of this volume. They include Mary Dilsaver, Terrie Weaver, and Carrie-Ann Biondi.

We wish to thank Executive Manager Kory Swanson, for his tireless administrative support; Publication Specialist Tamara Sharp, for her patient attention to detail; and Managing Editor Harry Dolan, for editorial assistance above and beyond the call of duty.

CONTRIBUTORS

Gerald F. Gaus is Professor of Philosophy and Political Science at the University of Minnesota, Duluth. In 1996–98, he was Professor of Ethics and Public Philosophy at the Queensland University of Technology at Brisbane. He is the author of *The Modern Liberal Theory of Man* (1983), *Value and Justification* (1990), and *Justificatory Liberalism* (1996). He is the coeditor of *Public and Private in Social Life* (with Stanley Benn, 1983) and, most recently, of a collection entitled *Public Reason* (with Fred D'Agostino, forthcoming). He is also an editor of the *Australasian Journal of Philosophy* and is currently completing two books, *Social Philosophy* and *Political Concepts and Political Theories*.

Robert Sugden is Leverhulme Research Professor of Economics at the University of East Anglia in Norwich. He has held positions at the University of York and at the University of Newcastle upon Tyne, and is the author of *The Economics of Rights, Cooperation, and Welfare* (1986). His research interests include liberal and contractarian approaches to social choice, the evolution of social norms, the scope and limitations of the theory of rational choice, and experimental economics.

Eric Mack is Professor of Philosophy at Tulane University. He has published numerous articles in moral, political, and legal philosophy, on such topics as moral individualism, natural rights and deontic restraints, property rights, Lockean provisos, distributive justice, contractual rights, liberal neutrality, bad samaritanism, and anarchism and the justification of the state. During the spring of 1997, he was a Visiting Scholar at the Social Philosophy and Policy Center, where he worked on a book tentatively entitled *Moral Individualism and Libertarian Theory*.

Daniel Shapiro is Associate Professor of Philosophy at West Virginia University. He received his Ph.D. from the University of Minnesota in 1984, and has held visiting appointments at Rice University, the University of North Carolina at Chapel Hill, and Bowling Green State University. He has published a variety of articles in social and political philosophy in such journals as *Philosophical Studies, Social Theory and Practice, Public Affairs Quarterly, Journal of Political Philosophy,* and *Law and Philosophy*. He is currently at work on a book in which he compares welfare-state institutions to more free-market alternatives, as judged by central values or principles in contemporary political philosophy.

N. Scott Arnold is Professor of Philosophy at the University of Alabama at Birmingham. He is the author of *The Philosophy and Economics of Market*

Socialism (1994) and *Marx's Radical Critique of Capitalist Society* (1990). He has been a Visiting Scholar at the Hoover Institution at Stanford University and at the Social Philosophy and Policy Center at Bowling Green State University.

Thomas W. Hazlett is Professor of Agricultural and Resource Economics at the University of California, Davis, and Director of the Program on Telecommunications Policy at the Institute of Governmental Affairs. He earned his doctorate in economics from UCLA in 1984, and was a Visiting Scholar at the Columbia University Graduate School of Business in 1990–91, the Chief Economist of the Federal Communications Commission in 1991–92, and a Visiting Scholar at the American Enterprise Institute in 1995–96. He has provided expert testimony on telecommunications policy in federal and state courts, before the Department of Commerce and the Federal Communications Commission, and before congressional committees. His book *Public Policy toward Cable Television* (coauthored with Matthew Spitzer) is forthcoming from MIT Press.

Daniel D. Polsby is Kirkland & Ellis Professor of Law at Northwestern University, where he has taught since 1976. He received his J.D. from the University of Minnesota in 1971. He is the author of over seventy scholarly articles and has taught courses in criminal law, First Amendment jurisprudence, family law, torts, broadcasting regulation, constitutional law, legislation, labor law, administrative law, sex discrimination, secured transactions, and debtor-creditor law.

James W. Child is Professor of Philosophy at Bowling Green State University and is also Chairman of the Aardvark Media Group, Inc., located in Findlay, Ohio. He is the author of *Nuclear War: The Moral Dimension* (1986), coauthor of *Two Paths toward Peace* (with Donald Scherer, 1992), and author of a number of articles appearing in such journals as *Analysis*, *Canadian Journal of Law and Jurisprudence*, *Ethics*, *The Monist*, and *Public Affairs Quarterly*. Child has held a Fulbright Lectureship and has been a research fellow at Pittsburgh's Center for Philosophy of Science and at St. Andrews Centre for Public Policy. He is presently working on a book entitled *Buy Low, Sell High: The Moral Foundations of Commercial Transactions*.

Robert Ehman is Associate Professor of Philosophy at Vanderbilt University. He earned his Ph.D. in philosophy from Yale University, where he taught for six years. His main areas of research are contemporary contractarian theories of ethics and the economic analysis of rights. He is especially concerned with the problems of determining initial property rights and the just distribution of income. His essays have appeared in such journals as *Public Affairs Quarterly*, *Journal of Value Inquiry*, and *Constitutional Political Economy*.

Roderick T. Long is Assistant Professor of Philosophy at the University of North Carolina, Chapel Hill, as well as Research Director of the Free Nation Foundation. He has published in the areas of moral and political philosophy, ancient philosophy, and philosophy of action, and is the author of a book manuscript entitled *Aristotle on Fate and Freedom*.

Loren E. Lomasky is Professor of Philosophy at Bowling Green State University. He was educated at Michigan State University, Harvard University, and the University of Connecticut, and has taught at the University of Minnesota, Duluth, and at the University of Connecticut at both the Hartford and Storrs branches. He is the author of *Persons, Rights, and the Moral Community* (1987), the coauthor, with Geoffrey Brennan, of *Democracy and Decision: The Pure Theory of Electoral Preference* (1993), and the coeditor with Brennan of a volume of essays entitled *Politics and Process: New Essays in Democratic Theory* (1989).

Jonathan R. Macey is J. DuPratt White Professor of Law and Director of the John M. Olin Program in Law and Economics at Cornell Law School. His research is in corporate finance, public choice, and the economics of regulation. In 1995, he was awarded the Paul M. Bator Prize for Excellence in Teaching, Scholarship, and Public Service by the Federalist Society of the University of Chicago; in 1996, he was awarded a Ph.D. *honoris causa* from the Stockholm School of Economics; and in 1997, he was elected to the Comitato Scientifico of the International Centre for Economic Research in Turin, Italy.

Richard A. Epstein is James Parker Hall Distinguished Service Professor of Law at the University of Chicago. He is the author of *Takings: Private Property and the Power of Eminent Domain* (1985); *Forbidden Grounds: The Case against Employment Discrimination Laws* (1992); *Bargaining with the State* (1993); *Simple Rules for a Complex World* (1995); and *Mortal Peril: Our Inalienable Right to Health Care?* (1997). He is an editor of the *Journal of Law and Economics* and a member of the American Academy of Arts and Sciences.

WHY ALL WELFARE STATES
(INCLUDING LAISSEZ-FAIRE ONES)
ARE UNREASONABLE*

By Gerald F. Gaus

I. The Welfare State versus the Liberal Rechtstaat

Liberal political theory is all too familiar with the divide between classical and welfare-state liberals.[1] Classical liberals, as we all know, insist on the importance of small government, negative liberty, and private property. Welfare-state liberals, on the other hand, although they too stress civil rights, tend to be sympathetic to "positive liberty," are for a much more expansive government, and are often ambivalent about private property. Although I do not go so far as to entirely deny the usefulness of this familiar distinction, I think in many ways it is misleading. In an important sense, most free-market liberals are also "welfare-state" liberals. I say this because the overwhelming number of liberals, of both the pro-market and the pro-government variety, entertain a welfarist conception of political economy. On this dominant welfarist view, the ultimate justification of the politico-economic order is that it promotes human welfare. Traditional "welfare-state liberals" such as Robert E. Goodin manifestly adopt this welfarist conception.[2] But it is certainly not only interventionists such as Goodin who insist that advancing welfare is the overriding goal of normative political economy. J. R. McCulloch, one of the great nineteenth-century laissez-faire political economists, was adamant that "freedom is not, as some appear to think, the end of government: the advancement of public prosperity and happiness is its end."[3] To be sure, McCulloch would have disagreed with Goodin about the optimal welfare-maximizing economic policy: the welfarist ideal, he and his fellow classical political economists believed, would best be advanced by provision of a legal and institutional framework—most importantly, the laws of property, con-

* I have greatly benefited from discussions with Julian Lamont. My thanks also to Fred D'Agostino and Bob Goodin for very helpful comments.
[1] For analyses focusing on this divide, see Edward Shils, "The Antinomies of Liberalism," in *The Relevance of Liberalism*, ed. Staff of the Research Institute on International Change (Boulder, CO: Westview, 1978), pp. 135–200; and Loren E. Lomasky, *Persons, Rights, and the Moral Community* (New York: Oxford University Press, 1987), ch. 5. See also my "Liberalism," in *The Stanford Encyclopedia of Philosophy* (online at http://plato.stanford.edu).
[2] Robert E. Goodin, *Utilitarianism as a Public Philosophy* (Cambridge: Cambridge University Press, 1995), ch. 1.
[3] J. R. McCulloch, *Principles of Political Economy*, 5th ed. (Edinburgh: Charles Black, 1864), pp. 187–88.

tract, and the criminal code—that allows individuals to pursue their own interests in the market and, by so doing, promote public welfare.[4] In general, what might be called the "classical-liberal welfare state" claims to advance welfare by providing the framework for individuals to seek wealth for themselves, while welfarists such as Goodin insist that a market order is seriously flawed as a mechanism for advancing human welfare and, in addition, that government has the competency to "correct market failures" in the provision of welfare.[5]

It may be objected that describing both these laissez-faire and state interventionist views as "welfare-state liberalism" is simply perverse: they are manifestly different doctrines. To be sure, on the familiar dimension of whether they favor more or less government intervention in economic life and provision of welfare, they do, of course, differ. But their agreement is also profound: both understand the government and the economy as instruments for the advancement of human welfare, and both make confident claims about what does and does not advance human welfare. For both, the primary justification of political institutions and government policies is that they effectively promote human welfare. The interventionists believe that they know what human welfare is, and (armed with welfare economics) why the market fails to advance it and why government can often do a better job; the free-market welfarists insist that the market does a superior job of promoting human welfare and (armed with public choice theory) tell us why government does badly at promoting welfare. While these are certainly significant disputes, especially for economists and political scientists, they are essentially social-scientific disputes within an approach to political economy that takes human welfare as the *summum bonum*. Understood thus, utilitarianism is the moral foundation of the welfare state, providing the basis for the classical political economists, neo-classical libertarian economists, and "government house" interventionists such as Goodin.[6]

The case for utilitarianism as a public philosophy, justifying the state and its policies, certainly seems overwhelming: at what else would a

[4] For an elaboration, see my "Public and Private Interests in Liberal Political Economy, Old and New," in *Public and Private in Social Life*, ed. S. I. Benn and G. F. Gaus (New York: St. Martin's, 1983), pp. 199–203.

[5] Robert E. Goodin, *Reasons for Welfare* (Princeton: Princeton University Press, 1988), pp. 11–12. President Franklin Delano Roosevelt recognized more clearly than most the broader ideal of the welfare state: "If, as our constitution tells us, our Federal Government was established among other things, 'to provide for the general welfare,' then it is our plain duty to provide for that security upon which welfare depends." Quoted in Amy Gutmann, "Introduction," in *Democracy and the Welfare State*, ed. Amy Gutmann (Princeton: Princeton University Press, 1988), p. 3.

[6] Regarding the term "government house," Goodin writes: "This is after all a term usually applied, usually derisively, to the closing chapters in [Henry] Sidgwick's *Methods of Ethics*, where he recommends that enlightened (implicitly, colonial) rulers govern according to utilitarian principles that are not necessarily . . . accessible to those subject to their rule" (Goodin, *Utilitarianism as a Public Philosophy*, pp. 61–62).

humane and rational state aim besides the welfare of its citizens? Perhaps in their private lives people may reasonably embark on courses of action that do not advance anyone's welfare, but to most observers this seems "simply perverse" and "irresponsible" when done by government.[7] Michael Oakeshott provides the clearest articulation of this apparently "perverse" alternative. Oakeshott repeatedly stresses that "[t]he civil condition is not an association in transactions for procuring the satisfaction of wants."[8] And because a civil association is not designed to satisfy wants or advance human welfare, "[t]he acknowledgment of the authority of a rule does not entail the recognition of the desirability of the conditions it prescribes."[9] The life of such an association is ordered by what Friedrich von Hayek calls "end-independent abstract rules of conduct."[10] As understood by Oakeshott and Hayek, then, the legal rules structuring a free society cannot be understood as means or instruments for achieving the good of human welfare, or indeed, as means for achieving a "desirable condition." They are noninstrumental rules of conduct. I shall call a political association ordered by such rules a Liberal *Rechtstaat*.[11] Here I follow Hayek, who depicted his own view as upholding the traditional *Rechtsstaat*'s idea of a general rule-based order.[12] However, as I understand the Liberal *Rechtstaat*, it is characterized not only by the rule of *law*, but by the rule of *right*, where it is not supposed that the right is justified simply as a means to produce the good.[13] It is this aspect of the Liberal *Rechtstaat* that seems irrational to many: what possible reason could we have to follow a rule of right that does not achieve a good result? Perhaps one might acknowledge that there is reasonable debate about whether the good result must be conceived solely in terms of human welfare—perhaps there are other goods too—but surely some good must be achieved by rules of right. As Ralph Barton Perry quipped, "It is certainly a doubtful compliment to the right to deny that it does not of itself do good."[14]

The widely shared perception, then, is that some form of welfarism is obviously rational, while the Liberal *Rechtstaat*, following rules that are

---

[7] *Ibid.*, pp. 10–11.

[8] Michael Oakeshott, *On Human Conduct* (Oxford: Clarendon Press, 1975), p. 156.

[9] *Ibid.*, p. 159.

[10] Friedrich A. von Hayek, *The Fatal Conceit: The Errors of Socialism* (Chicago: University of Chicago Press, 1988), p. 31.

[11] I vary the spelling from the traditional "*Rechtsstaat*" to indicate my slightly deviant use of the term. As I understand it, the traditional notion of the *Rechtsstaat* is consistent with rules of law that are justified as ways to achieve welfare. On the traditional view of the *Rechtsstaat*, see Hans Kelsen, *The Pure Theory of Law*, trans. Max Knight (Berkeley: University of California Press, 1967), pp. 312–13. The variation in spelling was suggested to me by Friedrich A. von Hayek, *The Road to Serfdom* (Chicago: University of Chicago Press, 1944), p. 88, n. 2.

[12] Hayek, *The Road to Serfdom*, ch. 6.

[13] In the terminology of ethics, the Liberal *Rechtstaat* is a deontological view of the state.

[14] Ralph Barton Perry, *Realms of Value* (Cambridge, MA: Harvard University Press, 1954), p. 107.

not justified simply in terms of the desirability of their outcomes, is irrational. As is commonly the case in philosophy, first appearances are deceptive: much closer to the opposite, I shall try to show, is true. I argue in this essay that, by and large, it is typically unreasonable or irrational to pursue policies seeking to achieve desirable social goals; when the goal is social welfare, this unreasonableness is striking. For most of the essay, then, I shall focus on the typical unreasonableness of the pursuit of any social goals, only at times pointing to the especially glaring unreasonableness of pursuing the particular goal of social welfare. In contrast to the unreasonableness of goal pursuit, I shall argue that reasonable legislators, taking up the public perspective,[15] will enact rules that cannot be reduced to mere instruments to achieve goals. The upshot of this argument is that a state whose laws are enacted by reasonable legislators will look much more like a Liberal *Rechtstaat* than a welfare state, of either the interventionist or laissez-faire variety.

II. Two Ways of Being Rational[16]

A. Goal rationality

Before we can evaluate the comparative rationality of the welfare state and the Liberal *Rechtstaat*, we need to reflect on the idea of a rational agent and her actions. The widely shared perception that some version of the welfare state must be rational, while the Liberal *Rechtstaat* is clearly irrational, stems, I think, from the dominant conception of reason in action, which I shall call *goal rationality*.[17] This theory, developed by Thomas Hobbes and later British empiricists, was basic to the emerging science of political economy, which split into political science and economics toward the end of the last century. The motivating idea has been articulated in a variety of ways. Some, following David Hume, argue that all rational action is intended to satisfy desires. Others put the point in terms of satisfying preferences, while yet others, more prevalent in political science, tend to talk of advancing one's interests. To call an economic agent a utility-maximizer is often taken to be much the same as saying

---

[15] Throughout I will be supposing that legislators, when deliberating about legislation, are taking up a genuinely public perspective, rather than using their public position to advance their private ends.

[16] For a fuller treatment, see my essay "The Conflict of Values and Principles," in *Conflicting Values*, ed. Thomas Magnell (Amsterdam: Rodopi, forthcoming).

[17] In addition to *ibid.*, see my essay "The Rational, the Reasonable, and Justification," *Journal of Political Philosophy*, vol. 3, no. 3 (September 1995), pp. 235–38; and Jean Hampton, "The Failure of Expected-Utility Theory as a Theory of Reason," *Economics and Philosophy*, vol. 10, no. 2 (October 1994), p. 198ff.

that she has "purposes that her action is designed to promote."[18] The basic idea is clear and simple: "If doing x would best serve a person's ends, then that person has reason to do x."[19] Goal rationality is at the heart of economics: the motor of market behavior is the pursuit of one's *"own* purposes which inspire one's actions and excite one's alertness."[20] We can get a little more precise about the nature of goal rationality by specifying four of its closely related features.

(F1) *More is better than less.* Faced with a choice between quantity p of goal G and quantity q, where $p > q$, a rational agent typically has reason to act to obtain pG rather than qG. Feature 1 is fairly straightforward: for almost any goal of mine, if I am given the option between satisfying it to a lesser or a greater extent, a goal-rational agent has reason to choose to satisfy it to a greater extent. If we interpret the goal G as "utility" or even "happiness," then F1 is true without exception. When we consider more specific goods, however, we can discover anomalies. Some goals, for example, manifest satiation; the goal of eating a big steak, for example, reaches satiation at some level of fulfillment; most of us prefer a two-pound to a ten-pound steak for dinner. Of course, in this case, if we redefine our goal in terms of, say, pleasure or satisfaction, then the anomaly is removed, for the bigger steak does not, presumably, bring about more pleasure. Although we need not adopt hedonism, it probably is the case that goal rationality conforms to F1 far better when goals are not understood as specific goods,[21] but as more abstract aims, ends, and states of being. Even if goals are interpreted as specific goods, however, it will generally be the case that a rational goal-pursuing agent does not have a hard time deciding whether to opt for more or less of a good.

(F2) *Decreasing marginal reasons.* One's reasons to obtain more of a goal increase (as stated by F1) as the amount of the goal to be achieved increases, but the rate of increase diminishes from the n to the $n + 1$ unit of a goal. The justification for this feature will differ depending on one's theory of value; on a subjective theory of value, for instance, it might be claimed that as one's G increases from the n to the $n + 1$ unit, one's rate of increased satisfaction slows. I shall avoid here any commitment to a sub-

[18] Geoffrey Brennan and Loren Lomasky, *Democracy and Decision: The Pure Theory of Electoral Preference* (Cambridge: Cambridge University Press, 1993), p. 9 (note omitted).

[19] David Schmidtz, *Rational Choice and Moral Agency* (Princeton: Princeton University Press, 1995), p. 7. As with Schmidtz, "I use 'end' and 'goal' ... interchangeably" (*ibid.,* p. 7n.). I have slightly altered Schmidtz's notation.

[20] Israel M. Kirzner, *The Meaning of Market Process: Essays in the Development of Modern Austrian Economics* (London: Routledge, 1992), p. 208. See also Philip H. Wicksteed, *The Common Sense of Political Economy,* ed. Lionel Robbins (London: George Routledge and Sons, 1946), vol. 1, pp. 170–83.

[21] If the goal is understood in terms of specific goods, "lumpiness" can also be a problem; it may well be that we only have use for goal G in certain "lumpy" increments, and an extra amount that does not get us to the next increment is of no use.

jectivist account of value;[22] for a theory of rationality, the important point is that other things equal, one's reason to x increases as one's amount of G achieved by x increases (F1), but this rate of increase slows down as one achieves more of the goal (F2). I shall treat decreasing marginal reasons as an empirical generalization rather than as a law.[23] Nevertheless, it seems to characterize almost all our goals. Suppose, for example, that one's goal is to become rich and famous. Although one always has some reason to choose being yet richer and more famous (F1), when one has become extremely rich and famous, one's reasons to seek yet more fortune and fame are going to be pretty weak. Again, we can imagine anomalous cases where someone not only "cannot get enough" in the sense that he or she is not satiated (which is consistent with F2), but where one's reasons to pursue a goal are just as strong no matter how much of it one obtains. However, cases like this often suggest an alternative explanation, in terms of neurotic rather than effective instrumental behavior; someone who "cannot get enough" in this sense may be looking for satisfaction where "it is not to be found," and thus his seeming obsession may well be an indication that he is not really achieving his goal at all.[24]

(F3) *Completeness of goal comparisons.* Fully goal-rational individuals possess a system of trade-off rates between all their goals. They are always able to determine whether q amount of G_1 is better than, worse than, or just as good as, p amount of G_2. This is equivalent to the standard requirement in decision theory that one completely rank one's preferences.

(F4) *Downward-sloping demand curves.* Given (F3), as the cost of G_1 (in terms of G_2) increases, goal-rational agents have less reason to undertake x acts seeking to bring about G_1. This is a gloss on the notion that the demand curve for G is downward-sloping.[25] A goal-rational agent, then, not only is able to resolve conflicts between his ends, but must do so through a system of trade-off rates (a utility function)[26] according to which the "demand" for a goal (or value, or end) decreases as its cost

---

[22] Although I have defended one elsewhere; see my *Value and Justification: The Foundations of Liberal Theory* (Cambridge: Cambridge University Press, 1990), Part 1.

[23] See Daniel M. Hausman, *The Inexact and Separate Science of Economics* (Cambridge: Cambridge University Press, 1992), p. 32. Cf. Ludwig von Mises's claim that "there is no question of any such thing as a law of increasing marginal utility" (i.e., marginal utility never increases over the range of possible quantities). Ludwig von Mises, *Human Action: A Treatise on Economics*, 3d ed. (Chicago: Contemporary Books, 1966), p. 125.

[24] See Sigmund Freud, "The Disposition to Obsessional Neurosis," in *On Psychopathology*, ed. Angela Richards (Harmondsworth: Penguin, 1979), pp. 134–44. Cf. Thomas Hill Green, "On the Different Senses of 'Freedom' as Applied to the Will and to the Moral Progress of Man," in his *Lectures on the Principles of Political Obligation and Other Writings*, ed. Paul Harris and John Morrow (Cambridge: Cambridge University Press, 1986), p. 228.

[25] Brennan and Lomasky, *Democracy and Decision* (*supra* note 18), p. 9. This is distinct from F2. According to decreasing marginal reasons, if we hold constant the cost of obtaining G, our reason to secure it decreases as we obtain higher levels; according F4, holding constant the level of G, our reasons for pursuing it decrease as the cost of obtaining it rises.

[26] For the present, these can be treated as synonymous, though in fact the idea of a utility function is usually interpreted in a way that is more demanding than a system of trade-off

relative to other goals (or values, or ends) increases. Again, anomalous cases occur, as with Giffen goods, for which demand increases as their costs rise.[27]

B. Rule rationality

A familiar picture emerges: A rational person has a system of goals and can make consistent choices among them. A person always has reason to act to pursue more of a goal rather than less, but her reason to keep on pursuing any particular goal lessens as the cost of achieving it increases; she generally also has less reason to seek an incremental increase when she has successfully achieved the goal than when she has yet to obtain it. To many, especially to economists and social scientists employing economic models, this (or something very similar) is the crux of all rational action. "Optimizing" and "rational" are pretty much synonymous terms to economists; one certainly cannot be the latter without being the former.[28] Even opponents of the optimizing model such as Herbert Simon tell us that "reason is wholly instrumental. . . . It is a gun for hire that can be employed in the service of whatever goals we have, good or bad."[29] Sociologists, lawyers, and moral philosophers, however, have generally taken far more seriously the idea that rationality can be expressed by action following from the acceptance of norms or rules.[30] As H. L. A. Hart stresses, in "any large group general rules, standards and principles" are the primary mode of regulating social life; the rules identify general classes of action and require or prohibit particular acts falling under these general descriptions.[31] This suggests an alternative notion of reason; let us say:

rates. See Stanley Benn, *A Theory of Freedom* (Cambridge: Cambridge University Press, 1988), ch. 3. See also my *Value and Justification* (*supra* note 22), p. 182.

[27] Sir Robert Giffen pointed out that when the price of bread rises, the very poor may purchase more of it; the increase in the price of bread has a significant effect on the real incomes of poor people, causing them to substitute bread for more expensive foods they can no longer afford, thus increasing the total amount of bread they consume. Status goods also can be considered as exceptions to downward-sloping demand—if they do not cost a great deal, they do not serve their purpose of showing that you can afford them. I am grateful to Julian Lamont for pointing these exceptions out to me.

[28] See, e.g., Gary Becker, *The Economic Approach to Human Behavior* (Chicago: University of Chicago Press, 1976), p. 3.

[29] Herbert A. Simon, *Reason in Human Affairs* (Stanford, CA: Stanford University Press, 1983), pp. 7–8.

[30] For the contrast between economic and sociological approaches, see Viktor J. Vanberg, *Rules and Choice in Economics* (London: Routledge, 1994), ch. 1. See Talcott Parsons's "classification of the sciences of action" in Parsons, *The Social System* (London: Routledge and Kegan Paul, 1951), p. 545ff. For analyses of rule rationality with a focus on law, see Gidon Gottlieb, *The Logic of Choice* (London: George Allen and Unwin, 1968); and Frederick Schauer, *Playing by the Rules* (Oxford: Clarendon Press, 1991).

[31] H. L. A. Hart, *The Concept of Law* (Oxford: Clarendon Press, 1961), p. 121. I shall not consider permissive rules here.

Alf has a *reason of fidelity* to (or not to) *x* if (1) Alf accepts some norm, principle, or rule *R*; (2) *R* requires (or prohibits) a type of action *X*; and (3) *x* is an instance of *X*.

This characterization of reasons of fidelity highlights three features of rule-following. *First*, an account of rational rule-following must clarify what is meant by embracing or internalizing a norm or a rule, a phenomenon that sociologists and psychologists have studied.[32] It is important to stress that rule rationality is not simply behavior in conformity to rules; it is action performed because rules are accepted. *Second*, rules are generalizations that identify types of actions;[33] because of this, *third*, a specific act required (or prohibited) by a rule stands to the rule in something like a token-to-type relation—to *x* because of a rule is to do it because it instantiates *X*, i.e., is an instance of it.[34] Together, the second and third points raise the standard problems about rule-following: How do we know that the correct way to "go on" with the rule—to instantiate *X*—is to perform this act rather than that? How do we know, for instance, whether a rule prohibiting vehicles in a public park provides a reason for leaving one's bicycle at the entrance?[35] I shall not plow these familiar philosophical and jurisprudential fields here; for present purposes what is worth stressing is that these are distinct philosophical problems raised by the idea of rule-following, problems that do not characterize goal pursuit. The very existence of these long-standing problems thus indicates that rule-following is an activity quite distinct from goal pursuit.

C. Why rule rationality is distinct from goal rationality

A common move in both philosophical ethics and decision theory is to reduce rule-following to goal pursuit. We follow rules, it is said, simply as a means to achieve goals. It is often the case that (1) because of lack of information, incentive structures, or strategic interactions, if each person sets out to achieve *G*, it will not be obtained. (2) In these sorts of cases (runs the reductionist argument), the best way to achieve *G* is through common acceptance of a rule *R*, which calls for actions of type *X*, where it is the case that *X* actions generally will lead to achieving *G*.[36] Therefore,

---

[32] See Parsons, *The Social System* (*supra* note 30), p. 207ff.; Vanberg, *Rules and Choice in Economics* (*supra* note 30), p. 14. See also Jerome Kagan, *The Nature of the Child* (New York: Basic Books, 1984), ch. 4.

[33] Schauer, *Playing by the Rules* (*supra* note 30), ch. 2; Vanberg, *Rules and Choice in Economics*, p. 16ff.

[34] Schauer, *Playing by the Rules*, pp. 54ff., 72, 77, 113; Benn, *A Theory of Freedom* (*supra* note 26), p. 24.

[35] This, of course, is Hart's famous example in *The Concept of Law* (*supra* note 31), p. 123ff.

[36] This is a familiar claim in a huge body of utilitarian literature. As Goodin puts it: "The best way to coordinate our actions with those of others, and thereby maximize the utility from each of our actions as well as from all of our actions collectively, is to promulgate rules (themselves chosen with an eye to maximizing utility, of course) and to adhere to them." Goodin, *Utilitarianism as a Public Philosophy* (*supra* note 2), p. 18.

(3) it is claimed, R is simply an indirect means of goal pursuit, and so the reason for x-ing based on R is, after all, an (indirect, to be sure) case of goal-pursuit rationality.

In their war against reductionist claims, advocates of rule rationality almost always choose the same battleground: a case where R instructs us to x but where x-ing does not produce G. To an advocate of pure goal rationality, it seems crazy to follow the rule here. As John Stuart Mill said, when such extraordinary cases occur, rules will be faulty guides to our goal; if we insist on x-ing, "we shall employ the means and the end will not follow."[37] Thus, says Mill, "the legislator, or other practitioner, who goes by rules rather than by their reasons . . . is rightly judged to be a mere pedant, and the slave of his formulas."[38] As I said, advocates of rule rationality such as Frederick Schauer have focused on these "recalcitrant experiences"—where x-ing does not produce G,[39] trying to show that (pace Mill) it is rational to x anyway, and if so, it must be the case that one's reason to x cannot be reduced to a means for attaining G.

Although I think Schauer's analysis of recalcitrant experiences is right, these sorts of arguments tend to be highly inconclusive. An advocate of goal rationality can plausibly maintain that a more subtle analysis shows that the goal really is advanced by sticking to the rule, or that an additional goal such as fairness is attained by obeying the rule in apparently "recalcitrant" cases.[40] And if no good at all comes from following the rule, a proponent of pure goal rationality may stick to a (seemingly) hard-headed anti-rule-worship line, and insist that one is a fool to follow rules in these cases. It is more useful, I want to suggest, to reflect on the cases where the rule does promote the goal. Schauer is convinced that these cases are not truly rule-governed: if rule R is justified because it mandates X actions, which bring about G, and if in this case x-ing does bring about G, it seems that the action dictated by the rule (instantiate X) is extensionally equivalent to the goal-directed action of bringing about G. In these cases, Schauer believes, the rule is "superfluous."[41] However, even when the rule agrees with the goal-based justification for it, rule rationality differs from goal rationality since it is not characterized by decreasing marginal reasons. Suppose I accept the rule that I ought to tell the truth. Even if I accept this because it will bring about good results, if I tell the truth because I accept the rule, my reasons to tell the truth do not decrease as I tell more and more truths. Suppose I tell the truth a lot—I am

---

[37] John Stuart Mill, A System of Logic (London: Longman's, 1947), Book VI, ch. xii, section 3.
[38] Ibid., Book VI, ch. xii, section 2. I consider Mill's view in depth in my essay "Mill's Theory of Moral Rules," Australasian Journal of Philosophy, vol. 58 (September 1980), pp. 265–78.
[39] Schauer, Playing by the Rules (supra note 30), ch. 3.
[40] See, e.g., Russell Hardin, "My University's Yacht: Morality and the Rule of Law," in NOMOS XXXVI: The Rule of Law, ed. Ian Shapiro (New York: New York University Press, 1994), pp. 219–22.
[41] Schauer, Playing by the Rules, p. 72.

thoroughly honest. If my actions were simply a manifestation of goal rationality, my reasons for telling the truth rather than seeking other goals should be declining.

In contrast to reasons that follow from goals, ends, and so on, reasons based on rules typically do not display any tendency to "decreasing marginal reasons." One's reason to tell the truth is simply that it instantiates truth-telling, not that one is accumulating instances of truth-telling in the world, or achieving more trust, or more cooperation, or whatever. This is the chief way that rule-following calls on drastically less information than goal pursuit. To recognize and evaluate one's reason to achieve a goal, one must know how much of the goal one has achieved, how much others are achieving, prospects for future attainments, and so on; to deliberate on one's reasons to follow a rule, one need only know that the act under consideration instantiates the type of act the rule addresses.

Now it might be replied that rule-following does, after all, usually exhibit decreasing marginal reasons. Suppose that I am a habitual truth-teller, and I am getting sick of missing out on the fun of lying. I try to keep on telling the truth, but the attractions of fibbing finally overcome me, and I tell a whopper. "One can't," I reason, "be an angel forever." This, however, is a case of *increasing costs* of following the rule: one's frustration builds up, and so do one's reasons to put aside the rule. I have not denied that the "demand curve" for rule-following is "downward-sloping," in the sense that as its cost increases, one has, overall, less reason to follow the rule. The important point is that one's reasons to fulfill the duty do not decrease as one is successful at living up to it—(F2) does not hold. However, it may seem that this does not accurately describe what are often called "imperfect duties." Charity or beneficence is characterized as an imperfect duty because we do not owe it to any particular person; as John Stuart Mill stressed, although we have a duty to be charitable, no specific person has a right to our charity.[42] Thus, it may seem that we have a less urgent reason to act charitably the more we have done so in the past; we do not wrong any particular person when we refrain from acting charitably, and as we have generally "done our duty" in the past, we can begin to relax and turn to other matters. One has, as it were, done one's bit, or near enough to it that one's duty does not press on one so urgently. This begins to look very much like decreasing marginal reasons to act charitably.

It may well be. I do not wish to insist that nothing we call a "duty" conforms to the goal-rationality model. It is not implausible to characterize an imperfect duty of charity as committing us to go a certain way toward achieving a goal of relieving suffering. We can have duties to work toward goals; if so, the closer we get to our goal, the closer we come to fulfilling our duty, and therefore the less urgent the duty is in our

---

[42] John Stuart Mill, *Utilitarianism* (Indianapolis: Bobbs-Merrill, 1957), pp. 61–62.

deliberations. Another analysis, however, is possible. We may have a duty to, say, instantiate the rule "Be regularly charitable." If that is how we understand imperfect duties, then decreasing marginal reasons does not seem to hold; I have a reason of fidelity to instantiate charity regularly. Suppose I have been a regular contributor to Oxfam, but for the last several years have forgotten. Can I claim that my reasons to give over the last several years were less urgent than they were in the past because in the past I had given regularly, and so already had achieved a good deal of the goal of relieving suffering in the world? It does not seem so; my reasons to act charitably were not weaker this year just because in the past I fulfilled my duty—what is crucial is that I have failed to meet my duty over the last few years. To be sure, if I have given to Oxfam in the last six months, it may well seem that I have less of a reason to give again, but that, I think, is not because reasons of imperfect charity are decreasing at the margins; rather, it is because it is unclear just what constitutes a "regular" contribution, and thus the reason to give may seem less urgent at six months than at a year, where it becomes clearer that one has not met one's duty.

Thus far I have not disputed step (2) of the basic reductionist argument, i.e., that rules are always intended to achieve goals. Even if we accept that the point of rules is always to achieve goals or eradicate evils, I have been arguing, rule rationality does not reduce to goal rationality.[43] Of course if we deny (2), the gap between rule rationality and goal rationality is much wider. S. I. Benn argued that principled reasons can be entirely divorced from a concern with optimizing value or producing good states of affairs: we can have reasons based on such principles "as freedom, justice, equal respect for person's rights, and fidelity to truth, inasmuch as we are committed to these principles in our dealings with any other person, and quite irrespective of the outcomes of our conforming to or departing from these principles."[44] The interest of this proposal is that the first, and most basic, feature of goal rationality is dropped: namely, that more is better. On Benn's view, I may embrace a principle that instructs me to tell the truth because that is required by my commitment to respect the moral personality of others. It does not follow, however, that I believe that the world is better off with more rather than less truth-telling, or more rather than less instances of respecting others. It does not even follow that I am committed to maximizing the number of times I respect others, or minimizing the instances where I fail to respect them. Such principled rationality accounts for reasons deriving from rights. If I respect your right, which implies a duty that I X, I will x rather than not x when the rule applies, but (1) I will not forgo x-ing today so that many *others* can X tomorrow, and (2) I will not forgo x-ing today even if doing so is neces-

---

[43] *Ibid.*, p. 26.
[44] Benn, *A Theory of Freedom* (*supra* note 26), p. 8.

sary for *me* to instantiate X more often in the future. On goal rationality these seem manifestly crazy: if my goal is either that we all instantiate X, or that I do so in my own life, then instantiating it today at the cost of many further instantiations in the future violates the "more is better than less" feature, and thus I am irrationally pursuing the goal. It seems likely that a morality of rights as side-constraints can only be rational if we reject this basic feature of goal rationality.

III. A RATIONAL AND REASONABLE ECONOMY OF REASONS

Despite the powerful case for rule rationality, there is considerable reluctance on the part of many philosophers (and almost all economists) to multiply types of rationality, and this is true for at least two reasons. One, I think, is a devotion to simplicity and elegance in theories: explanatory and normative theories based on a single notion of rationality are more elegant than those that resort to types of reasoning. This seems a misplaced devotion to aesthetics: if a theory is wrong and misdescribes the world, beauty ought to give way to truth. A second concern is more compelling: if we have multiple types of reasoning, there will be no way to bring them together. We would need some "super-reason" to decide when types of reasons clash. In order to decide whether to act on a rule-reason or a goal-reason, it seems we must have some standard on which both can be measured, and that drives us back to a monistic theory of reason. In the absence of super-reason, having multiple types of reasoning introduces incommensurable reasons. This not only seems to undermine the usefulness of reason as a tool for social science, but it undoes reason itself. For if reason requires coherence and consistency, and we possess incommensurable reasons, it seems that we cannot be rational.

The worry is unfounded: we do not require a third value, norm, or concept of reason in order to consistently decide between two competing ones.[45] What we do require is what I earlier called a system of trade-off rates. If we assume for simplicity's sake a system with only one rule and one goal, then for any given situation, a rational person must be able to rank the reason dictated by the rule and that dictated by the goal. It is important to stress that this will not be simply a matter of deciding whether the goal or the rule is more important. As Benn effectively argued, in different contexts both rules and goals may be "at stake" to different degrees.[46] This is so, *first*, because though the goal or rule may be relevant, it might be uncertain which action is called for. An important goal for any legislator, for example, is to reduce street crime; a legislator

[45] See Gaus, *Value and Justification* (*supra* note 22), pp. 175–85; Benn, *A Theory of Freedom*, pp. 47–50; and James Griffin, *Well-Being: Its Meaning, Measurement, and Moral Importance* (Oxford: Clarendon Press, 1986), pp. 89–92.

[46] Benn, *A Theory of Freedom*, ch. 3. I consider Benn's analysis in more depth in "The Conflict of Values and Principles" (*supra* note 16).

having to decide on a drug control policy may rightfully believe that this is a relevant goal. But we know so little about the linkages between street crime and drugs that it is impossible to predict with any significant degree of confidence what drug policies raise or lower street crime.[47] In this sense the goal is not highly salient in decisions about what to do. Much the same can happen with a rule. In Hart's famous example, a bicycle rider may know and embrace the rule prohibiting vehicles in the park. But to the extent that she is uncertain whether the rule applies to bicycles, the rule will be less salient for her than in cases where its requirements are clear.

A *second* type of variation in salience occurs in cases where a goal or rule is relevant, and one knows how one's action impacts on it, but the extent of this impact is modest. Thus, for instance, one can be highly confident that a Los Angeleno who stops driving his car will decrease the carbon monoxide level in the Los Angeles basin; it may be infinitesimal, but some vanishingly small improvement is likely. Nevertheless, the goal of decreasing carbon monoxide is not highly relevant when he decides whether to start his BMW or take the bus. A rule's salience may also vary in this way. Although I may well be committed to the rule that one ought not to lie, and I understand white lies to be lies, I may still regularly tell telemarketers that "Mr. Gaus is away for the next two weeks"; white lies are "unimportant" lies that do not seriously impinge one's commitment to telling the truth.

A rational resolution of a conflict between rule R and goal G will thus depend on two variables: (1) how weighty R and G are in your system of beliefs, rules, and goals, and (2) to what extent, in any situation, R and G are at stake. Figure 1 combines these variables. The x-axis represents variation of the salience of a rule (combining the two different sources of variation described above); the y-axis represents variation in the salience of a goal (again, combining both sources of salience variation). The curves represent the relative importance of the rule and goal; three different trade-off rates, A, B, and C, are depicted.

The points X_1, X_2, X_3, and X_4 on Figure 1 indicate four different decision situations in which a person has to choose between fidelity to R and pursuit of G. The trade-off indicated by C is that of a fairly devoted goal pursuer: in cases of conflict between R and G, C will act to promote G in all cases above line C. Only in case X_4, in which the goal is not highly salient but the rule is, will C decide in favor of the rule. In contrast, line B indicates a more rule-sensitive trade-off rate, acting on R in X_3 and X_4, but pursuing G in X_1 and X_2. Lastly, A is sort of a non-fanatical Kantian, strongly disposed to rules, but willing to pursue G when R is not salient (that is, only in case X_1 will A choose G over R).

---

[47] See Franklin E. Zimring and Gordon Hawkins, *The Search for Rational Drug Control* (Cambridge: Cambridge University Press, 1992), ch. 6.

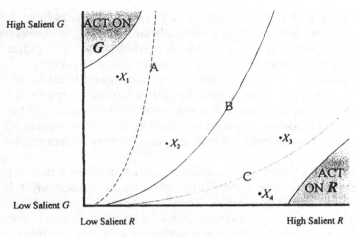

FIGURE 1. Three trade-off rates

A, B, and C are all rational in a fundamental sense: they represent
consistent trade-off rates.[48] However, they are also reasonable in the sense
that they acknowledge that both sorts of reasons are relevant to the decision. What would seem unreasonable is to simply deny that one or the
other reason carries any weight at all. For if, *ex hypothesi*, both goal-based
and rule-based reasons are relevant, then to so discount one that for all
practical purposes it vanishes is to ignore a relevant reason for action.
This, I think, explains our worry about those who give "absolute weight"
to some consideration, or insist on a strict lexical ordering of reasons.
Suppose we interpret the Rawlsian idea of lexicality to require that even
in cases where liberty is only salient in the most marginal possible way,
and where wealth is crucially and tremendously at stake, we should
choose liberty.[49] Brian Barry is right: on this formulation the idea is "out-
landishly extreme."[50] Indeed, it is fanatical: a fanatic is one who main-

---

[48] Note that a person with consistent trade-off rates can rationally choose "inconsistently,"
sometimes opting for R and sometimes for G. See Benn, *A Theory of Freedom*, p. 50ff.

[49] See John Rawls, *A Theory of Justice* (Cambridge, MA: Harvard University Press, 1971),
p. 61. A "lexical" order "is an order which requires us to satisfy the first principle in the
ordering before we can move on to the second, the second before we consider the third, and
so on. A principle does not come into play until those previous to it are either fully met or
do not apply. A serial [or lexical] ordering avoids, then, having to balance principles at all:
those earlier in the ordering have an absolute weight, so to speak, with respect to later ones,
and hold without exception" (*ibid.*, p. 43). In Rawls's theory of justice, the principle of liberty
is lexically prior to the principle dealing with economic justice. Rawls acknowledges that "in
general, a lexical order cannot be strictly correct" (*ibid.*, p. 45). As Elizabeth Anderson points
out, both Robert Nozick and Ronald Dworkin can be interpreted as offering lexical rankings.
See Anderson, *Value in Ethics and Economics* (Cambridge, MA: Harvard University Press,
1993), p. 67.

[50] Brian Barry, *The Liberal Theory of Justice* (Oxford: Clarendon Press, 1973), p. 60.

tains consistency by ignoring other relevant considerations and giving absolute weight to one factor. Some have argued that such fanatics can be rational as long as they are fanatical about only one thing, and their absolute commitments never clash;[51] it seems more accurate to say that they are unreasonable, and suffer from a defect in reasoning. A fanatic is one who is consistent but not reasonable; he suffers from a defect of reasoning, being a "hedgehog" who appreciates only one of the relevant considerations, as opposed to the "fox" who sees the plurality of relevant considerations.[52] If indeed plural considerations are relevant, one who construes things monistically is making a mistake, and thus suffers from a flaw of reasoning.

It might be replied that, on my account, the fanatic could reclaim his reasonableness simply by insisting that, after all, only one consideration is relevant; if only G is relevant, someone who only pays attention to G does not reveal himself to be a fanatic. Certainly this would move the dispute to a different issue: if we believe that both G and R are relevant, we probably would charge him with an epistemic error—failing to grasp a relevant consideration. But that is a deeper dispute—and a less obvious defect of reason—than that being considered here, for in the case we are considering the fanatic accepts that both are relevant to choice, but so weighs the two that any amount of G satisfaction, no matter how tiny, is preferred to any degree of R satisfaction, no matter how large. Here I think it is clear that we wish to say that the fanatic is being unreasonable. In a narrow sense he is still rational, as he demonstrates a sort of tunnel-vision consistency, but it is a consistency that is flawed from the perspective of reason itself, for he is effectively treating a complex situation as if it were a simple one. I think the epithet "unreasonable" is precisely the right one for this sort of defect of reason. A person who entertains an "outlandish" or "fanatical" devotion to one consideration when others are, from his own point of view, relevant, is not being reasonable.

If this is right, it follows that in something akin to area R in Figure 1— where rules are highly salient and goals are marginally at stake—a rational and reasonable trade-off rate must select the rule; in the neighborhood of area G, a rational and reasonable trade-off rate must choose the crucially important goal when it conflicts marginally with the rule. This allows for a great deal of difference among rational and reasonable people about how they are to decide in cases of conflict (A to C in Figure 1), but the range of reasonable decisions is limited. Summing up, then, let us say

[51] See Benn, *A Theory of Freedom*, pp. 56–59.

[52] Isaiah Berlin, *The Hedgehog and the Fox* (London: Weidenfeld and Nicholson, 1953). This understanding of fanaticism allows us to interpret R. M. Hare's famous fanatic as a special case: his fanatic cares only about one thing (say, his commitment to Nazism) and so ignores other relevant considerations, e.g., his own interests. See Hare, *Freedom and Reason* (Oxford: Clarendon Press, 1952), ch. 9. See also Lomasky, *Persons, Rights, and the Moral Community* (*supra* note 1), pp. 79–83.

that a *rational* agent's choices between rules and goals can be mapped somewhere on Figure 1, with a trade-off curve in the general shape of A, B, and C; a *reasonable* agent, in addition, possesses a trade-off curve that does not divide either area *R* or area *G* on Figure 1—if, that is, the agent acts on rules in area *R* and goals in area *G*, then I will say that the agent is *reasonable*.

IV. WHY GOVERNMENTS SPEND SO MUCH OF THEIR TIME IN AREA R

A. Radical uncertainty in the pursuit of public goals

A decision to implement a specific public policy *P* as a way to achieve any significant social goal *G*—reduction of crime, control of recreational drugs, reduction of poverty, economic growth, the national interest in foreign affairs, pollution control, public health, or the education of children—will be characterized by profound uncertainty as to whether *P* will in fact achieve *G*. This profound uncertainty has four sources.

1. Complexity of public policy goals. Almost all public policy goals are actually constellations of goals or objectives. Consider the problem of drug addiction. To use Ralph L. Keeney and Howard Raiffa's example, a mayor of New York would like to:

- Reduce the size of the addict pool (this is more complicated than it sounds since there are different types of addicts and trade-offs must be made between the sizes of these categories).

- Reduce costs to the city and its residents. Reduce crimes against property and persons.

- Improve the "quality of life"—whatever that may mean—of addicts and reduce their morbidity and mortality.

- Improve the quality of life of nonaddicts, make New York City a more pleasant place to live, and reverse the disastrous trends of in-and-out migration of families and businesses.

- Curb organized crime.

- Live up to the high ideals of civil rights and civil liberties.

- Decrease the alienation of youth.

- Get elected to higher office (perhaps the presidency?).[53]

[53] Ralph L. Keeney and Howard Raiffa, *Decisions with Multiple Objectives: Preferences and Value Trade-Offs* (Cambridge: Cambridge University Press, 1993), p. 3.

Decision theorists such as Keeney and Raiffa have displayed great ingenuity in developing a system of consistent trade-off rates for a single decision maker, allowing him or her to make consistent choices among these many competing desiderata. Even assuming all that can be done, it is important to stress that the complexity analyzed below is greatly magnified by the fact that public policy seeks simultaneous achievement of multiple aims.

2. *Conflicting hypotheses about relevant causes.* Almost every significant public policy goal requires extensive knowledge of the causes of social phenomena. If we want to reduce crime we need some idea of what causes it—so too with poverty, youth alienation, economic growth, technological innovation, migration from cities, and drug use.[54] It is an understatement to say that our social-scientific theories do not help much. Not only do the well-supported ones explain only a small part of the variance, but in almost every case we find ourselves confronted with rival plausible hypotheses deriving from rival plausible theories of the phenomenon. A decision theorist would like us to assign probability estimates to each theory and hypothesis, so that we could say that theory α about the causes of drug use has a .35 probability of being correct and theory β a .45 chance. But lacking any master theory, we are faced with radical uncertainty about which of these accounts is more likely to be right. As G. L. S. Shackle has pointed out: "To be uncertain is to entertain many rival hypotheses. The hypotheses are rivals to each other in the sense that they all refer to the same question, and only one of them can prove true in the event."[55] Proponents of each will have great confidence in their favored account, while observers may have little way to guess which is better.

The problems raised by our hopelessly inconclusive social sciences are fundamental, and can hardly be overemphasized. We should recall that the founders of utilitarianism, who offered it as the public philosophy of the future, were also early social scientists, being especially prominent in the emerging science of political economy. The organized pursuit of social welfare that utilitarianism embodies presupposes a social science that allows the policymaker to understand society. But in the last two hundred years we have come to see that the complexity of human behavior and social processes, coupled with the limits of our reason, has made a mockery of the confidence of the early utilitarian social scientists.

3. *Moderate and radical uncertainty in predicting the consequences of policies.* Not only are prospective policymakers seeking to solve problems the causes of which are deeply uncertain, but they are radically uncertain

---

[54] See Robert E. Goodin, *Political Theory and Public Policy* (Chicago: University of Chicago Press, 1982), pp. 7–38. Goodin argues that "incrementalism" does not obviate the need for such insight into the causes of social phenomena.

[55] G. L. S. Shackle, *Epistemics and Economics* (Cambridge: Cambridge University Press, 1978), p. 19.

about the consequences of their own policies.[56] We can distinguish moderate and radical uncertainty in forecasts about the future effects of one's actions.[57] A decision maker, let us say, is characterized by *moderate uncertainty* when, because of incomplete knowledge, he can only make probabilistic estimates of the effects of his policy. Modern decision theory has developed highly formal models of deciding under such uncertainty.[58] In principle, such uncertainty can be dealt with by accurate probabilistic estimates and suitable discounting of uncertain consequences. But it may be that even given perfect probabilistic reasoning, the likelihood of any set of consequences is very low. In this case, although there is a *best* thing to do, there may be no particularly *good* thing to do, since all the probabilities are very low. However, assuming that decision makers will accurately estimate the probabilities and act on them is unrealistic; a large body of psychological evidence indicates that decision makers are poor at estimating probabilities and, indeed, tend to ignore them even when they are presented.[59] Given this, a rational decision maker must question his own estimates, thus moving from moderate to radical uncertainty.

A decision maker is faced with *radical uncertainty* about the consequences of his actions when he is ignorant about what he does not know. This type of uncertainty is at the core of the "knowledge problem" analyzed by Austrian economists such as Israel Kirzner.[60] If we are ignorant about what we do not know, we cannot estimate the costs of finding it out, nor can we factor it into our probabilities. What I do not know that I don't know, I cannot discount or estimate. Suppose that our mayor of New York is deliberating on the merits of policy *P*. Utilizing all the preferred techniques for calculating probabilities, he determines that given his lack of knowledge about the relation between drug use and crime, there is only a .05 chance that *P* will achieve its goal. But entirely undreamt of by him or anyone else is a causal relation *C*, according to which *P* actually will increase criminal behavior. Because he is totally ignorant of the possibility of *C*, it was not factored into his initial estimate of the success of *P*. Because his uncertainty is deep and not moderate, it cannot

---

[56] "In actuality, the human being never has more than a fragmentary knowledge of the conditions surrounding his action, nor more than a slight insight into the regularities and laws that would permit him to induce further consequences from a knowledge of present circumstances." Herbert A. Simon, *Administrative Behavior: A Study of Decision-Making Processes in Administrative Organization*, 3d ed. (New York: Free Press, 1976), p. 81.

[57] See Goodin, *Political Theory and Public Policy* (*supra* note 54), ch. 9.

[58] See, e.g., J. B. Paris, *The Uncertain Reasoner's Companion* (Cambridge: Cambridge University Press, 1994).

[59] For a summary, see Paul R. Kleindorfer, Howard C. Kunreuther, and Paul J. H. Schoemaker, *Decision Sciences: An Integrative Perspective* (Cambridge: Cambridge University Press, 1993), pp. 87–100. See also *Judgment under Uncertainty: Heuristics and Biases*, ed. Daniel Kahneman, Paul Slovic, and Amos Tversky (Cambridge: Cambridge University Press, 1982).

[60] Kirzner, *The Meaning of Market Process* (*supra* note 20), chs. 9, 10. For the classic essay on this topic, see Friedrich A. von Hayek, "The Use of Knowledge in Society," in *Austrian Economics*, ed. Richard M. Ebeling (Hillsdale, MI: Hillsdale College Press, 1991), ch. 14.

be built into his calculations: he remains totally in the dark about what he does not know. And because the public policy maker is seeking to decide what will advance a goal among a large number of people for an indefinite future, he can reasonably suppose that, whatever his estimates, they overlook important factors about which he is totally ignorant.

4. *Uncertainty about implementation.* Although we have been picturing a single decision maker trying to make a reasoned choice between policies seeking to achieve goals, we need to remember that a public policy maker cannot perform the act "implement policy *P*." Just as the utilitarian fathers of the welfare state anticipated a powerful social science that would allow us to grasp the causes of social problems and predict the effects of our policies on them, so too did they suppose an efficient, public-spirited bureaucracy that would carry out these policies. But we know that the "utility function" of bureaucrats is not the same as that of their principals:[61] what the policymaker decides and what the bureaucracy implements are at best imperfectly coupled.

B. *An example: Reducing the risk of driving*

I am not claiming that governments can never rationally and reasonably pursue any goals. Governments can build schools (but it is more doubtful whether this can be said to increase the amount of education in society);[62] and it can build prisons for those who sell drugs (whether or not this reduces drug use or makes our streets safe). These are straightforward, uncomplicated (though not inexpensive) goals. But almost any public policy goal will be more complex, because the welfare state not only wants to do things, but do things that make people better off—that increase the welfare of its citizens. As soon as we make this move, uncertainty floods in. To see this, consider what would seem—in comparison to issues like reducing crime and poverty—a ridiculously simple goal: increasing welfare through mandatory seat belt legislation.

Just what is the policymaker seeking to accomplish? Suppose it is a very simple goal, such as a net saving of lives. If the goal is specified this simply, its public pursuit might be reasonable and rational. Writes Goodin:

> For example, consider the case of compulsory seat belt legislation. Policy-makers can say with some confidence that, on aggregate, more lives would be saved than lost if all automobile drivers and their

---

[61] See Alan Peacock, *Public Choice Analysis in an Historical Framework* (Cambridge: Cambridge University Press, 1992), pp. 74–79. See also Charles Wolf, Jr., *Markets or Governments: Choosing between Imperfect Alternatives*, 2d ed. (Cambridge: MIT Press, 1994), pp. 68–79; and Simon, *Administrative Behavior* (*supra* note 56), ch. 10.

[62] Evidence indicates, for example, that state investment in education tends to supplant rather than supplement private investment. See Becker, *The Economic Approach to Human Behavior* (*supra* note 28), p. 267n.

passengers were required to wear seat belts. As always, that aggregate conceals the fact that some gain while others lose. Some people would be trapped by seat belts in fiery crashes who otherwise would have been thrown to safety by the force of the impact, after all. The point is that policy-makers, contemplating seat belt legislation, have no way of knowing who those individuals are, exactly, or on what occasions, exactly, that might occur. All they can *know* is that, on aggregate, far fewer people would be saved than killed by being thrown clear of their cars upon impact.[63]

Goodin, like most of us today, supposes that it is obvious and uncontroversial that seat belt legislation has saved lives. A review of the research yields a much more ambiguous picture. The debate about the efficacy of seat belts began with Sam Peltzman's 1975 paper in which he argued that new cars subject to stricter safety regulations accounted for a significantly larger share of accidents than cars of similar age before safety regulations were implemented. Peltzman insisted that there was no evidence to show that seat belts saved lives.[64] The crux of Peltzman's analysis is the hypothesis of offsetting behavior: as cars become safer, drivers adjust their behavior and drive less safely, thus offsetting the effects of the increased safety provided by seat belts. The offsetting-behavior hypothesis is disputed in the literature: David J. Houston, Lilliard Richardson, Jr., and Grant W. Neely suggest that there is little evidence for it;[65] A. C. Harvey and J. Durbin, as well as David L. Ryan and Guy A. Bridgeman, report contradictory results,[66] while Christopher Garbacz's data provides strong support for it.[67] Steven Rhoads is confident that offsetting behavior occurs to some extent, though he acknowledges that noneconomists have trouble accepting the idea. Rhoads reports that in Sweden, for example, it was found that drivers with studded snow tires drive faster than drivers with regular tires when the roads are icy, but not when they are dry.[68]

---

[63] Goodin, *Utilitarianism as a Public Philosophy* (*supra* note 2), p. 63, emphasis added. See Steven Rhoads, *The Economist's View of the World* (Cambridge: Cambridge University Press, 1985), p. 57.

[64] Sam Peltzman, "The Effects of Automobile Safety Regulations," *Journal of Political Economy*, vol. 83 (August 1975), pp. 677–726.

[65] David J. Houston, Lilliard E. Richardson, Jr., and Grant W. Neely, "Legislating Traffic Safety: A Pooled Time Series Analysis," *Social Science Quarterly*, vol. 76 (June 1995), pp. 330–31.

[66] A. C. Harvey and J. Durbin, "The Effects of Seat Belt Legislation on British Road Deaths," *Journal of the Royal Statistical Society*, Series A, vol. 149 (1986), pp. 187–210; David L. Ryan and Guy A. Bridgeman, "Judging the Roles of Legislation, Education, and Offsetting Behaviour in Seat Belt Use: A Survey and New Evidence from Alberta," *Canadian Public Policy*, vol. 18 (1992), pp. 27–46.

[67] Christopher Garbacz, "Estimating Seat Belt Effectiveness with Seat Belt Usage Data from the Centers for Disease Control," *Economics Letters*, vol. 34 (1990), pp. 83–88; Christopher Garbacz, "Do Front-Seat Belt Laws Put Rear-Seat Passengers at Risk?" *Population Research and Policy Review*, vol. 11 (1992), pp. 157–68.

[68] Rhoads, *The Economist's View of the World* (*supra* note 63), p. 57.

If offsetting behavior does exist, the question in evaluating whether mandatory seat belt legislation saves lives turns on whether the gains through greater probability of surviving a crash are offset by more crashes, or crashes of greater severity, or other new fatalities resulting from riskier behavior. Again, the evidence is contradictory. Garbacz finds that in- creased fatalities by rear-seat passengers more than outweigh the gains of greater safety of front-seat passengers,[69] while Harvey and Durbin find some increased risk for rear-seat passengers, pedestrians, and cyclists, but argue that it is not significant, and certainly does not outweigh the gains to front-seat belt wearers.[70] Although most studies have concluded that the gains outweigh the costs,[71] it is noteworthy that the reported gains are almost always much more modest than earlier test crashes of dummies would have suggested, providing support for the offsetting-behavior hy- pothesis.[72] There is also a wide, though not a complete, consensus that mandatory seat belt legislation has made life more risky for pedestrians[73] and cyclists.[74]

As I said, an examination of the literature reveals a much more ambig- uous picture than the nearly universal perception that mandatory seat belt legislation saves lives. Alan Irwin's detailed study of the British debate on seat belt legislation is especially interesting in this regard. In 1979, a lecturer in geography, John Adams, published work claiming that mandatory seat belt legislation did not increase safety. His work spurred a number of studies—and personal attacks—reaching the opposite con- clusion; in response, Adams undertook further studies which supported his original claims. Partly because of the dispute, the United Kingdom undertook a "great experiment" in 1983: a three-year trial mandatory seat belt law. The evidence was reviewed in 1986; studies found a net safety advantage, though of considerably less magnitude than had been pre- dicted by proponents of the legislation—an observation made by *The Lancet*, generally a pro-compulsion journal.[75] For all practical purposes, however, the debate ceased, with Parliament overwhelmingly approving a renewal of the mandatory seat belt legislation. Irwin observes that,

[69] Garbacz, "Do Front-Seat Belt Laws Put Rear-Seat Passengers at Risk?"
[70] Harvey and Durbin, "The Effects of Seat Belt Legislation on British Road Deaths" (*supra* note 66).
[71] Rhoads, *The Economist's View of the World*, p. 57.
[72] Alan Irwin, "Technical Expertise and Risk Conflict: An Institutional Study of the British Compulsory Seat Belt Debate," *Policy Sciences*, vol. 20 (1987), pp. 339–64; Ryan and Bridge- man, "Judging the Roles of Legislation, Education, and Offsetting Behaviour in Seat Belt Use" (*supra* note 66), p. 32. For an exception, see M. N. Bhattacharyya and Allan P. Layton, "Effectiveness of Seat Belt Legislation on the Queensland Road Toll," *Journal of the American Statistical Association*, vol. 74 (September 1974), pp. 596–603.
[73] Rhoads, *The Economist's View of the World* (*supra* note 63), p. 239, n. 65.
[74] The Cyclists Touring Club and the British Cycling Federation opposed renewal of mandatory seat belt legislation in the United Kingdom in 1986. See Irwin, "Technical Ex- pertise and Risk Conflict," p. 359.
[75] *Ibid.*, pp. 359–60.

though the results of the trial were disappointingly ambiguous, the "paradox" of the trial was "its political success in closing debate *despite* its shaky methodological basis and the undeniable technical arguments that remained."[76] Irwin provides a sociological and institutional explanation of how public policy closure occurred despite the obvious *lack* of closure of the technical issue. Even pursuing an extremely simple goal with a relatively straightforward problem, we remain uncertain as to whether the public policy achieves its end.

My point here is twofold. First, there is indeed significant conflicting evidence about the effectiveness of mandatory seat belt legislation in saving lives, both concerning the direction of its net effects and the magnitude of any safety gains. Second, the fact that most advanced industrial societies have experienced a closure on this debate is not indicative of the extent of our knowledge, but, as Irwin argues, importantly depends on the perceptions of certain sorts of technical experts and the organizations supporting them.

And of course, "saving lives" is much too simple a policy goal. After all, if our ultimate goal was saving lives, we would probably prohibit all private cars, alcohol, contact sports, swimming, and wooden structures. There is more to welfare than not dying. Still, it seems that there is a clear and important welfare issue here: for most of us, dying is obviously welfare-decreasing. But even if we assume for now that seat belts save lives and this increases welfare, we are still confronted by the problem that mandatory seat belt legislation is a pure welfare loss to everyone who does not get into a serious auto accident. And without a doubt some welfare losses are involved in mandatory seat belt legislation: liberty is an important welfare interest that is clearly being sacrificed. The idea that the state can promote our interests and not count as a cost the blocking of our preferences drastically oversimplifies the problem: a cost of any paternalistic policy is that it forces people to do things for their own good, and so overrides their own choice. The welfare-state policymaker thus must be able to provide good evidence that in this case the number of lives saved justifies the overriding of many people's choices. But this seems impossible. First, as we have just seen, the net gain in lives saved from seat-belt legislation is extremely difficult to gauge. Secondly, although the people who die suffer huge welfare losses, and it is only a very tiny welfare loss to be forced to wear a seat belt, it seems quite impossible to compare the billions of tiny welfare losses (each car trip by each person that does not end in an accident) with thousands of huge welfare losses. It is an annoying arithmetical truth that the result of multiplying a very tiny number by a huge number can be greater than multiplying a huge number by a small number. I see no way to make this calculation or guess its outcome.

---

[76] *Ibid.*, p. 360.

A promising response is to focus on the *risk* of death rather than actual road deaths. If being exposed to risk itself decreases welfare, then every time a person travels without a seat belt, this decreases her welfare whether or not she is involved in an accident. And thus the billions of trips that do not result in accidents involve welfare losses too. Suppose, then, that the reasoning of the public policy maker runs something like this: (1) it is a clear welfare gain to decrease severe risks to citizens; (2) mandatory seat belt legislation does so, since it decreases deaths per thousand. There is considerable evidence that (2) is indeed the favored understanding of risk reduction by technocrats—that risk levels can largely be expressed in terms of deaths per thousand. However, citizens do not seem to perceive things so simply. Factor analyses of people's attitudes toward risk indicate two clear dimensions to risk perception: what Paul Slovic calls "dread risk" and "unknown risk." Dread risk involves an absence of control, potentially fatal or catastrophic consequences that are not equitably distributed; nuclear technology scores as very risky on this dimension. Unknown risk, in contrast, is characterized by "hazards judged to be unobservable, unknown, new, and delayed in their manifestation."[77] Electrical fields, DNA technology, and X-rays all rate as very "risky" on this dimension.

The upshot is that the goal of increasing welfare through risk reduction is by no means straightforward, as it is not at all straightforward just what constitutes a risk. Slovic reports that research demonstrates that lay people's risk perceptions are closely related to how high a risk scores on these two dimensions:

> Most important is . . . dread risk. The higher a hazard's score is on this factor . . . the higher its perceived risk will be, the more people will want to see its current risks reduced, and the more they will want strict regulation used to achieve the desired reduction in risk. . . . In contrast, experts' perceptions of risk are not closely related to any of the various risk characteristics or factors derived from those characteristics. . . . Instead, . . . experts appear to see riskiness as synonymous with expected annual mortality. . . . As a result, conflicts over "risk" may result from experts and lay people having different definitions of the concept.[78]

The very idea of risk is multidimensional, and thus any policy of reducing risk will have to weigh the various factors; but people disagree about the relative importance of the dimensions (e.g., policymakers and citizens), and thus there will always be uncertainty about whether any policy—

[77] Paul Slovic, "Beyond Numbers: A Broader Perspective on Risk Perception and Risk Communication," in *Acceptable Evidence*, ed. Deborah G. Mayo and Rachelle D. Hollander (New York: Oxford University Press, 1991), pp. 48–65.
[78] *Ibid.*, pp. 57–59.

about nuclear waste disposal, electrical fields, controlling DNA technology, nitrites, or reducing road deaths—actually reduces risk. There is no uncontroversial or clear case for any given policy linking risk reduction to welfare maximization. Citizens disagree among themselves, and their perceptions differ in systematic ways from those of the experts making policy. In the face of these uncertainties policymakers are apt to assert that the public is deluded, and that risk assessments and policies should be made on the basis of mortality rates. But this only supplants the reasonable views of citizens with a technocratic understanding of risk.

C. Approximations, rules, and other ways to cope with the "limits of reason"

It is commonly objected that all this is nit-picking: although there are disagreements about details, we know well enough, in a basic way, what promotes welfare. We know, for instance, that food, shelter, and medical care are crucial to welfare. Taking these rough measures, we can maximize *them*, knowing that they are usable rough-and-ready stand-ins or approximations for maximizing welfare.[79] Thus, it is said, by using devices such as rules and rough indexes, welfare-promoting public policy makers can operate within the "limits of reason."[80] The apparent reasonableness of such proposals is illusory. Because we have no reliable idea of what would maximize utility (or best promote social goals), we have no reliable estimates about what rules, policies, or institutions are good approximations of the goal. As Hayek has famously observed, this justification for rules presupposes just what it is trying not to presuppose: knowledge of what will promote utility.[81] For this rough-and-ready criterion of welfare to be useful, we still have to know that seeking some "stand-in" or proxy (e.g., providing shelter) is a fairly good way to maximize, or at least promote, welfare, W. But if we cannot get any workable handle on W and the likely W-consequences of various alternative policies, we have no basis for judging how well our various proxies for welfare serve us. If we were in the position to make intelligent judgments of the desirability of different proxies, we would not need them so badly, for we would have access to some reasonable way to calculate utilities. But if our problem is that we do not have access to W, it hardly can be solved by saying that we should seek stand-ins which are good approximations of W. Utilitarians generally assume that the goods we secure and the rules we follow are pretty good from a utilitarian point of view, while

---

[79] Griffin, *Well-Being* (*supra* note 45), pp. 121–24.
[80] See Goodin, *Utilitarianism as a Public Philosophy* (*supra* note 2), p. 17; Russell Hardin, *Morality within the Limits of Reason* (Chicago: University of Chicago Press, 1988).
[81] Friedrich A. von Hayek, *The Mirage of Social Justice* (Chicago: University of Chicago Press, 1976), p. 20.

James Griffin seems content to rely on legislators' "guesses" on these matters. Neither stance seems compelling.

Nevertheless, it might be insisted, we can make pairwise comparisons of social policies, even if we do not know the best. However, because we have no reliable idea of the total consequences of major social policies or social institutions, we are not even in a position to make accurate one-on-one comparisons. And even if we could reasonably conclude that P_1 is better than P_2, without having any clear idea about what would maximize social utility, we have no clear idea of whether these are two relatively bad options or two relatively good ones. If my aim is to get from Los Angeles to New York, knowing that route α takes me closer to New York than route β is hardly a guide to action if α gets me as far as San Bernardino, still beating β, which leaves me in Pasadena. Since neither really gets me any significant distance to my goal, I might as well do something else. Thus, we are seldom in a position to determine whether one option is "good enough," if this means that it does a relatively good job in getting us where we want to go.[82]

D. Political responsibility and doing one's best

All these problems are often duly noted, though seldom appreciated. Keeney and Raiffa begin their classic *Decisions with Multiple Objectives* by stating that "[i]n an uncertain world the responsible decision maker must balance judgments about uncertainties with his or her preferences for possible consequences or outcomes. It's not easy to do and, even though we all have a lot of practice, we are not very good at it."[83] Nevertheless, they insist that although "the methodological issues these points raise are devilish to work with ... decisions must be made."[84] To Goodin it is "almost indecent" for policymakers not to pursue welfare. He writes:

> It is in the nature of public officials' role responsibilities that they are morally obliged to "dirty their hands" —make hard choices, do things that are wrong (or would ordinarily be wrong, ...) in the service of some greater public good. It would be simply irresponsible of public officials (in any broadly secular society, at least) to adhere mindlessly to moral precepts read off some sacred list, literally "whatever the consequences." Doing right though the heavens should fall is not

---

[82] For a recent defense of this "satisficing" conception of reason, see Schmidtz, *Rational Choice and Moral Agency* (*supra* note 19), Part I. For a brief discussion, see my review of Schmidtz's book in the *American Political Science Review*, vol. 90, no. 1 (March 1996), pp. 179–80. The basic idea, of course, derives from Simon, *Administrative Behavior* (*supra* note 56).

[83] Keeney and Raiffa, *Decisions with Multiple Objectives* (*supra* note 53), p. 1.

[84] *Ibid.*, p. 20.

(nowadays, anyway) a particularly attractive posture for public officials to adopt.[85]

Keeney, Raiffa, and Goodin all invoke the idea of a "responsible" policymaker, echoing Max Weber's analysis in his famous essay "Politics as a Vocation." Weber contrasts what he (somewhat confusingly) calls the "ethic of ultimate ends" with the "ethic of responsibility." The ethic of ultimate ends "does rightly and leaves the results with the Lord,"[86] while the ethic of responsibility takes responsibility for the consequences of what is done. Weber and Goodin suggest that in politics the ethic of responsibility is appropriate: it is normally irresponsible in politics not to pursue the best consequences. We do not want squeamish politicians, acting according to their preferred moral principles and ignoring consequences. Thus, Weber and Goodin argue, whatever the problems of seeking the best consequences, politics offers no other options.

That we feel that we must do something does not show that it is reasonable to do anything. Responsibility should not be confused with wishful thinking. If we are not in a position to effectively act, it hardly is a sign of responsibility to act anyway. Of course, theorists and politicians believe they understand society and can predict the effects of their policies, but there is good reason to think they are simply deluded. The work of cognitive psychologists such as Amos Tversky and Daniel Kahneman indicates that people consistently ascribe high levels of probability to very faulty predictions. Indeed, they report that "subjects are most confident in predictions that are most likely to be off the mark."[87] "[P]eople are prone to experience much confidence in highly fallible judgments, a phenomenon that might be called the *illusion of validity*."[88] This, of course, does not show that their judgments are wrong, but it does indicate that the confidence with which policymakers act on their predictions of future events tells us very little, if anything, about whether those predictions are well grounded. Policymakers may believe it is necessary to make such judgments, and may convince themselves that they can, but this tells us little about the accuracy of (to use Griffin's description) their "guesses." Over the wide range of public policy—which includes much foreign policy, social policy, and, alas, economic policy—policymakers may be quite convinced that it is necessary to pursue good consequences, and may think they can do it, but nevertheless are apt to be quite deluded. In this sort of case it seems to me useless to say they *must* maximize good consequences.

[85] Goodin, *Utilitarianism as a Public Philosophy* (*supra* note 2), p. 10 (footnotes omitted).
[86] Max Weber, "Politics as a Vocation," in *From Max Weber: Essays in Sociology*, ed. H. H. Gerth and C. Wright Mills (New York: Oxford University Press, 1946), p. 120.
[87] Daniel Kahneman and Amos Tversky, "On the Psychology of Prediction," in *Judgment under Uncertainty* (*supra* note 59), p. 66.
[88] *Ibid.*

E. The salience of rules and principles

Although Weber stresses the importance of pursuing good consequences, he also appreciates that rules and principles are relevant: at
some point his politician proclaims, "Here I stand, I can do no other" —
something that Goodin's "government house utilitarian" never seems to
utter.[89] An appreciation of the radical epistemic limits of pursuing social
goals suggests that, *pace* Weber, it is rules and principles that are typically
salient in public life. We may have very little idea about how to control
drug addiction, but a commitment to individual liberty gives us a clear
direction. This is not to say that the principle of individual liberty is more
important than reducing addiction or controlling crime. Much the same
can be said about a wide range of policies, both domestic and foreign.[90]
The point is that once we appreciate how gross is our ignorance about
how to advance these goals, and thus how unlikely it is that we can
effectively promote them, we are pushed into area R on Figure 1, where
principled action is uniquely reasonable. It may well be that these goals
are vastly more important than the principles, and that in politics a trade-
off function along the lines of C on Figure 1 is demanded of the "responsible" politician. But even if we grant this much of the Weberian conception
of the vocation of politics, we still typically find ourselves in area R,
where even the reasonable goal-devotee must act on rules.

Up to this point the argument leads in the direction of principled,
rather than goal-oriented, government action; thus far the argument is a
general one, supporting the reasonableness of government action based
on Catholic principles rather than Catholic goals, Marxist principles rather
than Marxist goals, or liberal principles rather than liberal goals. Just
what sorts of principled action are justified is not only a matter for a
theory of reason in action, it also depends on moral theory, showing what
sorts of principles can be justified. I shall not try to provide such a theory
here, though elsewhere I have tried to justify liberal principles;[91] at least
in the context of an analysis of the problems of market liberalism, we can
take for granted that basic liberal principles such as the rights to liberty,
property, privacy, and bodily integrity have been justified. Now in public
life these liberal principles are almost always relevant. If so, then unless
a goal is salient, a reasonable legislator will act to respect these rights.
And, I have argued, since goals typically are not salient, reasonable liberal
legislators will normally act to respect rights rather than seek goals. This
is not because we know these rights are always more important than

---

[89] Weber, "Politics as a Vocation" (*supra* note 86), p. 127. See also Charles Larmore, *Patterns of Moral Complexity* (Cambridge: Cambridge University Press, 1987), pp. 144–53.

[90] For a foreign policy case, see S. I. Benn, "Deterrence or Appeasement? or, On Trying to Be Rational about Nuclear War," *Journal of Applied Philosophy*, vol. 1 (1984), pp. 5–19.

[91] See my *Value and Justification*, ch. 8 (*supra* note 22) and *Justificatory Liberalism: An Essay on Epistemology and Political Theory* (New York: Oxford University Press, 1996), ch. 10.

social goals and projects; it is because our uncertainty about the consequences of policy decisions renders most social goals not salient in the deliberations of reasonable legislators and "policymakers." This is not to say, of course, that we always agree on principles or that we never need to make trade-offs of one principle against another. I have argued elsewhere that these are precisely the sorts of disputes that characterize the politics of the Liberal *Rechtstaat*.[92]

It should be stressed that it is no part of my claim that governments can never reasonably pursue goals. If pursuit of a goal is normatively justified in our pluralistic societies, and if we can predict with a high degree of reliability what policies will further that goal, and if we can be confident that those assigned with implementing the policy will do so in an effective way, then the goal is justified and salient, and a moral, reasonable legislator may act on it—though we still have to consider what should be done if it conflicts with a principle. Some believe that these conditions are met quite often. I am skeptical, though of course I too accept that sometimes they are. Some goods may be truly public goods, and it may be manifest that policies to achieve these, and so promote the good of all, are reasonable.[93] The more modest our goals, the easier it is to act reasonably on them. Suppose our goal is not welfare, but simply economic growth; and suppose a state has a choice only between a Soviet-style command economy and a market economy. Here a reasonable politician will act to implement the latter. But when we consider the variety of goal-oriented policy disputes in advanced industrial societies today—about regulations to achieve health goals; policies to secure environmental goals; family policies to secure welfare; criminal law to secure safety and/or welfare; educational reforms (where it is often not clear just what the relevant goals are; apparently anything from beating the Japanese to achieving a satisfying life for the child); economic policies about micro-reforms in market economies to produce growth, or promote welfare—a reasonable legislator will, I think, usually put aside these goals and look instead to liberal rules of right to guide her.

V. THE MARKET, GOAL PURSUIT, AND WELFARE

It may seem that this conclusion constitutes a *reductio* of my analysis insofar as it seems always unreasonable or irrational to pursue goals, and thus we are always committed to acting on rules and principles. The absurd picture is conjured up of a starving Kantian—always acting on rules but never acting to pursue the goal of feeding herself. Surely goal pursuit is crucial to life.

[92] See my *Justificatory Liberalism*, Parts II and III.
[93] See *ibid.*, pp. 209–11.

Of course pursuing goals and values is central to life. What I have doubted is that it is typically a rational and reasonable activity when undertaken by the state. The rule of law structures the pursuit of goals by private individuals and associations, most notably in the market. As the classical political economists emphasized, the legal framework provides the rules within which the market operates. Agents acting in this framework operate in something like Area G on Figure 1—a moral-rule-free zone, in which rationality demands that they pursue their values.[94] In the market, people can effectively pursue their relatively specific personal or institutional goals because the market disperses information, allowing each person to obtain and use the information that will be useful in pursuing his particular goals. The market, as the Austrian economists have taught us, allows us to cope with our constitutional ignorance by dispersing information as well as "responsibility" for achieving specific goals. Admittedly individuals in the market also face uncertainty about the future and the consequences of their actions. But this uncertainty is typically much more limited or "bounded"—individuals are warranted in concluding that, despite the uncertainties they face, they can normally identify options that effectively achieve their goals.[95] This is not to say that individuals in a market order are always in a position to decide which options are rational and reasonable to pursue, much less that they always attain their goals. But the dispersion of responsibility for goal pursuit (making each the locus of decisions for her own goals) and the dispersion of relevant information, renders goal-directed action vastly more salient. Moreover, we have excellent grounds for believing that, in a rough way, the market allows for more efficient pursuit of goals than does any command economy or system where prices are set by central authorities. In general, in a market where prices are set by consumer demand, more people will achieve more of their goals than in alternative economic arrangements.

This said, we need to be very modest about the claims we can make concerning the welfare consequences of market order: sweeping judgments about the maximization of human welfare in certain sorts of markets seems a dubious enterprise indeed. For one thing, the constituents of human welfare are themselves complex, and there is reasonable dispute about the preferred conception of welfare. If, say, it is crucial to human welfare that people appreciate classical music, or become philosophers, then the market may not do a particularly good job at promoting human welfare thus understood. Moreover, even if we agree on what human welfare is, it is extremely hard to gauge the long-term consequences of our activity. Suppose we accept a mundane notion of welfare, as at least

[94] See David Gauthier, *Morals by Agreement* (Oxford: Clarendon Press, 1986), ch. 4.
[95] See Kirzner, *The Meaning of Market Process* (*supra* note 20), pp. 24-25. See also Simon, *Reason in Human Affairs* (*supra* note 29), pp. 19-23.

involving health, food, and security; and suppose further, as is by no means impossible, that there is indeed a greenhouse effect, and that it turns out to be surprisingly strong, such that human society in the next century experiences widespread and intense suffering because of climatic change. If this does happen, then a world of regulated economies that banned fossil fuel in the 1950s might have done better in pursuing welfare. As far as I can see, this is a possibility; and its realization would seriously undermine welfare claims about a free market. Of course, things may well turn out very differently. As is typically the case, we do not know.

Welfarist advocates of the market might reply to this that, if we put aside large-scale dynamic considerations, and look instead at a relatively static situation, we can at least say that the market is efficient at satisfying preferences, and therefore maximizes welfare understood *that* way. Now we can certainly say that a perfectly competitive market is efficient in the requisite sense, but the relevance of that axiom of economics to actual economies, with a variety of information constraints and restraints on competition, is not at all clear.[96] *Pace* neoclassical economics, we do not have any clear idea of what an optimum in our society would look like, and thus we could never know if we had come close to achieving it.[97] And if we do not have any clear idea about the goal, we have very little idea about what would approximate it, and so whether our actual market societies do a good job of achieving it.

Thus, although the market is indeed the realm of rational goal pursuit, and although the Liberal *Rechtstaat* provides the framework that allows individuals to pursue their "welfare" in this way, it is wrong to see the Liberal *Rechtstaat* as resting on the claim that it provides the structure for society to maximize welfare through the market. As I pointed out at the beginning of this essay, this too is a "welfare-state" claim. Although the state does not directly pursue interventionist policies to promote welfare, the claim is nevertheless that the laws of the liberal state are devices for welfare maximization. They are said to be the laws that are necessary for the political framework that allows the market to do its work. But this raises all the uncertainties I have been pressing in this essay. What we can say, I think, is that liberal principles of freedom and private property

---

[96] I am indebted here to Julian Lamont, whose forthcoming work on this topic promises to clear up a variety of confusions about efficiency judgments of real-world economies.

[97] I believe my views here are consistent with the "middle ground" of Austrian economics as well as the radical views of G. L. S. Shackle. For a defense of the middle ground, see Kirzner, *The Meaning of Market Process* (*supra* note 20), ch. 1. For Shackle, see his *Epistemics and Economics* (*supra* note 55), and his *Decision, Order, and Time in Human Affairs* (Cambridge: Cambridge University Press, 1969). See also Terence W. Hutchinson, "Philosophical Issues that Divide Liberals: Omniscience or Omni-nescience about the Future?" in *Subjectivism, Intelligibility, and Economic Understanding*, ed. Israel M. Kirzner (New York: New York University Press, 1986), ch. 10.

justify a market order,[98] and reasonable legislators will act to respect these rights; moreover, we have good grounds for thinking that if left to their own devices in the market, more people and institutions will achieve more of their specific personal and institutional goals than if government tries to direct their activity. This, I believe, is a morally powerful and reasonable case for a market order. To go "beyond" this, to insist that it is the best way to promote human welfare, and that the job of the liberal state is to protect and structure the market so that it can achieve its welfarist goals, is yet another route to irrational or unreasonable government action.

I have been granting up until now that laissez-faire and interventionist welfarism are distinct doctrines, though ones that share a common foundation. A closer examination, I think, shows that this common welfarist perspective tends to blur the distinction between the two. The classical-liberal welfarist argument paves the way for the common claim that "market failure" justifies state action.[99] The case for the classical-liberal welfare state presupposes that we can make rational estimates of human welfare, and can say that a market order promotes it. But if so, when the market is "disorderly"[100] there is at least a prima facie case for some adjustment in the rules to increase welfare. In their pursuit of welfare, even the classical political economists were willing to endorse a number of interventionist policies, such as the licensing of professionals,[101] health, safety, and fire regulations,[102] and banking regulations.[103] And Hayek too, in *The Road to Serfdom*, slipped into this welfarist reasoning, telling us that, when debating whether to introduce legislation to prohibit the "use of certain poisonous substances" or to "limit working hours," the "only question here is whether in the particular instance the advantages gained are greater than the social costs they impose."[104] Although they often disagree deeply about the facts, classical and interventionist welfare liberals concur about the aim of government and the justification of coercive

[98] See my "A Contractual Justification of Redistributive Capitalism," in *NOMOS XXXI: Markets and Justice*, ed. John W. Chapman and J. Roland Pennock (New York: New York University Press, 1989), pp. 89–121.

[99] "The principal justification for public policy lies in the frequent and numerous short-comings of market outcomes." Wolf, *Markets or Governments* (*supra* note 61), p. 17. Wolf, however, is far more aware than most that "the policy implications of market imperfections may be ambiguous" (p. 27).

[100] Kirzner, *The Meaning of Market Process* (*supra* note 20), p. 58.

[101] McCulloch, *Principles of Political Economy* (*supra* note 3), p. 228; Jean Baptiste Say, *A Treatise on Political Economy* (New York: A. M. Kelley, 1964), p. 181.

[102] McCulloch, *Principles of Political Economy*, pp. 129, 226–30. See also Lionel Robbins, *The Theory of Economic Policy in English Classical Political Economy* (London: Macmillan, 1961), pp. 88–93.

[103] David Ricardo, *On the Principles of Political Economy and Taxation*, ed. Piero Sraffa (Cambridge: Cambridge University Press, 1951), pp. 356–57; D. P. O'Brien, *The Classical Economists* (Oxford: Clarendon, 1975), pp. 274–75.

[104] Hayek, *The Road to Serfdom* (*supra* note 11), p. 43.

interventions; in a complex social world in which the facts of the matter are so murky, it can be surprisingly difficult to distinguish the two.

VI. CONCLUSION

Let me sum up this somewhat complicated argument. I began in Section I by distinguishing conceptions of the liberal state. The first, welfare-state view insists that the justification of the liberal state turns on its claim to achieve, either directly or indirectly, the goal of making humans better off. I stressed that this conception of the welfare state is considerably broader than that which occupies the traditional debate between classical and revisionist liberals, for classical liberals who maintain that a minimal state is justified because it provides the framework for the market to advance human welfare also qualify as welfare-state liberals; their liberalism is welfarist at its foundation. I contrasted this welfarist view to the Liberal *Rechtstaat*, according to which the liberal state is primarily guided by "end-independent" rules of right. As I pointed out, many believe this latter view is irrational or unreasonable: if the liberal state does not make us better off, how can it possibly be justified?

Section II explored the basis of this intuition: goal rationality. If rationality is characterized as goal pursuit, then a "goal-independent" rule will certainly seem irrational. After explicating this idea of goal pursuit, I contrasted it with another aspect of rationality—rule rationality—which, I have tried to show, cannot be reduced to the pursuit of goals. A rational agent must have some way to trade off goals and rules; a rational trade-off rate, I maintained in Section III, will take account of two factors: the relative importance of the rule(s) and goal(s) at stake, and their relative salience—to what extent each is "at stake" in a particular choice. In situations where both a goal and a rule are relevant, but one or the other is only marginally salient while the other is crucially salient, I argued that it is fanatical or outlandish—thus not *reasonable*—to act on the marginally or minimally salient consideration. Given this, I argued in Section IV that, because of the radical uncertainty of predicting the consequences of government policies designed to promote social goals, it is typically unreasonable for government to pursue them: the goals are much less salient than liberal rules and principles. To, as it were, drive this point home, I examined a policy goal which everyone seems to agree that government has attained: the reduction of traffic fatalities through mandatory seat belt legislation. Despite the apparent closure of this as a public policy issue, I tried to show that as a matter of social science the issue is not closed: not only the magnitude of the effect of such legislation, but the direction of its net effect, is still unclear. The closure of this issue, I indicated, is more of a sociological phenomenon than a scientific one. Now if even a simple, "closed" issue such as the effects of seat belt legislation on reducing traffic fatalities is unclear, it should not be surprising that the effects of hotly disputed practices, developments, and policies of today—economic policy, energy policy, DNA technology, ozone depletion, climatic change, street crime, pornography, minimum-wage legislation, educational policy—are deeply in doubt. It must be emphasized that I do not claim that we are uncertain about how to achieve all goals: if the goal is either broad and modest enough ("Do not cause immediate economic collapse") or specific enough ("Build more prisons"), we can achieve it. But if our goals are sophisticated—like improving human welfare, strengthening the family, making urban life safe—then it will typically be the case that they are not salient.

A rational and reasonable liberal state, then, should generally eschew the field of "public policy," understood as the government's pursuit of desirable social goals. This is not, of course, to say that goals should not be sought: as I argued in Section V, individuals and institutions can effectively pursue their specific goals in the market and in their private lives. Again, though, liberals should be cautious about the claims they make for the market. Claims that the market best advances human welfare or that our actual markets embody efficiency are open to the same epistemic doubts as are statist claims about government's ability to achieve good results. Because we live in a complex world, and because that complexity increases tremendously when we focus on society as a whole, the rational and reasonable legislator will normally do the right thing, leaving it up to individuals to seek their own goals in their own way.

Philosophy and Political Science, University of Minnesota, Duluth

MEASURING OPPORTUNITY: TOWARD
A CONTRACTARIAN MEASURE
OF INDIVIDUAL INTEREST*

BY ROBERT SUGDEN

I. INTRODUCTION

Liberals have often been attracted by contractarian modes of argument—
and with good reason. Any system of social organization requires that
some constraints be imposed on individuals' freedom of action; it is a
central problem for any liberal political theory to show which constraints
can be justified, and which cannot. A contractarian justification works by
showing that the constraints in question can be understood as if they
were the product of an agreement, voluntarily entered into by every
member of society. Thus, no one is required to give up his freedom for
someone else's benefit, or in the pursuit of someone else's conception of
the social good.

Contractarian arguments fit well with a Humean account of the primacy of passion over reason. From a Humean point of view, there are no
ends—whether for the individual or for society as a whole—that are
prescribed by reason. There are only desires. Thus, if we are to justify a
constraint to the person who is to be constrained, we need to show that
in some way the constraint helps him to satisfy his own desires. Contractarian arguments do this by showing that each person's acceptance of
certain constraints is a necessary part of a social scheme whose general
tendency is to satisfy everyone's desires. In this essay, I shall work within
a Humean framework, taking it as given that there are no rationally
prescribed ends.

This essay identifies a general problem in contractarian theory. The
usual strategy for showing that everyone could agree to a particular set of
rules is to show that, over the long run, those rules can be expected to
work in the interests of each individual. This requires some unit of account in which to measure an individual's interests or well-being. Most
economists, and some contractarian philosophers, have used each person's preferences as the fundamental measure of his or her well-being. I
shall argue that this strategy runs into serious problems if individuals'
actual preferences are unstable, or if they fail to satisfy the conditions of
"coherence" that economists usually assume. There are, I shall claim, no

* This essay was written as part of the Risk and Human Behaviour Programme of the
Economic and Social Research Council of the UK (award number L 211 252 053).

adequate *a priori* grounds for assuming preferences to be stable or coherent, and there is a lot of evidence to suggest that, in fact, the opposite is often the case.

The need for a measure of interest is quite obvious in explicitly contractarian theories, such as those proposed by James Buchanan and David Gauthier, which are based on principles of rational choice.[1] Less obviously, there are liberal theories that might be characterized as implicitly contractarian, which also depend on measures of interest.

For example, consider David Hume's account of why justice—by which he means the disposition to observe established rules of property—is a virtue. He notes that individual acts of justice, considered in isolation, are frequently contrary both to the private interest of the actor and to the public interest. Nevertheless,

> however single acts of justice may be contrary, either to public or private interest, 'tis certain, that the whole plan or scheme is highly conducive, or indeed absolutely requisite, both to the support of society, and the well-being of every individual. . . . Tho' in one instance the public be a sufferer, this momentary ill is amply compensated by the steady prosecution of the rule, and by the peace and order which it establishes in society. And even every individual person must find himself a gainer, on balancing the account; since, without justice, society must immediately dissolve, and every one must fall into that savage and solitary condition, which is infinitely worse than the worst situation that can possibly be suppos'd in society.[2]

Here, Hume is claiming that the rules of a free society can be expected to work in the interests of every individual; but he does not tell us how to measure those interests. He writes about "balancing the account"; but what account is being balanced? (Admittedly, Hume makes things easy for himself by suggesting that the only alternative to the rules of justice is a Hobbesian state of nature; but that move seems suspect.)

Or consider Friedrich von Hayek's argument for a free society in *Law, Legislation, and Liberty*. The second volume of this work opens with the words: "It is an axiom of the tradition of freedom that coercion of individuals is permissible only where it is necessary in the service of the general welfare or the public good." What, then, is the general welfare? According to Hayek, the role of public policy is to serve the general welfare by "creating conditions likely to improve the chances of all in the pursuit of their aims." The rules of a free society (Hayek calls it a Great Society) are justified because they create such conditions:

---

[1] James M. Buchanan, *The Limits of Liberty* (Chicago: University of Chicago Press, 1975); David Gauthier, *Morals by Agreement* (Oxford: Oxford University Press, 1986).

[2] David Hume, *A Treatise of Human Nature* (Oxford: Clarendon Press, 1978), p. 497, first published 1740.

Among the members of a Great Society who mostly do not know
each other, there will exist no agreement on the relative importance
of their respective ends. There would exist not harmony but open
conflict of interests if agreement were necessary as to which particular interests should be given preference over others. What makes
agreement and peace in such a society possible is that the individuals
are not required to agree on ends but only on means which are
capable of serving a great variety of purposes and which each hopes
will assist him in the pursuit of his own purposes.[3]

Hayek, like Hume, is claiming that the rules of a free society can be
expected to work to everyone's advantage, and thus can be justified as
principles on which everyone could agree.[4] As a unit of account for advantage, Hayek seems to be using some kind of metric of life chances; but
the nature of that metric is left unclear.

The object of this essay is to look for a measure of interest or well-being
which can be used in contractarian theories, and which does not depend
on untenable assumptions about individuals' preferences. However, I
shall begin with what may seem to be a digression.

Many recent discussions of well-being have been constructed as critiques of *welfarism*—the preference-based approach to normative analysis
that is conventional in economics. Because of this, it will be useful to start
with a critical look at the way that welfarism uses preference to measure
well-being. I shall then argue that some of the criticisms that can be made
of welfarism apply also to a preference-based contractarian measure of
well-being. Finally, I shall offer some suggestions about an alternative
approach, based on the idea of measuring opportunities. These suggestions will be much less concrete than I would like, but the problem of
measuring opportunity has only recently begun to be studied in any
depth.[5]

II. WELFARISM AND ITS PROBLEMS

Until fairly recently, there was a clear consensus about the proper way
to structure normative analysis within economics. The object of normative analysis, it was thought, was to compare alternative states of affairs
for a given society. Each such state of affairs was seen as giving some level
of individual welfare to each member of the society, and some level of

[3] Friedrich A. von Hayek, *Law, Legislation, and Liberty*, vol. 2: *The Mirage of Social Justice*
(Chicago: University of Chicago Press, 1976), pp. 2–3.
[4] I offer a general reading of Hayek's social theory as implicit contractarianism in Robert
Sugden, "Normative Judgments and Spontaneous Order: The Contractarian Element in
Hayek's Thought," *Constitutional Political Economy*, vol. 4 (1993), pp. 393–424.
[5] In a parallel paper, I review some of the main proposals that have been made up to now:
see Robert Sugden, "The Metric of Opportunity," *Economics and Philosophy* (forthcoming
1998).

social welfare to the society as a whole. The relationship between social welfare and the welfare of individuals was described by a "social welfare function"; social welfare was taken to increase as any individual's welfare increased (other things remaining equal). Each individual's welfare was identified with his or her utility, utility indices being understood as representations of the individual's preferences. This framework is usually interpreted as embodying two normative principles. First, society has no independent moral status: the good of society is nothing more than the good of the individuals who comprise it. Second, there is the principle that John Harsanyi calls *preference autonomy*: "in deciding what is good and what is bad for a given individual, the ultimate criterion can only be his own wants and his own preferences."[6]

This way of structuring normative analysis has come to be called welfarism. The intellectual roots of welfarism are clearly utilitarian; indeed, Kenneth Arrow has suggested the name "ordinal utilitarianism" as an alternative to "welfarism."[7] For a classical utilitarian, the good of society is nothing more than the sum of the goods of its component individuals: as Jeremy Bentham put it: "The community is a fictitious body."[8] This is what I have called the first principle of welfarism.[9] Further, classical utilitarians hold that in deciding what is good or bad for a given individual, the ultimate criterion must be his happiness. At first sight, this seems very close to the second principle of welfarism. Clearly, the classical and ordinal utilitarian versions of this principle would be equivalent if each individual always preferred those things that gave him most happiness.

However, first impressions are deceptive. The switch from using happiness to using preferences as the measure of goodness is a major change, which threatens to make the whole utilitarian framework incoherent. That this is so has been argued particularly clearly by Thomas Scanlon; related arguments are put forward by John Broome, James Griffin, and Daniel Hausman and Michael McPherson.[10] What follows is my own version of the argument, written from the perspective of an economist.

[6] John C. Harsanyi, "Morality and the Theory of Rational Behaviour," in *Utilitarianism and Beyond*, ed. Amartya Sen and Bernard Williams (Cambridge: Cambridge University Press, 1982).

[7] Kenneth J. Arrow, "Some Ordinalist-Utilitarian Notes on Rawls's Theory of Justice," *Journal of Philosophy*, vol. 7 (1973), pp. 245–63.

[8] Jeremy Bentham, *An Introduction to the Principles of Morals and Legislation* (London: Athlone Press, 1970), ch. 1, first published 1789.

[9] Strictly speaking, the utilitarian principle I have stated is stronger than the first principle of welfarism, since the latter does not require that the aggregation of individuals' goods is an arithmetic sum. Welfarism allows any increasing function of individual welfare levels to count as a social-welfare function.

[10] Thomas M. Scanlon, "The Moral Basis of Interpersonal Comparisons," and James Griffin, "Against the Taste Model," both in *Interpersonal Comparisons of Well-Being*, ed. Jon Elster and John E. Roemer (Cambridge: Cambridge University Press, 1991); John Broome, *Weighing Goods* (Oxford: Blackwell, 1991); Daniel M. Hausman and Michael S. McPherson, *Economic Analysis and Moral Philosophy* (Cambridge: Cambridge University Press, 1996).

Classical utilitarianism is based on an account of the nature of value: the only ultimate value is happiness. Once we have accepted this starting point, the utilitarian method of comparing social states is both coherent and natural. (Whether it can be made operational is another question: for that, we need a method for measuring happiness.) Since happiness is a mental experience, and since only sentient individuals can have such experiences, there can be no social good that is not the good of some sentient individual; and if happiness is the only source of value, the good of an individual can be nothing other than her happiness. What we have to ask is whether the corresponding principles of welfarism are correspondingly natural or coherent.

As a starting point, it is useful to consider why, from the early twentieth century, economists stopped using concepts of happiness or pleasure in their theories about what people *in fact* choose. The neoclassical economists of the late nineteenth century had built their theories of choice on the psychological assumption that each individual seeks to maximize his own pleasure.[11] They sometimes felt obliged to apologize for this assumption. It was not, they admitted, a universal truth, but it was supposed to be sufficiently realistic for the purposes of economics. For example, William Stanley Jevons accepted that there were "higher" and "lower" pleasures and that these were incommensurable; but, by virtue of its mundane subject-matter, economics could safely confine its attention to "the lowest rank of feelings."[12]

Why the need for apology? The reason, I think, is that nearly a century after Bentham's utilitarian theorizing, economists were no nearer to finding the one-dimensional metric of pleasure whose existence Bentham had assumed. The problem of "higher" and "lower" pleasures, which had so troubled John Stuart Mill (and which clearly worried Jevons), illustrates the difficulty. Mill wanted to be able to compare the pleasures of "Socrates dissatisfied" with those of "a fool satisfied."[13] Let us think of Socrates as dissatisfied because his life's work of philosophical inquiry has not met his own exacting standards, and of the fool as satisfied because, having been lucky with a bet, he can afford to get drunk. Considered purely as mental experiences, it is hard to see how the pleasures of doing philosophy can be made commensurable with those induced by lively company and alcohol. These seem to be different *kinds* of pleasurable experiences, with no natural common unit of measurement. At any rate, no such unit had been found when Mill was writing and, as far as I know, none has been found since.

[11] William Stanley Jevons, *The Theory of Political Economy* (Harmondsworth: Penguin, 1970), first published 1871; Francis Y. Edgeworth, *Mathematical Psychics* (London: Kegan Paul, 1881); Léon Walras, *Elements of Pure Economics*, trans. W. Jaffé (London: Allen and Unwin, 1954), first published in French 1889; Alfred Marshall, *Principles of Economics* (London: Macmillan, 1920), first published 1890.

[12] Jevons, *The Theory of Political Economy*, p. 93.

[13] John Stuart Mill, *Considerations on Representative Government* (London: Dent, 1972), pp. 259–60, first published 1861.

Perhaps Mill was also worried that, were a common measure to be found, it would give the wrong answer. Imagine that neuroscientists were to discover that all forms of pleasure were, in some chemical sense, of the same kind, differing only in quantity. And imagine that, as a result of this discovery, we were to have a reliable technology for measuring pleasure (say, by measuring activity along dopamine-transmitting pathways in the brain). Who would turn out to be having more pleasure, the modern-day dissatisfied Socrates or the satisfied fool? There is no way of knowing, but it would be rash to bet on Socrates.

Nevertheless, Mill was confident that almost anyone who had experienced both kinds of pleasure would *prefer* to be Socrates dissatisfied. Even if we are skeptical about this claim, we can take it that Mill himself had this preference. No doubt many philosophers do. The point of this example, then, is that there are cases where a person knows which experiences she prefers to which others, even though she knows no way of making those experiences commensurable. What is more, she would maintain her preferences even if neuroscience were to reveal that she was preferring less pleasure to more.

An economist might respond, as Jevons did, by claiming that Mill's difficulty is peculiar to higher pleasures: in the domain of economics, preferences and pleasures are closely correlated. But in the absence of any common unit for measuring even the "lowest rank of feelings," how can we possibly know whether Jevons is right?

The truth, I suggest, is that the early neoclassical economists had built their analyses on untenable psychological assumptions. Increasingly aware of this problem, they were groping for some alternative foundations. Eventually, Vilfredo Pareto had the inspiration which led to the modern interpretation of the theory of choice.[14] He showed how the formal structure of neoclassical economics could be maintained without the need for any explicit psychology. I shall call this move the *Paretian turn*.

Unlike his predecessors, Pareto does not begin consumer theory by speculating about the experiences that individuals derive from consuming goods. Instead, he starts with the concept of *indifference*. To say that a person is indifferent between two bundles of goods is simply to say that he would just be willing to exchange one bundle for the other. Indifference, Pareto claims, is "given directly by experience."[15] The properties of the indifference relation are open to direct empirical investigation: there is no need to inquire into the psychology that lies behind them.

Pareto assumes that, for any given individual, the indifference relation is such that we can identify *indifference curves*—sets of bundles of goods

[14] Vilfredo Pareto, *Manual of Political Economy*, trans. A. S. Schweir (London: Macmillan, 1972), first published in Italian 1906. It is difficult to assign credit for this "discovery," which was a natural progression of neoclassical economics. Some scholars give the credit to Irving Fisher, *Mathematical Investigations in the Theory of Value and Prices* (New Haven, CN: Yale University Press, 1925), first published 1892.

[15] *Ibid.*, p. 391.

among which the individual is indifferent. Preferences are (it is assumed) capable of being described by a family of indifference curves; these curves can be ordered, so that bundles on "higher" curves are preferred to bundles on "lower" curves. ("Preference," like indifference, describes choice behavior: a person prefers x to y if he is willing to take x in exchange for y, but not vice versa.) Given such a family of indifference curves, we may assign a numerical index to each curve. The mathematical function which assigns indices to indifference curves is a *representation* of the person's preferences. Although these indices are usually called indices of "utility" (Pareto would have preferred to use a different word), and although we may describe the person's behavior as utility-maximizing, it is a mistake to think that a particular bundle is chosen *because* that choice maximizes utility. Statements about utility-maximization merely provide a convenient language for expressing the idea that the person chooses in accordance with a given set of preferences. For Pareto, the great merit of this approach is that it eliminates the need to assume a common unit for measuring experiences, when no such unit is known to exist. If it is adopted, he says, the theory of economic science "acquires the rigour of rational mechanics; it deduces its results from experience, without bringing in any metaphysical entity."[16]

Pareto's analysis of preference and utility has been refined into what is now the standard economic theory of choice.[17] Roughly speaking, welfarism is what we get if we take classical utilitarianism and replace "happiness" with Pareto's preference-based concept of utility. This amounts to identifying the good of each individual with the satisfaction of her preferences, instead of with her happiness. The flaw in classical utilitarianism was that no one could find a satisfactory measure of happiness. The Paretian turn seems to resolve that problem, by substituting an observable entity for a nonobservable one. However, two new problems have to be faced. For reasons that will emerge shortly, these two problems are related.

The first problem is that the Paretian theory has to assume that each person's choice behavior has just the right structure to allow us to describe it *as if* that person were maximizing some measure of overall value — even though no theory of overall value is offered. What we are being given is an empirical hypothesis, open to refutation; but why we should expect that hypothesis to accord with experience is unclear. Recall that the original reason for supposing that choice behavior has a maximizing structure — the hypothesis that people seek to maximize pleasure — has been discarded as "metaphysical." The very *ease* of the Paretian turn — the claim that a complete change in the foundations of choice theory can be

[16] *Ibid.*, p. 113.

[17] Among the classic statements of the modern theory are: John Hicks, *Value and Capital* (Oxford: Clarendon Press, 1946); Paul A. Samuelson, *Foundations of Economic Analysis* (Cambridge, MA: Harvard University Press, 1947); and John Hicks, *A Revision of Demand Theory* (Oxford: Clarendon Press, 1956).

made without any significant change to the superstructure—is surely suspicious. We are entitled to be skeptical of Pareto's hypothesis until we see some supporting evidence.

The second problem is this: Is there a moral point of view from which it makes sense to identify a person's good with the satisfaction of his preferences? I take it that when an economist or philosopher writes about normative theory, he addresses the reader as a reasoning person. If the theory is utilitarian or welfarist, the reader is taken to be a reflective, morally concerned person, who has distanced herself from her personal interests—an *ethical observer*. She is invited to share the author's conclusions about what is good for individuals and for society. The modes of argument used by economists and philosophers presuppose that the aim is to convince the reader by giving her *good reasons* to accept the author's position. The aim is not simply to induce her to change her preferences. (To see this, compare a typical television commercial supporting a political campaign with a typical work of political philosophy.) Implicitly, the reader is taken to be someone who is trying to form considered, informed, and stable judgments about the social good. As part of that process, she has to make judgments about what is good for individual members of society. These judgments, too, should be thought of as considered, informed, and stable. Does it make sense to suppose that the ethical observer's considered judgments about the good of each individual should in each case coincide with that person's preferences?

The problem is that, on the Paretian interpretation, a person's (say, Joe's) preferences are simply whatever mental states are associated with his choices. We are not entitled to interpret them as any particular kind of *reason* for Joe's choosing one thing rather than another. However, the ethical observer is looking for reasons to ground her judgments about what is good for Joe.

I have said that the ethical observer is trying to form a considered, informed, and stable judgment about Joe's good. Joe's preferences themselves may have none of these properties.

We all know that many of our preferences are ill-considered and ill-informed. There is a huge amount of evidence from experimental psychology and from experimental economics to show that preferences are highly sensitive to the "framing" of decision problems (that is, to the context in which the decision maker perceives what, in terms of the conventional theory of rational choice, is a given problem). The phenomenon of *preference reversal* is one characteristic and well-attested example.[18] This concerns behavior in relation to two lotteries, roughly equal in attractiveness; one lottery offers a larger money prize than the other, but with a correspondingly smaller probability of winning. When people

---

[18] Paul Slovic and Sarah Lichtenstein, "Preference Reversals: A Broader Perspective," *American Economic Review*, vol. 73 (1983), pp. 596–605; Amos Tversky, Paul Slovic, and Daniel Kahneman, "The Causes of Preference Reversal," *American Economic Review*, vol. 80 (1990), pp. 204–17.

make straight choices between such lotteries, their apparent preferences are systematically different from those that they reveal when asked to say how much each lottery is worth to them. What seems to be happening is that people are using different "heuristics" or mental routines for tackling the two types of decision problem. When making a straight choice, they focus on the relative riskiness of the two lotteries, and tend to choose the lottery which gives the higher probability of winning. But when asked to put a money value on a lottery, they focus on the amount of money to be won, scaling this down in a rough-and-ready way to reflect the lack of certainty attached to it. In consequence, people tend to put higher money values on the lottery with the larger prize.

It is also well-established that people's preferences are strongly influenced by the "reference points" from which they view their options. People are less willing to trade than conventional theory predicts; it is as if the mere possession of an object creates a preference for it in relation to other things. (To give a personal example: Recently I did some work for which the payment was a case of vintage champagne. I would not have chosen to buy this champagne at its market price, but having received it—and even before tasting it—I did not want to sell it. The switch from a reference point at which I did not possess the champagne to one at which I did was sufficient to change my preference.) Such effects can be triggered by surprisingly small changes in the way a decision problem is described to people.[19]

There is growing evidence that the preferences of a typical individual should be thought of as stochastic rather than deterministic. That is, a person sometimes prefers one thing, sometimes another, with no apparent reason for the switch; to the extent that a person's preferences can be described as constant, the constancy is to be found in the relative *frequencies* with which different choices are made in a given decision problem.[20]

I could go on. The general picture seems to be that people's decision-making behavior shows many empirical regularities that are inconsistent with the hypothesis that preferences are stable and consistent. Many of the most convincing explanations of these regularities are offered by psychological theories which assume that individuals draw on a repertoire of heuristics; inconsistencies among preferences occur because different heuristics are used in different contexts.

It should be said that economists often assert that these experimentally observed "anomalies" in individuals' preferences will tend to be eroded

---

[19] Richard Thaler, "Toward a Positive Theory of Consumer Choice," *Journal of Economic Behavior and Organization*, vol. 1 (1980), pp. 39–60; Jack L. Knetsch, "The Endowment Effect and Evidence of Nonreversible Indifference Curves," *American Economic Review*, vol. 79 (1989), pp. 1277–84.

[20] John Hey and Chris Orme, "Investigating Generalizations of Expected Utility Theory Using Experimental Data," *Econometrica*, vol. 47 (1994), pp. 263–91; Graham Loomes and Robert Sugden, "Incorporating a Stochastic Element into Decision Theory," *European Economic Review*, vol. 39 (1995), pp. 641–48.

by experience of repeated trading in "real" markets. The idea is that the anomalous patterns of behavior are *mistakes* which, given sufficient experience, people will learn not to make. But little in the way of convincing evidence or theoretical argument has been advanced in support of this claim.[21] Notice that it is question-begging to assume that any behavior that contravenes the conventional theory of choice is a mistake. Nor are we entitled to assume the existence, for a given person, of some single scale of value which defines success for her. Thus, the mechanism by which experience is supposed to teach people to have consistent preferences is mysterious. In any case, many of the most important economic decisions we make—for example, choosing a career, choosing schools for our children, choosing among pension and insurance plans—are not made repeatedly, and therefore give us little opportunity to learn by our experience.

Faced with this evidence, each of us might still say that we are willing to live with the imperfect decisions that result from our apparently inconsistent preferences. It is one thing to say this, however, and quite another to say that someone else should endorse the outcomes of those decisions as good for us. For example, suppose Joe decides today, on the spur of the moment, not to wear his safety helmet when cycling. He is aware that this increases the risk of his being killed, but he has only a vague idea about the size of the risk; he also thinks that a cycle helmet projects an undesirably nerdish image. Usually he wears a helmet, but today the desire to make a good impression on other people is at the forefront of his mind. This is a stochastic preference formed on imperfect information and without much reflection. Many of our preferences are surely like this. Should an ethical observer judge that, today, wearing a cycle helmet is bad for Joe (although, had his spur-of-the-moment decision gone the other way, it would have been good for him)? It is hard to see why she must.

Notice that we are not discussing the morality of paternalism. The question is not whether anyone should interfere with Joe's decision, but whether he has chosen what is good for him. There are many strong arguments against paternalism which do not require us to believe that people always choose what is good for them. The most famous such argument, that of Mill, tries to show why, despite the fact that people sometimes choose what is bad for them, paternalistic interventions do not promote the long-run good of society.[22] (One of the reasons offered by

---

[21] Perhaps the most careful argument for interpreting anomalies as mistakes is Charles Plott's "discovered preference hypothesis": Charles R. Plott, "Rational Behavior in Markets and Social Choice Processes: The Discovered Preference Hypothesis," in *The Rational Foundations of Economic Behavior*, ed. Kenneth J. Arrow, Enrico Colombatto, Mark Perlman, and Christian Schmidt (New York: Macmillan, 1996). I think Plott's argument is question-begging. On this, see Daniel Kahneman's "Comment" in the same volume.

[22] John Stuart Mill, *On Liberty* (London: Dent, 1972), first published 1859.

Mill is that through the deliberation prior to acts of choice—even foolish ones—a person develops traits of character that promote his long-term happiness. Another reason is that choices that others would judge to be mistaken are a source of experiment; occasionally such choices lead to discoveries of great value to everyone.) This line of argument is possible for Mill because he has an account of an individual's good—his long-term happiness—which is logically independent of preference. Thus, Mill's conceptual scheme allows the possibility that people choose contrary to their own good. In contrast, welfarism has no way of formulating that possibility, since its conception of a person's good just *is* his preferences.

I have been discussing a case in which preferences are unconsidered, imperfectly informed, and stochastic. But what about a case in which preferences are not subject to any of those criticisms? Suppose Joe knows and understands the evidence on the safety benefits of wearing helmets when cycling. He also has a correct understanding of social norms: it is indeed true that people who wear cycle helmets are seen as nerds. In the light of this knowledge, he consistently chooses not to wear a helmet. This is a fully considered, well-informed, and stable preference. Must the ethical observer now conclude that wearing a helmet is bad for Joe?

I think not. We know that conflicting reasons bear on Joe's decision problem—reasons of safety, and reasons of image. Having taken the Paretian turn, we are not entitled to assume that there is any scale on which those reasons are commensurable. Thus, even given that Joe has thought carefully about the problem, that he is acting on good information, and that he consistently makes the same decision in similar circumstances, all we can infer from Joe's not wearing a helmet is that this is what Joe wishes to choose. We cannot assume that there is some overall, all-things-considered *reason* for this decision—a reason which will have force for the ethical observer. She too may be well-informed about the safety benefits and image costs of cycle helmets, but she may reach a different conclusion from Joe's about what is good for him.

Some writers are tempted by the idea that if a decision maker knew all the facts bearing on a particular decision problem, there would necessarily be a uniquely rational decision; any rational individual, given the same full information, would decide in the same way.[23] Harsanyi seems to take this position.[24] I suggest that it rests on an unwarranted act of faith. What grounds do we have to assume that rational decisions are always fully determined by information? It is understandable that a classical utilitarian might make this assumption, since the utilitarian could argue that every rational person seeks to maximize his own happiness (or

---

[23] A strict statement of this position would allow the possibility that, in some decision problems, rational deliberation leads to a tie between two or more equally rational solutions. The essential idea is that considerations of rationality fully determine the decision maker's ranking of the options open to him.

[24] Harsanyi, "Morality and the Theory of Rational Behaviour" (*supra* note 6), pp. 49–52.

alternatively, seeks to maximize the total happiness in the world). If all forms of happiness were commensurable, knowledge of all the relevant facts about happiness would indeed determine the rational utilitarian solution for any given decision problem. But if we take the Paretian turn, this kind of argument is no longer open to us: we do not have any criterion, independent of preference, with which to determine the rational solution to a decision problem.

The ungrounded claim that rational decisions are fully determined by information should not be confused with a much more modest claim: that if identical individuals face identical decision problems, they will make identical decisions. This second claim, which is close to being a tautology, differs from the first one by making no reference to rationality. (Whether it is a tautology depends on whether we admit the possibility that human behavior might be stochastic all the way down.) Again, take the case of Joe and the ethical observer. The ethical observer might recognize that if she were in Joe's position, complete with Joe's psychology, then she would choose exactly as Joe does. Whatever goes on in Joe's mind when he tries to reconcile the conflicting reasons for and against wearing a helmet would also go through her mind, were her mind identical to his. But this does not help her to resolve the problem she faces, which is to make *her own* judgment about what is good for Joe.

I draw the following general conclusion: Once we take the Paretian turn, there is no adequate general reason why an ethical observer, trying to form her own judgments about another person's good, should identify that good with the person's preferences—even if (which itself is questionable) those preferences are stable and consistent. But the identification of preference with individual good is one of the defining properties of welfarism. If I am right, then, welfarism is fatally flawed.

One way of responding to this critique of welfarism is to propose a substantive account of what the good or well-being of an individual is, and then to build the analysis on that account rather than on preference. This approach has found favor recently. Broome argues for using judgments about individual good in place of preferences, but does not propose a specific theory of good.[25] Griffin develops an account of well-being based on a list of "prudential values" which, he claims, are "valuable in any life."[26] Amartya Sen offers a theory in which any person's well-being depends on the achievement of certain broadly defined "functionings."[27] (Sen also explores the idea that value might be associated with *sets* of functionings, which he calls "capabilities." This idea is closer to the approach I shall be suggesting.) The proponents of these theories claim that,

[25] Broome, *Weighing Goods* (*supra* note 10).
[26] James Griffin, *Well-Being: Its Meaning, Measurement, and Moral Importance* (Oxford: Clarendon Press, 1986), and Griffin, "Against the Taste Model" (*supra* note 10). The quotation is from p. 64 of "Against the Taste Model."
[27] Amartya Sen, *Inequality Reexamined* (Cambridge, MA: Harvard University Press, 1992).

after due reflection, reasonable people will find they agree on the main dimensions of well-being and, to some degree at least, on how to make comparisons across dimensions. But why should we expect this kind of agreement? Sen does not give a direct answer to this question, but flirts with an Aristotelian notion of the good life.[28] Griffin suggests that the concept of value may be irreducibly social. To see something as valuable, he says, we have to see it as something that is generally intelligible as valuable for any normal human being. Since basic prudential values are embedded in language, people from the same language community will have these values in common.[29]

I remain skeptical. To me, it seems most improbable that we can reach a consensus on an answer to the question of what makes a good life, with sufficient precision to be able to say anything useful about real social questions. (Of course, we might be able to agree on an anodyne mission statement for humanity, but what use would that be?) One of the most attractive features of welfarism is that it does *not* assume any particular theory of human well-being. This feature of welfarism is encapsulated in Harsanyi's principle of preference autonomy, with its suggestion that we should work with each individual's *own* conception of what is good for her. We might hope to find a coherent form of normative economics which retained this principle, or something like it.

III. Preference as a Contractarian Measure of Interest

Contractarianism provides a possible escape route from the problems which beset welfarism. Contractarian arguments work with each individual's own conception of what is good for her, but do not require that conception to be endorsed by anyone else. These arguments are not addressed to an ethical observer, and do not aim to show what is good for society as a whole. The contractarian writes as if from the position of the chairman of a meeting, or of the mediator in a dispute. He addresses his arguments separately to each individual member of society. The aim is to recommend particular rules or practices as the terms of an agreement to which each individual can rationally give his assent. To each person, what is being said is this: An agreement on these terms will benefit you; and, recognizing that other people have their own interests and are as rational as you are, you cannot reasonably expect to reach an agreement that is any more favorable to you than this.

This strategy allows there to be as many different understandings of what is good as there are people. Suppose that different individuals make different judgments about what makes a life good—not just for themselves, but for anyone. For example, Griffin believes that accomplishment

---

[28] *Ibid.*, pp. 5, 45.
[29] Griffin, "Against the Taste Model," pp. 50–52, 66–67.

is an important part of anyone's good, and finds it hard to accept that there is any value in "just frittering away" one's life.[30] Nevertheless, someone who has a more happy-go-lucky outlook may find value in taking the pleasures of life as they come, and not see the point of accomplishment. Consider a society which contains both people like Griffin and people who are happy-go-lucky; each person's preferences reflect his own judgments about what is good in life. An ethical observer will not be able to endorse *both* types of judgment, and therefore she must reject at least some people's preferences as measures of those people's good. In contrast, a contractarian can work with each person's judgments, without trying to reconcile them. The contractarian's task is merely to propose the terms of an agreement which each person can accept as good for him, viewed from his own perspective.

However, contractarian arguments are like welfarist ones in that they are addressed to reasoning persons. The writer of a contractarian theory proposes the terms of an agreement and then tries to give each reader *good reasons* to accept those terms. Implicitly, then, the reader is taken to be someone who is trying to form considered, informed, and stable judgments about her own good. In most contractarian theories, individuals are modeled as reaching agreements about the fundamental rules of their society—agreements that are to stay in place for many years. (Recall the importance of the long run in the arguments of both Hume and Hayek: it is only over the long run that the rules of a free society can be claimed to benefit everyone.) So the supposition must be that each individual is making a considered and informed judgment about his long-term good. We must now ask: Can we identify each person's judgments about his long-term good with his preferences?

Part of the difficulty here is that a reasoning person may not be able to endorse *his own* future preferences as a measure of his good. The "contracting party" of a contractarian theory—reflective, reasonable, well-informed—will know that his own future preferences are likely to be ill-considered, ill-informed, and volatile. He cannot assume that those preferences will be based on some coherent set of reasons that he can now endorse. Thus, in thinking about his future preferences, the contracting party is in much the same position as the welfarist ethical observer is in when she thinks about other people's preferences. Preferences cannot be taken uncritically as measures of a person's good—not even by the person himself.

Perhaps all we can say is that a person's *current* preferences—including his current preferences about future states of affairs—constitute his current judgments about what is good for him. This, in essence, is the position taken by Gauthier in what is perhaps the most careful attempt to construct a preference-based measure of value, adapted to a contractarian

[30] *Ibid.*, pp. 59–61.

approach.[31] Gauthier starts from a conception of preference that is essentially the same as Pareto's. While denying that observations of choices provide the only possible source of information about preferences, Gauthier insists that choices always reveal some kind of preference. He denies the existence of any concept of value (candidates might be happiness, interest, or prudence) in terms of which preferences can be justified: the content of preference, he says, is not subject to rational assessment. He defends this approach by appealing to Hume's principle that reason is and ought only to be the slave of the passions. The idea, I take it, is that preference is a passion or (to use a Hobbesian word which Gauthier quotes with approval) an appetite. As a passion, preference has a status that is superior to that of reason.

Although desires are not subject to rational assessment, they can be influenced by reason. For example, my desire to smoke (never very strong) has been greatly reduced by my learning that smoking causes lung cancer. In Humean terms, it is reason that tells me that smoking has this effect. This element of reasoning interacts with my present desire for a long life and generates a desire not to smoke. Notice, however, that reason does not tell me that, given that my desires are as they are, I ought not to smoke: to say that would be far too uppity for a slave. My desire not to smoke is simply another passion. For Hume, there are no irrational passions: "a passion must be accompany'd with some false judgment, in order to its being unreasonable; and even then 'tis not the passion, properly speaking, which is unreasonable, but the judgment."[32] Thus, although reason may constrain the beliefs I hold about the relationship between smoking and lung cancer, it imposes no constraints on my desires themselves. There is no presumption that desires are commensurable, or that reason can pick out the action which maximally satisfies a person's desires. In this sense, the Humean approach is compatible with the Paretian turn.[33]

Gauthier follows a Humean line by defining preferences *relative to subjective beliefs*. Thus, a person's choices reveal her current preferences, not over the actual outcomes of her potential acts, but over what, at the moment of choice, she believes the outcomes of those acts will be. In this way, Gauthier separates passion (represented by preferences) from reason (which directly bears on beliefs). As a contractarian, Gauthier takes each person's preferences as given, but offers his readers reasons for holding particular beliefs (for example, about the bargaining behavior to be ex-

---

[31] Gauthier, *Morals by Agreement*, pp. 21–59.

[32] Hume, *A Treatise of Human Nature*, p. 416.

[33] Robert Sugden, "Rational Choice: A Survey of Contributions from Economics and Philosophy," *Economic Journal*, vol. 101 (1991), pp. 751–85; Jean Hampton, "The Failure of Expected-Utility Theory as a Theory of Reason," *Economics and Philosophy*, vol. 10 (1994), pp. 195–242.

pected of other rational people). However—again following Hume—Gauthier allows that each person's preferences can be influenced by reason. Since he is addressing his readers as reasoning persons, he is concerned with the preferences that they hold after careful thought. He defines a person's *considered preferences* as those preferences that are "stable under experience and reflection," and that the person would, in acts of speech, endorse as her preferences. Such preferences, Gauthier argues, reveal each person's conception of value. They are the right sort of data for a contractarian analysis.

So far, I think, Gauthier's analysis is broadly right. But he then makes the further claim that the considered preferences of a rational person satisfy the axioms of expected utility theory. Among the requirements of these axioms are that preferences are complete and transitive. Notice that here Gauthier is ruling out the possibility that considered preferences might be stochastic. Completeness requires that, between every pair of options, the individual has a preference (or is exactly indifferent between them); and by Gauthier's definition, considered preferences are stable. In claiming that preferences are (at least) complete, transitive, and nonstochastic, Gauthier is following a precedent set by almost all those economists who have taken the Paretian turn. Nevertheless, we may ask whether that claim is well grounded.

What reason do we have to suppose that, with experience and reflection, a person's preferences will converge to some stable pattern? Having taken the Paretian turn, we cannot appeal to any one-dimensional standard of value which lies behind and justifies preferences. Were there such a standard, we might expect experience and reflection to produce convergence on that standard. For example, if pleasure was the standard of value and if all pleasures were commensurable, we might be able to argue that it was uniquely rational to maximize expected pleasure, assessed in relation to "objective" probabilities. A person might fail to maximize expected pleasure as a result of an error in calculation, or as a result of false beliefs about the relationship between consumption and pleasure. Still, the extent of errors should tend to decrease with greater reflection and experience. That argument is no longer open to us, however. There is no standard of value to converge to.

If reason is the slave of the passions, it cannot be a requirement of reason that the passions are stable, or that they have any particular mathematical structure. Suppose I find that on some days I feel a strong desire that my life (not just on that day, but in general) should lead to career achievements, while on other days I feel no such desire at all. Perhaps these different desires are like mood changes, triggered by chemical changes in my body; to me, they appear as random shifts in my desires. Neither pattern of desires is accompanied by any false belief: it is not that I don't know what achievement is, or what it feels like; it is just that I sometimes want it and sometimes don't. Then, on a Humean analysis, I am not irrational. Or suppose (to use an example of Broome's)[34] that if I am offered a choice between staying at home and going on a mountaineering holiday, I prefer mountaineering; if the choice is between staying at home and going on a holiday to Rome, I prefer staying at home; and if the choice is between mountaineering and Rome, I prefer Rome.[35] Broome — who has not taken the Paretian turn, and who does not claim to be a Humean — supposes that, if I am to claim to be rational, I must give special reasons for these apparently nontransitive preferences. But from a Humean point of view, no reasons are required. If my desires happen to take this form, that is just a fact about my passions, to which reason must accommodate itself.

I suggest that there are no satisfactory *a priori* grounds for assuming that each person has a set of stable and coherent preferences, which can be discovered by experience and reflection. Whether such preferences exist is ultimately an empirical question. And, as I pointed out in Section II, the evidence is not encouraging.

How does Gauthier deal with these difficulties? Rather cursorily. He says that on his account, value is identified with utility. Utility is not a standard for preference: it is a measure of preference. The standard axioms of coherence ensure that this measure exists, and thus that rationality can be identified with the maximization of expected utility:

> Were value a standard, then reason might have a role in determining this standard which would then go beyond mere maximization. Were there neither standard nor measure, then reason would have no practical role whatsoever; there would be nothing to maximize. The theory of rational choice sets its course between the dogmatism of assuming a standard for preference and the scepticism of denying a measure of preference.[36]

Notice that Gauthier gives us no reasons for thinking that individuals' considered preferences are in fact coherent in the sense that he requires. He merely says that if they were not, there would be no role for reason. But that is not a decisive argument: perhaps there *are* decision problems in which reason has no practical role.

What does seem clear, however, is that any contractarian argument presupposes that reason has some role in decision making: recall that the

[34] Broome, *Weighing Goods*, pp. 100–104.

[35] There is some evidence that people's preferences over certain kinds of lotteries are cyclical in this way: we can find lotteries A, B, and, C such that people prefer A to B, B to C, and C to A. See Graham Loomes, Chris Starmer, and Robert Sugden, "Observing Violations of Transitivity by Experimental Methods," *Econometrica*, vol. 59 (1991), pp. 425–39.

[36] Gauthier, *Morals by Agreement*, p. 26.

point of such an argument is to show that individuals have good reason to make and to comply with a particular agreement. It is difficult to see how contractarian arguments could get off the ground without assuming some minimally coherent conception of individual well-being or interest. (I say "minimally" because we may not need to insist on all the axioms which underpin expected utility theory.) If a person's preferences are to be used as the measure of her well-being or interest, as judged by herself, then we do seem to need those preferences to be minimally coherent. So how can we proceed? I suggest that we need to look for a different measure.

IV. Opportunity

In decision theory, individuals have preferences over outcomes (or over the actions which generate those outcomes). A decision problem consists of a set of mutually exclusive outcomes—an *opportunity set*. One and only one of the outcomes in the opportunity set must be chosen. According to conventional theory, a rational individual has coherent and stable preferences over all possible outcomes; from any opportunity set, he chooses the outcome that he most prefers. In welfare economics, the individual's preferences are taken as a measure of what is good for him. In Gauthier's version of contractarianism, the individual's (considered) preferences are taken as a measure of his judgments of value. I have argued that both these interpretations of preference lead to problems.

I shall now consider an alternative approach to contractarian economics, which sees opportunity sets, and not individual outcomes, as the carriers of value. The fundamental assumption is that each individual prefers his opportunity set to be larger rather than smaller. Clearly, this is a contestable empirical claim about human preferences; but I think it is consistent with many of the most significant economic trends of at least the last hundred years. Think of the continuous flow of migrants, almost everywhere in the world, from rural areas to large cities. Think of the pressure of potential migrants to all the successful capitalist economies— from Mexico to the U.S., from Eastern Europe and North Africa to the European Union, from Vietnam to Hong Kong. Think of the increasing participation of women in the labor market in all rich countries. Think of the continuous growth in the range of goods on sale in shops, in the range of television channels, in the range of financial services being offered, and consider why firms have found it profitable to put all those goods and services on the market. Needless to say, the issue is not whether these trends promote human happiness, but what they tell us about human preferences. I suggest that they tell us that there is a pervasive preference for increases in opportunity.

A person's preference for opportunity *might* derive from his preferences over outcomes, as conventional choice theory would imply. Nothing in the argument that follows denies that possibility. However, a preference for opportunity does not *have to* be explained in that particular way. My approach will not refer to a person's actual preferences over outcomes. By following this approach, we may be able to evaluate opportunity sets even when preferences over outcomes are ill-informed, ill-considered, incoherent, or volatile. Since the individual's preferences over outcomes would lie outside the domain of analysis, there would be no need for anyone to endorse those preferences as measures of value. However, paternalistic interventions would not be licensed. The whole point of such interventions is to restrict the set of opportunities open to the individual; if opportunity has value, paternalism detracts from that value.

To see the intuition behind this proposal, consider the problem of providing for one's retirement. Suppose I think about the problem of providing for my retirement by trying to form preferences now over alternative consumption possibilities in, say, 2020. As a first step, I try to predict what my preferences over consumption possibilities will be in 2020. But the further I look into the future, the more difficult it is for me to predict what my preferences will be. This is partly because I know less and less of the relevant facts about the environment in which I shall be living (assuming that I shall be living at all), but also because I do not know what kind of desires I shall then have. (When I am in my seventies, will I want to travel around the world, or will I prefer to sit in my garden?) At best, I can make intelligent guesses about the general properties of my 2020 preferences, based on the evidence of my own and other people's present preferences. Among the predictions that I can make fairly safely is that many of my 2020 preferences will be ill-considered, ill-informed, and volatile. But I am not now in a good position to judge whether or not to endorse any specific instance of those preferences: however considered my present judgments about the future may be, they are necessarily inexperienced and ill-informed. Nevertheless, despite my deep uncertainty about my future preferences, I have a clear preference now that my opportunity set in 2020 should be larger rather than smaller. I want it to be the case that in 2020 I have plenty of room for the exercise of whatever preferences I turn out to have. I want this, even though I know very little about what those preferences will be, and even though I cannot be confident that they will be considered, well-informed, or stable. Further, my general preference for opportunity *is* a considered one, in Gauthier's sense: it is stable under reflection and experience.

Or consider a case in which the possible options are less significant for my life. Suppose it is a hot day at the seaside and I am thirsty, but have not decided exactly what I want to drink. I am midway between two shops, each quite a long walk away, and neither of which I have been to before. One is a small convenience store, which I can expect will stock a very limited range of drinks; the other is a large supermarket, which I can expect will offer a much wider range. I would choose to go to the super-market, because it offers more opportunity. Of course, an economist might want to interpret this choice as the rational maximization of expected utility—as the most efficient means for me to satisfy my as yet uncertain preferences. But it is not obvious that it *must* be interpreted in this way. If my preferences over drinks are unstable and inconsistent, it may not be possible to define a concept of expected utility which my choice can be said to maximize. Nevertheless, I may still have a clear and considered preference for the shop offering the wider range.

Someone who subscribes to a substantive theory of the good might expect me to give reasons for this preference for opportunity. Why (she might ask) is it good for me to have more opportunity? If my preferences are unstable and inconsistent, what good does it do me to have more options on which to exercise those preferences? Does my having a wider range of choice make me any happier in the long run? But I am working within the Humean and Paretian approach, in which no substantive theory of the good is postulated. On this account, there is nothing beyond con-sidered preferences: my considered preferences *are* my values.

Of course, my preference for opportunity is influenced by my beliefs. (Or, if one prefers Gauthier's formulation, my preference is held in rela-tion to given beliefs.) For example, I have certain beliefs about the likely motives of would-be paternalists, about how much they are likely to know about my particular circumstances, and about how strongly they will care about my interests; those beliefs have influenced my desire not to be subject to paternalistic interventions. One may ask whether those beliefs are well-founded. But my preference for opportunity is ultimately a passion, which does not have to be justified in terms of any theory of well-being.

Remember that I am looking for a *contractarian* measure of individual interest. It is an essential feature of the contractarian approach that it does not appeal to contestable claims about what is good for people. Instead, it appeals to each person's considered preferences, without asking what lies behind those preferences. If most people do in fact have a considered preference for more opportunity rather than less, that is all we need to know.

If my proposed strategy is to be followed through, we need a measure of opportunity. At this point, it is worth recalling what the purpose of such a measure is. The contractarian theorist wishes to recommend par-ticular general rules as the terms of an agreement that it is in each indi-vidual's interest—as judged by the individual himself—to make and to keep. Now the theorist cannot hope to know exactly what judgments each individual will make about his own interests. The best the theorist can do is to present a *model* of those judgments. Because that model is to be used to generate recommendations in a larger contractarian theory, the modeled judgments must be coherent and stable. If the theory as a whole is to persuade, the model must be recognizable as an adequate approximation to the truth. That is, for most people, the judgments that the model attributes to them must not be too different from the judgments they actually make.

It may also be important that the model has the property that game theorists call *salience*. Roughly, the idea is that for certain kinds of inter-action between individuals, what each person should do (and what each should expect each other person to do) is underdetermined by ordinary assumptions about rationality. In such cases, people can coordinate their expectations by focusing on those solutions which are salient—which "stick out." To see the relevance of this idea for contractarian theory, notice that such a theory starts by conceiving of individuals who are seeking to agree on the terms of their association. Let us call this starting point, prior to agreement, the *baseline*. The baseline defines a bargaining problem. A contractarian theory recommends the terms of an agreement which, it claims, it would be rational for each individual to accept. Now it is an open question in game theory whether every well-defined bar-gaining problem has a unique "solution," which fully rational bargainers would recognize. Clearly, if the baseline bargaining problem has such a solution, the task of a contractarian theory is simply to identify it. My own view, however, is that bargaining problems typically do *not* have unique rational solutions.

The idea that rationality alone is insufficient to resolve bargaining prob-lems derives from Thomas Schelling and David Lewis; the origins of this line of thought can be found in Hume's *Treatise of Human Nature*.[37] Schell-ing and Lewis model bargaining problems as noncooperative games with many equilibria. That is, for a typical bargaining problem there is a range of alternative viable agreements. Each of these potential agreements has the property that it is rational for each bargainer to concede just enough to settle on the relevant terms, provided he expects the other bargainers to do the same. Thus, a bargaining solution can be understood as a set of mutually consistent expectations—in Lewis's terms, as a *convention*. To explain how such expectations are formed, we need to consider how people draw on their common understandings of precedents and analo-gies. For example, there is often a common expectation that disputes over resources will be resolved in favor of the status quo, or in favor of the current or first possessor. These expectations are encapsulated in such maxims as "finders keepers" and "possession is nine points of the law."

[37] Thomas Schelling, *The Strategy of Conflict* (Cambridge, MA: Harvard University Press, 1960); David Lewis, *Convention: A Philosophical Study* (Cambridge, MA: Harvard University Press, 1969). I explore the implications of Schelling's and Lewis's analyses for contractarian theory in Robert Sugden, "Contractarianism and Norms," *Ethics*, vol. 100 (1990), pp. 768–86. I discuss Hume's treatment of these issues in Robert Sugden, *The Economics of Rights, Co-operation, and Welfare* (Oxford: Blackwell, 1986).

Anyone who has been a member of a committee which allocates a budget will recognize the significance of the status quo in bargaining problems. The property of standing out as an "obvious" or "natural" solution, in a way that is commonly understood but not embodied in formal or explicit rules, is salience.

If this account of bargaining is correct, contractarian theories cannot coherently be addressed to actors who are conceived as ideally rational, but lacking any experience of an ongoing social life: such abstract individuals would be unable to form the mutually consistent expectations which allow bargaining problems to be solved. Viable contractarian arguments must be made from within an ongoing society: we cannot pretend that we are making the world anew.

Thus, if a contractarian theory is to recommend a particular set of rules as the terms of an agreement, it has to draw on preexisting conceptions of salience. It does this by imposing some conceptual structure on the underlying bargaining problem (or, perhaps better, by finding some structure in that problem), such that when the problem is viewed in terms of that structure, a particular solution appears "obvious" or "natural." For example, if a problem can be conceptualized so that one possible agreement is represented as the status quo, that agreement may gain salience.

I have suggested that a contractarian theory might begin from the idea that each person values opportunity. This amounts to imposing a particular conceptual structure on the bargaining problem. If this strategy is to work, the structure must be one that people can recognize as natural—not merely as a description of their own judgments, but also of other people's. What we need, then, is a workable, salient, and reasonably realistic model of people's judgments about opportunity.

One possible model is offered by John Rawls's concept of *primary goods*.[38] It should be said straightaway that Rawls does not treat justice as a matter of convention. In the "original position"—Rawls's baseline—the contracting parties are stripped of any knowledge of their personal features and endowed with the ideal rationality which (according to Rawls) characterizes men "as free and equal rational beings." The idea is that the principles of justice are moral laws that all men can rationally will. This form of social contract theory owes much more to Kant than to Hume.[39] Nevertheless, Rawls's method of analysis provides some important suggestions that a Humean might adapt.

[38] John Rawls, *A Theory of Justice* (Cambridge, MA: Harvard University Press, 1971). Primary goods are defined on p. 62.

[39] Rawls explains the Kantian nature of his theory on pp. 251–57 of *A Theory of Justice* (the quotation is from p. 252). In his later work, Rawls puts less emphasis on ideal rationality, and more on the need to secure agreement among individuals with incompatible moral or religious beliefs: see John Rawls, "Justice as Fairness: Political not Metaphysical," *Philosophy and Public Affairs*, vol. 14 (1985), pp. 223–51. This later work is closer to the contractarian tradition in which I am working.

Rawls begins from a theory of the good which he calls "goodness as rationality": a person's good is determined by what for that person is "the most rational plan of life."[40] Rawls supposes that if a person could choose with perfect "deliberative rationality," that is, with full information and without error, then he would find "the objectively rational plan," and this plan would determine his "real good."[41] Here Rawls seems to be relying on something like the same act of faith as Harsanyi does. Unlike Harsanyi, however, Rawls denies the commensurability of different individuals' conceptions of the good.[42] In denying this, he is recognizing what is wrong with welfarism.

Rawls wants his theory of justice to be neutral with respect to different conceptions of the good. If these are incommensurable, neutrality cannot be achieved by the welfarist method of a neutral aggregation procedure: there is nothing to aggregate. The problem that Rawls faces here is formally similar to that of finding some measure of an individual's interest when she is uncertain about her future preferences, or if those preferences are stochastic. In each case, the problem is to find a single ranking of states of affairs when we have many different and incommensurable ways of valuing them, and when we wish to be neutral between those different valuations.

In Rawls's theory, neutrality is to be found in the idea that there are certain goods that normally have a use whatever a person's rational plan of life happens to be, and thus that every rational person can be presumed to want. These are primary goods.[43] A person's *expectations* are defined by an index of primary goods; it is assumed that everyone prefers more rather than less primary goods, as measured by this index. Rawls's theory of justice does not "look behind" primary goods to try to measure the satisfactions individuals achieve from those goods: the requirements of justice are satisfied if the distribution of expectations is fair.[44] We might hope to follow a similar strategy to construct a Humean measure of an individual's interest. Instead of considering rational plans of life, we should consider the range of preferences (rational or irrational) that an individual might come to have. We might then try to identify goods which have a use whatever a person's preferences, and assume that each individual prefers more rather than less of those goods.

Rawls describes the strategy of focusing on primary goods as a "simplifying device" and as representing an agreement on "the most feasible way to establish a publicly recognized objective measure" of people's situations.[45] The idea seems to be that the index of primary goods is a

---

[40] Rawls, *A Theory of Justice*, p. 395.
[41] *Ibid.*, p. 417.
[42] *Ibid.*, p. 174.
[43] *Ibid.*, p. 62.
[44] *Ibid.*, pp. 93–94.
[45] *Ibid.*, p. 95.

simple and workable model of individuals' judgments about their interests, which is neutral with respect to alternative plans of life. In supposing that people would agree to use this index to determine the claims they may make against one another, Rawls seems to be appealing to some notion of salience: this part of his theory, at least, requires something more than ideal rationality, detached from social experience.

To an economist, the most significant of Rawls's primary goods are "income" and "wealth." Rawls usually treats these two goods as if they were different ways of talking about the same thing: perhaps he has in mind the economist's understanding of wealth as the capitalized value of a flow of income.[46] To simplify the discussion, I shall focus on income. Although Rawls discusses the problem of combining the various primary goods into a single index,[47] he does not seem to see any problem in measuring income itself. He treats income as if it were a physical object like coal, with a natural unit of quantity; just as coal can be used to promote life plans that involve being warm, so income can be used to promote (a wider range of) life plans.

I think this analysis of income is mistaken: income is not a physical object. The usual unit of account for income is money, but money in itself is worthless. Money has value to the extent that it represents *purchasing power*—that is, to the extent that it can be exchanged for other goods. Rawls's fundamental idea, I take it, is that any rational plan of life will require some goods of the kind that are normally traded in markets; thus, a general power to buy such goods is valuable across all life plans. An individual's real income should be understood as an opportunity set—as that set of consumption bundles he can afford to buy, given the prices prevailing in the market. By treating opportunity sets rather than consumption bundles as the carriers of value, we may be able to avoid the need to refer to each individual's preferences when evaluating his situation.

Unfortunately, once we recognize that income is just another word for opportunity, we must also recognize that Rawls has not told us how opportunity is to be measured. At first sight, it might seem that income has a straightforward measurement in money: isn't a person's income just the amount of money he is able to spend? But even if we restrict our attention to economies with well-functioning price systems, and even if we ignore those public goods which cannot be traded on markets, there is no simple and meaningful money measure of opportunity.

Of course, if all prices are held constant, the amount of money a person has to spend *is* a good index of the size of her opportunity set: if there is

---

[46] For example, if I own shares in a company, the value of those shares on the stock market is (part of) my wealth. The dividends I receive from the shares is income. But the market value of a share is just the capitalization of the expected flow of future dividends. Income and wealth are just different ways of describing the same underlying source of value: I can realize the capital value of my shares only by forgoing the dividends.

[47] Rawls, *A Theory of Justice*, pp. 93–95.

an increase in the amount of money she has to spend, she is able to buy everything she could buy before, and she has new opportunities in addition. The case of constant prices is relevant if we wish to make comparisons between individuals in a given economic regime. For example, if we want to ask whether all individuals in a given society have equal opportunities when they are all able to buy goods at the same prices, then it is sufficient to compare their money incomes. That, in essence, is the logic of Ronald Dworkin's "clam shell" auction as a criterion of equality of resources. Dworkin asks us to imagine an original position in which resources are unowned. A fixed stock of some unit of account—say, clam shells—is divided equally among all individuals, and then all resources are sold by auction, payments being made in clam shells. We can expect different individuals to buy different bundles of resources, depending on their abilities and preferences; but since everyone has had the same opportunities to acquire resources, Dworkin claims the resulting allocation of resources satisfies an egalitarian principle of fairness.[48]

In a contractarian theory, however, such comparisons between individuals have no real significance. Recall that the object of a contractarian argument is to recommend particular social rules as the terms of an agreement to which each person can rationally assent. What matters to each person is how the consequences for her of those recommended rules compare with the consequences for her of other possible rules on which everyone might agree. Thus, a contractarian theory has to compare the consequences of different economic regimes for each individual taken separately. It has no need to compare the consequences for different individuals of a given regime.

Once we make comparisons across economic regimes, we run into the problem that prices are not constant. In essence, this is the "index-number problem" of economic statistics. For example, if we wish to compare a person's real consumption in two periods, we need some constant set of "weights" to apply to the array of goods that the person consumes, so as to generate a one-dimensional measure. The usual method is to weight each good by its market price. The difficulty is to decide *which* prices to use: those prevailing in the first period, or those prevailing in the second? Either choice is arbitrary, but it may make a big difference which we choose. (Think of comparing living standards in 1998 and 1978: in evaluating the increase in consumption of products which embody information technology, should we use 1998 or 1978 prices?) There are similar problems in comparing real consumption across countries. (Think of comparing living standards in Hong Kong and Australia: in evaluating differences in the consumption of housing space in the two countries, should we use Hong Kong or Australian housing prices?)

---

[48] Ronald Dworkin, "What Is Equality? Part 2: Equality of Resources," *Philosophy and Public Affairs*, vol. 10 (1981), pp. 283–345.

Nevertheless, I think Rawls's fundamental strategy is the right one for a contractarian to follow. If preferences tend to be unstable and to lack the properties of internal coherence that rational choice theory assumes, then we need some other measure of a person's long-term interest. The idea of looking for a measure of opportunity is, I suggest, the most promising strategy available to us. This measure of opportunity cannot be based on the actual preferences of the person in question, since that would take us straight back to the problem with which we started—the instability and incoherence of individual preferences. Neither can our measure of opportunity be based on any substantive account of individual good, independent of preference: that would be incompatible with the logic of the contractarian approach. But we have to have some way of imposing a one-dimensional metric on the space of opportunity sets, where each opportunity set is a set of multidimensional bundles of commodities. What seems to be needed is a measure of the desirability of an opportunity set in relation to the range of desires that a person *might have*. This "might have" must encompass counterfactual desires, since the measure we are looking for is not to be based on each person's actual preferences; and it must not appeal to any substantive conception of the good to filter out "illegitimate" or "unreasonable" desires.

However crudely, market prices do reflect the relative desirability of different commodities to people in general, without presupposing any particular conception of the good. Some kind of income-based measure may be the best we can hope for. Even if no such measure can be justified as uniquely correct, we may be able to find a measure that can be defended as a simple and salient model of people's judgments about opportunity.

V. Conclusions

I fear that many readers with liberal or contractarian sympathies will not have liked my argument. The concept of opportunity is essentially the same as "effective freedom," and liberals often regard the latter as a suspiciously collectivist idea—and as an illegitimate hijacking of the word "freedom." In addition, my emphasis on the instability and incoherence of individuals' preferences might be seen as opening the way to paternalistic arguments for the state to interfere in people's lives. I think both these objections are mistaken.

Of course, effective freedom must not be confused with negative freedom. Effective freedom or opportunity is a concept of "freedom to," while a person has negative freedom to the extent that he is free *from* interference by others. The value of negative freedom is built into the fundamental structure of contractarian theory, by virtue of the principle that constraints are justified only if the person who is constrained has consented to them. However, we still need some conception of each person's interests—of what each person is seeking to achieve from social cooperation. It is in no way contrary to the principles of classical liberalism to claim that each person is seeking to maximize the extent of his opportunities. Notice that the claim is not that society ought to be so arranged as to maximize some aggregate of everyone's opportunity. The aim is to recommend social arrangements to which each person, seeking to maximize his own opportunity, can consent.

I can understand why liberals might wish it to be the case that individuals have stable and coherent preferences. A demonstration that preferences have those properties would indeed help to counter some paternalistic arguments. Nevertheless, we must live with the world as it is. I believe the evidence supports the hypothesis that preferences are often unstable and inconsistent. I recognize that not everyone shares my interpretation of that evidence. If ultimately that interpretation is proved wrong, then much of the argument of this essay will have been unnecessary. If my interpretation is right, however, liberals will have to bite the bullet.

I have tried to show that contractarianism does not need the assumption that individuals have stable and coherent preferences over all possible states of affairs. It would be sufficient if we could find some measure of opportunity such that everyone can be assumed to prefer more opportunity to less. But how such a measure is to be constructed, and, indeed, if any satisfactory measure can be constructed at all, remains to be discovered.

Economics, University of East Anglia

DEONTIC RESTRICTIONS ARE NOT
AGENT-RELATIVE RESTRICTIONS*

By Eric Mack

I. Introduction

The primary purpose of this essay is to offer a critique of a particular program within moral and political philosophy. This program can be stated quite succinctly. It is to account for agents' being subject to *deontic restrictions* on the basis of their possession of *agent-relative reasons* for acting in accordance with those restrictions. Needless to say, the statement of this program requires some further explication. Specifically, two claims require explanation: (1) the reasons individuals have for or against engaging in particular actions are, at least to a very significant extent, *agent-relative* rather than *agent-neutral*; and (2) agents' conduct toward others is subject to *deontic restrictions*. Finally, (3) I need to explain why an agent's possession of agent-relative reasons for performing or refraining from certain actions may be thought to explain that agent's being subject to certain deontic restrictions.

1. To explicate the idea of agent-relative reasons and the contrasting idea of agent-neutral reasons, let us begin with the closely related ideas of agent-relative and agent-neutral *value*. If a certain condition has agent-relative value, the value of that condition is its value for some particular agent who stands in some special relation to that condition. If, for example, the value of a given agent's integrity is agent-relative, the value of that condition is its value for the agent whose integrity it is. Because the value of the integrity is its value for this particular agent, that value as such provides only the agent for whom it obtains with reason—agent-relative reason—to promote that condition. Other persons can readily acknowledge that this integrity has value for the agent whose integrity it will be and provides that agent with reason to achieve and sustain it, while denying that the value of this condition provides them with any comparable reason for promoting this agent's integrity. If the value of a given agent's integrity is agent-relative, that instantiation of integrity is, in effect, a private good—a good which, as such, provides its prospective subject with reason for its promotion, but does not, as such, provide

* I thank Ellen Frankel Paul for her valuable editorial advice and the other contributors to this volume for their helpful comments.

61

others with reason to promote that instantiation of integrity.[1] And agents do, it seems, have agent-relative reasons—for example, reasons to attain (their own) sensorial pleasure, reasons to complete (their own) life-defining projects, and reasons to sustain (their own) integrity.[2]

In contrast, if some condition has agent-neutral value, its value is not specifically value for some particular agent who stands in some special relationship to that condition. If an agent's integrity has agent-neutral value, then its value is not its value for the agent whose integrity it would be. The integrity has, so to speak, value for the universe at large. It has public value that provides everyone equally with reason—agent-neutral reason—to promote it.

If an agent has agent-relative reason for bringing about a certain condition within his life, his having that reason will be consistent with his not having comparable reason to bring about similar conditions in other persons' lives. For those similar conditions in other persons' lives directly provide them, but not him, with reason to bring them about. Suppose that instantiations of integrity have agent-relative value and, for this reason, each prospective instantiation specifically provides the agent whose integrity it will be with reason to achieve and sustain it. Then, if an agent is faced with a choice between achieving or sustaining his own integrity and others' loss of their integrity, he will, everything else being equal, have reason to choose the former course of action. Similarly, if an agent has agent-relative reason to avoid the performance of a certain sort of action within his life, his having reason to see to his nonperformance of actions of that sort will be consistent with his not having comparable reason to see to the nonperformance of similar actions within other people's lives. If that agent is faced with a choice between avoiding his performance of an action of that sort and preventing others from performing actions of that sort, he will, everything else being equal, have reason to avoid his performance of the action.

2. Deontic restrictions are moral prohibitions against inflicting certain forms of treatment upon others. They are prohibitions that obtain even if violating those prohibitions would have valuable results—because the prohibitions do not acquire their directive force from the value of compliance with them. Consider the deontic restriction against killing the innocent. This is a prohibition that has directive force for me even if killing an innocent person would enhance the balance of agent-neutral value in society, enhance the balance of my agent-relative value, or even enhance the balance of the innocent person's agent-relative value (as it

---

[1] The recurrent "as such" is my device for sliding past the various ways in which the promotion of an agent's agent-relative value can have vicarious value for another agent.

[2] Although I have focused on agent-relative reasons that are reflective of agent-relative value, I have not excluded the possibility of an agent's having agent-relative reasons for or against performing certain actions without those reasons being reflective of the agent-relative value or disvalue of those actions for that agent.

would if that innocent person would be better off dead). An interesting mark of the fact that the wrongfulness of violating a deontic restriction is not the disvalue of the violation is that, if I am under a deontic restriction, I ought not to violate it even if doing so will decrease the number of violations of that restriction that will occur. If I am deontically bound not to kill the innocent, then I ought not to kill innocent A even if doing so will prevent Z from killing innocents B and C. But if it were the disvalue of killing innocents that makes it wrong, then in this special case I ought to minimize that disvalue by killing A.

3. We can now see how the program of accounting for an agent's deontic restrictions in terms of his agent-relative reasons emerges naturally from belief in the existence of agent-relative reasons and deontic restrictions. We can see this most readily by restating more precisely the final sentence of the last paragraph: If it were the *agent-neutral* disvalue of killing innocents that normally makes my killing A wrong, then in the special case I ought to minimize that agent-neutral disvalue by killing A. In the special case in which I can prevent two killings by performing one, I will, all things considered, have *agent-neutral reason* to engage in the killing of an innocent. If my reason not to kill is agent-neutral, then I have reason myself to avoid killing only when this behavior minimizes the killing of innocents.

If one presumes that I am, nevertheless, under a deontic restriction not to kill innocent A even when doing so would prevent Z from killing innocents B and C, and that, therefore, I have reason not to kill A even in these special circumstances, then it is natural to infer that this reason must be *agent-relative*. After all, it seems natural to say that what I have reason to avoid is *my killing* of A. It is not that *my killing* A is agent-neutrally worse than Z's killing B and C. *Other people* may very reasonably favor my killing A over Z's killing B and C. It seems to be the special disvalue or wrongfulness of *my killing* that is involved in my being deontically bound not to kill A. So, the natural conclusion is that the reason that underlies this deontic restriction—the reason that provides a justifying account of my being subject to this moral restraint—is an *agent-relative reason*. This conclusion launches the project of identifying the agent-relative reasons on the basis of which individuals are subject to various deontic restrictions.

Two points must, however, be made about the inference to this conclusion. The first point is that the inference from a reason's not being agent-neutral to its being agent-relative presumes that all reasons are either agent-neutral or agent-relative. However, it is not too difficult—at least for someone prepared to accept the existence of deontic restrictions—to envision how there could be reasons that are neither agent-neutral nor agent-relative. All one has to do is to suppose that: (a) an agent-relative reason is one that arises in connection with the directive force of agent-relative value (or disvalue); (b) an agent-neutral reason is one that arises in connection with the directive force of agent-neutral value (or disvalue); and (c) deontic restrictions do not obtain in virtue of the value of compliance with them (or the disvalue of noncompliance with them). Since the reason for performing (or refraining from) an action that an agent has in connection with his being subject to a deontic restriction does not obtain in virtue of either the agent-relative or the agent-neutral value of compliance with it (or the agent-relative or agent-neutral disvalue of noncompliance with it), that reason will itself be neither agent-relative nor agent-neutral. In short, if "agent-relative" and "agent-neutral" apply only to reasons that obtain in connection with the directive force of some value or disvalue, the premise that an agent's reason is not agent-neutral will not warrant the conclusion that the agent's reason is agent-relative.[3] The second point is that an agent may have an agent-relative reason to act in accordance with some deontic restriction to which he is subject without that agent-relative reason being the explanation of that deontic restriction. I shall recur to both of these points in the course of my critique of the program of providing a justifying account of an agent's deontic restriction on the basis of that agent's agent-relative reasons.

I shall proceed by tracing the emergence of this program and critically examining two attempts to carry it out. Tracing the emergence of this program through important essays by Bernard Williams and Samuel Scheffler provides evidence that it is a mistake to construe deontic restrictions as agent-relative phenomena, while also explaining how this misconstrual has developed.[4] A critical assessment of the attempts by Thomas Nagel and Stephen Darwall to carry out the program confirms that deontic restrictions ought not to be thought of as grounded in agent-relative reasons possessed by the subject of those restrictions. I should emphasize that my purpose is to explain why this *program* ought to be rejected. It is not merely that attempts to carry out this program have be unsuccessful. Rather, it is a misguided strategy for explaining deontic restrictions. While I offer criticism of attempts, such as Nagel's, to carry out this strategy, I am no less critical of others, such as Scheffler, who see the difficulties faced by this program as undermining the last best hope for accounting for deontic restrictions.

[3] This inference is no better than the inference from its not being an agent-relative reason to its being an agent-neutral reason.

[4] A similar denial of the agent-relative character of deontic restraints can be found in the later sections of Frances Kamm's "Non-Consequentialism, the Person as an End-in-Itself, and the Significance of Status," *Philosophy and Public Affairs*, vol. 21, no. 4 (Fall 1992). In the present essay, I provide a much more extended account of the genesis of this mistaken characterization of deontic restraints. I also suggest how an appeal to agent-relative value may undergird and motivate the invocation of persons' "status" as ends-in-themselves through which Kamm seeks to account for deontic restraints (see *ibid.*, pp. 386–89). The thesis that deontic restrictions are "victim- rather than agent-focused" (*ibid.*, p. 385) is anticipated in my "Moral Individualism: Agent-Relativity and Deontic Restraints," *Social Philosophy and Policy*, vol. 7, no. 1 (Autumn 1989), p. 105.

Indeed, I should emphasize that my special interest in the program under examination arises from the fact I have a warm philosophical regard for *both* agent-relative reasons and values *and* deontic restrictions—in particular, those restrictions that are correlative to persons' moral rights. Moreover, I believe that there are important connections between, on the one hand, the agent-relativity of value and of our value-oriented reasons for action and, on the other hand, our possession of rights that are correlative to deontic restraints on others' behavior toward us. My ultimate complaint about the program under examination, then, is not that it attends to both agent-relative reasons and deontic restrictions or that it attempts to reveal an illuminating connection between the two. Rather, it is that this program attempts to connect agent-relativity and deontic restraints in the wrong way. I hope in the course of my critique to provide some intimations of what the more illuminating connections between agent-relativity of reasons and values and deontic restrictions may be.

Before proceeding, however, I must record a qualification of the thesis expressed in my title. My primary interest is in a certain subclass of deontic restrictions—the subclass of restrictions that are correlative to other agents' rights. There may be duties that are genuinely deontic but do not involve others' correlative rights—perhaps because they are fundamentally self-regarding. I am not concerned with such duties here. In particular, I am not concerned with whether such duties, if they exist, can be vindicated in terms of the agent-relative reasons of the agents who are subject to them.[5] My purpose in this essay is to deny the agent-relative character of rights-correlative deontic restrictions. This more focused thesis still has considerable bite because those who have looked for or even advocated agent-relativist explanations of deontic restrictions have taken rights-correlative restrictions as prominent among the restrictions that are supposed to be explained.[6]

II. THE CONFLATION OF PARTIALIST AND DEONTIC OBJECTIONS

The primary proximate source of the program under examination is Bernard Williams's highly influential essay "A Critique of Utilitarianism." The

[5] Kamm is probably correct to deny that even these "duty-based" restrictions are agent-relative. She says, "I believe that duty-based theories are agent-focused but not agent-relative, in that the constraint supposedly arises from the content of what the agent is doing, not from his (versus others') doing it" ("Non-Consequentialism," p. 382).

[6] Thus, Scheffler's search for a rationale for deontic restrictions takes place explicitly within the context of assessing Robert Nozick's ascription to persons of rights that impose side-constraints on others' behavior. See Samuel Scheffler, *The Rejection of Consequentialism* (Oxford: Clarendon Press, 1982), p. 82; and Robert Nozick, *Anarchy, State, and Utopia* (New York: Basic Books, 1974), pp. 26–33. And, when he introduces the topic of deontic reasons, Nagel speaks of them as stemming from "the claims of other persons not to be maltreated in certain ways" and as a man's relative reasons "not to maltreat others himself, in his dealings with them (for example by violating their rights, breaking his promises to them, etc.)." Thomas Nagel, *The View from Nowhere* (Oxford: Oxford University Press, 1986), p. 165.

central theme of that essay is the clash between, on the one hand, integrity, and on the other hand, the demand for impartiality that is at the core of utilitarianism and all kindred doctrines that require agents to promote what is taken to be the impersonally best outcome. Integrity is a matter of adherence to one's own projects and commitments; it is a matter of being true to oneself as the particular person one is in virtue of one's central, life-defining allegiances. Because each person's allegiances significantly determine what his self and life are about, each person has special reason to act in accordance with his own central projects and commitments. But the demand for impartiality at the core of utilitarianism requires that one give equal weight to all projects and commitments of comparable magnitude no matter whose projects and commitments they are. When an agent decides on the basis of such impartiality,

> [h]is own substantial projects and commitments come into it, but only as one lot among others—they potentially provide one set of satisfactions among those which he may be able to assist from where he happens to be. He is the agent of the satisfaction system who happens to be at a particular point at a particular time. . . .[7]

But such a conception of rational choice ignores who the committed agent is and what his life is about.

> It is absurd to demand of such a man, when the sums come in from the utility network which the projects of others have in part determined, that he should just step aside from his own project and decision and acknowledge the decision which utilitarian calculation requires. It is to alienate him in a real sense from his actions and the source of his action in his own convictions. It is to make him into a channel between the input of everyone's projects, including his own, and an output of optimific decision. . . .[8]

Similarly, it would be absurd for this man or any coalition he might join to demand that any other agent alienate herself from her own life-defining projects and make herself into a channel for the optimal processing of everyone's projects.

Although Williams does not employ the vocabulary of agent-relativity and agent-neutrality, his position can be restated as the contention that each individual's life-defining projects and commitments provide that individual with agent-relative reasons to abide by and promote them. Though each individual must acknowledge that others' projects and com-

---

[7] Bernard Williams, "A Critique of Utilitarianism," in *Utilitarianism: For and Against*, J. J. C. Smart and Bernard Williams (Cambridge: Cambridge University Press, 1973), p. 115.
[8] *Ibid.*, p. 116.

mitments provide those others with reasons for action, this in no way requires that the agent himself be impartial among all these projects and commitments. Focusing on the importance for individuals of maintaining their allegiance to and fulfilling their projects and commitments, the integrity critique takes aim at the impartialist (agent-neutralist) conception of the good according to which each person's good provides all persons with like reason to devote themselves to its promotion. The integrity critique upholds the rationality of an agent's partiality toward his own projects and commitments by maintaining that these projects and commitments provide the agent with agent-relative reasons for action.

The integrity critique of utilitarian-like doctrines is, therefore, fundamentally distinct from the justice critique of such doctrines. For the justice critique focuses, not on the impartialist conception of the good, but rather on the consequentialist thesis that whatever action produces the greatest good is right. The justice critique challenges this thesis by invoking deontic restrictions that provide agents with reasons against certain ways of treating others even if that treatment yields what, for the sake of argument anyway, is taken to be the greatest good. Although the anti-utilitarian appeal to the rationality of the agent's partiality to his own projects and the anti-utilitarian appeal to the agent's being subject to deontic restrictions are entirely consistent, they represent quite distinct individualist objections to utilitarianism and kindred doctrines.[9]

Unfortunately, the particular examples that Williams employs, especially his famous example of Jim and the Indians, obscure the line between the two anti-utilitarian critiques: the critique that insists on the rationality of partiality to one's own projects and on the recognition of agents' agent-relative reasons, and the critique that insists that there are deontic restrictions against even optimizing conduct. In Williams's example, Jim, who we must presume is deeply committed to not killing innocents, wanders into a South American village where the evil commandant Pedro is about to kill twenty innocent Indians. In honor of Jim's arrival, Pedro announces that if Jim will himself kill one of these villagers, Pedro will spare the remaining nineteen. And it is clear to Jim that his only options are to kill the one—in which case Pedro will indeed spare the nineteen—or allow Pedro to proceed with the twenty killings. We should note that Williams's view is not that it is clearly wrong for Jim to kill the one. Rather, his view is that Jim's killing the one would be deeply morally problematic and any doctrine that implies that it is clearly right for Jim to kill the one is, for that reason, fundamentally defective.

This renowned example obscures the line between the integrity and justice critiques, because what really renders Jim's killing one of the vil-

---

[9] Williams announces at the outset that his purpose is to offer a critique of utilitarianism that, instead of dealing with justice, will be "concerned with something rather different, integrity" (*ibid.*, p. 82).

lagers morally problematic is Jim's being subject to a deontic restriction against killing the innocent. At the core of Jim's moral dilemma is the conflict between his belief that in some sense it is better for one person to be killed than twenty and his belief that he is morally precluded from bringing about this better outcome by the deontic restriction against killing the innocent. The example, however, is taken by Williams to reveal the deficiency of any doctrine that requires Jim to be impartial between his own projects and the projects of others and, hence, the deficiency of any doctrine that ignores the agent-relative importance of Jim's projects. We have an example in which the real work in rendering the action morally problematic is done by a deontic restriction and, yet, what is taken to lead Jim astray is his failure to appreciate the rationality of special allegiance to his own projects. The suggestion that emerges is that what explains the morally problematic character of Jim's killing the one villager—what explains what is in fact the deontic defect of Jim's killing the one—is Jim's having agent-relative reasons to advance his own projects.

The implausibility of this suggestion is masked by two features of the situation. First, Jim presumably does have partialist (agent-relative) reason not to kill the one, and second, Jim presumably has this reason in connection with his sense that he is under a normative restraint against killing the innocent. Presumably, Jim has committed himself to abide by the restriction against killing the innocent—he has made a project of compliance with this restraint—because of his sense of the injustice of killing innocents. Jim's resulting project of abiding by this norm may then play an important role in structuring his life and constituting Jim's sense of himself. As a consequence, Jim may acquire strong agent-relative reason to abide by this principle. It may even be true that Jim will be motivated to comply with the restriction only if he has so internalized his affirmation of it. Nevertheless, this agent-relative reason derives its force and its respectability from Jim's prior belief that he is subject to a deontic restraint of justice.

Suppose that Jim's reluctance to kill the one villager is merely reflective of a deep-seated *distaste* on Jim's part for the gritty task of killing. We would then be drawn to the charge that Jim's refusal to kill the one is merely unadmirable self-indulgence.[10] That self-indulgence charge may be dismissed if and only if Jim's aversion to killing innocents derives either from his sense of the agent-neutral badness of innocents' being killed (in which case, Jim should overcome his personal aversion so as better to serve agent-neutral value) or from his sense of the deontic wrongfulness of killing innocents. Jim's possession of agent-relative reason not to kill the one villager should not obscure the prior deontic reason—

---

[10] See, e.g., Bernard Williams, "Utilitarianism and Moral Self-Indulgence," in *Contemporary British Philosophy*, 4th series, ed. H. D. Lewis (London: George Allen and Unwin Ltd., 1976), pp. 306–21.

which I would suggest is *neither* agent-relative *nor* agent-neutral—from which Jim's agent-relative reason derives.[11]

The derivative, agent-relative reason for Jim's abiding by the constraining norm takes center stage within Williams's discussion; there is no acknowledgment of the prior, deontic, justice-oriented norm. This of course has to be Williams's focus if the intuitive force of the case of Jim and the Indians is to be drafted into the service of the integrity critique rather than the justice critique. Yet the effect of this focus and Williams's inattention to the underlying deontic norm "Do not kill innocents" is to create the appearance of there being an explanation of the likelihood of Jim's being bound not to kill the one in terms of Jim's agent-relative reasons. Williams's admixture of an example whose anti-utilitarian force in fact derives from deontic restrictions, with his rejection of utilitarianism on the grounds of its failure to acknowledge agent-relative reasons, suggests that such restrictions are in fact agent-relative phenomena.

III. SEARCHING FOR RESTRICTIONS IN ALL THE WRONG PLACES

Samuel Scheffler's examination of agent-centered restrictions in his *The Rejection of Consequentialism* provides one of the main pillars of the view that, if the claim that an agent is subject to deontic restrictions is to be made plausible, it must be on the basis of identifying that agent's agent-relative reasons for abiding by those restrictions. Scheffler's discussion begins with the purportedly paradoxical character of deontic restrictions. This is the fact—readily noted by every advocate of deontic restrictions— that the upshot of an agent's compliance with such a restriction may be the more extensive violation of that very restriction. For example, the upshot of Jim's compliance with the restriction "Do not kill innocents" is the more extensive violation (by Pedro) of that very restriction. As Scheffler sees it, if anything about the *victims* of the violation of a restriction against K-ing makes K-ing wrong, it must be the agent-neutral disvalue of persons being subjected to K-ing. If there is a moral requirement against K-ing, it must be a function of the agent-neutral disvalue of being K-ed. Or it must be a function of "the possession of some allegedly significant property by the victims of violations" in virtue of which "it is undesirable for persons to be victimized."[12] But according to Scheffler, any appeal to

[11] I have set aside a number of complicating features of the case. Among these are the fact that the one who Jim would kill would be among the twenty Pedro would otherwise kill and the fact that all twenty of the villagers are begging Jim to kill one of them. My guess is that Williams includes the latter feature in order to derail the thought that the key anti-utilitarian consideration is the *injustice* of Jim's killing one of the villagers. The problem for Williams is that if we really attend to this stipulated fact, then it becomes pretty clear that Jim ought to kill one of the villagers. His refusal to do so would merely be a matter of self-indulgence. For, given this authorization, the otherwise crucial deontic restriction against killing innocents will no longer apply.

[12] Scheffler, *The Rejection of Consequentialism*, p. 102.

"the disvalue of violations of such restrictions" or to "the victims' possession of some property" is an

> appeal to a consideration that simply makes all violations of the restrictions seem equally objectionable, and which thus appears to militate in favour of permitting, rather than prohibiting, the minimization of total overall violations.[13]

Scheffler's conclusion is that one ought not to attempt to account for deontic restrictions by focusing upon the victims of violations. Instead, it is better to approach this task by focusing on "the possession of some significant feature by the agents who commit violations."[14] According to Scheffler,

> [t]he question is not: what is it about people that makes it objectionable for them to be victimized? But rather: what is it about a person that makes it impermissible for him to victimize someone else even in order to minimize victimizations which are equally objectionable from an impersonal standpoint?[15]

This is an extraordinary thought. For surely the central intuition of the advocate of deontic restraints is that some morally considerable fact about other persons precludes one from (mal)treating them in certain ways. While, of course, moral side-constraints apply to one as an agent, it is something about the existence of other persons that imposes those constraints upon one's agency. But for Scheffler, this extraordinary thought is quite natural. Since deontic restrictions, if they exist, are presumed to be

> an agent-centred component [in] moral theory ... it is natural to suppose that the identification of a rationale for them must take the form of a demonstration that they represent a rational response to the agent's possession of *some* feature.[16]

However, Scheffler is quick to discover that he can locate no feature of the agent that subjects the agent to deontic restrictions. The only feature of the agent that has any agent-relative force is the independence of the agent's personal point of view—the agent's disposition to view and assess the world through his own desires, interests, and projects. According to Scheffler, this feature provides a rationale for an agent-centered prerogative which allows the agent not to promote the agent-neutrally best

---

[13] *Ibid.*, p. 103.
[14] *Ibid.*, p. 102.
[15] *Ibid.*, p. 100.
[16] *Ibid.*, p. 102.

outcome if doing so would be disproportionately costly to that agent. The prerogative provides the personal point of view of the agent with some modest protection against the demands of impersonal optimality. But does the independence of the *agent's* personal point of view provide a rationale for deontic restrictions upon *that agent*? Not surprisingly, Scheffler answers in the negative. Such restrictions would amount to the requirement that the agent always exercise his prerogative against unduly personally costly subordination to the impersonal standpoint. Yet making the exercise of the agent's prerogative mandatory hardly increases, and arguably decreases, protection of the agent's personal point of view. Of course, what is extraordinary here is the idea that if some special protection or value is afforded by an agent's being subject to deontic restrictions, it will be afforded *to that agent*, rather than to that agent's prospective victims. (Indeed, the focus has so completely shifted away from the victim and to the agent that the restriction considered by Scheffler is one which other individuals would rather not have obtain. For it is a restriction against the agent's imposing costs on himself for the sake of achieving an overall optimal outcome.)

This key argument against deontic restrictions suggests that, if there were an agent-relative basis for such restraints, it would be the agent-relative *value* of the agent's compliance with those restraints. Perhaps, however, there can be agent-relative reasons for an agent's compliance with deontic restrictions that are not a matter of the agent-relative *value* of abiding by those restraints. Scheffler does not explicitly differentiate between reasons that reflect relative values and those that are agent-relative because in some other way they reflect the personal perspective of the agent. Nevertheless, he does go on to consider what may be described as agent-relative reasons that do not reflect agent-relative values. In particular, he examines the ideas that "an agent is specially responsible for what he does, and responsible only secondarily, if at all, for what he fails to prevent others from doing," that "human beings have the capacity to directly cause harm to other human beings," and that "people have the capacity to *intentionally* cause harm to others."[17] However, I will not review his arguments against grounding deontic restrictions upon any of these non-value agent-relative considerations. For a much more explicit and illuminating discussion of this grounding of restraints is offered by Thomas Nagel.

IV. AGENCY AND RESTRICTIONS

In *The View from Nowhere*, Nagel acknowledges the existence of agent-relative values and reasons. According to Nagel, although some states, such as states of sensorial pleasure, have agent-neutral value and provide

[17] *Ibid.*, pp. 102, 104, and 106.

everyone with reason to promote them, other states, such as my fulfilling my project of climbing Mount Kilimanjaro have (only) agent-relative value and provide (only) agent-relative reason for their promotion. Although I have reason to carry through on this project, others may very well have no reason to assist me. The recognition of such agent-relative values and reasons amounts to something like Scheffler's agent-centered prerogative. Insofar as particular states have significant agent-relative value for an agent, that agent has reason to bring about a world in which those states are more fully realized than they would be in the agent-neutrally best world.[18] Nagel, however, explicitly treats deontological reasons as a *second* type of reason that is "relative in form, and whose existence seems to be independent of impersonal values." In contrast to Scheffler, Nagel insists that this second type of reason "stems from the claims of other persons not to be maltreated in certain ways." Considerations of agent-relative *value* "limit what we are obliged to do in the service of impersonal values. Deontological reasons . . . limit what we are *permitted* to do in the service of either impersonal or [agent-relative values]." Yet deontic reasons are not neutral reasons. For neutral reasons would mandate that maltreatment be minimized, whereas these reasons mandate that "each individual not . . . maltreat others *himself*, in *his* dealings with them."[19] Thus,

> deontological constraints . . . are agent-relative reasons which depend not on the aims or projects of the agent but on the claims of others. . . . [T]he relative reason does not come from an aim or project of the individual agent, for it is not conditional on what the agent wants. Deontological restrictions, if they exist, apply to everyone: they are mandatory and may not be given up like personal ambitions or commitments.[20]

But this, according to Nagel, makes the idea of deontic restrictions so puzzling as to suggest their nonexistence. On the one hand, they stem from outside the agent, and Nagel presumes that the only thing that can have normative force from outside the agent is agent-neutral value or disvalue. On the other hand, they do not call for the minimization of maltreatment—so these reasons cannot be reflective of the disvalue of the maltreatment.

Nagel attempts to resolve this puzzle by an ingenious, but I think not ingenious enough, melding of the two factors involved—the agent-

---

[18] Nagel's counterpart to Scheffler's prerogative is more than a mere permission. For Nagel, it would be unreasonable for an agent to sacrifice agent-relative value in the single-minded pursuit of the agent-neutrally best. In contrast, Scheffler seems to want to say that it would not be unreasonable to forgo exercising one's prerogative.

[19] Nagel, *The View from Nowhere*, p. 165, emphasis added to the pronouns.

[20] *Ibid.*, pp. 175 and 178.

neutral disvalue of what befalls the victim, and some property of the agent's perspective. Imagine that my friends have been seriously injured in a car accident and need medical assistance. I rush to an isolated farmhouse and ask the elderly woman who lives there if I can borrow her car to go for help. My desperate appeal panics her and she grabs the car keys, runs to the bathroom, and locks herself in. But I can get her to open the door and surrender the car keys by painfully twisting the arm of her sweet little granddaughter who is also in the house. Nagel takes me to be under a deontic restriction not to twist the child's arm. This moral restraint may not be absolute. It may even be overridden in other cases in which my friends more urgently need medical attention or in which two or three carloads of people need medical attention as much as my friends do in the present case. But even if the restraint is nonabsolute and overridden, its existence will be manifest in the fact that my decision will be much more difficult than it would be were the relevant consideration only which of the actions available to me will yield the better results.

For Nagel, the most plausible candidates for deontic restrictions are restrictions against *intentionally* harming others in one way or another. For it is the intending of a harm that can render its intentional production wrongful even if the agent-neutral disvalue which attaches to that harm is less—perhaps very much less—than the disvalue that would have been prevented by producing that harm. Since the pain of the granddaughter would be my intended means, while the greater harm that the friends will suffer if I do not twist her arm would merely be foreseen, I ought not to twist that child's arm. I ought not to do so even though "*things* will be better, what *happens* will be better," if I do. But why is it worse to intentionally bring about a relatively small agent-neutral disvalue (the child's pain) than to allow or even nonintentionally bring about a relatively large agent-neutral disvalue? Nagel's answer is that, within the perspective of the agent, intention magnifies the (agent-neutral) disvalue of what is intentionally produced.

> When I twist the child's arm intentionally I incorporate that evil into what I do: it is my deliberate creation and the reasons stemming from it are magnified and lit up from my point of view. They overshadow reasons stemming from greater evils that are more "faint" from this perspective, because they do not fall within the intensifying beam of my intentions even though they are consequences of what I do.[21]

It is not the agent-relative disvalue (for me) of the child's pain or of my causing the child's pain that, added to its agent-neutral disvalue, outweighs the disvalue of my friends' suffering. Rather, what makes the twisting wrong is that the magnified *agent-neutral* disvalue of the child's

---

[21] *Ibid.*, p. 180, emphasis added.

pain is greater than the nonmagnified disvalue of the friends' suffering. Nagel's imagery of magnification and intensification suggests that, within the agent's perspective, the disvalue of what is intended gets multiplied and the action in question is wrong if and only if the resulting multiple of disvalue is greater than the disvalue associated with the agent's alternative action or inaction. (Read somewhat differently, Nagel's imagery of the intended evil being lit up and overshadowing more faint nonintended evils suggests that intention gives a type of salience or even lexical priority to the intended evil, so that the disvalue of what is intended becomes, within the agent's perspective, the relevant factor in evaluating the action. This would seem to make the restrictions absolute—not to be violated whatever the nonintended consequences.)[22]

Against Nagel's magnification account, it is natural to wonder why intention does not similarly magnify good results. Specifically, although if I forbear from twisting the child's arm, my friends' lack of medical attention will be merely foreseen, if I do twist the child's arm, their receiving medical attention will be the intended consequence of my action. So if I were to proceed to inflict that pain as an intended means, shouldn't the magnified disvalue of the child's pain be overbalanced by the magnified value of my friends' getting medical attention? Or if intention bestows salience, shouldn't the child's loss and my friends' gain have equal salience—with the greater original magnitude of my friends' gain overbalancing the lesser original magnitude of the child's loss? In anticipation of this sort of objection, Nagel insists that intention is selective in what it magnifies.[23] To intentionally do evil is to swim "head-on against the normative current." It is to push "directly and essentially against the intrinsic normative force" of your proper goal, to serve and protect the good.[24] This focus on what one is directly doing rather than on what will or might happen is appropriate because each of us is "a particular person with a particular perspective."

> [F]rom the internal point of view, the pursuit of evil in twisting the child's arm looms large. The production of pain is the immediate aim, and the fact that from an external perspective you are choosing a balance of good over evil does not cover up the fact that it is the intrinsic character of your action.[25]

---

[22] In either case, Nagel's account seems to violate his own requirement that deontic restraints "not themselves be understood as the expression of neutral values of any kind" (*ibid.*, p. 177).

[23] Nagel does not address the issue of the magnification of the value of intended good *ends*. But he does deny that intention would magnify the value of an intended means (*ibid.*, p. 181).

[24] *Ibid.*, p. 182.

[25] *Ibid.*, p. 183.

Unfortunately, none of this seems to explain why *intentionally* securing medical attention for my friends should not similarly loom large. If it is especially bad within my perspective as a particular agent to swim directly against the normative current, why isn't it also especially good within that perspective to swim directly with the current—as I would be insofar as the purpose of my behavior is to get my friends that needed medical assistance?

Perhaps a crucial role is supposed to be played by the *immediacy* of my intentional infliction of pain on the child. Since *that* is what I am doing, that is what I must evaluate (or what I must give multiplied negative weight in my evaluation). Even though I am *also*, albeit less immediately, intentionally getting valuable medical assistance for my friends, the reasons that speak on behalf of my doing this cannot overbalance the discrete evaluation of my immediate act of intentionally twisting the child's arm. Perhaps, then, Nagel's position is this: actions are differentiated by the intentions they involve; when there is an intended means to an intended end, the agent must discretely evaluate the action that is identified by the intended means and the action that is identified by the intended end; and the agent may not proceed if either of these discrete evaluations is negative. In effect, one may not intentionally do evil even if doing so is a means to intentionally doing greater good. Unfortunately, it is not at all clear why the discrete positive evaluation of my securing that medical assistance should not be weighed against the discrete negative evaluation of my twisting the child's arm. What is it about having a particular perspective, having an internal point of view, that precludes one's performing an action with a bad intrinsic character as a means to performing an action that both has a good intrinsic character and eliminates significantly more agent-neutral disvalue than the bad action engenders? Again, this weighing could be allowed and an anti-consequentialist conclusion still drawn, if there were any good reason to think that swimming directly against the normative current is especially bad, whereas swimming directly with it is not especially good. For then the greater good of getting help for my friends would still be overbalanced by the lesser evil of twisting the child's arm. But there is no apparent reason to believe in this normative asymmetry.

In the present context, what is more fundamentally troublesome about Nagel's account is that the deontic character of restraints is entirely the creature of the agent's perspective and seems to have its existence entirely within that perspective. This contravenes the idea that the deontic character of restraints "stems from the claims of other persons"[26] or from something about *those persons* that grounds these claims. To see how on Nagel's perspectival account the deontic character of the constraint against

---

[26] *Ibid.*, p. 165.

twisting the child's arm resides within the agent, consider whether a third party would be justified in forcibly preventing me from twisting that child's arm.[27] Surely if what is at stake is *the wronging of the child*, the infringement upon *her rights*, then (absent special complicating factors) it must be at least permissible for that prospective defender to forcibly suppress my assault on the child. However, the only cost to the child that can provide any rationale for the third party's intervention is the nonmagnified agent-neutral disvalue of her pain. And, against this, a Nagelian third party must weigh the far greater agent-neutral disvalue of my friends' not getting medical assistance. It seems as though, viewed externally, any prospective Nagelian defender must take my twisting of the child's arm to be for the best. Is there any way in which the defender's internal perspective can be brought into play? Is there any moral cost, residing within the defender's perspective, that can overbalance this external assessment? The prospective defender cannot justify her interfering on the grounds that she must interfere in order to avoid suffering her own, perspectivally induced, moral cost. For it cannot be plausibly argued that, in not intervening, this third party would be intentionally bringing about the child's pain. Nor does it seem that the third party's allowing the twisting to take place brings the agent-neutral evil of the child's pain within the scope of that party's agency — with the result that this evil is perspectivally magnified.[28] So it cannot plausibly be thought that this pain would be magnified or lit up within the perspective of the defender.

Of course, on Nagel's account, *I* ought not to twist the child's arm because of the moral cost to me of swimming directly against the moral current — a cost which we will presume would not be overbalanced by the moral gain of swimming directly toward the value of medical assistance for my friends. However, it is difficult to see why the prevention of that moral cost to me should, in the prospective defender's deliberations, be more weighty than the agent-neutral gain that will result from my twisting the child's arm. Suppose, however, that the prevention of that moral cost to me would justify the prospective defender's intervention against me. It would, nevertheless, be the wrong sort of justification. For the defender's intervention would not be vindicated as a defense of the child but rather as an act of moral paternalism on *my* behalf.

One may even wonder whether, on Nagel's account, the *child* would be justified in forcibly suppressing or even escaping from my attack. After

---

[27] The argument over the next couple of paragraphs assumes that some level of injurious force is justified to suppress an aggressor's violation of rights. Nagel himself endorses this view — on the very principle of double effect that is central to his account of deontic restrictions. See Thomas Nagel, "War and Massacre," *Philosophy and Public Affairs*, vol. 1, no. 1 (Winter 1972), pp. 123–44.

[28] If it did, then any choice to allow certain benefits to occur that also involved allowing certain evils to occur would involve a magnification of those evils.

all, the child too, as objective self, sees that it would be better that she undergo the pain than that my stranded friends suffer to a greater extent. In what way can the child have more justification for resisting my attack than the third-party defender would? Nagel does assert, almost as an afterthought, that "there is also something to be said about the point of view of the victim."[29] Indeed, two things can be said. The first is that the victim will have reasons reflective of her agent-relative values for resisting my optimizing action. If I am about to kill someone in order to save the lives of five other people, the person I am about to kill need not accede to my actions as she would have to "on a purely agent-neutral consequentialist view." Yet this consideration does not provide the target of my optimizing strategy with anything like a deontic objection to my actions; and it provides each of the five prospective beneficiaries of that strategy with their own agent-relative reasons to support my action and suppress the target's resistance to it. The second thing to be said about the point of view of the target is that she *also* gets to magnify the disvalue of her loss and to count that magnified disvalue in her evaluation of my action. Why? Nagel's explanation seems to be that the target is entitled to draw upon her intentional attacker's magnification of the disvalue of that attack:

> The deontological constraint [that] permits a victim always to object to those who aim at his harm . . . expresses the direct appeal to the point of view of the agent from the point of view of the person on whom he is acting. It operates through that relation.[30]

I cannot myself see why, within the parameters of Nagel's position, the victim is entitled to this "direct appeal to the point of view of the agent." What is significant, however, is that Nagel's need to invoke this appeal is a further indication of his failure to accommodate the idea that the constraints on the agent stem from the prospective victim, that they are reflective of claims of this victim which have some reality outside of the perspective of the wrongdoing agent. The same failure is indicated if we consider optimizing actions, such as the twisting of the granddaughter's arm, carried out by God or some equally objective saint. Since such an agent will have no particular perspective, will view the world from nowhere, the harm he directly does will not be magnified or lit up. There will be no point of view of the agent for the victim to appeal to, and there will be no perspective for a deontic restriction to reside in. Indeed, on Nagel's account, the more any agent transcends his subjective self, the less moral inviolability others will possess against that agent's optimizing

---

[29] Nagel, *The View from Nowhere*, p. 183.
[30] *Ibid.*, p. 184.

impositions. This, again, reveals that, on Nagel's analysis, the victim's rights are entirely in the eye of the subjective agent.[31]

When Nagel does conclude his discussion of deontic restrictions with remarks that suggest that those restrictions are not merely creatures of the agent's perspective, he seems to go beyond the bounds of his own perspectival account. Thus, Nagel says that

> [t]he victim feels outrage when he is deliberately harmed even for the greater good of others, not simply because of the quantity of the harm but because of the assault on his value of having my actions guided by his evil. What I do is immediately directed against his good: it doesn't just in fact harm him.[32]

Indeed. But this claim seems to have nothing to do with magnification and, even more assuredly, nothing to do with appealing to the point of view of the agent—except in the sense that it is the intentionally harmful act of the agent that is seen as *wronging* the victim. Here the direction of argument seems to move from the wrongfulness of subjecting the victim to an "assault on his value," through an intentional harm constituting such an assault, to the conclusion that an intentional harm wrongs the victim and, hence, is a wrongdoing on the part of the agent. And notice that, while this is the direction of argument one wants as a vindicating account of rights-correlated deontic restrictions, it does not at all appeal to the agent's agent-relative reasons. Similarly, there is no appeal to the point of view of the agent when Nagel contrasts the "appeal" that the five persons who I could save by killing the one can make to me in terms of the agent-neutral value of their lives, with the "protest" that the one can make to me "as the possessor of the life I am aiming to destroy."[33]

To make my survey a bit more complete, I will say a word or two about Stephen Darwall's attempt to provide an agent-relativist account of deontic restrictions in his very interesting essay "Agent-Centered Restrictions from the Inside Out."[34] As his title suggests, Darwall seeks a vindicating explanation in the only place he thinks it can possibly be found—in a morality that begins with the agent and his moral responsi-

---

[31] I do not mean to suggest that Nagel is unaware of his focus on the agent rather than the victim. He says, "I have concentrated on the point of view of the agent, as seems suitable in the investigation of an agent-relative constraint" (*ibid.*, p. 183). But I do think he fails to connect how this focus—which is dictated by the program of providing an account of restrictions in terms of the agent's agent-relative reasons—precludes accommodating the intuitions about others' claims and inviolabilities that largely motivate the deontic disposition.

[32] *Ibid.*, p. 184.

[33] *Ibid.*

[34] Stephen Darwall, "Agent-Centered Restrictions from the Inside Out," *Philosophical Studies*, vol. 50 (1986), pp. 291–319.

bilities rather than with the intrinsic value of states of the world. The key feature of such a morality is the "duty not to compromise one's moral integrity."[35] The problem is that this duty is second-order; whether this duty will ever give one reason to forgo performing an optimizing action will depend upon whether any of one's first-order duties have a deontic character. If one's specific first-order duties all involve maximizing the good or minimizing the bad, then such maximization or minimization will be essential to one's moral integrity.

The difficulty of making a non-question-begging move from the second-order duty to maintain moral integrity (or moral purity) to first-order deontic norms is almost perfectly stated by Horacio Spector.

> [T]he fact—if it is a fact—that an agent sacrifices his moral purity in transgressing a deontological restriction, even though it may be a means of minimizing transgressions of the same type, is due to the existence of moral considerations *independent of moral purity* that establish the agent-relative nature of the deontological restriction in question: otherwise, why should my moral purity have to be affected if I commit a violation of a deontological restriction and *not* if I let others commit a larger number of violations of the same sort?[36]

And Darwall grants that "there is a serious question whether any rationale can be mounted from [the premises of the inside-out approach] for any specific theory of right, in particular for a theory of right with specific agent-centered restrictions."[37] Furthermore, Darwall's own most-favored route to first-order deontic norms—a Rawlsian approach in the manner of *A Theory of Justice*—seems ill-suited to yield such a theory of right. For whatever duties appeal to Rawlsian contractors behind a veil of ignorance, those contractors will always favor individuals and/or institutions being bound to minimize violations of those duties rather than their being bound never themselves to violate those duties. (The argument for this is the same as Robert Nozick's argument for why the contractors will always favor end-state principles over historical principles.)[38]

---

[35] *Ibid.*, p. 311.

[36] Horacio Spector, *Autonomy and Rights* (Oxford: Clarendon Press, 1992), p. 168, first emphasis added. Cf. also Shelly Kagan, *The Limits of Morality* (Oxford: Oxford University Press, 1989), p. 31:

> It is clear that no argument [against killing one to prevent the killing of two or more] based on the loss of moral integrity can succeed . . . unless killing the one does actually involve a sacrifice of the agent's integrity. But if killing the one to save the two is justified—as the [opponent of constraints] believes—then it is no sacrifice of moral integrity for the agent to do so.

[37] Darwall, "Agent-Centered Restrictions," p. 314.

[38] Nozick, *Anarchy, State, and Utopia*, pp. 198–204. For the Rawlsian approach, see John Rawls, *A Theory of Justice* (Cambridge: Harvard University Press, 1971).

V. One Last Misleading Factor

Before concluding with an attempt to draw a positive lesson about the grounds for rights-correlated deontic restrictions, I want to discuss briefly a common motivation for the search for agent-relative reasons for deontic restrictions. This is the idea that it is one thing for there to be a moral requirement—indeed, a deontic restriction—against *K*-ing; but it is something *further* for that restriction to have what Spector refers to as an "agent-relative nature." If *I* must comply with the requirement against *K*-ing even if *my* compliance leaves others to engage in more extensive violations of that same restraint, then, as Frances Kamm expresses the idea, it must be because of "some special disvalue or prominence for the agent in his own violation of [that restriction]."[39] Yet what is described as the agent-relative nature of the deontic restraint against *K*-ing is simply a consequence of its being a deontic restraint. The point is not that all one has to do is *declare* a requirement to be a deontic restraint and then hit *save* on one's word processor. Rather, if one has a reasonable argument for some requirement being a deontic restraint—as Nagel and Spector think they do—then one needs no further explanation of why each person should *herself* abide by that restraint. After all, one's argument has, we are supposing, led one to the conclusion that *K*-ing violates a moral side-constraint, rather than the conclusion that *K*-ing is something whose occurrence should be minimized. Each of us is subject to this constraint, in contrast to being subject to a requirement to minimize violations of the constraint. Kamm makes this point nicely when she writes:

> [I]t would be simply self-contradictory for it to be morally permissible to minimize violations of the constraint itself for the sake of showing concern for *it*. . . . The agent's own act is special only in that it makes him come up against the constraining right.[40]

In fact, to their credit, authors who describe themselves as offering an account of the agent-relative character of restraints often are doing something else which is more sensible. Thus, Spector cites the fact that we are, each of us, separate agents—beings who act as our discrete selves and not as everyone. "We are separate persons too in the crucial sense that we are separate agents." In pointing to this fact, Spector is not so much explaining "the agent-relative nature of the duties bound up with libertarian rights,"[41] as he is indicating the satisfaction of a precondition for our each being constrained by those rights. Similarly, Darwall's focus on respon-

---

[39] Kamm, "Non-Consequentialism," p. 382. As previously noted, Kamm rejects this agent-relativist understanding of deontic restrictions. Note that I exploited this "last misleading factor" in my introductory explication of the program under examination.

[40] Kamm, "Non-Consequentialism," pp. 384 and 385.

[41] Spector, *Autonomy and Rights*, p. 178.

sible agents can more profitably be understood as indicating the presence of apt addressees for deontic restrictions—restrictions which Darwall himself takes to enjoy an independent Rawlsian rationale.

VI. CONCLUSION

Part of the appeal of the program of providing an agent-relativist account of deontic restrictions is the initial plausibility of the idea that a moral system that rejects (agent-neutralist) consequentialism by denying that people are always obligated to perform (what is taken to be) the agent-neutrally best action will also reject consequentialism by insisting that people are sometimes bound not to perform (what is taken to be) the overall best action. A moral system that holds that consequentialism demands too much *of* people in the way of service to the overall agent-neutral good will also hold that consequentialism allows too much to be done *to* people—in ways that violate deontic restrictions—in the service of that purported good. It is obviously desirable to identify some unifying link between these two components of the full rejection of consequentialism. Since the recognition of agent-relative reasons is essential to the first component, it is natural to seek unity in the form of an agent-relativist account of deontic restrictions. We have seen, however, that it is not plausible to construe deontic restrictions upon an agent as reflective of that agent's agent-relative reasons. Deontic restrictions are not, in this way, agent-relative restrictions. And while the agent-relative disvalue for the victim of an agent's violation of the restriction will provide the victim with reason to evade or suppress that violation, this agent-relative disvalue will not provide a reason for the agent to comply with the restriction.[42]

Does this mean that we cannot connect the two components of systematic anti-consequentialism through the medium of agent-relativity? I want to close by *suggesting* two ways in which the fact that value is agent-relative, not agent-neutral, or implications of this fact, make the affirmation of deontic restrictions reasonable.

1. The more pervasive agent-relative value is on the normative landscape and the less prominent agent-neutral value, the more robust will be each person's agent-centered prerogative (to use Scheffler's term) to serve her projects and commitments rather than (what might be taken to be) the impersonally best. But there would be something conceptually odd about a normative system that ascribed to each person a robust prerogative and at the same time did not assert any restrictions on interference with persons' exercise of those prerogatives. As Darwall puts it:

---

[42] Any standard appeal to the agent-neutral disvalue of the violation points to the minimization of violations. For *nonstandard* appeals to agent-neutral value, see Spector, *Autonomy and Rights*, pp. 152–78; and Kamm, "Non-Consequentialism," pp. 382–89.

The idea of a prerogative suggests the idea of a morally protected
sphere of personal action, but without an accompanying restriction
on the acts of others, the sphere will not be protected against morally
sanctioned interference.[43]

Indeed, the more robust persons' prerogatives are, the more the point of
their affirmation will be defeated, and the more they will be rendered
practically nugatory, in the absence of restrictions upon interference with
their exercise. Hence, the more robust the prerogatives that are affirmed
within a moral system, the more this affirmation requires that restrictions
against interference with the exercise of those prerogatives also be affirmed within that normative system.

2. Deontic restrictions on our treatment of others are often said to reflect
their status as ends-in-themselves. Since others are ends-in-themselves, it
is not reasonable to treat them (as one would treat natural resources) as
means to one's own ends—no matter how valuable those ends are. Constraint in our behavior toward others manifests in practice our recognition of them as ends-in-themselves. Here the agent-relativity of value
enters into the explication of persons' status as ends-in-themselves and
enters into the explanation of why that status yields side-constraints upon,
rather than goals for, our conduct. Each person is an end-in-herself because each has in *her own* life and well-being an end of ultimate value in
its own right. A person's own life and well-being can be an end of ultimate value in its own right only if her life and well-being is not one
among many ultimate values with anything like comparable directive
force for her. And of course it is not that, for each person's life and
well-being, there is *someone somewhere* for whom that life and well-being
has special noncomparable directive force. Rather, for each person, the life
and well-being which is or may be hers is what has ultimate value in its
own right and unique directive force *for her*. But this can be the case only
if the value of each person's life and well-being is agent-relative. So it is
because of the agent-relativity of value that persons are ends-in-themselves.
Moreover, recognition of the agent-relative character of the value of each
person's life and well-being confutes any suggestion that an appreciation
of the ultimate value of others' lives and well-being reveals that they are
ends that one is bound to promote. The agent-relative value of others'
respective lives and well-being provides them with reasons—value-based

---

[43] Darwall, "Agent-Centered Restrictions," p. 304. Darwall ultimately rejects this argument. His reason is that the agent-relative disvalue for the victim does not provide the agent
with reason for noninterference. This is correct but irrelevant to the argument at hand. For
this argument focuses on the purported incompleteness of an ethical theory that affirms
strong prerogatives but no restrictions that protect the exercise of any of those prerogatives.
For a more extended statement of this sort of argument (and the next one to be discussed
in the text), see my essay "Personal Integrity, Practical Recognition, and Rights," *The Monist*,
vol. 76, no. 1 (1993).

reasons—for the promotion of these ends; but it is the fact that they are beings with reasons of this sort that makes it unreasonable for me to treat them as means to my own ends.

I have traced the development and offered a critical assessment of the program of explaining an agent's being subject to deontic restrictions on the basis of that agent's agent-relative reasons for acting in accordance with those restrictions. Such a program reflects a failure to distinguish sufficiently between two different components of the critique of utilitarianism and kindred consequentialist doctrines—the affirmation of agent-relative reasons and values against impartialist conceptions of the good, and the affirmation of deontic restrictions against the consequentialist doctrine that the optimal promotion of the good is always right.

At the core of advocacy of this program is the following argument.

(a) If *Y* is subject to a deontic restriction *R* on her behavior toward *A*, that restriction cannot obtain in virtue of the agent-neutral disvalue of *Y*'s violating *R* with respect to *A*.

(b) Nor can it obtain in virtue of the agent-relative disvalue for *A* of *Y*'s violating *R*.

(c) Therefore, the restriction must obtain in virtue of some agent-relative reason possessed by *Y*.

We have seen, however, that no agent-relative reason possessed by *Y* can account for *Y*'s being under a deontic restriction *R*. From this we might conclude, as Scheffler does, that *R* is unaccountable and that we should resist its intuitive appeal. Or we may believe, as one should antecedently expect of deontic restrictions, that the reasonableness of *Y*'s constraining her conduct toward *A* is based on neither the agent-relative nor the agent-neutral value of that constraint. What, then, might it be based upon such that the restraint stems from *A* or some morally fertile property of *A*? I have *suggested* a couple of ways in which the reasonableness of *Y*'s constraining her conduct may stem from the *fact* that *A*, the prospective recipient of *Y*'s action, is a being with ultimate, agent-relative values of his own and, hence, has the status of a moral end-in-himself.

Philosophy, Tulane University

WHY EVEN EGALITARIANS SHOULD FAVOR MARKET HEALTH INSURANCE*

By Daniel Shapiro

I. Introduction

Socialism is dead, though many of its academic proponents take no notice of its demise. With its death, private property in the means of production is not generally in dispute, and the action in political philosophy centers on the justification of the welfare state. The heart of the welfare state is social insurance programs, such as government managed and subsidized health insurance, retirement pensions, and unemployment insurance.[1] The arguments about health insurance will arguably be among the most ferocious, difficult, and important of the welfare-state debates: Ferocious, because proposals to alter government managed or subsidized health care strike at people's fears and concerns in a way matched by few other proposals. Difficult, because people can often not even conceive of a (genuine) market alternative to the status quo in health insurance, and there is no real existing alternative to hold up as a model. Important, because if an intellectually solid case for market health insurance can be established, then supporters of the welfare state should be on the defensive, since social health insurance is an institution central to their vision of the just or good society.

Suppose one wishes to argue for market health insurance. How should this be done? Two strategies come to mind, which can be used here or in political philosophy when comparing market institutions with welfare-state institutions. First, one can argue that the normative principles and viewpoints used by defenders of the welfare state—e.g., egalitarianism, communitarianism—are mistaken. This method accepts the opponents' view that their principles, if correct, would provide good reasons for supporting certain institutions, and focuses attention on problems with the principles. I call this an external strategy, because it argues from a

* I would like to thank N. Scott Arnold, Richard A. Epstein, Ellen Frankel Paul, Jeffrey Paul, and David Schmidtz for comments on an earlier draft of this essay. Part of the research for this essay was done while I was a Visiting Scholar at the Social Philosophy and Policy Center, Bowling Green State University, during the 1995-1996 academic year. I would like to thank the directors of the Center, Fred D. Miller, Jr., Ellen Frankel Paul, and Jeffrey Paul, for their support and encouragement, and for their provision of an ideal place to work.

[1] In popular parlance, "welfare" refers to means-tested programs, such as Aid to Families with Dependent Children in the U.S. However, means-tested programs make up a small portion of the budget of contemporary welfare states.

standpoint outside the views, as it were. An alternative way of arguing is an internal strategy. Here one argues that the principles that opponents take to support welfare-state institutions do not in fact do so, because these institutions do not work the way egalitarians (or communitarians, or others) think that they do, or because egalitarians and other defenders of the welfare state have misunderstood the implications of their principles, or both.

Most political philosophers, regardless of their normative viewpoints, use an external strategy. My hunch, though, is that the alternative of an internal strategy is underappreciated. Internal strategies have a number of virtues. First, if one can show that a certain institution is supported by all or virtually all plausible normative principles, then that institution will have a far more solid justification than if it were supported by only one principle or viewpoint. I have adapted this point from one that philosopher Loren Lomasky makes concerning the best way to support a certain view of basic rights.[2] Lomasky notes that rather than looking for the fully adequate moral theory to support a certain view of basic rights, it makes more sense to show that this view can be supported by any plausible moral theory. If, for example, there are five plausible or reasonable moral theories, but we are not positive which is correct but believe that one of them is, the warrant or support for a certain view of rights is much higher if that view is compatible with or entailed by most of them (the warrant is 100 percent if it is compatible with all of them, assuming we are correct in believing that one is true). Analogously, support for certain market institutions over welfare-state institutions is significantly strengthened if the former institutions are compatible with or entailed by most plausible normative principles in political philosophy, for example, with libertarian, egalitarian, and communitarian views of justice.

A second virtue of the internal strategy is a practical one. I suspect it is harder to convince critics that their fundamental principles in political philosophy are mistaken than to argue that they have misunderstood the implications of their principles or that their understanding of the way certain institutions actually work is defective.

There is a third virtue as well: the internal strategy helps to shift the terms of the debate. Suppose one can show that market alternatives to welfare-state institutions are supported by most or all plausible normative principles in political philosophy.[3] Then the debate will, or should, no

---

[2] Loren E. Lomasky, *Persons, Rights, and the Moral Community* (New York: Oxford University Press, 1987), p. 13.

[3] I am at work on a book, tentatively called *Justice, Efficiency, and Community: Can the Welfare State Be Justified?*, where I aim to do just that. Elsewhere I have argued that government provision and management of retirement pensions, or what I call old-age social insurance, is inferior to compulsory private pensions (e.g., the system in Chile) on the basis of virtually all principles or values predominant in contemporary political philosophy. See my essay "Can Old-Age Social Insurance Be Justified?" *Social Philosophy and Policy*, vol. 14, no. 2 (Summer 1997), pp. 116–44. A system of compulsory private pensions would not, in my

longer focus on the welfare state versus those alternatives, but on what forms of market institutions are the best. My aim in this essay is to argue for market alternatives with regard to health insurance. I shall argue that egalitarian principles, usually considered to provide strong support for social health insurance, or national health insurance, as it is popularly called, in fact support market health insurance. Since it is quite clear that libertarianism would support market health insurance over social or national health insurance, my arguments show that at least two prominent viewpoints in political philosophy converge on supporting market health insurance over national health insurance. While I do not have space to show that this convergence holds for all the major viewpoints in political philosophy—e.g., I will not address the question of what communitarian principles imply on this matter—my hunch is that if it can be shown that egalitarians should support market over national health insurance, the same result can be demonstrated with regard to other viewpoints and principles in political philosophy that have often been taken to support national health insurance. (Henceforth I will use the more popular term "national health insurance," rather than "social health insurance," since the former is used by virtually everyone who writes on this topic.)

In the next section, I explain the differences between national and market health insurance. In Section III, I explain how egalitarians typically argue for the former. Sections IV and V show why egalitarians are mistaken in their belief that their principles support national over market health insurance.

My arguments in this essay do not focus on the question of how present-day national health insurance systems should move toward market health insurance. That is an important matter, but space limitations prevent me from addressing it.

II. The Institutional Alternatives

A. National health insurance

National health insurance (henceforth "NHI") consists of the following key features.[4]

---

view, be the most preferred institution, since I believe that voluntary private pensions would be more desirable. Nevertheless, adopting the former would mean the end of a central welfare-state institution.

[4] My information comes from William Glaser, *Health Insurance in Practice: International Variations in Financing, Benefits, and Problems* (San Francisco: Jossey-Bass Publishers, 1991), chs. 1–4 and appendix A; and Joseph White, *Competing Solutions: American Health Care Proposals and International Experience* (Washington, DC: The Brookings Institution, 1995), ch. 2. Glaser's focus is on Germany, Switzerland, Holland, Belgium, and France; White's is on Germany, France, Canada, the UK, Japan, and Australia.

First, there is universal or near-universal coverage, which is achieved by compulsion.[5] Individuals are forced to pay taxes to cover their own and other people's health care. Governments either provide the insurance (e.g., Canada) or manage a national health service (e.g., Britain, Sweden, New Zealand), or require that one purchase health insurance from a nonprofit sickness fund or a private company (e.g., Germany,[6] France, Belgium).

Second, NHI is not market, actuarial insurance. Even in countries with NHI that allow private insurance companies and nonprofit sickness funds, these companies or funds are forbidden to engage in the raison d'être of market insurance, namely risk rating. Premiums are not allowed to vary according to risk, with a few mild exceptions, such as by age. The intent of the premiums or the taxes paid is to redistribute or cross subsidize: in general, those with low risks of using health services are supposed to subsidize those with high risks. Now, market insurance does involve risk sharing as well as risk rating; one is grouped with a class of people with *similar*, but not identical, risks. However, in a competitive market significant gains are made by limiting the extent to which different risks are charged the same premium, and whatever "redistribution" is achieved within a class of risks charged the same premium is not by intent.

Third, there is limited choice of plans within NHI. Governments mandate that all plans offer a certain common set of benefits. Choice is slightly augmented for those who can purchase supplemental insurance that typically provides better benefits than NHI.[7]

The features discussed so far—compulsion, non-actuarial insurance, limited choice of policies or plans—are the typical features of social insurance, such as retirement pensions, unemployment insurance, and workers' compensation. But crucial to understanding NHI is a fourth feature: NHI is an example of a comprehensive service plan, not casualty insurance.[8] Service plans provide coverage for the consumption of medical or health-care services, not necessarily for being ill or undergoing an adverse event; this is why coverage is typically comprehensive in the sense that everything from routine doctor visits to hospital care is covered. However, casualty insurance (for example, auto and homeowner's insur-

[5] Switzerland is a special case. Only a few cantons require that one purchase health insurance. Universal coverage is achieved by subsidies to the sickness funds. Glaser, *Health Insurance in Practice*, pp. 4, 61, and 561.

[6] In Germany, around 10 percent of the population—made up of those above a certain income—is not required to purchase health insurance. Virtually all of them choose to purchase private health insurance. *Ibid.*, pp. 6 and 504.

[7] In some countries, e.g., Canada, private insurance is only allowed for benefits not covered by NHI. White, *Competing Solutions*, p. 66.

[8] For a clear discussion of the differences between these, see John C. Goodman and Gerald L. Musgrave, *Patient Power: Solving America's Health Care Crisis* (Washington, DC: The Cato Institute, 1992), pp. 178–82; and Susan Feingenbaum, "Body Shop Economics: What's Good for Our Cars May Be Good for Our Health," *Regulation*, vol. 15, no. 4 (Fall 1992), pp. 25–31.

ance) insures against adverse events, so that one is reimbursed for some identifiable loss one suffers; typically, then, one is insuring against catastrophes and payment goes to the insured (unlike service plans, which usually reimburse the providers). Thus, casualty insurance is not comprehensive. While market insurance could and does involve comprehensive service plans, for reasons I shall discuss later there is good reason to believe that these plans would not dominate a market insurance system.

The difference between casualty-catastrophic insurance[9] and comprehensive service plans is crucial; since NHI falls into the latter category, this means that the government is directly or indirectly involved in virtually all facets of health-care markets. Casualty insurance, by contrast, does not have that much of a spillover effect in the broader market for services. Since it is not comprehensive, and since the insured typically decides how or whether to spend his or her payment for losses incurred,[10] casualty insurance's effects on the broader market for services—e.g., automobile insurance's effects on the market for automobile services or products—is necessarily limited. Normal commercial exchanges between buyers and sellers govern those markets. Once insurance is comprehensive, however, and once the government has a role in almost all consumption decisions, then the effects of national health insurance necessarily dominate and structure all health-care markets.

Once government finances or subsidizes most decisions to consume or purchase health-care services, it is virtually inevitable that it will be involved in production decisions as well. Health-care services, in advanced industrial societies, involve significant expenditures of resources; since subsidization increases demand, a decision to subsidize those services inevitably means that a significant percentage of a government's budget will be devoted to health-care resources—making it virtually inevitable that governments at some point will take steps to control those costs. Either governments must then stop subsidizing demand, which would really defeat the purpose of NHI, or they must control supply. Hence we

[9] I combine casualty and catastrophic insurance in this hyphenated expression to emphasize that casualty insurance, since it insures against adverse events and does not reimburse one for services consumed, is usually just insurance against catastrophes. However, it is important to notice that the connection between casualty insurance and catastrophic insurance does not hold with equal strength in both directions. That is, while casualty insurance is almost always catastrophic-only insurance, catastrophic-only insurance need not be based on the principles of casualty insurance; that is, it need not be limited to reimbursement for identifiable losses or illnesses. For example, one could take out a high-deductible policy which covers all of one's medical expenses above a certain amount, regardless of whether those expenses were incurred due to some loss or illness. This would be catastrophic-only insurance in the sense that a high level of medical expenditures often indicates the occurrence of a medical catastrophe; however, reimbursement for a high level of medical expenditures is not casualty insurance, since the reimbursement is for the consumption of medical services, not for some identifiable loss or illness.

[10] Sometimes casualty insurers will place limits on the insured's discretion. Auto insurers, for example, sometimes place limits on how and when you fix your car after a wreck.

arrive at the fifth feature of NHI, the limited role for genuine market prices. Some countries have a global budget which limits the total yearly amount spent on health care or for hospitals and/or certain procedures. All NHI systems place controls on capital expenditures by hospitals, either through global budgets or through requirements that private hospitals seek permission from a governmental body before making these, or certain types of these, expenditures. Those controls tend to squeeze investment in expensive high-tech equipment. As for doctors' fees, they are either set by the government (price controls) or are set by negotiation between doctor alliances or groups and sickness funds and/or the government (either national or provincial).[11] In most of these negotiations, the sickness funds or the government tend to have the upper hand, and doctors have come reluctantly to accept a yearly expenditure cap or, more often, a target which can be adjusted downward the following year if spending is above the target for a particular year. Similar situations exist with pharmaceutical prices. Global budgets plus fee regulation and/or expenditure caps/targets are the chief mechanisms by which NHI puts a brake on subsidized demand.

Sixth, all NHI systems engage in nonmarket and nonprice forms of allocation, that is, government rationing. This is both a consequence and cause of the absence of genuine market prices. This rationing leads to waits in various sectors of the system.[12] Sometimes the wait is for a doctor, usually for a specialist or a hospital-based physician, rather than one's primary-care physician. Sometimes it is for a place in the hospital;

[11] Sometimes, as in Australia, the government sets no fee, but then the government forbids private insurance from reimbursing above what Medicare (Australia's ambulatory NHI program) does. Since Medicare pays 75 percent of doctor fees, this amounts to de facto government fee regulation. See White, *Competing Solutions*, p. 97.

[12] Because some countries do not keep any records of waits, and because there is rarely a national waiting list (as opposed to a regional or provincial list), it is often hard to get reliable information about the extent of waits. For an unusually detailed study, see Cynthia Ramsay and Michael Walker, *Waiting Your Turn: Hospital Waiting Lists in Canada* (Vancouver: The Fraser Institute, 1995). Countries with a national health service tend to have the worst problems. As Robert Baker notes, the British National Health Service is sometimes dubbed the "British National Health Shortages," given its extensive waits for many operations and procedures. See Baker, "The Inevitability of Health Care Rationing: A Case Study of Rationing in the British National Health Service," in *Rationing America's Medical Care: The Oregon Plan and Beyond*, ed. Martin Strosberg, Joshua M. Wiener, Robert Baker, with I. Alan Fein (Washington, DC: The Brookings Institution, 1992), p. 208. Some countries with national health services have requirements for maximum waiting time; that these requirements fail to work is noted by Jo Lenaghan, "Health Care Rights in Europe," in *Hard Choices in Health Care*, ed. Jo Lenaghan (London: BMJ Publishing Group, 1997), pp. 188–89. Glaser, *Health Insurance in Practice*, p. 250, claims that waits are not a problem in countries that have private insurance companies and nonprofit sickness funds. But this claim is belied by *Choices in Health Care*, a report by the Netherlands' Government Committee on Choices in Health Care (Rijswijk: Ministry of Welfare, Health, and Cultural Affairs, 1992), pp. 97–98, and by an admission of the German government in 1993 that waiting lists were about to become more common. See Timothy Harper, "Rationing: What We Can Learn from Europe," *Medical Economics*, September 13, 1993, p. 140.

other times it is for equipment needed for a diagnosis or an operation. But wherever the rationing occurs one thing is a virtual constant—specific rationing decisions are not made publicly and democratically. They are made, with little public input or awareness, by administrators, local health authorities, and doctors.

Seventh, patients pay little out of pocket and have little awareness of (monetary) costs. In service plans, the provider bills the carrier or insurance fund, which then pays the bills; usually the patient pays, at most, relatively small co-payments or has to meet a minimal deductible. Thus, there is little incentive for her to know what health-care services cost, or for providers to communicate that information to her. This lack of information and incentive to acquire that information extends to the insurance premiums as well, though the lack of information varies somewhat with the type of system (for example, patients are more aware of premiums that they pay themselves than of those that are paid solely by employers or by taxes).

Finally, in NHI the patient is not generally treated as, nor is she in fact, a consumer. The patient does not directly purchase or pay for services; she is not given information about price, quality, or availability, is not encouraged to shop around for better offers, and does not directly negotiate with the seller of services. Of course, in other forms of insurance, the insurance company acts as an intermediary between seller and buyer; the whole point of insurance is that when risky events occur, there is another party besides oneself and the seller. But what is striking about NHI is the virtual elimination, from all aspects of the medical system, of the insured's role in monetary transactions with providers.

To summarize, then, NHI contains the typical features of social insurance—compulsion, non-actuarial insurance, limited choice of plans—with a form of payment for consumption of comprehensive medical care that characterizes service plans. As a result, NHI requires significant government intervention and domination of the broader market for health-care services, via fee regulation, expenditure caps/targets, global budgets, and rationing—and not surprisingly, in such a system the patient is not a consumer and has little awareness of monetary costs.

B. Market health insurance: What it is not

The usual contrast with NHI is the private health insurance market in the United States. However, this is a grave error, since it is *not* an example, nor even an imperfect exemplar, of market health insurance, as I argue below.

First, the number of insurance mandates has been increasing in the last fifteen years or so. Insurance companies are increasingly compelled, usually by state governments, to offer certain benefits (for example, alcoholism and drug treatment programs, mental-health benefits, well-baby care, mammography screening, chiropractic services), a practice which limits consumer choice, in particular the choice of a "no-frills," purely catastrophic insurance policy that would not cover many of these benefits. Not only are insurance companies forbidden to offer such policies, but the mandates drive up the cost of insurance, making it less affordable.[13]

Second, risk rating is increasingly forbidden by law. Congress recently banned insurance companies from excluding preexisting conditions when people change insurance companies,[14] and state laws prescribing community rating—the same rate for all or most subscribers—are on the rise.[15]

The changes noted above have been relatively recent. The most significant fact about the U.S. private health insurance market, however, is that it is dominated by employer-provided and employer-sponsored service plans, and this domination was not achieved through market means. Some remarks about how this was achieved are in order.[16]

During the 1930s, service plans offered by Blue Cross and Blue Shield—the former a hospital service plan begun by nonprofit hospitals, the latter a physician service plan begun by doctors—achieved market dominance over commercial insurance companies by a number of government-assisted techniques.[17] (A) They achieved exemptions from most taxation that their commercial rivals had to pay. (B) State insurance commissions permitted them to avoid keeping reserves which commercial insurance companies needed to have, in order to have adequate funds to pay out benefits (in effect, the Blues were allowed to operate as a pay-as-you-go scheme, and in return they were required to serve the entire community by charging a rate low enough that low-income people could afford to pay it). (C) In a number of states, commercial insurers were subject to minimum premium/rate regulations, while the Blues were not. (D) There was an incestuous relationship, as it were, between professional medical

---

[13] See Goodman and Musgrave, *Patient Power*, ch. 11.

[14] See Steve Langdon, "Health Insurance Law," *Congressional Quarterly Weekly Report*, vol. 54, no. 37 (September 14, 1996), pp. 2619–23.

[15] For example, such laws have been passed in New York, New Jersey, and Florida. For a discussion of these laws, see Richard A. Epstein, *Antidiscrimination in Health Care: Community Rating and Preexisting Conditions* (Oakland: The Independent Institute, 1996), pp. 5–7.

[16] See Terree Wasley, *What Has Government Done to Our Health Care?* (Washington, DC: The Cato Institute, 1992), pp. 47–57; Goodman and Musgrave, *Patient Power*, pp. 156–61; and Joseph A. Califano, Jr., *America's Health Care Revolution* (New York: Simon and Schuster, 1986), pp. 40–47.

[17] The reason hospitals began offering Blue Cross was that the Depression was taking a toll on the hospitals' business. Service plans, with their "first dollar coverage" (i.e., no deductibles, but with limits on total expenses covered) were a way of stimulating business. See Wasley, *What Has Government Done to Our Health Care?*, pp. 47–50; and Califano, *America's Health Care Revolution*, pp. 41–42. Blue Shield was introduced after commercial insurers introduced plans to compete with Blue Cross.

associations, hospitals, and the Blues, from which commercial rivals were excluded. As already mentioned, hospitals themselves started the Blues, and they instituted a method of reimbursement known as "cost-plus," meaning that they would use the hospitals' costs as a guideline for reimbursement and thus add some amount on top of this. (For physician services, they used the notion of a customary and reasonable amount.) Cost-plus reimbursement guaranteed the hospitals' survival and produced no incentive to economize; in fact, it produced the opposite incentive: the higher the costs, the greater the reimbursement. Not surprisingly, then, the hospitals were happy to give the Blues some discounts in the early days, enabling these service plans to attract more customers than their commercial rivals; and doctors and hospitals were encouraged to place American Medical Association (AMA) approved ads for the Blues in their waiting rooms (this during a time when competitive advertising by doctors was forbidden by the AMA).[18]

The result of all of this was that by 1940 the dominance of the Blues was already in place: half of those with hospital insurance had coverage from the Blues.[19] No one commercial insurer could provide a significant challenge to the Blues, and commercial insurance policies started to take on more and more of the characteristics of the Blues: service plans, not casualty insurance, and cost-plus reimbursement (although, unlike the Blues, commercial insurers used risk rating, not community rating, and they still made payment to the insured rather than to hospitals or doctors). At this point we have the domination of service plans, but not employer-provided service plans. That was brought about by the second crucial transforming

[18] Furthermore, prior to the 1930s the AMA took action to squash *consumer*-based service plans. Starting in the early part of the twentieth century, a number of industries, mutual aid societies, and consumer cooperatives also provided service plans for low monthly or annual fees which covered both hospital and physician services, but these were different from the Blues in a crucial respect. The cooperatives, mutual aid societies, or industries provided the care without the insurance companies: they hired company doctors who were paid a fixed salary, and/or they owned the hospitals or clinics themselves. The AMA eventually eliminated all of these by lobbying successfully for state laws which effectively required all medical service plans to obtain AMA approval. See Lawrence C. Goldberg and Warren Greenberg, "The Emergence of Physician-Sponsored Health Insurance: A Historical Perspective," in *Competition in the Health Care Sector*, ed. Warren Greenberg (Germantown: Aspen Systems Corporation, 1978), pp. 288–321; and Goldberg and Greenberg, "The Effect of Physician-Controlled Health Insurance: *U.S. v. Oregon State Medical Society," Journal of Health, Politics, Policy, and the Law*, vol. 2, no. 1 (Spring 1977), pp. 48–78.

[19] However, hospital insurance was still confined to a small group, around 9 percent of the population. Around 12 million had hospital insurance, while the total population was around 132 million. The Blues never held less than around 45 percent of the entire private health insurance market until the early 1980s. As of 1993, the latest year for which I have been able to obtain figures, the Blues held around 36 percent of the market. See Health Insurance Association of America, *Sourcebook of Health Insurance Data, 1988* (Washington, DC: Health Insurance Association of America, 1988), tables 1.2 and 1.3; and Health Insurance Association of America, *Sourcebook of Health Insurance Data, 1995* (Washington, DC: Health Insurance Association of America, 1996), table 2.5.

event: tax policy in the early 1940s. The Internal Revenue Service (IRS) declared that fringe benefits up to 5 percent of wages were exempt from wage and price controls during World War II. In addition to excluding employer-provided health insurance from wages, the IRS shortly thereafter ruled that employers could exclude health insurance from taxable business income and that employees getting employer health insurance did not have to include the value of their benefits in calculating taxable income. Thus, there was a double tax exemption for employer-sponsored health insurance. This, combined with the fact that insurance premiums paid by individuals were not tax-deductible (and those paid by the self-employed only received a small tax deduction), gave a considerable push to employer-sponsored health insurance. When high marginal income tax rates became a permanent feature of American life during and after World War II, the value of the double tax exemption for employer-sponsored health insurance and the disadvantage of consumer-bought health insurance became virtually overwhelming. When employers started to offer health insurance (partly under pressure by unions, which in 1949 won the right to bargain over health benefits), they offered the product that was available in the market, which was not casualty insurance, but service plans. Hence, by the end of the 1940s, the U.S. market for health insurance was dominated by employer-provided service-plan insurance, with cost-plus reimbursement,[20] and community rating (most large employers followed the Blues' lead and charged a uniform premium for all workers).

While the domination of employer-sponsored comprehensive service plans still continues in the U.S., in the last fifteen years that market has changed in an important respect. Explosive rises in health-care costs made cost-plus reimbursement economically unfeasible, and employers during the 1980s required insurers to actively control their health-care costs.[21] This rise in managed care, as it has come to be called, took a variety of forms.[22] No longer did insurance companies passively reimburse claims; instead, they conducted utilization reviews to identify unnecessary or wasteful services and procedures, required prior authorization for certain procedures and pharmaceuticals, required second opinions for surgeries and other expensive procedures, provided incentives for patients to participate in so-called wellness programs that stressed preventive care, in-

[20] The cost-plus reimbursement system was reined in during the 1980s, as I discuss below.

[21] Some of this pressure occurred when large firms began self-insuring. In this way, companies established their own rules and procedures; the insurance company's role, if any, was simply limited to processing the claims. Once a significant segment of large employers began to self-insure and engage in cost-control techniques, these techniques rapidly spread through the U.S. health-care market. See Goodman and Musgrave, *Patient Power*, pp. 195–201.

[22] See *ibid.*, pp. 201–8; White, *Competing Solutions*, pp. 180–83; and Richard A. Epstein, *Mortal Peril: Our Inalienable Right to Health Care?* (Reading, MA: Addison-Wesley Publishing Company, 1997), pp. 420–30.

creased employee deductibles and copayments, and so forth. These measures were attempts to make providers and patients more aware of costs, and to provide incentives for them to reduce their use of health-care services. The most important aspect of managed care has been the rise in health maintenance organizations, or HMOs. HMOs integrate the financing and delivery of medical care by contracting with selected doctors and hospitals (the former usually paid on a salaried basis, rather than fee-for-service) to provide comprehensive care to members who pay a fixed monthly fee (plus, in some cases, minimal copayments and deductibles); members who obtain care from doctors and hospitals that are not part of the HMO network are not covered or must pay a greater amount out-of-pocket. HMOs provide strong incentives for providers and patients to constantly keep their focus on costs, and the cost savings that they achieve are supposed to make them attractive to patients despite the restriction of freedom in choosing doctors and procedures. However, while the rise of managed care and the demise of cost-plus reimbursement is obviously an important change in the U.S. health-care market, managed-care plans are still comprehensive employer-sponsored service plans, and the tax policies that favor such plans are still in place. Thus, the dominance of managed care in the private U.S. health insurance market does not affect the point that this market is dominated by comprehensive service plans, and that casualty-catastrophic insurance plays only a small role.

I have argued that employer-provided service plans achieved their domination of the health insurance market by government assistance. The argument, however, does not show that such domination could not occur by free-market means, and it is that counterfactual claim that is of greater importance here in light of my earlier claim that service plans will not be the dominant form of health insurance in a free market. The counterfactual claim can be supported by three points:

1. Employer-provided service plans cause significant labor-mobility problems: certainly many people would prefer to own their own policy, as this would make health insurance portable and would eliminate any worry about job-lock. This point indicates why it is unlikely that employer-sponsored plans would dominate in a free market, but it does not address the comprehensive versus casualty insurance question, which is addressed in the next two points.

2. In the absence of tax disadvantages and other government obstacles, casualty insurance has a secure place, because of its cost advantage. Comprehensive service plans are likely to require higher premiums than casualty-catastrophic insurance, particularly for those in a relatively low risk pool.

3. An additional reason to think casualty insurance has a secure place in a free market for health insurance concerns a difference between casualty insurance and service plans that I did not stress earlier. Casualty

insurers are liable for damages from the time of the risky or adverse event, even if it takes years to assess the damage, while service plans are liable only so long as the insured pays premiums; if the policy is canceled, the insurer can cease paying benefits even if losses from a risky event are continuing. I did not mention this when I explained how NHI is an example of a service plan, because in NHI there are sometimes no premiums, and whether one receives services is, to a considerable degree, independent of whether one has paid or is paying taxes. But this difference is applicable to comparing casualty insurance and service plans in a free-market system, and it is that comparison that is relevant right now. Certainly many consumers would prefer a policy that covered damages for the adverse event, even if those losses occurred many years after the event or after one has switched or canceled policies.

Thus, for all these reasons—no job-lock, cheaper premiums for low risks, payment of damages so long as there are losses stemming from the adverse event—it is reasonable to believe that casualty insurance (that is not owned and sponsored by employers) will have a home in a free market.

So far I have argued in this section that private health insurance in the U.S. bears only a remote resemblance to market health insurance because of state insurance mandates, federal and state restrictions on risk rating, and, most importantly, because that market is dominated by comprehensive service plans, a domination achieved by government policies and unlikely to exist without it. Yet another reason why private health insurance in the U.S. should not be confused with genuine market health insurance has to do with the effects of Medicare and Medicaid, which are the U.S. versions of social insurance—the former a federal government program for senior citizens, the latter a joint federal and state government program for the indigent. These population groups are large enough that these programs have a strong tendency to influence and structure the private health insurance market. In 1983, the federal government abandoned its cost-plus procedures for Medicare part A (the part that covers hospital care), for the same reason businesses did (namely, the explosion in health-care costs), and instituted reimbursement for diagnostic related groups, or DRGs. The DRG system sets a price for services and surgical procedures, set independently of supply and demand, and it forbids hospitals to charge more even for patients willing to pay more. Many state governments also adopted the DRG system for their share of reimbursements for Medicaid. Now a significant percentage of all hospital revenue comes from both programs, and private insurers have adopted the DRG method;[23] thus, the nonmarket pricing system set out by DRGs

[23] On the DRG system, see White, *Competing Solutions*, pp. 44–45; and Goodman and Musgrave, *Patient Power*, pp. 55, 60–62, and 302–11.

has had a significant impact. Furthermore, the DRG system appears to lead to the rationing of new medical technology; if the DRG reimbursement is too low—and it generally is for new expensive technologies—the technology will not be made available to those who might be willing to pay for it.[24]

One final respect in which the private health insurance market in the U.S. should not be confused with market health insurance is that hospitals do not charge anything that could be called a recognizable price. This is in part a remnant of the cost-plus reimbursement system. When cost-plus reimbursement reigned, around 90 percent of a hospital's revenues were reimbursed on this basis;[25] thus, hospitals had incentives to inflate costs, and "prices" on a bill had little relationship to supply and demand. Patients had no incentive to shop around for the best price, since there was no best price—only lists of thousands of items, many of them not recognizable to an average patient. The same practice still largely exists today: hospitals rarely offer a fixed preadmission price per diem or per procedure, and most people cannot make sense of hospital bills.[26] In a real market for health insurance, catastrophic-casualty insurers would have enormous incentives to bargain for fixed preadmission prices, perhaps even pressing for a combination of hospital and surgeons fees into a single fixed preadmission price (or, for exploratory surgery, a "not to exceed" price).[27] Furthermore, as I shall discuss later, for noncatastrophic expenses or procedures, hospitals would be competing for patients' own money, which would make them far more consumer friendly than they are today, since the need to attract customers would provide a good incentive for attractive services and comprehensible prices.

To summarize this section, then, U.S. private health insurance deviates significantly from market health insurance vis-à-vis some restrictions on risk rating, enormous government bias in favor of comprehensive service plans, a noncompetitive pricing system, and, in the case of hospitals, an

[24] Goodman and Musgrave, *Patient Power*, pp. 60–62 and 303–16.

[25] *Ibid.*, pp. 163–67.

[26] Why does the same practice exist even after the demise of cost-plus reimbursement? I am not entirely clear on the answer, but some of the reasons seem to be the following. First, a significant percentage of hospitals' revenues are from Medicaid and Medicare, and, as is often the case with government financed and managed programs, they do not have the same incentives as insurance companies in a genuine market to press for comprehensible prices. Second, the DRG system used by Medicare and Medicaid, and increasingly by private insurers, is still in a sense cost-plus, but with a time lag: DRGs reimburse hospitals not on the basis of present costs, but on the basis of last year's average costs (that is how the figure for reimbursement is arrived at). This still gives hospitals an incentive to inflate costs rather than to compete over price. Third, even cost-conscious employers are not as good at bargaining as patients would be themselves if they paid for hospital expenses out of their medical savings accounts or insurance plans. (Medical savings accounts are tax-free accounts designed to pay for deductibles and small medical bills. See the discussion in Section IIC.) On the first two points, see Goodman and Musgrave, *Patient Power*, pp. 306, 311.

[27] *Ibid.*, pp. 53–55.

absence of comprehensible prices. While it is true that U.S. private health insurance is not universal, and that some aspects of the market do engage in risk rating, this is far from sufficient for it to merit being described as market health insurance.

C. Market health insurance: What it would look like

Genuine market health insurance does not exist in any contemporary industrialized democracy today.[28] For the most part, a description of its essential features can be generated by contrasting it with NHI—indeed, in most respects, market health insurance (henceforth "MHI") is the opposite, or almost the opposite, of NHI. I shall rely for the most part upon a comprehensive and detailed proposal for MHI, offered by policy analysts John Goodman and Gerald Musgrave, that is tailored for the U.S.[29]

Recall that, as a form of social insurance, NHI is compulsory, bans most risk rating, and restricts choice of insurance plan; by contrast, MHI is voluntary, allows risk rating, and does not mandate any particular set of benefits.[30] Recall also that what distinguished NHI among social insurance programs was that it provided comprehensive service plans, not casualty-catastrophic insurance. Thus, MHI would allow casualty insurance to freely compete with service plans. Accordingly, the heart of the Goodman-Musgrave proposal is to alter tax policy so as to end the strong bias in favor of employer-provided service plans. All purchasers of health insurance, whether individuals, employers, or the self-employed, would receive a tax credit. All premium payments would be included in the gross income of the insured, who would receive a tax credit for a certain percentage of the premium. For individuals who pay no income tax, this credit would be refundable, and this subsidy would enable them to purchase health insurance. In this way, MHI would be personal and portable; even if purchased by an employer, it would be the insured's property.

The tax credit would be available only if one purchased high-deductible catastrophic insurance. The reason for the limitation on the tax credit is that were the credit available for all kinds of insurance, including comprehensive service plans with low deductibles, there would still be a strong tax bias in favor of such plans. The premiums for such plans would appear not to be more expensive than catastrophic insurance with a high

---

[28] Singapore has certain features of market health insurance, and thus is a possible exception, if one considers it a democracy. See Thomas A. Massaro and Yu-Nig Wong, *Medical Savings Accounts: The Singapore Experience* (Dallas: National Center for Policy Analysis, 1996).

[29] Goodman and Musgrave, *Patient Power: Solving America's Health Care Crisis* (supra note 8). Regina Herzlinger, *Market-Driven Health Care* (Reading, MA: Addison-Wesley Publishing Company, 1997), provides a useful elaboration (and, to some degree, alteration) of the Goodman-Musgrave proposal.

[30] But see pp. 99–100 for why I think the first and third conditions must be modified.

deductible, which in a market is typically not the case.[31] As for noncatastrophic expenses not covered by the deductible, tax-free medical savings accounts (henceforth "MSAs") could be used. MSAs are accounts into which individuals and families, or employers acting on their behalf, can deposit pretax dollars (on an annual basis, about the amount for an average deductible for a catastrophic-only policy)[32] and then use them to pay for small bills. These accounts would be the property of the insured individuals or families (even if the deposits were made by employers), and money withdrawn from them to pay for medical bills (the simplest way would probably be with a debit card) would not be taxed, whereas money withdrawn for nonmedical purposes would be fully taxed. Tax-free MSAs, along with the change in the tax code discussed above, would provide incentives for many people to self-insure for small bills and choose high-deductible insurance. Furthermore, since MSAs would allow one to accumulate the money deposited each year over a lifetime, they would help one budget for post-retirement expenses (unlike flexible savings accounts, which are today's analogue of MSAs, but which require one to forfeit any money deposited that is not spent at the end of the year).

The other features of MHI follow pretty much straightaway from eliminating government's role in subsidizing demand for comprehensive service plans. Whereas NHI sharply restricts (or even eliminates) free-market prices and requires nonmarket forms of rationing, MHI lacks either of these features. Much of the population would use their MSAs for noncatastrophic expenses, and thus prices would be formed by the normal interaction of buyers and sellers, with a limited role for third parties. For catastrophic and large hospital bills, the absence of cost-plus reimbursement or one-price-fits-all DRGs would create incentives for hospitals to have genuine pre-admission prices for procedures and surgery. And, finally, the central role of noncomprehensive private health insurance would increase significantly

[31] Present tax policies encourage people to choose low-deductible rather than high-deductible insurance, even when the cost of the more expensive premiums for the former outweighs the savings achieved by choosing the lower deductible. Since the premiums paid receive the double tax deduction described in the text, but the money paid out-of-pocket or put toward savings for the bills not covered by the deductible is paid in after-tax dollars, there is a strong incentive to choose the lower deductible. For example, suppose a $1,000 deductible policy costs $800 a year less in premiums than a $250 deductible policy (which may be the case, if one is middle-aged and lives in a high-cost area). Assuming a standard insurance policy that pays 80 percent of medical bills covered by the policy, the higher-deductible policy yields $600 less of health insurance coverage. This is far less than the $800 extra one has to pay in higher premiums; yet since the premiums are excluded from the employee's gross income, while the money paid for bills not covered by the deductible is fully taxed, for many people choosing the low-deductible policy is more rational (particularly if they are in a high tax bracket). See Goodman and Musgrave, *Patient Power*, pp. 44–46 and ch. 8.
[32] Goodman and Musgrave leave this matter somewhat open, suggesting at one point that some groups (the young, those living in a low-medical-cost area) might be allowed to make larger annual deposits to their MSAs. See *Patient Power*, p. 258.

the amount paid for by savings or out-of-pocket, would maximize the insured's awareness of costs, and would make patients consumers, in the way that they are in other forms of noncomprehensive private insurance—all the opposite of NHI.

I have described MHI as virtually the opposite of NHI. However, this has to be qualified to some extent, because on the matter of the voluntary purchase of insurance and the absence of mandated benefits, it is unclear that the stark contrast is accurate. The reason for this has to do with the fact that some people will choose not to purchase health insurance. Goodman and Musgrave propose that rather than being required to purchase health insurance, nonpurchasers be taxed and the money be used to compensate institutions that provide them with free health-care services — for example, during medical emergencies.[33] But for this to be a feasible proposal, the people who do not purchase health insurance must have enough income to pay taxes, which may not be the case. This aspect of the Goodman-Musgrave proposal thus seems adequate only for the nonindigent[34] who are also nonpurchasers of health insurance. One solution to this problem is to force the indigent to take the refundable tax credit and purchase health insurance, which eliminates the voluntary nature of MHI.

Furthermore, some specifications will need to be given regarding what kind of health insurance the indigent must purchase, which raises the question of mandated benefits. While the specification here can be rather loose—along the lines of "high-deductible catastrophic insurance, with a certain limit on total expenses incurred by the insured"—there will still need to be some kind of specification, particularly on questions such as whether "catastrophic insurance" must include long-term care to cover nursing-home expenses and the like. (Concerns about the indigent's ability to pay for routine and noncatastrophic care will be addressed later.)

The same problem arises, though in a somewhat different form, for the question of uninsurable risks. For various reasons, the probability that genuine market insurance will be offered for most of these risks is low.[35] MHI

---

[33] *Ibid.*, pp. 68–69.

[34] Or, more precisely, the nonindigent who are not wealthy. The wealthy can generally afford to pay their health-care bills whether or not they purchase health insurance.

[35] The reasons stem from the economics of insurance. Markets for insurance exist because there are gains from trade from pooling risks. On the demand side, consumers who have some degree of risk aversion gain from paying a certain amount each year to reduce the chance of a loss in any particular year. On the supply side, companies gain because they are reasonably confident that their payouts to insureds who suffer losses in any given year will be more than made up by income received from insureds who suffer no loss. However, there are no gains from trade for consumers who will suffer certain losses. Since the losses are certain, insurance companies cannot make money by using income obtained from policyholders in a similar risk class who will not suffer a loss—for there are none. Thus, the company will have to offer "insurance" priced at a rate equal to the loss plus the company's profit and overhead, and no rational consumer would have a demand for such insurance (why pay, for example, $1,500 a year to "insure" against a certain loss of $1,200?). Of course, insurance companies could charge consumers who face certain losses the same premium as those with a low probability of facing losses, and use the income from the latter to subsidize

would mitigate the problem of uninsurable risks, since some of these risks arise after one already has insurance; and since insurance would be portable, switching jobs after one has acquired the adverse condition would not cause a loss of one's health insurance. (Note that in life insurance there is a market for guaranteed annual renewable insurance, and it seems reasonable to expect something similar with MHI.)[36] Furthermore, to some extent the problem of uninsurable risks is functionally equivalent to a lack of income to treat the condition, because if one had enough savings to treat it, one would not need insurance. To some extent MSAs would handle this problem, if the problem were a chronic one which involved the use of relatively routine medical services (e.g., mild diabetes). However, though MHI would mitigate the problem of uninsurable risks, it would not eliminate them, and for the ineliminable cases, proponents of MHI propose using tax funds to subsidize the premiums of a high-risk pool. But again this raises the question of nonpurchasers—even with a subsidy, some high-risk individuals may not purchase insurance—and we are back to the same problem of compulsion and mandated benefits.

One additional feature of MHI needs to be highlighted: the proposal that everyone will get the same tax *credit* for a certain percentage—Goodman and Musgrave suggest 30 percent—of their health insurance premiums. The reason for a credit rather than a tax *deduction* is because the latter, but not the former, is regressive.[37] One could go further and propose a sliding scale for the credit, and thus enable those with lower income to receive as a credit a greater percentage of the premium, reducing the percentage as income rises. Along the same lines, one could propose that the minimum amount of the deductible in a catastrophic policy that makes one eligible for the tax credit also be on a sliding scale, so that those in lower income brackets could obtain the credit with a somewhat

---

the former; but given the strong tendency in a competitive market for insurers to charge different premiums for different degrees of risk, this is unlikely to occur.

[36] Goodman and Musgrave, *Patient Power*, pp. 98–99. They also note (pp. 96–97) that even as late as the 1950s in the U.S. consumers could purchase guaranteed renewable health insurance. Since this was at a time when employer service plans were not quite as completely entrenched as they are today, this may provide some evidence that, in a free market, the demand for such insurance would be considerable, and that insurers would meet the demand.

[37] A tax credit for health insurance premiums means that one can reduce one's tax bill by the amount of the credit; for example, if one would otherwise pay $3,500 a year in taxes, and one's health insurance premiums are $3,000 a year, a 30 percent tax credit would cut one's tax bill from $3,500 to $2,600. A tax credit is not regressive; if two people pay the same amount of health insurance premiums, then they get the same reduction in their tax bill. A tax deduction, on the other hand, means that a certain percentage of one's gross income is shielded from taxes; for example, if one is taxed on gross income of $30,000, but one can deduct 30 percent of one's $3,000 health insurance premiums, then one would be taxed on an income of $29,100. Tax deductions for health insurance premiums are regressive; that is, the value of the exclusion of the premiums from taxable income is more valuable for those in the higher income brackets. Nine hundred dollars excluded from taxation is less valuable for someone who is not in a very high marginal tax bracket than for someone who is in such a bracket. For more details, see *ibid.*, pp. 41–43.

lower-deductible catastrophic policy, while the amount of the deductible that makes one eligible for the credit rises as one's income rises.[38] While these additions are not essential to the basic idea of MHI, they are not incompatible with it, and since my aim is to show that MHI should be favored by egalitarians, I will add these features to my comparison of NHI with MHI.

Since MHI will likely involve a requirement to purchase health insurance as well as some specification, even if very minimal, of the benefits offered by that insurance, I have referred to it as *market* health insurance, not *free*-market health insurance. The latter would have no elements of government compulsion, government subsidy, or mandated benefits, and would rely upon voluntary organizations, such as charities and/or mutual aid societies for those who are unable and/or unwilling to purchase health insurance. While I believe that free-market health insurance would be superior to market health insurance, defending this view is a separate project that must be left to another time.

III. How Egalitarians Argue for National Health Insurance

A. Egalitarianism: Some basic distinctions

Strictly speaking, egalitarian principles of justice are those which value equality *as such*, that is, consider it a noninstrumental value.[39] Thus, an egalitarian, when comparing (1) a redistribution from the better off to the worse off (however these terms are defined) and (2) identical gains for the worse off with equal (or even greater) gains for the better off, will rank the former as better, since there is less inequality between the better and worse off. (The ranking will be defeasible, since sensible egalitarians will not view equality as the *only* value.) However, "egalitarian" is commonly predicated of principles of justice, such as John Rawls's difference principle, which states that social and economic inequalities are to be arranged so that they are to the greatest benefit of the least advantaged.[40] The difference principle yields no preference for either distribution described above, since the absolute position of the worst off (least advantaged) in both cases is identical. For purposes of this essay, the term "egalitarianism" will be used broadly, to refer both to views that consider equality a noninstrumental value, and to views that require that significant weight be given to improving (at the limit, maximizing) the plight of

---

[38] This is suggested by Herzlinger, *Market-Driven Health Care*, p. 258.

[39] On this conceptual or terminological matter, I have been influenced by Larry S. Temkin, *Inequality* (New York: Oxford University Press), pp. 7–8.

[40] John Rawls, *A Theory of Justice* (Cambridge: Harvard University Press, 1971), p. 302; Rawls, *Political Liberalism* (New York: Columbia University Press, 1993), p. 291.

the worst off, and are only concerned with equality per se as a means to improving the lot of the worst off.

All egalitarians must answer the question: "Equality of *what?*" That is, in what aspect of people's lives should people be made more equal or should the worst off's position be improved? Most egalitarian theories are either *welfarist*, which means that the relevant metric for equality is happiness, satisfaction, or some desirable psychological state of the person, or *resourcist*, which means that the relevant metric of equality is resources, opportunities, capacities, and the like.[41] A resourcist egalitarian theory, when applied to the topic at hand, would focus on inequalities in health care, while a welfarist one would focus on inequalities in health. Most egalitarian arguments for NHI focus on equalizing access to health-care *services* rather than on equalizing *health* outcomes (differences in mortality, disability, disease, etc.) and thus follow resourcist egalitarianism, which shall be my focus as well. (Reasons for the focus on equalizing access to health-care services rather than on equalizing health outcomes will be discussed below.)

A crucial feature of virtually all egalitarian theories is that they incorporate some kind of responsibility or choice condition, so that inequalities in resources require rectification or compensation only to the extent that one's condition does not arise through some present or past fault or choices of one's own.[42] An alternative way of putting this point is that "the primary egalitarian impulse is to extinguish the influence on distribution of . . . [bad] brute luck,"[43] brute luck being the kind of luck or risks

[41] Two helpful summaries of the "Equality of what?" literature are G. A. Cohen, "On the Currency of Egalitarian Justice," *Ethics*, vol. 99, no. 4 (July 1989), pp. 906–44; and Amartya Sen, *Inequality Reexamined* (Cambridge: Harvard University Press, 1992).

[42] Rawls's difference principle is the great exception here: his conception of the worst off does not incorporate a responsibility or choice condition. But post-Rawlsian egalitarianism invariably incorporates such a condition, for reasons I discuss in Section IV. In any event, though Rawls's difference principle does not incorporate a responsibility or choice condition, the distinction between those who are and are not responsible for their choices is recognized by Rawls in other parts of his theory and writing, particularly in his argument that justice does not require that one subsidize voluntarily acquired expensive tastes. For a valuable discussion of how Rawls does recognize a distinction between voluntary and involuntary inequalities, despite the wording of the difference principle, see Will Kymlicka, *Contemporary Political Philosophy: An Introduction* (Oxford: Clarendon Press, 1990), pp. 73–76.

[43] Cohen, "On the Currency of Egalitarian Justice," p. 908. I added the modifier "bad" before brute luck, because it is not an essential part of egalitarianism that the effects of good brute luck must be extinguished or modified. See Peter Vallentyne, "Self-Ownership and Equality: Brute Luck, Gifts, Universal Dominance, and Leximin," *Ethics*, vol. 107, no. 2 (January 1997), pp. 330–31. The distinction between brute and option luck originated with Ronald Dworkin, who played the crucial role in contemporary egalitarianism's incorporation of a responsibility or choice condition. See Dworkin, "What Is Equality? Part 2: Equality of Resources," *Philosophy and Public Affairs*, vol. 10, no. 4 (Fall 1981), p. 283. There is, unfortunately, no canonical definition of the brute luck/option luck distinction. Dworkin originally defined it so that option luck is luck that results from a deliberate or calculated gamble, but later egalitarians have modified this, probably because Dworkin's definition seems too restrictive—the key intuition behind the distinction is whether choices significantly influence one's outcomes, and choices can play a significant role even where one does

that one could not reasonably avoid having or undertaking (as opposed to option luck, which is luck or risks one reasonably could take into account in one's past or present choices).

This responsibility or choice condition is of utmost importance for our discussion. Egalitarians divide up their approach to justice into two parts: where people generally make genuine or uncoerced choices, principles of individual rights—particularly basic *negative* rights[44]—apply and markets are usually appropriate, but where such choices are generally absent, or at least are generally absent under present circumstances, no such rights apply and markets are inappropriate and/or must be corrected by state action. Egalitarians support NHI by arguing that most health-care choices, or at least health-care choices under present circumstances, fall into the latter category. The qualification "or at least under present circumstances" is necessary because one explanation for why egalitarians focus on inequalities in health care rather than inequalities in health is that, under fair institutional arrangements, they view the latter as a person's own responsibility.[45]

I shall focus on two prominent egalitarian arguments for NHI. Norman Daniels uses a principle of fair equality of opportunity to argue for NHI, while Ronald Dworkin argues that NHI provides roughly the same results that would exist in an ideal fair market where unchosen circumstances play little role in health-care allocations.

B. Daniels and fair equality of opportunity

Daniels uses John Rawls's theory of justice to support his view about justice in health care. Rawls defends two principles of justice. One is a principle of equal liberty, which is essentially a principle that contains a list of basic (largely negative) rights.[46] Rawls defends these rights as necessary to give people the freedom to pursue and revise their diverse conceptions of the good life. This is a typical egalitarian way of justifying basic rights.[47] It is not, however, this principle that Daniels uses. Rather, he focuses on Rawls's second principle, which not only contains the above-mentioned difference principle (that social and economic inequal-

---

not deliberate or calculate. My use of the distinction comes from Vallentyne's gloss on Dworkin's distinction.

[44] All rights imply that someone other than the right-holder has duties to respect the right. Negative rights imply duties to refrain from some action; positive rights imply duties to do something. Basic rights are rights which have a considerable degree of moral weight, so that they typically defeat claims of aggregate utility or individual well-being.

[45] Another possible explanation is that fixing inequalities in health care is more feasible than fixing inequalities in health.

[46] Rawls, *A Theory of Justice*, pp. 60–61; Rawls, *Political Liberalism*, p. 291.

[47] For a discussion of the main lines of argument many egalitarians use to defend basic rights, see Daniel Shapiro, "Liberalism, Basic Rights, and Free Exchange," *Journal of Social Philosophy*, vol. 26, no. 2 (Fall 1995), pp. 104-5 and my references therein.

ities should be arranged to the greatest benefit for the least advantaged) but also contains the principle that offices and positions should be offered to all under conditions of fair equality of opportunity. Fair equality of opportunity means, roughly, that people with similar talents and skills and motivation should have the same opportunities.[48] Rawls did not apply his second principle to access to health-care services, but Daniels does by noting that meeting health-care needs is a way of protecting our opportunities, and if we are obligated to protect those opportunities, we are obligated to meet those needs. More specifically, Daniels argues that institutions that affect the allocation of health-care resources should be arranged so that each person enjoys his or her fair share of a normal opportunity range for individuals in his or her society. A normal opportunity range for a given society is the full set of individual life plans that it would be reasonable for individuals in that society to pursue, if they enjoyed "normal species functioning." Daniels believes there is an objective sense of "normal species functioning," and while he does not do much to flesh out this concept, for our purposes what is vital is that disease, illness, and disability reduce this functioning. Thus, Daniels's view is that since health-care resources function so as to prevent, minimize, or compensate one for departures from normal species functioning, and since departures from that functioning—disease and disability— constitute one important barrier to fair equality of opportunity, it follows that ensuring fair equality of opportunity requires a set of health-care institutions that enable us to function as normally as possible.[49]

It is unsurprising, then, that Daniels argues in favor of universal health insurance with comprehensive benefits and against market, actuarial insurance. Health insurance for all is necessary as a way of meeting the obligation to remove barriers to normal functioning, and the benefits of the insurance must be extensive, since there are a variety of services necessary to restore or maintain full functioning (routine and preventive care, hospital care, long-term care for the elderly, services designed to maintain and restore our mental as well as physical health, etc.). Daniels says that his views imply that the freedom to purchase private insurance that provides benefits above the amount NHI offers would be justified, since justice requires access to services that restore or maintain, to the extent that this is possible, normal functioning, not that we need guaranteed access to services designed to *enhance* normal functioning. So on Daniels's view it is permissible for people to purchase supplemental insurance to obtain private rooms in a hospital, cosmetic surgery, etc. However, he rejects the idea that justice requires only that the state provide

[48] Rawls, *A Theory of Justice*, p. 73.

[49] Norman Daniels, *Just Health Care* (New York: Cambridge University Press, 1985), chs. 2 and 4. Basically the same account is given, in a more compressed manner, in Norman Daniels, Donald W. Light, and Ronald L. Caplan, *Benchmarks of Fairness for Health Care Reform* (New York: Oxford University Press, 1997), pp. 19–22.

access to a bare-bones, minimal level of care, for such an approach would exclude a whole range of services needed to restore or maintain normal functioning. Thus, Daniels argues that a two-tiered system of health insurance is acceptable only to the extent that the basic tier provides for those services needed to restore and maintain basic functioning (and only to the extent that the existence of the supplemental tier does not undermine support for the basic tier of the NHI system).[50]

As for actuarial insurance, Daniels condemns it as doubly unjust: not only does it provide barriers to full coverage, but it is unfair to charge people according to expected risk, since "most health risks are not affected by choices, and others are so only somewhat and in ways of which we are not aware."[51]

This account is not complete as it stands, because the argument so far only focuses on the demand or consumption side of health care, and Daniels (and anyone offering a theory of just health-care institutions) must explain how the subsidization of health-care needs can avoid being the equivalent of a black hole that sucks out resources devoted to all other goods. This is not just a practical problem, but a requirement of justice on Daniels's account, for if excessive resources are devoted to health care, less is left for people to pursue the goals that are part of their life plans, as well as for other government programs that egalitarians take to be required by justice. Daniels's account seems particularly vulnerable to this problem, because enormous resources could be expended on certain individuals and yet their illnesses, diseases, or disabilities would not be removed or even significantly lessened.[52] Furthermore, not only do health-care needs compete with other needs for resources, they compete with each other—some criteria for ranking various kinds of health-care needs or medical services is obviously required.

Daniels does attempt to address these issues. He notes that the scope of the right to health care must be constrained by facts about scarcity and technological feasibility within a particular society, and that there is no obligation to provide access to services whose chances of being effective are low or speculative. He also says that the health-care services that are most pressing are those that make the greatest contribution to restoring one's range of opportunities, rather than those which play a relatively minor role in doing so.[53] Still, as Daniels himself notes, these are quite vague requirements, and do little to show how, in allocating resources designed to restore or maintain normal functioning, we could avoid the problem of a medical "bottomless pit," or how one should make specific choices between different kinds of health-care services. Daniels's real

---

[50] Daniels et al., *Benchmarks of Fairness*, pp. 27–28 and 43–44.

[51] *Ibid.*, p. 46.

[52] As noted by Allen Buchanan, "Health-Care Delivery and Resource Allocation," in *Medical Ethics*, ed. Robert Veatch (Sudsbury: Jones and Bartlett, 1997), pp. 347–48.

[53] Daniels et al., *Benchmarks of Fairness*, pp. 25–26.

answer to these problems is government rationing. This constrains demand, and a global budget enables us to make explicit trade-offs with other government programs (ending the "bottomless pit" problem); furthermore, any rationing procedure must implicitly or explicitly provide some ranking of, or some way of making choices between, various kinds of services. Concerning the latter, Daniels maintains, for reasons I will discuss in Section V, that the principle of fair equality of opportunity does not really provide any determinate guidance for these choices, and for this reason, as well as to maintain accountability, he argues that this should be a matter for democratic, public deliberation. Thus, he criticizes present NHI programs whose criteria for rationing, as I shall discuss in Section V, are generally invisible to the average citizen.[54]

Thus, Daniels's account rationalizes the major features of NHI. The requirement of fair equality of opportunity for access to health-care services is used to support universal provision of comprehensive benefits with few out-of-pocket expenses, and the elimination of most forms of risk rating. The indeterminacy of fair equality of opportunity vis-à-vis the ranking of medical services, and the requirement of justice that resources devoted to health care not swallow up resources for other welfare-state institutions, are used to support the rationing and global budgets that structure the supply side of NHI. But what about the restriction, if not virtual elimination, of the role of the patient as a consumer? In one sense, of course, Daniels must and does approve of this restriction, since awareness and negotiation about prices and a wide range of choices of health plans would restrict access to the level of services he thinks justice requires. Yet he *also* argues that a system is more fair when it respects autonomous choices, and that such choices help to ensure the quality and efficiency of care. Thus, a requirement of justice is that, within the limits necessarily required by NHI, consumer choice of providers (both primary-care physicians and specialists) and procedures must be maximized. Or to put matters another way: wherever choice is appropriate, it should be maximized. However, on Daniels's view, choice only has a limited place in health-care policy.

C. Dworkin and the results of an ideal, fair market

Dworkin has only recently turned his attention to the issue of justice in health care.[55] His arguments depend upon his more fundamental theory

---

[54] *Ibid.*, pp. 57–58. Daniels's critical description of proposals in the U.S. Congress for NHI (none of which even mentioned the issue of rationing) as using "doublespeak," shows that he would be critical of present-day NHI secretive criteria for rationing. See *ibid.*, pp. 116–19.

[55] See Ronald Dworkin, "Justice in the Distribution of Health Care," *McGill Law Review*, vol. 38, no. 4 (1993), pp. 883–98; and Dworkin, "Will Clinton's Plan Be Fair?" *New York Review of Books*, January 13, 1994, pp. 1–8.

of justice, which he has developed over the last twenty years or so, in particular his view about justice and markets.[56]

On the one hand, Dworkin argues that markets are essential for justice. To show respect and concern for people with different (peaceful) views of the good life, different ambitions, preferences, etc., justice mandates that individuals have the right to act in accordance with those views and have the freedom to pursue, revise, and realize their ambitions and goals. Furthermore, such respect requires that one be held responsible for one's choices and the costs of those choices. It would be unfair to require those under an obligation to respect individual rights to refrain from interfering with the right-holder's choices and to subsidize the costs of the right-holder's choices. Hence, a system which allows one to make choices, gives one information about the costs of the choices so these choices can be informed, and holds one responsible for these costs is just. Markets do all three. If we lived in a world in which we all began in roughly the same circumstances, then any inequality in wealth and income that resulted would be just, for it would simply reflect people's choices about how to live their lives as revealed by their trade-offs of work for leisure, their trade-offs of savings and investment for consumption, their rates of time preference (i.e., the extent to which they discount the future), their occupational choices, and so forth.

Of course, we do not live in that world. In the real world, people find themselves in unchosen circumstances of varying degrees of disadvantage or advantage. When markets reflect or compound unchosen disadvantages resulting from one's natural endowments, or one's race, sex, or social or family background, markets do not embody justice but injustice. Dworkin argues that welfare-state policies which interfere with markets are justified to the extent that they correct for unchosen disadvantages while still allowing people to act on their peaceful ambitions and conception of the good. We need not go into detail about what policies he thinks would most closely embody justice—for our purposes what is essential is that he thinks that the present inequalities of income and wealth that exist in the U.S. are clearly unjust. While people do voluntarily choose to save or invest different amounts, make different work-leisure trade-offs, etc., compensation for unchosen disadvantages would narrow considerably the range of present-day inequalities in the U.S.

Dworkin uses his views about a just distribution of wealth and income to argue against free-market health insurance, where there are no subsidies and no bias in the tax code distorting people's decisions to purchase or not purchase varying kinds of health insurance. Dworkin says that this

[56] The key pieces are Dworkin, "What Is Equality? Part 1: Equality of Welfare," *Philosophy and Public Affairs*, vol. 10, no. 3 (Summer 1981), pp. 185–246; Dworkin, "What Is Equality? Part 2: Equality of Resources," *Philosophy and Public Affairs*, vol. 10, no. 4 (Fall 1981), pp. 283–345; and Dworkin, "What Is Equality? Part 3: The Place of Liberty," *Iowa Law Review*, vol. 73, no. 1 (1987), pp. 1–54.

policy would be unjust, for a person's decision not to purchase such insurance would likely not be a reflection of her view of the good life, but rather a reflection of her inability to afford it, an inability due to the background injustice in the distribution of wealth and income. But would a free and unsubsidized market for health insurance be just if there were a more or less just distribution of wealth and income? No, says Dworkin. Patients' information about the value, cost, and side effects of medical procedures—what a good doctor knows—is quite limited and inaccurate, and therefore decisions to purchase insurance based on such information would not really reflect patients' views of the good life but instead would reflect, in part, brute luck. Furthermore, in a free and unsubsidized market with a fair distribution of income and wealth, insurance companies would have information about a person's antecedent risk of being ill or diseased, and since such risks are unchosen,[57] it would be unfair to charge high risks a higher price than is charged to low risks.

Thus, a just market in health insurance would be one where (1) wealth and income is distributed fairly, (2) patients possess roughly the kind of medical knowledge doctors have, and (3) insurance companies lack information about antecedent health risks. Whatever insurance prudent[58] people would purchase in such a market constitutes justice in health care in both a macro sense (whatever level of aggregate resources was devoted to health care would be morally appropriate) and in a distributive sense (however health care was distributed in such a society would be just). Summarizing his views, Dworkin says that conditions (1) through (3) "follow directly from an extremely appealing assumption: that a just distribution is one that well-informed people create for themselves by individual choices, provided the economic system and distribution of wealth in the community in which these choices are made are themselves just."[59]

But since there is not and could not be any market that fits Dworkin's version of an egalitarian market, how are we to determine what insurance it would be prudent for, say, the average citizen in a contemporary welfare state to purchase? Though Dworkin notes that "what is prudent for someone depends on that person's own individual needs, tastes, personality and preferences,"[60] he thinks that nevertheless we can make some judgments with a fair amount of confidence concerning what the average

[57] Dworkin does acknowledge in a note that this is not true of all risks; he mentions that it would seem fair to charge smokers more than nonsmokers. As I shall argue in the next section, this concession helps to undermine Dworkin's defense of NHI. See Dworkin, "Will Clinton's Plan Be Fair?" p. 4, note 10.

[58] It is not entirely clear why Dworkin introduces the concept of prudence at this point. Perhaps the reason is that he is working within the contractarian tradition in moral and political philosophy, where justice is determined by seeing what rational, prudent people would choose under certain conditions.

[59] Dworkin, "Will Clinton's Plan Be Fair?" p. 4.

[60] *Ibid.*, p. 5.

prudent citizen would purchase in such a market—and it turns out to be functionally equivalent to NHI. He thinks such a person would purchase insurance covering both routine and preventive medical care as well as hospitalization. This corresponds to NHI's being compulsory, universal, comprehensive insurance. On the other hand, Dworkin argues that some health-care decisions would almost certainly be imprudent—for example, insurance coverage for expensive care during dementia or for heroic and expensive treatment that would only prolong life for a few months. He also argues that at some point our confidence runs out concerning what an average person would purchase, and thus that justice requires that people have the freedom to buy supplemental insurance. The elimination of risk rating is, of course, equivalent to the lack of information insurers would have in Dworkin's thought experiment about an ideal market. As for NHI's restriction on supply via rationing, global budgets, and the like, Dworkin sees them as the inevitable result of universal coverage combined with a prudential commitment to controlling costs. Like Daniels, he also believes democratic input on rationing decisions is required, though he says little about this matter.

Thus, although Dworkin, far more than Daniels, stresses that justice in health care flows from a view of equality that is "dynamic and sensitive to people's differing convictions on how to live,"[61] they both end up supporting roughly the same kind of policies. This is because a view that (most) health-care decisions do not reflect genuine choices and a view that they would only reflect them under conditions that could not exist, reach the same conclusion: that a market under present, actual circumstances compounds and reflects unjust inequalities rather than reflecting the choices of individuals with different preferences, ambitions, or views of the good life.

To summarize the discussion in this section: Daniels argues for universal, comprehensive health insurance with no risk rating and limited choice of plans, because he sees justice in health care as requiring the removal of barriers that prevent one from achieving (to the extent that this is possible) normal functioning. His emphasis upon a health-care policy that removes barriers (to fair equality of opportunity), rather than one which respects choices that reflect people's different views about how to live their lives, stems from his belief that most health-care risks are not voluntarily assumed and that most health-care decisions in a market do not reflect genuine choices. Dworkin argues for the same kind of NHI as Daniels because Dworkin believes that (real) markets constitute unfair barriers rather than reflecting individuals' different choices and preferences, though he does not invoke the notion of fair equality of opportunity, and instead uses a thought experiment about an ideal fair market as a way of showing that NHI would lead to roughly the same result as such

---

[61] Dworkin, "Justice in the Distribution of Health Care," p. 898.

a market. As for NHI's rationing, global budgets, and other constraints on subsidized demand, Daniels and Dworkin approach this in two ways. In part, these constraints are justified as inevitable results of a commitment to providing universal coverage joined with a commitment to controlling costs and preventing health-care resources from becoming a drain on other resources. In part, they are also justified as necessary for making trade-offs between different kinds of medical services, while democratic input on these trade-offs is seen as necessary to maintain accountability and to give some determinate criteria for making these trade-offs that egalitarian principles are unable to provide.

IV. Risks, Choices, and Moral Hazard

As we have seen, NHI differs from MHI in the way it structures both the consumption or demand for health-care services, and the production or supply of such services. Egalitarian arguments that support NHI over MHI are also composed of two sides, as it were. In this section, I examine the consumption-side arguments and show why egalitarians should support, not oppose, risk rating and a wide choice of health-care plans; and in the next section, I examine the production or supply of health care, and argue that egalitarians should support markets over government rationing of health-care services.

Recall that egalitarians argue that risk rating and a widespread choice of health-care plans are unfair, because differences in health-care risks are largely involuntary and because choices to forgo comprehensive service plans are due to present background inequalities that are unjust. Hence NHI, which eliminates risk rating and compels everyone to pick similar comprehensive plans (with limited purchase of supplemental insurance) is much fairer than MHI.[62] I first discuss health-care risks and then proceed to the question of choices to purchase different kinds of health-care policies.

A. Health-care risks

Some health-care risks—that is, risks of premature mortality, morbidity, illness, and injury—are completely beyond one's control. If one has the gene for Huntington's disease, for example, one will get ill and then die from it, no matter what one does. Most health-care risks are not matters of brute bad luck like this. Indeed, among the important causes of health-care risks are "lifestyle" decisions or activities, such as tobacco use, diet and patterns of physical activity, alcohol use, sexual behavior, the care-

---

[62] I will not discuss the issue of compulsory coverage, since as I noted in Section II, the Goodman-Musgrave proposal for MHI may not fully eliminate compulsion for the provision of some very minimal set of health-care benefits.

fulness of one's driving (e.g., whether one uses seat belts regularly or drives while intoxicated), and the use of illegal drugs.[63] In general, it is not a matter of brute luck if one gets injured, becomes ill or diseased, or dies prematurely from these activities or behaviors. I shall now argue that these behaviors should be classified as generally belonging on the voluntary side of the voluntary-involuntary continuum.

Egalitarians believe that choices such as how much work to trade off for leisure, how much savings to trade off for consumption, what line of work to pursue, and the like are, in general, voluntary, because they reflect and are constituted by different ambitions and views of the good life (recall Dworkin's argument). However, the same relationship holds

---

[63] See J. Michael McGinnis and William H. Foege, "Actual Causes of Death in the United States," *Journal of the American Medical Association*, vol. 270, no. 18 (November 1993), pp. 2207–12. I thank Robert S. Sade, M.D. for directing me to this reference. This article surveys and synthesizes articles published between 1977 and 1993 that discussed the causes of death in the U.S. The authors estimate that around 40 percent of all deaths in the U.S. are due to tobacco use, alcohol consumption, sexual activity, motor vehicle accidents, and the use of illegal drugs. A longitudinal study of 6,928 adult males in Alameda County, California, from 1965 to 1974, is also suggestive: it shows that good health practices (not smoking, moderate or no use of alcohol, seven to eight hours regular sleep, regular physical activity, proper weight, eating breakfast, not eating between meals), and not the initial health status of the survey respondents, were responsible for significant differences in mortality. See Lester Breslow and James E. Enstrom, "Persistence of Health Habits and Their Relationship to Mortality," *Preventive Medicine*, vol. 9 (September 4, 1980), pp. 469–83. I have not located any studies that attempt to quantify the effects of lifestyle choices on mortality in Europe, but since a greater percentage of the population smokes in most European countries than in the U.S., it is not unlikely that a higher proportion of deaths in those countries could be attributed to "lifestyle" choices. See U.S. Congress, Office of Technology Assessment, *International Health Statistics: What the Numbers Mean for the United States* (Washington, DC: U.S. Government Printing Office, November 1993), pp. 70–71 and 83–84.

It is important to stress two limitations of the above articles. First, their focus is on premature deaths, not morbidity, illness, or injury. That lifestyle risks cause a certain percentage of premature deaths does not mean that they cause the same percentage of morbidity, illness, or injury. For example, women generally have greater morbidity than men, but tend to live longer. See Mildred Blaxter, "A Comparison of Measures of Inequality in Morbidity," in *Health Inequalities in European Countries*, ed. John Fox (Aldershot: Gower Publishing, 1989), p. 199. Second, the first article cited above does not discuss how much of the *differences* in premature mortality is due to lifestyle factors.

Studies that do attempt to determine how much of differential premature mortality was due to lifestyle factors, as opposed to other influences such as years of schooling, relative income, and occupational status, have found that lifestyle factors played a role, but not the most significant role. The most famous of these is probably Michael Marmot's longitudinal study of four occupational classes of British civil servants working in the same office, which showed that the civil servants' occupational status had a stronger correlation with mortality from coronary heart disease than did lifestyle factors such as smoking. See Michael Marmot, "Social Inequalities in Mortality: The Social Environment," in *Class and Health*, ed. Richard G. Wilkinson (London: Tavistock Publishing, 1986), pp. 21–33. Other longitudinal studies that show a stronger correlation between health and income and/or education than between health and lifestyle factors are discussed by Mary N. Haan, George A. Kaplan, and S. Leonard Syme, "Socioeconomic Status and Health: Old Observations and New Thoughts," in *Pathways to Health: The Role of Social Factors*, ed. John P. Bunker, Deanna S. Gomby, and Barbara H. Kehrer (Menlo Park: Henry J. Kaiser Family Foundation, 1989), pp. 83–86. For reasons I discuss in note 71, however, all of these studies must be viewed with great caution and have various methodological and conceptual problems.

for "lifestyle" risks. Consider the following, all of which reflect and constitute one's "lifestyle" risks:

A. One's rate of time preference: Those with higher rates of time preference, that is, those who place a high value on present goods over future goods, will engage in more risky behavior, including behavior which might increase their chances of becoming ill or diseased, or dying prematurely.

B. One's choice of occupation: For example, firefighting is a more risky profession than teaching.

C. One's epistemic values: The extent to which I assess and am open to evidence, the value I place on discovering the truth, the degree to which I desire to hold coherent beliefs, etc., will play a role in determining whether I should care about health-care risks or believe what scientific evidence or scientific methods tell us about the risk of certain behaviors or ways of life. These epistemic values are in part affected by one's non-epistemic values: given one's aims in life, commitments, and so forth, it can be rational for different people to devote different amounts of time and effort to learning and absorbing information about health-care risks.

D. One's moral and metaphysical views or values: One's views about the meaning and value of life and death, enjoyment and happiness, suffering and pain, will play a role in one's degree of risk aversion, and that degree of risk aversion is, in turn, also reflected and constituted by (A) through (C).

It is clear, then, that one's conception of the good life—which includes one's metaphysical, epistemic, and moral values— to a significant extent influences one's assumption of "lifestyle" risks (and vice versa). Since choices to pursue and revise one's ambitions, one's conception of the good life, etc., are considered by egalitarians to be sufficiently voluntary that inequalities resulting from such choices are regarded as just, it follows that egalitarians should in general consider "lifestyle" risks to be sufficiently voluntary.

It may be objected that even if the initial assumption of such risks is sufficiently voluntary, this diminishes over time, so that subsequent behavior becomes more and more involuntary. This argument might be applied to such risks as the use of legal and illegal drugs. While, for example, initial decisions to smoke are sufficiently voluntary, subsequent decisions are not, as the smoker becomes addicted and thus it becomes difficult to quit. For this kind of argument to succeed, it must be true that the difficulty in quitting is not due, principally, to smoking's becoming for many people a central activity or being well-integrated into many facets of one's life. Central activities are always difficult to alter, and if egalitarians were to declare that continued participation in risky central activities was indicative of involuntariness, then much of life, indeed much of what matters in life, would be labeled as involuntary. I have argued elsewhere, however, that the difficulty in quitting smoking *is* in large part due to smoking's being a central activity for many people.[64] More generally, the pharmacological model of addiction—that (some) people have difficulty in ceasing or modifying repeated drug use largely because of the pharmacological effects of repeated use of the drug—does not fit the evidence very well for either legal or illegal drugs.[65] The same point applies to the more popular arguments that people who repeatedly engage in harmful behavior that has adverse effects on their health and well-being (e.g., gambling, promiscuity, etc.) are addicts who are genetically or biologically unable to help themselves.[66]

So far I have discussed relatively clear-cut kinds of influences on health-care risks. Other causes of differential health-care risks are much harder to classify. Consider, for example, differences in education, income, and wealth (in general, the more years of education and the greater one's wealth, the better one's health).[67] Clearly, young children have extremely limited choice concerning how much and what type of schooling they receive; but as they approach adulthood and become adults, they do have such choices. One's level of income and wealth are viewed by egalitarians as to some extent chosen, since they are partly the result of decisions about how to lead one's life, and to some extent due to unchosen circumstances such as family background, one's race and sex, etc.

Similar remarks apply to psychological characteristics of the person, such as one's sense of self-efficacy, one's ability to cope with adversity, and one's general outlook on life (e.g., one's degree of optimism or cheer-

---

[64] Daniel Shapiro, "Smoking Tobacco: Irrationality, Addiction, and Paternalism," *Public Affairs Quarterly*, vol. 8, no. 2 (April 1994), pp. 187–203.

[65] See my "Addiction, Responsibility, and Drug Policy," unpublished, May 1997. See also Richard J. DeGrandpre and Ed White, "Drugs: In Care of the Self," *Common Knowledge*, vol. 5, no. 3 (Winter 1996), pp. 27–48 and the references cited therein.

[66] For a good critique of such views, see Stanton Peele, *The Diseasing of America: Addiction Treatment Out of Control* (Boston: Houghton Mifflin, 1991).

[67] On the relationship between education and mortality, see Tapani Valkonen's longitudinal study of seven European countries, "Adult Mortality and Levels of Education," in *Health Inequalities in European Countries*, ch. 7, pp. 142–72. In "Socioeconomic Status and Health: An Examination of Underlying Processes," in Bunker et al., eds., *Pathways to Health*, p. 19, David Mechanic says that "[e]ducation is one of the most consistent predictors of measures of mortality, morbidity and health behavior." In "Socioeconomic Status: A Personal Research Perspective," in *ibid.*, p. 141, Michael Grossman and Theodore J. Joyce say that education has been shown to be a more important causal determinant than occupational status or income. Leonard A. Sagan also argues that education is a more important causal determinant of morbidity than wealth; see Sagan, *The Health of Nations: True Causes of Sickness and Well-Being* (New York: Basic Books, 1987), pp. 176–78.

Of course, even if education is a better causal determinant or predictor of mortality and/or morbidity than income, this does not mean that income level is unimportant. For some studies that stress the effect of income on mortality, see G. Pappas, S. Queen, W. Adden, and G. Fisher, "The Increasing Disparity in Mortality between Socioeconomic Groups in the United States, 1960 and 1986," in *New England Journal of Medicine*, vol. 329 (1993), pp. 103–9, cited in Oliver Fein, "The Influence of Social Class on Health Status: American and British Research on Health Inequalities," in *Journal of General Internal Medicine*, vol. 10, no. 10 (October 1995), pp. 577–86; and Haan et al., "Socioeconomic Status and Health," p. 84.

fulness), which also affect one's health.[68] To the extent that these characteristics are largely determined in childhood and are very difficult to change thereafter, they should be placed on the involuntary side of the spectrum. To the extent that one can, as an adult, develop and/or alter these characteristics, they should be placed on the voluntary side of the spectrum. Some of these characteristics are probably largely determined in childhood (one's cheerfulness?) and others are more under one's control (one's sense of self-efficacy?); overall, then, it is hard to give a general answer concerning these types of influences.[69]

One could continue with an elaboration of other influences that affect differential health-care risks; however, the general difficulty is now apparent. Unless it can be shown that most health-care risks are due to matters of brute luck, like getting Huntington's disease, or due to lifestyle choices such as smoking, excessive alcohol use, and the like, egalitarians can provide no determinate answer to the question: "Are most health-care risks voluntarily or involuntarily assumed?" And this is what cannot be shown. Few health-care risks are merely matters of brute luck. A significant but indeterminate number are due to lifestyle risks. A significant but indeterminate number are due to mixed causes. Furthermore, most of the causes of health-care risks interact with each other—e.g., the more affluent and more educated tend to follow less risky "lifestyles"[70]—and the causal interactions between most of the factors influencing one's health-care risks are quite complex and difficult to measure. As a result, it is difficult if not impossible to firmly support a conclusion about the extent to which health-care risks are or are not voluntarily assumed.[71]

---

[68] On self-efficacy, see Albert Bandura, "Self-Efficacy Mechanism in Physiological Activation and Health-Promoting Behavior," in *Neurobiology of Learning, Emotion, and Affect*, ed. John Madden IV (New York: Raven Press, 1991), pp. 229–69; Herzlinger, *Market-Driven Health Care*, pp. 60–62 and the references cited therein; and Sagan, *The Health of Nations*, pp. 187–94. Sagan also discusses the role of hope and coping skills on pp. 180–81 and 184.

[69] Cohen, "On the Currency of Egalitarian Justice," pp. 930–31, discusses the example of a cheerful person and says that, in conversation, Dworkin viewed cheerfulness as a borderline case.

[70] For discussion of the relationship between education and lifestyle choices, see Sagan, *The Health of Nations*, p. 179; Raymond Illsley, "Comparative Review of Sources, Methodology, and Knowledge [of Health Inequalities]," *Social Science and Medicine*, vol. 31, no. 3 (1990), p. 230; and Mechanic, "Socioeconomic Status and Health" (*supra* note 67), p. 19. There are a number of studies showing a relationship between socioeconomic status and risky lifestyles, but for reasons discussed in note 71, such studies are of limited use, since socioeconomic status, as typically defined, combines education with other influences, such as occupational status and income.

[71] Studies that show a correlation between one influence (e.g., lifestyle or income) and another (e.g., mortality or morbidity), or that show differing degrees of correlation between different influences and a certain measure(s) of health, are always vulnerable to the "third variable" problem: correlation is not proof of causality. Studies that show a correlation between socioeconomic status—defined as a combination of income and/or occupational status and/or education—and health outcomes are particularly problematic, if the correla-

What should egalitarians conclude from this? Were they to use the fact of this "mixture" as a basis for arguing that health-care risks belong on the involuntary side of the voluntary-involuntary continuum, this would imply that *nothing* belongs on the voluntary side of the continuum. Since life is a mixture of choices and unchosen circumstances, an egalitarian cannot infer from the notion that health-care risks are also a mixture that these risks are involuntary, for then the egalitarian view that justice requires that involuntary disadvantages or inequalities be rectified implies that all inequalities must be rectified—a view which would make egalitarianism intuitively implausible, and which is contrary to the way egalitarians argue. Furthermore, such a view would undermine any protection for individual rights that egalitarians want to defend—for example, the right to free speech, freedom of religion, and privacy—since one's communicative, religious, and personal and intimate choices are also affected, in some cases significantly, by unchosen circumstances. For example, those who are inarticulate or not terribly literate will be at a competitive disadvantage vis-à-vis their exercise of their right to free speech, as compared with the way the articulate will exercise that right and the way that right will help the articulate achieve their goals. (Indeed, in some cases, the inarticulate person's overall position is worsened because of the presence of the articulate.) And while the extent of one's literacy and articulateness depends in part on one's choices, it is also a function of unchosen circumstances (family background, genetic makeup, etc.). If the egalitarian principle of correcting for unchosen disadvantages were to be applied to the realm of communication, it would likely eviscerate if not eliminate any sort of basic right to free speech. In principle, correcting for such disadvantages might mean regulating communications to make sure the inarticulate and illiterate's situation was not being worsened and/or preventing the articulate from communicating when such communication threatened to provide them with competitive advantages—and it is quite

---

tion between the various factors making up socioeconomic status is not that high, as Victor Fuchs points out in "General Comments of Conference Participants," in Bunker et al., eds., *Pathways to Health*, p. 226. Furthermore, some studies are not longitudinal, which raises the suspicion that the relationship found is a temporary one. Many studies are of only one country, which makes them of limited use. Morbidity studies are particularly tricky, since (a) authors often use different notions of morbidity (is it defined in terms of some objective signs of pathology, or in terms of self-reported symptoms, or by an inability to perform certain "normal" tasks?) and (b) there is a big gap between actual morbidity and reported morbidity. On different concepts of morbidity, see Blaxter, "A Comparison of Measures of Inequality in Morbidity" (*supra* note 63), pp. 206–21. On the gap between reported and actual morbidity, see Illsley, "Comparative Review of Sources, Methodology, and Knowledge," p. 233.

Finally, the factors being measured are notoriously difficult to measure accurately (e.g., diet and physical activity). One reason "years of schooling" may show up as a better predictor of mortality or morbidity than other factors is simply that "years of schooling" is relatively easy to measure.

hard to see what would be left of a basic right to free speech if such interventions were considered legitimate.[72]

Since there are good reasons for egalitarians not to label or categorize most health risks as involuntary, they should view most of these risks as voluntary, and favor a system with risk rating, namely MHI. At this point, it might be suggested that there could be a middle ground between the absence of risk rating in NHI and the risk rating in MHI (which, subsidies to the indigent to one side, only subsidizes uninsurable risks). Couldn't NHI have some selective risk rating, for example, taxes on products, such as tobacco and alcohol, whose repeated use increases one's health-care risks? Perhaps. However, a middle ground is not really a live issue. The aim here is to compare real institutions, and an essential feature of NHI is that it almost completely avoids risk rating. Furthermore, an essential feature of the egalitarian argument for NHI over MHI is the absence of risk rating in the former. Most importantly, taxes in NHI will not really perform the same function as risk rating. Taxes are determined by political considerations, and it is quite doubtful that the level of tax paid would be proportional to increased risks of mortality or morbidity.

Another consideration strengthens my argument that egalitarians should favor risk rating. A health insurance system which has a comparative advantage on communicating information about one's health-care risks will be *ceteris paribus* justified on egalitarian grounds, because the degree to which individuals are or can be made cognizant of the various risks they assume makes the assumption of those risks more voluntary. I have so far stressed that egalitarians believe one should be held responsible for one's choices and the cost of one's choices, but responsibility is not just a backward-looking issue, a question of whether one is or should be held responsible for what one *did*. It is also a forward-looking issue, that is, a question of how people can be given incentives to *be* responsible in the future. Communication of information about one's health-care risks does this; thus, even if health-care risks are not as voluntary as other kinds of decisions that egalitarians believe are voluntary, a comparative superiority of one kind of system of health insurance in communicating information about health-care risks probably compensates—perhaps more than compensates—for the diminished responsibility in acquiring those risks

[72] Perhaps an egalitarian might reply that where basic rights are at stake, egalitarian principles simply do not apply. Since there is a basic right to free speech, the egalitarian principle, whether it be correcting for unchosen inequalities or correcting for inequalities per se, would not apply. However, this reply begs the question. Egalitarians who justify a basic right to free speech do so by arguing that there are communicative *choices* vis-à-vis the exercise of one's conception of the good that need to be protected. If egalitarians acknowledge that communicative activities are influenced by a mixture of choices and unchosen circumstances—but they nevertheless, despite this mixture, defend a basic right to free speech and inequalities resulting from the exercise of this right—then the same kind of defense should apply to health insurance systems.

in the first place. The risk rating in MHI provides that information, while the abolition of risk rating in NHI eliminates it.[73]

Furthermore, it is the poorly educated who need risk rating the most. I already noted that rates of mortality and morbidity drop as education increases, and part of the reason for this is that the more educated engage in less risky "lifestyles" or behaviors.[74] A system which gives the less educated an obvious and direct way of learning that their actions have a negative effect on their mortality and morbidity—and which gives them an obvious incentive to act on this information[75]—would appear to be a necessity on egalitarian grounds, and risk rating does just this. After all, the more educated and affluent have less need of risk rating: they are likely to be informed, and to have access to information, about the effects of various "lifestyle" choices. The absence of risk rating in NHI is a clear injustice, since it removes a mechanism by which those with greater unchosen disadvantages can increase their sense of personal responsibility and their ability to make informed choices in the future.[76]

B. Choice in health plans

I turn now to the other demand-side feature that distinguishes NHI from MHI: namely, that the former allows fewer choices among health plans than the latter—in particular, choices to forgo comprehensive coverage. As the reader will recall, Daniels and Dworkin both argue that present choices to forgo comprehensive coverage are due to background inequalities (in wealth and/or opportunities) that are unjust. Strictly speaking, this is a separate issue from risk rating, for even if the egalitarians are

[73] Economist Robert Sugden has raised an objection to this argument, noting that risk rating is based, to some degree, upon unalterable or virtually unalterable characteristics of an individual (e.g., upon age or sex). That one's premiums are based in part on such characteristics provides no incentive for more responsible behavior, since one cannot alter (or can only alter with great difficulty) such characteristics, and one is not acting responsibly or irresponsibly by simply having such characteristics. However, the arguments in this essay are *comparative* ones. That risk rating is based only in *part* on characteristics or behavior that one can alter is still an improvement (vis-à-vis acting responsibly in the future) over the absence of risk rating, since the former provides more information than the latter concerning the cost of one's (partially) alterable behavior.

[74] See note 70.

[75] Knowledge about some risky activities, such as smoking, is widespread. But it is one thing to know this in the abstract and another to have this information communicated in a direct and powerful way. Public health campaigns about the risks of smoking may not be as effective as health insurance that raises one's premiums based on one's behavior. For evidence that smokers, at least in the U.S., are not ill-informed about the risks of smoking, see W. Kip Viscusi, *Smoking: Making the Risky Decision* (New York: Oxford University Press, 1992), pp. 77–78.

[76] Notice also that the combination of medical savings accounts plus risk rating not only provides a way for people to become informed about the effects of different lifestyle choices, but encourages them to budget over time to reap the benefits of healthy lifestyle choices or pay the costs of unhealthy ones. See Goodman and Musgrave, *Patient Power*, p. 251.

wrong that egalitarian justice requires the elimination of risk rating, they might be right that justice requires that there not be a widespread choice of health-care plans (and, in particular, that people not have the choice to forgo comprehensive coverage). However, the arguments about health-care risks in the previous section pretty much carry over to the question of choices in health-care coverage. Individuals' differing ambitions and conceptions of the good life affect their choice of health-care plans. The choice of plans is affected by one's rate of time preference: the higher it is, the more likely one is to trade off expenditures on long-term and catastrophic care in favor of other kinds of insurance or other goods. Obviously, one's choice of occupation makes a difference: certain occupations are riskier and call for different kinds of health insurance and different ways of allocating savings over time. One's epistemic values play a role, since my views about whether I should care about health-care risks will play a role in determining what kind of insurance, if any, I desire. And moral and metaphysical values play an essential role, since questions about the meaning and value of life and death will influence one's views about the appropriateness of various kinds of lifesaving or life-prolonging procedures, contraception, abortion, physician-assisted suicide, euthanasia, and so forth.

Indeed, the relationship between one's conception of the good and widespread choice in health-care plans is probably stronger than in the case of the assumption of health-care risks. The latter are often assumed nondeliberatively and implicitly, while health-care plan choices and health-care budgetary decisions are often made explicitly and deliberately. To the extent that deliberate and explicit decisions are more reflective of one's conception of the good, the connection between one's ambitions, conception of the good, etc., and one's health-care plan choices throughout life is even stronger than the connection between one's ambitions, etc., and one's assumption of health-care risks.

I have already argued that egalitarians should support risk rating, because health-care risks are based upon a mixture of voluntary choices (e.g., lifestyle risks) and unchosen circumstances (e.g., genetic makeup), and because there are good arguments that egalitarians should place such a "mixture" on the voluntary side of the voluntary-involuntary continuum. I have now argued that the choice side of this "mixture" is greater vis-à-vis the choice of health-care plans than it is vis-à-vis the assumption of health-care risks. Thus, the reasons that give egalitarians grounds for supporting risk rating give them, *a fortiori*, grounds for favoring widespread choice in health-care plans, and, in particular, the choice to forgo comprehensive coverage.

C. Moral hazard

The arguments in this section can be strengthened by an examination of moral hazard. Moral hazard occurs when the provision of insurance or compensation for an adverse event or a loss produces an increase in the probability or size of the loss. For example, auto insurance makes some people less careful drivers and thus increases their accident rate as compared to what it would be if they lacked insurance. Moral hazard arises because the incentive of the insured to prevent or control her losses after purchasing insurance diminishes, since the extent to which one's lack of loss prevention affects one's premiums diminishes with the existence of numerous other policyholders, and since it is costly for the insurer to monitor the insured's behavior.[77] The principle, endorsed by egalitarians, that it is unjust to subsidize people's voluntary choices, supports a health insurance system that, *ceteris paribus*, has a comparative advantage on reducing moral hazard, since moral hazard implies that one is foisting upon others the costs of one's deliberate or negligent action and provides incentives to continue to do so in the future.

Now moral hazard can be intentional (i.e., fraud) or nonintentional. Since the former is the less important phenomenon,[78] I shall turn my attention to showing why MHI has a clear advantage on nonintentional moral hazard, focusing first on the matter of the insured influencing the probability of the loss, and then on the question of the insured influencing the size of the loss.

Concerning the former, casualty-catastrophic insurance has an advantage, because the cost to the insured of influencing the probability of the occurrence of an adverse event or a catastrophic illness is often considerable: even if I am completely reimbursed for my catastrophic medical expenses, the psychic costs and physical suffering I may have to undergo are considerable. On the other hand, in comprehensive service plans the loss is simply the occurrence of medical expenses, and, particularly in the case of routine care, influencing the probability of one's needing such care may involve little or no psychic costs or physical suffering. I lose relatively little by not taking sufficient care to avoid going to the doctor, and indeed for some people the visit might be a net benefit (they get to talk to an educated person about their health, which a lot of people enjoy; they get a routine check of some health problem that may be of concern; and so forth). Since comprehensive service plans play a smaller role in MHI than in NHI, the former has a comparative advantage in this regard.

As for influencing the size of the loss, in MHI some people will use part of their accumulated funds in their MSAs to pay for their expenses, in

[77] Much of my argument in the text concerning the relationship between insurance and moral hazard is indebted to Kenneth Abraham, *Distributing Risk: Insurance, Legal Theory, and Public Policy* (New Haven: Yale University Press, 1986), ch. 2.

[78] Neither NHI nor MHI has an obvious advantage on the issue of combating intentional (fraudulent) moral hazard. Many policies in MHI will pay the insured directly, which will give some of them an incentive to commit fraud; on the other hand, companies which are lackadaisical in combating fraud are at a competitive disadvantage. NHI does not pay the insured directly, which removes that incentive for fraud; but payment to health-care providers can provide the same kind of incentives, particularly with fee-for-service medicine.

which case they have obvious incentives not to increase the size of the loss. Other people in an MHI system will use casualty insurance to pay for such losses, and this kind of insurance provides a mechanism which limits the extent to which the policyholder influences the size of the loss: reimbursement is based on diagnosis of the loss suffered or adverse health event, not on services rendered or treatment costs. Just as auto and homeowner insurance companies usually evaluate or estimate the value of the loss before they provide payment, a similar process can exist with casualty health insurance. Before the insured seeks medical care,[79] the insurance company can conduct claims appraisals based on diagnostic and treatment cost information (either generated by their own diagnosticians or by outsider reviewers). The company would then pay the insured directly on this basis, and the insured could use the money as she wished: either for expensive treatment or cheap treatment or no treatment. This method of reimbursement gives the insured an incentive to reduce the size of the loss, because once he receives the payment, seeking treatment not covered by the payment will mean more out-of-pocket expenses. In service plans, on the other hand, the insurer's payment, which is usually made to providers, not to the insured, is related to consumption/treatment decisions, and thus the feature of casualty insurance which provides both the insurance company and the insured with incentives to limit the size of the loss is absent.

However, while that feature is absent, service plans are able to use insurer-*provider* incentives to hold down costs, and thus such plans would seem to hold down the ability of the insured to influence the size of his insured loss. NHI's cost-control techniques can have considerable teeth, in virtue of government's coercive power and the establishment of global budgets, expenditure caps and targets, and the like.

It is a mistake, however, to conclude that the existence of NHI's cost-control techniques provides good reason to believe that it is at least as good as MHI in combating moral hazard vis-à-vis the size of the insured's losses or the incurring of medical expenses. This is the case due to epistemic and motivational reasons. The epistemic point is that cost control does not equal reduction in moral hazard. Reducing moral hazard does not mean simply reducing costs; it means reducing costs or losses that come about *because* the insured has paid *insufficient* attention to loss prevention. Thus, from the existence of a sizable loss one cannot infer that its size is due to moral hazard. In MHI, however, risk rating gives one a method, albeit quite an imperfect one, to help determine whether this insufficient attention has occurred. If one is placed in a relatively low-risk class, but one incurs much higher losses than the average member of that

---

[79] By definition, my analysis in the text does not apply to emergencies. Even here, casualty insurance has a built-in incentive to limit moral hazard, namely, that it would not pay for a trip to an emergency room per se, but would only pay if something serious was uncovered.

class, then these losses are evidence that one is under-allocating to loss prevention. On the other hand, there is little evidence of moral hazard in the case of an insured who pays relatively high premiums and who suffers considerable losses due to inattention or neglect of loss prevention, if the premium charged was designed to cover the relatively high losses of a relatively high-risk group. Thus, risk rating gives one at least some basis for determining how much the insured "should" be devoting to loss prevention and how much to insurance, but cost-control techniques in the absence of risk rating do not.

The motivational point is that when both parties to a relationship have similar incentives to achieve a certain goal, or at least do not have conflicting incentives, that goal is more likely to be achieved than when the parties are in conflict. In casualty insurance, once it has been determined that there has been a loss, neither the insured nor the insurer has an incentive to expand the size of the loss by seeking expensive treatment — the insurer, obviously, since its financial interest is in minimizing the size of the loss, and the insured, because (as I have already noted) once he gets the settlement, it is his money to do with as he wishes and he will not receive any more funds from the insurance company by seeking expensive treatment. However, in service plans, while the first motive is obviously present and is employed to try to influence providers to provide low-cost treatment, the second is not, since the insureds do not get benefits for health-care losses, but make prepayments for the consumption of care. Notice, also, that the first motive gets quite diluted in service plans, since providers often resent pressure by insurers to provide low-cost treatment — they view it as interfering with their professional autonomy — and may thus resist the insurer's attempt at cost control.[80]

Of course, there will be some service plans in MHI. The point, however, is that not all medical expenses in MHI are paid for by service plans, while virtually all such expenses are paid for by service plans in NHI.

To summarize the discussion of nonintentional moral hazard: MHI has an advantage as far as influencing the probability of the loss, since, with catastrophic losses, there is little incentive to increase the probability of being sick or ill; as far as the insured influencing the size of the loss, there is little basis for concluding that NHI's cost-control measures provide it with a comparative advantage in this area. Thus, overall, MHI has a comparative advantage on reducing moral hazard. And since egalitarians should favor a health insurance system that has a comparative advantage in combating moral hazard, we get another strong reason why they should favor MHI over NHI.

---

[80] On the difficulties NHI systems have faced historically in getting doctors to accept expenditure targets, see William A. Glaser, "How Expenditure Caps and Expenditure Targets Really Work," *The Milbank Quarterly*, vol. 71, no. 1 (1993), pp. 97–127.

V. Rationing, Visibility, and Middle-Class Capture

My argument in the previous section that egalitarians should favor markets as the chief mechanism for allocating demand or the consumption of health-care services suffices to show that they should favor markets over government rationing on the supply or production side as well. This is because the main reason egalitarians favored government rationing was to put a brake on subsidized demand in NHI, but once market forces predominate on the demand side, there is little subsidized demand to brake — there is market demand which can be adjusted to supply by normal market means. However, it is useful to address the production/supply-side issues separately, because the view that egalitarians should favor government rationing may seem obvious, and it is worth showing why egalitarians should favor market "rationing"[81] over government rationing.

A. The egalitarian criteria for fair rationing

Egalitarians believe fair rationing must be done in a public, democratic manner. Publicity means something like the following: that the fact of government rationing must be acknowledged and made widely known; that the exclusion or inclusion of certain health services in the basic health-care package, or at least the criteria used for their exclusion or inclusion, must be made public; and that the reasons for specific rationing decisions at the clinical level must be made known to patients or consumers. The aim of public rationing is to create a visible chain of accountability[82] from governments (federal, state, and/or local) down to the clinical level, so that the reasons for denials of care, waits, limits on the availability of equipment, and so forth are openly and plainly stated. As for the "democratic" part, this means that the list of medical priorities must not be made solely by the legislature or medical professionals, but must be based on or influenced by public input of some sort—such as public forums, surveys, and citizen juries.[83]

One way NHI could ration care in a democratic, public manner— henceforth called "visible rationing"—is by incorporating a substantive

---

[81] "Rationing" is an ambiguous concept. In any system where all wants or preferences cannot be satisfied—that is, any system in the real world—some method or procedure is used to determine which wants or preferences get satisfied. In that sense, both markets and governments ration. However, as Ellen Frankel Paul has pointed out to me, rationing also means the division of a fixed supply with fixed shares. In that sense, it is quite misleading to say that markets ration, since, over time, markets expand the resources or supply available (while government per se cannot expand resources).

[82] I adopt this phrase from a description of Oregon's rationing system, which I discuss below. See Martin A. Strosberg's introduction to *Rationing America's Medical Care: The Oregon Plan and Beyond*, ed. Martin A. Strosberg, Joshua M. Wiener, Robert Baker, with I. Alan Fein (Washington, DC: The Brookings Institution, 1992), p. 3.

[83] A citizen jury is a "trial" whereby those responsible for health-care allocation decisions are "cross-examined" by experts, after which citizens on the jury deliberate and offer their assessment of those allocation decisions.

right to a specific set of services (as opposed to merely a right of access to the system or a right to fair procedures), using public forums and the like to arrive at a decision about what does and does not belong in this right. Such a right might seem to help to establish what Daniels calls "democratically developed, unambiguous" criteria for allocation.[84] No present NHI system actually incorporates such a right, a point to which I will return later.[85] The closest approximation that exists is the Medicaid program in the state of Oregon. After a series of highly publicized forums, meetings, and telephone surveys to determine citizens' views about the criteria that should govern the ranking of health-care services, the publicly appointed Oregon Health Services Commission ranked 709 condition-treatment pairs (e.g., appendicitis-appendectomy) and presented the list to the Oregon legislature. The legislature was forbidden by statute to alter the list and could only decide the location of the cut-off point for funding (it excluded those below number 587).[86] For reasons I shall discuss later, it is not obvious that egalitarians should actually favor such a procedure for NHI—indeed, Oregon-type rationing has been discussed but rejected in the UK, Sweden, and New Zealand[87]—but it does provide one way to give some bite to the requirement of visible rationing.

Egalitarians favor visible rationing for two reasons, which were briefly mentioned in Section III. First, visibility is a way of maintaining accountability. If those making rationing decisions do not have to state the reasons for their decisions or justify their actions, then they are not accountable to the public; and without such accountability, we distrust their ability to make just decisions.[88] Second, egalitarian principles of distributive justice are indeterminate on the question of ranking medical services and the proper trade-offs between health care and other goods, and making these trade-offs and rankings is part of the point of rationing (the other part is to limit overall demand). Neither fair equality of opportunity (Daniels) nor the prudent insurance ideal (Dworkin) will provide much help in making rationing decisions. Concerning the former, while Daniels at one point argued that we could rank different health-care schemes in terms of the extent to which they curtailed a normal opportunity range,[89] he has abandoned this idea. Even assuming we could determine the extent to which different life plans are restricted by different health-care schemes—

[84] Daniels et al., *Benchmarks of Fairness*, p. 57.

[85] See Jo Lenaghan, "Health Care Rights in Europe: A Comparative Perspective," in Lenaghan, ed., *Hard Choices in Health Care* (*supra* note 12), p. 188.

[86] See Strosberg's introduction to Strosberg et al., eds., *Rationing America's Medical Care*, pp. 3–7; and J. Kitzhaber and A. M. Kemmy, "On the Oregon Trail," *British Medical Bulletin*, vol. 51, no. 4 (October 1995), pp. 813–17.

[87] See C. Ham, "Synthesis: What We Can Learn from International Experience," *British Medical Bulletin*, vol. 51, no. 4 (October 1995), pp. 821–28. In Holland, a government commission proposed something similar to Oregon's rationing system, but so far this has had no effect on public policy. See P. M. M. van de Ven, "Choices in Health Care: A Contribution from the Netherlands," *ibid.*, pp. 785–88.

[88] Daniels et al., *Benchmarks of Fairness*, p. 58.

[89] Daniels, *Just Health Care*, p. 35.

which is quite dubious, since comparing life plans likely involves comparing incommensurable activities and goals[90] —we would have to compare whether it was better that disease and disability should greatly restrict a few life plans or slightly restrict a large number of them. There is also the not insignificant matter of deciding to what extent, if any, we should focus on the worst off, that is, the persons whose diseases and disabilities are such that they are furthest from the ideal of having a full range of life plans that it is reasonable for them to pursue.[91] As for Dworkin, his argument depends on determining what most prudent people, or an average prudent person, would purchase in a hypothetical market, but, as he recognizes, what is prudent depends upon one's values, preferences, and tastes; and even if we were to accept his claim that certain health-care schemes would clearly be imprudent, this would not tell us what would be prudent in many cases.

Although egalitarians favor visible rationing because of the indeterminacy of egalitarian principles, there are limits to this indeterminacy. Egalitarians do not think that a visible system of NHI is an example of pure procedural justice, that is, that any result or outcome resulting from a visible rationing process in NHI is just. This is why a second egalitarian criterion, avoiding obviously inegalitarian outcomes, is needed. Suppose the middle class or the relatively healthy received a significantly greater amount of the benefits of rationing than did the poor or relatively unhealthy. This result, which I shall call "middle-class capture," is clearly inegalitarian. Almost as regrettable would be a situation where the poor did use health-care services more than the middle class, but not enough to compensate for their greater needs, or where the costs that people faced in getting access to health services were higher for the poor than for the affluent, which kept the poor from receiving the services that they needed.

I shall now compare NHI with MHI with respect to visibility of rationing and avoiding middle-class capture or other obviously inegalitarian outcomes. I shall argue that MHI wins on both counts and that this gives egalitarians strong reasons to favor MHI.

B. Visibility and rationing

Rationing occurs at three levels. At a macro level, rationing places limits on the total amount spent on nonsupplemental health care, or the total amount spent for particular services or for certain providers. At a

---

[90] See Ezekiel J. Emmanuel, *The Ends of Human Life: Medical Ethics in a Liberal Polity* (Cambridge: Harvard University Press, 1991), pp. 130–33, for some cogent arguments along this line.

[91] Daniels mentions both of these problems, along with some others, in "Four Unsolved Rationing Problems: A Challenge," *Hastings Center Report*, vol. 24, no. 4 (July–August 1994), p. 28.

middle level, rationing involves the allocation of resources to particular forms of treatment (or particular geographical areas), as well as decisions concerning what to include or exclude in a basic health-care package. At the clinical or micro level, rationing involves decisions made by providers concerning treatment and procedures for individual patients.

At the macro level, NHI is fairly invisible to the average citizen. Most people are unaware of global budgets. In general, most people are fairly ignorant of the details of government budgets, and a budget limit which is not a limit on one's own personal budget is not terribly visible. The expenditure caps or targets, and other government-imposed or negotiated limits on reimbursements for providers, are also fairly invisible to patients, since it is the providers who are primarily aware that these limits lead to the denial of care.

Furthermore, the global budgets and/or expenditure caps primarily affect capital investment, particularly in high-tech equipment. This means that new, potentially innovative equipment and techniques are being rationed; and by the nature of the case, when some change in present practices does not occur, no one except those who had tried to develop and/or use it are cognizant of this fact. In addition, the average person — indeed, even a person with some sophisticated medical knowledge — has little understanding of technological advances in medicine: capital investment is not something the typical consumer in any field knows much about — only specialists do.

By contrast, in MHI there are no global budgets; it is one's own visible budget that matters (except for those whose health insurance is subsidized). And while insurance companies will try to limit reimbursement to providers, as NHI does, the extent to which this occurs will be less, because a significant percentage of consumers will not use insurance for small bills and/or will purchase casualty insurance which reimburses the insured, not the providers. The average person's ignorance about capital investment and high-tech procedures will of course remain; but unlike NHI, which restricts incentives to modify existing technologies or invent new ones, markets tend to encourage innovation, and thus the issue of patients being unaware of the rationing of new innovative techniques and procedures is basically a moot point.

At the middle level, the same kinds of considerations apply, albeit with a few more qualifications. In NHI systems which have a national health service, allocation of resources to particular forms of treatments (or geographical areas), or decisions to include or exclude certain services, are as invisible as macro decisions, since they are not made by the patient, but by a national or local government, or by hospital administrators or local health authorities. In NHI systems with competing sickness funds and/or private insurance, decisions about what to include or exclude in the basic insurance package are influenced by consumer choice — but within strict limits set by the government's requirement that all insurance plans have a similar set of benefits.[92] Furthermore, rationing at the macro level has an obvious effect at the middle level: if a sickness fund and/or private insurance company promises to cover a certain treatment which is getting pinched because of global budgets and/or expenditure caps, then the insured may be completely unaware that a promised treatment will not be forthcoming.

In MHI, however, allocating resources to various forms of treatment, and inclusions and exclusions in one's health insurance policy, are largely market decisions, and as such are more under the direct control and awareness of the patient or consumer. Of course, hospitals will continue to make their own allocation decisions, which are affected in part by reimbursement policies of insurance companies, but the issue is a comparative one; the fact that, under MHI, consumers make these allocation decisions and choose, within broad limits, the type of health policy they desire, makes MHI far more visible vis-à-vis these middle-level decisions.

My argument about middle-level rationing decisions has compared *present-day* NHI with MHI. What if NHI adopted what some egalitarians recommend—a right to a specific set of services—and what if this list were derived from some sort of democratic input? It is worth pointing out that it is unclear whether such a right is feasible. To establish such a right requires overcoming politicians' nervousness about bearing responsibility for the denial of care, physician's resentments about the limitation of their clinical discretion, and the public's reluctance—since the public may want doctors to have the freedom to make specific rationing decisions (figuring that they trust doctors more than a group of strangers and/or politicians). These obstacles may explain why no present-day NHI system has adopted this kind of rationing. But even if we suppose this kind of right could be instantiated, NHI would still be worse than MHI at this middle level of rationing. A health-care package designed by consumer choice is still more visible than one which is the outgrowth of a democratic process, for the same reason that one's own budget is more visible than a global budget—one is clearly more aware of the shape of a health-care package one purchases with one's own funds, than of a health-care package produced by collective decisions in which one may have had little or no input.

Turning now to the clinical or micro level, it might seem that there would be little difference between NHI and MHI, because the extent to which doctors, nurses, etc., make patients or consumers aware of the basis of their decisions to pursue or not pursue certain courses of action is a matter of their preferences plus patient input. However, this is misleading at best. Patients are more likely to spend their own money and to have paid for their own insurance policy in MHI than in NHI, and thus

---

[92] Furthermore, in some NHI systems with sickness funds, one has limited choice in picking the fund. In Germany, for example, members of the 90 percent of the population that must stay within NHI are often assigned sickness funds on the basis of their occupation and/or region. See Glaser, *Health Insurance in Practice*, pp. 502–3.

in MHI patients have more control and influence over micro decisions. Furthermore, the effects of rationing on the macro and middle level trickle down to the micro or clinical level. For example, a primary-care physician's referral to a specialist in an NHI system is not infrequently shaped by assumptions about what volume and type of cases a referral unit can handle, which depends in part on rationing decisions and the extent to which they produce waits at various points in the system. Indeed, the waiting list itself acts as a deterrent to primary-care physician referrals.[93] While a primary-care physician can tell a patient that he or she cannot recommend a certain course of treatment because of rationing or political decisions beyond the physician's control, doctors tend to want to make decisions based on their view about what is best for the patient, and thus there is significant potential for self-deception and dissembling: a doctor may tell a patient (or give him the impression) that a decision not to pursue a certain treatment is based on a clinical judgment about the effectiveness of that treatment when in fact the judgment is based on the unavailability of the treatment. (This occurred in the British National Health Service, when doctors told people over fifty-five with kidney failure that there was nothing that could be done for them, and did not mention the fact that age rationing by the National Health Service made renal dialysis unavailable for those patients.)[94] While masking the basis for micro decisions could also occur in MHI in service plans or managed care, it would be far less prevalent than in NHI, since service plans or managed care would be unlikely to dominate a genuine market in health care, and since, with fewer waits in the system, clinical decisions would be less likely to be based upon a physician's assessment of whether a person would have to wait for care.

Would the advantage of MHI over NHI regarding the visibility of micro rationing decisions be ended if the latter adopted a right to a specific set of services? Only if such a right eliminated all clinical discretion—which is doubtful, due to inherent uncertainty and vagueness in the definition of services, and the inevitable clash between global budget decisions and a specific list of services provided. Concerning the former, note that, in Oregon, ten thousand medical diagnoses were squeezed into 709 condition-treatment pairs,[95] which leaves, to put it mildly, a lot of room for clinical discretion; concerning the latter, note that limits on total health-care spend-

[93] As noted in R. J. Maxwell, "Why Rationing Is on the Agenda," British Medical Bulletin, vol. 51, no. 4 (October 1995), p. 765; and S. Harrison, "A Policy Agenda for Health Care Rationing," ibid., p. 892.

[94] See Henry J. Aaron and William B. Schwartz, The Painful Prescription: Rationing Hospital Care (Washington, DC: The Brookings Institution, 1984), pp. 101–2. That this still occurs in Britain is argued in R. Klein, P. Day, and S. Redmayne, "Rationing in the NHS: The Dance of the Seven Veils—In Reverse," British Medical Bulletin, vol. 51, no. 4 (October 1995), pp. 769–70. That most patients in Britain accept the doctor's views that no further treatment is warranted is argued in Harrison, "A Policy Agenda for Health Care Rationing," p. 892.

[95] Henry J. Aaron, "The Oregon Experiment," in Strosberg et al., eds., Rationing America's Medical Care, p. 109.

ing mean that unless one assumes an omniscient legislature or one with virtually unlimited funds, the services that are supposed to be funded will not be funded at a level sufficient to accommodate all of the subsidized demand.

C. Middle-class capture or avoiding inegalitarian outcomes

I now examine whether NHI has avoided obviously inegalitarian outcomes, and then discuss how MHI's outcomes would compare with NHI.

The evidence on the egalitarian effects of present-day NHI seems to be indeterminate, for a number of reasons.[96] First, many studies measure the extent to which different socioeconomic groups, often defined in terms of occupations, use various services, but the definitions and members of these groups vary over time and among different countries. Second, studies that measure the use of services cannot reveal to what extent the actually sick or diseased visit doctors, as opposed to those who report illness and disease. And third, the studies are sometimes confined to a small section of the population. Having said all that, within the limits of these studies the results seem to indicate that in many countries with NHI, "it seems likely that lower socio-economic groups make more use of medical services (though not necessarily enough to compensate for their higher needs) but that upper groups make more varied and informed use of services."[97] As noted earlier, this seems to be an outcome egalitarians would at least regret.

Even if NHI has outcomes which egalitarians would regret, the key issue is whether there are good reasons to believe MHI would be less inegalitarian. There are indeed, and they are hinted at by the above quote: the more knowledgeable make better and more informed use of services that are rationed by nonmarket means, and the middle-class or affluent are more knowledgeable than the poor. In my arguments to follow, I will set aside the ability of the middle-class or affluent to purchase supplemental health insurance. Even if there were no supplemental insurance, NHI would be more inegalitarian than MHI.

MHI has fewer waits than NHI. The price mechanism quickly eliminates shortages and surpluses, that is, gaps between supply and demand, while nonprice mechanisms rely on the sluggish process of waits. Now getting on a waiting list, and getting to the top of that list, is not a mechanical process. One has to be motivated enough to go to a doctor and present oneself as sick. Since doctors can sometimes jump one near the top of the list if one is considered in greater need, one may have to be willing to press one's doctor to do this. One may need to seek out information about other hospitals or other specialists where there may be

---

[96] In what follows, I rely on Illsley, "Comparative Review of Sources, Methodology, and Knowledge" (supra note 70), p. 233.

[97] Ibid., p. 231.

fewer waits, and this kind of information may depend upon connections. In all of these matters the prize goes to the motivated, knowledgeable, and connected, all areas in which members of the middle class dominate the indigent. By contrast, in an MHI system with subsidies for the indigent and those with uninsurable conditions to purchase catastrophic health insurance, most of these barriers are absent (that one must be motivated and knowledgeable enough to seek medical care in the first place, however, is a given in any system).

It might be said, in reply, that since the affluent make more money than the poor, they give up more by spending time away from work to wait for and seek care. Thus, *ceteris paribus*, the affluent have greater opportunity costs in waiting for care, and so their advantage in jumping through the queues merely counterbalances their disadvantage in bearing these greater costs.

However, it is a mistake, albeit a natural one, to believe that the affluent have greater opportunity costs in this matter.[98] The affluent tend to be salaried, not paid on an hourly basis as is typical with the poor, and the former can vary their hours at the margin without loss of pay. Furthermore, the poor have greater costs of travel: they are less likely to use cars than the affluent, and cars have a lower marginal cost and are quicker than the alternatives. Some of the factors that make people poor in the first place, such as disability and single-parenthood, raise the costs of travel. These higher costs of travel of the poor are quite important when considering the issue of waits, for jumping through queues requires the ability and willingness to travel to distant hospitals with shorter waiting lists. Notice, finally, that the poor's greater cost is independent of distance; if they have to travel a greater distance than the affluent, this will compound the problem. And they may have to do so in at least some NHI systems which centralize certain types of care in certain locations.[99]

Besides the issue of waits, the arguments I gave earlier about the greater visibility in MHI also provide reasons to believe MHI will be less inegalitarian. At the micro level, recall that I argued that there is a greater potential for dissembling and self-deception in NHI by clinicians making rationing decisions. Members of the more knowledgeable and motivated middle class are much less likely than the poor to accept a doctor's decision that care is not warranted on clinical grounds, and it is human nature for a doctor to interpret (or reinterpret) the illnesses of those patients whose backgrounds are similar to the doctor's own (i.e., affluent) in such a way that these patients are seen as better candidates for treatment

---

[98] The following paragraph is much indebted to Robert E. Goodin, Julian Le Grand, and D. M. Gibson, "Distributional Biases in Social Service Delivery Systems," in *Not Only the Poor: The Middle Classes and the Welfare State*, ed. Robert E. Goodin and Julian Le Grand (London: Allen and Unwin, 1987), pp. 131-32.

[99] Systems with a national health service tend to centralize care within a certain region, while, in a market, services are typically dispersed throughout a city or country. See Goodin et al., "Distributional Biases in Social Service Delivery Systems," pp. 128-30 and 133-38.

than those patients who are from a dissimilar background.[100] At the macro and middle levels, political decisions about global budgets and the geographical distribution of funding in NHI are likely to benefit the better organized, knowledgeable, and motivated middle class, while MHI will be less subject to such political considerations.

So far I have set out a variety of considerations indicating that nonmarket rationing benefits the more affluent—due largely to their superior motivation and knowledge, which enables them to work the system, as it were, to their advantage. An egalitarian could respond that the price barriers confronting the poor in MHI more than outweigh the disadvantages for the poor in NHI, and that, in the final analysis, these barriers give grounds for the egalitarian to rank NHI higher on the issue of avoiding inegalitarian outcomes. However, the MHI proposal discussed here incorporates subsidies for the indigent (and those with uninsurable risks) to obtain catastrophic health insurance, thus muting these barriers. And since it is largely at the level of catastrophic care that NHI engages in nonmarket rationing, MHI clearly has fewer barriers here.

Still, the egalitarian may press his point, noting that MHI does not provide subsidies for the indigent to cover noncatastrophic expenses or small bills. Even if the tax credit for health insurance premiums were completely refundable for the indigent, and even if that subsidy covered a somewhat lower-deductible policy than the tax credit for the affluent, the poor would still have to pay for their out-of-pocket expenses prior to meeting the deductible.

I can think of two replies to this objection, but neither will completely allay the egalitarian's worries. One reply is to point out that the indigent could save some of the tax credit for catastrophic health insurance and put it in a medical savings account. However, the most likely way to accrue such savings is by choosing a somewhat higher-deductible policy, and this may not occur since the poor tend to have a higher rate of time preference than the affluent and thus would prefer policies with as low a deductible as possible.[101] Another reply is to alter the details of MHI so that a refundable tax credit for the indigent is allowed for a comprehensive policy. However, the heart of the proposal for MHI is to reduce the extent to which health insurance is comprehensive; thus, a proposal to subsidize comprehensive insurance for the indigent is (arguably) incompatible with the spirit of MHI.

[100] Julian Le Grand presents evidence that this occurred in the British National Health Service, i.e., that middle-class capture occurred; see Le Grand, *The Strategy of Equality: Redistribution and the Social Services* (London: G. Allen and Unwin, 1982), ch. 3. For an opposing viewpoint, and an argument that Le Grand used inappropriate methodology to measure the extent to which the British National Health Service allocated resources equitably, see Owen O'Donnell and Carol Propper, "Equity and the Distribution of UK National Health Service Resources," *Journal of Health Economics*, vol. 10 (1991), pp. 1-19.

[101] Paul Menzel, *Strong Medicine: The Ethical Rationing of Health Care* (New York: Oxford University Press, 1990), p. 143.

Let us assume, then, that it is likely that a significant number of the poor under an MHI system will have skimpy or nonexistent MSAs that limit their ability to pay for small medical bills and routine care, and let us also assume that there are limits to the extent to which a defender of MHI is willing to alter the proposal to mollify egalitarian concerns. Given these two assumptions, I think we have arrived at the egalitarian's best argument: that MHI provides a barrier to noncatastrophic care (e.g., preventive care, small-scale expenses, etc.), based on price,[102] that does not exist in NHI, since the latter tends to provide ample subsidies in this area and primarily rations expensive and catastrophic care. However, it would be quite a stretch to conclude from this that NHI produces less-inegalitarian outcomes than MHI. The bulk of health-care expenses arise from catastrophic care and large bills, rather than noncatastrophic care and small bills. If one has to choose which kind of care it would be better for the poor to have access to—and the egalitarian must choose, since NHI does not give the poor better access to both kinds of care—it seems clear that it is better for them to have access to catastrophic care.[103] Of course, faced

[102] Furthermore, the egalitarian could point out that the relative disadvantage for the poor in getting access to preventive care gets worse over time, since MSAs that are used to pay for such care are tax-free over one's lifetime, and are more valuable for those in a high tax bracket than for those in a low or zero bracket.

[103] It might be objected that from an egalitarian point of view, it is more important for the poor to have routine and noncatastrophic care rather than catastrophic care, since having the former prevents the need for much of the latter. Under MHI, the poor may very well not have access to routine and noncatastrophic care in two kinds of cases: illnesses which must be paid for out-of-pocket or out of one's savings under the terms of a high-deductible policy; and preventive care, which is not covered by casualty insurance when there is no adverse event or loss.

As for the former, it would be less inegalitarian to provide better access to such care than to catastrophic care only if the bulk of catastrophes resulted from such low-cost illnesses. However, this is not the case. Most catastrophic illnesses result from chronic degenerative conditions that start in middle and old age. Furthermore, it is worth reiterating a point already made in the text, that under MHI, the poor will get a (refundable) tax credit for a somewhat lower-deductible policy than would be available with a tax credit to the non-indigent.

The issues relating to preventive care are more complex, but the argument does not hold here either. First, some preventive care involves expensive diagnostic, high-tech equipment (CAT scans, mammograms, etc.); thus, NHI's rationing of high-tech equipment affects access to preventive care. Second, the higher rate of time preference of the poor suggests that they will not take advantage of preventive services, even if such services are available (I have found no data on whether the poor under NHI take good advantage of preventive care, so this remains a theoretical point, rather than an empirical one). Third, and most important, even if we were to suppose that the poor will take advantage of subsidized preventive services, and that these will not be rationed by NHI, the logic of the argument is suspect. For preventive care to be effective, it must cover most or all of the relevant population. Thus, for an egalitarian to plausibly argue that it is fairer for the poor to have better access to preventive care than catastrophic care, he must argue that it is better to treat all of the poor—most of whom are healthy now and only some of whom will later have the disease we are seeking to prevent—than it is to treat a smaller group, who will actually be sick later. There is little in egalitarianism that would support such a conclusion; on the contrary, focusing resources on people now who are in acute need seems to be more in keeping with the spirit of egalitarianism.

with a choice of how to spend their limited income, the poor may very well prefer to avoid budgeting for long-run problems and catastrophes. In that regard, MHI's policy (requiring the poor to purchase insurance) is definitely paternalistic. But egalitarians cannot use that as an objection, since their endorsement of NHI is based upon, to a significant extent, something other than people's present health-care preferences as expressed in a market.

Thus, MHI defeats NHI on both egalitarian criteria for a fair system of rationing: visibility and avoiding clearly inegalitarian outcomes. Thus, even apart from the argument in Section IV concerning the demand or consumption side of health insurance, on the production or supply side egalitarians should support MHI.

VI. Conclusion

Egalitarians have excellent grounds to support MHI over NHI. This is very significant. NHI is a central welfare-state institution, and egalitarianism is generally thought to provide one of the strongest, if not the strongest, grounds for supporting NHI. My arguments here show that egalitarians should actually agree with libertarians that MHI is superior to NHI. Suppose that the conclusions reached here can be replicated for most plausible viewpoints in contemporary political philosophy; they all should believe that MHI is superior. Then the usual presumption that exists today in contemporary political philosophy, that it is opponents of the welfare state who bear the burden of proof, will be turned on its head, at least with regard to this central welfare-state institution.

Philosophy, West Virginia University

AFFIRMATIVE ACTION AND THE DEMANDS OF JUSTICE*

By N. Scott Arnold

This essay is about the moral and political justification of affirmative action programs in the United States. Both legally and politically, many of these programs are under attack, though they remain ubiquitous. The concern of this essay, however, is not with what the law says but with what it should say. The main argument advanced in this essay concludes that most of the controversial affirmative action programs are unjustified. It proceeds in a way that avoids dependence on controversial theories of justice or morality. My intention is to produce an argument that is persuasive across a broad ideological spectrum, extending even to those who believe that justice requires these very programs. Though the main focus of the essay is on affirmative action, in the course of making the case that these programs are illegitimate, I shall defend some principles about the conditions under which it is appropriate for the state to impose on civil society the demands of justice. These principles have broader implications for a normative theory of social change in democratic societies.

I. AFFIRMATIVE ACTION PROGRAMS

Affirmative action programs exist in a variety of institutional settings. They can be found as a part of the policies that govern hiring, promotion, and retention (in both the public and private sectors); the awarding of contracts; and admissions to training programs, universities, and professional schools. All such programs can be classified in two broad categories, what can be called "outreach efforts" and "preferential treatment programs." Outreach efforts are intended to broaden the search for the best talent, where "best" is defined by reference to the institution's goals and objectives. One purpose of such programs is to seek to reassure women and minorities that the institution in question does not discriminate on the basis of race, gender, or ethnicity, and that the institution is genuinely concerned to recruit the best talent or award the contract to the most deserving firm. Such programs include advertising in minority-targeted media (e.g., black-owned newspapers), taking extra time and effort to examine the credentials of minority applicants (time and effort

* I would like to thank Ellen Frankel Paul, Daniel Shapiro, and David Schmidtz for helpful comments on earlier drafts of this essay.

that would not be extended to majority applicants with identical records), and setting up or attending special job-fairs or minority-owned business exhibitions to get acquainted with talent that firms and organizations would otherwise not be aware of. Some may complain about these programs on the grounds of unfairness to those not targeted, but such complaints are not widely voiced and are not the subject of the main controversy over affirmative action.

Preferential treatment programs are another matter. These involve taking race, gender, or ethnicity[1] into account as a positive factor in the awarding of contracts, in hiring, or in admissions. It may be a small factor, breaking ties between otherwise equally qualified applicants or contractors, or it may be a rather more important factor, which operates to give preference to the minimally qualified or the less qualified over the more qualified applicants or contractors. Let us consider the various categories of preferential treatment programs in a bit more detail:

1. *Minority set-asides.* Minority set-aside programs require or encourage government agencies or general contractors who do business with the government to set aside a certain percentage of the total dollar value of a contract for minority-owned (or women-owned) businesses. This may involve an inflexible requirement, or there may be financial incentives for general contractors to do this, or there may even be a form of "bid-rigging" by government agencies to ensure that minority firms are awarded the contract.[2]

2. *Preferential hiring.* Hiring policies in the public sector or in the private sector sometimes take race into account as a positive factor in hiring decisions. The operation of preferential hiring programs results in the hiring of members of minorities who would not be hired if race were not a non-negligible factor in the decision. Those doing the hiring may have in mind target percentages that they would like to meet for minority hires ("goals," as they are sometimes called), or they may be operating with relatively hard quotas. The line between goals and quotas is never a clear one, however; few quotas are insensitive to (other) qualifications, and few goals are mere aspirations. What makes something a quota is that those doing the hiring will not seriously consider nonminority candidates for a position or a range of positions for an extended period of time while they search for suitable minority candidates. The mind-set is to find the best qualified minority person for the job. A nonminority candidate would be

---

[1] In this essay the term "race" will generally be used as shorthand for "race, gender, or ethnicity." This is done purely as a matter of terminological convenience. In a similar vein, I shall use the term "minority" to cover women, even though they are not in the minority in most reference populations.

[2] Terry Eastland reports that the Defense Department added 10 percent to the bid submitted by Kay & Associates, Inc., a nonminority firm, so that they could be "underbid" by a minority-owned firm. For an account of some of the methods employed by the federal government in set-asides, see Terry Eastland, *Ending Affirmative Action* (New York: Basic Books, 1996), p. 136.

considered only if no minimally qualified minority candidate could be found at a reasonable search cost.

Quotas are of dubious legality in most settings, since Section 703(j) of Title VII of the 1964 Civil Rights Act states:

> [N]othing contained in this subchapter shall be interpreted to require any employer . . . to grant preferential treatment to any individual or to any group because of the race, color, religion, sex, or national origin of such individual or group on account of an imbalance which may exist with respect to the total number or percentage of persons of any race, color, religion, sex, or national origin employed by any employer . . . in comparison with the total number or percentage of persons of such race, color, religion, sex, or national origin in any community. . . .[3]

However, in some settings quotas have been upheld.[4] Indeed, the courts have sometimes ordered hiring by the numbers as a remedy in discrimination suits.[5] In any event, the dubious legality of quotas does not prevent them from being used. If a manager is in part evaluated and rewarded on the basis of his contribution to his organization's affirmative action goals, minority status will be an important factor in his hiring decisions. As historian Herman Belz has written, describing preferential treatment programs developed in the private sector:

> Many corporations used an equal employment opportunity measurement system that offered rewards and penalties intended to change the behavior of managers, showing them how to arrive at an "ideal" number of minorities in the work force. . . . [C]ompany executives increasingly included equal employment opportunity performance along with traditional business indicators as a standard in overall evaluation.[6]

An important subcategory of preferential treatment programs in the private sector are what might be called *defensive preferential hiring programs*. Firms that do business with the U.S. government and have more than fifty employees, or contracts with the government worth more than

---

[3] 42 U.S.C. 2000e-2(j).

[4] Kaiser Aluminum had a training program that used racial preferences for blacks over whites, which was upheld by the Supreme Court in *United Steelworkers of America v. Weber*, 443 U.S. 193 (1979).

[5] See, e.g., *Morrow v. Crisler*, 491 F.2d 1053 (1974), and *NAACP v. Allen*, 493 F.2d 614 (1974).

[6] Herman Belz, *Equality Transformed* (New Brunswick, NJ: Transaction Publishers, 1991), p. 105. See also Theodore V. Purcell, S.J., et al., "What Are the Social Responsibilities of Psychologists in Industry? A Symposium," *Personnel Psychology*, vol. 27 (Autumn 1974), p. 436.

$50,000, are required to submit elaborate affirmative action plans, complete with minority hiring goals and timetables within which those goals are to be achieved.[7] Failure to meet these goals according to the timetables can result in an investigation by the Office of Federal Contract Compliance Programs (OFCCP). This in turn can mean enormous administrative burdens for the firm, lawsuits, and/or the loss of the contract. To avoid these burdens, risks, and the sheer intrusiveness of the bureaucracy, very often the rational thing for firms to do is to hire by the numbers.[8] This is certainly more efficient than designing and implementing ever more elaborate outreach programs whose prospects for success are uncertain.

Another situation in which defensive preferential hiring programs are used is to avoid what are called "disparate impact lawsuits." Anytime a company with fifteen or more employees (whether or not it is a government contractor) has job requirements, uses tests, or has hiring practices that have a negative "disparate impact" on minorities, it is risking a discrimination lawsuit from disappointed job applicants or from public-spirited lawyers who recruit clients to bring these suits. For example, suppose that 12 percent of the relevant population is African American and the use of a test or job qualification results in hiring only 6 percent African Americans. This test or job qualification is said to have a (negative) disparate impact on African Americans and can serve as a basis for a lawsuit. The company can still use the test or qualification, but it faces certain hurdles. It can argue that the definition of the reference population that serves to define the disparate impact should be restricted to those with certain job-related qualifications or to those who actually applied for the position, or it can contest the definition of the firm's workforce (e.g., does the workforce include other divisions of the firm located elsewhere?). Perhaps most importantly, the company can argue that the test or qualification that produced the disparate impact is job-related and consistent with business necessity. This can defeat a claim of discrimination based on disparate impact. For example, if one is hiring physicians, applicants must be licensed to practice medicine, and if this requirement has a disparate impact on a protected minority population, that would be legally acceptable. Once the business necessity of the challenged practice has been established, it is then open to the plaintiff to argue that there are other selection criteria that would have a less disparate impact which the employer could have used in place of the challenged practice.

---

[7] This is required by Executive Order 11246, signed into law in 1965. See 30 *Federal Register* 12319. The exact rules and regulations can be found in 41 C.F.R. 60-1, as amended. As of 1990, over 27 million people were employed by firms that did business with the government. See Farrell Bloch, *Antidiscrimination Law and Minority Employment* (Chicago: University of Chicago Press, 1994), p. 84.

[8] For a horror story about the enormous burdens and administrative intrusiveness of the civil-rights bureaucracy in the life of a small contractor, see Tama Starr, "The 7.63 Percent Solution," *Reason*, February 1995, pp. 30–35.

The way the law is currently interpreted has had some perverse effects. It is often very difficult or expensive to establish that a test or requirement is in fact a business necessity, at least given the stringent way the courts have interpreted this.[9] Consequently, it is often rational for companies to drop the requirement or practice before it is challenged and hire by the numbers as best they can, so as to ward off a disparate-impact lawsuit. Or they can continue to use the practice that has a disparate impact and bundle it with a more subjective screening device (e.g., an interview) and use the latter to get the numbers to "come out right." Although the government does not mandate these strategies—and indeed specifically prohibits them in Section 703(j), as quoted above—these strategies are clearly encouraged by the way Title VII of the Civil Rights Act has been interpreted to allow hiring practices with disparate impact to serve to get a lawsuit started.

3. *Preferential admissions.* Colleges, universities, professional schools, and training programs have often used preferential admissions policies. Justice Lewis Powell's majority decision in the *Bakke* case stated that achieving diversity in the composition of the student body was a substantial interest that could permit admissions committees to use race, gender, or ethnicity as a "plus factor" in their admissions decisions.[10] This has been interpreted to prohibit separate admissions committees for minorities; theoretically, every candidate has to be in competition with every other candidate for every seat. In practice, however, universities can and do employ quotas that are about as rigid (or even more so) as those used in public or private sector hiring.[11]

This essay deals with preferential treatment programs in contracting and hiring. It argues that most such programs are unjustified. Typically, opponents of such programs say that the programs treat people differently on account of race or gender, factors which are morally irrelevant. Preferential treatment, they say, is just as wrong as discrimination against minorities. On the other hand, proponents of such programs say that there are important differences between discrimination against minorities

---

[9] See Richard Epstein, *Forbidden Grounds: The Case against Employment Discrimination Laws* (Cambridge, MA: Harvard University Press, 1992), pp. 212–22. For a careful discussion of some empirical evidence of the coercive impact of federal civil-rights legislation on hiring practices, see Alison M. Conrad and Frank Linneham, "Formalized HRM Structures: Coordinating Equal Employment Opportunity or Concealing Organizational Practices?" *Academy of Management Journal*, vol. 38 (1995), pp. 787–820.

[10] *Regents of the University of California v. Bakke*, 438 U.S. 265, 312–19 (1978).

[11] An example of this is the now-defunct minority admissions program at the University of Texas Law School, as described in *Hopwood v. State of Texas*, 78 F.3d 932 (1996). Although this program could have been ruled unlawful under the *Bakke* criteria, the fact of its existence indicates how deeply entrenched the belief in preferential treatment is, at least in this corner of the academic community. There is widespread anecdotal evidence that relatively hard quotas are in place elsewhere in the academic community, but this issue will not be explored in this essay. For reasons that will become apparent later, academic employment and admissions create special complications for the main argument this essay advances.

and preferential treatment programs. They argue that the former practice stigmatizes and/or expresses contempt for minorities, whereas preferential treatment programs do not have that symbolic function vis-à-vis white males. More generally, they claim that factors such as race and gender *are* morally relevant, perhaps because of past injustices suffered by disadvantaged groups or because preferential treatment programs correct for the present effects of past discrimination. However, what is morally relevant or not morally relevant depends on one's theory of justice or theory of morality, and therefore the dispute usually founders on these deeper questions.

This essay offers a rather different argument against preferential treatment programs. I want to begin by discussing a relatively rare variant of these programs—purely voluntary preferential treatment programs in publicly traded corporations in the private sector. These programs are *not* defensive in nature but are voluntarily instigated by senior management. For example, the Disney Corporation instituted a set-aside program for minority contractors in the planned expansion of its California facilities. There seems to have been no pressure on the firm to do this from any layer of government, but they decided to set aside $450 million for minority contractors out of a total budget of $3 billion.[12] Similarly, a corporation might have a preferential hiring program that is voluntary in the sense that it would remain in place even if the law were changed so that firms did not need to maintain such programs in order to receive government contracts or to avoid lawsuits. Although there may be few such programs in either hiring or contracting, a discussion of them will prove a useful preliminary to a discussion of the much more common mandated set-asides and defensive preferential hiring programs. More specifically, the next section argues that, subject to some qualifications and exceptions, these voluntary set-asides and hiring programs are wrong; subsequent sections apply the same reasoning to more common types of preferential treatment programs that are mandated or encouraged by the government.

II. The Problem with Purely Voluntary Preferential Treatment Programs

The argument to be advanced in this section is a moral one, not a legal one. The law introduces complications that will be addressed shortly, but the main argument of this section concerns the morality of purely voluntary preferential treatment programs in contracting and hiring. The first premise is that management has a fiduciary responsibility to its shareholders to act in the firm's best financial interests, subject to the con-

---

[12] Chris Woodyard, "Disney to Boost Minority Builders," *Los Angeles Times*, June 16, 1992, p. D2. Subsequently, the planned expansion was significantly scaled back.

straints imposed by the law. There may be exceptions to this general principle, and thus it is a rebuttable presumption, but typically when a board of directors hires a chief executive officer (CEO) or a management team, there is a shared understanding that management will act in the firm's best financial interests. This shared understanding is the basis of the fiduciary responsibility (and thus the moral obligation) of the CEO or management team. Possible exceptions to one side, there is an ambiguity in the concept of what constitutes the firm's best financial interests. Is it maximizing profits in the near term? Increasing market share? Maximizing shareholder value? Or some combination of these? Answers to these questions can be variable and indeterminate, though they may be addressed at the time the board hires the CEO or management team. Nevertheless, as agents for the firm's principals (i.e., the stockholders), management's primary goal and responsibility is to advance the financial interests of the firm. However the ambiguity about the firm's best financial interests is resolved, there is the further difficulty of identifying which policies will actually further that goal. Management's moral responsibility to the shareholders does not require perfection in the choice of policies, but it does require that managers act according to their best judgment about what will advance the financial interests of the firm. One thing this implies is that managers are not permitted to further their own conception of justice by instituting programs such as Disney's, at least when they foresee that this is not financially advantageous to the firm.[13]

Contractors who lose out in bidding on Disney contracts or job applicants who have been shut out by a corporation's voluntary preferential hiring program have a morally legitimate complaint against the corporation's managers on the grounds that the latter have not followed procedures they agreed (implicitly or explicitly) to follow when they were hired by the board of directors, who in turn represent the interests of shareholders. The moral wrong in Disney's minority set-aside program (and comparable hiring programs) is to be found in the violation of management's obligation to its shareholders to act in the best financial interests of the firm, subject to the constraints imposed by the law. Such programs may not cause serious harm, since the actual costs, including the possible negative effects on morale within the company, might not be enormous. Indeed, compared to other ways in which corporate officers waste money and otherwise act as poor agents for their principals, these harms may be comparatively minor, though they are not negligible. Nevertheless, it is the principle of the thing, and the principle implies that

---

[13] By contrast, defensive preferential treatment programs are morally justified and indeed morally required, given the legal exposure firms face from disparate-impact lawsuits. It is generally not in a firm's financial interests to be vulnerable to disparate-impact lawsuits. Whether or not firms should face that exposure is a separate question and indeed is the subject of the argument in subsequent sections of this essay.

managers violate their fiduciary obligations to the firm's owners when they follow their own conception of justice at the expense of the firm's financial interests.

Just because this moral obligation exists does not mean that it is, or even should be, legally actionable. The state gives fairly wide latitude to corporate officers in matters of business judgment by insulating them from legal liability in all but the most egregious cases. Part of the reason for this is that shareholders (and the boards of directors who are their agents) have a variety of ways of dealing with managers who do not act in the firm's best financial interests, ways that are more effective and efficient than what could be accomplished through the courts. For example, shareholders can sell their shares in the company, and boards of directors can discipline or fire the CEO, who often works without a written contract.

Now for the exceptions and complications. Note that this argument does not apply to privately held firms owned and managed by one individual. An owner of such a firm might decide on his own to implement a preferential treatment program; if there is anything morally objectionable about this, it is not because the managers have violated a fiduciary obligation to the owners. Similarly, the owners of a closely held corporation might jointly agree to order management (which might consist of one or more of their number) to institute a preferential treatment program not required or encouraged by law. Finally, there could be cases in which the owners of a privately held company announce, upon making an initial public offering of stock, that the company will pursue such programs as a matter of company policy, even if it is detrimental to the firm's financial interests. Or they could go before the shareholders at the annual shareholders' meeting and announce their intention to pursue preferential policies that are not in the firm's financial interests, detailing their best estimates of the costs and benefits (both financial and otherwise) of these policies. Under those circumstances, shareholders would have no grounds for complaint. Let us suppose, however, that a firm's management does not do either of these things. Suppose instead that they simply decide, perhaps with the acquiescence of the board of directors, to pursue a social-justice agenda (or an environmental agenda, or a charitable-giving agenda) that foreseeably harms the firm's financial interests.[14] They do not tell the shareholders about it, or if they do, they do so after the fact and mislead them about its costs and benefits. Under such circumstances, they have violated their fiduciary obligations to the shareholders and thus have acted wrongly.

[14] Perhaps there is a *de minimus* level of financial harm below which moral condemnation is inappropriate or at least of little moral significance. No one seriously maintains, however, that preferential treatment programs are comparable, in terms of their net costs, to taking home some office supplies, or even to modest affirmative action outreach efforts of the sort described at the beginning of this essay.

One objection to this argument would be to charge that purely voluntary preferential treatment programs in contracting and hiring really are in a firm's best financial interests. Proponents of affirmative action often claim that a diverse workforce is in the company's best financial interests, and indeed can point to an array of diversity programs that large corporations have instituted and an army of diversity consultants whom companies have hired to run them.[15]

It is difficult to evaluate this objection for the simple reason that it is difficult to determine how many preferential treatment programs in contracting or hiring are truly voluntary in the sense that they would persist in the absence of any legal pressure to maintain them. The proliferation of diversity programs does not prove very much in this context for at least two reasons. First, and most obviously, antidiscrimination law is extremely far-reaching in its coverage. As I noted above, disparate-impact lawsuits can be brought against any firm with more than fifteen employees. As for set-asides, an estimated 27 million people work for firms that do business with the federal government.[16] Executives have learned to speak the language of diversity, whether or not they believe in it. As diversity consultant David Jamieson has said, "CEOs have learned to speak PC [political correctness] so well we can't tell if they are genuinely interested in diversity or not."[17] An expensive and elaborate diversity program is part of a well-conceived defensive preferential treatment program for large companies.

Second, diversity programs include much more than preferential programs in hiring and contracting. They often include attempts to achieve a more harmonious and effective workforce by sensitizing workers to cultural and gender differences. They also try to prevent, or at least insulate the company from, other types of lawsuits (e.g., those arising from the Americans with Disabilities Act, sexual harassment lawsuits). For these reasons, the percentage of preferential hiring and contracting programs that would continue to exist in the absence of threats of Title VII litigation or the loss of government contracts is impossible to determine. For the sake of argument, however, let us grant that there could be purely voluntary preferential treatment programs which management reasonably believes are in a firm's best financial interests; the above argument would not apply to such programs, if in fact they do exist. The focus of the argument of this section is on voluntary preferential treatment programs in hiring or contracting that would clearly not be in a firm's financial interests in the absence of government-induced threats. These are the ones that are in place because it is thought to be the socially responsible thing to do, or because the firm claims to value diversity for its own

[15] For a thorough discussion of the "diversity industry," see Frederick Lynch, *The Diversity Machine* (New York: The Free Press, 1997).

[16] See note 7 above.

[17] Quoted in Lynch, *The Diversity Machine*, p. 19.

sake, or because the firm's managers believe that the demands of justice require such programs.

A second objection to the argument against preferential treatment programs presented above is based on the idea that some theories of justice or morality are better than others. Sometimes economists make an argument similar to the one given above and blithely assume that all such theories are equal, or that all moral judgments are merely expressions of personal feelings and that following the demands of justice is nothing more than imposing one's own subjective preferences on others. However, not all theories are equal, and unless a radical subjectivism about morality or the meaning of moral language is correct, moral judgments are not merely expressions of feelings. Philosophers would insist, moreover, that some theories are true and some are false, or at least that some are defensible and some are indefensible. Now if the theory of justice that, for example, the Disney management is operating with—call it "the Mickey Mouse theory"—is indeed the right one, then Disney is simply doing what justice requires. The argument set out above looks persuasive only to the extent that it assumes that managers are imposing their own *views* or *conceptions* of justice on the company, but maybe more than that is going on. They may be imposing what justice does in fact require. In this essay, I have tried to avoid passing judgment on which theory of justice is correct, but a critic might charge that this simply cannot be done. If the Mickey Mouse theory of justice is correct or is the most defensible theory, then voluntary programs such as Disney's set-aside program are justified. Otherwise, they are not.

The reply to this objection is that it shows at most that there could be a conflict of duties for the managers of firms such as Disney's. The demands of justice conflict with their fiduciary duties to shareholders, but that does not show that the former and not the latter should be followed.[18] So, even on the assumption that the Mickey Mouse theory of justice is the correct theory, it does not follow that Disney's program—and other programs like it—are justified, all things considered. In other words, this objection does not succeed without a further premise to the effect that when the demands of justice conflict with fiduciary duties, the demands of justice always take precedence. And that premise, as I shall argue in the next section, is false.

---

[18] The fiduciary duties may themselves be conceived of as demanded by justice, on the grounds that violating those duties violates the moral rights (property rights) of the principals and that justice requires that people's moral rights be respected. If that is so, the conflict is a conflict of claims of justice, with one of those claims being a rights-claim and the other being a claim of distributive (or perhaps compensatory) justice. A comprehensive theory of justice would systematically resolve such conflicts; what follows in the next section could be thought of as taking the first steps toward such a theory. However, an alternative way of describing this conflict is the way it is done in the text, namely, as a conflict between fiduciary duties and the demands of justice. The problem then is to determine what one's moral duty is, all things considered.

III. Nonvoluntary Preferential Treatment Programs: The Perotian Argument and the Demands of Justice

The argument of Section II does not address the most common types of preferential treatment programs that are currently in force—those which the state mandates or encourages. These include minority set-asides and preferential hiring programs involving government contractors, as well as defensive programs in the private sector that are instituted to avoid disparate-impact lawsuits. When people talk about the affirmative action controversy, these are the programs (along with similar programs in higher education) that they are talking about.

It seems that an argument parallel to the one set out above could be mounted against these programs as well. Government bureaus are analogous to firms, with citizens occupying a role analogous to that of shareholders. Because former presidential candidate Ross Perot reminds us that in a democracy the citizens own their government, let us call this "the Perotian Argument."[19] Whether or not citizens literally own their government as Perot maintains, it is clear that they have a legitimate expectation that the government will try to get the best mix of quality and price in the goods and services that it buys from the private sector. They also have a legitimate expectation that the government will not gratuitously impose added costs or reduced quality on goods and services exchanged in purely private business dealings. Of course, the legitimacy of these expectations is purely moral, not epistemic. Only the very naive believe that governments generally meet these expectations. Most citizens are well aware that governments very often do not. But they should. By mandating and encouraging preferential treatment programs, however, the government violates citizens' legitimate expectations about how their government will behave.

There are two premises in this argument: that the citizens of a democracy have a legitimate expectation that the government will not act in such a way as to raise the price and/or reduce the quality of goods and services in both the public and private sectors; and that nonvoluntary preferential treatment programs violate this expectation. The first is hard to argue with, at least as a general proposition. It is simply a demand that government act efficiently in procuring goods and services and in affecting the private sector. There are undoubtedly exceptions to this general proposition, and thus it is a rebuttable presumption; indeed, proponents of preferential treatment programs may insist that in this area an excep-

---

[19] Or is it the taxpayers who own the government? Not all citizens are taxpayers and not all taxpayers are citizens, though the two groups substantially overlap. Since I do not wish to claim that anyone literally owns the government, this complication need not be pursued. All that is claimed in what follows is that citizens or taxpayers have a principal-agent relationship with their government analogous to shareholders' relationship to management, at least when it comes to the government's dealings in the economy.

tion should be made because of the demands of justice. This claim will be taken up in due course, but for now it is sufficient to note that those who control the government in a democracy do not own the resources they control. They have a fiduciary relationship with the citizenry that closely parallels the relationship between corporate officers and shareholders; this serves as the basis for the legitimate expectations just mentioned.

Consider now the other premise, namely, that preferential treatment programs mandated or encouraged by government raise the cost and/or lower the quality of goods and services produced by firms or government bodies that are subject to them. There is ample evidence that nonvoluntary preferential treatment programs substantially raise the costs of doing business. The economist Farrell Bloch reports that the compliance costs and the productivity losses among private firms doing business with the federal government have been calculated to be as high as $40 billion per year. As for the other costs associated with preferential treatment programs (including hiring), Bloch writes:

> Neither comparable estimates of the impact of EEOC [Equal Employment Opportunity Commission] regulation nor overall administrative costs . . . have been similarly calculated, although the roughly $210 million and $55 million annual budgets of the EEOC and OFCCP [Office of Federal Contract Compliance Programs] . . . clearly provide floors for program administrative expenses. Additionally, direct litigation and, more speculatively, employers' efforts to avoid it, each has been estimated to cost about $100 million per year.[20]

Some of these costs would be incurred even if government enforced only those laws that prohibit intentional discrimination and did not mandate or encourage preferential treatment programs. It is clear, however, that government-mandated or -encouraged preferential hiring programs have imposed enough additional costs to substantiate the crucial premise that these programs have imposed nontrivial costs on the taxpayers and the businesses that are subject to them.

Proponents of these programs might agree with all this and yet insist that even though these programs do impose real costs, that is simply the price of justice. Justice, John Rawls asserts, is the first virtue of social institutions.[21] If justice requires preferential treatment programs, so be it. This is essentially the same objection raised against the purely voluntary programs considered in the last section. It is now time to give it full consideration. I shall argue that even if the demands of justice require

---

[20] Bloch, *Antidiscrimination Law and Minority Employment*, p. 112.
[21] John Rawls, *A Theory of Justice* (Cambridge, MA: The Belknap Press of Harvard University Press, 1971), p. 3.

preferential treatment programs, the government is not justified in requiring or encouraging them. In other words, the argument that follows grants, for the sake of discussion, that justice requires preferential treatment programs, and yet concludes that these programs are, all things considered, unjustified.

This argument starts with some suggestive parallels with Locke's observations about the problems of a state of nature. Recall that a state of nature is a pre-political society in which people have various natural rights, including the rights to life, liberty, and property. In addition, they have the right to punish those who violate their other rights. All this gives rise to what Locke calls the "inconveniences of a state of nature." These include the following: Some people cannot enforce their rights. Some people do not correctly apply the natural law, or they tend to be biased when judging in their own cases, or they tend to mispunish, overpunish, etc. They use the demands of justice as a cloak to further their own interests and/or the interests of their friends at the expense of others and at the expense of justice. This worry is a special case of the central worry of Western political philosophy, at least in the liberal tradition: How is government to be limited? Whether or not one believes in Lockean rights, there is no doubt that the state faces a permanent threat—very often realized—of being hijacked to serve private interests. Historically, state power has been used to advance private interests at the expense of the public interest, including the demands of justice, however one understands these concepts.

This problem has become especially acute in the United States and almost all industrial democracies over the past 150 or so years, as the scope of government activity has grown unremittingly. A principal way in which this growth has manifested itself is by increasing restrictions on, or interferences with, freedom of contract. From wage and hour legislation to health and safety regulations to anti-trust legislation, governments have increasingly intervened in the market economies of the world by restricting freedom of contract. Furthermore, most of these restrictions have had significant primary or secondary redistributive effects, substantially benefiting various groups and individuals who were not the officially intended beneficiaries of the relevant legislation at the expense of other groups and individuals. For example, Gabriel Kolko has argued persuasively that much of the anti-trust legislation that was passed around the turn of the century had as its primary beneficiaries existing corporations who wanted to restrict competition from upstarts and outsiders.[22] The entire subdiscipline of public-choice economics is founded on the presumption that legislation is a product that interest groups "buy" and politicians "sell." Though one may question the explanatory scope of

[22] Gabriel Kolko, *The Triumph of Conservatism* (New York: Free Press of Glencoe, 1963).

public-choice explanations, or public-choice explanations for particular phenomena, there is no denying that they give important insights into the workings of modern governments.

These observations motivate two plausible requirements that must be met if the power of the state is to be used to further some conception of the demands of (distributive or compensatory) justice:[23]

(i) Proponents of state action must get a political consensus for doing what justice requires. A political consensus does not require unanimity among the people or their elected representatives, but it does require that supporters of government intervention make their case publicly and get an on-the-record vote from the legislature or from the electorate through a referendum. Let us call this the *Public Justification requirement*. This requirement does not demand that proponents of state action demonstrate that justice does in fact call for what they propose to do; it only requires that they publicly make an intellectually serious case for that proposition. To discharge this responsibility, it is not enough to identify some social evil and simply assert that the proposed legislation will eliminate or ameliorate it; in other words, it is not enough to recite good intentions. The social evil the legislation is intended to address must be identified, and there must be an explanation of how the implementation of the law will deal with it. Typically, this will involve identifying not only the intended beneficiaries but also the intended victims[24] of the legislation. As will be shown in detail in Section V, a paradigm case of the satisfaction of this requirement can be found in one form of intervention in freedom of contract in the Civil Rights Act of 1964. There was extended public debate in Congress on this, which was thoroughly reported in the press; and members of Congress, who had to face the voters, had to take a stand and vote for or against it. In the debate, the social evil of discrimination was identified and an explanation was given about how the law would ameliorate the problem. The intended beneficiaries were women and minorities who had been excluded by discriminatory hiring policies, and the intended victims were employers and hiring agents who had been permitted to practice this discrimination.

Because of the importance of precedent both in the law and in the formulation of public policy, it is especially important that this require-

---

[23] In what follows, the demands of justice are limited to the demands of compensatory or distributive justice, the grounds on which affirmative action programs are typically defended. There are other forms of justice (e.g., retributive), and there are rights-claims that may not be best conceptualized in terms of justice (e.g., rights to free speech or to religious liberty). It is unclear under what circumstances, if any, the two requirements I set forth should apply in conflicts between fiduciary obligations and these other demands. For example, if honoring a fiduciary responsibility involved perpetuating slavery, it is doubtful that these requirements would apply. But that is not what is at issue here.

[24] "Victims" is a morally loaded term in most contexts, though not all (e.g., "victims of disasters"); unfortunately, there is no simple morally neutral antonym for "beneficiaries." Consequently, as the term is used in this essay, "victims" means simply those whose interests are adversely affected and carries no implication that they have been morally wronged.

ment be met when it is first proposed that the state intervene in a new way in the private sector on the grounds of justice. Once a mode of intervention is established, it is common to justify new applications of this mode by reference to precedent.

(ii) Proponents of state action must explain how and why their proposal will not permit state power to be systematically abused to further private interests at the expense of those disadvantaged by the policies in question. Very often, proposed legislation will foreseeably but unavoidably help groups and individuals it is not intended to help at the expense of groups and individuals it is not intended to harm; if this is so, that fact has to be made public and a case has to be made that this is a cost worth paying. For example, the Civil Rights Act of 1964 required personnel to enforce it, and it created work for attorneys representing both plaintiffs and defendants. These personnel would be foreseeable but unintended beneficiaries of the legislation. The foreseeable but unintended victims would be primarily the taxpayers who would have to fund the enforcement machinery and who would not directly or indirectly benefit from it. Because this requirement is intended to prevent legislation from being hijacked to serve some private interests which it is not ostensibly intended to help at the expense of those which it is not intended to harm, let us call this the *Anti-Hijacking requirement*. Like the Public Justification requirement, the Anti-Hijacking requirement does not demand that the argument actually succeed. All that is required is an intellectually serious attempt to meet the concerns that this requirement reflects.

On the face of it, both of these requirements seem quite reasonable, though the threshold the arguments must meet to be intellectually serious requires further articulation. This will be done in the next two sections, in the course of making the case that existing minority set-aside and preferential hiring programs mandated or encouraged by the government fail to satisfy one or both of these requirements. Section VI considers challenges to these requirements, including the charge that these requirements are unjustifiably conservative, giving undue respect to the status quo and to the legislature. It might be argued that they unnecessarily hamper the judiciary and the executive in making progress on important social problems for which there is no legislative consensus. An investigation of this and related charges will both permit and require a discussion of the deeper rationale for the Public Justification and Anti-Hijacking requirements.

IV. MINORITY SET-ASIDE PROGRAMS

The main question this section and the next will address is whether minority set-aside programs and nonvoluntary preferential hiring programs satisfy the two requirements. Let us begin with the former. Minority set-asides began in 1968 with the Small Business Administration. The SBA served as prime contractor for other government agencies, awarding procurement contracts to small businesses. It interpreted its statutory authority to allow it to set aside a certain percentage of its contracts to businesses owned by "socially and economically disadvantaged" individuals, which was further interpreted to apply primarily to "minority business enterprises" (MBEs). The first set-aside program legislated by Congress was included in the 1977 Public Works Employment Act (PWEA).[25] It required each prime contractor to set aside 10 percent of the dollar value of the contract for MBEs, which were explicitly defined as businesses at least 50 percent owned by members of minority groups; or, if the business was a joint stock company, at least 51 percent of the stock had to be owned by minorities. Targeted minorities included African Americans, Hispanics, Asians, Native Americans, Eskimos, and Aleuts. The PWEA contained a provision to suspend the requirement if there were no available minority firms. In subsequent years, state and local governments instituted their own minority set-aside programs modeled on federal programs. Other set-aside programs at the federal level were introduced piecemeal, either by executive order or as part of other legislation.

Do minority set-aside programs meet the Public Justification requirement? Set-aside programs instituted by the executive branch (such as the SBA's program) were not subject to any public debate and discussion in Congress; they were simply imposed by the executive branch, so they clearly do not meet the requirement. The case of set-asides mandated by Congress is not as simple, since set-aside provisions can be found in many pieces of legislation that Congress passed and that the president signed into law. The crucial issue is the legislative history of a given set-aside provision.

The first of these provisions—the one included in the PWEA—is especially important, since it set the precedent; proponents of subsequent programs appealed to it as conferring presumptive validity on their proposals. One would expect that the first modern attempt to introduce race-conscious programs by legislation would occasion considerable congressional debate and discussion, but in fact that did not happen. There were no committee hearings or reports relating to the minority set-aside provision in the PWEA, probably because the provision was offered as a floor amendment in the House of Representatives. It passed on a voice vote and was accorded similar treatment in the Senate.

Representative Parren Mitchell, a leading minority legislator who sponsored the amendment, gave a number of reasons in support of it. He cited the fact that the bill under consideration targeted a number of other groups (e.g., Native Americans, the unemployed in states with high rates

---

[25] Information in this and subsequent paragraphs on the set-aside provision in the PWEA comes from the *Congressional Record*, 95th Congress, 1st session (1977), pp. 5327–30.

of unemployment). He also cited the precedent of the SBA's set-aside program targeted at minorities, which had been instituted by executive order. These reasons hardly rise to the level of serious arguments. At one point, however, he did approach this level:

> [A]ll this amendment attempts to do is to provide that those who are in minority businesses get a fair share of the action from this public works legislation. . . . The average percentage of minority contracts, of all Government contracts, in any given fiscal year is 1 percent—1 percent. . . . Why should the minority enterprise people not go on a competitive basis? The answer is very simple: We cannot. We are so new on the scene, so relatively small, that every time we go out for a competitive bid, the larger, older, more established companies are always going to be successful in underbidding us.[26]

All of the above makes it possible to reconstruct Mitchell's argument. It is based on the supposition that minority contractors must have been (and continue to be) the victims of discrimination. This discrimination, which has deprived them of their "fair share," may have taken the form of simple bias in the awarding of contracts by government agencies and private general contractors who hire subcontractors, or it may be that the number and size of minority contractors have been held down by other forms of discrimination. In other words, the supposition seems to be that but for the effects of discrimination, minority participation in government contracting would have been much greater than 1 percent—indeed, at least ten times greater. The proposal would rectify that situation for government contractors. In the language of affirmative action, the claim is that minority contractors have been "underutilized."

The problem with this argument is that the key factual claim about discrimination, and the corresponding counterfactual claim about what minority participation would have been in the absence of discrimination, are simply unsubstantiated. There was no finding by Congress of discrimination in the construction industry. Nor did the Supreme Court rely on any empirical evidence when it upheld the set-aside provision of the PWEA when it was challenged in the courts. In his concurring opinion on this challenge in *Fullilove v. Klutznick* (1980), Justice Powell found the 10 percent figure acceptable because it was "roughly halfway between the present percentage of minority contractors [4 percent] and the percentage of minority group members in the Nation [17 percent to 18 percent]."[27]

Principles of justice are contentious, and it may be asking too much for a lowly congressman (or even a Supreme Court justice) to produce a good argument, or indeed any argument at all, in support of whatever princi-

---

[26] *Ibid.*, p. 5327.
[27] *Fullilove v. Klutznick*, 448 U.S. 448, 512 (1980).

ple of justice he subscribes to. But this does not excuse the failure to address the empirical questions about discrimination against minority contractors. This is something that could be established by empirical investigation, resources for which are available to the Congress.

In *City of Richmond v. J. A. Croson Co.* (1989) and *Adarand Constructors v. Pena* (1995), the Court moved toward the view that minority set-asides by government bodies (at any level) are constitutionally permissible only if there has been a finding that general contractors or governmental bodies have actually discriminated against minority contractors.[28] These two opinions are consistent with, and indeed give judicial expression to, the demands of the Public Justification requirement—demands that were not satisfied in the debate on the PWEA. In the *Croson* case, if the city of Richmond had demonstrated that public-works MBEs had been discriminated against by the city and/or general contractors to whom the city awarded contracts, then city officials would at least have had the factual predicate to make the case that their minority set-aside program was needed to address a problem of discrimination. As George LaNoue has written:

> Nothing like the judicial record of finding discrimination in voting, education, and housing exists regarding public contracting. Indeed, there may be *no* modern cases where a public agency has been found guilty of not awarding a contract to a qualified minority low bidder.[29]

In response to this, it might be claimed that although there is no evidence that low-bidding MBEs were not awarded contracts, various patterns and practices have had a disproportionate negative impact on MBE firms (e.g., qualifying procedures, old boy networks, etc.). The charge of discrimination, then, would depend on the counterfactual claim that but for the effects of these practices, minority participation would have been much higher than it is. This is something many people might be inclined to believe; it is easy to conjure up stereotyped images of racist politicians and contractors, especially in the South, conspiring to cut out minority-owned enterprises. As opponents of racism remind us, however, stereotypical images do not count as evidence. More generally, economist Thomas Sowell has shown that many factors influence occupational choices by various racial and ethnic groups,[30] and there is simply no reason to be-

---

[28] *City of Richmond v. J. A. Croson Co.*, 488 U.S. 469 (1989); *Adarand Constructors v. Pena*, 115 S.Ct. 2097 (1995).

[29] George LaNoue, "The Disparity Study Shield: Baltimore and San Francisco," in *Racial Preferences in Government Contracting*, ed. Roger Clegg and Walter H. Ryland (Washington, DC: National Legal Center for the Public Interest, 1993), p. 72, n. 14.

[30] Thomas Sowell, *Preferential Policies: An International Perspective* (New York: W. Morrow, 1990); and Thomas Sowell, "The Presuppositions of Affirmative Action," in *Discrimination, Affirmative Action, and Equal Opportunity*, ed. Walter Block and Michael Walker (Vancouver, BC: Fraser Institute, 1982).

lieve that members of the designated minorities would have become successful public-works contractors at a rate that would result in their getting at least ten times the dollar value of contracts they were currently receiving.

Defenders of set-asides might want to base their case on broader claims of societal discrimination. Women and minorities, so the argument goes, have been the victims of discrimination in ways that have reduced their socioeconomic status relative to what it would have been absent such discrimination. Set-asides are a way of rectifying that maldistribution, so there is no need for detailed empirical investigation of the construction industry.

There are three difficulties with this argument. First, even if this discrimination was present, set-asides may have little or no effect on the overall distribution of wealth and income between white males and minorities—and not because of the relatively small amounts of money involved. Set-asides reward already-successful minority contractors, and they may disproportionately attract to the contracting business minorities who are already successful in other lines of work or would have succeeded in other endeavors. More generally, there is no guarantee that a program benefiting minority contractors will set up a ripple effect throughout the minority community. The series of nested counterfactuals that would have to be true are too many and too speculative to sustain the proposition that the distribution of income and wealth between minorities and nonminorities would be favorably changed as a result of the set-aside program. Once again, an argument turns on empirical considerations that have not been investigated.

Second, claims about the effects of general societal discrimination would seem to support much wider redistributive efforts. At the very least, they would seem more appropriate in support of proposals for across-the-board set-asides or for allowing disappointed minority contractors to sue governments and private businesses on grounds of disparate impact. Judicially imposed disparate-impact theory in employment discrimination had been in place for about five years at the time of the PWEA; supporters of set-asides could have proposed a similar law covering contractors. But no such proposal was made in 1977 (or in 1991 when the Civil Rights Act of 1866 was amended), and congressionally mandated set-asides have never been across-the-board. The closest thing to the latter is the SBA's program, which was imposed by the executive branch.

Third, as Jeffrey Rosen has pointed out, MBEs have now been favored by set-aside legislation for about twenty years, so it is hard to see how it could be claimed that they have been the *victims* of discrimination by the government or by government contractors who award subcontracts to other firms.[31]

Since the *Croson* decision applied only to state and local governments, in the aftermath of this decision governmental bodies other than Con-

---

[31] Jeffrey Rosen, "The Day the Quotas Died," *The New Republic*, April 22, 1991, pp. 21–27.

gress have spent enormous sums in an attempt to establish that minority contractors have been underutilized, but the studies they have commissioned are deeply flawed. For example, most disparity studies rely on a simple head count of MBE and non-MBE firms and do not take into account that MBEs tend to be newer and smaller, often lacking even the capability to do the larger jobs that non-MBE firms get. This results in an overstatement of the availability of MBEs. On the other hand, attempts to control for qualifications, and to segment the market properly, make statistically significant comparisons difficult, if not impossible.[32] Finally, a considerable portion of the dollar value of government contracts goes to large corporations (e.g., defense contractors) that have no particular racial or ethnic identity. The majority of their stockholders on any given day may very likely be white, but it seems odd to describe them as majority-owned firms, perhaps because they do not directly compete with minority-owned firms. Properly targeted legislation would restrict set-asides to contracts typically bid on by MBEs and their smaller competitors.

The flaws in the disparity studies are instructive; because they are restricted to particular metropolitan areas, it is difficult to get enough of the right kind of data to substantiate a claim that minority contractors have been "underutilized." This is just the sort of data that could be gathered if Congress chose to commission larger, nationwide studies. The fact that Congress has not done this suggests that congressional supporters of set-asides are not at all confident about what they would find or that their ideology dampens their curiosity about the facts. In the end, the argument for set-asides seems to run something like this: "Everyone knows women and minorities have suffered discrimination. Therefore, minority contractors probably have been discriminated against (or would have been discriminated against had they existed) in trying to win government contracts. Therefore, set-asides should be instituted to help them." For the reasons indicated, this argument is seriously flawed, but in any case it was not explicitly made.

When one turns to a consideration of the Anti-Hijacking requirement, there is even less to recommend set-aside programs. Rarely does Congress carefully consider all of the unintended beneficiaries and victims of its legislation. The taxpayers who were not also contractors might be counted as (recognized) unintended victims, since they foot the bill for these programs. Although Congress sometimes makes an effort to find out how much a program will cost, that seems not to have been done in the case of set-asides. As for unintended beneficiaries, there are the additional bureaucrats needed to run these programs; presumably, Congress knows about this and foresees that these bureaucrats will benefit, though once again there seems to have been little thought given to how much this would cost.

---

[32] LaNoue, "The Disparity Study Shield," p. 109.

There are also unintended beneficiaries and victims who occupy that status because of the perverse ways in which set-asides operate. For example, as noted above, the vast majority of government contracts (defined in terms of total dollar value) go to large, publicly traded companies such as defense contractors. To meet set-aside quotas, the government must often completely shut out nonminority firms in entire industries or sub-industries (e.g., construction) in different regions or states. For example, virtually all the road-building contracts at the White Sands military facility in New Mexico go to MBEs so that the Defense Department can meet the national goals of the Small Business Administration's Section 8(a) program. In ten states, more than 40 percent of all construction contracts to small businesses went to MBEs.[33] Moreover, large, successful MBEs which can compete on an equal footing with other firms do not have to underbid their competitors to win government contracts, and thus can reap additional profits from the program. One particularly egregious example of this was a provision in communications legislation giving tax breaks to MBEs that purchased media outlets. A group of minority businessmen purchased and then resold a group of radio and television stations, reaping a $40 million windfall.[34] Careful fact-finding and appropriately tailored legislation might have prevented many of these apparent injustices. Alternatively, defenders of set-asides could have simply argued that these apparent injustices are not genuine injustices or that they simply represent the price of justice. It may be reasonably doubted, however, that the legislation would have survived a full airing of these problems.

V. Preferential Treatment in Hiring

Though minority set-asides are an important form of preferential treatment, preferential hiring programs are more significant. They impact many more people and seem to have provoked more passionate debate. The vast majority of preferential hiring programs are mandated or encouraged by the government and would likely not exist but for that pressure. They fall into three categories: (1) those mandated by the courts in response to successful discrimination suits; (2) defensive preferential hiring programs encouraged by the executive branch for contractors doing business with the federal government; and (3) defensive preferential hiring programs undertaken to ward off disparate-impact lawsuits. Let us consider each of these in turn to see if the Public Justification and Anti-Hijacking requirements were satisfied when these programs were instituted.

1. *Court-ordered preferential hiring programs.* Courts occasionally order hiring (or promotions) by the numbers in response to successful lawsuits

---

[33] Rosen, "The Day the Quotas Died," pp. 25–26.
[34] Eastland, *Ending Affirmative Action*, p. 178.

brought under Title VII of the 1964 Civil Rights Act.[35] Section 706 of Title VII gives a court considerable discretion in ordering remedies for discriminatory practices. In response to a finding of discrimination, Section 706(g)(1) says,

> the court may enjoin the respondent from engaging in such unlawful employment practice and may order such affirmative action as may be appropriate which may include but is not limited to reinstatement or hiring of employees, with or without back pay . . . or any other equitable relief that the court deems appropriate.[36]

Though it is doubtful whether "quota relief" is consistent with Section 703(j) of Title VII, the courts have assumed that it is and have on occasion ordered hiring or promotion by the numbers. They have forced employers to hire a certain percentage of minorities against whom no discrimination has been proven or even alleged. Typically, these remedies are imposed on employers who seem particularly racist or sexist in their policies and practices. This remedy fails to satisfy the Public Justification requirement, even if it is legally permissible, since nowhere in the Civil Rights Act is this remedy explicitly mentioned. Congress never debated and sanctioned hiring or promotion by the numbers as a remedy for discrimination, no matter how egregious. The fact, if indeed it is a fact, that Congress somehow left the door open for quota remedies is irrelevant for the purposes of the Public Justification requirement, since this requirement imposes burdens on the legislature. This form of affirmative action is relatively rare, however, in comparison to the next two types to be considered, so perhaps we should not make too much of this failure.

2. *Preferential hiring under various executive orders.* In 1965, President Lyndon Johnson issued Executive Order 11246, which created the Office of Federal Contract Compliance (later renamed the Office of Federal Contract Compliance Programs) and led to the establishment of defensive preferential hiring programs by government contractors. Later, President Richard Nixon extended preferential hiring requirements to cover the civil service in Executive Order 11478. The story of the development of this policy has been told elsewhere.[37] The "goals and timetables" approach to hiring was inaugurated under these executive orders, which remain in effect to this day. The OFCCP has considerable power over firms doing business with the government. Many such firms do business exclusively (or nearly exclusively) with the government and can ill-afford to walk away from government contracts. Though firms are nominally prohibited from hiring by

---

[35] See note 5 above.
[36] 42 U.S.C. 2000e-(g)(1).
[37] See Belz, *Equality Transformed*, pp. 31–40.

the numbers, they must submit an affirmative action plan, complete with goals and timetables. The failure of so-called "good faith efforts" to yield the right hiring numbers can bring the OFCCP down on a contractor with a vengeance. This office has much more power than the EEOC, since it can deny contracts without a court finding that a company has been guilty of discrimination. OFCCP officials can simply refuse to certify a company as able to bid on contracts. Although this sanction has seldom been applied, the threat of it is usually sufficient to get compliance. As one contract compliance officer reportedly said: "All that is needed is to take an employer to the cliff and say, 'Look over, baby.' "[38] It is disingenuous to suppose that preferential hiring programs undertaken in response to these threats are truly voluntary. Managers of firms doing business with the government who did not hire by the numbers would be guilty of gross neglect of their fiduciary duties to stockholders.

Since Congress did not legislate preferential hiring programs by government contractors, there was no debate on either the intended or the unintended beneficiaries and victims of such programs, so neither the Public Justification requirement nor the Anti-Hijacking requirement was met. Whatever its drawbacks, the legislative process permits (though, as can be seen in the case of the PWEA, it does not guarantee) an airing of the costs and benefits of proposed programs. Opponents will be eager to argue that there are significant numbers of unintended beneficiaries and victims; proponents of the legislation can rebut those claims or argue that this is the price that must be paid. Programs imposed by the judiciary and the executive branch face no such test and do not receive the close scrutiny that is likely to be given to a proposed piece of legislation.

3. *Other defensive preferential hiring programs.* Defensive preferential hiring programs among firms not doing business with the federal government came into existence in response to judicial interpretation of Title VII of the 1964 Civil Rights Act. In *Griggs v. Duke Power* (1971)[39] and subsequent cases, the Supreme Court ruled that hiring practices and policies having a disparate impact on minorities were prima facie suspect and could be grounds for a Title VII lawsuit. Moreover, the EEOC has made it clear that it will not bring disparate-impact lawsuits against employers who abide by what is called "the 80 percent rule."[40] This rule states that if the percentage of women or minorities a firm hires is at least 80 percent of their percentage in the relevant populations, the firm will not ordinarily be subject to an investigation and a disparate-impact lawsuit. Rational firms have responded to these pressures by instituting preferential hiring programs to reach safe harbor from such lawsuits. In 1989, the

[38] Quoted in *ibid.*, pp. 31–32.
[39] 401 U.S. 424 (1971).
[40] Uniform Guidelines on Employee Selection Procedures (1978), 29 C.F.R. Section 1607.4D (1989).

Supreme Court pulled back from the standards imposed by *Griggs* and its progeny in *Ward's Cove Packing Co. v. Antonio.*[41] It lessened the pressure on businesses to engage in preferential hiring by redistributing the burden of proof in disparate-impact cases. In response to the Court's ruling in *Ward's Cove*, Congress reimposed the *Griggs* standards in the Civil Rights Act of 1991. Were the Public Justification and Anti-Hijacking requirements satisfied for preferential hiring programs anywhere in this series of events? Let us begin with the original legislation: Title VII of the 1964 Civil Rights Act.

If one purpose of Title VII was to foster preferential hiring programs, proponents of the law would have had to make clear that employment practices that have a disparate impact on minorities create a rebuttable presumption of discrimination. Under this construal of Title VII, the intended beneficiaries would be the women and minorities who successfully sued, as well as those who would be hired to avoid such suits, and presumably other women and minorities who might indirectly benefit from preferential hirings and promotions. The intended victims would be the owners of the businesses who, for whatever reason, used employment practices (or hired managers who used such practices) that created a disparate impact. Others in the firm, such as other managers who would have to struggle with affirmative action regulations and other employees who would be negatively affected in a variety of ways, might also count as intended victims of the policy, though that depends on how the argument is framed. The argument would have to be made that the benefits of the law, as so interpreted, outweigh the costs.

What about the unintended beneficiaries and victims? The Anti-Hijacking requirement stipulates that they have to be identified as well. The main unintended victims are, of course, the nonminority candidates who otherwise would have gotten the jobs. Academic defenders of preferential hiring are quick to point out that their being excluded is not a result of stereotyping and does not stigmatize them in the way ordinary racial discrimination would. Moreover, if there were ways to solve the underlying social problems without hurting these people, defenders of preferential hiring programs would probably embrace them. All this makes the victim status of disappointed majority job candidates unintended, however foreseeable their plight is. However, they are still adversely affected, and whatever the demands of justice, the lack of stigmatization is cold comfort to someone who did not get a job or promotion because of his or her race or gender. The unintended beneficiaries of preferential hiring programs are a little harder to identify. Clearly, government bureaucrats and lawyers in the equal employment opportunity/affirmative action industry count as foreseen though unintended beneficiaries. In addition,

---

[41] 490 U.S. 642 (1989).

the private sector has its affirmative action officers, "diversity consultants," and others who profit from attempts to eliminate (perceived) social injustice.

The above identifies the intended and unintended beneficiaries and victims of preferential hiring programs, an identification essential to satisfying the Public Justification and Anti-Hijacking requirements. The main problem for defenders of preferential hiring programs is that legislators supporting Title VII never made this case. Opponents of the legislation as it was originally proposed argued that preferential hiring would be encouraged as a way of avoiding lawsuits; they also expressed worries about the meaning of "discrimination."[42] These critics had identified many of the potential unintended victims and beneficiaries of the legislation catalogued above, but proponents of Title VII explicitly denied that the scenarios they envisioned would occur. Indeed, Section 703(j) (quoted near the beginning of this essay) was inserted specifically to address this concern.

Moreover, in answer to a question about the definition of discrimination, Senator Hubert Humphrey, the Senate's leading supporter of the bill, clearly indicated that he understood it in terms of disparate treatment (so-called "intentional discrimination"), not disparate impact. He said to one of the bill's opponents:

> [I]f the Senator can find in Title VII . . . any language which provided that an employer will have to hire on the basis of percentage or quota related to color, race, religion, or national origin, I will starting eating the pages one after another because it is not there.[43]

An interpretive memorandum on Title VII inserted into the *Congressional Record* by Senators Joseph Clark and Clifford Case said:

> There is no requirement in Title VII that an employer maintain a racial balance in his workforce. On the contrary, any deliberate attempt to maintain a racial balance, *whatever such balance may be* [emphasis added], would involve a violation of Title VII because maintaining such a balance would require an employer to hire or refuse to hire on the basis of race.[44]

---

[42] *Congressional Record*, 88th Congress, 2d session (1964), pp. 2571, 2576, 2605.

[43] *Ibid.*, p. 7420. See also *ibid.*, pp. 5864, 6000. Humphrey also said he was "disturbed" by a ruling by the Illinois Fair Employment Practices Committee that invoked a precursor of disparate-impact theory to hold that a minority-group member had been the victim of discrimination.

[44] *Ibid.*, p. 7312. On the same page, Senators Clark and Case explicitly deny the disparate-impact interpretation of discrimination, though not by that name.

On the House side, Representative John Lindsay explicitly denied that quotas would be permissible.[45] Although the term "disparate impact" was not used, the concept was thoroughly discussed; both opponents and proponents understood that discrimination was to be conceived of in terms of disparate treatment only and not in terms of disparate impact.

It should be noted in passing that these considerations do not presuppose any comprehensive theory of statutory interpretation, though they do impose some constraints on such theories, at least when questions of distributive or compensatory justice arise. The Public Justification and Anti-Hijacking requirements simply say that when the demands of distributive or compensatory justice are being imposed, those doing the imposing are to be legislators and are required by political morality to be up front about what they are doing. They cannot leave their dirty work to the courts or the executive. The next section considers some challenges to these requirements, but for present purposes, the central fact about the debate on Title VII is that there was no shared understanding that disparate impact would count as discrimination; indeed, there was a shared understanding that disparate impact would *not* be considered a form of discrimination.

The debate on Title VII is illuminating in other respects. A good case can be made that this debate really did meet both the Public Justification requirement and the Anti-Hijacking requirement for disparate-treatment ("intentional") discrimination. A widely (though not unanimously) shared principle of justice employed in the debate was something to the effect that people should not be treated differently in the employment relation because of their race, gender, and so on. This bill prohibited that and spelled out the enforcement mechanisms by which this goal was to be achieved. The intended beneficiaries were those who would have suffered discrimination (understood in terms of disparate treatment) in the absence of this law; the intended victims were employers who would treat people differently because of their race or gender and the white males who would have benefited if discrimination continued to be permitted.

When we turn to the unintended beneficiaries, there was a clear recognition that these laws would have to be enforced by the bureaucracy and the courts, thereby brightening the employment prospects for bureaucrats, court personnel, and attorneys who would litigate these matters. The main concern of opponents of the legislation concerned other unintended beneficiaries and, perhaps more importantly from their perspective, unintended victims. They worried that less-qualified minority-group members would be hired as part of a quota so that employers could avoid discrimination lawsuits. They further worried that white males would be unjustly denied employment opportunities because employers would be pressured into hiring by the numbers. In other words, the

---

[45] *Ibid.*, p. 1540.

concerns about hijacking were clearly voiced. Proponents responded by making clear that disparate impact would not be grounds for lawsuits and that the effective burden of proof would always remain with the plaintiffs. It was in response to these concerns that Section 703(j) ("nothing contained in this subchapter shall be interpreted to require any employer ... to grant preferential treatment ...") was inserted into the bill.

The fact of the matter, of course, is that it did not turn out that way. The courts interpreted Title VII in a way that clearly violated the shared understanding of proponents and opponents of the legislation. Proponents of Title VII cannot be responsible for that, even if, in the event, some of them were pleased by what the courts did. The Public Justification and Anti-Hijacking requirements do not demand that the relevant arguments actually succeed, either in terms of the truth of the underlying principles of justice or the factual predictions about the effects of the policy; they only require that an intellectually respectable case be made that justice requires passage of the proposed legislation and that the costs associated with unintended victims and beneficiaries are worth paying. These burdens were successfully discharged in the 1964 debate on Title VII, at least with respect to the disparate-treatment interpretation of discrimination. The fact that the courts created large classes of unintended beneficiaries and victims in defiance of the shared understanding achieved in the legislative process is unfortunate but irrelevant to the question of whether these two requirements had been satisfied. To summarize, both the Public Justification and Anti-Hijacking requirements were satisfied in the debate on Title VII of the 1964 Civil Rights Act insofar as the Title is interpreted to prohibit discrimination, understood in terms of disparate treatment. Neither requirement was satisfied on the disparate-impact interpretation of discrimination.

There are two more incidents related to preferential hiring programs that have to be considered. One is the attempt by Senator Sam Ervin to dismantle these programs in 1972, and the other is the legislative response to *Ward's Cove* in the Civil Rights Act of 1991.

In the 1972 debate on amending Title VII, Senator Sam Ervin tried to end preferential hiring and the minority set-asides instigated by the Office of Federal Contract Compliance. This was the first straight up or down vote on preferential treatment programs in the Congress, and Ervin's amendments were defeated. Although the Public Justification requirement demands a favorable vote by the legislature, it also demands an intellectually serious argument in support of it. What argument was given? Senator Jacob Javits responded to Senator Ervin's contention that preferential treatment was inconsistent with Title VII. Senator Javits's argument consisted of the following observations:[46] The Third Circuit Court of Appeals had upheld a preferential hiring program imposed by

[46] *Congressional Record*, 90th Congress, 2d session (1972), p. 1665.

the Nixon administration on government contractors, and thus the executive branch was legally entitled to impose such programs. Moreover, the courts had ordered hiring and promotion by the numbers in other cases. Senator Ervin's amendment would have prevented both these developments. This was why it should be defeated. Senator Harrison Williams added that the amendment would deny the executive and the judiciary "all power to remedy the evils of job discrimination."[47]

These are not serious arguments. Senator Williams's claim is simply false, since the judiciary still had the power to order injunctive and make-whole relief in disparate-treatment cases. Perhaps he was exaggerating a valid concern, but a serious argument does not indulge in that. Senator Ervin deserved a more adequate response, whether or not he or any other opponent would have been persuaded. Senator Javits's argument amounts to nothing more than saying that preferential treatment programs are currently legal, a point which Senator Ervin not only conceded but which he himself used as a key premise in his argument in favor of the amendment! He wanted to change the law, and a reply that simply cites the current law is a completely inadequate response.

Over the next twenty years, preferential hiring programs became ubiquitous as the scope of government contracting grew and as private individuals and the EEOC successfully pressed disparate-impact lawsuits. Proponents of preferential hiring programs might concede that such programs had originally been imposed by executive and judicial fiat. Nevertheless, they might argue, Congress finally faced the issue squarely when it considered and passed the 1991 Civil Rights Act, which was signed into law by President George Bush. This reimposed the *Griggs* standards and thereby gave legislative sanction to preferential hiring programs. But did the legislative debate on this bill actually satisfy the Public Justification and Anti-Hijacking requirements?

To answer this question, some background is in order. In 1989, a majority of the Supreme Court seemed to have some doubts about affirmative action as it had developed over more than two decades. Their ruling in *Ward's Cove Packing Co. v. Antonio* significantly lessened the pressure on firms to hire by the numbers by tightening and rearranging the burdens of proof in disparate-impact cases. In this connection, the three most important changes or clarifications made by *Ward's Cove* were these:[48]

1. The plaintiff must identify a specific employment practice that has a disparate impact; she cannot focus on the "bottom line" percentages of minorities and nonminorities within the firm or within any of its divisions.

Perhaps the most important changes introduced by *Ward's Cove* were related to the business-necessity defense that companies could offer once

---

[47] *Ibid.*, p. 1676.
[48] See 490 U.S. 642 (1989). The summary that follows is drawn from Henry H. Perritt, *Civil Rights Act of 1991: Special Report* (New York: John Wiley and Sons, 1992), pp. 91–92.

disparate impact had been established. In this connection, the Court set out two conditions:

2. The company need only articulate a legitimate business basis for the challenged practice; it need not prove that the practice is strictly necessary for the operation of the business.[49] For example, fast-food restaurants may require basic literacy and numeracy skills, which could have a disparate impact on minorities. They could do this even though their cash registers automatically calculate change, and there are little pictures of the food on the buttons of the register. A basic literacy and numeracy requirement could probably survive the "legitimate business function test" because the restaurants could argue that the requirement allows them to screen out people who could never be promoted and would be unlikely to perform well, even though employees do not actually have to have basic literacy or numeracy skills to do the job. Though the employer has the burden of production (i.e., to produce a reason and any relevant evidence) and cannot say just anything, the Court's *Ward's Cove* opinion suggests that the burden is not onerous:

> [T]here is no requirement that the challenged practice be "essential" or "indispensable" to the employer's business to pass muster: this degree of scrutiny would be almost impossible to meet, and would result in a host of evils we have identified above.[50]

3. The plaintiff must be given the opportunity to show that the challenged policy is not reasonably necessary for the operation of the business. In practice, about the only way this can be done is to show that there is another employment practice the employer could have used which would have had less disparate impact on minorities. This practice would have to be roughly comparable in terms of its effectiveness and costs.

There seemed to be widespread agreement that this case effectively overturned *Griggs*. Though disparate-impact cases could still go forward, *Ward's Cove* imposed a heavier burden on the plaintiff to establish disparate impact, and it relaxed the "business necessity" defense that employers could use to override the claim of disparate impact. In terms of larger social policy, it significantly attenuated the incentives businesses had to hire or promote by the numbers, since their chances of being successfully sued on these grounds were greatly diminished because of the heavier burden of proof that plaintiffs bore and the relative ease with which their case could be rebutted. Had *Ward's Cove* been allowed to stand, it likely

---

[49] Some critics of *Ward's Cove* claimed that this weaker requirement would permit employers to discriminate because of customer preference or employee morale. These concerns are specious, however, since a person denied a job or promotion under these circumstances could sue under the disparate-treatment construal of discrimination.

[50] 490 U.S. 659 (1989).

would have significantly diminished the number of defensive preferential hiring programs in the private sector.

The legislative response to *Ward's Cove* was to overturn it. Liberal Democrats and the civil-rights lobby had been content to let the courts do the heavy lifting in encouraging preferential hiring via the decision in *Griggs* and its progeny. When the Supreme Court became uncomfortable with what it had wrought and redefined the rules, proponents of preferential treatment correctly believed they had enough political muscle to restore the status quo ante. The 1991 Civil Rights Act did that and more.

The relevant amendments to Title VII contained in the 1991 Civil Rights Act had the following implications:

1. *The use of statistics.* The 1991 act did not clarify how statistics were to be used to establish disparate impact. In particular, the question of what population should be used to calculate the percentage of minorities who would have been hired or promoted in the absence of the suspect practice remained contestable. Data from actual applicants are best from the plaintiff's point of view, but the courts have allowed general workforce and even general population data to establish the prima facie case of disparate-impact discrimination in certain circumstances. There is also a question of how to define the geographical area from which the workforce is to be drawn. The size of that area can be variously defined by reference to the immediate neighborhood, the city in which workers or potential workers live, or the Standard Metropolitan Area.[51] Although this issue had been a contentious one in case law under *Griggs*, the 1991 act did not address it.

2. *The particularity requirement.* The new law did require the plaintiff to identify a particular employment practice that produces disparate impact unless "the elements of the respondent's decision-making process are not capable of separation for analysis."[52] Thus, if an employer uses a test and an interview to make hiring decisions but leaves it to the discretion of the hiring officer how to weight these requirements, the two requirements would be treated as one practice for purposes of proving disparate impact.

3. *The business-necessity defense.* The 1991 act said that for a challenged practice to be sustained, it has to be "job-related and consistent with business necessity."[53] An interpretive memorandum inserted into the *Congressional Record* said that these concepts were to be understood as enunciated in *Griggs*.[54] This shifted the effective burden of proof fully back to the employer; it tightened the job-relatedness requirement so that only the ability to do the job for which the person is hired is relevant. No longer could an employer reject someone because he believed that the applicant would not be likely to progress and be promoted in the firm.

---

[51] See Perritt, *Civil Rights Act of 1991*, pp. 129–36.
[52] The wording comes from Section 703 (k)(1)(B)(i) of Title VII. See *Congressional Record, Daily Report*, 102d Congress, 1st session (1991), p. S15274.
[53] *Ibid.*, p. S15503.
[54] *Ibid.*, p. S15276.

4. *Alternative practices.* Under the 1991 act, the business-necessity defense can be overturned only if the plaintiff can identify another employment practice that had less disparate impact and would serve the same ends, but the act removed a requirement that such alternative practices had to be comparable in terms of effectiveness and cost. Regarding the latter, according to Congressman Don Edwards's interpretive memorandum, the employer had to expend resources and effort in search of alternative practices with less disparate impact approximately in accordance with (i) the number of persons disparately impacted, (ii) the degree of adverse impact, and (iii) how feasible it would be, both financially and otherwise, for that particular employer to find alternatives (this implies that more will be demanded of large, successful firms than of smaller or weaker firms). Absent a favorable finding for the employer on all of these scores, the business-necessity defense would fail and the disparate-impact analysis would be dispositive.[55]

There are many other provisions in the 1991 law, but they are tangential to the concerns of this essay. What is crucial and undeniable is that Congress clearly sanctioned the disparate-impact theory of discrimination; but how did it fare in meeting the demands of the Public Justification and Anti-Hijacking requirements? These requirements demand not only that the legislature vote on the proposed policy, but also that the intended and unintended beneficiaries and victims of the legislation be identified and that a serious argument be made to the effect that the benefits of the legislation outweigh the costs, all things considered.

Opponents of the 1991 bill raised concerns relevant to these requirements when they labeled the proposed legislation a "quota bill." For example, Senator Jesse Helms made reference to an article in *Newsweek* (June 3, 1991) in which representatives of Fortune 500 companies admitted to hiring by quotas.[56] The Bush administration had objected to earlier versions of the bill on these grounds. The concern about quotas is primarily a concern about the existence and fate of unintended victims of the proposed legislation, namely, more-qualified nonminority candidates who would not be hired as a result of a company's defensive preferential hiring program.

How did proponents of the legislation respond to these concerns? The short answer is: Not well. Senator John Danforth, one of the bill's sponsors, responded to Senator Helms by saying that a prohibition on preferential hiring (which Senator Helms had introduced as an amendment) "interfered with voluntary efforts to remove discrimination."[57] Now in one sense this is perfectly true—if discrimination is understood in terms of disparate impact—but of course this is just the understanding that Senator Helms was challenging. Senator Ted Kennedy said: "[I]t is not an issue of quotas. . . . [C]urrent laws do not force employers to provide

---

[55] *Congressional Record, Daily Report*, 102d Congress, 1st session (1991), p. H9528.
[56] *Ibid.*, p. S12755.
[57] *Ibid.*

preferential treatment to any employee or applicant."[58] Senator Dennis
DeConcini clearly stated the potential problem (that employers would
use quotas defensively), but his response was simply to deny that the
proposed legislation was a quota bill and then to disparage President
Bush's concerns by attacking his motives.[59] Much was made of the fact
that the "leading" opponent of the bill was the Republican nominee for
governor of Louisiana, David Duke, a former Ku Klux Klansman and a
barely disguised racist. Debate over the bill in the House was equally
dismal, consisting mostly of denials that it was a quota bill and an attack
on the motives of the bill's opponents.[60]

Proponents of preferential treatment may object that too much is being
made of what was essentially a non-debate by the time the bill reached the
floor. The real work on these bills is done in committees and in private
meetings among legislators. The response to this objection is that the Public Justification and Anti-Hijacking requirements demand that the arguments be made in full public view, in the kinds of debates that the
Congressional Record records. Private understandings among proponents or
even between proponents and leading members of the opposition do not
count, nor should they. The idea behind these requirements is that if legislators are going to impose the demands of justice on some members of
the population to benefit others, they have to do it in public. There might
be a case for permitting discussions held in committees and subcommit-
tees to count, since these are often open to the press and the public. Two
committees of the House of Representatives, the Education and Labor Committee and the Judiciary Committee, issued substantive reports.[61] Neither
report, however, included any transcripts of what was said. Moreover, although the minority reports for each committee raised the question of
whether the law would encourage hiring by the numbers as a way of avoiding disparate-impact lawsuits, the majority reports did not seriously address this concern.[62]

Perhaps more importantly, if one looks at the actual provisions of the
amendments to Title VII, it is clear that each of the relevant features of the
bill identified above *increases* the incentives to hire less-qualified minorities at the expense of more-qualified nonminorities:

---

[58] *Ibid.*, p. S12775-76.
[59] *Ibid.*, p. 15337.
[60] See, e.g., Representative Jack Brooks's remarks on the quota question at *ibid.*, p. H9525.
[61] H.R. Rep. No. 40(I), 102d Congress, April 24, 1991 (Education and Labor Committee);
and H.R. Rep. No. 40(II), 102d Congress, May 17, 1991 (Judiciary Committee).
[62] The minority report of the Education and Labor Committee (*supra* note 61) raises this
issue on pp. 125-39. See especially p. 138. See also Representative Dick Armey's remarks on
pp. 162-64. The minority report of the Judiciary Committee (*supra* note 61) also raises this
issue on pp. 56-60. The majority report of the Education and Labor Committee summarily
dismisses these concerns on p. 44, and the Judiciary Committee's majority report simply
fails to address the issue. Compare this cavalier treatment of what is perhaps the central
civil-rights issue of this bill with both reports' careful discussion of the issue of the recovery
of expert-witness fees and attorney's fees, which goes on for many pages.

1. *The use of statistics.* The fact that the use of statistics to establish disparate impact was never clarified in the language of the 1991 law is significant. The reference class against which the class of those hired is to be measured may only be established if the case comes to trial. An employment practice that does not have a disparate impact on minorities if the reference class is the Standard Metropolitan Area may well have a disparate impact if the reference class is defined as those living in the inner city. What all this means is that even if an employer seeks to avoid employment practices that have a disparate impact, he may not be able to know whether or not he has done so until and unless he is haled into court. This, together with other uncertainties in the law, gives employers an incentive to hire as many minority-group members as possible, which presumably is just what some proponents of the law wanted. However, this point was not made in congressional debate on the bill. No one got up on the floor of the House or Senate and said: "We're going to leave the determination of the reference class in disparate-impact suits up to the courts, since that will increase employer uncertainty about the application of the law. We seek to have as many employers as possible hire as many minority-group members as possible, and the best way to achieve this is to create real indeterminacy in the law."

2. *The particularity requirement.* The impact of the particularity requirement is uncertain. Originally, some members of Congress wanted to dispense altogether with the requirement that plaintiffs in disparate-impact suits identify the particular practice or practices which caused a disparate impact. If they had done so, all the plaintiff would have to show is that the "bottom line" was not right. If the firm's bottom-line numbers were not right, the firm would have to attempt to make a business-necessity defense. Given the stringent way this had been interpreted, employers would have had virtually no choice but to institute quotas. However, the compromise language of the final bill required that the plaintiff identify the practice that caused the disparate impact—but it allowed an exception: if the decision-making process did not permit disaggregation of different practices, they could all be treated as a single practice. It is hard to know if this exception guts the particularity requirement and significantly encourages quotas without knowing if it is usually possible to disaggregate decision-making processes that result in offers of employment. Congress made no effort to find out what the effect of this provision would be. Once again, Congress showed little interest in materially important matters of fact.

3. and 4. *The business-necessity defense and alternative practices.* The tightening of the business-necessity defense by restricting acceptable requirements to those directly relevant to the job clearly increased the incentive for firms to hire by the numbers. Moreover, the interpretive memorandum's reference to *Griggs* hardly clarified the concept of business necessity, since the Supreme Court's decision in that case did not really define

"business necessity." Once again, Congress chose language that is highly indeterminate. The effect of this can only be to increase employer uncertainty, further strengthening the incentive to employ quotas as a prophylaxis against Title VII litigation. No effort was made to determine how common disparate-impact practices were or how feasible it would be for companies to devise race- or gender-neutral alternatives. Given the premises of the 1991 bill's proponents concerning the important negative effects of discrimination on women and minorities, it would be very common for facially neutral hiring practices to negatively affect the prospects of women and minorities. And by 1991, it was clear that it would be difficult to validate tests and hiring practices in a way that would satisfy the requirements of the business-necessity defense.[63] To say that the resulting legislation "is not a quota bill" is just disingenuous.

It is important to remember what is at stake. It is reasonable to suppose that proponents of this legislation favored preferential hiring policies (a term they would probably prefer to the more emotionally loaded "quota"), and they were crafting the law to encourage employers to adopt them. Now, there are perfectly respectable arguments in favor of preferential hiring based on considerations of distributive or compensatory justice, but—and this is the crucial point—none was offered. To the extent that the bill's proponents recognized the issue at all, they simply denied that the bill encouraged preferential hiring by denying that it was a quota bill. This is not an argument; it is an evasion of their responsibilities as legislators.

Why weren't proponents of the legislation more forthcoming about their intentions? Two obvious reasons suggest themselves. First, many Americans, including many voters, think preferential hiring is just wrong. Members of Congress might be reluctant to vote in favor of this bill if it were publicly recognized as a major piece of public policy encouraging a kind of preferential hiring that many Americans think is wrong, and not just a technical correction of some Supreme Court decisions. (For this to be a factor, one need not suppose that voters were listening to the debate; the legislators' political opponents almost certainly were listening or would at least consult the record before the next election.) Second, squarely facing this issue would have required, as a practical matter, rewriting Section 703(a) of Title VII, which states:

[I]t shall be an unlawful employment practice for an employer—
    (1) to fail or refuse to hire or to discharge any individual . . .
        because of such individual's race, color, religion, sex, or national origin.[64]

---

[63] For a thorough discussion of this point and an entrée into the empirical literature on the difficulties involved in validating testing in a way that would satisfy the requirements of the business-necessity defense, see Epstein, *Forbidden Grounds*, pp. 206–26, 236–41.

[64] 42 U.S.C. 2003e-(a)(1).

Rewriting this prohibition would have involved explicitly exempting discrimination against some groups. It would have also required rewriting the first sentence of Section 703(j), which now reads, "nothing contained in this subchapter shall be interpreted to require any employer ... to grant preferential treatment. ..."[65] The requisite change would involve dropping the first three words of this sentence. If proponents of the 1991 act wanted to be honest about the fact that they were encouraging preferential hiring, they would have revised Sections 703(a) and (j) to make it clear that only some forms of discrimination are legally prohibited. This would have made explicit the race- and gender-conscious intent of the relevant sections of the amended version of Title VII and would have exempted from litigation companies that engaged in the "right" kind of discrimination. The fact that they did not make these changes makes their lack of intellectual honesty transparent. It also makes it clear that they either failed to meet the Public Justification requirement or failed to meet the Anti-Hijacking requirement, depending on whether the main victims and beneficiaries of the act are conceived of as intended or unintended.

At this point it would be useful to restate and summarize briefly the main argument about preferential treatment programs in hiring and contracting mandated or encouraged by the government:

(1) Public officials are justified in imposing the demands of justice on a society in violation of their fiduciary obligations to citizens and/or taxpayers only if they meet the Public Justification and Anti-Hijacking requirements.

(2) Public officials of the U.S. government either did not meet the Public Justification requirement or did not meet the Anti-Hijacking requirement (or both) for preferential hiring programs and minority set-asides they have instituted or encouraged.

Therefore,

(3) Public officials were not justified in imposing on American society the demands of justice in the form of preferential hiring programs and minority set-asides.

Recall that the Public Justification requirement has two parts: (a) there must be a vote by the legislature to implement the program, and (b) an intellectually honest case has to be made that the relevant legislation will have its intended effect by helping its intended beneficiaries and harming its intended victims (if any). The Anti-Hijacking requirement demands that those who are imposing a program make an intellectually honest

---

[65] 42 U.S.C. 2000e-2(j).

effort to identify and to take into consideration the unintended beneficiaries and victims of their proposal.

Premise (2) asserts that one or both of these requirements were not met
in government-mandated or -encouraged preferential treatment programs
in American society. The case for premise (2) has been made in this section
and the last, and can be briefly summarized as follows: Preferential treatment programs in government contracting and in hiring were first imposed or encouraged by the executive and judicial branches. Set-asides were
first imposed in 1968 by the Small Business Administration, an agency of
the executive branch. The first preferential hiring program was also imposed by the executive branch when President Johnson issued Executive
Order 11246 in 1965. The Supreme Court created significant incentives for
preferential hiring among companies that were not government contractors in its 1971 ruling in *Griggs v. Duke Power*. Only after preferential hiring
and minority set-asides had become entrenched in American society did
the legislature get involved. In the first instance, it was on the issue of set-
asides. Legislators casually inserted set-aside provisions into a number of
pieces of legislation in the late 1970s and thereafter, without having made
any effort to determine the extent of discrimination in the awarding of contracts. In the case of preferential hiring programs, proponents of affirmative action were content to let the courts and the executive branch do the
heavy lifting until the 1989 *Ward's Cove* decision, which attenuated the incentives for preferential hiring in the private sector. Congress reacted by
reinstituting the *Griggs* standards in the Civil Rights Act of 1991, which restored and increased the incentives for preferential hiring. While legislators were doing this, they repeatedly claimed they were not doing anything
of the sort. Strong-arm tactics and disingenuousness have been woven into
the history of affirmative action in this country. The next section considers
whether the two requirements I have described place legitimate restrictions on the tactics that may be used by proponents of affirmative action
and other social policies, or whether these requirements unduly burden legislators in their pursuit of a more just social order.

VI. The Two Requirements Revisited

Much has been made in this essay of the fact that affirmative action
programs in contracting and hiring were not instituted by the legislature
after honest debate, as required by the Public Justification and Anti-
Hijacking requirements. However, a critic might challenge these requirements on a number of different grounds. This section considers some of
these criticisms and explores some of the larger implications of these
requirements.

Perhaps the most obvious objection to these requirements is that, if
followed, they would hinder progress toward justice. The demands of
justice often conflict with the self-interest of the majority and, not coinci-

dentally, with many citizens' views on what justice requires. A critic might charge that if a certain policy or program is what justice demands, why does it matter that the Public Justification and Anti-Hijacking requirements have not been met?

There are a number of reasons why it matters. The first begins with the observation that it is very difficult to know what justice does in fact require. Principles of justice are notoriously controversial. Men and women of high intelligence and good will can differ profoundly about which principles of justice are correct or most defensible. Moreover, even if there is agreement about principles, there can be reasonable disagreement about how they are to be applied to any particular public policy issue.[66] If the principles are mistaken or incorrectly applied, it is fair to say that those instituting the policy are doing no more than coercively imposing their own preferences on society at large, since there is in fact no larger purpose being served. (This is true even if their intentions are wholly honorable.) Though some economists falsely reduce all claims about justice to nothing more than personal preferences, they are right to be concerned about those cases in which the principles are in fact false or are misapplied. To say all that matters are the demands of justice is to be insensitive to the difficulties involved in knowing the truth about justice.

A second reason why it matters that these requirements are met is that the best argument in favor of some policy very often will crucially depend on empirical claims that need to be substantiated. This was the case with minority set-asides, which depended on some claims about the underutilization of minority-owned contractors. A full airing of the argument will expose its proponents to a challenge on the facts, which they may not be able to meet. Alternatively, answering that challenge might serve to stimulate research that will ultimately vindicate those factual claims.

Third, very often claims about justice mask a hidden agenda, in part because of their inherent indeterminacy. Consider proposals to increase the minimum wage, often advanced on the grounds of justice or fairness. Unintended (or perhaps intended) beneficiaries of these proposals include union members whose wages are tied directly or indirectly to the minimum wage. Unintended victims include young people who are denied employment to the extent that the demand for unskilled labor is downward-sloping. An honest effort to identify fully the unintended ben-

---

[66] For example, there is disagreement over whether Rawls's two principles of justice imply that the economic system of advanced industrial democracies should be free-market capitalism or some form of socialism. For an argument in favor of the former, see Daniel Shapiro, "Why Rawlsian Liberals Should Support Free Market Capitalism," *Journal of Political Philosophy*, vol. 3 (1995), pp. 58–85. For arguments in favor of the latter, see Barry Clark and Herbert Gintis, "Rawlsian Justice and Economic Systems," *Philosophy and Public Affairs*, vol. 7 (1978), pp. 302–25; Gerald Doppelt, "Rawls' System of Justice: A Critique from the Left," *Noûs*, vol. 15 (1981), pp. 259–307; Arthur Di Quattro, "Rawls and Left Criticism," *Political Theory*, vol. 11 (1983), pp. 53–87; and David E. Schweickart, "Should Rawls Be a Socialist?" *Social Theory and Practice*, vol. 5 (1978), pp. 1–28.

eficiaries and victims of this policy may cause some legislators to conclude that the gains associated with raising the minimum wage do not offset the losses, all things considered. On the other hand, they might conclude that the gains do outweigh the losses. Gains and losses need not be narrowly construed in terms of monetary costs and benefits but may also include considerations of justice or fairness. Regardless of the outcome, those who are imposing these policies will have a better understanding of what they are doing if the Public Justification and Anti-Hijacking requirements are met.

More general considerations in favor of a full airing of the reasons behind a particular policy are familiar to readers of John Stuart Mill's case for freedom of thought and expression in the second chapter of On Liberty.[67] Mill argues that one does not really know the truth unless one has considered what can be said against one's point of view. In a scenario in which the Public Justification and Anti-Hijacking requirements are satisfied, proponents will have to consider objections to their views, and/or opponents of the policy will get a chance to present the other side. This makes it more likely that public policy will be guided by knowledge instead of mere opinion.

According to Mill, if an opinion is not subject to challenge, it can become a "dead dogma." At first, the reasons behind the opinion are forgotten and ultimately the meaning of the opinion itself is lost. Mill illustrated this point by reference to belief in Christianity in nineteenth-century England, but the point can be equally well illustrated in late twentieth-century Washington. Wealthy and well-connected women and minorities get rich from sheltered competition for public contracts. So-called "diversity consultants" in human resource management light like mosquitoes on corporate bodies. What started out as an attempt to give victims of segregation a little extra help has suffered significant abuses and declining respect.[68] Support for these programs has hardened into a kind of dogma; proponents of "diversity" have trouble explaining what it is or why it is a good thing. In addition, the celebration of diversity among the relatively well-to-do has obscured the plight of the minority underclass and dissipated support for measures to help the latter. A full airing of the redistributive aims behind various affirmative action policies in the context of legislative debate might have led to provisions that would have diminished the number of unintended victims and beneficiaries of affirmative action. For example, sunset provisions, which auto-

[67] John Stuart Mill, On Liberty [1859], ed. Elizabeth Rapaport (Indianapolis: Hackett Publishing Co., 1978).

[68] Prior to joining the Clinton administration, Labor Secretary Alexis Herman came under scrutiny for having a $500,000 ownership stake in a real-estate venture for which she put up none of her own money. She served as an affirmative action consultant for the project and was taken on as a limited partner (a so-called "face partner," in the language of minority set-asides) in the deal. See The Birmingham News, February 15, 1997, p. 14A.

matically terminate programs after a certain period of time, could force Congress to investigate whether or not discrimination in contracting persists or has been essentially eliminated.

Similar considerations apply to Mill's observation that sometimes the truth lies between two contending sides. A policy such as set-asides that has produced so many unintended victims and beneficiaries might have had lower costs, both human and financial, if these programs (especially the precedent-setting SBA program imposed by executive order) had been subject to legislative debate.

Of course, there is no guarantee that any of these good consequences would flow from a real debate on the policy. The above discussions of legislative debate on the PWEA in 1977 and on the 1972 amendments to Title VII of the Civil Rights Act indicate that very often these good consequences do not follow, but it does seem that they would be more likely to be secured through open and honest debate than through its absence.

A critic might charge that at most these considerations support open and honest debate but not necessarily in the legislature. Why is the legislative arena particularly suited to discharging the responsibility of making a public case for the demands of justice? Proponents of judicial activism see the courts as an especially effective tool for progress toward social justice, in part because judges are immune from majoritarian pressures. The executive has less immunity from these pressures but does have real flexibility and freedom of action in comparison to the legislature, at least in the American system of separation of powers where the president is elected by the people and not by the ruling party.

The need for debate in the legislative arena has a number of distinct rationales. One of these can be appreciated by a comparative institutional analysis of the three branches of modern American government. The judicial branch is ill-suited to the task of adjudicating conflicting claims about distributive justice for a number of reasons. First, at the appellate level and at the level of the Supreme Court, the courts' central task is statutory or constitutional interpretation. However much some of these judges may conceive of their task as determining the demands of justice, their primary task is to determine what the law or the Constitution says. While it is often claimed that activist judges effectively rewrite the law, they are not starting from a blank slate in the way that legislators are. For example, when the Court upheld set-asides in *Fullilove v. Klutznick*, it was not in a position to address the abuses of these programs. Indeed, most of Chief Justice Warren Burger's majority opinion turned on procedural considerations about whether or not Congress had the authority to set up these programs, instead of on whether or not the legislation was wise or just.[69] Perhaps more importantly, although the process of judicial review is adversarial, judges are essentially answerable to no one. If they make

---

[69] *Fullilove v. Klutznick*, 448 U.S. 448 (1980).

a mistake, their rulings can be overturned at a higher level, but they are in no danger of losing their jobs, unlike members of Congress. Even the threat of having their rulings overturned on appeal is removed at the level of the Supreme Court. At most, they risk the obloquy and condemnation of people they generally neither respect nor admire. Moreover, at this level, justices need only seek the concurrence of four other people, whereas legislators answer to broad constituencies and need to line up the support of enough other legislators, as well as the executive, to pass a bill. This often allows and requires them to take more serious notice of opposition to their own views than the judiciary must.

What about the executive? Of course, the executive has to sign or veto legislation that passes both houses of Congress, but the issue here is unilateral executive action to implement the demands of justice as he sees them. The main obstacle to a full and fair hearing in the executive branch is that there is no institutionalized opposition to executive policy within this branch. Since high-level bureaucrats are hired to carry out policy, they obviously have an incentive to keep any doubts they might have about it to themselves. Unlike members of minority parties in Congress, who cannot be fired by the leadership of their own party, high-level bureaucrats serve at the president's pleasure. Moreover, presidents are free to submit legislation embodying social policy changes they favor to the Congress. If the requirements defended in this essay are observed, they will do this, rather than acting unilaterally.

Perhaps the most compelling reason to require the legislature to impose the demands of justice has to with the character of ownership rights in productive assets in the late twentieth century. Over the past century, the state has asserted limited ownership rights in all of society's productive assets, including its human capital, through the expansion of government's regulatory powers, tax powers, and fiscal and monetary policy. One of the main avenues of this socialization is through the simple growth in government expenditures. However much classical liberals may regret it, the state has socialized private property along many margins. For the most part, these state ownership rights have been asserted in the public interest. Whether members of the public in their role as taxpayers retain some residual ownership rights in the assets that have been socialized (as those on the political right are inclined to believe), or whether members of the public are conceived of as collective owners of these assets (as those on the left are inclined to believe), the public is the principal. If the public is the principal, the legislature (or the legislature in conjunction with the executive) is the most plausible candidate for the agent. The agent owes the principal an explanation of what it is doing with these assets when the agent seeks to violate its fiduciary duties in the name of justice—just as corporate officers owe the stockholders an explanation when they do something similar. For all these reasons, the legislative arena is the proper forum for formulating and implementing the demands of justice.

Having responded to the objection that the Public Justification and Anti-Hijacking requirements would, if followed, hinder progress toward justice, I turn now to a second objection: that the requirements ask too much of the legislature. There are two grounds on which this might be advanced. One is that it is asking too much, morally speaking, for proponents of a piece of legislation to detail all the people they are going to hurt with their bill, which is what the Anti-Hijacking requirement demands. Legislation is almost always presented as providing a Pareto-superior alternative to the existing order (i.e., an alternative in which some people are made better off and no one is made worse off), and while everyone recognizes that this is not really accurate, it is asking too much of the morally frail people we elect to public office to display fully the financial and human costs of their bills.

Perhaps this is true, but the burden of these requirements is collectively placed on the legislature, which includes the opposition. The latter certainly has substantial motivation to identify the unintended beneficiaries and victims, and indeed this was done, more or less clearly and forcefully, in the case of a number of the bills discussed in this essay. All one can ask of proponents of a given policy is that they take seriously the arguments of the other side when those arguments are made. Proponents of a policy are not, in the manner of academics, being asked to formulate objections to their own proposals. The dismissive attitude exhibited by liberal Democrats toward the opposition in the debate over the 1991 Civil Rights Act contrasts sharply with the respect Senator Humphrey and other liberal Democrats accorded their opponents in 1964, some of whom were racists and segregationists.

A second reason why it might be claimed that the Public Justification and Anti-Hijacking requirements ask too much is more cognitive than moral. Few individuals, it might be argued, are in a position to identify all the intended and unintended beneficiaries and victims of a proposed policy and to argue persuasively that the benefits of a piece of legislation outweigh its costs, all things considered. These requirements invite the practice of studying social problems to death in order to clear up doubts about the efficacy of the proposed legislation. Having to meet these requirements would place too heavy an argumentative burden on elected officials.

In considering this objection, it is important to distinguish the proper standards of debate from the question of expertise. Regarding the former, the standards really are quite modest. An intellectually serious argument does not engage in any of the following practices: (1) attacking the motives of the opposition; (2) assuming in one's premises the very thing to be proved in the conclusion; (3) making sweeping factual claims without any supporting evidence; or (4) denying the conclusion or a key premise in the opposition's argument without giving any reason why it is mistaken. There are undoubtedly other shoddy practices that should be avoided as well, many of which are learned on the campaign trail. However, elected officials need to wash after the election to remove the mud from their hands. When they step into the legislative arena, the intellectual standards are higher—but not excessively high. The overall standards of argumentation are no more than it is reasonable to expect of someone who has had a decent secondary school education, which most college graduates have. As to the question of expertise, the Congress has vast resources at its disposal and can and does avail itself of a variety of research services. In addition, to make a rationally persuasive case for something, it is not, strictly speaking, necessary to identify all of the beneficiaries and victims. Some categories of each may be partially or completely unknown and unknowable. It is possible for a legislator to acknowledge that the unintended beneficiaries and victims are not fully known. He can insist, however, that the costs are worth paying; and while such a claim may be hard to prove outright, it may nevertheless be reasonable to accept in a world in which all the facts will never be in. All that is required is that legislators try to identify as fully as is practicable the intended and unintended beneficiaries and victims of their policies.

As further evidence that the Public Justification and Anti-Hijacking requirements do not impose unreasonable demands, one need only look at the debate on Title VII of the Civil Rights Act in 1964. Opponents of the legislation as it was originally proposed raised concerns about unintended victims and beneficiaries that proponents made serious efforts to address. It might be doubted that the legislators of 1964 were more intelligent or virtuous than their 1991 counterparts. It is just that they had a tougher legislative row to hoe and actually had to persuade some other legislators to support them. Indeed, it would not be surprising to find that intellectually serious debate takes place only when there is no decisive voting majority on the issue. Politics is about power, and when one has the power, arguments are superfluous. However, this does not relieve legislators of their responsibilities to those who own society's productive assets, namely, the taxpayers and/or society at large.

A final objection to these requirements is that they are unjustifiably conservative because they put the burden of proof on those who advocate social change to meet the demands of justice, a burden that is not required of those who favor the status quo. The existing distribution of wealth and income is accepted as given, but it too requires justification. If defenders of the existing order bear no special burden of proof, neither do proponents of change. The problem with this objection is that it misconceives the context in which these requirements are proposed. That context is a normative theory of moderate social change, not a fundamental political philosophy. The scope and ambitions of the former are more modest than those of the latter. A political philosophy seeks to justify state institutions from the ground up, so to speak. It takes seriously the possibility that anarchism is the correct view about the moral and political justification of the state, and it may serve as a logical precursor to a radical theory of social change. A radical theory would have something to say about the circumstances under which revolutionary change is morally or politically justified, and about what means it might be permissible to employ in that struggle. On the other hand, a normative theory of moderate social change is about what ought to be done to modify—not destroy—existing institutions. As such, it takes existing institutions as given and seeks answers to questions about the legitimacy of social change within that framework. In other words, a moderate theory accepts the basic framework of the existing order (e.g., private ownership of the means of production) as morally legitimate and seeks to determine the circumstances and conditions under which nonradical change is justified. Some parts of this theory may engage larger issues in political philosophy, but other parts may not. The two requirements defended in this essay are parts of a normative theory of moderate social change which do not directly engage these larger issues. Although the aims of the theory as developed in this essay are relatively modest, it has obvious practical implications that more comprehensive political philosophies often lack. For all the intellectual grandeur of the comprehensive political philosophies of the twentieth century, few of them have readily identifiable practical implications. This apparent lack of practical implications supports a frequently voiced charge of irrelevance made against these theories.

The (partial) normative theory of social change presented in this essay implies that those who wish to abolish affirmative action now bear the burden of proof, given the existing realities of the law. They wish to change the distribution of wealth and income in the name of justice by eliminating minority set-asides and by repealing the offending sections of the 1991 amendments to Title VII of the Civil Rights Act. However, they must do so in a way that meets the Public Justification and Anti-Hijacking requirements. This would take a modest amount of political courage, but if their view of the matter is correct, justice demands nothing less.

Philosophy, University of Alabama at Birmingham

THE DUAL ROLE OF PROPERTY RIGHTS IN
PROTECTING BROADCAST SPEECH

By Thomas W. Hazlett

Congress shall make no law . . . abridging the freedom of speech, or
of the press. . . .

First Amendment, U.S. Constitution

Freedom of the press is guaranteed only to those who own one.

A. J. Liebling[1]

I. Who Should the First Amendment to the
U.S. Constitution Constrain?

The connection between property rights and free-speech rights has
most often surfaced in conflicts between the two. In his classic formulation of the problem, journalist A. J. Liebling mocked the First Amendment's free-press clause by noting that ownership of a printing press was
required in order to actually enjoy the constitutional protection. In an
important case decided in 1980, *Pruneyard Shopping Center v. Robins*,[2] the
U.S. Supreme Court ruled that a group wishing to circulate political pe-
titions at a shopping center had a constitutional right to do so. There the
Court found that such governmentally enforced access to private property did "not amount to an unconstitutional infringement of [the shopping center owners'] property rights under the Taking Clause of the Fifth
Amendment. . . ."[3]

In either of the two examples, Liebling's much-quoted aphorism or the
Supreme Court's adjudication of a real-world conflict, the concern expressed is that free speech may be limited by "private censorship." Where
those who own property used for communication (whether printing
presses, radio or television transmitters, cable TV plant, software, telephone or computer networks, sidewalks in a shopping mall, or satellite
facilities) are free to exercise editorial control over what "content" is
communicated, the argument is made that affirmative government action

---

[1] Quoted in Richard Kluger, *The Paper: The Life and Death of the NY Herald Tribune* (New
York: Alfred A. Knopf, 1986).

[2] *Pruneyard Shopping Center v. Robins*, 447 U.S. 74 (1980).

[3] The Fifth Amendment to the U.S. Constitution reads, in part: "[N]or shall private property be taken for public use, without just compensation." This protection of individual
property rights against state action is a crucial component of civil liberty. See Richard A.
Epstein, *Takings* (Cambridge, MA: Harvard University Press, 1985).

is required to limit the editorial discretion of the owner. While this might seem, at first blush, to violate the First Amendment's protection of freedom of the press, or to constitute a taking of private property, the argument is made that the spirit of the First Amendment is best served by government regulation which counters "private censorship."[4]

This rationale for regulation has recently been re-endorsed by the U.S. Supreme Court in *Turner Broadcasting System, Inc., et al. v. Federal Communications Commission et al.* (1997).[5] Here the Court found that Congress did not violate the First Amendment rights of cable TV systems by mandating that such systems carry all local, over-the-air broadcast TV signals to subscribers ("must carry" rules), even though such a mandate indisputably crowds out competing cable TV networks. Since the federal government specifically argued that it sought to protect broadcasting stations (licensed in the "public interest") due to the informational content, and diversity of expression, that such stations brought to viewers, the Court's decision upholding "must carry" rules legitimized regulation which protects some forms of expression over others, as ranked by Congress's estimate of the "public interest."[6]

This approach to enforcing First Amendment protections for Americans is fraught with hazard, as the practical outcome of the "must carry" episode convincingly demonstrates. The marginal TV stations that are granted cable-system carriage via "must carry" rules typically offer duplicate programming (virtually all network signals are carried at least once by cable systems voluntarily), sitcom reruns (as is the case with little-watched independent stations), or home shopping, all services which elicit little interest from actual viewers. (Indeed, if the channels did elicit viewer interest, they would not need "must carry" rules to convince cable operators to include them on system program menus.)[7] On the other hand, the cable television networks which have been dislodged to make room for such viewing fare include such popular viewing alternatives as Discovery and C-SPAN, a public-affairs channel which lost carriage (either full or part-time, counting C-SPAN1 and C-SPAN2) in 7 million

[4] Cass Sunstein, a leading proponent of this school, argues in favor of a "New Deal for speech." This entails a First Amendment which is not seen as an impediment to government regulation of speech; rather, he sees "the possibility that government controls on the broadcast media, designed to ensure diversity of view and attention to public affairs, would help the system of free expression." Cass Sunstein, *Democracy and the Problem of Free Speech* (New York: The Free Press, 1993), p. xix.

[5] *Turner Broadcasting System, Inc., et al. v. Federal Communications Commission et al.*, 117 S.Ct. 1174 (1997).

[6] The case did not concern the takings aspect of the "must carry" rules, despite the appropriation of private property (channel capacity on cable TV systems created and owned by private investors). Rather, the constitutional issue concerned the First Amendment rights of the broadcasters seeking carriage versus the First Amendment rights of the cable TV operator.

[7] "It is undisputed that the broadcast stations protected by 'must carry' are the 'marginal' stations within a broadcast market," wrote Justice Sandra Day O'Connor in her dissenting opinion in *Turner*.

households following the 1992 Cable Act (in which the "must carry" rules in question were enacted). Hence, the Court's ruling effectively embodied a preference for the expression broadcast in the older medium and against the discourse featured in the newer. This peculiar revealed preference (favoring old sitcom reruns and home shopping over the diverse and often public-affairs-oriented programming of new cable networks) made the empirical basis of the decision ironic.[8]

In the conventional discourse it is possible to identify two distinct views of the First Amendment as applied to electronic media. The view now dominant[9] on the U.S. Supreme Court finds that property interests are subordinate to free-speech interests, and that the free-speech rights of owners of property used to supply communications are legitimately subject to extensive government regulation. The issue was framed as follows in the 1997 *Turner* decision. When reviewing a government regulation concerning speech or expression, the Court's inquiry first decides what level of scrutiny the law (enacted by the legislature or an administrative body) should receive. The highest standard is one of "strict scrutiny," meaning that the law must serve a "compelling state interest" and be narrowly tailored to achieve that goal. The Supreme Court is very likely to strike a law down as unconstitutional when it applies this "strict scrutiny" test. As a practical matter, this standard is triggered when the regulation in question is found not to be "content-neutral," meaning that it favors some forms of expression over others. The one categorical exception is broadcasting, which receives a lower level of constitutional protection from government regulation due to the Court's "physical scarcity" doctrine, the belief that the use of radio waves for communications presents unique problems for policymakers.[10]

Broadcast regulations are examined by the Court under a less rigorous "intermediate scrutiny" test. Here, "[a] content neutral regulation will be sustained under the First Amendment if it advances important governmental interests unrelated to the suppression of free speech and does not burden substantially more speech than necessary to further those interests."[11] One important aspect of this standard is that the Court has shown

---

[8] Thomas W. Hazlett, "The Cubic Zirconia Court," *Reason*, vol. 29, no. 2 (June 1997), p. 66.

[9] The view is only marginally dominant, since *Turner* was decided by a slim 5-to-4 majority. Moreover, the author of the dissent, Justice O'Connor, has made clear her opposition to the burden which the majority opinion placed on private market institutions to provide a "multiplicity" of voices. In dissenting to the previous decision rendered in the *Turner* case by the Supreme Court in 1994, she wrote: "But the First Amendment as we understand it today rests on the premise that it is government power, rather than private power, that is the main threat to freedom of expression; and as a consequence, the Amendment imposes substantial limitations on the Government even when it is trying to serve concededly praiseworthy goals." *Turner Broadcasting System, Inc. v. FCC*, 114 S.Ct. 2445, 2480 (1994).

[10] *NBC v. United States*, 319 U.S. 190 (1943); *Red Lion Broadcasting Co. v. FCC*, 395 U.S. 367 (1969). See also Thomas W. Hazlett, "Physical Scarcity, Rent-seeking, and the First Amendment," *Columbia Law Review*, vol. 97, no. 4 (May 1997), pp. 905–44.

[11] *Turner Broadcasting System, Inc., et al. v. Federal Communications Commission et al.*, 117 S.Ct. 1174, 1186 (1997).

a willingness to define as "content-neutral" rules which clearly favor some speakers (and speech) over others. In the *Turner* case, the majority opinion "referred to the 'unusually detailed statutory findings' accompanying the Act, in which Congress recognized the importance of preserving sources of local news, public affairs, and educational programming."[12] This clearly stated congressional preference for broadcast speech over cable-cast speech did not, to the Court, breach content-neutrality.

While the Court majority in *Turner* claimed to apply "intermediate scrutiny," the decision reveals how quickly even that soft standard can give way once the government regulation in question comes to be viewed as *economic* regulation, rather than as a question of free speech. With economic regulations, the Court almost always applies only a "rational basis" test, the least restrictive standard of constitutionality. This level of scrutiny makes it virtually impossible to overturn a regulation, since the Court is highly deferential to Congress's determination that the regulation serves a legitimate governmental purpose, and the Court does not engage in its own, independent inquiry. The Court limits its review, under this most lenient test, to whether the means Congress chose could reasonably be thought to further the end. As Justice Anthony Kennedy wrote for the majority: "The question is not whether Congress, as an objective matter, was correct to determine must-carry is necessary to prevent a substantial number of broadcast stations from losing cable carriage and suffering significant financial hardship. Rather, the question is whether the legislative conclusion was reasonable and supported by substantial evidence in the record before Congress. . . ."[13]

Supreme Court doctrine is even more confusing than this, because the Court has not adopted universal standards for free-speech cases across different media. With respect to government controls on the content of traditional media such as books, magazines, and the print press, even content-neutral rules will be quickly dismissed as unconstitutional.[14] Yet when the speech is relayed via the airwaves or cable, the Court is much more agreeable to congressional regulation. The Court has overruled the 1996 Communications Decency Act as overbroad in regulating speech over the internet,[15] a very interesting finding in that the transmission technology involved spans telephone, cable television, and radio (wireless) frequencies—a fact that, in other contexts, has led to substantially reduced constitutional standing. While *Turner* does not settle the law, then, it loudly broadcasts the Court's willingness to entertain a "broad"

[12] *Ibid.*, dissenting opinion of Justice Sandra Day O'Connor, p. 1206, quoting the 1994 *Turner* opinion by the Supreme Court (114 S.Ct. 2461).

[13] *Turner Broadcasting System, Inc., et al. v. Federal Communications Commission et al.*, 117 S.Ct. 1174, 1196 (1997).

[14] In the 1974 *Miami Herald* decision, the Court found arguments regarding market power in the newspaper business to be beside the point: government was barred by the plain language of the First Amendment from imposing equal-time rules on newspapers. *Miami Herald Publishing Co. v. Tornillo*, 418 U.S. 241 (1974).

[15] *Reno v. ACLU*, 117 S.Ct. 2329 (1997).

view of the First Amendment that makes large exceptions in the "Congress shall make no law" mandate for rules which can be characterized as "only" economic. As Justice Kennedy wrote: "Judgments about how competing economic interests are to be reconciled in the complex and changing field of television are for Congress to make. Those judgments 'cannot be ignored or undervalued simply because [appellants] cas[t] [their] claims under the umbrella of the First Amendment.'"[16] Hence, the freedom of cable television operators to exercise editorial control over the programming offered on their systems can be "abridged," so long as the government is able to state a plausible case that the regulations it imposes have some public purpose.

The underlying premise of this legal and philosophical construct is that the danger presented by "private censorship" can and should be remedied by state action,[17] even if such action clearly abridges the free speech of some citizens, and even if the attempted intervention results in policies which demonstrably fail to achieve stated goals.[18] (The regulatory undertakings need only be "reasonable.")[19] This view is strongly held by politically disparate factions: conservatives sympathetic to legislative action and hostile to judicial review,[20] Galbraithian advocates of big government as a counter to private market power,[21] and leftist critics hostile to the for-profit basis of American organs of the press, particularly in broadcasting.[22]

---

[16] *Turner Broadcasting System, Inc., et al. v. Federal Communications Commission et al.*, 117 S.Ct. 1174, 1203 (1997) (end of Justice Anthony Kennedy's opinion); quoting *Columbia Broadcasting v. Democratic National Committee*, 412 U.S. 103 (1973).

[17] In the *Turner* case, the "private censorship" involved the decision by cable operators to favor cable-originated programming over broadcast TV stations. The Court found that such choices would significantly deprive broadcasters of market share, and thereby endanger the choices of viewers who wanted to watch broadcast TV—especially in those 30 percent of U.S. households that do not subscribe to cable or satellite TV services.

[18] The Court was not swayed (or even heavily influenced, it seems) by the government's own study of the "must carry" matter. Analysts at the Federal Trade Commission found that consumers were well-served by abolition of the "must carry" rules (which had been struck down by two federal appellate courts in the 1980s). Rather than use their market power to exclude rivals for audience (and advertiser) share, cable systems which dropped broadcasting signals in the wake of "must carry" deregulation were found to be primarily searching for programming more in demand by the viewing public. See Michael G. Vita and John P. Wiegand, "Must-Carry Regulations for Cable Television Systems: An Economic Policy Analysis," *Journal of Broadcasting and Electronic Media*, vol. 37 (Winter 1993), pp. 1–19.

[19] While the *Turner* decision strikes a pose for a higher standard early on, claiming to be subjecting the government's "must carry" rules to "intermediate scrutiny" demanding narrow tailoring to provide content-neutral remedies, the standard of review actually employed closely resembles a "rational basis" test—as would be used in a straight economic regulation case.

[20] See, e.g., the recent volume by conservative legal scholar Robert Bork, *Slouching Towards Gomorrah: Modern Liberalism and American Decline* (New York: Regan Books, 1996), which endorses more-ambitious government regulation of movies, records, and television programs.

[21] The most detailed legal argument for government regulation of the U.S. press, a case made generically for print and electronic media, has been published by Jerome Barron; see, e.g., Barron, "Access to the Press—A New First Amendment Right," *Harvard Law Review*, vol. 80 (1967), pp. 1641–78.

[22] See, e.g., Thomas Streeter, *Selling the Air* (Chicago: University of Chicago Press, 1996).

I noted earlier that there are two main views of the First Amendment in the conventional discourse. The second view adheres to a more literal meaning of the First Amendment, and strikes a libertarian pose against government regulation of the press. The position, while grounded in a strict-constructionist approach to constitutional law, ironically has not been most associated with "strict constructionists." Indeed, the late Supreme Court justices William O. Douglas and Hugo Black are typically associated with this "absolutist" school.[23] "No law," observed Justice Black as he eyed the First Amendment, "means no law."[24] Wrote Douglas: "The purpose of the Constitution and Bill of Rights, unlike more recent models promoting a welfare state, was to take government off the backs of people. The First Amendment's ban against Congress 'abridging' freedom of speech . . . create[s] a preserve where the views of the individual are made inviolate."[25]

This position has a number of utilitarian adherents, analysts who have essentially given up on the ability of broadcast regulation to actually achieve "public interest" outcomes.[26] It has thus been influential with economists who have analyzed the actual policies crafted in the "public interest," as well as the performance of regulated broadcast markets.[27] In addition, a Madisonian argument in favor of interpreting the First Amendment as a property right has recently reemerged from the legal literature.[28] This perspective cites both philosophical and practical arguments for equating property rights and speech rights in a "leveling up" process

---

[23] See Sunstein, *Democracy and the Problem of Free Speech*, p. 7; and Ithiel de Sola Pool, *Technologies of Freedom* (Cambridge, MA: Harvard University Press, 1983), p. 55. It is safe to say that Justices William O. Douglas and Hugo Black, in that order, were the *bêtes noires* of American conservatives in the 1950s through the 1970s. The conservative critique was that "activist" judges (such as Douglas and Black) were making their own law, and ignoring—or striking down—that of duly elected legislatures. See Bork, *Slouching Towards Gomorrah*, pp. 96–102.

[24] *Smith v. California*, 361 U.S. 147, 4 L.ed. 2d 205, 80 S.Ct. 215 in concurrence.

[25] *Schneider v. Smith*, 390 U.S. 17, 25 (1968).

[26] Henry Geller, a former FCC General Counsel and Assistant Secretary of Commerce, is a well-known exemplar of this view. Writes a chastened Geller, a onetime champion for aggressive regulation of the content of broadcasting and cable companies: "In my view, the public trustee scheme has failed. It has not been effective in achieving its goals and has engendered serious First Amendment concerns." Geller, "The Role of Future Regulation: Licensing, Spectrum Allocation, Content, Access, Common Carrier, and Rates," in Eli Noam, ed., *Video Media Competition* (New York: Columbia University Press, 1985), p. 296. See also Pool, *Technologies of Freedom*; and Thomas G. Krattenmaker and Lucas A. Powe, Jr., *Regulating Broadcast Programming* (Cambridge, MA: MIT Press, 1994).

[27] Ronald Coase, "Evaluation of Public Policy Relating to Radio and Television Broadcasting: Social and Economic Issues," *Land Economics*, vol. 41 (1965), pp. 161–67; Bruce M. Owen, Jack H. Beebe, and Willard G. Manning, Jr., *Television Economics* (Lexington, MA: Lexington Books, 1974).

[28] John O. McGinnis, "The Once and Future Property-Based Vision of the First Amendment," *University of Chicago Law Review*, vol 63 (Winter 1996), pp. 49–132. Sunstein (in *Democracy and the Problem of Free Speech*) also attempts a Madisonian reconstruction of First Amendment law, but it is a linear extrapolation of Madison's utilitarianism (free speech is healthy for democracy) which ignores Madison's outspoken endorsement of the free-speech clause as an "absolute reservation" (James Madison, *Writings*, ed. Gaillard Hunt [New York: G. P. Putnam's Sons, 1906], p. 39).

that affords the former the higher level of protection afforded the latter under prevailing precedents.[29]

This essay will specifically deal with one quintessentially important information media: the broadcast press. Wireless communications have been a key concern of federal regulators in the United States since even before the 1927 Radio Act,[30] and television and radio broadcasters continue to attract substantial attention from policymakers today. Such stations, licensed according to "public interest, convenience, or necessity," are the most heavily regulated organs of the press, since the courts have carved out special rationales for why the use of radio waves reduces traditional First Amendment protections for "electronic publishers."[31] Because the distinct treatment of broadcast speech has opened up opportunities for government to regulate all manner of electronic communications (to wit, the "must carry" regulations imposed on cable TV systems, which do not transmit over radio frequencies in the "air"), and because all forms of electronic speech are likely to become far more important practically and economically in the years to come, analyzing the rights afforded to those who communicate via radio waves focuses the analysis on a key aspect of public policy in the information age. As the late MIT political scientist Ithiel de Sola Pool identified the fundamental policy choice in the conclusion of his classic 1983 treatise *Technologies of Freedom*:

> Will public interest regulation, such as the FCC [Federal Communications Commission] applies, begin to extend over the conduct of the print media as they increasingly use regulated electronic means of dissemination? Or will concern for the traditional notion of a free press lead to finding ways to free the broadcast media and carriers from the regulation and content-related requirements under which they now operate?[32]

The practical argument characterizing property rights as integral to the protection of free speech (abstracting from the philosophical libertarian defense of individual rights) rests on the positive social consequences

[29] McGinnis approvingly cites Steven Shiffrin, "The Politics of the Mass Media and the Free Speech Principle," *Indiana Law Journal*, vol. 69 (1994), p. 716, as "concluding that the free speech principle is more 'solidly anchored' in our culture than ever before" (McGinnis, "Once and Future," p. 50).

[30] The 1927 Radio Act established the system of spectrum allocation and licensing "according to public interest, convenience and necessity." This regulatory system yet prevails in the United States, although the Federal Radio Commission (authorized in the 1927 act) was replaced by the Federal Communications Commission (with authority broadened to include interstate telephony and other wireline communications) in the 1934 Communications Act.

[31] The most important Supreme Court cases are *NBC v. United States*, 319 U.S. 190 (1943); and *Red Lion Broadcasting Co. v. FCC*, 395 U.S. 367 (1969).

[32] Pool, *Technologies of Freedom*, p. 251.

flowing from decentralization of influence and economic decision-making.[33] The decentralization view advocates a property-rights approach to free broadcast speech as proper in that it allows competitive forces to deliver information which consumers actually demand, while blocking the government's penchant for controlling information.[34] The power-decentralization rationale stands in stark contrast to the alternative view that "public interest" licensing of electronic media can improve social life, since such a regime depends on administrative processes to deduce, mandate, and enforce specific market outcomes.

The importance of decentralization will be illustrated by examining the nature and historical construction of property rights to radio spectrum in the United States. The history of such rights shows how the system of "public interest" licensing developed in the Radio Act of 1927, and continued essentially intact ever since, intentionally preempted the common-law spectrum rights then emerging. A natural experiment was effectively conducted in the U.S. radio market in the years immediately following the shift from a quasi-property-rights regime (1920–1927) to one relying on central administration of airwave access (post-1927), an experiment which reveals the relative hospitality of the alternative regimes toward a multiplicity of viewpoints. Specifically, the economic success of nonprofit radio broadcasters under the newly enacted "public interest" standard can be examined to gauge the degree to which radio-station licensing fostered diverse sources of expression.

After stating a normative case for property rights in the radio spectrum based upon the results of a positive analysis, I will attempt to draw out a rich irony which appears to have escaped notice: the current system, which severely truncates *de jure* property rights over communications media, results in excessively generous *de facto* property rights.[35] Thus,

---

[33] This view is well articulated in McGinnis, "Once and Future." McGinnis argues strongly that additional rationales favor a property-rights approach, including the strong influence of John Locke and natural law on James Madison, who crafted the First Amendment.

[34] Whether unregulated markets will be sufficiently competitive to deliver the full benefits of decentralized decision-making is a matter for study (and often intense debate) in particular sectors. Yet it is widely conceded that generic policy remedies exist (most notably, antitrust as it is called in the United States, competition policy as it is often called elsewhere) and may be applied separate and apart from any direct regulation of speech.

[35] The extent to which this important point causes confusion in contemporary analyses can be seen in a recent paper by Kristilyn Corbett, "The Rise of Private Property Rights in the Broadcast Spectrum," *Duke Law Journal*, vol. 46 (December 1996), pp. 611–50. The article is correct to note that the U.S. courts have long held that "[t]he policy of the [1934 Communications] Act is clear that no person is to have anything in the nature of a property right as a result of the granting of a license" (quoting from the Supreme Court's decision in *FCC v. Sanders Brothers Radio Station*, 309 U.S. 470 [1940]). It is also correct to note that in recent years, parties holding FCC licenses have petitioned for and sometimes won targeted rule changes which effectively relax government regulation of licensee behavior. But the analysis seriously errs in taking this development as synonymous with an increase in private property rights and a decline of the "public trust" system. That is because a policy regime switch to private property rights in the radio spectrum would allow entrants—not just licensed incumbents—to access radio waves where such entry did not interfere with existing uses. Not only does the system

too-lucrative properties are held by licensed media firms—firms which voluntarily divest themselves of their First Amendment rights, engaging in "gains from trade" with policymakers. These gains are embedded within the "social compact" regulators establish with broadcast licensees, an implicit contract that shields incumbent interests from competitive entry. This outcome not only lessens the free-speech rights of potential entrants who are denied access to markets, but also lessens those of incumbents, who operate under incentives not to engage in types of expression held to be controversial by policymakers. Government control of speech is furthered, while consumer welfare is lessened. In a dynamic world, specially configured property rights for electronic media invite aggressive rent-seeking[36] by private interests attempting to profit by influencing regulation (decided on a case-by-case basis, where the general rule of law has been abandoned). While the social costs of rent-seeking can be substantial, the most damaging outcome of departing from a property-rights-based regulation of electronic speech (as clearly demonstrated in the case of the broadcast press) is that private interests become adept at crafting regulatory deals with policymakers in which free speech is traded for economic protection.

The central policy conclusion of this essay is of immense importance in ongoing efforts to liberalize telecommunications policy: Expanding the private property rights held by communications service providers (that is, wireless licensees) will, ironically, tend to have a *negative* impact on asset values of such service providers. In other words, broadcasters could suffer a windfall loss if they were to be suddenly awarded (even free of charge) complete use of the radio spectrum assigned to their service.[37] This is because an expansion of licensees' effective property rights to utilize radio waves will increase the amount of competition faced by incumbent licenses (both from other incumbents and from new entrants). This is both a powerful argument in its favor normatively, and a powerful

---

of "public interest" regulation still prohibit free entry into wireless markets, that system is strongly supported by broadcasters (and other current FCC licensees) which benefit from the entry barriers in place. Hence, the rights which incumbents seek to expand are not, strictly speaking, private property rights, but greater latitude under rules crafted in the "public interest."

[36] Rent-seeking is a subset of economic competition; specifically, competition for a fixed pie. This is in contrast to more traditional market competition, where rivals compete by offering customers better prices and/or higher quality. Rent-seeking involves rivalry to obtain a monopoly or special economic position; a classic rent-seeking example would involve competition between potential radio broadcasters to procure a government-issued radio license. See Anne O. Krueger, "The Political Economy of the Rent Seeking Society," *American Economic Review*, vol. 64 (June 1974), pp. 291–303.

[37] This would, in essence, give private broadcasters flexibility to do anything with the bandwidth assigned to radio or television service so long as it does not interfere with other transmissions. Currently there exist severe restrictions placed on what types of signals broadcasters emit; vast bandwidth—within the "broadcasting band"—is protected from use by any party; and business practices (including editorial control) are regulated in detail by the Federal Communications Commission.

positive argument against liberalization actually being realized. While the introduction of competition will clearly stimulate the free flow of information, the incentives for potential entrants to lobby for such reform are clearly weaker than the incentives of incumbents to lobby against it. This paradox of public policy is not an unusual state of affairs. What is unusual is the popular and scholarly misunderstanding within the policy debate that extending *de jure* property rights would result in a beneficial "windfall" to industry incumbents.

II. THE EMPIRICAL CASE FOR DECENTRALIZATION VIA DE JURE PROPERTY RIGHTS IN U.S. RADIO

A. Replacing priority-in-use property rights with "public interest" licensing

The United States government has not asserted ownership of radio spectrum. Indeed, the late Senator Clarence C. Dill (D-WA), author of both the 1927 Radio Act and the 1934 Communications Act,[38] thought the issue quite irrelevant: "[I]t makes no difference who owns the air or who claims to own channels in the air. The thing that is really controlling is the right to use apparatus which sends the radio impulses into the air."[39] The Federal Radio Commission quickly adopted the position that the government could not even define the spectrum resource, much less assert ownership: "The ether is an hypothetical medium. There is no satisfactory definition of it. It is not even known to exist."[40]

The justification for regulation proceeds not from the premise of government ownership of the allegedly indefinable "ether," but from the assertion that the airwaves are owned collectively by the people of the United States. The government merely regulates access to the "public's airwaves" as a protection against the chaos which would result from unrestricted signal interference. As Senator Dill stated the case for regulation in congressional debate just days prior to the enactment of the 1927 Radio Act:

> The Government does not own the frequencies, as we call them, or the use of frequencies. It only possesses the right to regulate the

[38] These acts established the current regime in the United States, where an independent regulatory agency of the federal government issues broadcasting licenses according to "public interest" criteria. It should be noted that FCC license auctions, authorized by Congress in 1993, are used *only* for nonbroadcast services such as cellular telephones and paging. See Thomas W. Hazlett, "Assigning Property Rights to Radio Spectrum Users: Why Did FCC License Auctions Take 67 Years?" paper delivered at the Marconi Center Conference on the Law and Economics of Property Rights to Radio Spectrum (July 1996).

[39] *Congressional Record*, vol. 68 (February 3, 1927), p. 2871.

[40] Federal Radio Commission brief in *General Electric Co. v. Federal Radio Commission*, 58 Appeals DC 386 (1929), p. 148; cited in General Electric's brief to the U.S. Supreme Court in response to a request for writ of certiorari filed by the Federal Radio Commission (December 1929), p. 47.

apparatus, and that right is obtained from the provision of the Constitution which gives Congress the power to regulate interstate commerce.[41]

The abundant use of the terms "spectrum auctions" and "spectrum rights" as descriptors of current (circa 1998) government policy reveals not a semantic problem, but an analytical mistake. Because the Federal Communications Commission (FCC) does not allow spectrum to be allocated by market forces, we do not observe market prices for spectrum. Instead, the FCC auctions operating licenses for various (nonbroadcasting) wireless services, where bidders offering the highest dollar prices obtain the right to use assigned frequencies according to the terms specified in the license. This is distinct from an auction of spectrum property rights, where winning bidders would determine the use of frequencies. Spectrum would then be allocated by market forces, and not according to "public interest" regulation.

The confusion over the difference between "spectrum rights" and the "use permits" issued by the Federal Communications Commission is a confusion of substance. That is, the regulatory path chosen by Congress in the 1927 Radio Act, and repeated in the 1934 Communications Act, was to explicitly reject a system of private property rights, opting instead for licenses configured as operating permits in place of a system of spectrum rights.[42] The key concern of Congress in passing these two acts was, in fact, to avert the courts from applying common-law principles which would have granted broadcasters legally enforceable property rights.[43] This was certainly the view expressed by the author of both pieces of legislation, Senator Dill, as revealed in a book he wrote upon retiring from the U.S. Senate.[44]

Dill's description of the events leading up to the Radio Act of 1927 is a most valuable source regarding the legislative history of spectrum-access licensing. Dill noted that the original radio-station broadcasters were protected in their frequency assignments by a "long established principle of law that if a citizen openly and adversely possesses and uses property for a long period of time without opposition, or without contest, he acquires

---

[41] *Congressional Record*, vol. 68 (February 3, 1927), p. 2870. Note that this rationale for regulation is consistent with the "collective ownership" rationale in that "public ownership" is distinct from "government ownership."

[42] Despite the "ceiling to attic" rewrite of the 1934 Communications Act which was enacted as the Telecommunications Act of 1996, spectrum allocation was not reformed in any substantial aspect. Indeed, broadcasters won further protections against auctions for TV or radio licenses.

[43] See Thomas W. Hazlett, "The Rationality of U.S. Regulation of the Broadcast Spectrum," *Journal of Law and Economics*, vol. 33 (April 1990), pp. 133–75.

[44] Clarence C. Dill, *Radio Law: Practice and Procedure* (Washington, DC: National Law Book Company, 1938), pp. 77–81.

title by adverse possession."[45] Dill called this "property by right of user." Dill described how these rights were being asserted by radio broadcasters and had been recognized in an important common-law decision granting a private property right to a radio broadcaster protecting its airspace from interference.[46] The motive of Congress in passing the Radio Act in February 1927 is described in a section entitled "Why Congress Became Aroused on Subject":

> The development of these claims of vested rights in radio frequencies had caused many members of Congress to fear that this one and only remaining public domain in the form of free radio communication might soon be lost unless Congress protected it by legislation. It caused renewed demand for the assertion of full sovereignty over radio by Congress.[47]

The response of Congress to the burgeoning legal reality was to legislate away "these claims of vested interests," first in a resolution (December 1926) that all broadcasters must waive any and all vested rights, and then in the Radio Act (which became law on February 23, 1927). As detailed in a law review article some years later, the congressional legislation

> required a licensee to sign a waiver indicating that "there shall be no vested property right in the license issued for such station or in the frequencies or wave lengths authorized to be used thereon." . . . The Commission, fearful that licensees would assert property interests in their coverage to the listening public, has inserted elaborate provisions in application forms precluding the assertion of any such right.[48]

The concern over vested rights in radio frequencies was widespread. In noting that Congress explicitly rejected a proposed amendment to the Radio Act which would have paid existing radio broadcasters monetary compensation for frequencies taken away under enactment of "public interest" licensing, Dill notes that the measure (and its rejection) "shows that the purpose of Congress from the beginning of consideration concerning broadcasting was to prevent private ownership of wave lengths or vested rights of any kind in the use of radio transmitting apparatus."[49]

[45] *Ibid.*, p. 78 (footnote omitted).
[46] *Tribune Co. v. Oak Leaves Broadcasting Station, Inc.* (Cir. Ct., Cook County, Ill. 1926), reprinted in *Congressional Record*, vol. 68 (1926), p. 216.
[47] Dill, *Radio Law*, p. 80.
[48] Paul M. Segal and Harry P. Warner, "Ownership of Broadcasting Frequencies: A Review," *Rocky Mountain Law Review*, vol. 19 (1947), pp. 113, 121.
[49] Dill, *Radio Law*, p. 81.

The system of regulation adopted was to enlist private capital as an expedient, but to maintain strict federal authority over the airwaves. As Dill's book sums up the result (in a section entitled "The Alpha and Omega of Radio Law"):

> Instead of establishing government owned and government oper-
> ated radio stations as most other great nations have done, Congress
> has adopted a policy of permitting private individuals to own and
> operate radio stations. But Congress provided that these privately
> owned and privately operated radio stations should be subject to a
> system of government regulation.
>
> Congress desired to secure the use of private funds and, most of
> all, the benefit of individual initiative for the more rapid develop-
> ment of the radio art, but all of this development to be kept under
> government control.
>
> The means and method of administering and enforcing this sys-
> tem of government control is the radio license.[50]

The regulatory story comes full circle, for the control which Dill details as Congress's essential motivation, could only be accomplished via a licensing scheme which focused on the physical transmitting equipment itself. Hence, Dill finds the regulatory approach adopted to be a utilitarian outcome dictated by Congress's desire to control radio broadcast content. In discussing the "right to use radio apparatus," he is careful to differentiate between spectrum rights (which Congress determined can only belong to the people of the United States as a whole) and the use of, or access to, the spectrum resource. To wit:

> The right to use radio apparatus is often popularly termed "the use
> of the ether." In this sense "the ether" has been called the last public
> domain belonging to the people of the United States. Congress has
> been extremely desirous of retaining control of that public domain,
> but the only way to do that has been to control the use of radio
> apparatus.[51]

Hence, just as the contemporary debate is confused by the reference to "spectrum auctions" or "spectrum licenses" or "spectrum rights," the popular language in Dill's era was given to "the use of the ether." Dill specifically notes that the way Congress chose to control the communi-cations medium generally was to control each piece of transmitting equip-ment quite specifically, through the FCC license. The radio spectrum itself

[50] *Ibid.*, p. 127.
[51] *Ibid.*, pp. 126–27.

was not considered the property of private citizens, nor of the state; indeed, oil leases and rights to other tangible goods "can not be considered as analogous to the use of radio apparatus."[52] The result was a highly inefficient, centrally planned allocation system—a system of spectrum regulation which the United States still experiences today. It is fundamentally important to understand that this regulatory paradigm was chosen due to its political attributes, not due to economic efficiency. In particular, the commonly asserted view that federal licensing under the 1927 Radio Act was initiated to quell radio broadcasting interference, and that reform of current institutions to provide for greater market competition would again lead to chaos in the airwaves, is merely a seemingly persuasive myth.[53]

B. Public interest advocates choose government over the market

In the debate surrounding the "public interest" licensing regime enacted in the 1927 Radio Act, three major interest groups have been identified as influential: incumbent radio-station owners, key radio policymakers (including Secretary of Commerce Herbert C. Hoover and Senator Dill), and "public interest" advocates.[54] While the degree to which the public advocates influenced the legislative outcome is unclear, what is well-documented is the degree to which those who championed regulation as a remedy for "private censorship" selected a public policy strategy of licensing in the "public interest." Indeed, legislation was helped through Congress by pressure from the nonprofit sector, after two rival measures (one sponsored by Senator Dill, the other by Representative W. H. White, Jr. [R-ME]) became stalled. At this point, the Association of College and University Broadcasting Stations "tried to profit from the deadlock . . . [via] preferential treatment in the assignment of wavelengths and the division of time."[55] When this group, like the great majority of nonprofit lobbyists, endorsed the Dill bill, it was enacted into law. With the advantage of hindsight and an excellent historical account of the period just following the Radio Act,[56] we can now judge how well the strategy paid off in terms of the goals which the public interest advocates themselves set for the policy.

[52] Comments of Senator C. C. Dill, *Congressional Record*, vol. 68 (February 5, 1927), p. 3027.
[53] See Thomas W. Hazlett, "Physical Scarcity, Rent-Seeking, and the First Amendment," *Columbia Law Review*, vol. 97, no. 4 (May 1997), pp. 905–44.
[54] Hazlett, "The Rationality of U.S. Regulation of the Broadcast Spectrum" (*supra* note 43), pp. 152–65.
[55] Philip T. Rosen, *The Modern Stentors: Radio Broadcasters and the Federal Government, 1920–34* (Westport, CN: Greenwood Press, 1980), p. 99.
[56] Robert W. McChesney, *Telecommunications, Mass Media, and Democracy* (New York: Oxford University Press, 1994).

Perhaps the most succinct manner in which to appropriately frame the issue is to focus on the position and supporting arguments advanced by the American Civil Liberties Union. The ACLU was extremely active in the debate in the 1920s over radio policy, and its general counsel Morris Ernst wrote (and testified) widely on the matter.[57] Important leaders of the organization were informed and outspoken on virtually all aspects of the broadcasting regulation question.

It is also instructive that the ACLU endured a tense debate over the issue within its ranks. As Ernst noted: "Nothing has ever divided believers in the Bill of Rights as sharply as the question of radio."[58] The ACLU fault line ran along the jagged edge dividing "private censorship" from government control: "As early as 1926," communications scholar Robert W. McChesney writes in his 1994 book *Telecommunications, Mass Media, and Democracy*,

> the ACLU was sympathetic to criticisms of commercial and private broadcasting as being inimical to the open, robust, and freewheeling debate that a democratic society needed from its media system. . . . [Yet] the ACLU could never quite reconcile itself to the role the government would seemingly have to play to counteract the domination of the airwaves by a handful of powerful corporations supported by commercial advertising.[59]

The ACLU, however, quickly learned to live with its misgivings concerning the perils of state regulation of speech, despite "its original mandate as defending political dissidents from government persecution and harassment in the wake of the First World War."[60] Ernst led the ACLU into a campaign against private property rights and limits on state action, in favor of "public interest" licensing. Indeed, Ernst's critique of the explicitly anti-property Radio Act (with its waivers of all claims of vested rights forced upon licensees) was that it did not go far enough in cleansing the system of decentralized decision-making. He strenuously argued in Senate testimony, for instance, that allowing radio licenses to be traded freely in the marketplace was a mistake because "you are increasing your difficulty in making a change."[61] The premise was that even quasi–property rights, such as those exercised in buying and selling licenses, would limit the regulators' freedom—an outcome Ernst firmly opposed. Ernst and Forrest Bailey (Director of the ACLU) also championed extensive record-

---

[57] See, e.g., Morris Ernst, "Who Shall Control the Air?" *The Nation*, vol. 122 (April 21, 1926), pp. 443–44; and Ernst, "Radio Censorship and the 'Listening Millions'," *The Nation*, vol. 122 (April 28, 1926), pp. 473–75.

[58] As quoted in McChesney, *Telecommunications*, p. 80.

[59] *Ibid.*, p. 81.

[60] *Ibid.*

[61] *Ibid.*

keeping requirements for radio licensees, including details as to what "types of broadcasting, such as jazz, opera, speeches, etc." were being aired,[62] so that the public and its governmental representatives could closely monitor broadcast content.[63]

The endorsement of "public interest" regulation was made in tandem with a proposal that freedom of expression (and, hence, the First Amendment) was best served by licensing rules favoring nonprofit broadcasters, a group whose motives were seen by the ACLU and other public interest advocates as more conducive to the dissemination of valuable information and the sponsorship of healthy, democracy-enhancing discussion. Certainly, lobbyists for nonprofit organizations which had gone into the broadcasting business in the early 1920s (including labor unions, municipalities, educational institutions, and churches) envisioned clear economic benefits from such a regulatory bias. But it is difficult (and unnecessary) to discount the ideological (i.e., noneconomic) motive for this position on the part of many who seemingly stood to gain little materially from the "public interest" position they advocated.

A natural experiment is created by the imposition of "public interest" licensing in the Radio Act of 1927. From 1920 to February 1927, prior to imposition of "public interest" regulation, radio licenses had been issued on a first-come, first-served basis by the U.S. Department of Commerce. While the Department had limited the amount of spectrum devoted to AM radio broadcasting, and had designated only a fixed number of slots to issue to private users,[64] it exercised relatively little discretion in assigning individual licenses. This, in fact, was precisely what Secretary of Commerce Hoover complained of in advocating (from 1921) the need for new legislation allowing greater regulatory discretion over license assignments and broadcasting content. It is interesting, then, that when common-law property principles (such as "right of user") were used to define and

---

[62] See Ernst, "The 'Listening Millions'," p. 474.

[63] The ACLU resolved its position so clearly in favor of governmental control that it was attacked in 1934 by Louis G. Caldwell, "the foremost commercial broadcasting attorney in the United States" (McChesney, *Telecommunications*, p. 240), for "advocating what seems to me an inconsistent and indefensible view on radio censorship. The evil to be avoided—if we have any regard for the lessons of history—is *governmental* restraint on liberty of expression, whether imposed by hereditary monarchs or democratic majorities" (*ibid.*, emphasis in Caldwell's speech).

[64] The Department of Commerce could easily have increased the bandwidth allocated to radio broadcasting, or reduced the minimum separation between license assignments, or resorted to increased use of frequency time-sharing, thereby increasing the AM band's intensity of use. Such proposals, in fact, were voted down by the Federal Radio Commission—in the face of heavy lobbying against them by commercial broadcasters—in the first substantive decisions rendered by the FRC in 1927. A radio trade journal wrote at the time: "Broadening of the band was disposed of with a finality which leaves little hope for the revival of that pernicious proposition; division of time was frowned upon as uneconomical. . . . [T]he commissioners were convinced that less stations was the only answer" (Hazlett, "The Rationality of U.S. Regulation of the Broadcast Spectrum," p. 155).

allocate rights to radio spectrum, nonprofit stations actually prospered without preferential treatment: "Literally hundreds of [nonprofit] stations commenced operations between 1920 and 1926."[65]

C. The "public interest" result: Nonprofit stations expropriated of de facto radio rights

Yet by 1935, just as the Federal Radio Commission was ending its reign so as to pass the regulatory baton to the Federal Communications Commission, an article in the *Harvard Business Review* gave the following summary of the FRC's work:

> [T]he point seems clear that the Federal Radio Commission has interpreted the concept of public interest so as to favor in actual practice one particular group. While talking in terms of the public interest, convenience, and necessity the commission actually chose to further the ends of the commercial broadcasters. They form the substantive content of public interest as interpreted by the Commission.[66]

McChesney's book documents this episode more fully than previous research. The key regulatory decision he identifies is the FRC's General Order 40, announced in August 1928. This ruling reallocated the broadcasting rights (changing frequency, time of operation, location, or power) for 94 percent of U.S. radio stations—exempting only the 6 percent owned by or affiliated with the two broadcasting networks of the time, NBC and CBS. In making its assignments, the Commission expressed an explicit preference for a general-audience commercial broadcast station "over a propaganda station,"[67] as radio broadcasters evincing a point of view were characterized. As McChesney observes: "This interpretation of the public interest, convenience, or necessity was a clear endorsement of the private commercial development of the airwaves. . . . Numerous nonprofit stations would fall victim to this logic and see their hours reduced and the time turned over to capitalist broadcasters, often affiliated with one of the two networks."[68]

Despite the onset of the Great Depression, commercial broadcasting enjoyed its golden age in the years following the Radio Act of 1927. The years 1928 to 1933 were marked by "prosperous, almost triumphant expansion"[69] in the radio industry. The for-profit broadcasting sector serves as a handy control sample during this period, and it indicates that de-

---

[65] McChesney, *Telecommunications*, p. 254.

[66] Quoted in Eric Barnouw, *A Tower in Babel* (New York: Oxford University Press, 1967), p. 219.

[67] McChesney, *Telecommunications*, p. 28.

[68] *Ibid.*

[69] *Ibid.*, p. 30, quoting Rosen, *The Modern Stentors* (*supra* note 55).

mand for radio services was robust. The collapse of the nonprofit broadcasting sector, by contrast, is not readily explained except by the regulatory regime switch. As McChesney describes this part of the picture:

> The other side of the same coin, however, was reflected in the equally dramatic decline in the role played by nonprofit broadcasters. . . . The number of broadcasting stations affiliated with colleges and universities declined from ninety-five in 1927 to less than half that figure in 1930. The number of overall nonprofit broadcasters would decline from over 200 in 1927 to some sixty-five in 1934, almost all of which were marginal in terms of power and impact. By 1934 nonprofit broadcasting accounted for only 2 percent of total U.S. broadcasting time. For most Americans, it effectively did not exist.[70]

In essence, the nonprofit sector was driven to extinction by the technical rulings of the Federal Radio Commission. (The FRC did not typically revoke a license; it merely imposed such onerous restrictions on the license as to make it exceedingly uneconomic for the licensee to comply with its terms.) While under a common-law property rights system such broadcasters had, if not prospered, at least peacefully coexisted with the commercial broadcasting sector, the advent of "public interest" licensing — and an explicit abnegation of the right of a broadcaster to occupy radio space that it had productively used to provide service to the public — effectively expropriated "public interest" broadcasters. Looked at from the standpoint of an honest advocate of government regulation, this outcome must be head-spinning. Indeed, it is to McChesney, who appears perplexed by the fact that "some still characterize the Radio Act of 1927 as some sort of 'progressive victory' that was 'passed in the best interest of the citizenry.'"[71]

D. How the broadcasters concocted "supra-property" rights

There are at least two striking elements regarding this experiment in the effectiveness of government regulation to enhance free speech in a democracy. The first is that advocates of regulation as a strategy to counteract "private censorship" were so badly fooled in endorsing the "public interest" licensing approach, an approach which devastated nonprofit broadcasting. At a minimum, it is clear that the prevailing 1927 status quo would have been a healthier state for nonprofit stations. But in their quest to advance a system containing preferential treatment for noncommercial speech, advocates of such an outcome emerged with virtually no noncommercial speech at all.

---

[70] *Ibid.* (footnote omitted).
[71] *Ibid.*, p. 254.

The second stunning fact is that commercial broadcasting interests appear to have perfectly forecast the results associated with "public interest" licensing.[72] This is seen in the advocacy of the "public interest" — arguing for a move away from priority-in-use property rights—by major broadcasters for many years prior to the 1927 Radio Act. Indeed, the idea of instituting a "public interest" standard came directly from the broadcasters, according to the Radio Act's author, Senator Dill (in a section of his book entitled "How Broadcasters Suggested 'Public Interest' Test"):

> An interesting fact in this connection is that the broadcasters themselves suggested the inclusion of the words "public interest" in the law as a basis for granting licenses. They did this by a resolution which the National Association of Broadcasters passed in 1925.
>
> A resolution submitted to the Fourth National Radio Conference declared: "That in any Congressional legislation . . . the test of the broadcasting privilege be based upon the needs of the public served by the proposed station. The basis should be convenience and necessity, combined with fitness and ability to serve."
>
> One of the provisions which the Fourth National Radio Conference adopted read: "That public interest represented by service to the listener shall be the basis for the broadcasting privilege."[73]

While it is evident that the larger radio interests (enrolled in the National Association of Broadcasters) recognized their financial self-interest early on, it is perhaps a bit more impressive to learn that smaller commercial stations correctly foresaw trouble on the horizon in the form of the Radio Act. A group of small, independent broadcasters, fearing they would receive substandard assignments under a regulatory agency dominated by major broadcasting interests, opposed both the bill offered by

[72] The implicit assumption here is that pressure groups tend to advocate policies which advance their financial self-interest. This is not an ambitious assumption; it is often employed in the economics and public choice literature. See Gary Becker, "A Theory of Competition among Pressure Groups for Political Influence," *Quarterly Journal of Economics*, vol. 98 (May 1983), pp. 357–85. That the advocacy of "public interest" licensing by representatives of the nonprofit sector seemingly backfired has been previously explained by the weakly monitored agency relationship between such policy advocates and their economic constituencies (Hazlett, "The Rationality of U.S. Regulation of the Broadcast Spectrum," p. 168). To the extent that the nonprofits' cause was advanced in some measure by purely ideological arguments—a much likelier possibility than in the for-profit sector (where firm managers have a fiduciary responsibility to stockholders to maximize stock value)—the nonprofit principal-agent problem becomes further exacerbated.

[73] Dill, *Radio Law*, p. 89, emphasis in original. It is most instructive to observe herein that the largest radio incumbents were quite anxious to convert their property rights established under priority-in-use into mere "privileges." It is clear that a *privilege* implies less legal standing than a *right*. The Supreme Court has been quick to note this, of course, and bases its lessened protection of broadcast speech (versus printed communications, for instance) on the premise that access to the radio waves is not a right but a privilege. (Note that the *Red Lion Broadcasting* opinion is peppered with the term "privilege.") This gets to the irony of property rights discussed in Section III.

Senator Dill and the alternative measure sponsored by Representative White.[74] Since the large radio chains were to wholly dominate the reallocation process engineered by the FRC, such fears proved well-founded. As McChesney reports:

> Whereas NBC had twenty-eight affiliates and CBS had sixteen for a combined 6.4 percent of the broadcast stations in 1927, they combined to account for 30 percent of the stations within four years.... When hours on the air and the level of power are factored into the equation, NBC and CBS accounted for nearly 70 percent of American broadcasting by 1931. One study estimated that by the mid-1930s some 97 percent of total nighttime broadcasting, when smaller stations were often not licensed to broadcast, was conducted by NBC, CBS, or their affiliates.[75]

E. Why the "public interest" is politically popular

Regulation, when sought by an industry, must yet be delivered by self-interested policymakers. What's in the "public interest" licensing scheme for regulators? In a word: lots.

Start with government influence over broadcast speech. It is not a difficult point to make that political authorities enjoy press licensing—for all the reasons, for instance, that the Bill of Rights included a "free press" clause prohibiting it.[76] Radio and television licensing in the United States, however, has more of a payoff for incumbent officeholders than that associated with censorship of material deemed hostile to the incumbents' political interest. It turns out that various forms of government regulation of broadcasters are exceptionally popular with the electorate; indeed, in recent years, American audiences have witnessed heated rivalries as the great political parties compete in Hollywood-bashing contests.[77] Regulation of sex and violence on television, promotion of screening devices

[74] Rosen, *The Modern Stentors*, pp. 96–97.
[75] McChesney, *Telecommunications*, p. 29.
[76] Pool, *Technologies of Freedom* (*supra* note 23), p. 16, writes: "American legislators and the courts rejected these three abuses which publishing had suffered in their country of origin [Great Britain]: licensing of the press, special taxes on the press, and prosecution for criminal libel. The unconstitutionality of licensing, which the American courts referred to as 'previous' or 'prior restraint,' was decided as early as 1825." Pool cites *Commonwealth v. Blanding*, 3 Pick 304, 15 Am. Dec. 214, as the precedent.
[77] In the 1996 presidential election cycle, for instance, both major-party candidates took turns criticizing television programming. President Clinton (joined by Vice President Al Gore and Attorney General Janet Reno), complained that TV shows displayed excessive violence, and advocated that the government force cable and broadcast networks to develop a system of violence ratings, while requiring TV stations to air minimum levels of educational programming for children in order to gain license renewals. Republican nominee Robert Dole also denounced Hollywood for its emphasis on violence and vulgarity, singling out Time Warner's more lurid movies and sensational "gangsta rap" music recordings for opprobrium.

such as the so-called "v-chip," providing free time for political candidates, banning liquor or beer commercials, airing educational programs for children—each of these content-related demands has occasioned a good deal of the "photo op" activity in recent election cycles for federal candidates.

Having broadcasters licensed in the "public interest" provides both a formal forum in which such demands can be levied and an incentive for broadcasters to at least appear publicly responsive to policymakers' demands. Under a *de jure* property rights system, both these features would disappear. What is especially appealing about this highly visible platform on which to engage a motivated and politely obsequious (so long as the regulator holds the "public interest" adjudication hostage) private broadcaster, is that eliciting even a string of broken promises from the licensees works to impress the relevant audience. That is, where broadcasters make ambitious commitments to provide a public service such as children's educational programming, the publicity is favorable and votes are potentially won. Where the commitment is made but not delivered (some years later), the publicity is still favorable: the policymaker is then in a position to conduct tough investigative hearings, to "hold the licensee's feet to the fire," to champion the "public interest" even more sternly than before.

In the broadcast-licensing game, this cycle of promise-renege-promise-renege is many decades old. Children's educational programming, for instance, has been explicitly mandated of TV station licensees since 1960, yet a 1995 FCC study found that thirty-five years of "kidvid" regulation had produced no positive results.[78] This, of course, only encouraged the FCC to step up its efforts and to engage in a new major kidvid rulemaking, one which successfully received front-page publicity in newspapers around the country in July 1996.[79]

In other instances, licensees actually respond to FCC regulations, but in ways that are entirely perverse. For instance, a recent study found that strong statistical evidence indicating a "chilling effect" was imposed by the Fairness Doctrine, a policy instituted by the FCC in 1949 to promote the coverage of controversial issues from balanced perspectives. When this doctrine was abolished by the Commission in 1987, the number of informational formats offered on AM and FM radio stations skyrocketed.[80] Yet policymakers responsible for the counterproductive rules (i.e., the Fairness Doctrine) were not punished by voters. The policies instituted by regulators clearly failed to achieve the goals announced as being

[78] Federal Communications Commission, *Notice of Proposed Rulemaking*, MM Docket No. 93-48, FCC 95-143 (released April 7, 1995). See also Laurence H. Winer, "Children Are Not a Constitutional Blank Check," in Robert Corn-Revere, ed., *Rationales and Rationalizations* (Washington, DC: Media Institute, 1997), pp. 69–124.

[79] See, e.g., Kathy Lewis, "Networks Agree to Boost Kids' TV Standards; Clinton Praises Plan to Offer Three Hours of Programs Weekly," *Dallas Morning News*, July 30, 1996, p. A1.

[80] Thomas W. Hazlett and David W. Sosa, "Was the Fairness Doctrine a 'Chilling Effect'? Evidence from the Postderegulation Radio Market," *Journal of Legal Studies*, vol. 26, no. 1 (January 1997), pp. 307–29.

in the "public interest"—and no political feedback loop exacted a price from the responsible parties. Such an open-ended failure suggests systemic malfunctioning of the licensing regime in broadcasting.

III. How Less Is More: Why Incumbent FCC Licensees Oppose "Property Rights"

A. FCC licenses regulate the "apparatus," police the wireless cartels

As discussed above, the rights to access radio spectrum which the federal government issues to private parties are not best labeled "spectrum rights," but rather "use permits." The actual right granted is to use specified transmitting equipment for certain purposes and according to certain standards. Hence, a U.S. wireless license is entitled: "Radio Station Authorization." Embedded within this operating permit will be an assignment of radio spectrum, allocated to the license by the Federal Communications Commission.

The reason this does not constitute a spectrum right, per se, is that the licensee has no right to reallocate spectrum from one use to any other or, in fact, to deliver a given service not specified in the license. Thus, when the FCC allocated cellular telephone licenses in the 1980s to 1,468 licensees (two in each of 734 geographic markets), recipients of the authorizations could only deliver cellular telephone service, and could only do so using analog technology, with a particular technical standard (Advanced Mobile Telephone Service, or AMPS).[81] There were myriad other rules regulating licensee behavior, very few of which were related to interference (the one issue on which an actual spectrum license would focus).

Hence, by the very nature of the FCC license, competition between licensees is thwarted: unless potential competitors have been affirmatively authorized to compete, they are prohibited from doing so. This creates an effective entry barrier around each wireless service (e.g., radio, television, cellular phone service, etc.) for which the FCC has allocated spectrum space (and an impenetrable entry barrier blocking those services for which it has not allocated space). This effectively assists in the creation of wireless cartels in various bands along the electromagnetic dial.

The standard problem in organizing a cartel in the open marketplace is the prisoner's dilemma: while all members of an industry share a collective interest in restricting output so as to raise price (all the way to the monopoly level), each member (and any potential entrant) individually has an incentive to cash in on whatever price increases can be forged by increasing output and, thereby, profits. The cartel tends to suffer from incentive incompatibility.

---

[81] This mandate was relaxed in 1988, after cellular systems in large metropolitan areas had already been built. See George C. Calhoun, *Digital Cellular Radio* (Norwood, MA: Artech, 1988).

Federal control of the radio spectrum in the "public interest" eliminates this dilemma. Potential entrants into wireless markets must first effect a new spectrum allocation, and must then obtain a license. Adjudicating either issue in the "public interest" is likely to be both difficult and time-consuming. Examples of regulatory lag are legion, and it is widely recognized that FCC regulation tends to foreclose much profitable entry.[82] On the other hand, industry incumbents are themselves held in check by FCC rulemakings which set technical parameters: by setting input specifications in the operating license, firms can be constrained from competing too vigorously against one another.[83]

An illustration of the economics of this policy is offered in a 1992 FCC study.[84] There, the question was asked: What would be the effect on consumer welfare if a single UHF TV station[85] in Los Angeles, California were to go dark, reinventing itself as a cellular telephone company in the spectrum space thereby made available? The answer to the question was that the gains to "voluntary reallocation" of the spectrum space would be enormous (between $500 million and $1 billion in the one instance studied alone), but the analysis reveals much more of relevance for our inquiry: the FCC report specifically notes that Commission rules had never allowed such a reallocation to occur in the private sector. Spectrum use is designated by "public interest" rulemakings via the government's administrative process, not according to profit considerations of competitive wireless service providers.[86]

The inaccessibility of radio spectrum without an FCC license, combined with the rigidities embodied in licenses actually issued, protects incumbent licensees from upstart competitors. Because industry incumbents have overwhelming advantages in lobbying agency officials for favorable rulings versus potential entrants, the spectrum allocation process can be

---

[82] See, e.g., Harvey J. Levin, *The Invisible Resource* (Baltimore: Johns Hopkins Press, 1980).

[83] Hence, a technically inferior technology (say, analog cellular) may be pushed as a condition of the FCC license, because an alternative (say, digital cellular) would increase industry output to the point of decreasing profitability. (Where this sort of thing occurs depends, of course, on the profit function, which incorporates the demand function.)

[84] Evan Kwerel and John Williams, "Changing Channels: Voluntary Reallocation of UHF Television Spectrum," Federal Communications Commission, OPP Working Paper No. 27 (November 1992). This study can be characterized as part of a two-decades old effort by some FCC staff to liberalize the rights issued by the Commission, using license flexibility to improve the allocation of radio spectrum. This constitutes a move in the direction of property rights, but within the "public interest" regulatory framework. (Even former FCC Chairman Reed Hundt has endorsed this liberalization, at least for nonbroadcast services. See Reed E. Hundt and Gregory L. Rosston, "Spectrum Flexibility Will Promote Competition and the Public Interest," *IEEE Communications Magazine* [December 1995], pp. 40–43.) As a practical matter, however, the position remains highly controversial; indeed, the Kwerel and Williams study was embargoed for some months by the FCC, and only released to the public in November 1992—after the November elections determined that the Bush Administration would soon be leaving office.

[85] The UHF (or ultrahigh frequency) TV band encompasses channels 14 through 69.

[86] Some cracks in the rigidity of the FCC allocation policy have recently begun to appear. They are summarized in Thomas W. Hazlett, "Liberalizing Radio Spectrum Policy," unpublished paper (October 1997).

used as a rather formidable cartel-enforcement device. The ironic outcome is that truncating property rights can result in more lucrative operations for incumbent firms than would be available to them under a more far-reaching set of private property rights.[87] This result obtains wherever the cost which any one firm suffers from the limits imposed on its use of spectrum is more than offset (in discounted present value of profits) by the advantage it derives from being protected against potential competitors' expanded use of radio spectrum.

The historical scenario sketched out above, wherein *de jure* property rights for radio spectrum were abandoned by major commercial radio broadcasters in favor of severely truncated broadcasting "privileges," is readily explicable in a framework where actors rationally pursue policies that bring financial benefit. Broadcasters were able to reap a greater share of the market (and, hence, higher profitability) because interpretation of the "public interest" was severely biased in favor of the interests of the commercial sector. Under a common-law framework similar to that prevailing in the U.S. prior to "public interest" licensing, economic agents are permitted to establish rights to a resource by "adverse possession" or "squatter's sovereignty." Hence, rivals from the nonprofit sector (as well as additional commercial entrants) may not be so easily excluded from the market. Indeed, radio broadcasters sought, and procured, "public interest" regulation to (successfully) restrict access to airwaves.

B. Standard misunderstandings of the "less is more" principle

Historically and currently, those who hold the most economically valuable rights issued by the FCC are firmly opposed to a regime of private property rights for radio spectrum. The proposal for "public interest" licensing put forth prior to the 1927 Radio Act by the National Association of Broadcasters has already been noted. In a more recent episode, a study group released a 1995 report advocating a liberal regime of private property rights in radio spectrum.[88] The *Wall Street Journal* reported that "industry groups didn't rush to embrace the report." Most pointedly, "broadcasters and companies planning elaborate satellite-communications projects have already resisted the idea of 'dezoning' the spectrum in a

---

[87] This, of course, would not be ironic to economists from Adam Smith to Karl Marx to Milton Friedman. The classical argument for unregulated competition has often been mischaracterized by modern critics of capitalism as springing from an innate trust of (or affection for) business interests. Yet Smith was quite clear in his belief that such interests would surely attempt to conspire against competitive market forces, but typically be defeated by the pervasive force of self-interest. Marx was even more insistent that competition would defeat capitalists' own attempts to maximize profit, and in fact lead to the ruination of the entire class. Friedman and other modern economists condemn industrial policy as "corporate welfare," and argue for free-market competition (including unfettered international trade) to counter business interests.

[88] *The Telecom Revolution: An American Opportunity* (Washington, DC: Progress and Freedom Foundation, 1995). I served on a Working Group that assisted on the report.

way that would make them compete with other industries for blocks of spectrum."[89]

Yet the scholarly literature is littered with confusion on this topic. Most glaring, perhaps, is a recent book by sociologist Thomas Streeter, *Selling the Air*.[90] The central thesis of this volume is that the broadcasting business in the United States has become dominated by private, for-profit corporations because the ideology of "corporate liberalism" emerged triumphant in enacting the Radio Act of 1912.[91] Asserting that "property is inherently political,"[92] Streeter categorizes the entire institution of property rights—including broadcasting for profit—as a scheme crafted by large corporations intent on dominating the radio sector. Rather than limiting or banning such business forms in favor of amateur users and nonprofit organizations desiring to access radio waves, U.S. public policy has resulted in capitalists "selling the air," which, in turn, produces crass commercialism and social misuse of the radio spectrum resource.

This analysis could not be more wrong. It is not the case that public policy permits "selling the air"; the great advantage sought, and gained, by broadcasting interests in the 1927 Radio Act was that airwaves were *not* to be treated as property.[93] Rather than lying at the root of the problem imagined by Streeter, "selling the air" would form the root of the solution. By permitting the common principles governing right of first appropriation to prevail, perhaps with some statutory streamlining (involving adjudication efficiencies, as with patent disputes which are sent for resolution to an expert Patent Court), competitive forces could provide a wide panoply of amateur and nonprofit services—precisely the services whose absence Streeter cites as evidence of the failure of the system of "selling the air."

[89] Daniel Pearl, "Think Tank Linked to Gingrich Urges Ending FCC, Privatizing Spectrum," *Wall Street Journal*, May 21, 1995, pp. A3, A6.

[90] Streeter, *Selling the Air* (*supra* note 22).

[91] To be distinguished from the 1927 Radio Act. The 1912 legislation gave the Secretary of Commerce and Labor the duty to assign radio licenses so as to "minimize interference." That broadcasting policy was, for all intents and purposes, settled by the 1912 Radio Act is a case made unconvincingly by Streeter. More compelling work in this area, including that by authors presumably sympathetic to Streeter's self-described "neo-Marxist" analysis (for instance, McChesney's *Telecommunications, Mass Media, and Democracy*), all focus on the 1920s radio market as the venue for fundamental decision making on broadcasting policy. Indeed, most of *Streeter's* book is devoted to showing how events well after 1912 shaped the modern broadcasting marketplace.

[92] Streeter, *Selling the Air*, p. 252.

[93] Streeter is aware of the explicit provision, dating to a resolution passed just before passage of the Radio Act of 1927, which forces broadcasters to waive any claim to a vested right in order to receive a license. But he considers it a mindless contradiction of a confused system: "[T]he vigorous pursuit of the principle of property has led to a series of dilemmas. The fact that our law simultaneously has forbid ownership of the airwaves and invited their purchase and sale for more than sixty years is only the most glaring of these" (*ibid.*, p. 254). This is upside down. Since 1927, the regulatory regime has explicitly overruled the "principle of property" in favor of a "public interest" licensing scheme. By truncating rights—and mandating that no one can buy or sell the "airwaves"—the regime has ensured that incumbent corporate interests have been well served. Cartels have been created and enforced all along the radio dial. No confusion there.

Common-law rules of property were kryptonite to Streeter's mighty capitalist broadcaster, and it was only after alert industry lobbyists disposed
of them through the legislative process that the nonprofit broadcasters—so
active under the property rights regime—were effectively vanquished.
Hence, this analysis wholly misses the role of property rights in facilitating competition and, more provocatively, promoting diverse, out-of-the-
mainstream speech.

C. Pirate radio and captive broadcasters

To evaluate the free-speech merits of the "public interest" regime against
the property rights alternative, one can, fortuitously, observe the actions
of disparate parties that are currently challenging the existing licensing
structure. A series of FCC enforcement actions is now in the federal courts,
as the Commission has—in its mandated authority under the 1934 Communications Act—been authorized to shut down unlicensed stations trans-
mitted in the AM or FM bands. These stations are generically called
"pirate radio."[94]

The fact is that "micro" radio stations, transmitting at between one-half
watt and thirty watts of power, can be set up for miniscule dollar amounts
(in some cases, under $200). Community organizations and alternative
music listeners are anxious to take advantage of such low-power transmissions, which are extremely localized (both in terms of geography and
product space). Yet, the FCC refuses to license stations with less than 100
watts (outside of Alaska), a change which went into effect in 1978 (up
from ten watts minimum). In keeping lower-powered stations off the air,
the Commission determined that more stations at higher wattage could
be licensed—a policy that the Corporation for Public Broadcasting, whose
affiliates stood in line to receive many of the higher-powered station
permits, lobbied for.[95]

Hence, amateur, nonprofit stations are informally springing up in a sort
of black market of the air: as many as a thousand radio "pirates" are
currently on the air in communities across the country. The most famous,
perhaps because of the litigation the Federal Communications Commission has brought against it, is Radio Free Berkeley. Its program format
ranges from offbeat musical arrangements to political commentaries judged
too controversial to be aired by commercial or public radio stations. It
also specializes in international reports from pirate radio sources outside
the U.S.

---

[94] See Jesse Walker, "Don't Touch That Dial," *Reason*, October 1995, pp. 30–35; and Julie
Lew, "Radio Renegade Fights FCC Rules," *New York Times*, December 8, 1997, p. D12.
[95] Walker, "Don't Touch That Dial," p. 32. The Corporation for Public Broadcasting dis-
penses federal subsidies for programs appearing on public stations. Its role is to promote
programming which would not be aired by commercial broadcasters—precisely the niche
which "pirate radio" stations aim to fill.

The question arises: Is Radio Free Berkeley—transmitting at low-power so as to leave all surrounding wireless communications undisturbed—exercising its First Amendment right to air its form of audio expression? Under a property rights regime, there is no question: so long as the radio entrant occupies space not used by others, it acquires a propertied interest by putting that space into useful service. Likewise, under a "public interest" licensing regime, there is no question: so long as the potential applicant has not been issued an FCC license to broadcast, it is illegal for it to access the airwaves. And since the FCC has determined that low-powered radio stations are not in the "public interest," the people or organizations wishing to express themselves via radio had better save up for a station which costs many times what a pirate radio station costs. These communicative folks are forced to fight politically to gain what, under traditional property law, would clearly be theirs.

As "Radio Free America" (a website providing information on "pirate" stations) has summarized the issue:

> The people involved in micro radio at this site have a lot of things in common. We are all united in the fight to protect our first amendment rights at virtually any cost. We are not a group of law breakers as the FCC wants to place us. We are a group of American citizens that would stake nothing less than our life on the values this country is based on. In this country there is a branch of the Federal Government which is operating outside the law. They are shutting down radio stations which speak for their small communities and giv[ing] them no opportunity to be on the air. The FCC will not [award] a broadcasting license to anyone in low wattage radio. . . . We have few rules, other than making certain that our stations do not interfere with any emergency bands or any other commercially or privately used frequencies.[96]

Contrast this bombastic challenge, and the resultant court actions to rein in pirate radio stations, with the meek response to far more costly (in dollar terms) rulings foisted on the major commercial broadcasters. In a recent series of regulatory initiatives, TV broadcasters lost at least three major battles: (1) the v-chip was mandated in the 1996 Telecommunications Act (signed February 8, 1996); (2) kidvid, where the FCC set a quantitative standard—three hours per week per station of educational programming[97]—was imposed in July 1996;[98] and (3) all five major broad-

---

[96] "Radio Free America" website, formerly at: http://pages.prodigy.com/RFAmerica/KCILState.html. (Apparently the website has been discontinued.)

[97] The devil, as usual, is in the details. Although sold as a hard standard, it is soft in the sense that stations may meet the letter of the law without airing three hours of educational programming for children per week. And, of course, the issue as to what constitutes educational programming is to be hammered out over time.

[98] Lewis, "Networks Agree" (*supra* note 79).

cast networks (NBC, CBS, ABC, Fox, and PBS) reluctantly agreed to provide free time for presidential candidates to speak directly to voters during
the 1996 campaign. In each of the three cases, commercial broadcasting
executives issued plaintive wails that such commitments would violate
the First Amendment rights of TV station owners. In each instance, TV
stations ended up quietly acquiescing to the policy. Indeed, in the latter
case, broadcasters "voluntarily" donated time to the campaigns of Bill
Clinton, Bob Dole, and Ross Perot. In no case did a single U.S. TV station
(of about 1,500) assert its First Amendment rights to operate free of government content controls.

The incentives of the broadcast licensees to cooperate with political
authorities severely temper any urge to flamboyantly assert constitutional
rights, particularly during a period when between $12 billion and $70
billion in new digital television licenses are being awarded to incumbent
broadcasters.[99] This, then, is where the award of licenses in the "public
interest" delivers us: to a market in which entry is severely restricted,
creating lucrative profit opportunities for licensees that are selected on
vague "public interest" criteria, and that have every economic incentive
to get along with incumbent policymakers. This, I argue, does not respect
the letter, let alone the spirit, of the First Amendment.[100]

IV. PROPERTY RIGHTS AS DUAL FIRST AMENDMENT PROTECTION

February 23, 1997 marked seven decades of "public interest" licensing
in the U.S. broadcasting sector. The behavior of regulators, the incentives
of radio and TV licensees, and the performance of actual markets in
satisfying consumer demands are all now clearly observable. Policymakers use the "public interest" licensing process to engage in a "fake wres-
tling match" with broadcasters, "signifying nothing."[101] But, as with its
pseudo-sport cousin, such "matches" do inspire audiences: the public
will cheer a good performance. Policymakers can make virtually vaude-
villian displays of concern for the content promulgated by those licensed

[99] Thomas W. Hazlett, "The 'Public Interest' Fraud," Wall Street Journal, May 6, 1996,
op-ed page.
[100] Reed Hundt, chairman of the FCC from 1993 to 1997, has testified that broadcasters are
not likely to bring suit against the government for infringing on their First Amendment
rights because—if successful—such a suit would bring down the entire licensing scheme
which protects the market value of their broadcast properties (i.e., shields them from competitive entry). Hence, broadcasters prefer retaining (or, in the case of new awards such as
digital TV licenses, obtaining) extremely valuable broadcasting rights and are quite willing
to trade away their constitutional rights in the bargain. On the other side of the deal,
policymakers are eager to make this exchange, as it allows government to bridge the First
Amendment wall and exercise direct influence over "free speech." Hundt, for instance,
earned a reputation as an activist FCC chairman on "content" issues, frequently reminding
broadcasters of their "public interest" obligations with respect to children's educational
programming, free time for political candidates, viewer ratings for violent content, maintaining a years-old agreement not to air liquor ads, etc.
[101] As FCC Member Glen O. Robinson described the process in Cowles Florida Broadcasting,
Inc., 60 FCC2d 371, 439 (1976).

to use the "public's airwaves"—the regulatory system offers a stable platform from which abundant publicity may be garnered, a stage upon
which the political entrepreneur poses as a champion of the public, fiercely
standing up to the broadcasting interests.[102] Broadcast licensees can live
with that—quite comfortably, in fact. For they use the "public interest"
just as profitably, obtaining licenses without charge—an arrangement which
continues for broadcasters even though, in 1993, *nonbroadcast* licenses
issued by the Commission began to be assigned via competitive bidding.[103] (Thus far, such license auctions have generated over $23 billion in
revenues for the U.S. Treasury.)[104] By accepting "public interest" obligations, broadcasters avoid paying market value for their station permits.

Indeed, there is a bonus: broadcasters can use "public interest" rulemakings to deny entry to competitive firms, thus protecting and enhancing license values. An ongoing, high-profile example illustrates how this
is achieved. In 1997, every TV station in the United States won the right
to a new, second TV station license. These licenses will be used to provide
digital television in radio spectrum originally set aside for television broadcasting service in the FCC's TV Allocation Table of 1952. What was this
spectrum being used for during the previous forty-five years? Essentially,
nothing: it was blocked off from use by other firms, and was not utilized
to create additional competition in the TV business. The "public interest"
spectrum-allocation process made this restraint of trade (withholding a
valuable input—a radio license—from potential entrants into wireless-
communications markets, including broadcasting) possible. For instance,
in the mid-1980s, cellular telephone and wireless paging companies requested access to fallow (unused) spectrum in the TV band. After a "public interest" proceeding, it was determined that these firms could not
access such radio waves, as the spectrum was to be used (at some future
date) for high definition television (HDTV).[105] As journalist Thomas Donlan wrote in a 1991 book:

> In January 1987, broadcasters tried to rent a monster called HDTV to
> do a little dirty work. Then they were surprised when the monster
> did not go back into its cage.
> The broadcasters were trying to head off a power play against
> them at the Federal Communications Commission. The people who

[102] See also Thomas W. Hazlett, "Sham Regulation as an Equilibrium Solution in FCC
Broadcast Licensing," unpublished manuscript (June 1996).

[103] In the 1993 federal budget, Congress finally approved (after decades of requests by
various parties, including the executive branch) the use of auctions for assigning nonbroadcast FCC licenses. In the comprehensive Telecommunications Act of 1996, broadcasters
again escaped auctions when their licenses were specifically exempted from auctions. See
Thomas W. Hazlett, "Explaining the Telecommunications Act of 1996: Comment on Thomas
G. Krattenmaker," *Connecticut Law Review*, vol. 29 (Fall 1996), pp. 217-42.

[104] See: http://www.fcc.gov/wtb/auctions/.

[105] High definition television can be provided via analog or digital transmission formats.
What is called "digital TV" may or may not be "high definition."

make and sell beepers, pagers, and portable telephones were trying to get the FCC to give them more room on the airwaves for their services. Their target was several channels in the UHF band allocated to television broadcasting. . . .

When anybody suggests to the FCC that some part of the radio spectrum is not being put to its highest and best use, those who have been assigned those channels react immediately to protect themselves. If they are unable or unwilling to use what they are trying to protect, they are all the more vicious and vehement in defense—like the dog in the Aesop's fable. . . .

Edward Fritts, president of the NAB [National Association of Broadcasters], proudly demonstrated the wonderful pictures and high-fidelity sound to regulators and lawmakers. He said if UHF channels were taken from the broadcasters, that would "preclude America's broadcasters from developing HDTV as a free over-the-air service to the nation. It is a fact that consumers will be able to enjoy this improved broadcast technology in the near future. The question is whether the FCC will let them."[106]

Now a decade has passed and no American enjoys high definition television—except those subscribing to satellite television, which shows that UHF frequencies were not "technically" required for the service (and, hence, need not have been set aside for the purpose). Indeed, even though the broadcasters have, in 1997, won the right to claim new digital television licenses, there is no assurance that they will be used for HDTV (that is, broadcasters may use their new digital licenses to "simply" supply more TV channel choices to customers, rather than enhancing signal quality to high definition).[107] But the effect of the "public interest" process is

[106] Thomas G. Donlan, *Supertech* (Homewood, IL: Business One Irwin, 1991), p. 4. One key, if subtle, aspect to this passage is that the interest group lobbying for entry into the market is identified as the *makers* of various wireless devices. The cellular and paging companies that actually provide services, i.e., incumbent FCC licensees, do not typically have an interest in promoting new entry. Those equipment suppliers who sell the inputs to competitive service providers are the business interests most likely to promote additional market rivalry and, hence, consumer welfare.

[107] ABC announced in summer 1997 that it would not broadcast high definition programs with its new digital TV licenses, while other broadcasters studiously avoided committing to HDTV. (See "There's No Stampede to HDTV," CMP Media Inc., August 20, 1997; CMP is an online news service available at: http://www.newspage.com.) This is hugely ironic, because the digital TV licenses were allocated to broadcasters, without charge, in a ten-year-long FCC rulemaking which reserved spectrum and preferential treatment in the award of such licenses (including the no-charge provision) due to the stated importance of this new technology (HDTV) to the "public interest." The technology acted as a place-marker reserving special opportunities for U.S. broadcasters. However, at the eleventh hour, the FCC reconsidered its imposed HDTV standard, and liberalized its rules—TV stations receiving the new licenses would be required only to transmit digital (not necessarily high definition) TV signals. Taken alone, this flexibility in the FCC allocation is a very good thing, which the computer industry—largely shut out of the FCC's pro-broadcaster standard-setting process for HDTV—lobbied to achieve. (See Thomas W. Hazlett, "Industrial Policy for Couch Potatoes," *Wall Street Journal*, August 7, 1996, p. A14.) But the global picture is that the FCC's

now clear: no use of valuable UHF radio waves has been made, as incumbent TV licensees have successfully blocked those who would productively use such resources to provide additional service to the public. And the TV licensees received a handsome payoff: in awarding new TV licenses, the FCC assigned one license to each existing (analog) licensee without charge, thereby subsidizing an upgrade to digital service. What is even more striking, perhaps, is that the restriction of output continues well beyond the current allotment of new digital TV licenses: there will continue to be vast bandwidth unutilized in the so-called TV band (402 MHz, or sixty-seven channels of six MHz each). Given the advent of efficient digital compression techniques and spread spectrum,[108] it is economically possible to provide a plethora of additional services in the TV band—including competitive TV programming, cellular and paging service, and high-speed internet access, to name but a few—even after digital television broadcasts begin in late 1998.[109]

While the "public interest" standard facilitates the political bargain which regulators and licensees strike, it serves the consuming public very poorly. By truncating competitive entry, entry that would be legally invited under a property rights regime, regulation reduces the opportunity for low-cost communications to serve the more disparate and commercially marginal demands of the marketplace. The disastrous experience suffered by nonprofit radio broadcasting during the transition (after the 1927 Radio Act) from a property rights regime to one operating under the "public interest" standard, so starkly detailed in existing historical work, is a graphic demonstration of the tendency of such regulation to pinch diversity of expression in precisely the same motion as it limits economic competition. The current battle in which pirate radio stations, often arising as spontaneous efforts by radio amateurs or community activists, are excluded by the "public interest" spectrum-allocation process is a simple confirmation of the tendency for history to repeat itself. The dynamic at the heart of the "public interest" standard proffered by the National Association of Broadcasters in 1925 is alive and well today.

Thus, the empirical basis of the standard property rights arguments, which see such rights as promoting experimentation through decentralization of decision making, appear compelling. More competitive systems emerge from the property rights framework, and this serves the consumer—as well as the health of democracy.

What is additionally clear, however, is that *de jure* property rights would protect us not only from inefficient and antidemocratic bureaucratic de-

---

stated rationale for foreclosing competitive use of the UHF band for the past decade has now been revealed as an empty bag, in that an HDTV mandate for broadcasters has been determined by the Commission to no longer be in the "public interest."

[108] These technologies allow much greater communications capacity over (or through) a given frequency range.

[109] Paul Baran, "The Myth of Spectrum Shortage Exposed," *Computer Technology Review, Supplement,* Summer/Fall 1995, pp. 18–20.

cision making, but from the commercial interests which now dominate many of the broadcasting markets. If rules of priority-in-use were restored, wireless rivals would not be so easily blocked in their attempts to offer competitive communications services. Moreover, broadcasters would face fewer incentives to curry favor with regulators, and would face stronger incentives to engage in controversial programming. The scene of politicians pandering to the press presents an ugly picture; the view is uglier still when key organs of the press pander to the politicians. Yet, the "public interest" regime motivates just such behavior, while additionally encouraging socially wasteful competition (rent-seeking) by firms wishing to deny Americans access to new communications services. In the absence of such incentives, markets would predictably offer yet a greater array of opportunities for diverse expression.

The late D.C. Circuit Court of Appeals judge David Bazelon wrote as thoughtfully as any legal mind on the nexus between FCC regulation and freedom of speech. While initially a supporter of the status quo, he progressed to the following position: that the "public interest" spectrum-allocation system, in reliably depriving the public of communications which market competitors are willing and able to provide, engages in unconstitutional conduct. Focusing specifically on televised speech, he wrote:

> My point . . . is that this concept of scarcity is not a result of the limitation on frequencies but rather the market power gained by VHF licensees through FCC policies on allocation of frequencies and relative development of alternative technologies. My suggestions for reform . . . attempt to meet these policies head on, rather than through regulation of speech. But if such reform efforts do not move ahead, I can perceive an argument that past FCC allocation and development policies are themselves a denial of the free press rights of those whose demand for frequencies cannot be met under the present scheme.[110]

By moving to a simple rule of entrant liability, under which a wireless service provider has the presumptive right to provide communications so long as liability is assumed for any damage to existing communications (via airwave interference) thereby incurred, the anticompetitive and arguably unconstitutional prohibitions on electronic speech now practiced in the daily course of operations at the FCC could be eliminated. Such a policy would unleash a multiplicity of diverse voices, would empower consumers to select from a far broader array of programming choices, would end the broadcast licensees' willingness to shade behavior to favor incumbent policymakers, and would deliver to the public heretofore un-

[110] David L. Bazelon, "FCC Regulation of the Telecommunications Press," *Duke Law Journal*, vol. 1975, no. 2 (May 1975), p. 226.

seen opportunities in the exciting information-technology sector. But what property rights to radio spectrum would also do would be to expropriate the *de facto* property rights held by broadcast licensees, rights which effectively permit incumbents to exclude competitive entrants, and which convey to privileged commercial enterprises undue power over the free-speech rights exercised by American citizens. This is the second, less obvious payoff, embodied in moving to a liberal regime of private property rights in radio spectrum. The dual role of property rights in protecting broadcast speech is both to shield the electronic publisher from governmental interference and to protect the marketplace from undue control by incumbent firms or technologies. Hence, A. J. Liebling was more right, and less ironic, than he knew when he pointed to the link between ownership and constitutionally protected free speech: a truly robust First Amendment would guarantee a free press—for printing papers or propagating radio waves—to anyone who owned one, whether or not such an interest was adjudged in accordance with "public interest, convenience, or necessity."

Economics and Telecommunications Policy, University of California, Davis

REGULATION OF FOODS AND DRUGS AND LIBERTARIAN IDEALS: PERSPECTIVES OF A FELLOW-TRAVELER*

By Daniel D. Polsby

I. Introduction

For one with libertarian sympathies, the official regulation of foods and drugs is presumptively a bad thing. One is most accustomed to seeing the argument in debates about legalizing marijuana and other hedonic drugs. And it remains a very good if by now well-trafficked question, which will be more well-trafficked still by the time this essay ends, why government should be in the business of telling people what sorts of chemical mood-enhancers they may take. But as the criminologist James Jacobs has pointed out, to ask this question is to put in play matters far larger and more important than marijuana.[1] What business is it of government to say what medicines may be sold and by whom they may be sold? Why should certain chemical agents be available to willing buyers only with a doctor's scrip, and other agents, such as unproved drugs or devices, forbidden to all, even with medical permission? If libertarians answer these questions impatiently, then admirers of the administrative welfare state ("statists") will be happy to play rope-a-dope with them, chattering on about the endearing eccentricities of libertarians' assumptions and avoiding the challenge to articulate and defend their own increasingly shabby-looking principles. Those principles are much in need of defense. Food and drug laws are among the most well-established offices of regulatory government. They are complicated, hypertechnical, mysterious, and expensive to administer and maintain. One is entitled to suspect that a number of them are carried on more out of habit and routine than out of any authentic conviction that they are the best way, or among the better ways, to provide for the welfare of citizens.

It seems to me that there are a number of food and drug problems that it is perfectly sensible to manage in the public sector. Where third-party harms are the issue—injuries and risks imposed on people who do not consent to them literally or constructively—libertarians should acknowl-

* Thanks are owed to the research assistance of Kent Pflederer, Nathan Linn, and James Fitzpatrick, M.D. Thanks also to several colleagues for helpful comments, in particular Robert W. Bennett, Anthony D'Amato, Mayer Freed, Andy Koppelman, and Gary Lawson, all of whom are held harmless hereby. Acknowledgment is also due to the Kirkland & Ellis Research Fund, which subsidizes the author's research activities.

[1] James B. Jacobs, "Imagining Drug Legalization," *The Public Interest*, vol. 101 (1990), p. 31.

edge the respectability of public control in some form. The problem with these ought-to-be straightforward cases is not the matter that they present directly, but their adjacency to slippery slopes which can involve libertarian arguments in great perplexity. Beyond the problem of externalities (and related to it) is the problem of paternalism. Libertarians are against paternalistic laws because they deny that the "nanny state" knows best for adults. Let it be stipulated that any number of food and drug laws are vulnerable to this reproach. Still, there remain some domains in which at least some paternalistic concerns, and the regulations that they yield, are arguably permissible in libertarian terms.

I should make clear that I intend the limited justification for public regulation of foods and drugs offered here to impeach the practically unlimited regime that currently governs the area. Such bills of impeachment have to justify themselves first of all. After all, life is short. Knowledge, especially of the practical kind, is limited and usually expensive to come by. Institutional arrangements of all kinds economize on the scarcity of time and information, making it possible for people to do things with their lives other than the most basic things that allow survival. It is an effort to rethink such matters as whether a federal Food and Drug Administration is the best way to tackle the range of problems at which it is aimed. Tinkering around the edges of institutional practice to redress some perceived imperfection is one thing, but radical changes such as getting rid of most of the functions of a big administrative agency, because the premises on which the agency chiefly rests have led far down a mistaken path, is a hard sell. It might often be simple common sense for even a committed libertarian to take as given much of the whole embedded apparatus of the modern administrative welfare state, and to expend libertarian energy in the margin—litigating a certain case of bureaucratic adventurism or opposing the adoption of an overreaching agency rule— where such activity could make more of a difference and do more good.

Though acknowledging the difficulties, the argument here is that, nevertheless, it is a wise investment of time and energy to subject the regulation of foods and drugs by government to a hard look, in order to understand what government's proper functions should be in this endeavor and, in the process, to get a handle on what limits on its activities government ought to be asked to respect. What drives the argument is not the sense that we have lost our way in a forest of bureaucratic inertia. While that is undeniable, it is not where I think emphasis should be placed, because that sort of diagnosis usually leads down the garden path of reformist nostrums—streamlining an agency's internal processes, or modernizing or otherwise reinventing them. The argument here is that, with some workable exceptions, current government efforts to police the chemical-ingestion behavior of the population is, in concept and in principle, a first-scale public policy disaster that is beyond any reform short of abandonment. A good bit of this case is fairly common currency by now. For example, that the U.S. government's war on drugs touched off a homicidal crime wave for eight or nine years following its big ramping-up in 1984 is now reasonably well-established, perhaps even conventional wisdom, among criminologists.[2] More will be said about this evident state of affairs and what its relevance may be to normative theories of human liberty, but there are much bigger, and more usually overlooked, fish to fry when one considers the performance and effects of the U.S. Food and Drug Administration (FDA).

The case for strictly regulating drug manufacture and marketing begins with a recognition of the obvious, that these substances can be dangerous to human beings—indeed, are usually dangerous in one way or another, sometimes mortally so, if they are used unwisely. To the libertarian's favorite rhetorical gambit, "Why should the government regulate people's choice of the medicines they want to use?," the statist has a rhetorical rejoinder: "Why should people be left at large to harm themselves when regulation can protect them? What do we have government for if not to facilitate the prevention of preventable harms?" Over the course of the past several generations, the statist's rejoinder, and the parade of implied horror stories that it conjures, has seemed much more formidable to the public than abstract libertarian talk of people's rights. But, perhaps as a by-product of the AIDS epidemic, in recent years there has been a growing recognition that undue caution with respect to allowing people to exercise their rights of choice has some formidable costs of its own.

General food and drug regulation began in the United States with the Food, Drug, and Cosmetic Act, which was passed in 1938, at the height of the New Deal. At that time, it may have seemed natural to speak, as Justice Felix Frankfurter later did, of an "innocent public who are wholly helpless" when faced with the complexities of foods and drugs in the marketplace.[3] But in a world of literate, sharp-penciled, label-reading shoppers, the metaphysical helplessness of consumers no longer rings true. It is possible, in practice as well as in theory, for people to protect themselves from risks that are in excess of those they choose to bear. The nub of the problem, indeed, is that when looked at closely and against a background of the right to choose one's own poison, the whole idea of uniform risk-management and the parade of horror stories along with it begins to look more and more unreal. The regulation of foods and drugs against a benchmark of risk presupposes something that is quite abstract. "Risk," or the probable safety of a substance, either in relation to some criterion of its efficacy or absolutely, is not an entity in and of itself, but a term of relation. That all ingestable chemicals carry with them both risks and benefits is an evident truism, and is indeed one of the chief principles

---

[2] Alfred Blumstein, "Youth Violence, Guns, and the Illicit Drug Industry," *Journal of Criminal Law and Criminology*, vol. 86 (1995).

[3] *United States v. Dotterweich*, 320 U.S. 277 (1943).

upon which regulatory approval and practical medicine proceeds. But there is a large subjective component to both the notion of risk and the notion of benefit, which, quite appropriately, leads people to exhibit considerable variability ("the right to choose"); and this means that *in principle* no one answer to the question of risk can possibly be correct. At the end of the regulatory day, the decision to approve a given drug or device makes an assumption about the amount of risk that potential purchasers of the product can accept. The decision may be too bold for some tastes, not aggressive enough for others; but on average, if people are average, it will be just right, or should aim to be so. But a one-size-fits-all framework is a dubious way to approach a matter as personal as what value to attach to a potential benefit, and what sort of discount table to use in assessing whether a given risk is worth running.

It may be useful to think for a moment of what we know of risk,[4] and how we deal with it, in investment theory and practice, where the matter has been much studied and where a relatively much higher level of sophistication in public conversation is evident. Investors differ widely in what they will agree to pay for a given asset, and much of the reason for this difference is simply a reflection of the reality that their capacity to tolerate risk varies widely. Though to some extent this variation can be written down to individual differences in temperament—the gamut that human personalities run from the swashbuckling to the bashful—one could still count on people to exhibit great differences in how much risk they were willing to accept in connection with a certain investment decision even if their personalities were just alike. People late in their seventh decade of life have less time to recoup the losses that the normal ups and downs of securities markets may bring than people late in their third decade of life. Therefore, old people are more risk-avoidant. People with extensive and diversified holdings of property can afford to take a flier on an initial public offering that sensible investors of more modest means will probably wish to shun. People with greater uncertainties about what their family obligations will be, or how secure their basic income is, should be expected to seek less-risky parking places for their savings than people who have these loose ends tied down. All these extraneous differences in circumstances pulling one way and another would serve to locate people's risk preferences along a continuous function rather than at a single point, even if (as is, of course, not the case) people's taste for adventure and willingness to tolerate stress were absolutely identical. It follows that it is not merely incorrect but usually not even meaningful to think of a given security as "risky" or "too risky" or "not risky enough," and in the real world securities are seldom spoken of in this way, because the concept of risk draws all its force from context—the wide and changing array of personal factors and contingent circumstances that are not

---

[4] A superb treatise on this subject is: John G. U. Adams, *Risk* (London: UCL Press, 1995).

identical for any two people. One size *cannot possibly* fit all. To think of risk as an absolute is absolutely to misunderstand the concept.

For the regulation of drugs and medical devices, the problem is quite similar. No one can meaningfully say, for example, "the risk of this silicone breast implant has not been established as justified," without knowing how a given individual solves her own, highly personal equation embodying trade-offs between cosmetic advantages, the probability that connective tissue dysfunctions or other complications may follow, the expenses and other consequences of alternative courses of action (including doing nothing), and, what is easily overlooked but highly relevant, the period of time—the depreciation schedule, so to speak—over which the decision will operate. Some people exhibit a large degree of indifference toward the conventions of fashion and personal presentation, while other people's very self-definition seems to hang upon them. Some people expect to die within a year or two in any event, while other people can reasonably expect to live fifty or sixty years more. Some people have a limited budget to devote to reconstructive surgery, and other people have an effectively unlimited budget. Some people tolerate hospital discomforts rather well, others not well at all. It is not meaningful to speak of the risk of silicone breast implants as though the safety characteristics of the product were some sort of free-floater operating independently of all these contextual particularities. It should be expected that a regulatory regime based on contrary assumptions about risk would routinely arrive at arbitrary results, for its assumptions would blind it to the human condition. This is precisely how the laws require the Food and Drug Administration to proceed. It is not the bureaucrats within the agency but rather the members of Congress who deserve the blame for this state of affairs. Yet we must still answer the question of what the agency's role should be in policing the supply of foods, drugs, and devices that reach the marketplace. I shall argue that, in principle, there ought to be at least a few cases of justifiable regulation, and perhaps more than a few, that the libertarian critique does not reach. And then there is the rest. Someone else will have to defend and justify that.

II. Public Goods and Externalities

Some drugs are criminogenic. The use of anabolic steroids and certain central nervous system stimulants (including some commonly abused ones, such as cocaine and amphetamine) is evidently linked to increased irritability and aggression, which in turn sometimes leads to assaultive behavior. A question therefore arises as to whether substances with these properties should be excluded from a libertarian aspiration to deregulate the sale of drugs.

Anabolic steroids build muscle mass. They are extremely effective at doing so. Therein lies a dilemma for athletes especially, because, other things being equal, someone who does not use this drug is at a competitive disadvantage to someone who does. Sports leagues and sanctioning committees are alert to the problem and have done what they can to discourage steroid use, which is probably less extensive now than once was the case. Nevertheless, countless football players, bodybuilders, track athletes, and other competitive performers for whom strength, muscle mass, and stamina are crucial have shown themselves to be prepared to tolerate the significant personal hazards associated with using these drugs. Supposing anabolic steroids were legal and freely available, no doubt their use would increase significantly. If this occurred, one should not look for the aftermath only among athletes. Narcissistic yuppies in their quest for perfect abs—obviously a competitive activity in and of itself[5]—would quickly tumble to the reality that their hours of thankless conditioning on the Nautilus machine could actually be quite redeemed from a pill bottle. We should also assume that adolescents, combining inherent insecurity about the acceptability of their bodies with a bizarre aptitude for discounting future consequences, would read the benefits of anabolic steroid use in pica and the dangers in agate.

There are substantial social costs associated with the use of anabolic steroids. If more anabolics were used, which we would anticipate if the drugs were available over-the-counter, these costs would increase. The best documented reasons for concern involve matters that are borne internally, by the users of these drugs themselves, in the form of endocrine and cardiac disorders. The libertarian instinct would be to treat the choice to accept these costs in return for a benefit as a personal one, as with the choice to smoke. Though the prisoner's dilemma that arises on account of the "zero-sum" nature of athletic competition complicates the analysis somewhat, most libertarians would probably say that this is finally a problem for the sports leagues to sort out for themselves, that it does not justify regulation by the state at all, let alone by means of criminal laws. But the criminogenic aspects of anabolic steroids are another matter entirely. Here is rather clearly an epidemiological risk, with reports of increased aggressiveness, assault, and domestic violence associated with daily use of anabolic compounds.[6] The drug itself does not make violence "compulsory" in any morally commanding sense, nor does it remove the

---

[5] David Buss, *The Evolution of Desire* (New York: Basic Books, 1994).

[6] N. C. Pope and D. L. Katz, "Affective and Psychotic Symptoms Associated with Anabolic Steroid Use," *American Journal of Psychiatry*, vol. 145 (1988); P. Perry, K. Anderson, and W. Yates, "Illicit Anabolic Steroid Use in Athletes: A Case Series Analysis," *American Journal of Sports Medicine*, vol. 18 (1990); K. Brower, F. Blow, J. Young, and E. Hill, "Symptoms and Correlates of Anabolic-Androgenic Steroid Dependence," *British Journal of Addiction*, vol. 86 (1990); N. C. Pope and D. L. Katz, "Homicide and Near Homicide by Anabolic Steroid Users," *Journal of Clinical Psychiatry*, vol. 51 (1990); see also W. E. Buckley et al., "Estimated Prevalence of Anabolic Steroid Use among Male High School Seniors," *Journal of the American Medical Association*, vol. 260 (1988), pp. 3441–45.

capacity for choosing to refrain from acting upon a violent impulse as the criminal law conceives of choice.[7] It merely disposes a subject toward violence. Still, an externality is an externality. The trick with externalities is usually in agreeing about what they are and whether to notice them, but violence toward others is a noticeable externality if anything is, and no libertarian principle should demand that the regulation of what all can agree are weighty externalities must necessarily be limited to the criminal punishment of those who most directly caused them.

All of the problems of anabolic steroid use are magnified in the context of amphetamines and cocaine. Both drugs, when taken at high (but not rare) dosage levels, markedly increase a subject's disposition to aggression.[8] The ferocity of the war on drugs (concerning which I will have more to say later) must have done a great deal to suppress the popular use of cocaine, particularly, given its cachet in the entertainment industry. Legalization of all drugs would certainly boost cocaine use; how much is anyone's guess. Guessers, however, should remember that in a world with legal cocaine, one would not merely see more of the same of the current way of consuming cocaine (snorting and smoking) but large-scale commercial uses as well, in soft drinks, wine coolers, chocolate or coffee confections, and many other prepared food products where, as with caffeine currently, a bitter flavoring and stimulant effect are valued. I am prepared to grant, at least for the sake of the present argument, that this might actually be a better world. Nevertheless, it is all but guaranteed to produce more edgy, angry people, people more disposed to committing impulsive acts of violence. And though someone might reasonably think that, all things considered, the benefits would redeem the costs of such an environmental change, it does not seem persuasive to say that one *must* accept the superiority of that sort of world—that it is the sort of question that should not be put to a vote.

The criminogenic pitfall of cocaine might well turn out to be child's play next to amphetamine in its many forms. Indeed, it seems quite possible that, in head-to-head competition, amphetamine might single-handedly rout our society's flirtation with cocaine once and for all. Amphetamine is the more powerful stimulant. People who take it can stay awake for days in a row without discomfort or fatigue. Like cocaine, amphetamine produces a pleasing euphoria, which means it is a satisfactory substitute for cocaine as a party drug. Amphetamine has much more potent anorexic properties than cocaine. Major, effortless weight loss is among the most commonly reported side effects of amphetamine use

[7] Hence, an "anabolic steroid" defense against a charge of assault would probably be useless.

[8] See, e.g., Stuart Yudofsky, Jonathan Silver, and Robert Hales, "Cocaine and Aggressive Behavior: Neurobiological and Clinical Perspectives," *Bulletin of the Menninger Clinic*, vol. 57 (1993).

(indeed, often this is the primary object of such use). Far better than cocaine, amphetamine focuses one's attention and facilitates the performance of repetitive, routine tasks like housecleaning or the sort of boring homework that requires drill and review. There are, accordingly, many good reasons to take this drug along with several good reasons not to— costs of the internalized kind (such as risks of brain toxicity, hypertension, heart disease, and miscellaneous psychiatric complaints) but also externalities. One well-documented side-effect of chronic amphetamine use at high and increasing daily dosage (the drug habituates, so increasing dosage is necessary to maintain a desired effect) is micropsychotic rages, in which subjects become combative, assaultive, and unreasoning. To say that, on principle, one should acquiesce in having more of this sort of thing in the world implies strong principles indeed.

It is, of course, a non sequitur to say that if society tolerates alcohol, which is probably even more criminogenic than amphetamine, then it can tolerate these other criminogenics just as well. The question is not, after all, whether one is prepared, for the sake of libertarian principle, to embrace a society with a few million additional amphetamine addicts. The question is whether libertarian principle does in fact require this embrace, remembering how amphetamine addicts behave toward other people, including, perhaps, oneself. The answer to that question appears to be "no." And while one may always argue prudentially that in this or that context the regulation game is not worth the candle, on neither side of that argument is there an obviously libertarian point of view.

Teratogenic drugs (that is, drugs that cause birth defects) make up a different class of potential externality-imposers—one that comes, however, in a more conceptually untidy package than criminogenic drugs. Teratogens cause their harm not to the (usually female) persons who take them, but in the next generation, to the persons-to-be whose exposure is in utero. Thalidomide is the most famous teratogen. The drug is a tranquilizer, evidently innocuous to those who take it; but if taken by pregnant women, it is capable of causing terrible limb-formation defects to their unborn children. Thalidomide claimed a number of victims in Europe in the late 1950s, but none in the United States because its approval was held up by Dr. Frances Kelsey of the FDA, whose actions made her a folk heroine even though her suspicions about the drug—she believed that it might induce peripheral nerve damage—turned out to be unfounded.[9] For those old enough to remember the incident (which received extensive publicity at the time), the entire case for aggressive FDA regulation of untested drugs is probably encapsulated by the picture of the

---

[9] Because of her work on thalidomide, Dr. Kelsey was awarded the President's Gold Medal for Distinguished Service. See Sam Kazman, "Deadly Overcaution: FDA's Drug Approval Process," *Journal of Regulation and Social Costs*, vol. 1 (1990), p. 36.

intrepid Dr. Kelsey, like Horatio at the bridge, barring the way to thalidomide's introduction in the market.[10] Similarly, DES (diethylstilbestrol), an anti-miscarriage remedy that used to be given to pregnant women in the late 1940s and 1950s, turned out to seriously increase the risk of congenital reproductive-tract abnormalities (adenosis) and cancer (adenocarcinoma) in these subjects' female offspring.[11] It might be argued that in the case of drugs that carry such risks (and there is even a class of generation-skipping teratogens, whose bad effects are felt in the generation of the subject's grandchildren),[12] the patient herself is an imperfect agent for the rights of the unborn child, which in many arguments would lead to the conclusion that regulation is necessary (or, at a minimum, permissible).

In public debate over policy, this situation is vexing for several reasons. First, it violates the norm of political correctness that discourages the assumption that risks might follow an attribute classification like sex, because it singles out women, and pregnant ones at that, as objects of regulatory attention. Second, it takes explicit account of the rights of persons who are as yet unborn, thereby summoning all the Furies that have stalked debates about abortion. Third, it asserts that mothers-to-be, as imperfect agents of the rights of their unborn children, are also inferior agents to the regulatory regime that might displace what would otherwise be discretionary decisions concerning what drugs they might choose to take.

Nothing in libertarian theory would seem to dictate an answer to the question of whether an unborn child constitutes a rights-bearing person, although in the case of a child-to-be *that had not even been conceived*, one would have to suppose that libertarians would have to deny that such a virtual entity could have rights.[13] Nevertheless, limiting oneself to the case of an already-conceived but as yet unborn child, suppose that one had decided, on nonlibertarian grounds, that conception rather than live-birth-at-term is the proper line of demarcation between who does and who does not qualify as a bearer of rights; in that case, the regulatory

[10] Thalidomide still remains a substantial mystery. One researcher has stated: "There were 800 studies after the thalidomide disaster, but teratologists still do not know how that one drug causes limb reduction in the human embryo. They haven't even found the active part of the molecule in thalidomide or determined where it strikes during gestation." Mark Dowie, "Teratology: The Loneliest Science," *American Health*, June, 1990, p. 58.

[11] Some abnormalities in boys were also reported. DES has spawned a great deal of litigation and made some important law on the subject of joint causation and liability. See, e.g., *Sindell v. Abbott Laboratories*, 607 P.2d 924 (California Supreme Court, 1980); and *Hymowitz v. Eli Lilly & Co.*, 539 N.E.2d 1069 (New York Court of Appeals, 1989).

[12] C. M. Stinton, "Preliminary Indications that Functional Effects of Fetal Caffeine Exposure Can Be Expressed in a Second Generation," *Neurotoxicology and Teratology*, vol. 11 (July–August 1989), pp. 357–62.

[13] Otherwise, occasions for governmental intervention in any person's behavior would multiply without limit, on the ground that a given regulation was nothing more than a protection for the rights of persons unborn and unbegotten.

question would not be a simple one to answer. I do not propose to solve this problem here, because from the standpoint of drug regulation it seems more a special case than a general one. If one believes that "fetuses are persons," then the problem is one of regulating the behavior of women who are pregnant; teratogens are not of peculiar interest here, because there are many drugs women can take (cocaine being a well-known example), and also many non-ingestive behaviors in which they can engage (for example, skydiving), that create risks to the fetus. Libertarians should be comfortable with the social consensus that has emerged. For the most part it has been accepted that, even though mothers-to-be are not perfectly dependable brokers for the welfare of their offspring (and the same is true, for that matter, of parents of both sexes of already-born children), there is little chance that alternative institutions, such as regularized state supervision of pregnant women (or families), would improve matters, on net, over the run of cases. We have always been prepared to fudge this general principle on the tail of the distribution—hence abortion restrictions and actions to terminate parental rights in extreme cases of neglect or abuse—but these are rightly considered as rare and exceptional situations that do not represent the norm.

There is a different, perhaps less-apparent way that a regime of unregulated drug distribution could lead to the creation of external harms. Taking this problem seriously exposes what I take to be a remarkable rift in the libertarian position. Recently the readers of a national newspaper were greeted with a startling, front-page headline: "How Antibiotics May Be Making You Sicker: Overuse of the Drugs Can Create Dangerous 'Superstrains.' "[14] The body of the story goes on to describe the declining effectiveness of amoxicillin, still the treatment of choice for strep throat, some kinds of pneumonia and ear infections, and many other bacteriogenic diseases. It seems that more than 150 million prescriptions for this drug are written annually. The laws of large numbers thus give the probabilistic Darwinian laws of natural selection of genetic mutations an ample field of play, and bacteria that medicine cannot easily kill develop rapidly. Amoxicillin-resistant streptococci are already beginning to appear in significant numbers. It is a continuing challenge for medical research to keep one step ahead, and there is, of course, no guarantee that it will be successful.

There is a well-known connection between the effectiveness of an antibiotic drug and how commonly it has been used.[15] The amoxicillin phe-

---

[14] *Investor's Business Daily*, February 10, 1997.

[15] See generally Henry Blumberg, David Rimland, Donna Carroll, Pamela Terry, and Kaye Wachsmuth, "Rapid Development of Ciprofloxacin Resistance in Methicillin-Susceptable and -Resistant Staphylococcus aureus," *Journal of Infectious Diseases*, vol. 163 (1991); Mitchell Cohen, "Epidemiology of Drug Resistance: Implications for a Post-Microbial Era," *Science*, vol. 257 (1992); and Harold Neu, "The Crisis in Antibiotic Resistance," *Science*, vol. 257 (1992). See also, among many other authorities, Robert Muder, Carole Brennen, Angella

nomenon has been observed with ciprofloxacin, an antibiotic generally administered by intravenous infusion to hospitalized patients. After its introduction in the market, it swiftly became the favored means of controlling the hospital-borne bacterium *S. Aureus*, against which it was at first 100 percent effective. By the time ciprofloxacin had been in use for only a year, 80 percent of *S. Aureus* bacteria were found to be resistant. Because of overuse, the value of the drug had largely disappeared.

Antibiotics are prescription drugs. Willing buyers and willing sellers may not by law transfer them without a doctor's order. Whatever the original purpose (if any) of this legal restriction, it can certainly be justified as a means of solving what would otherwise be an intractable public-action problem that touches a matter of great seriousness—indeed, of life and death. The concern is that, in the absence of this regulation, individuals might self-medicate with antibiotics on medically inappropriate occasions, that is, when a bacterial infection was not serious enough to justify treatment at all or when a medical complaint originated from a nonbacterial source, such as colds and influenzas, which are caused by viruses and therefore cannot be treated with antibiotics. In fact, the great majority of illness in the population (though not nearly all) is viral in origin. Yet it is usually hard to tell viral and bacterial infections apart, because they typically have about the same clinical symptoms. Physicians can sometimes differentiate between them through physical examination, but lab tests ordinarily are necessary to confirm the diagnosis.

This is a libertarian conundrum that may have no satisfactorily libertarian solution. It is futile to hope that people could be educated not to try to use antibiotics against viruses, or that, if lab tests are necessary to obtain a differential diagnosis, then people, as individuals, could certainly be trusted to order and pay for such lab tests for themselves. We should not expect any such thing. In a world where antibiotics were available over the counter, rational consumers should not care whether their disease was bacterial or viral in origin. If bacterial, then the antibiotic will kill the infection unless it is caused by a resistant mutation. If viral, then little or no harm done—except the harm of overuse, an infinitesimal marginal harm to the community as a whole, which would swiftly have to learn to come to grips with resistant bacteria in any event. The harm sought to be averted—the development of resistant strains of bacteria—will occur irrespective of what any one individual may choose

---

Goetz, Marilyn Wagener, and John Rihs, "Association with Prior Fluoroquinolone Therapy of Widespread Ciprofloxacin Resistance among Gram-Negative Isolates in a Veterans Affairs Medical Center," *Antimicrobial Agents and Chemotherapy*, vol. 35 (1991); Robert Gaynes, Robert Weinstein, William Chamberlin, and Sherwin Kabins, "Antibiotic-Resistant Flora in Nursing Home Patients Admitted to the Hospital," *Archives of Internal Medicine*, vol. 145 (1985); Barbara Murray, "New Aspects of Antimicrobial Resistance and the Resulting Therapeutic Dilemmas," *Journal of Infectious Diseases*, vol. 163 (1991); and Thomas O'Brien et al., "Resistance of Bacteria to Antibacterial Agents: Report of Task Force 2," *Reviews of Infectious Diseases*, vol. 9 (1987).

or do. In the prisoners' dilemma, it is rational to "defect" no matter what the other prisoner does. And so it is here.

Loren Lomasky has suggested[16] that a nongovernmental solution for this problem might be to extend manufacturers' property rights in antibiotic drugs, so that they would have both an incentive and a means of preventing the overuse of their products. Such a property right might be quite similar in practice to an ordinary patent, except that it would not be limited in duration. Manufacturers would have to control the distribution of their product quite carefully, because the result of piracy would not merely be lost profits, but potentially the loss of the product itself. Similar medicines produced by competing manufacturers could lead to a cartel problem—that is, cheating by a cartel member whose time horizon is, for some reason, shorter than that of the average member of the cartel. Such cartel problems might well be overcome, and if they were, all to the good; but this is a solution to a superficial problem (the clunkiness of public regulation) rather than the deep libertarian problem of whether the community is justified in asserting the common ownership of the immunological characteristics of its individual members.

Without regulatory mechanisms of some kind, it seems that decontrolling the distribution of antibiotic drugs would lead to more such drugs being taken than currently, followed by a rapid diminution in the efficacy of the existing inventory of such medicines. There would be a corresponding increase (to which one could assign an actuarial present value, in order to clarify how expensive such a policy would be) in the dangers and costs to which each member of the community would then be exposed because resistant bacteria require stronger, higher-priced drugs to treat, are more likely to require hospitalization, and are much more likely to kill the subjects they infect. The Centers for Disease Control in the U.S. have estimated that, for patients infected with antimicrobial-resistant salmonella, hospitalization is necessary more than twice as often as it is for patients who are afflicted with the susceptible strain—57 percent as compared to 24 percent. Antimicrobial-resistant salmonella infections have *seventeen times* the mortality rate that susceptible-bacteria infections do— 3.4 percent compared to 0.2 percent.[17]

Suppose we reject this outcome and accept that the immunological status of the community as a whole is to be regarded as a public good, to which people are appropriately coerced to contribute. This was, arguably, the import of the holding of the U.S. Supreme Court in *Jacobson v. Massachusetts*,[18] decided in 1905. Jacobson's argument was that—on religious grounds, among others—he should be excused from compulsory small-

---

[16] In discussion.

[17] Scott Holmberg, Steven Solomon, and Paul Blake, "Health and Economic Impacts of Anti-Microbial Resistance," *Reviews of Infectious Diseases*, vol. 9 (December 1987), pp. 1065-77.

[18] 197 U.S. 11 (1905).

pox vaccination. Of course, if everyone else in the community is vaccinated against smallpox, the chances of the last, unvaccinated individual getting it nearly vanish, and what is the state's interest in using coercion to extinguish a practically negligible risk? Furthermore, if a person has refused vaccination and does come down with smallpox, who has a right to complain about it, given that all the others, having been vaccinated themselves, are going to be quite immune?

Though it had never heard the term "free-rider," the Supreme Court knew one when it saw one, and it had no difficulty brushing off Jacobson's claim. Being in an unvaccinated condition made Jacobson a vector for smallpox. He was therefore what amounted to an ambulatory nuisance. It was just as though he was keeping a malarial swamp—what we would nowadays call a wetland and strictly safeguard from improvement. Try as they might, public health authorities will never immunize every single person in a community. Some vaccinations do not take; new people are being born and must not be vaccinated for a time; susceptible people drift in from other places; some people live in such isolation that they do not know anything about smallpox and have no idea that they are supposed to be vaccinated; others live in such obscurity that the public health department cannot find them or does not know they are there. Let the bubble of unvaccinated people get larger and the risk to public health expands still faster. Hence, no one whom public health authorities can possibly reach may be allowed a free ride.

Libertarians must surely find this turn in the argument unsettling. Of course, no one is going to carry a brief for killer bacteria, but if one owes one's antibodies to the community, what does one not owe? Where is the stopping place for this duty to others? It would seem that answering this question would require a distinctively libertarian account of public goods—an account of what sorts of publicly beneficial activities are worth allowing a little (or a lot of) coercion, and how we can tell. As my colleague Gary Lawson points out, however, libertarians are interested in rights rather than public goods; hence, they prefer to leave such easily abused subjects as common property to one side in order to zero in on the question of when coercion can be used without violating someone's rights. This probably disqualifies me from full membership in the tribe (hence the subtitle of this essay), because it seems to me to beg the central question of what rights people ought to be free to claim if they want to live with other people. It is idle to object to coercion when it comes to the creation of jointly consumable, non-excludable goods like an environment free of deadly diseases. Thus, if the very composition of a person's bloodstream is a public good, it would seem to follow that coercing that person (in order to achieve certain public-health goals) is proper simply because he is alive.

Such a conclusion allows the camel's nose of the statist argument, and the rest of the camel along with it, to get not merely under the tent-flap but almost the whole way to the bedroll of libertarian ideals. Lacking some better way to say what is and what is not a public good, there is nothing left but mediating institutions, in other words, a democratic political process where citizens vote on how much of other people's stuff the nanny state will allow them to keep. Of course, notoriously, mediating institutions are poor respecters of rights; precisely what they usually mediate is the transformation of A's rights into B's subsidy. If libertarians continue to insist that this is a conversation in which they want no part, they abandon the field to those whose deepest intellectual commitments involve the proposition that the good consists in what the gods of mediating institutions generate. If there are no rights, everything is permitted, and so, because mediating institutions have the power to produce them, public goods are everywhere and damn the owl-hating, wifebeater-loving, baby-starving philistines who stand in the merry way of creating more. Nothing, not bottles of urine with crucifixes within, nor passenger trains that hardly anyone will ride, nor university research on the reproductive habits of tree frogs, nor anything else in human imagination fails the test of being a public good, because there is no test—and, for that matter, in the statist endgame, no good either in any self-respecting metaphysical sense, but only a public with an unstructured, insatiable appetite. In this state of affairs, the only rights that can have much meaning are the rights to organize a pirate ship of one's own. Everything is on the table and the libertarians are sulking in their tents, solving syllogisms with axiomatic rights as their major premise, and refusing even to entertain the possibility of a libertarian restatement of public goods.

III. PATERNALISM

Paternalism involves the claim that a person is, in some respects, in a sort of agency relationship with himself, and furthermore is, for some reason, a comparatively inadequate or untrustworthy agent of his own welfare. Much food and drug regulation, perhaps most, is essentially paternalistic. And if there is one thing libertarians know for sure, it is that they are against paternalistic laws. The following discussion is meant as a plea for a bit more nuance in this antipaternalistic reflex. The problem of paternalism exasperates libertarian theory as seriously as does the public-goods problem, and for a similar reason. Both are what might be called boundary issues that concern how one draws the line between oneself and the larger world. The one-clause claim of libertarians against paternalistic laws is: I am a fitter decision-maker for my own welfare than some committee of which I am not even a member. This claim makes two crucial assumptions. The second assumption, concerning what counts as membership in the law-making body, involves the issue of representation—when one can be taken as having constructively "consented" to laws to which one did not in fact consent, and to which one may in fact object. That problem I set to one side as beyond the scope of the present discussion. The first assumption in the libertarian claim is that one knows (and can answer for) the identity of "I." It is no small matter. Without some kind of account of who "I" is, it will not be possible to pin down the boundary between where a particular "self" stops and where the community of others begins. And the very idea of what, after all, a "self" actually *is* abides in ambiguity.

Most of us share a common perception that, from day to day, there is a continuity in human personalities. A given person's tastes, temperament, character, and so on, will fluctuate only so much, and somewhere in that narrow band of variance, the person, himself, is to be found. But this is simply an assumption. Many observers, even those with decidedly libertarian sympathies, will recognize the "loosely integrated self" of which Jon Elster has written.[19] A clear illustration of the problem can be seen if one views a "self" over an appreciable timescale. Is a nine-year-old boy for all intents and purposes the same person he will be when he is nineteen or forty-nine or seventy-nine? It is a reasonable guess that not many forty-nine-year-olds could honestly deny that they are better off now because certain choices were foreclosed to them back when they were young and stupid.

But even if long timescales are not in question, it seems to be the case that a person's "self" is a complicated, nested, self-contradictory beast. The mental faculties one brings to bear on the making of choices must operate on various levels of generality. What should we say of a "choice" to eat our cake and have it too (one of the more common "choices" people make as citizens, as when they insist on lower taxes and more public services)? People who backslide on self-improvement campaigns experience the same conflictual relationship with their "selves." Some justification has to be offered for counting the revealed preference as the "choice" (as in, "He chose to eat the brownie") rather than counting the reflective desire (as in, "I wish I could lose some weight"). Libertarian critiques of regulatory programs have to take these complexities seriously, because regulatory programs are often based on the (charitably reconstructed) premise that people will often, for some good reason, "choose" to limit their own choices.

The prohibition on heroin (a drug which does not produce aggressive behavior) is an example of a paternalistic law. Nonpaternalistic justifications for such laws are hardly more than aerobics for the lips. It is labored and implausible to justify heroin prohibition as a regulatory control on externality-creation (let's say, because heroin users may drive their cars under the influence) or as the solution to free-riding (because—ain't it the truth?—everyone would like to be the lone junkie in an otherwise orderly,

[19] Jon Elster, ed., *The Multiple Self* (New York: Cambridge University Press, 1986), p. 3.

drug-free world). The real reason we ban heroin is because it is bad for people to use it (or so the authorities believe), and because people who think otherwise are mistaken. The question, then, should be: What is it that junkies are mistaken about? Whether it feels good to use heroin? The *nature* of the good? The essence of their own self-interest? The relationship between hedonic activities, reason, and the duties that go along with membership in the community? What supports the claim that, at least sometimes, ordinary people are incompetent agents of their own welfare in comparison to public authorities?

Evidently we are not dealing with some sort of information deficit as we normally speak of such things. Paternalistic regulation is not primarily based on the theory that heroin users lack "information"—in other words, that they don't know things about heroin that the authorities know. If that were the problem, then we could simply tell them, and they *would* know. Heroin regulators are hardly content to leave matters there, because they appreciate that some people with full information about heroin go ahead and use it anyway. Inasmuch as we try to prevent this bad choice even when it is an informed choice, a non-information-based justification for regulation must be at work. We are asserting and enforcing a certain human good, a Socratic set-up if there ever was one. Tell us what you know of the Good, Senator, we are hungry to learn from one so wise.

In passing laws that seek to prevent bad choices from being made, we are behaving as parents do toward their children. One of parents' main jobs is guiding and limiting the choices of their children, which means ruling out certain choices altogether. The problem of children's preferences is inherently a difficult one for libertarian theory. The choices of children do not count; they are a special case. But why should we say so? It is arrantly a fiction to say that children are "incapable" of consent. Anyone who has ever been well-acquainted with a two-year-old knows that the capacity-in-fact to form preferences, and strong ones at that, over a wide assortment of subjects, develops early on in life. Surely the proposition that children "cannot consent" is merely a shorthand way of expressing the thought that they are chronically short on information and the wherewithal to process it: information about who they are, what is and is not in their own interest, how one can get the things that one wants, who other people are and what they're for, and so forth. But, of course, children are not the only ones who lack perfect information on these matters. Everyone is in that position to a greater or lesser extent. It is part of the human condition. Something more is required in order to preserve the asserted "specialness" of the case of children from question-begging.

There is, of course, something more. What is "special" about the case is not the innate limitations of children's reason but rather the nature of the familial relationship. There is an excellent theory about why parents might be superior to their children as decision makers over a range of choices, but no obvious cognate theory about why the state might similarly be superior to individuals with respect to the same sorts of decisions. Very little of this theory of intrafamilial paternalism can be transferred to the state's paternalism toward its citizens. It is unintelligible to speak of the state's "altruism" toward individuals, and question-begging in its own right—to say nothing of being at odds with common experience—to say that public authorities ordinarily have a grasp of human happiness that is systematically superior to that of those whose behavior they presume to regulate. It is not that individuals are so wise in managing their own affairs. The real point is that there is no good reason to credit the assertion that a perfect stranger, or a committee of perfect strangers, has a better comprehension than oneself about such crucial questions as what risks should be taken in pursuit of one's own welfare, or how individual risk preferences translate into a prescription about how one should behave.

Yet it is not quite true that the case for paternalistic regulation is thus refuted. Paternalism comes in more than one variety. The concept that Thomas Schelling has called "self-paternalism" is probably the most formidable objection to the libertarian argument against paternalistic law.[20] The idea of self-paternalism capitalizes on the commonplace observation that people have limited intertemporal control over their own behavior, know that they do, and often wish they could do something about it. Quite often people act in a certain way in the present in order to increase the probability of being able to do something else in the future. Putting one's alarm clock on the other side of the room before one goes to sleep at night is a self-paternalistic act. The person one is tonight—the "tonight person"—is thus trying to prevent the "tomorrow morning person" from oversleeping, even though (as one can foresee the night before) the "tomorrow morning person" will *want* to oversleep, and may even, when the alarm goes off, be annoyed by the "last night person's" accurate foresight of this fact and effective precaution-taking against it. Placing a padlock on the refrigerator door as an adjunct to a diet, or giving away one's cigarettes at the office in a very public way on the day one quits smoking, are other, familiar self-paternalistic acts mentioned by Schelling. All involve the same idea: that in order to accomplish certain objectives, one must often behave in a way that will defeat the behavioral consequences that flow from future fluctuations in one's schedule of preferences. Some people may maximize their freedom to quit smoking for the rest of their lives only by finding ways of subverting their freedom to change their mind and smoke a cigarette.

It is only trivially paradoxical to say that "freedom" may be enhanced by the existence of visibly binding constraints on freedom. The law of contract, and the freedom of contract that it largely aims to protect, is not

[20] Thomas Schelling, "The Intimate Contest for Self-Command," *The Public Interest*, vol. 60 (1980).

paradoxical in any morally interesting way. The entire project of social cooperation, to which we owe almost all of the material goods we possess, is made possible by people being able to make credible promises in the present about how they will be obligated to behave in the future. We give legal significance to one concept of what it means to "choose" rather than to another. This is no more a paradox than it is paradoxical to go to one movie instead of another.

The concept of agency and self-ownership is a complicated one. Even a doctrinaire libertarian might be fearful about, and wish to take precautions against, oscillations in his own risk preferences. Though a person might be able to answer for himself 99.9 percent of the time, sooner or later some great sleepless worry might overwhelm one's usual self, and then a trip to the (legal) heroin dispensary, if there were one, might seem the most sensible thing to do *at that particular moment*. Voting for a world in which heroin is illegal (and therefore relatively hard to get) need not, in other words, be based on A's fear that B will use heroin, but may be based on A's knowledge that his *own* heroin-related predilections are not invariant, but may fluctuate depending on circumstances. And of course, part of the reason one refrains from using an addictive substance is simply that it *is* addictive, meaning that a choice to use heroin for the first time today will make it more difficult to refrain from using it—which is to say, to exercise the choice not to use it—tomorrow and habitually. It would diminish any incentive one might have to refrain from using heroin right now if one thought that sooner or later, when the great sleepless worry did befall (as inevitably one must), one would probably go out and get oneself hooked on the drug anyway—so what the hell, why not save time?

In our world—and perhaps this is one of its more libertarian characteristics—there exist few institutions that allow a binding effect to be given to the promises one makes to oneself. One cannot simply hire an insurance company or a valet-cum-enforcer to make sure one does not cheat on one's diet or backslide on one's decision to quit smoking cigarettes. We cannot indenture ourselves; slavery, even on a leasehold basis limited to certain purposes, is not really an option this side of having ourselves committed. Thus, external public regulation, rather than contract or other private-sector devices, has been the most straightforward way, and in many cases it does seem the only feasible way, to put self-paternalisms in place.

The libertarian critique of paternalistic laws is weaker for failing to recognize the moral significance of the self-paternalistic choices people might make for themselves. To give those choices a pugnaciously libertarian spin, one might say that people have a right to make such choices—we might even say an inalienable, God-given right to make them. Saying so, we shall of course be reinventing a very old wheel, for this is no more than to say that people have a right to form governments to further their own welfare, a task which can be carried on only institutionally—and if those institutions are democratic, then they must be of the mediating kind, which, as libertarians know, leads on to perdition.

But not directly. Once libertarians have lost the argument about whether paternalistic institutions should exist at all, they should not retire to their cells for the life of fasting and prayer. After all, the field of action in which self-paternalistic drug regulation makes any sense is quite limited, and someone needs to point this out. It is one thing to say: "For the sake of my own weakness and stupid, risk-taking curiosity, all heroin must be locked up." It is something quite different to make the same claim about ulcer medicine, blood pressure medicine, prostate medicine, angina medicine, and so on. With prescription drugs, the concern is that people will take these drugs improvidently, will self-diagnose incorrectly, and will self-medicate dangerously. Let us not be too quick to say "What if they do?" because, after all, why *would* people do such a thing? It is only a distraction to pretend that one answers this question by imagining the immediate effects—what would happen this afternoon, let us say, if Congress suddenly repealed Durham-Humphrey—the 1951 amendment to the 1938 Food, Drug, and Cosmetic Act that prohibited over-the-counter sale of medicines which could not safely be used without medical supervision. The question is: How would we expect people to behave if there were adequate lead time to accustom them to taking greater responsibility for their own safety? In the current dispensation, what government *allows* people to do is information about what they *may* safely do (or so people have been led to believe). But nothing like this is necessary; this reliance, to the extent that it exists, is largely an accident of the monopoly that government exercises over what may and may not be legally sold for a person's own good. In this instance, the harm against which the government means to defend is one against which people could easily defend themselves. If they understood that, hereafter, self-protection would be up to themselves, wise people would take only the medicines they were familiar with or that their doctor, or some other source they regarded as reliable, told them to take. Let us not kid ourselves that in such a regime, there would not be foolish people who fell through the cracks. But it is foolish in itself to insist on the moral inevitability of a social order that is a padded room for fools. Liberty favors the wise, in this as in most other instances. There is ordinarily no reason to coerce people to be wise—in other words, to act in their own interests. For the vast majority of strictly regulated substances and the vast majority of people, self-paternalism is nearly an irrelevant concern.

IV. Libertarianism as a Critical Theory

It seems to me that libertarian ideals, best understood, bear about the same relationship to public policy that bay leaves do to a pot of soup: a

228 DANIEL D. POLSBY

flavor but not a source of nutrition. I do not see this as a definitive put-down but as a reminder of the practical limits of the libertarian argument. When deployed as a critical theory rather than as a means of generating a political organism in its own right, the argument comes into its own. It does not need good answers if it has good questions for those who assume to wield the coercive power of the state. As a method of criticism, the whole enterprise of libertarianism loses its burnish of utopian ardor and begins to look like ordinary American common sense. In tactical terms, one might compare the transformation to that of going from the defensive over to the offensive (which, come to think of it, is something that most libertarians of my acquaintance have quite an aptitude for). Let the talk be not of theory but of actual cases and it is statists who must acknowledge that they have no good limiting principles for their idea of public goods, and that their theory of social progress implies, acquiesces in, or insists upon a public sector of constantly increasing size at the expense of private lives. Rather than trying to defend the questionable proposition that all paternalisms are bad, libertarians can change the subject to whether a given use of state power depends on the laughable proposition that all paternalisms are (at least contingently) good. If many of the existing food and drug regulations can be justified to a libertarian sensibility, most could scarcely be justified to *any* rational sensibility. Most give evidence of a bureaucratic and political process that has taken on a life of its own, moving more and more resolutely away from any sensible uses of regulatory power toward a steady state of unwarranted, mindless puttering with other people's affairs.

Under current law, the FDA must approve a new drug as safe and effective before it may be marketed. Food additives, unless they are "generally recognized as safe," must be demonstrated to be safe. Should a drug be developed that effectively treats a disease to some degree but carries side-effects, it is likely that the FDA will delay or refuse to approve marketing. Even terminally ill patients may be prevented from obtaining drugs which they hope may prolong their lives. The Supreme Court in 1979 rejected the claim of terminally ill cancer patients that they were entitled to an exception from FDA approval for Laetrile.[21] Even a patient at death's door is not allowed to purchase a drug unless it has been found both safe and effective by the FDA.[22] More recently the FDA delayed approval of Tacrine, a drug designed to treat Alzheimer's disease.[23] Where,

[21] *United States v. Rutherford*, 442 U.S. 544, 551–52 (1979).

[22] However, the FDA has suspended its policy of seizing nonapproved drugs imported from other countries, so a patient with sufficient resources may be able to obtain the desired medication from abroad. Peter Hutt, "The Regulation of Pharmaceutical Products in the U.S.A.," in *Pharmaceutical Medicine*, ed. Denis M. Burley et al., 2d ed (London and Boston: E. Arnold, 1993), pp. 216–17.

[23] Gina Kolata, "Sharp Debate on Value of an Alzheimer's Drug," *New York Times*, April 4, 1991, p. B1. Tacrine was eventually approved in September 1993 (*FDA Electronic Bulletin Board*, September 9, 1993).

precisely, is the externality here against which the public must be protected? None can be articulated that does not involve silliness. All that appears to be at work here is a heavy-handed paternalism that expresses an illiberal value: those without hope should not, for their own good, be permitted false hope. (And a hope is false unless it has been shown to be safe and effective by adequate and well-controlled experiments and tests in human subjects.) Where does the Food, Drug, and Cosmetic Act speak of hope or of what one may hope? This is a value that has no roots in any intelligible philosophy of consumer protection; there is nothing in the statute that it meaningfully reconstructs. This approach on the part of the FDA manifestly speaks of the good of a person as though it knew the good—as if to close its eyes to the reality that the real "good" being protected here is the sweeping administrative discretion that the Supreme Court will allow the agency to exercise.

The FDA's recent adventures with the ersatz dietary fat Olestra (sucrose polyester) is a snapshot of destructive government in a similar, perhaps even more ridiculous posture. Obesity is linked to multiple health problems, principally cardiovascular diseases (by far the leading cause of mortality in the United States) and diabetes (the sixth leading cause of mortality).[24] It is common knowledge that excess fat consumption contributes to obesity. Olestra can be used in many products where other fat-substitutes cannot—for example, baked foods like cake mixes, or fried products like potato chips—and it is aesthetically superior to other fat-substitutes (or so its manufacturer says) in salad dressings, ice-cream type products, and many other applications. Olestra is valuable because it allows a given volume of food to be consumed with much less fat and many fewer calories than if regular, digestible fat were used. Procter & Gamble began seeking approval for use of Olestra as a fat-substitute in 1987.[25] In November 1995, eight years later, a divided FDA advisory committee voted to recommend approval of Olestra as a food additive,[26] and the FDA has finally approved its use in salt snacks such as potato chips and for other limited purposes, though not more generally—for example, as a substitute for Crisco or margarine, where its greatest usefulness probably lies.

The hold-up has been that Olestra has known side-effects. Some users get diarrhea and some may experience a diminished uptake of fat-soluble vitamins. It seems to strain credulity that any such trade-off could have been taken seriously. Millions, literally, of obese customers, praying for the least crutch to help them with their problem, are put on hold for twice

---

[24] *Statistical Abstract of the United States, 1995 National Data Book* (Washington, DC: Government Printing Office, 1995), p. 92, table 125.

[25] Eben Shapiro, "Fat Substitutes: The Long, Hard Quest for Foods That Fool the Palate," *New York Times*, September 29, 1991, p. C5.

[26] Marian Burros, "FDA Advisory Panel Backs Approval of a Fat Substitute," *New York Times*, November 18, 1995, p. A11.

as many years as it took to win World War II because a bureaucracy believes they must not be allowed to take even easily managed, easily reversible risks. It is very well to speak in general of the importance of controlling externalities, but in this particular case, there is no externality to be controlled. No one has to consume Olestra involuntarily. No one need consume it at all. Similarly, one can grant paternalism an honorable place in public policy as a limited generality, but let us be specific. This paternalism prevents people from taking risks that are minor, risks of which they can easily be fully and fairly informed beforehand, risks that make utter sense not only in helping them work out judicious life-plans for themselves but also as a means of helping diminish the huge risks of disease and death, *to which they do not "consent,"* that are connected with their predicament.

And then there was the strange case of the home drug-testing kit. For more than a year, the FDA held up over-the-counter sale of this product, even though it was based on technology that has long been used in industry, insisting that it must clear through the arduous process required for the approval of a Type-III medical device. This was a situation in which the agency did indeed have discretion to decide that the kit was a Type-III medical device, but also had discretion to decide whether or not it needed to go through the long-form approval process. Why did the FDA prefer the longer path in this case? Though it soft-pedaled the reasoning in its public statements, the agency disclosed its real concern in a private conference with an industry attorney: if parents were allowed to use industrial drug-surveillance techniques to monitor their children's possible drug use, this might contribute to familial "coercion and discord." It is a jurisprudentially interesting question whether, if the agency has statutory discretion to treat the kit as a Type-III device, it must observe any limits on exercising its statutory discretion to waive the long-form approval process. The kit would be unavailable still, except that somehow a copy of the attorney's memorandum of his meeting with the agency leaked, and the agency's underlying motives were ratted out. Bipartisan jeering in Congress obliged the agency to take into account the ultimate nonstatutory criterion for the exercise of discretion and it relented, approving the sale of the kit.[27] But this is a faux-happy ending for the story. Heaven knows how much equally airheaded mischief is being done out of the public's gaze. Congress has not acted to refine and focus the FDA's mission, and there is no reason to suppose that the agency will not persist in its ways.

Lest it be thought that a large indictment hangs on only a few short stories, one should make clear that the foregoing are not isolated incidents but are part of an established pattern of activity for which the agency makes no apology, a pattern which flows from the very structure

[27] *Washington Post*, February 2, 1997, p. F13.

of incentives under which the agency necessarily operates. Some additional illustration is in order. William Wardell, a Nobel laureate in medicine, estimated that FDA delays in the approval of beta blockers to treat heart-attack victims, delays that went on for years after the beneficial effects of these drugs had become generally accepted in the scientific community, cost seventy to eighty thousand lives.[28] Wardell and Louis Lasagna noted that the "introduction of a new drug that produced fatalities anywhere approaching this magnitude would be regarded as a major disaster, but the undoubted occurrence of deaths through failure to introduce a drug has so far gone unremarked."[29]

In the early 1970s, the FDA rejected the new drug application (NDA) of Levamisole, a drug designed for the treatment of worms, ostensibly because other effective treatments for worms were available. Its real reason, according to some observers, was different—a fear that once the drug was approved and available to doctors to use at their discretion, they would seek to use it for a nonapproved purpose, namely to treat colon cancer. Levamisole was finally approved for use in treating colon cancer in 1989.[30] When the investigational application for valproate sodium, which is now used in the treatment of epilepsy, was first filed in the 1970s, it was already recognized abroad as the drug of choice for many epileptics. However, the FDA initially classified valproate sodium's investigational application as not meriting the fast-track approval process.[31] Misoprostol was already available for the treatment of gastric ulcers in forty-three other countries when the FDA finally got around to approving it for use in the United States. Gastrointestinal ulcers are common among users of aspirin and other nonsteroidal anti-inflammatory drugs, and at the time the NDA for misoprostol was submitted to the FDA, these ulcers caused approximately 10,000 to 20,000 deaths per year. One researcher estimates that, based on the 94 percent effectiveness of the drug and the FDA's nine-month review of misoprostol's NDA, 8,000 to 15,000 lives were lost due to FDA review during the NDA period alone.[32] Streptokinase and TPA, two drugs used to open the blocked arteries of heart-attack victims both had the potential to save the lives of the 11,000 heart-attack victims who die in hospitals each year. The FDA's approval of streptokinase did not occur until two years after its NDA was filed (and six months after an FDA advisory panel had recommended approval), thus costing a possible 22,000 lives.[33] TPA, a synthetic version of streptokinase, was thought by

[28] William M. Wardell, "A Close Inspection of the 'Calm Look'," *Journal of the American Medical Association*, vol. 239 (1978), p. 2010.

[29] William M. Wardell and Louis Lasagna, *Regulation and Drug Development* (Washington, DC: American Enterprise Institute, 1975), p. 77.

[30] H. Schwartz, "A 'Miracle' Drug That Languished among the Worms," *Wall Street Journal*, July 18, 1989, p. A22.

[31] Wardell, "A Close Inspection," p. 2010.

[32] Kazman, "Deadly Overcaution" (*supra* note 9), p. 47.

[33] *Ibid.*, p. 49.

many experts at the time of the filing of its NDA to be even more promising in treating heart-attack victims than streptokinase. However, the same advisory panel which eventually recommended approval of streptokinase recommended against approval of TPA's NDA. The drug was later approved, but news reports indicated that the initial vote not to approve TPA's NDA was based largely on jurisdictional disputes between one FDA bureau responsible for drugs and another responsible for genetically engineered products.[34] The hypnotic Nitrazepam, which is used in lieu of much-riskier barbiturates for the treatment of sleeping disorders and anxiety, was approved in the United States five years after its approval in Great Britain. Wardell and Lasagna estimate that it would have saved thousands of lives in the United States in the interim.[35]

Of course, the FDA *must* make its mistakes on the far side of caution. If the agency approved a drug that turned out to be unsafe and resulted in even a hundred deaths, it would provoke national headlines, extended congressional investigations, a drive-by shooting by a *60 Minutes* camera crew, and, for the FDA's management, professional disgrace. However, the FDA's lengthy delays in approving drugs which in many cases are known (to officials in other countries and experts in the American medical community) to be effective treatments are met with silence, because the victims of these delays are, in most cases, unaware of the existence of the potential treatment.[36]

If one is attached to theories of false consciousness, this is a very good place to start using them. We know it is a human tendency, robust and often observed, to give short weight to the costs we cannot see and to overweigh the costs we can. The very purpose of institutions founded on explicitly paternalistic premises is to help us overcome what we accept as defects in our own judgment and foresight. But the FDA is an institution designed to exacerbate the astigmatism instead of correcting it. No servile extenuations about the temperance of self-paternalism or correctives to intrinsically faulty human judgment will answer for any of the foregoing examples. They bespeak a pathology of administrative government, no more and no less. It may well be that bad decisions are sometimes made because of mistaken judgments by the personnel of the agency or its

---

[34] "TPA: The Tip of the Iceberg," *Wall Street Journal*, December 2, 1987, p. A12.

[35] Wardell and Lasagna, *Regulation and Drug Development*, pp. 72–73.

[36] When a class of victims is organized and alert, as AIDS victims have been and cancer patients have become, they can, of course, often win special, fast-track concessions from the agency. See generally Elizabeth Larson, "Unequal Treatments," *Reason*, April 1992, p. 48; Gina Kolata, "Trial of Experimental AIDS Drug to Be Continued, with Revisions," *New York Times*, March 9, 1990, p. 1. It is an unusual situation when a disease strikes largely at a class of people who have pre-constituted themselves into a vocal, well-funded interest group, but lucky for those who have that disease rather than some other, equally serious or more serious disease whose victims have no political juice. See Morton Kondracke, "How Diabetes Plan Was Hatched—And Why It Is Not Enough," *Roll Call Online*, http://www.rollcall.com/commentary/kondracke.html.

adjunctive committees. But to locate the problem in this officer or that doctor, rather than in the very structure of the institution, is crudely to miss the point. Without a change in the structure of accountability and incentives under which the agency operates, and some firmer boundaries on what its proper scope should be, we have the best FDA we are going to get.

V. Some Utilitarian Considerations

Because libertarian thinking tends to be normative thinking, some justification must be offered for inserting a positive account of the costs of a regulatory regime into a libertarian conversation. It seems to me that in a world where everything good is scarce, it is self-evident if not axiomatic that costs impinge on persons and also on their rights—either the rights that they "have," or at least the ones they will be in a position to exercise—and that pointless, foolishly incurred, or cruelly incurred costs are the hardest kind of all to bear. If this premise underrates the stoutheartedness of libertarian attachment to purely normative rights discourse, apologies beforehand are hereby tendered.

A. The FDA

Congress budgets about $100 million per year for FDA drug reviews, a number that can, as these things go, be regarded as trifling. Manufacturers must spend much larger sums to develop new products and see them through the approval process. A 1990 study put the expected research and development costs for each approved drug at $231 million (in 1987 dollars).[37] Eventually, consumers pay these costs, no doubt more than they should, for the drug industry is quite oligopolistic, consisting of a few giant concerns hunkered down behind high entry barriers which the FDA obligingly furnishes, and hence more likely to merge with one another than to face competition from a start-up firm.[38]

The FDA's monopoly on new drug approvals means the process is isolated from market forces which would give balance to safety concerns. The agency's drug-approval performance has been deteriorating, as compared with both its own previous record and that of similar agencies in

---

[37] J. A. DiMasi et al., "Cost of Innovation in the Pharmaceutical Industry," *Journal of Health and Economics*, vol. 10 (1991), p. 126. The study estimated the probable range of costs to be between $197 million and $287 million.

[38] The high research-and-development costs mandated by government approval have been cited as a reason for market consolidation and merger activity. See *ibid.*, p. 108. During the late 1980s, several mergers within the pharmaceutical industry occurred, including SmithKline-Beecham, Bristol Myers-Squibb, and Merrell Dow-Marion Laboratories. See *ibid.*, p. 108, n. 5.

other countries.[39] The FDA's average review time for new drug applications increased from an average of seven months during the 1962 to 1967 period (immediately after the Food, Drug, and Cosmetic Act was amended to require testing for efficacy as well as safety, but before the FDA had fully embraced its new task) to thirty months in the late 1980s.[40] The slowness of this average approval time is highlighted by comparison to approval times in Great Britain: in 1984, median approval time of new drugs in the U.S. was 31.1 months; in Great Britain it was 12.0 months.[41] The FDA claims it has improved its approval times recently, to a median of 26.7 months in 1993 and 19.0 months in 1994,[42] but it seems a reasonable guess that the 1994 improvement in approval times was the result of a rash of approvals in late 1994 meant to deflect criticism from the incoming Republican congress.[43]

Comparison of the average approval times of drugs introduced in both the United States and Great Britain also illustrates the FDA's growing inertia. In the period between 1962 and 1965, drugs that were approved in both countries were approved an average of six months quicker by the FDA than by its British counterpart. In the period from 1966 to 1971, the FDA's lead had been reversed, and new drugs became available in Great Britain an average of fifteen months earlier than in the U.S.[44] A similar statistic indicates that the American agency's performance did not improve in the 1980s: 114 of the 204 new drugs introduced in the United States between 1977 and 1987 were available first in Great Britain, with an average lead time of five years. Of the 186 new drugs introduced in Great Britain during the same period, forty-one were available first in the United States, with an average lead time of two and a half years.[45] Robert Hahn and John Hird, updating a 1973 study by University of Chicago economist Sam Peltzman, have estimated that in 1990, FDA regulations gave

[39] Both of these comparisons probably understate the FDA's inefficiency, since they are comparisons against other bureaucratic monopolies rather than against competitive reviewing agencies.

[40] Sam Peltzman, *Regulation of Pharmaceutical Innovation* (Washington, DC: American Enterprise Institute, 1974), p. 18; Kazman, "Deadly Overcaution," p. 38.

[41] See J. R. Crout, "Objectives and Achievements of Regulations in the U.S.A.," and J. P. Griffin, "Objectives and Achievements of Regulations in the U.K.," in *International Medicines Regulations: A Forward Look to 1992*, ed. Stuart R. Walker and John P. Griffin (Dordrecht: Kluwer, 1989), pp. 73, 87, 117, 130.

[42] Statement of FDA Commissioner David Kessler, Hearings before the Senate Subcommittee on Labor and Human Resources, 104th Congress, 1st Session (1995).

[43] Henry I. Miller, "FDA and Regulatory Reform," *San Francisco Chronicle*, March 10, 1995, p. A23; Benjamin Wittes, "Has FDA Gotten Its Act Together?" *Legal Times*, March 20, 1995, p. 5.

[44] Peltzman, *Regulation of Pharmaceutical Innovation*, p. 18.

[45] Kaitlin et al., "The Drug Lag: An Update of New Drug Introductions in the United States and in the United Kingdom, 1977 through 1987," *Clinical Pharmacology and Therapeutics*, vol. 46 (1989). The differences in speed of approval were the same for the first period in the study (1977-1982) as they were for the second period (1983-1987), indicating that the FDA was not improving relative to its British counterpart. See *ibid.*, p. 135.

rise to a dead-weight loss to the U.S. economy of between $1.5 and $3.0 billion.[46]

Of course, these are only the easy-to-count numbers. What might the tally be if we could accurately measure the good that would flow from a competitive, consumer-driven drug industry? The regulatory burden that drug companies bear amounts to a tax both on new products and on potential new entrants, a tax which affects the structure of the industry, the nature and number of the products that will be developed, and hence the sort of world in which we shall live. It is open to someone, at this point, to make the Luddite move and say that, yes, this is precisely the point, we have to take control of the world in which we live lest the onrush of consumer demands change it for the worse. The real question is where the probabilities lie, and of course there is no definitive answer to this other than faith. In this case, however, faith is not blind. Someone who doubts this should reflect on what the computer industry would look like today, the home-computer segment especially, if, in the mid-1960s, the Federal Communications Commission (or some analogous federal agency) had successfully asserted jurisdiction over the computer business in order to make sure that products offered for sale to the public were compatible with one another, that they measured up to a certain standard of quality, and that only equipment with a worthwhile purpose, which was not prone to facilitating mischief, and whose probable benefits outweighed its probable costs, could be introduced for sale in interstate commerce.

Of course, because it is a thought experiment, one is free to make it come out in any way one sees fit. My version of the experiment, suggested to me by the economist Robert Crandall, ends with this morning's *Wall Street Journal*, which would show IBM and Control Data dividing most of the American computer market of 3,500 large mainframes per year between themselves. There would be no desktop computers, laptop computers, or personal digital assistants at all, nor any internet or modern telephony, nor any of the myriad of superior, chip-controlled products that console modern life. Bill Gates, having dropped out of Harvard, would be selling Oldsmobiles in Framingham, Massachusetts. Last year Steve Jobs would have succeeded Willard Scott as the weather guy on the Today Show. And today at Marshall Field's, handheld four-function calculators would still weigh in at seven ounces each and retail for $340. The "Federal Computer Commission" would issue a press release, taunting its kooky libertarian critics with the revelation that, though the consumer price index had tripled in the past thirty years, the price of those calculators had gone up hardly at all.

---

[46] Robert W. Hahn and John A. Hird, "The Costs and Benefits of Regulation: Review and Synthesis," *Yale Journal of Regulation*, vol. 8 (1991), pp. 276–77; see also Peltzman, *Regulation of Pharmaceutical Innovation*.

The point of the foregoing is to emphasize what is perhaps obvious: that the regulatory environment in which an industry operates always affects, and at the margin determines, the structure of that industry, the kinds of customers the industry will solicit, the kinds of products it will develop, and the kind of personnel it will recruit. Large, mature, oligopolistic industries tend to produce different products from small, fluid, started-in-the-garage industries. The latter make more different kinds of products, and more successful products, if more failures also. They will also tend to be more oriented toward consumers, including consumers who do not yet identify themselves as such, which was, of course, at one time the condition of *all* current owners of personal computers born before 1950.

In order to think accurately about the costs of a particular regime, then, the point upon which to focus is the opportunity costs, not the out-of-pocket ones. If these opportunity costs are unknowable, they are not imponderable. It seems probable that in a pharmaceutical world that more nearly resembled today's consumer-electronics industry, there would be fewer fat people, bald men, and acne-afflicted teenagers than there are now. No one knows how many; no one can make an authoritative guess about how much additional, attributable morbidity and mortality there would also be, though there would certainly, in gross, be some to counterbalance the probably even greater gains on the other side of the ledger. The people who would have been drawn into drug development and manufacturing would be a larger, more diverse, and differently motivated assortment than those in the business now. It seems almost fanciful to suppose that with their energy, ingenuity, and lively taste for money, they would not have had a considerable, beneficial impact on ordinary human lives. But who can speak of magnitudes? Drawing on the parallels to the personal-computer industry, it should be apparent that the benefits of consumer choice even in the intermediate future will be mostly invisible to those in the starting blocks. Hardly anyone saw with clarity the vast, nearly universal improvement of living standards that the silicon revolution would bring about. Had some political structure intervened to quash that revolution in its infancy, or to freeze the industry in the shape into which it appeared to be maturing thirty years ago, we would hardly be in a position to speak, thirty years on, of what the costs had been.

These are matters that ought to concern libertarians. It is not credible to think of the rights that people have in a way that is abstracted from the choices they are in fact capable of making to order their affairs. The existence of at least a minimal material surplus is a precondition to the meaningful exercise of choice, and, as a first approximation, the more surplus the better. Nor does there seem to be any good reason to think of the question in static terms, as though the only meaningful choices there were related to choosing among opportunities already in existence rather than making choices about institutions meant to affect the future and the patterns of living, not now available, that might be on offer there.

B. *The war on drugs*

Public efforts to suppress marijuana smoking and other forms of non-medicinal drug use can be thought of as the much more famous and tele-genic elder sibling of conventional food and drug regulation. Surely hundreds of commentators have discussed the problem (myself included), many of them from one or another ostensibly libertarian perspective. The field is too well-plowed to merit another plenary plowing, so I will devote myself largely to the positive side of the problem: what the costs of waging the war have been. But I begin this excursion on the normative side.

As indicated earlier, I think there is, in principle, a plausible case to be made for restricting heroin on self-paternalistic grounds, and cocaine, amphetamine, and steroids because of their criminogenic, externality-pregnant potentials. I am far from being satisfied, however, that an adequate case has *actually been made* for such regulation with respect to any of these drugs. There needs to be a much firmer grasp of what the facts are: How addictive is heroin, actually? How many of the observed social pathologies of many junkies, which are conventionally written down in heroin's account, are in actuality a reflection of unrelated, indwelling personality deficits of these junkies themselves, deficits that may predis-pose them to desire heroin but which heroin does not exacerbate? How marked is the criminogenic effect of cocaine or amphetamine? How clear are we, after all, that these substances are indeed the "but-for" causes of all the evils conventionally attributed to them, rather than simply the accidental companions of some bad behavior? The case for regulating these substances turns on whether one is convinced by the relevant evidence currently available. But if one were convinced (and let it be noted that others seem to think the evidence is stronger than I do), then regu-lation, including prohibition, should not be absolutely out of the question. The "externalities" case for regulating marijuana and hallucinogenics such as LSD, as near as I can make out, seems to involve the claim that they are, in effect, a solvent of republican virtue—that a self-governing nation cannot be a nation of pot- or acid-heads. Though there is surely a great deal of truth in this claim, such harms are far too marginal, and the embedded concept of public good far too general and unbounded, to support any serious regulatory effort beyond keeping the ingestion of these drugs out of public places; certainly the potential harms associated with these drugs do not justify their management by criminal law. Re-publican democracy beats out its competition only if one does not insist on brutal coercions aimed at ensuring that everyone will be mentally competent to participate.

Indeed, it is impossible to protect a decent idiom of representative democracy by indecently harsh means. The implication is that pursuing the problem of drug abuse as a species of Wilsonian war ("to make the world safe for democracy") is fraught with contradictions and has led, predictably, to a very nearly incoherent public response to the problem. Consider what this war has meant to American life. We have become beasts. Life in prison for first offenders.[47] The lethal needle for "kingpins."[48] No effort to be spared to stem the tide. Fifteen billion dollars in the 1997 federal budget for interdiction and law enforcement;[49] fifty-plus thousand men and women serving time in U.S. Department of Corrections facilities for drug offenses;[50] state budget aggregates and penitentiary censuses undoubtedly even higher; and no end in sight.[51]

One could leave recriminations about prohibitionist drug policy there and have a worthwhile case against it, but the democratic dilemma is far deeper than attempting to foster the values of an open society by harshly repressive means. For not only does government remorselessly punish drug abuse, *it subsidizes it at the same time*. For example, in *Nisperos v. Buck*,[52] the plaintiff, an attorney, was fired from his job at the Immigration and Naturalization Service, because (among other things) he had been arrested for cocaine possession and hospitalized for addiction. The court found no doubt that under the federal Rehabilitation Act of 1973[53] (which applies both to the federal government and to private employers who are grantees or contractors thereof) a narcotics addict was a "handicapped person," and thus entitled not to be discriminated against in employment. His attachment to cocaine was, for this plaintiff, a source not only of criminal liabilities but of civil rights.

Current drug users are excluded from this statute's definition of "handicapped person," which under *Burka v. New York City Transit Authority*[54] is

---

[47] This is not hyperbole, unfortunately. See *Harmelin v. Michigan*, 501 U.S. 957 (1991).

[48] See, e.g., the front-page story in the Sunday edition of the *Montgomery* (Alabama) *Advertiser*, February 11, 1996.

[49] The Clinton administration has requested $16 billion for the war on drugs for the 1998 fiscal year, an increase of $800 million over the 1997 appropriation. *Chicago Tribune*, February 26, 1997, section 1, p. 14.

[50] *1995 Sourcebook of Criminal Justice Statistics* (Washington, DC: U.S. Department of Justice, Bureau of Justice Statistics, 1995), p. 492.

[51] Admittedly the foregoing numbers are not solid. Significant portions of the nominal budgets go toward dual-purpose items; for example, coastal-surveillance assets paid for by the war on drugs are useful in other budget lines without being reflected in them. Most of the criminals serving time for drug offenses are in prison on negotiated pleas, so that we cannot be certain what, exactly, they actually did to get into trouble. Few of them are Boy Scouts in any event, and might be locked up for something else if not for this. But though we should discount the numbers somewhat, they do give at least a rough feel for the edge of hysteria that this subject seems to provoke.

[52] 720 F.Supp. 1424 (N.D.Cal. 1989).

[53] 29 U.S.C. sections 701-795(i).

[54] 680 F.Supp. 590, 600 (S.D.N.Y. 1988).

construed to mean drug abusers who are "rehabilitated or rehabilitating." The same exclusion is found in the Americans with Disabilities Act (1990),[55] which regards drug addiction (though not "current use") as a handicap, thus giving persons with a history of drug abuse negotiating leverage with an employer that is not possessed by individuals without such a record. Yet the entire question of when drug use is "current" and when it is past history is inherently uncertain. And one thing that becomes certain in the presence of such uncertainties is litigation. There is also the matter of "reasonable accommodation," something employers are legally required to offer drug addicts (because they are disabled persons), though no such obligation exists with respect to ordinary employees. In *Burka*, for instance, the defendant-employer was said to have a duty to show that it could not "reasonably accommodate" itself to the plaintiff's medical condition. Seldom if ever can one dispose of matters of this kind with motions, and when the costs of a trial are taken into account, the ante may seem too steep to make it seem attractive to a rational employer to press even a likely-to-be winning hand. So the value of the subsidy to drug abuse is considerable. Moreover, all sorts of employer actions have been insisted upon by courts as "reasonable accommodations" of an employee's disability: extra sick days; counseling; special extenuations for nonperformance; or assignment to different duties[56]—all "rights," obviously valuable, that employees with clean records would not be allowed to claim.

Construing New York's Human Rights Law, *Doe v. Roe Co.*[57] held that a trial was required to determine whether an employer had discriminated against the plaintiff because it believed he was a drug addict, a statutorily protected "disability." What had happened was that this plaintiff failed his preemployment physical examination because opiate molecules were found in his urinalysis. Was this an example of discrimination by the employer against a protected category of person? It would depend on the employer's intentions—specifically, on whether the failure to hire was based on a "legitimate, non-discriminatory reason" rather than a statutorily illegitimate one. The effect of the court's decision, as in *Burka*, is that the legal question of discrimination cannot be disposed of on motions (which is to say that it cannot be disposed of cheaply). The matter must go to trial; the employer must expend tens or hundreds of thousands of dollars to establish its bona fides. But if we searched the trunk of that same man's car, we might find a stash—obviously he had a stash somewhere, the source of the molecules that were detected in his blood—sufficient to send him to prison, under New York's pioneering, ultraharsh Rockefeller drug law, for the rest of his life.[58]

[55] 29 U.S.C. section 1201, et seq.
[56] See generally 22 ALR Fed 111 (1997).
[57] 539 N.Y.Supp.2d 876 (1989).
[58] See, e.g., *New York v. Jones*, 350 N.E.2d 913 (N.Y.Ct.App. 1976).

What, then, does the state of New York believe about drugs, and when did it start believing it? We have already seen and acknowledged the extent to which individual decision-makers may be imperfect agents for their own "selves." But here is the reason why that earlier-made concession to the incomplete coherence of individual "selves" cannot be converted into a general justification for paternalistic public regulation. It must be very unusual to find an individual "self" so scattered that it is prepared both to imprison for life and to bestow valuable presents upon a person for one and the same behavior. Yet this is a perfectly routine state of affairs for the collective, public self as expressed by legislation. Courts judge such legislation to be "rational." If an individual exhibited similar purposive disintegration, we would be fully justified in suspecting psychosis.

It is increasingly evident, moreover, that the *war* on drugs must have inflicted far more damage upon civil society than the drugs themselves could ever begin to do. An admittedly conjectural but nevertheless persuasive account of what has happened can be sketched briefly.[59] In 1984, more or less coincident with the great escalation of the war on drugs, crack cocaine, which had previously been a relatively marginal part of the drug trade, began to assume a significant place in the market. Crack was a marketing innovation, but it is pharmacologically no different from any other cocaine. Its distinguishing feature is that crack is sold in small batches, a dose at a time. An ounce of cocaine in the hands of a distributor will yield thirty to fifty retail sales if the product is powder (depending on how much it is cut) but ten to twenty times as many smaller transactions in the form of crack. Multiplying the number of retail transactions produced a burgeoning demand for retail help. In some cases this resulted in the best economic opportunities potential jobholders could soon, or ever, expect to see. Many of the recruits were what we should properly call children—fourteen-, fifteen-, and sixteen-year-old boys. Classical economics gives the reason that children were being drawn into the drug trade: the principle of comparative advantage. Drug hysteria was driving legislatures at every level of government greatly to aggravate punishments for drug crimes, even as drug-specific law-enforcement activity, often with the encouragement of escalating federal financial support, increased dramatically. Punishments in the juvenile justice system did not escalate as much, if at all.

No one anticipated what seems to have followed from that. Rather quickly, incentive patterns for an entire class of potential adult offenders had changed as well. The public penalties for dealing drugs had skyrocketed; those for armed robbery stayed about the same. That change alone would open up a new margin in which it would make sense to substitute

---

[59] A more extended account of what follows is given in Daniel Polsby, "Ending the War on Drugs and Children," *Valparaiso Law Review*, vol. 31 (1997).

the robbing of drug dealers for dealing drugs oneself as a means of getting money. Changes in private incentives also pushed in the same direction, because juvenile drug dealers, considered as potential targets of predation, will tend to be less physically formidable than their adult counterparts, while their numbers and dispersion will make it harder for their employers to protect them. Changes in the legal ground rules had contrived to make these retail clerks sitting ducks, and so their behavior changed to compensate. They increased their demand for guns to enable them to protect themselves, their receipts, and their inventories. Those who meant to prey on them had to get guns in response, tit for tat. The resulting murder epidemic was so terrible that it convinced the country that we were experiencing a great crime wave through a decade when crime rates were, in fact, steadily declining for the population as a whole. Almost the entirety of the disaster was visited on young males in minority neighborhoods. Rates of mortality by criminal victimization more than doubled among the most at-risk age cohorts of the African-American population. What is as bad, for the first time since records began being kept, victimization data began to include large numbers of younger teenagers, who had previously been no more at risk for being murdered than people in their parents' age group. It is a reasonable extrapolation from U.S. Justice Department figures that the excess mortality directly attributable to the war on drugs must have been in the range of ten to twenty or so thousand dead, concentrated in black populations, in the ten-year period ending in 1994.

All of the story just told is the result of regulation. Those costs dwarf anything that can be reasonably feared of the inherent, pharmacological liabilities of cocaine to excite aggression and thus contribute to crime. And of course, even here the cost-counting is not complete, because the criminal activity that prohibitory drug laws underwrite operates, even more than FDA regulation in that other drug domain, as a tax—in this case on the capital, human and physical, of the neighborhoods in which the drug trade flourishes. What pops out at the other end of this law-and-economics morality tale is boarded-up and broken-down places, inhabited mainly by those who are too old, too young, or not resourceful enough to leave. Though libertarians may not like to dwell on the concept of social costs, here are some incalculably large ones created by the failure of government to respect people's liberty.

One should not leave this problem without confronting the "utilitarian" shrug that libertarians use to brush off narratives of social cost like the one recounted above: It is a sad enough story, all right, but putting it at the center of an argument leads straight on to the serpent-windings of utilitarianism. What is its possible relevance to *libertarian* theory? Of course, the general form of this question is whether God is a utilitarian, an old conundrum and one whose unwinding is well beyond the pay grade of the present author. But even one who does not want to close with the

question of what the ultimate relationship may be between utilitarian
considerations and the Good must be struck by considering the particularities of the case before us. The root, first cause of the problem with the
war on drugs is that it exceeds "the limits of the criminal sanction."
People want to get high. They know it is against the law, but they do not
go along with that law; they want to exercise at least this much dominion
over their world and they are going to do it—and hang the law. By failing
to offer a rationale strong enough to command respect, laws of this kind,
which have thin backgrounds in customary manners and practice (in
other words, laws against acts which are *mala prohibita*), make their way
in the world with impaired moral claims to obedience. People who believe they have a right to do what they want to do—who believe that they
own their own bodies and have a right to put in them pretty much
whatever they please, so long as they don't harm anybody else by so
doing—are going to be hard cases for the state to control, whoever they
are. What has led the state into its present predicament is a utilitarian
miscalculation to be sure, but the meaningfully libertarian angle to the
story is how it shows that even mighty Leviathan cannot with impunity
forget the boundary between public and private life. People, even the
bottommost poor, can be forced only so far once they think that they
know that boundary—that is, once they believe they have rights.

Law, Northwestern University

PROFIT: THE CONCEPT AND ITS MORAL FEATURES

By James W. Child

I. Profit as an Essentially Contested Concept[1]

Profit is a concept that both causes and manifests deep conflict and division. It is not merely that people disagree over whether it is good or bad. The very meaning of the concept and its role in competing theories necessitates the deepest possible disagreement; people cannot agree *on what profit is*. Still, simply learning the starkly different sentiments expressed about profit gives us some feel for the depth of the conflict. Friends of capitalism have praised profit as central to the achievement of prosperity and to civilized modern life. Calvin Coolidge, that silent sentinel of American business, said, "Profit and civilization go hand in hand."[2] F. A. Hayek tells us that

> in the evolution of the structure of human activities, profitability works as a signal that guides selection towards what makes man more fruitful; only what is more profitable will, as a rule, nourish more people, for it sacrifices less than it adds.[3]

Peter Drucker, a well-known management theorist, says that "profit is just another name for rationality."[4] On the other hand, socialists and related thinkers have excoriated profit with ferocity. Pierre-Joseph Proudhon is typical when he announces:

> Products are bought only by products. . . . [P]rofit is impossible and unjust. Observe this elementary principle of economy and pauperism, luxury, oppression, vice, crime, and hunger will disappear from our midst.[5]

Can Proudhon possibly be talking about the same thing as Coolidge, Hayek, and Drucker? As it turns out, no. They are referring to quite

[1] See W. B. Gallie, "Essentially Contested Concepts," *Proceedings of the Aristotelian Society 1955–56*, vol. 56, pp. 167–98.
[2] In a speech in New York City, November 27, 1920.
[3] F. A. Hayek, *The Fatal Conceit: The Errors of Socialism* (Chicago: University of Chicago Press, 1988), p. 46.
[4] Peter Drucker, *The Concept of the Corporation* (New York: John Day, 1946), p. 234.
[5] Pierre-Joseph Proudhon, *What Is Property?* (New York: Howard Fertig, 1966), p. 286.

different things, and we will soon be able to see what and how. My concern, in this essay, is twofold. First, I analyze some of the various sources of these differing, but related and contesting, notions of profit. To do this will require discussions of the nature of economic value, theories of exchange, and theories of price. Remember, this is just to analyze *what profit is*. Second, I seek to answer a question which follows directly from the analysis of profit: *Is profit a good (or bad) thing?* That is, *what are its moral features?* Is it conducive to civilization, prosperity, and economic growth, or is it, as Proudhon, Marx, and others believed, the moral equivalent of theft, which leads to exploitation, injustice, and pauperism on one hand, and greed, luxury, and corruption on the other? In short, the aim is to *analyze* the concept of profit and then *morally* assess it. Although carrying out that project for all possible notions of profit would take far more space than I have, it is possible to begin this dual task with one particularly important notion of profit. That is the goal of this essay. The notion of profit that concerns me here is *the profit that results from a single commercial transaction*. When a merchant sells something, he or she intends to make a profit, that is, to gain more than he or she gave up. In the language of contemporary economics, this is often called *gains from trade*. In rational choice theory, it is called *pure surplus* or *transaction surplus*. The questions addressed in this essay will be: What does all this mean? Where does the "surplus" come from? What happens to the other party to the transaction? Is the whole process moral or immoral? As we shall see, there are two predominant theories (or, at least, points of view) that shape our answers to these questions.

Why begin with this simple transactional notion of profit? There are at least four important reasons why. First, it is very simple and the issues are uncomplicated compared to those in, for example, entrepreneurial profit, monopoly profit, speculative profit, profits from arbitrage, etc. Second, this kind of profit does not presuppose (although it is quite consistent with) full-blown markets and all their complicated institutional foundations and side-effects. Third, for this reason, it is the kind of profit Aristotle, Aquinas, and all those who wrote before the dawn of capitalism discussed—precisely because they could not talk about notions of profit that had to await the birth of genuine market institutions. Fourth, this kind of profit, in this kind of transaction, is like an atom in the fine structure of markets and all other forms of profit. In short, all other forms of profit contain, in some important way, this notion of profit.

First, we must clear away some underbrush and refine our terms. If we take the accounting definition of profit and simplify it as much as possible, we might get one of two possible formulations. It is at this point that we face our first major ambiguity. We might define profit as:

$$output - input = profit$$

After all, as Ludwig von Mises taught, economics is about purposive human activity.[6] This means that all relevant human action is geared toward some output.

To rein in the definition a bit, we might say that "output" and "input" apply to anything connected to what might, in the broadest possible terms, be called *economic production*. This means that if Brown lives on a subsistence farm, then his labor, the use of his implements, his seed, etc. are inputs. The tomatoes he grows are the output, and the net value of the tomatoes, less the value of the inputs, represents the profit, even if he eats all the tomatoes himself. Likewise, all the output of Brown's farm, minus all the inputs over a year, gives us the annual profit of the farm as a productive economic unit. This approach has distinct advantages. It captures the great generality of economic activity. It can be used to describe subsistence economies (or economic units) as well as activity in fully planned economies. Although measurement is a serious problem, there is no reason in principle why what business types call "profit centers" could not be used in planned economies, where output and the relevant input can be matched and a "profit" computed.[7] This is, in fact, a highly interesting concept and one which has a great deal of conceptual and moral relevance to the problem at hand. Still, to adopt it would make my job too easy. Socialists and their friends would have a hard time criticizing this sort of "profit." Indeed, Marx explicitly recognized at least a society-wide notion of "social surplus" which seems to be aggregated "profit" in this sense. In a collectivized economy, such a surplus is unobjectionable for Marx. Indeed, it is the source of economic growth and social investment. Moreover, this broad notion of profit divorces the issue from production for exchange, markets, private ownership of capital, and the so-called cash nexus; and for a socialist, that is to miss the whole point of a critique of capitalist profit. So, let us refer to this very important notion of "output minus input" as *gain* and introduce a narrower notion of profit.

A Dictionary for Accountants defines profit as, *inter alia*:

> A general term for the excess of revenue, proceeds or *selling price* over related costs ... [or] ... as any pecuniary benefit arising from a *commercial* operation, ... or from *one or more individual transactions*. ...[8]

---

[6] Ludwig von Mises, *Human Action*, 3d rev. ed. (Chicago: Contemporary Books, 1966), ch. 1.

[7] See Eric L. Kohler, *A Dictionary for Accountants*, 5th ed. (Englewood Cliffs, NJ: Prentice Hall, 1975), entry under "profit center," p. 380.

[8] *Ibid.*, entry under "profit," p. 379 (emphasis added). To appreciate just how complex the notion of profit can be in accounting, see William Paton, *Corporate Profits* (Homewood, IL: Irwin, 1965). The entire volume is pertinent, but chapter 2 is especially on point.

The reader will note that "selling price," "commercial operation," and "transaction" do limit profit to a commercial concept. (Why it does not necessarily involve a full-fledged concept of "the market" depends upon the importance of the phrase "one or more individual transactions" and will emerge below.) Another source (Benjamin Newman and Martin Mellman's *Accounting Theory: A CPA Review*) defines profit as a *net* concept referring to "the balances after the deduction from *revenues* of cost of goods *sold*, expenses and losses."[9]

In short, this kind of definition ties profit intimately to exchange and, less intimately but still typically, to private ownership of factors of production and goods and services produced and sold. That is, it ties profit to the results of *transactions*, i.e., bartered exchanges, or the sale of privately owned goods or services for money. Notice one important thing: since profit results from each transaction, the moral status of profit, at least prima facie, is tied one-to-one to the moral nature of the transaction which produces it. Let us call this perspective the *micro-ethics* of transactions, in contrast with the *macro-ethical* perspective of market institutions or an entire economy made up of markets, namely, a *market economy*. This difference shapes the whole nature of the present inquiry. Lastly, cumulative notions like annual profit, profit margin, etc. become derivative upon this simple notion of *a gain through the acquisition and sale (or exchange) of a single product or service*.

II. The Macro-Ethics of Institutions and the Micro-Ethics of Actions and Transactions

A. Macro-ethical arguments about markets as institutions

The first class of macro-ethical arguments to be discussed here are anti-market arguments based upon the immorality of the market system generally and of its consequences.[10] These systemic arguments include the claim that such a system produces a vast inequality of resources among people and that it visits severe externalities upon society, including unsafe products, pollution, and other ecological costs. Yet another argument is that monopolies inevitably emerge under a market system and subvert the market itself. A very important anticapitalist argument is that the market does not serve true human well-being, because it manipulates and creates artificial desires and wants. This, in turn, creates a

---

[9] Benjamin Newman and Martin Mellman, *Accounting Theory: A CPA Review* (New York: John Wiley and Sons, 1967), p. 58 (emphasis added).

[10] See, for example, David Schweickart, *Against Capitalism* (Boulder, CO: Westview Press, 1996), esp. chs. 3, 4, and 5; and, for a more evenhanded view, Allen Buchanan, *Ethics, Efficiency, and the Market* (Totowa, NJ: Rowman and Allanheld, 1985), chs. 2 and 3, esp. pp. 19–36, 55–59, and 87–101.

superficial, consumerist society, characterized by selfish, shallow, and ultimately unhappy and alienated people.[11]

While many arguments against the market system are based upon its aggregate features and consequences (that is, upon what I have called the macro-ethical perspective), it is also true that many important arguments in its behalf rest on the same foundation. Foremost among these is the utilitarian (or sometimes merely consequentialist) argument that the very genius of capitalism is its ability to harness human greed, selfishness, and general wickedness for the common (aggregative) good.[12] This argument, admittedly in a mild form, is familiar to us from Adam Smith and is captured in a famous quote:

> It is not from the benevolence of the butcher, the brewer or the baker, that we expect our dinner, but from their regard to their own self interest. We address ourselves, not to their humanity but to their self love, and never talk to them of our own necessities but of their advantages.[13]

Yet it is through this "self love" that,

> by directing that industry in such a manner as its produce may be of the greatest value, he [the individual producer in a market] intends only his own gain, and he is in this, as in many other cases, led by an invisible hand to promote an end which was no part of his intention.[14]

Indeed, if Smith's *argument* for capitalism is remembered at all today, it is almost always this consequentialist argument featuring a wholly self-interested economic actor. This is not to say that Smith offered only these kinds of arguments. He was, I believe, also dedicated to a concept of "natural liberty" and deployed arguments of that sort as well.[15]

This strategy of argument accomplishes its task if that task is *to defend the market system*. Yet the concerns of this essay are not those of Smith; ironically, they are closer to those of Aristotle and Thomas Aquinas (I say "ironically" because I disagree with their conclusions). Unlike Smith and virtually all who came after him, Aristotle and Aquinas were not interested in aggregate (macro) effects and markets as institutions. They were interested, as I am, in individual transactions, their motivations, and their moral qual-

---

[11] See Herbert Marcuse, *One Dimensional Man* (Boston: Beacon Press, 1968), and J. K. Galbraith, *The New Industrial State*, 2d ed. (New York: Mentor, 1970), which jointly form the *locus classicus* of this argument.

[12] In its most unvarnished form, this argument is found in Bernard Mandeville, *The Fable of the Bees*, 2 vols. (Oxford: Oxford University Press, 1924); see also F. B. Kaye's long and very helpful introduction.

[13] Adam Smith, *The Wealth of Nations* (New York: Random House, 1937), p. 14.

[14] *Ibid.*, p. 423.

[15] See Ellen Frankel Paul, *Moral Revolution and Economic Science* (Westport, CN: Greenwood Press, 1979), ch. 1, esp. pp. 22–25.

ity. My goal is more consonant with Aristotle and Aquinas than it is with the concern of Smith and his followers for the market. The goal is to ask whether market activity, that is, the *making of profits in individual transactions,* is inherently morally offensive or whether it is inoffensive and even perhaps commendable. Defending market activity by appealing to beneficial, aggregate side-effects of morally objectionable conduct is like deciding to keep the bathwater because there is a baby in it. True, we might, as a society, make a choice to keep a market system if the by-products of greed and selfishness are worth enough, but we could not feel too good about it. For the critics of business would still be correct in their belief that market activity or business is *essentially* driven by unattractive motives and it would be *unusual among human activities* in having that feature. Subsistence farming, government service, family life, religious activities, pursuing noncommercial hobbies, and operating in a planned economy would all be essentially different and morally preferable. The only other practice falling into the category of unattractive human activities might be war, with which market activity is often compared.

Particularly today, under the force of neoclassical economics, it is almost impossible to exaggerate how quickly and unconsciously most thinkers, including very powerful ones, find themselves unable to sustain talk about the nature and moral assessment of a micro-level transaction. Many analysts begin here and soon end up discussing aggregated numbers of actions, their collective characteristics, and the institutions which govern these numerous activities on a large scale, namely, markets and their externalities. A classic example is a paper by Allan Gibbard entitled "What's Morally Special about Free Exchange?" He begins with a question of the sort we shall examine: "Is there anything special about free exchange?" But, by the second paragraph, he has converted that question, without discussion and apparently unconsciously, to a systemic macro-issue:

> My chief question, then, is what, if anything, is morally special about *a system* of pure free exchange, as opposed to other *economic orders* that yield *a system of prices?*[16]

It is not that Gibbard is to be singled out for criticism. For virtually all authorities who begin or seem to begin at the micro level end soon enough at the macro, systemic level. Others fail even to see that there *is* a micro level to be considered.

B. *Micro-ethical arguments about market transactions as intentional human actions*

The kind of argument most pertinent to the concept of profit, and the one which I shall investigate in this essay, is not of the macro-institutional

---

[16] Allan Gibbard, "What's Morally Special about Free Exchange?" *Social Philosophy and Policy,* vol. 2, no. 2 (Spring 1985), p. 21 (emphasis added).

kind. Instead, it focuses upon that atom of market systems, the individual market transaction. This approach passes moral judgment upon that transaction, the parties to the transaction, their actions, their motives, and the immediate consequences of that single transaction.

It is worth noting that while I will end up agreeing, in *substance*, with Adam Smith and contemporary economics, in *method* I am closer to Aristotle and Aquinas. That is, my concern will be with the individual transaction first, and only then with the issue of aggregated transactions, i.e., a market. The argument is that (unless one accepts a rigorous consequentialism) we should morally analyze the motives, intentions, knowledge, etc. of the individual agents engaging in a transaction. Neither Smith nor (especially) contemporary economists are interested in normative issues, so the micro perspective is not as significant to them. On the other hand, Aristotle and Aquinas are definitely interested in the normative questions and, as such, look at the micro picture first, as shall I.

A micro versus macro approach might be demonstrated in a simple area of ethics. A macro approach would ask about a practice or a convention as a social norm. Thus, "Must one keep one's promises when they do not pay off consequentially?" or "What moral postulates lead to the conclusion that we ought to keep our promises when they do not pay off consequentially?" are typical macro questions.[17] On the other hand, questions about specific promises in specific circumstances are typically micro questions—for example: "If I promise to deliver to you a serviceable car, how good a shape does it have to be in?" or "Should I make a promise which I know I only have a 60 percent chance of being able to carry out?" These last questions are about specific, intentional human actions or action types; they are not about (or are only derivatively about) norms, conventions, or institutions. My task here, then, is an analysis—pro or con—of what I shall call the *micro-ethics* of market transactions, the ethics of the individual market transaction, and, of most relevance to the present inquiry, *the micro-ethics of profits and profit-making* in individual transactions.

Certainly, the micro perspective, which finds what is morally objectionable in the individual transaction, is vastly important in history and in the popular mind. Success in business, and the making of profit, generally, is thought to lie in "screwing people," i.e., taking advantage of others in such transactions. Merchants, from time out of mind, have been presented as greedy schemers, uniformly selfish and inherently dishonest. In all cases, these undesirable character traits are made manifest paradigmatically in market transactions, that is, in individual acts of buying and selling in pursuit of profit, an expression of pure greed.

Throughout history (and long before the "capitalist system" was born), people found commerce, trade, and exchange for profit wrong, or disrep-

---

[17] This micro-macro distinction is essentially the distinction John Rawls set out in "Two Concepts of Rules," reprinted in *Ethics*, ed. Judith Thomson and Gerald Dworkin (New York: Harper and Row, 1968), pp. 104–35.

utable, or exploitive, or unfair in some never too clearly articulated way. They were not objecting to the aggregate effects of markets, to inequality or alienation or pollution. They were objecting to what merchants and business people *actually do* when they do business, that is, primarily when they engage in acts of buying and selling for profit. The criticism of the market system which most clearly captures this perspective holds that if we transact, and I "get a good deal," you must have lost something. I have gained only by your losing and I have gained what I gained from you.

III. The Zero-Sum Theory of Exchange and Profit

If market transactions themselves are, by their very nature, immoral, or at least morally suspect, then each transaction is a pair of acts (one by each party) of attempted "taking advantage" of the other. If I gain in a transaction with you, I did so at your expense. I "got the best of you" or "screwed you." Commerce, then, becomes nothing but a series of these efforts to take advantage or benefit at another's expense. A market is just an organized institution where such transactions go on.

Profit, in its simplest form, is the gain realized in such a trade or exchange. Since my efforts are to gain by taking advantage of you, any profit I make must come at your expense. On this view, two parties cannot both profit from a transaction, though one can be deluded into thinking that he did, while the other really did. Profit from an ongoing business, then, is just an accumulation of such gains at the expense of others. It follows that if my business makes much profit and I grow rich, I have been very successful at taking advantage of others. This tendency, especially as enhanced by my talent at it, clearly says something about my *character*, something pejorative. Merchants have been so judged throughout history, as have bankers, brokers, speculators, industrialists, and entrepreneurs—all those who engage professionally and successfully in market transactions, in the broadest possible terms.

Let us refer to this view of commercial transactions as a *zero-sum* view. It is zero-sum in that my gain is your loss. Indeed, if I gained five dollars in an exchange, you must have lost the same amount, so it is formally zero-sum.[18] As we shall see, when we set the view out completely, it does allow for the possibility of "fair exchanges" in which no one might have come out ahead. But it is hard to see how one could trade successfully as

---

[18] Of course, the more typical expression in game theory is that a *game* is zero-sum. But the idea that gains and losses sum to zero, and thus cancel each other out, can easily be extended to a single transaction. (Indeed, a transaction can be treated like a two-by-two game, where each player can elect to trade or not to trade, giving rise to four possibilities in a four-celled [two-by-two] matrix. However, since the zero-sum theory is wrong, the transaction will not come out to be zero-sum.) In any case, for now, I will use the term a little loosely and go no further into game theory.

a business person and still engage only in such "fair trades," for, by definition, there can be no gains from such trades.

IV. The History of the Zero-Sum Perspective

One cannot point to a complete formulation of the zero-sum view in the history of economic thought. This is, in part, due to the general fact that notions of value, price, exchange, and utility, among others, were not fully understood until late in the nineteenth century. The notions of games and zero-sum games were not understood until almost the middle of the twentieth century. This is the main reason why I will not refer to zero-sum theory but, rather, to the zero-sum view or conception of transactions. Indeed, we can find contradictory formulations of concepts like value and exchange within the work of the same author, for example, Aristotle or Smith. Nonetheless, ideas, perspectives, and notions connected to the zero-sum view abound and work themselves together to form a *theme* or a way of thinking about business which, if never quite a coherent theory, still managed to form a powerful traditional understanding of business and business transactions.

A. Aristotle

Generally, the Greeks adopted a monadic and objective theory of economic value. Plato propounded the famous water-diamond paradox.[19] Water is enormously useful, indeed, indispensable to life; yet it has little economic value per unit. Diamonds are of minimal use, yet are enormously valuable. How can this be so? Notice that, to someone trained in modern micro-economics, the grip of this "paradox" is weak, its paradoxical character vague. One key reason is that we see value as relational (indeed, subjective) and, as such, subject to change *relative* to supply. Moreover, the other key to value in modern economics is demand, which is determined by the aggregated utility functions of the buyer. A utility function, in turn, is a function (in the technical, mathematical sense of the term) mapping a preference ordering into the real numbers (where both the range, i.e., the preference ordering, and the domain, i.e., the real numbers, are subject to certain conditions). But consider: If one sees value as *in* the object (i.e., as a feature of the object alone), the water-diamond paradox is indeed paradoxical. Value does not seem to depend upon human preference, or demand (both relational, subjective notions), or even utility measured by how people understand and feel their own needs. It must be something else.

---

[19] Plato, *Euthydemus*, 304, in *The Dialogues of Plato*, trans. Benjamin Jowett (New York: Random House, 1937), p. 167.

Did Aristotle believe that there was an objective value upon which to pin a just price? The answer is not clear. At the beginning of a very difficult passage in the *Nicomachean Ethics*, he tells us: "All goods must therefore be measured by some one thing. . . ."[20] Immediately below this passage, however, he tells us that this "one thing" is *demand*, a relational notion.[21] Yet, a few lines later, he introduces a cost-of-production theory of value, one which is surely objective, and seemingly monistic, i.e., nonrelational. Then later in the passage, he again connects value to demand. For our purposes, however, even within this difficult passage, one thing is clear. Exchange requires the *equalization* of the two items being traded. Money does this. But it is not merely a matter of setting a market or bargained-for price. It is a process of making both items *equal in value*. This certainly suggests that there must be some objective, measurable quantity which can be equalized. Moreover, this quantity seems to be a simple feature of the item being traded, that is, a feature designated by a monadic predicate, rather than a relational property between the item and the trader designated by a dyadic predicate. Just how "demand" would work here is unclear, at best.

While Aristotle's views on value are equivocal and confusing, he clearly articulates a zero-sum conception of exchange. He begins his discussion of exchange in the *Politics*, with yet another foray into the theory of value. He tells us that there are two ways to value something: its use value and its exchange value. He then tells us that the use value is the proper one and that the exchange value is "improper or secondary." For him, "retail trade" (we might say "commerce") is not a part of the natural art of producing wealth. Thus, it seems that commerce does not increase wealth or the value of things. The natural production of wealth is through production *for use*. Still, exchange which occurs only to satisfy "man's natural wants" is not "contrary to nature." Engaging in exchange to maintain a household is both natural and proper. However, exchange through "retail trade" has as its purpose the unlimited accumulation of riches in the form of money. What Aristotle condemns in the *Politics* is what we would call capital accumulation. Thus, money as a medium of exchange to facilitate trade for immediate use by the household, to satiate natural wants, is acceptable. But trade to accumulate wealth, even if one's purpose is what we would call "reinvestment," is condemned. Thus, it seems that trade *for its own sake* is improper. Retail trade is trade for its own sake carried out by merchants, not householders. Those who earn a living only through trade must be morally suspect. But why? What is it about trade itself, or trade to facilitate more trade in the future, or trade for money, that is morally condemnable or, at least, morally suspicious? Aristotle says that

---

[20] Aristotle, *Nicomachean Ethics*, ed. and trans. Richard McKeon (New York: Random House, 1941), 1133a26, p. 1011.

[21] *Ibid.*, 1133a–1133c, pp. 1010–12. Below, I shall argue that Aristotle's view, even if based on demand and relational in nature, cannot be truly subjective. Still, in contemporary economics, we naturally think of demand as based upon subjective preference. For us, demand *just is* aggregated preference, and preference must be subjective.

it "consists in exchange justly censured; for it is unnatural, and a mode by which men gain from one another."[22] Thus, exchange is gaining from others and at their expense. This sentiment fits quite well with further comments Aristotle makes in the *Nicomachean Ethics*:

> These names, both loss and gain, have come from voluntary exchange; for to have *more than one's own* is called gaining and to have *less than one's original share* is called losing, e.g. in buying and selling and in all other matters in which the law has left people free to make their own terms; but when they get neither more nor less but just what belongs to them, they say that they have their own and that they neither lose nor gain.
>
> Therefore the just is intermediate between a sort of gain and a sort of loss. . . . [I]t consists in having *an equal amount before and after the transaction*.[23]

Note that "more than one's own" clearly suggests that one has acquired someone else's property unfairly or without adequate moral claim; that is, it suggests a zero-sum exchange. On the other hand, "less than one's original share" clearly speaks of a loss due to the transaction; however, it does not imply that the loss had to come as the result of another's gain. One could lose part or all of one's original share by accident, through one's own negligence, or in many other ways, which may not involve zero-sum exchange and another's taking it. Aristotle's concern with a failure to square gains and losses, that is, with having "an equal amount before and after the transaction," is illustrative of a very deep confusion about *just what exchange is*, and it shall occupy us at some length below.

There is a vast literature on Aristotle's views on economic value, price, demand, and exchange. As with most matters of scholarship, the issues are hotly contested. I am not an Aristotle scholar, but I believe I detect a strong majority who tend to characterize Aristotle's views in the following way: (1) Retail trade is an activity that gives rise to no completed state and, therefore, is a form of unlimited, unending desiring (which is both irrational and immoral).[24] (2) Retail trade is a zero-sum game where one

---

[22] *The Politics of Aristotle*, ed. and trans. Ernest Barker (Oxford: Clarendon Press, 1946), Book I, ch. X, 1258a38–40, p. 28.

[23] Aristotle, *Nicomachean Ethics*, 1132b18–20, pp. 1009–10 (emphasis added).

[24] See, for example, Henry William Spiegel, *The Growth of Economic Thought*, 3d ed. (Durham, NC: Duke University Press, 1991), pp. 24–27; Eric Roll, *A History of Economic Thought*, 4th ed. (London: Faber and Faber, 1973), pp. 31–35, esp. pp. 32–33; Odd Langholm, *Wealth and Money in the Aristotelian Tradition* (Bergen: Universitetsforlaget, 1983), ch. 4, esp. pp. 50–53; and Thomas J. Lewis, "Acquisition and Anxiety: Aristotle's Case against the Market," *Canadian Journal of Economics*, vol. 11 (1978), pp. 69–90. It should be noted that Lewis believes his own contribution to the case for Aristotle's anti-commerce point of view lies in having shown that anxiety about livelihood and the destruction of friendship and citizenship counts against market transactions. Nonetheless, Lewis also concurs completely with the more canonical interpretation of Aristotle's critique based upon the unending pursuit of money in retail trade. See pp. 73–77.

person wins a profit and the other incurs a loss.[25] (3) Perverting money, a natural medium for household exchange, simply to make money unendingly, is a violation of the true nature of money.[26]

It is true that Joseph Schumpeter, in his *History of Economic Analysis*,[27] disagrees with almost every element of my description of Aristotle's views. Although space does not permit a point-by-point refutation, it is sufficient to note several items: (1) Schumpeter manages, by his sweeping views on value theory, exchange, and price, to demonstrate disagreement with the vast majority of Aristotle scholars, even though they often do not agree with each other. (2) His interpretation rests not on close textual analysis but on broad surmise, such as: "It is not farfetched to equate ..." and "[T]here is nothing strange in the conjecture.... "[28] (3) He indulges in a disparaging attack against the possibility of Aristotle's subscribing to an objective value theory rather than a market value theory (referring, for example, to "some mysterious Objective or Absolute Value of things"). (4) He mounts a related attack against people with "philosophical propensities," as opposed to his heroes: "people of a more 'positive' type of mind." (Presumably, he considers Aristotle to be one of the latter.)[29] This is an instance of a great economist doing intellectual history and not quite getting it right. It is reminiscent of the great physicists of the early twentieth century, Ernst Mach or P. W. Bridgman, for example, trying to write on the history of physics and ending up in diatribes against metaphysics and unscientific speculation, because some poor scientist of the past (e.g., Ptolemy or Kepler) might not have practiced rigid empiricism or positivism to their satisfaction.

Aristotle's manifest equivocation (not to say confusion) about whether value consists in cost of production (or some part of cost of production, like labor) or in demand, should not cloud another matter. Although we cannot be sure, there is every reason to believe that even when he spoke of "demand," he did not mean to refer to a subjective state of the valuer. Likewise, when Aristotle spoke of the "use value" of a thing, he did not mean the subjective value the user placed upon it. (This would be Carl

[25] See Antony G. N. Flew, *The Politics of Procrustes* (Buffalo: Prometheus Press, 1981), pp. 148–54; Fred D. Miller, Jr., *Nature, Justice, and Rights in Aristotle's "Politics"* (Oxford: Clarendon Press, 1995), p. 321 (in fairness to Miller, he suggests that this interpretation, while legitimate, "requires considerable speculative unpacking"); and Scott Meikle, "Aristotle and Exchange Value," in *A Companion to Aristotle's "Politics"*, ed. David Keyt and Fred D. Miller, Jr. (Oxford: Blackwell, 1991), pp. 156–81. Meikle has other, more original, interpretations of some of Aristotle's views on trade, but he makes it clear that, in addition, he adheres to the interpretation of Aristotle which sees trade as inherently zero-sum. See esp. pp. 163–64.

[26] See Langholm, *Wealth and Money*, p. 55, and especially Odd Langholm, *The Aristotelian Analysis of Usury* (Bergen: Universitetsforlaget, 1981). Although the whole book is pertinent, chapter 4, entitled "The Teleology of Money," pp. 54–69, is most directly on point.

[27] Joseph Schumpeter, *History of Economic Analysis* (Oxford: Oxford University Press, 1954), pp. 60–62.

[28] *Ibid.*, p. 61.

[29] *Ibid.* "Positive economics" is that part of economics which is capable of empirical confirmation and which does not engage in value judgments or normative claims.

Menger's advance and, as we shall see, it would never be clear until his time, i.e., the late nineteenth century.)[30] When Aristotle used these terms, he was tied to his own metaphysics. All things, but especially artifacts, had a *proper* or *appropriate use*. For Aristotle, that proper use is an objective fact. After all, it is the outcome of the thing's formal and final cause. One *must* value shoes, for example, due to the way they function when they are worn as a protective cover over or on the foot. That is what they were designed for; it is their *formal* cause. It is also their purpose, their *final* cause. One is simply *mistaken* if one values them as ornamental objects to be hung from one's ears. To be sure, this is a case of a relational value, in that the shoes have value *to* people, but it is an *objective relational* value, not a merely felt or subjective one.[31]

It is true that Aristotle does introduce the notion of demand and does relate it to price.[32] Moreover, demand is clearly not related, in any way, to cost of production or any objective part or ingredient of the product. However, to the extent that what Aristotle puts forth as based upon demand is a kind of proto-market price conception, it is a remarkable anticipation of a more modern conception. It seems to divorce price from cost, and that is a major advance. Still, it will do us no good for our own inquiry because demand, even in Aristotle, is an aggregate concept; that is, it involves many buyers and many sellers. For the purpose of the present inquiry, we seek the subjective assessment of value of a single buyer and a single seller in a micro-situated single transaction. The notion of a *market price* with respect to a single transaction is an *objective* notion. That is, I can charge you the market price for my used car (as determined by the much-celebrated "blue book" guide, let us say), or I can charge you an over-market price, if you are willing to pay it based upon your subjective preferences. The former is objective—look it up in the blue book. Thus, the market price gives rise to a standard which can be used to judge the *justice of a price* and, therefore, the moral propriety of an exchange. Therefore, *the cost-of-production theory of value or the long-run market-price theory of value are equally objective theories of value*, so far as the *individual exchange* is concerned. Clearly, it is true that when disaggregated, the concept of market price depends upon many people's subjective preferences in a way that the cost of production does not. By hypothesis, however, that is true only when *disaggregated*. As an aggregate, long-run market

---

[30] I believe this is true despite Sir Ernest Barker's claim that, for Aristotle, "value depends upon demand, *felt* utility" (emphasis added); see Barker, *The Political Thought of Plato and Aristotle* (London: Methuen, 1906), p. 379, n. 2. This claim seems fatuous, a case of reading modern conceptions back onto Aristotle, much like Schumpeter's points. Given Aristotle's notion of use as *proper use* in accord with his notions of formal and final causes (see below), a "felt utility" is either an empty notion or an exiguous one. It is also anachronistic in the extreme. Indeed, although it would take us too far afield to pursue the matter further, I do not believe that Aristotelian (or Platonic, for that matter) philosophy of mind could give rise to a modern notion of subjective preference. For that, we need Descartes, Locke, Hume, et al.

[31] See Aristotle's discussion of his four causes and what point each serves in *Physics*, Book II, chs. 7–9, and *Metaphysics*, Book VII, chs. 7–9, in McKeon, *The Basic Works of Aristotle*.

[32] See Aristotle. *Politics.* Book I. ch. 11. and *Nicomachean Ethics.* Book V. ch. 5.

price is a fact, a datum. The price set in an individual transaction is equal to, above, or below, this market price. Market price is, by hypothesis, a *fact* beyond the control of any two transacting parties. Thus, from the perspective of the individual seller asking, "Did I set a fair price?," the answer is as objective as it is in a cost-of-production model. Furthermore, as one can easily see, the notions of a just price and a zero-sum exchange can be developed using a long-run market-price theory of value. This will become even more clear with the medievals, some of whom seem to develop these notions using both kinds of theories, but with more clarity than Aristotle.

B. *Aquinas and the medieval perspective on exchange and profit*

The medieval churchmen inherited from Aristotle a rather confused picture of value but a firmly negative view of commerce and commercial transactions as carried out by those in the profession of business for the purposes of gain. Moreover, they inherited perhaps an even more negative view of commerce from the Bible (at least from those parts emphasized by the Christian tradition and the Church Fathers). In Ecclesiastes 27:2, we read: "As a nail sticks between the joining of the stones, so does sin stick also between buying and selling." In Mark 10:23–25, Jesus says that it is "easier for camel to go through the eye of a needle than for a rich man to enter the Kingdom of Heaven." He tells the rich man who wishes to be his disciple that he must first give away all his money, and reminds us that we cannot serve two masters, God and man.[33] The saying "All riches come from inequity and unless one has lost another cannot gain" is attributed to St. Jerome.[34]

That there is a strong thrust in early Christianity against commerce, wealth, and profit-making is obvious. That St. Thomas Aquinas and the schoolmen were the heirs to this tradition is also obvious. Nonetheless, the Aristotelian objection that trading for gain is the beginning of a chain of transactions which has no natural end (and which is therefore irrational and morally debasing) is one that Aquinas finds incomplete. While, for Aquinas, trade implies no necessary good, it also implies nothing necessarily bad or wrong. One must, instead, investigate what motivates a trade (even in what Aristotle disparagingly called "retail" trade). If one's aim is to purchase something for one's household (Aristotle's conception), or to pay one's workers, or to assist the needy, or to serve the public by trading, then not only is trade acceptable, but so is "moderate gain." Still, Aquinas believes that trade for profit—where profit is both substantial and sought for the sake of gain itself, or to accumulate capital and expand trade or expand the enterprise—is wrongful or, at least,

---

[33] Matthew 19:21 and Matthew 6:24.
[34] Quoted in *The Great Thoughts*, compiled by George Seldes (New York: Ballantine Books, 1985), p. 210.

morally distasteful: "greed for gain, which knows no limit, is deserving of blame" and "debasing." Thus, Aquinas may be somewhat more friendly toward trade than Aristotle, but is certainly ambivalent and not supportive of trade dedicated to profit-making, capital accumulation, and growth. The sort of free-wheeling trade characteristic of vigorous, entrepreneurial capitalism would clearly not be welcome. But let us be more specific. What is Aquinas's view of value and price, and, from that, what sort of theory of exchange does he adopt?

C. Aquinas on value and price

There is a long and tortured debate as to whether Aquinas adopts a cost-of-production theory of value or a long-run market demand based theory of value. We do know that, whatever his theory of value, it is true without question that he adopted a notion of a just price. There is good textual evidence that Aquinas's theory of value might have been one based loosely upon a cost-of-production model (though not clearly upon the cost of labor).[35] This, of course, would make his theory of value objective in the crucial sense. If this were true, then a just price would reflect cost of production and would be the morally proper price which *both parties* would be obligated to arrive at. Such a transaction, in turn, would yield a zero-sum view of exchange, since the just price and objective value would allow no room for gain on either side. Either the exchange would take place at the just price and neither party would gain, or one party would profit at the expense of the other. However, there is a more recent view among scholars which holds that Aquinas based his notion of value upon demand (in some loose, but clearly aggregated, sense)[36] and his theory of just price on long-run market price.[37] Perhaps the best approach is to admit that Aquinas is none too clear and that his is a mixed view.[38]

At first blush, a demand-based theory of value would seem to destroy the possibility of Aquinas's having a zero-sum theory of exchange. For if you recognize the market as a legitimate arbiter of price, then the market allows differential gains on the part of the buyer and seller, and we have a much more trade-friendly notion of transactions. Correct? Unfortunately, it is not! For, whatever else may be true of him, Aquinas does not

[35] See, *inter alia*, Roll, *A History of Economic Thought*, p. 46; Ronald L. Meek, *Studies in the Labor Theory of Value* (London: Lawrence and Wishart, 1973), pp. 12–14; and R. H. Tawney, *Religion and the Rise of Capitalism* (New York: Harcourt Brace, 1937), p. 37.

[36] Alejandro A. Chafuen relates demand in Aquinas to "common estimation"; see his *Christians for Freedom: Late-Scholastic Economics* (San Francisco: Ignatius Press, 1986), p. 95 and ch. 7 *passim*.

[37] See *ibid.*; David O. Friedman, "In Defense of Thomas Aquinas and the Just Price," *History of Political Economy*, vol. 12, no. 2 (1980), pp. 234–42; and Barry Gordon, "St. Thomas Aquinas," *The New Palgrave: A Dictionary of Economics* (New York: Macmillan Press, 1987), pp. 99–100.

[38] See a very persuasive argument to this effect in Samuel Hollander, "On the Interpretation of Just Price," *Kyklos*, vol. 18, no. 4 (1965), pp. 615–34.

provide us with a modern theory. There is no hint of subjective value (nothing based upon preference), nor of the price being freely negotiated. Rather, for him the long-run market price must be a just price, that is, a normatively sanctioned price. Moreover, since the just price is a determinable, long-run market price, it is *objective*. It is the "common estimation" of the value of the object by the community, and that is an objective fact. No subjective pull can influence the price and no bargaining or negotiation can open an opportunity for true profit (i.e., transaction surplus) in the micro-level transaction. Since the market price is the *just* market price, it is not clear whether Aquinas allows room for a market-permitted profit or not. Moreover, the nature of that "profit" is unclear, for, at different times, Aquinas talks about profit as compensation for the merchant's costs (labor, transportation) or about allowing profit where one party *needs* to gain (profit) from the transaction to make up for past losses, or to help the community, or to feed and clothe his family. One thing is clear, however: the dominant paradigm is the zero-sum transaction:

> Therefore if either the price exceeds the amount of the thing's *worth*, or, conversely, the thing exceeds the price, there is no longer the equality of justice, and consequently to sell a thing for more than it is worth or to buy it for less than its worth, is in itself unjust and unlawful.[39]

I shall conclude with two points. First, Aquinas's text radically underdetermines its possible interpretations. His work is open to a hybrid interpretation between the cost-of-production value/just price theory and the demand-based value/market price theory. For neither is a universal, consistent theory which will hold. It is pretty clear, then, that Aquinas simply was not consistent. This is the position of Samuel Hollander in his essay "On the Interpretation of Just Price,"[40] and his seems overwhelmingly the most cogent presentation in the literature.

Second, to a large extent, it does not really matter which interpretation of the value and price theory we accept. Either way, Aquinas is left with a zero-sum theory of transactions and, inevitably, the view that true profit (i.e., gain on a single transaction seen as a transaction surplus, and based only upon the willingness of the buyer to pay and the seller to exchange) is illegitimate.

D. Adam Smith's view

It is ironic that Adam Smith, the "father of capitalism" and the great partisan of free markets, should have held a zero-sum theory of commer-

---

[39] Aquinas, *Summa Theologica*, II-II, question 77, in *St. Thomas Aquinas on Politics and Ethics*, ed. Paul Sigmund (New York: Norton, 1988), pp. 73–74.
[40] Hollander, "On the Interpretation of Just Price" (*supra* note 38).

cial transactions. Yet he did. Indeed, his work is perhaps the clearest demonstration of the close conceptual tie between an objective theory of value and a zero-sum theory of commercial transactions. As is well-known, Smith espoused a labor theory of value—although, under that broad theoretical umbrella, he sometimes seemed to hold a labor quantity theory, sometimes a labor cost theory, sometimes a labor command theory. Moreover, sometimes demand played a role. In short, it is possible that relational and even subjective elements crept into Smith's notion of economic value. Nonetheless, he boldly began his discussion of value in Book I, Chapter V of *The Wealth of Nations* with a clear and robust statement of a theory of labor as objective value: "Labor, therefore, is the real measure of the exchangeable value of commodities."[41] That this implies, at least in Smith's mind, a zero-sum view of commercial transactions is made clear in his famous example at the beginning of Chapter VI: "If among a nation of hunters, for example, it usually costs twice the labor to kill a beaver which it does to kill a deer, one beaver should *naturally exchange* for or *be worth* two deer."[42] Here we get the clearest connection of objective value (i.e., a beaver is worth two deer) with a zero-sum view of commercial transactions (i.e., one beaver is appropriately exchanged for two deer). Indeed, though at this stage Smith himself does not even hint at a moral point, it seems clear that a deer hunter who inveigled a beaver hunter into a one-for-one swap would have "taken advantage" of him. The deer hunter would be unfairly ahead one deer, and the beaver hunter would have lost the equivalent of the worth of one deer. Obviously, this is a zero-sum transaction.

To complete the case for Smith as zero-sum theorist, we have only to quote from Chapter V, a few lines down from his first introduction of the labor theory of value: "They [money or goods] contain the value of a certain quantity of labor which we *exchange* for what is supposed at the time to contain *the value of an equal quantity*."[43] And again: "Labor alone, therefore, never varying in its own value, is alone the ultimate and real standard by which the value of all commodities can at all times and places be estimated and compared. It is their real price. . . ."[44]

Why, then, does Smith believe that a market economy is so amazingly productive? It cannot be from aggregated mutual gains from market transactions. (Or, to put it another way, it cannot be from aggregated Pareto im-

---

[41] Smith, *The Wealth of Nations* (*supra* note 13), p. 30.

[42] *Ibid.*, p. 47 (emphasis added).

[43] *Ibid.*, p. 30 (emphasis added). Thorough discussions of Smith's labor theory of value may be found in Samuel Hollander, *The Economics of Adam Smith* (Toronto: University of Toronto, 1973), ch. 4; and Meek, *Studies in the Labor Theory of Value*, ch. 2. Hollander, in a judicious discussion, gives fair weight to those places where Smith seems to use demand, utility, and other concepts related to contemporary neoclassical economics, yet concludes that Smith is, at heart, a partisan of some sort of labor theory of value.

[44] Smith, *The Wealth of Nations*, p. 33. See also a similarly categorical statement on p. 36.

provements, moving the whole economy toward Pareto optimality.)[45] Smith simply does not ever say or imply that, nor does he have the conceptual machinery to think it. Scholars who insist that he grasped gains from trade in the narrow technical sense (i.e., the idea of a transaction surplus) clearly are practicing interpretation by hindsight with a vengeance.[46]

Whence, then, the remarkable increases in standard of living provided by markets? Smith tells us frequently and clearly that these increases result from specialization, division of labor,[47] and technological improve-

---

[45] *The Dictionary of Modern Economics*, 2d ed. (Cambridge, MA: MIT Press, 1983) defines "Pareto optimality" as that state "when the economy's resources and output are allocated in such a way that no reallocation makes anyone better off without making at least one person worse off" (p. 332). It defines a "Pareto improvement" as "[a] reallocation of resources which makes at least one person better off without making anyone else worse off" (*ibid.*). Obviously, an ethical exchange makes both parties better off (or, in the limit, leaves one of them unchanged in his utility) and makes no third parties worse off, so such an exchange is Pareto-improving. Exchange is a kind of "reallocation of resources" referred to in the definition. On Paretian conditions generally, see Andrew Schotter, *Free Market Economics* (New York: St. Martin's, 1985), chs. 1 and 2 and p. 134.

[46] There is one very limited exception to this blanket assertion. But first let me remind the reader what I mean by "gains from trade." I mean this as a term of art for those gains realized by individuals who exchange as recognized by formal economics, either through the notion of consumer and producer surplus or through the Edgeworth Box (an economic model for analyzing exchange which presupposes a world of two traders, where they possess reciprocal preferences and there exists a bilateral monopoly). For a typical treatment, see Jack Hirshleifer, *Price Theory and Applications*, 3d ed. (Englewood Cliffs, NJ: Prentice Hall, 1984), pp. 210–26 (consumer surplus) and pp. 400–410 (the Edgeworth Box). All this sounds very fancy, but it really only means that if I have an apple and I love oranges far more than apples, and you have an orange and have a confirmed preference for apples, we will both gain from the exchange simply because of our reciprocal preferences. That is *gains from trade* or what I earlier set out as *pure surplus* or *transaction surplus*.

However, I do *not* mean for the expression "gains from trade" to refer to the more general improvement of position due to market transactions in all conceivable circumstances. For example, Smith *does* realize that when the city trades with the country, both benefit (*The Wealth of Nations*, p. 356)—although he attributes the gain to division of labor, not to the mere act of exchange in the context of reciprocal preferences. Moreover, he clearly recognizes that free international trade benefits all countries involved, for without this assumption, his war against mercantilist regulation and tariffs on trade makes no sense. Again, however, everything he says indicates that he bases this mutual improvement (as in the case of trade between city and country) on division of labor, or even on a vague glimpse of comparative advantage, but not on an aggregation of individual "gains from trade" that come from transactions alone.

One must, of course, carefully differentiate (1) "gains from trade" which arise exclusively because of reciprocal preferences of individual transactors, and which result in an improvement in each individual's situation, from (2) more general improvement in the position of two *collective* parties (countries or regions) engaged in aggregations of transactions, resulting from specialization and division of labor. The necessity of making this distinction with great care was made clear to me in a very helpful conversation with Robert Sugden.

[47] Smith, *The Wealth of Nations*, pp. 4–5. Smith's famous example of the pin factory makes the point well. If one man makes one whole pin at a time, he may only make a few in a day, as there are a variety of operations he must go through. Even if you add workers, where each makes a whole pin, gains in production are merely additive. If, however, you break down the task and have one man draw the wire, one man cut it, one man sharpen it, another make the head, another attach it, etc., you will get multiplicative increases in production. In Smith's pin factory, the division of labor provides 240 times the productive power of the same number of individual pin-makers each making one whole pin at a time.

ments. (This last is promoted by the first two.)[48] These three, in turn, come from the "power of exchanging," which is really only the market's efficiency bootstrapping itself by extending specialization and division of labor, as trade both spreads geographically and becomes more intense.[49]

V. MARX: THE FRUITION OF THE ZERO-SUM VIEW

A. General Marxian exploitation

We can usefully divide Marx's views into those he held as a young man, especially at the time he wrote the *Economic and Philosophic Manuscripts of 1844*, and the mature work, especially *Capital*. Even in his early work, the mode of production, not exchange or distribution, is central to the nature of an economic system. The key characteristic of capitalism is that production occurs for exchange. (This is contrasted with production for use, virtually the same distinction made by Aristotle.) For Marx, production for use characterizes, in different ways, both primitive economies and advanced socialist (especially communist) economies. Production for exchange then gives rise to the central notions of commodities, wage labor, capital, the labor theory of value (at least as instantiated in capitalism), and the "cash nexus." It is clear in Marx's early work that he saw production for exchange (and the subsequent exchange itself) as zero-sum and as a process of almost warlike, mutually aggressive efforts. He tells us:

> Each of us sees in his own product [when produced for exchange] only his *own* objectified self interest and the product of another person, *another* self interest which is independent, alien and objectionable. . . . My *social* relationship with you and my labor for your want is just plain *deception*. . . . Mutual pillaging is its base. Its background is the intent to pillage, to defraud. Since our exchange is selfish on your side as well as mine and since every self interest attempts to surpass that of another person, we necessarily attempt to defraud each other. . . . Our mutual acknowledgment of the mutual power of our objects is a battle and the one with the more insight, energy, power and cleverness is the winner.[50]

Never was a zero-sum view of market exchange more clearly or passionately set out—and all of this is, viewed one way, a struggle for profit, that is, gain from the other party to the transaction, who has, then, suffered a loss.

[48] *Ibid.*, pp. 9–10.
[49] See, *inter alia, ibid.*, pp. 11–12 and 17–18.
[50] Karl Marx, "Free Human Production," in *Writings of the Young Marx on Philosophy and Society*, ed. Loyd Easton and Kurt Guddat (Garden City, NY: Doubleday, 1967), pp. 278–79.

Allen Buchanan interprets the foregoing passage (quite correctly, I believe) in so perspicacious a way as to make his remarks worth quoting at some length. He compares the passage to other points in Marx's works, both early and late:

> Like the passage in *The German Ideology* in which Marx describes all bourgeois relations as relations of harmful utilization for gain, it shows that *Marx did not restrict the term "exploitation" to relationships between classes, much less to the wage-relationship between capitalist and worker.*
>
> More importantly, Marx's general conception of exploitation is *broad enough to apply to relationships between persons who are not producers. For it applies with equal force to more sophisticated exchange-relationships between members of the bourgeoisie in fully developed capitalist society.* Even though two merchants or two bankers, for example, are members of the same class, even though both have property in means of production and stand in no wage-relation to one another, they nonetheless exploit one another in their transactions. Each harmfully utilizes the other as a mere means to his own advantage. Each views the *needs* and *desires* of the other not as needs and desires, but rather as levers to be manipulated, as weaknesses to be preyed upon.[51]

Thus, if Buchanan is correct, there is a sense of Marxian exploitation broader than the technical sense employed in *Capital*, where exploitation is seen as existing exclusively between labor and capital and as featuring the expropriation of surplus value by the capitalist. This broader kind of exploitation typifies all transactions (and other human activities and institutions, as well).

Indeed, it turns out that, with minor variations, this is the regnant view of what Marx meant by exploitation. N. Scott Arnold explicates Marx by distinguishing two general categories of exploitation:[52] parasitic exploitation and property-relations exploitation. *Parasitic exploitation* is the most general kind of exploitation; it possesses (as do all forms of exploitation) two definitive features:

(1) The exploiter takes unfair advantage of the exploited person, and the exploiter is getting something for nothing.[53]
(2) The exploited person is forced, in some way, to deal with the exploiter.[54]

---

[51] Allen Buchanan, *Marx and Justice* (Totowa, NJ: Rowman and Allanheld, 1982), p. 39; for Buchanan's full account of exploitation, see generally ch. 3.

[52] N. Scott Arnold, *Marx's Radical Critique of Capitalist Society* (Oxford: Oxford University Press, 1990), chs. 4 and 5 *passim*. To clarify, Arnold is not a Marxist; rather, he is a strong critic of Marx. Nonetheless, Arnold's analytic rubric for exploitation is highly original and one of the most helpful in the literature.

[53] *Ibid.*, pp. 91 and 97.

[54] *Ibid.*, p. 90; cf. Buchanan, *Marx and Justice*, p. 38.

Within parasitic exploitation (as a subset), there is *surplus-value exploitation*, which is the Marxian notion of the exploitation of the individual laborer by the Marxian capitalist (more on this later). The second of the two main categories, *property-relations exploitation*,[55] takes place between *classes* in society, for example, the proletariat and the capitalists.

Parasitic exploitation, then, explains what happens when anyone profits from a commercial transaction, based upon the zero-sum view. Furthermore, surplus-value exploitation explains an identical kind of exploitation in a special case of commercial transactions: the commercial transaction of employment for a wage. Here, obviously, the capitalist takes advantage of the worker, benefiting at his expense (because of the former's ownership of the workplace and tools, and for monopolistic reasons as well).

Two other important commentators, far more sympathetic to Marx than Arnold, are Jon Elster and John Roemer. Elster has delineated a general notion of exploitation which includes commercial transactions: "Being exploited is being 'taken advantage of,' a much subtler form of suffering harm than being the object of physical coercion."[56] Elster generally believes, along with Roemer, whom he cites, that exploitation can arise in commodity and credit markets as well as in labor markets, and that there is a "logical possibility of exploitation arising through the exchange of commodities, without labor-power itself being a commodity."[57]

Thus, we can safely conclude that important contemporary interpreters of Marx believe that exploitation in a genuinely Marxian way does (or at least can) occur between transacting parties in all markets in capitalism, wherever a profit is made. The most coherent interpretation of Marxian exploitation between laborer and capitalist is that it is a zero-sum transaction (as we shall see below), and that it fits nicely with a view that classifies *all* transactions in which a profit is made the same way. But let us look at typical Marxian wage exploitation (what Arnold calls "surplus-value exploitation"). Is it best described as zero-sum in the relevant sense?

B. Surplus-value exploitation[58]

Recall that Marx holds fast to a labor theory of value. It is not enough to say that alone, however; for labor determines not one, but at least two,

---

[55] Arnold, *Marx's Radical Critique*, pp. 90–91.

[56] Jon Elster, *Making Sense of Marx* (Cambridge: Cambridge University Press, 1983), p. 167. For Elster's coverage of exploitation more generally, see especially ch. 4.

[57] *Ibid.*, p. 181. See also John Roemer, *A General Theory of Exploitation and Class* (Cambridge, MA: Harvard University Press, 1982), pp. 39–40 and ch. 3 generally.

[58] This explication of the narrow notion of Marxian exploitation draws on Karl Marx, *Capital* (New York: Charles Kerr and Co., 1906), esp. vol. 1, Part III, ch. 7. Secondary sources include: Buchanan, *Marx and Justice*; Arnold, *Marx's Radical Critique*; Elster, *Making Sense of Marx*; Roemer, *A General Theory of Exploitation and Class*; Susan Himmelweit's entry "Exploitation" in *A Dictionary of Marxist Thought*, ed. Tom Bottomore (Cambridge, MA: Harvard University Press, 1983), pp. 157–58; and Paul Craig Roberts and Matthew Stephenson, *Marx's Theory of Exchange, Alienation, and Crisis* (New York: Praeger, 1983).

labor values for a commodity. The *labor power* needed to produce the commodity has a price and, therefore, a value. It is just what the capitalist has to pay to get the worker to produce the commodity for him. In most mature labor markets, the price the capitalist has to pay to buy sufficient labor power to get the commodity made (assume one worker per commodity) is the worker's wage. He must, after all, provide the worker with a sufficient wage so that he will have energy to come to work. However, the worker's subsistence costs less than the worker can produce; therefore, per unit, each commodity is worth more in labor value than the labor/subsistence-cost to produce it. Since the commodity is worth more than subsistence-cost, and since *labor value* measures the real worth of the commodity, it is, to use Marx's term, "embodied labor." The difference between what the capitalist has to pay the worker (labor power to produce the commodity), and what he can get for the commodity on the market (its value in labor terms), is surplus value. This difference should belong to the worker. After all, it is his embodied labor, given value only by his labor. But it is expropriated by the capitalist.[59] Now, we must not tie this exploitation exclusively to labor and, indeed, Marx himself does not. In the third volume of *Capital*, he talks about exploitation through rent, taxes, and credit, i.e., other kinds of transactions.[60] Moreover, as we have seen above, many contemporary Marxists and Marx scholars hold that exploitation can be generalized to cover almost any market transaction. We have also seen that this generalized notion of exploitation fits very well with the zero-sum model.

VI. The Zero-Sum View in Detail

The zero-sum view holds that there are only three possible outcomes to a market transaction between merchant A and customer B. Either A gains at B's expense, or B gains at A's expense, or neither gains from the sale. Moreover, the only way merchant A makes a profit is by taking advantage of B. The only way A grows rich is by doing this to as many other Bs as possible with whom he does business. This view contains some kind of objective theory of value, some notion of a just price (except on Marx's version, since he forswears normativity), and a zero-sum theory of transactions. I will sketch these one at a time in a generalized form.

A. An objective theory of value

The zero-sum view typically begins with a conception of economic value. Value is, the view holds, objective, and even more basically, it is

---

[59] Things get more complicated than this for a variety of reasons. Labor differs in quality, intensity, and required training, so a notion of "abstract labor" must be formulated. That leads to further complications. For our purposes, however, the foregoing simple sketch will do.

[60] See Karl Marx, *Capital* (New York: International Publishers, 1967), vol. 3, pp. 594–97 and 609.

monadic; that is to say, it is not relational. Value is a property, like Newtonian mass or Platonic beauty. It is referred to by a one-place predicate, because it is determined only by the object which possesses it. Such a monadic property would be expressed as Px, where x is a variable or a logically proper name.

Obviously, if economic value is not relational, then it is the same for all people. Just as the ball is not merely this (Newtonian) mass in this part of the universe (or as measured in this reference frame, or for this particular person), so Alcibiades is not beautiful merely to Socrates alone. That is, the predicate is not relational in that it relates Alcibiades, beautiful, and Socrates and might be written in logic "sBa" ("Socrates finds Alcibiades beautiful"). Instead, Alcibiades is beautiful, or the mass of this billiard ball is .25 kilograms—period, full stop. On this view, it is the same with economic value. The value to you of a head of lettuce in the marketplace is the same as the value to me of that same head of lettuce. The nonrelational (i.e., monadic) character of value has two powerful consequences. First, economic value cannot be subjective, for subjectivity is relational. Not all relational properties are subjective, but all subjective properties are relational. They relate me as a subject to some object. A relational property that is objective rather than subjective is "to the north of";[61] another would be "has a mass greater than" (using Newtonian mass, again). But many relations *are* subjective. *I* find Picasso's *Les Demoiselles d'Avignon* ugly (however important it is in the history of painting) and Thomas Gainsborough's *The Honorable Mrs. Graham* beautiful. These are relational claims, each relating a particular painting to me. They are also subjective in that the relationship is one of my feeling, my impression, that is, a state of my mind, as related to something else. Other people, just in virtue of their being different *subjects* with different states of mind, would have different answers to questions about the beauty of the two paintings. However, these claims are just like objective relational ones in that they relate two entities, and, in the same way, they need a two-placed predicate to do it, for example, xBy ("Person x finds painting y beautiful"). Yet if economic value is neither relational nor subjective, it follows from the nonrelational (and nonsubjective) property of economic value that it is objective. But much else follows, as well. Let us see.

B. Just price

It follows that if a commodity has an objective value, then as we denominate that value in money terms, that monetary value is its appropriate price upon exchange. Imagine we are at a medieval fair and a certain merchant is selling heads of cheese. If the cheese has a value of

---

[61] This particular example comes from Bertrand Russell, *The Problems of Philosophy* (Buffalo: Prometheus Books, 1988), pp. 97–98; for his discussion of relations generally, see chs. 9–13 *passim*.

two shillings, then the merchant overcharges his customer if he sells it for three shillings. He has taken advantage of his customer by one shilling. If you will, he *harms* or *costs* the customer one shilling. We might most appropriately describe the extra shilling as a *taking* without compensation. The merchant *took* the difference without compensation. On the other hand, if a customer somehow inveigles the merchant into selling the cheese for one shilling, the merchant is taken advantage of by that amount. Both of these transactions, under this view, are wrongful.

It is typically true that the merchant has a near-monopoly on information about the commodity and about relevant market conditions. Indeed, he might even have something like a transitory local monopoly over supply. So he will more often take advantage or, even if he does not, he will be accused of it or thought to have done it by suspicious peasants. Thus, he acquires his dubious reputation.

C. *Profit*

What of the notion of profit in a transaction? What of the merchant's profit of one shilling on the cheese? We saw that the shilling constituted a wrongful taking. On the zero-sum view, profit on a transaction is just the measure of the wrongful taking and, thus, of the wrongfulness of the transaction and the merchant's action in engaging in it. Of course, the nature of the actions of the transacting parties and the surrounding circumstances can cause the *degree of wrong* to vary. If merchant A failed to realize he would profit at customer B's expense, the profit might be a windfall to A, and he might not have done anything *wrong*; but the transaction would still be *unfair*. However, the typical case is where A *intends*, indeed premeditates, reaping the profit, and that makes it his *intentional wrong*—as much a wrong, this would imply, as larceny. In addition, there are other issues: B's need, the nature of the product (whether it is a necessity or not), B's level of capacity, his knowledge of the product, the availability of alternatives, etc. would add or detract from the degree of wrongness of A's act. Thus, the transaction can go from unfair to monstrous, but it can never be rightful, nor can its consequence be good. Certainly, if merchant A has expended labor to acquire the cheeses and transport them to the marketplace, if he takes his own time and energy to work the stall during the fair, he is entitled to payment for that service, but not to anything more. Here, as was often the case in medieval and early modern times, the "wages of the merchant" might be thought of as a moderate *fair* profit.

D. *Zero-sum exchange*

If each commodity has an objective value and a consequent just price, exchange is necessarily barren. If the merchant sold his cheese for its just price of two shillings, he parted with a cheese worth two shillings and acquired two shillings in coin. The customer, on the other hand, parted with her coins, but acquired a cheese worth two shillings. Since neither party gained or lost, as they must not in a "fair exchange," the transaction is appropriately described as zero-sum. Indeed, it can be compared to a game of cutthroat (two-party) poker, where each party started with $20 and ended with the same amount.

As an example of exchange as analyzed by this theory, imagine that Smith has a stereo which he is considering selling to Jones. Some possible transactions are set out in Table 1. The figures in Table 1 reflect the fact that, on this view, a gain (a profit) is made only through the other party's loss. The just price ($370) in this case provides neither party with a gain (a profit). The sum of gains and losses (even if there are none at the just price) always amounts to zero.

E. Conclusion

The zero-sum view of economic gain (and its subspecies profit) is now about as clear as it can be made (given the position's internal problems of rationality). The key is that, on this view, economic gain is often (and profit is always) taken from one economic agent by another, enriching the latter. This is not enough to show that economic gain is wrong or evil. It surely is enough, however, to set up a presumption against it, requiring moral justification—for example, "I found it in nature" or "I made it for my own use" or "He gave it to me." Since, by definition, profit cannot have such a justification, it must always be wrong or bad or both.

Is there something wrong with the zero-sum view and the arguments based upon it? Of course, but exactly what? Almost everything. First, its basic concepts (value, price, market transaction, etc.) are at complete odds with contemporary neoclassical economics. Second, the view lacks any account of a rational motive to engage in trade. As we shall see, however, this view has deeper problems, and in discovering what they are, we might understand the real moral foundation of economic gain, profit, and market transactions. Hopefully, we shall be able to draft a view which would turn the moral assessment of commerce promoted by the zero-sum view completely on its head.

TABLE 1. *The Theory of Zero-Sum Transactions*

Assume Smith's stereo has an objective value of $370:			
Selling Price	Smith's Gain/(Loss)	Jones's Gain/(Loss)	Sum
$300	($70)	$70	0
$400	$30	($30)	0
$370	0	0	0

VII. GAIN, GAINS FROM TRADE, PROFIT, AND THE PROFIT MOTIVE

Robert Heilbroner, in his enormously successful, popular economic history *The Worldly Philosophers*, begins with a discussion of the development, in nascent capitalism, of the notion of gain and "the struggle" for it:

> The absence of the *idea of gain* as a *normal guide for daily life*—in fact the positive disrepute in which the idea was held by the Church—constituted one enormous difference between the strange world of the tenth to the sixteenth centuries and the world that began, a century or two before Adam Smith, to resemble our own.[62]

He also tells us: "The profit motive as we know it is only as old as 'modern man.' Even today the notion of *gain for gain's sake* is foreign to a large portion of the world's population."[63] Later, Heilbroner describes the advent of full-fledged capitalism in this way: "Transactions, transactions, transactions, and gain, gain, gain provided a new and startlingly powerful motive force."[64]

Heilbroner's discussion is typical of many popular books and academic texts.[65] Unfortunately, it is typically vague and equivocal as well. Given Heilbroner's usage of the term "gain" (and in response to others who use the term "profit" in much the same way), we are well-advised to ask: "Gain from what (or from whom)?" and/or "Gain with respect to what?" At times, "gain" means profit from a single market transaction; that, of course, only forces us back to the question of the nature of profit. At other times, "gain" seems to mean upward mobility in society. Sometimes, it means the accumulation of wealth over time. Often, as I noted above, it is related to some sort of a "struggle" (with what or whom? over what?). In the discussion from which I have quoted, Heilbroner never clearly says that gain is to be wrested *from others at their expense*, though this interpretation is always open and sometimes positively invited. What else would a struggle be for?

In another work, Heilbroner is much more specific:

> Profits take on different forms under capitalism. Initially, they arise as the gains from trade made by merchants. . . . The possibility of trading profits depends on unequal positions of strength, whether

---

[62] Robert Heilbroner, *The Worldly Philosophers* (New York: Simon and Schuster, 1980), p. 24 (emphasis added).

[63] *Ibid.*, p. 22 (emphasis added).

[64] *Ibid.*, p. 34.

[65] Some volumes that take this approach are actually pro-capitalist. See, for example, George Brockway, *Economics* (New York: Harper and Row, 1985), ch. 2. Most, however, take Heilbroner's highly critical position. See, for example, Gerald Cavanaugh, *American Business Values*, 3d ed. (Englewood Cliffs, NJ: Prentice Hall, 1990), chs. 1, 2, and 3; and Barry Schwartz, *The Battle for Human Nature* (New York: Norton, 1986), chs. 3, 6, 9, and 10.

based on political subjugation, or the possession of knowledge, or a monopoly of buying or selling power enjoyed by the trader: if strength were equal on both sides of the market, there is no reason why a merchant should be able to buy "cheap" and sell "dear."[66]

Here, the picture is clear. Power and coercion (information is also power) allow the merchant to profit by extracting a "good deal" from the customer. Although a few technical loopholes prevent this from being a canonical statement of the zero-sum view of transactions and profit, it is about as close as popular literature, phrased as loosely as Heilbroner writes, can come.

The chapter in *The Worldly Philosophers* from which I have quoted is typical of any number of discussions of gain or profit. They usually combine a stress upon how terribly important the idea of gain or profit is to capitalism with a variety of uses of the term which are carelessly mixed up and ill-defined. Many of these uses, but not all, suggest some vague form of zero-sum gain or profit. Whether intentionally or inadvertently, this often gives the impression that gain, and the motivation to do things for gain, is morally dubious or worse. After all, gain under this interpretation makes someone else worse off. To be motivated by gain is, then, just to be motivated to make someone worse off. At the very least, this makes many feel a moral ambivalence about the propriety of profit or gain, a moral ambivalence that has haunted the history of commerce. Thus, we would do well to unpack the several uses of this notion of gain analytically and explore them carefully, for a great deal turns on the term's use.

A. Gain and economic interaction—Solitary gain

When Roberta Crusoe sets out on her otherwise deserted island to find a breadfruit tree, she does so from a "gain motive," and when she finds one, she has gained. What did she gain? A supply of breadfruit! From whence did that gain come? The tree, the island's flora, nature variously. Most important, however, we must ask: Gain with respect to what? For gain means an increase in some quantity or number, as where (alas) I gain weight or (more happily) the Boston Celtics gain a (rare) victory. Here, the meaning is quite clear: Roberta's welfare (or utility, or preference satisfaction, etc.) gained or increased from t_0, when she started her search, to t_1, when she found the breadfruit. So, one clear meaning of economic gain, and that which motivates it, is a gain in welfare from t_0 to t_1, that is, a *gain over time* in one individual's situation. This often comes from productive effort, as it does here. Roberta was engaged in the most primitive of all human productive activity, *gathering*. If she builds a hut, she gains

[66] Robert Heilbroner, *The Nature and Logic of Capitalism* (New York: Norton, 1985), pp. 65-66.

from her labor, her know-how in hut construction, etc., i.e., from production. Of course, her gain could have come from a windfall. Perhaps she went into the forest only to get a better look at a colorful macaw and happened serendipitously upon the breadfruit tree. Here, there was no gain motive and no effort, but she gained nonetheless. None of this matters right now. Our only point, a terribly elementary but vastly important one, is that her gain is *over her own situation at an earlier time*. Notice that this kind of gain need have nothing to do with taking from others or with *any* economic interaction with others at all. It can be both morally neutral and without moral (i.e., interpersonal) relevance at all.

We are now in a position to see the patent silliness of a claim like Heilbroner's quoted earlier. How could only "modern man" be concerned with "gain for gain's sake"? Or, even more oddly, how could only modern man treat gain as a "normal guide for daily life"? Gain, understood this way, is a fundamental element of life, indeed of survival, for *anyone* in *any* society at any time. To fail to pursue the "gain motive" in this elemental sense would be to foreclose survival, if not now, or next week, certainly during the next winter or the next drought. Recall that Roberta accomplished her gain in a completely solitary context. No other human beings were around. Note also that in some uninteresting and certainly not pejorative sense, Roberta's motives were egoistic. How could she be concerned with anyone else?

Now, suppose there is another person—let us say, Thursday—on the island; but in this case Roberta and Thursday, while knowing of each other's existence, have no social interactions of any kind. We shall make two assumptions: (1) There are plenty of breadfruit trees, though finding any one and gathering its fruit takes some effort. Thus, Locke's proviso is in effect: there is "enough and as good" for all members of the society, in this case.[67] Another way of saying the same thing is that there is no condition of scarcity. (2) Thursday, perhaps in virtue of (1), does not bother to follow Roberta as she searches for a tree, and Roberta does not tell Thursday when or where she discovers one. Having no social relations with him, she would have no occasion to do so. Certainly, under these assumptions, Thursday is in no way affected either positively or negatively by Roberta's gain. Roberta's gain is still only over her own previous position; she has in no way at all gained *from* Thursday, has not taken anything from him (even an opportunity) or worsened (or improved, for that matter) his situation in any way. Indeed, despite Thursday's physical presence on the island, Roberta's gain is as solitary as it was when she was all alone, as in our first case.

---

[67] John Locke, *Second Treatise*, in Locke, *Two Treatises of Government* [1690], ed. Peter Laslett (Cambridge: Cambridge University Press, 1960), ch. 5. The Lockean proviso is formulated several times and in several different ways in the *Second Treatise*. The two clearest, most explicit, and most famous formulations are in section 27, where "enough and as good" is used, and in section 33.

For gains to involve other people in any way that could possibly be morally relevant, we must first have causal, intentional, and normatively significant relations between or among them. In short, what I shall call "interactions" ("transactions" are a special subclass of interactions) involve people *affecting each other causally through intentional action in ways that influence things they value in their lives.* An alternative formulation is that interactions *affect the economic situation* of those interacting, where that is broadly construed and measured in utility, preference satisfaction, welfare, or some similar measure.[68] Note again that Roberta's egoistic motive is in no way objectionable, although now there is another person in the general vicinity.

B. Gain from economic interaction

From Roberta's perspective, there are three broad classes of ways in which she can be affected by economic interactions with Thursday. Obviously, she can *gain, lose,* or *be left undisturbed.* She can, in turn, gain in four ways. First, Thursday can *give* her something, without consideration. Second, she can *take* something from Thursday by force or stealth. Third, she can benefit from a *positive externality* resulting from some otherwise solitary action of Thursday. (Suppose Thursday fells a breadfruit tree to make his hut, leaving some breadfruit on the forest floor. Roberta's gain of the breadfruit is a positive externality. She gained from a spillover effect which had no effect, positive or negative, on Thursday.) Fourth, Roberta can *exchange* or *transact* with Thursday. This last we shall consider shortly.

As for the remaining forms of economic interaction, Roberta can interact while being left undisturbed only where she imposes an externality, positive or negative, on Thursday. She can lose in cases where Thursday takes from her or where he imposes a negative externality upon her. Suppose, for example, that in the course of his otherwise solitary hut-construction, he fells a tree that lands on her hut, smashing it.

Notice that among the four ways Roberta can gain, two clearly make Thursday worse off. If Thursday gives her a breadfruit, he is worse off by that one breadfruit. If Roberta steals or robs a breadfruit from Thursday, he is clearly worse off by that breadfruit. Here, Roberta's gain really is

---

[68] Throughout, I have used these three expressions as if they were synonymous. Of course, they are not. Utility in the canonical formulation is a mapping of a preference ordering into the real numbers—that is, a *function* in the technical, mathematical sense, where both the range and the domain are subject to a variety of limitations. Preference satisfaction is the psychological basis for utility maximization. However, welfare is the term that differs most from the others, for it (typically and at least prima facie) suggests "objective" elements of undesired needs and unrecognized constituents of well-being. That is, I may need a medicine for my welfare but not know it, or I may know it, but not prefer it or desire it. For our purposes, however, the three terms can be used interchangeably.

Thursday's loss. She gains a breadfruit, he loses one, a classic zero-sum interaction.

In the case of theft, it is important to realize the great risk of equivocation over the word "gain." On the one hand, Roberta gains *from* Thursday by and through his loss. In another quite different sense, she gains over time from t_0, before she stole the breadfruit, to t_1, after it is in her possession. The former sort of gain, i.e., gain from another, is unique to theft, gifts, and closely related interactions. It is *this* sense of gain which is the result of a zero-sum interaction. As we shall see, gain in the second sense, i.e., over time from one's situation at t_0 to one's situation at t_1, is clearly not the result of such interaction.

Roberta also gains *from her own otherwise solitary activity* when she imposes a negative externality upon Thursday. The cost imposed upon Thursday does not directly provide Roberta with a gain as it did in the case of theft or gift; it is instead a *causal by-product* of her gainful (to her) activity, a true *spillover effect*. Note that, since this is not a direct transfer of value from Thursday to her, his loss does not have to equal her gain. It might be much greater or might be minimal to the point of triviality.

The case where Roberta is the recipient of a positive externality through Thursday's felling a breadfruit tree to make a hut (and leaving the fruit to her as a windfall) is an interesting one. For, here, new value or utility is actually created. Thursday is making himself better off by felling a breadfruit tree for his hut. He gains between t_0, when he has no timber for his hut, and t_1, when he has some. Meanwhile, Roberta *also gains* breadfruit over time, breadfruit that otherwise would have taken additional time, energy, and bother to gather. Both parties are net gainers, as compared to their respective starting positions, over time. Note what is so obvious that we might stumble over it: in this situation, there is no mysterious zero-sum principle in operation which says that for one to gain, the other must lose. Now, recall that no one else is affected in any way. After all, this is an otherwise deserted island. Economists have a term for an activity or an interaction (including an exchange) that benefits all parties or leaves them undisturbed. We have met it before. By the terms of this case, Thursday's activity is *Pareto-improving*. He helped himself and Roberta, and harmed no one else.

C. Competition

Before I go on to discuss the case of exchange, one point must be briefly mentioned. I have assumed until now that the world has no ultimate scarcity. Food, shelter, etc. are not "there for the picking," in that obtaining them is not free; it takes effort, know-how, and even, perhaps, ingenuity. But, given the exercise of these capacities, there is no shortage. That is just the force of Locke's proviso. Assume, for the moment, that breadfruit is scarce; that is, let us drop the proviso. If Roberta finds a breadfruit tree, she must make sure Thursday does not find that one. She may take great care not to be followed; she may lay false trails. A breadfruit tree that he finds is one she can, at best, harvest only part of the time. Whoever reaches the tree first after the fruit has ripened wins, and the other loses out. Again, as in the theft case, one breadfruit more for Roberta is one breadfruit less for Thursday. It is, of course, a "lost opportunity cost" for Thursday, because he never actually possessed it, but the zero-sum principle is very much in force.

The word "competition" has all sorts of vague associations with market exchange and markets, but here it is obviously unrelated to any such thing. It is closer to Hobbesian competition in a state of nature. Indeed, if we think of possible things Roberta could do to secure her breadfruit (for example, guard the trees, lay traps, even ambush and kill Thursday), we see that their situation just *is* Hobbes's state of nature.

Have these two unfortunates any alternatives to falling into Hobbesian war in the face of scarcity? Of course they do. They can innovate: discover other food plants, develop agriculture, etc. They can specialize: Roberta gathers breadfruit, Thursday gathers bananas. Innovation and specialization lead naturally to exchange. Roberta and Thursday can enter into economic transactions where, of course, *both can gain*.

D. Mutual gains from trade

Suppose that Thursday begins to specialize in gathering wild bananas, while Roberta continues to gather breadfruit. This could eventuate from scarcity, or from the discovery that bananas are a tasty and nutritious food, or from Thursday's possession of greater innate talent at banana-gathering than at breadfruit-gathering, or from any combination of the three. That does not matter. What does matter is that under conditions of scarcity, this specialization is an *alternative* to competition, and an implicitly *cooperative* one, though it requires no mutual planning, nor even an explicit agreement ahead of time. Adam Smith, in his famous examples, assumes that specialization—or at least its long arm, the division of labor—is a product of a more or less full-blown market. But that need not be so. As it does here, specialization can precede the development of a free exchange in a sort of proto-market, arising as a direct reaction to scarcity.

Soon, however, Thursday will have all the bananas he wants and will no doubt long for the occasional breadfruit. Roberta will be likely to have reciprocal preferences for bananas, from time to time. To satisfy their preferences they could return to competition or they could *cooperate further*; that is, they could exchange. It is very important to realize that, while the desire for gain (i.e., making yourself better off than you were before) can produce competition in the Hobbesian case, the desire for gain can also produce exactly the opposite outcome—cooperation. Cooperative outcomes include specialization and exchange; together these form a so-phisticated, and relatively complex, social response to the desire to improve one's lot. Thus, the motive or *desire for gain in one's own situation, over time,* can produce social cooperation and interdependence through specialization and exchange. Indeed, that is precisely what happens in the development of early capitalism, a fact seemingly lost on Heilbroner, and on the popular writers of his persuasion, but not on serious economic historians.[69] Ultimately, such social cooperation leads to the exquisite patterns of cooperation, specialization, and global interdependence characterized by advanced capitalism.

What assumptions must we make to get exchange off the ground? We must assume that, at the margin, Roberta prefers a banana to her nth breadfruit and Thursday prefers a breadfruit to his nth banana. This, in turn, must presuppose a subjective (or at least agent-relative) theory of value. Roberta's valuation of breadfruit and Thursday's must differ at the margin. Moreover, each must impose a notion of diminishing marginal utility on their respective stocks of fruit; that is, each must ascribe less value to their nth fruit than to their first, or second, etc. For either one of them, then, a given kind of fruit ranges over a set of diminishing values, depending on how many of those fruits that person has. It may be that some objective theory of value can account for all this, though it would have to be tortured and *ad hoc* in nature. By comparison, a *subjective theory of value*, whether it is based upon a personal utility function or, perhaps more basically, a preference ordering, or something else, fits the situation like a glove.

Armed with such a subjective theory of value, we can characterize the prospective trade between Roberta and Thursday in beautifully simple terms. "Use value" and "exchange value," though antedated in modern economics, serve well for our present purpose.[70] Assume Roberta places value V^r on her nth breadfruit, if she could utilize it in a trade to get a banana. We will call this the *exchange value* V^r_e of her nth breadfruit. She could also *use* her nth breadfruit, i.e., store it and eat it before it spoils; for that purpose, it has a *use value* to her of V^r_u. Now, it is clear, by hypothesis, that:

$$V^r_e > V^r_u$$

[69] See, for example, Fernand Braudel, *The Wheels of Commerce* (New York: Harper and Row, 1979); Nathan Rosenberg and L. E. Birdzell, *How the West Grew Rich* (New York: Basic Books, 1988); and E. L. Jones, *The European Miracle* (Cambridge: Cambridge University Press, 1981).

[70] The same point could be made in a couple of ways using the concepts of contemporary economics. One approach is that of consumer and producer surplus. A different perspective that, nonetheless, makes the same point is the example of the two traders in the Edgeworth Box. See note 46 *supra*.

On exactly similar reasoning, if Thursday's nth banana has values V_e^t and V_u^t, then:

$$V_e^t > V_u^t$$

Now, an exchange between Roberta and Thursday will yield a gain *over their respective previous positions* of:

$$V_e^r - V_u^r$$

for Roberta and

$$V_e^t - V_u^t$$

for Thursday. Note that the gain has nothing to do with the effects of the exchange on the other exchanging party. The gain is only with respect to their own previous positions. Note, also, that neither party worsens the position of the other. In that sense, the gain here is very like solitary gain. Of course, it is also Pareto-improving.

E. Egoistic and nonegoistic considerations in simple barter

Given what I have said, Roberta and Thursday could each be *exclusively egoistic* in their motives to exchange—although perhaps neither could be selfish, or at least *too selfish*, for a reason we shall see below. They could and would engage in exchange based solely on considerations of their own welfare. However, they would not have to be egoists, or at least egoists in anything like the way that egoism is typically defined. A typical libertarian ethic requires that one take care of oneself, subject to the constraints of respect for the rights of others. Now, if that is egoism, it is a highly constrained version, because it requires the respect of moral rights of others. This, in turn, means considering others in situations where not considering them would maximize your own welfare, and thus means accepting less than the maximum for yourself precisely because you respect the rights of others. That surely is regarding them as morally considerable subjects—dare we say, as "ends of themselves."[71] It certainly sounds like it, and if this is so, it is *surely* not egoism in the pejorative sense. Let us call this the *rights respecting rule*. This is an odd egoism, if it is one at all. But here we could introduce an even stronger nonegoistic constraint on exchange (although this would be beyond the standard libertarian morality). Roberta *could* adopt a rule which says: "I will do the best I can for myself so long as I *in no way worsen* Thursday's situation (his welfare)"—a far stronger constraint than prohibiting rights violations.

---

[71] See Robert Nozick's elegant last paragraph in *Anarchy, State, and Utopia* (New York: Basic Books, 1974), pp. 333–34, for an implicit, but powerful, appeal to Kantianism in this form of rights-based libertarianism. Even more clear is the undeniable moral, as opposed to egoistic, foundation of the position.

Perhaps we should call this the *weak Paretian rule*. Indeed, subject to some additional, quite plausible, assumptions, Roberta could invoke an even stronger welfare criterion. She could adopt a *strong Paretian* rule: "I will not exchange unless I positively improve, at least a little, Thursday's situation.[72] So, I will improve his situation, even as I improve mine."

There are more-stringent moral rules that Roberta could impose upon herself, or which could be imposed by an outside party. Roemer, for example, believes that the transaction surplus must be justly divided between the parties, whatever that means.[73] Let us call an obvious version of Roemer's requirement the *egalitarian rule*. This rule creates all sorts of logical and epistemological problems, including providing great incentives for the strategic misrepresentation of preferences, difficulty in actually measuring a utility function, and even, perhaps, requiring the interpersonal comparison of utilities. An even stronger rule might be called the *altruistic rule*. For Roberta, it simply goes like this: Give everything you gained in the transaction to Thursday. But, then, since the same rule pertains to Thursday, the transaction must be reversed, so why transact? Is this a coherent rule? With transaction costs included, it is probably not.

In any case, all this shows is that the Paretian rule (in its weak or strong version) is sort of halfway between a Hobbesian state-of-nature rule and an altruistic rule fit only for angels. The Paretian rule requires serious moral restraints and more than a little moral consideration for the other party, if not for the actual amount of his or her transaction surplus. At least at first glance, then, profit-making subject to a Paretian rule is so morally restrained as to be morally permissible under any reasonable code of ethics.

I have not yet fully integrated this notion of mutual benefit into a true theory of market exchange. Rather, I have been analyzing the world of two traders and a bilateral monopoly. After all, a single banana exchanged for a single breadfruit is hardly a market transaction, though it surely is a sort of proto-market transaction.[74] But before extending the

---

[72] Although the mathematics of contemporary economics does accept the case where the improvement in Thursday's situation approaches zero in the limit, I reject it on practical and psychological grounds. Just as, in the zero-sum view, exchange at a "just price" was intentional action without motive, so exchanging where your gain "approaches zero in the limit" makes no sense as regards motivation or practical reasoning, for you are also approaching indifference in the limit.

[73] John Roemer, *Free to Lose* (Cambridge, MA: Harvard University Press, 1988), p. 59.

[74] It fails to be a market transaction because there is no market (there are not multiple traders of bananas and breadfruit). Rather, this is a case of "bilateral monopoly," with each trader having one kind of item and reciprocal preferences. However, this does not offer the threatening associations that usually go with "monopoly." There is not, indeed there cannot be, coercion, for example. Each trader, but for lacking special knowledge and skills, has access to the other's source of products, and each trader can live quite well (as they did in the pre-trade world) without the other's product.

Return to the market point again for a moment. Usually we think of a market as requiring money, if for no other reason than to generate *enough* exchange to be a market. For our purposes, it can remain a moot point whether a market requires money, for we do not really need a fully developed market.

discussion to genuine market transactions, let us consider the whole normative picture in a single Pareto-improving exchange.

F. Necessary normative constraints on exchange

As I have noted, in addition to being concerned with her own welfare, Roberta could be concerned with not worsening Thursday's situation, or even with bettering it (at least by a very small amount). There are, however, some normative constraints which each trader *must* impose upon him- or herself. I use the term "normative" to include both prudence and morality, because they often go together in justification and even perhaps in the evolution of social norms.

Indeed, the norms necessary to get trade off the ground are obvious, and I have adumbrated them already. But let me make them explicit and precise. Both Roberta and Thursday must abstain from attacks upon each other's person. Without personal security, one cannot engage in specialized economic activity over a sustained period of time; one spends all one's time on guard, looking for a safe place to sleep or obtaining minimal sustenance. Similarly, there must be a simple system of property rights and those must be respected. Otherwise, exchange makes no sense, and an exchange economy with specialization deteriorates again into a Hobbesian state of nature. Although I have severe doubts above deriving a prohibition against fraud from rights to security of person and property, that prohibition is usually included at this point.[75] I would argue that it must be introduced as an independent moral postulate. In any case, there must be a moral prohibition against fraud, whether derived or independent. There seems to exist no need for respect for contracts and the discharging of them in a world of immediately executed transactions, but to the extent that contracting occurs, it imposes yet another norm.

I will not inquire into the puzzling question of how much these norms can be based upon rational self-interest and bargaining, and how much they must finally rest on irreducible moral commitment. I will only add that until a definitive reduction of personal rights and property rights to self-interested bargaining is provided, there will remain some admixture of morality at the base of these norms.[76] That is fine by my lights, for that means that exchange, at least in this simple two-person world, must be based upon moral commitment. Thus, we have a cooperative response to the gain motive that requires for its effectiveness moral commitment to moral restraint.

---

[75] See my essay "Can Libertarianism Sustain a Fraud Standard?" *Ethics*, vol. 104, no. 4 (July 1994).

[76] Hobbes is, of course, the *locus classicus* for this approach. By far the most important effort in contemporary theory is David Gauthier's *Morals by Agreement* (Oxford: Oxford University Press, 1986), although most would agree that Gauthier does not quite succeed in a complete reduction of morals to self-interest.

VIII. PROFIT AND THE PROFIT MOTIVE

A. Profit as gain per unit of time: A real-world illustration

What is profit? In a very loose and elementary way, it is the revenue associated with some economic activity minus the costs associated with producing that revenue. What, then, is profit as calculated for a business enterprise—the annual profit of a firm, for example? Assume that Jones is a sole proprietor. He manufactures and sells widgets. A very simple income (or profit and loss) statement for Jones would look like Table 2. Note first that the income statement is for *a period of time*. Thus, as in the simple model of gain on Roberta's island, there is a t_0 and a t_1. In this case, t_0 is January 1, 1997 and t_1 is December 31, 1997. Sales revenue is what comes into the business, i.e., payments for widgets. Costs, obviously, are what goes out. Net income or net profit is what is left, which *just is* the net gain experienced over one year of business activity.

Where does the gain come from? Well, first of all, it makes no sense to think that it is *taken from someone* in a zero-sum transfer. It is not profiting (gaining) at someone else's expense, at least this is not typically the case (and not the case at all when the business is run ethically). Of course, one's gain can be at the expense of others if one's business is extortion or theft. In the usual case, however, it comes by making others at least a little better off and making no one worse off—that is, through engaging in Pareto-improving transactions (in this case, selling widgets to those who are willing to pay at least the sales price for widgets). This occurs when value is added to raw materials through the use of factors (land, labor, capital) to produce a product for which people are willing to pay more than it costs to produce. The buyers of widgets gain from the exchange, or else they would refuse to engage in it. Likewise, the suppliers of raw materials and factors of production gain, or else they would not transact. A moment's reflection makes this as clear as it was in the case of the trade of breadfruit for bananas that Roberta and Thursday engaged in.

TABLE 2. *Jones Widgets—Net Profit for 1997*

Sales revenue	$100,000
Cost of goods sold (raw materials, direct labor, direct power)	−$ 60,000
Gross profit	$ 40,000
Cost of sales (advertising, promotion, etc.)	−$ 2,000
Administrative costs (telephone, insurance, accounting)	−$ 8,000
Net profit	$ 30,000

The entrepreneur, in this case Jones, brings together the materials and factors and manages the process in such a way that he too gains. After all, the costs are paid out of revenue, and he is the residual claimant who gets what is left over (if anything). That is Jones's profit—his gain realized over a certain period from the business activity. And he obtains it by making everyone with whom he transacts (from whom he buys or to whom he sells) just a little better off, and leaving no third parties worse off (that is, he generates no pollution or other negative externalities).

One should note that a great deal of time has been spent by neoclassical economists, as well as by Marxists, trying to account for profit arising in the production process. However, the most interesting work has been done by the Austrian economists, particularly by Joseph Schumpeter[77] and Israel Kirzner[78] on entrepreneurial profit. Nonetheless, we must remember that profit, as I (and almost all economists) have defined it, can only arise in a market and after exchange. Therefore, so long as the Paretian theory of exchange is correct and the zero-sum view is wrong, then profit must ultimately appear as gains from trade, that is, through buying and selling in a market—although much profit of the kind I have *not* considered here has its *cause*, not in gains from trade, but in production efficiencies, production and product innovation, new markets, etc. (Recall Smith's view of the division of labor, and see the works of Schumpeter and Kirzner.) *Still, all profit is ultimately realized as gains from trade.*

What, then, is the profit *motive*? It is the gain motive, where we understand gain to be improvement over time in one's position, with one important addition: that the gain is pursued through transactions with others rather than through, say, solitary economic activity or positive externalities. It is true that these gains (benefits) might be realized by predation, that is, gains or profits as understood by Aristotle and Marx (gains "at the expense of other men"). Thus, they can be simultaneously gains in one's situation and gains extracted from other people. But extortive or larcenous profits are criminal and, as we have seen, their prohibition is a prerequisite to market exchange—and likewise with fraud or exploitation of incapacity (dealing with a minor or a severely retarded person).

Less clearly illegitimate, but still zero-sum in character, are profits that are made in part by externalizing costs, that is, by imposing costs which should rightfully fall upon the producer upon others without their consent or without compensation to them. But this is also something a system of market exchange must prevent or at least accommodate by some means of rectification (usually through a tort system), though I have not shown

[77] See, for example, Joseph Schumpeter, *The Theory of Economic Development* (New Brunswick, NJ: Transaction Books, 1983), ch. 4.
[78] Among several works, perhaps the one most on point is Israel Kirzner, *Perception, Opportunity, and Profit* (Chicago: University of Chicago Press, 1979), esp. Part 3; but see also his *Competition and Entrepreneurship* (Chicago: University of Chicago Press, 1973).

that. Suffice it to say here that some stable system of property rights is surely necessary, and that some system of penalties and/or enforced compensation is necessary to internalize negative externalities. Typically, the imposition of serious negative externalities tends to become tortious (and occasionally criminal) when discovered and appreciated as harmful (for example, toxic dumps or exotic new pollutants).

As we have seen, it is possible to conceive of solitary economic activity generating gains over time. Roberta might keep books on the number of breadfruit gathered during a specific period, for example. Thus, a market transaction is required as part of the accounting definition of *profit* (and as part of the economic/philosophical concept) but not as part of the concept of gain. The very notion of profit, what it is and why we have it, is to *express one party's portion of the mutual gain realized in Pareto-improving transactions*. As we saw, commercial transactions, if they go as they should, provide gain to both parties and thus provide profit to both parties. When Jones, the widget manufacturer, sells his widgets to Smith, the widget wholesaler, Smith's payment is Jones's revenue, which, after the deduction of costs, is Jones's profit. The same payment is one of Smith's primary costs, and he deducts it from *his* revenue to get *his* profit.

As we have seen, the Paretian rule that Roberta, Thursday, or Jones could follow ("Only increase my welfare by economic interaction if I can help, if only a little, someone else") is perfectly consistent with market exchanges. (Remember, we leave aside, as a practical impossibility, the limiting case where the gain of one transacting partner approaches zero in the limit.) Are market transactors altruists? Of course not. First, they are helping themselves, too. Indeed, that may be the *sole motive* and still the market player could live in accord with the moral rule cited above. Indeed, to learn more, let us set the commercial world in motion around this rule. (Note, however, that I have space enough only to sketch this much more complicated world. The brunt of the essay has been to use simpler examples to build concepts necessary to deal normatively with this more complicated world on another occasion.)

B. Transactions in a fully developed competitive market

Here, competition takes over, so the portion of the Paretian surplus (or transaction surplus) the merchant can keep will fall as he must give more and more to the customer to make the sale. Soon, when the merchant's incremental cost per unit equals his incremental price, his profit will have reached zero. Then, he must become more efficient, must innovate, or must find supply bottlenecks (à la Kirzner), etc. The point is, the market colludes with the Paretian moral rule to force the merchant (never mind his motives) to give more and more of the transaction surplus to his customer.

C. Transactions in negotiated sales[79]

If A and B negotiate over the price of a house, two things are clear. First, assuming that A and B are rational and that neither is misrepresenting the situation (i.e., committing fraud), then, whatever price they arrive at, there will be a transaction surplus and both will get some of it (i.e., both will gain). Notice, though, that both A and B want as much of the transaction surplus as possible. This gives rise to a two-rule system, with the rules sequentially applied:

(1) Economically interact not only so that my own economic welfare is increased but so that the economic welfare of the person I transact with is also increased, if only a little.
(2) Once I have assured myself that (a) there is a transaction surplus and (b) my transaction partner will get at least a little, then I may act through bargaining to get as much as possible of the transaction surplus for myself, leaving for my partner only enough to continue to rationally motivate the transaction.

Thus, the "helping others" requirement has to be amended (but not eliminated) in the case of the negotiated sale and bargaining. Even in negotiated sales, one must not harm or impose a net cost on one's transaction partner (much less violate his rights), and one must actually make him at least a little bit better off. Of course, since one is required to help one's transaction partner so little, the moral force of the rules does not lie in *helping*. The moral force lies, instead, in virtue of the marginal help actually required, in having to *lean over backward not to harm* one's transaction partner. Now, it is true that Rule 2 is an egoistic rule; but Rule 1 is not. Indeed, it represents a severe moral limitation on the egoism expressed in Rule 2, and it insists that a transaction partner be treated as a morally considerable being whose welfare counts.

IX. Conclusion

All of this has an ironical ring: that profit in the canonical case can *only* be realized by participation in mutually beneficial transactions. Com-

---

[79] A "negotiated sale" involves only one (or one lot) of something versus the vast quantity required for a true market with nearly perfect competition. It does not involve repetitive purchases and sales to many parties. There is no market price set by supply and demand and no assurance that the market will "clear." Indeed, in this case, that could only mean that the item will be sold; but there is no assurance of that. Lastly, the actual transaction price is arrived at through bargaining.

Treatments of negotiation, where the points set out here are discussed in detail, may be found in Roy J. Lewicki and Joseph A. Litterer, *Negotiation* (Homewood, IL: Irwin, 1985), ch. 4; and in an outstanding book by Howard Raiffa, *The Art and Science of Negotiation* (Cambridge, MA: Harvard University Press, 1983), *passim*, but esp. pp. 35–65.

merce can only exist successfully where all the actors are treated as morally considerable. It sounds like Chamber of Commerce treacle, but it is nonetheless quite true. Let us finally face it: Aristotle and Marx were wrong; the Chamber of Commerce is right. The making of profit is consistent not only with rigorous rules prohibiting harm or net costing, but actually with even stronger rules requiring mutual (if minimal) benefit. If there were space to consider repeat business, reputation effects, and other dimensions besides price by which one can benefit one's transaction partners (e.g., customer service, credit terms, consistency and assurance of supply, product quality, etc.), we might well find that the benefit provided to the buyer by the seller in order to make a transaction go will not remain marginal. It will be context-dependent, and difficult for technical economics to capture, but, nonetheless, real and significant for all that. *One makes profits by benefiting those one transacts with, while benefiting oneself and leaving others undisturbed.* It seems ironic in the face of two thousand four hundred years of zero-sum propaganda and the wider anti-commerce and anti-profit bias based upon it. But there it is!

Philosophy, Bowling Green State University

NATURAL PROPERTY RIGHTS: WHERE THEY FAIL

By Robert Ehman

I. Introduction

For classical liberals, natural property rights are the moral foundation of the market and of individual freedom. They determine the initial position from which persons legitimately make contracts and assess the validity of collective action. Since they establish the initial conditions of legitimate agreements, they cannot be dependent upon agreements. Persons possess these rights apart from social institutions. Natural rights typically not only prohibit interference with a person's body and mind but also forbid interference with a person's appropriation of unowned natural resources and with his freedom to do as he chooses with the products that he makes from them, so long as he does not infringe upon the equal rights of others. These rights prescribe, as Locke put it, that persons be free "to order their Actions, and dispose of their Possessions, and Persons as they think fit . . . without asking leave, or depending upon the Will of any other Man."[1]

In this essay, I argue that natural rights may fail to adjudicate the disputes that arise when one person's exercise of rights imposes costs that interfere with other persons' exercise of their rights. I also argue that natural rights may be incompatible with the non-unanimous collective decision-making procedures that are often necessary to provide a satisfactory level of public goods.

My discussion proceeds in three parts. In Section II, I consider how Locke might deal with the challenge to property rights raised by rights conflicts and by goods that require collective action. In Section III, I examine Robert Nozick's and David Gauthier's approaches to these issues. I find that they are no more successful than Locke in answering the questions raised by rights conflicts and public goods. In Section IV, I explore the question of how to protect individual liberty and establish a legitimate foundation for market transactions where natural property rights fail to do so.

II. Locke on Rights Conflicts and Public Goods

For Locke, the natural equality of men means that they are not to be subordinated to one another without their consent. However, in the orig-

---

[1] John Locke, *Second Treatise*, in Locke, *Two Treatises of Government* [1690], ed. Peter Laslett (Cambridge: Cambridge University Press, 1960), ch. 2, section 4.

283

inal condition of life prior to society, men require natural resources to provide materials for the labor by which they satisfy their needs. If men are to be able to live without being subordinate to others, they must have a right to use these resources without the consent of others. For if they needed this consent in order to provide for their lives, they would be subject to the will of others. The natural right not to be subordinate to others therefore implies a right to appropriate natural resources apart from the consent of others. But the nonconsensual use of natural resources raises a problem. These resources are not originally the property of any given individual, but are available to all. How, apart from the consent of others, can we legitimately appropriate, as our own private property, resources that are held in common for all?

Locke's answer is that we can do so because in the original conditions under which we live, the appropriation leaves "enough and as good" in the common for others. For this reason, no one can object that appropriation on the part of others interferes with his appropriation of the resources needed for his own life. However, this "enough and as good" proviso no longer holds once we have fully appropriated the common. Hence, full appropriation might appear to invalidate nonconsensual appropriation.

There are a number of conflicting interpretations of Locke on the validity of nonconsensual appropriation when no natural resources remain in common. Jeremy Waldron argues that Locke's "enough and as good" proviso is not a constraint on appropriation but simply a fact about original appropriation. Hence, for Waldron, the proviso does not call into question appropriation that does not satisfy it.[2] But John Tully maintains that natural property rights no longer hold once there is no longer "enough and as good" natural resources available for appropriation. On Tully's interpretation of Locke, once all resources have been appropriated we must appeal to collective action and consent to validate property rights.[3] In contrast to these positions, A. John Simmons holds that for Locke natural property rights remain valid once the common has been fully appropriated so long as the appropriation did not violate the proviso at the time of the original appropriation.[4] And Gopal Sreenivasan finds that Locke's proviso permits full appropriation so long as those who have appropriated the resources fulfill a duty to employ those unable to appropriate, so that the latter may live without appropriation.[5]

[2] Jeremy Waldron, *The Right to Private Property* (Oxford: Clarendon Press, 1988), pp. 210–18.

[3] James Tully, *A Discourse on Property* (Cambridge: Cambridge University Press, 1980), p. 146.

[4] A. John Simmons, *The Lockean Theory of Rights* (Princeton: Princeton University Press, 1992), pp. 297–98.

[5] Gopal Sreenivasan, *The Limits of Lockean Rights in Property* (New York: Oxford University Press, 1995), pp. 100–102.

For Locke, as Sreenivasan points out, market transactions make it possible for persons to fulfill their needs by selling their labor and buying what they need with the wages they earn from their labor. The market thereby frees them from dependence on appropriation from the common for the comfort and preservation of their lives. Since, as Locke argues, persons consent to the market exchanges by which they sell their labor for wages, it is reasonable to conclude that, in so doing, they waive the claim to the common that the proviso expresses. The proviso appears to hold only where persons need to appropriate natural resources from the common for their livelihood and where they do not consent to obtain what they need for their lives apart from the common.

The acceptance of money in exchange for goods expands trade and industry. For Locke, this leads to a scarcity of natural resources to appropriate. However, the inability to appropriate natural resources does not, on Locke's view, lead to a scarcity in the means to the preservation and comforts of life. For the expansion of industry and trade makes possible more of the comforts and conveniences of life than are obtainable from natural resources remaining in common apart from trade and industry. The "enough and as good" proviso does not limit appropriation in the early stages of civilization when there is more in the common than we can use for our preservation and comfort; likewise, it does not do so in the more civilized parts of the world when the benefits of commerce and industry provide more of the goods that we need for our lives than we could attain from the common.

Sreenivasan's position that the proviso no longer limits appropriation when we can earn a living apart from the common is consistent with Locke's account of the consensual basis and mutual benefits of the monetary economy that replaces the self-subsistence economy of the original common. However, in order to reconcile the proviso with full appropriation, we need not, as Sreenivasan does, admit a duty to employ those who are no longer able to appropriate. For when persons are no longer able to appropriate from the common, they either can make a living from the market without appropriation from the common or else they can claim support from others by virtue of the duty that, according to Locke, each person has to preserve the lives of those who cannot do so on their own.

But although we may be said to waive the "enough and as good" proviso when we consent to earn a living by market transactions rather than by original appropriation, we cannot thereby be said to consent to the interference in our own exercise of our rights that results from the costs others impose on us when they exercise their rights. The benefits of trade and industry do not eliminate the need to adjudicate the disputes that arise from conflicts in the exercise of rights.

For example, consider Ronald Coase's classic case of two neighboring landowners, one of whom raises cattle and the other of whom raises corn.[6] The cattle damage the corn unless someone bears the cost of a fence or the rancher raises fewer cattle. When the rancher raises all of the cattle his land will support, he appears legitimately to exercise his property rights. But in so doing he prevents the farmer from raising all of the corn he would be able to raise in the absence of the rancher. Hence, the rancher interferes with the farmer's exercise of his property rights.

Locke maintains that it is the task of the state to "settle" property rights and boundaries. He appears to mean that the state is needed to decide cases of this sort. But what is the criterion of the decision? Do natural property rights prescribe state action, or does the state decide these cases on some basis other than natural rights?

In order to respect natural property rights in conflicts of this sort, a Lockean might argue that the party that causes the loss ought to compensate for that loss, since that party infringes on the property rights of the other. On this principle, the rancher ought to pay for the damage to the corn, because his cattle trespass on the land of the farmer and trample his corn. For the farmer has a right not to have cattle trespass upon his land unless he consents to this. He might consent to the trespass in order to promote cooperation with his neighbors, but he need not do so as a matter of respecting his neighbor's right to raise all of the cattle that he could apart from the presence of a neighboring farmer. On this position, the rancher has no right to raise cattle that damage his neighbor's property unless he compensates his neighbor or his neighbor agrees to permit the damage.

But why protect the farmer's right to raise all of the corn that he can apart from the presence of the neighboring rancher and not protect the right of the rancher to raise all of the cattle he can in the absence of the neighboring farmer? The two situations appear symmetrical. The farmer might reply that they are symmetrical in the costs that are imposed, but are asymmetrical in that the cattle damage the farmer's crop while the corn does not damage the cattle. The question is: How relevant is the physical causality?

The point of claiming an ownership right is not simply to fix certain physical boundaries that are not to be crossed without permission, but to realize the value of the exercise of the right. The value of a property right is the use to which we can put the property or the income we can earn from it. To restrict the use or reduce the income decreases the value of the

---

[6] Ronald Coase, "The Problem of Social Cost," *Journal of Law and Economics*, vol. 3 (1960), p. 1. The problem that I am raising with respect to social costs is not the problem with which Coase is concerned. Coase raises the problem of efficiently allocating social costs. He rightly recognizes that unless there are no transaction costs, the decision as to whether or not to shift these costs affects the overall level of social cost. He proposes to decide on the liability for these costs by reference to cost-minimization and economic efficiency. In this essay, unlike Coase, I assume initial natural rights and am concerned with social costs only when they arise from conflicting exercises of these rights and interfere with the exercise of them.

right and, in this sense, interferes with the exercise of the right. If a boundary crossing does not have these consequences, it does not constitute a meaningful interference with the right.

The fact that preventing cattle from straying, or paying compensation for the damage the cattle cause, imposes costs that diminish the value of the rancher's property means that these demands interfere with his property rights in the same sense that the damage from the cattle to the farmer's property interferes with the farmer's property rights. The rancher-farmer case must be distinguished from a case in which a homeowner objects to the development of neighboring land because the development makes it unavailable to him for fishing or hiking. The homeowner's fishing or hiking is not a use of his own land, but a use of another's land. The rancher might appear similarly to use his neighbor's land by allowing his cattle to stray upon it. On the assumption that we are making, however, the rancher is not using the farmer's land to expand his herd beyond what he would raise apart from the farmer's land. He is simply declining to bear the cost of compensating the farmer for the damage, building a fence, or reducing his herd to prevent damage to the farmer's land. He is no better off as a result of the cattle's trampling the farmer's land than he would be if the farmer built a fence to keep the cattle out.

Rights conflicts do not arise only with regard to a marginal exercise of rights; they also arise with regard to the full value of the rights. For example, suppose that the chemicals needed to grow corn at a profit poison the water and make it unprofitable to raise cattle on the adjoining land. The parties to the dispute in this case cannot both profitably use their land. One might argue that the losing party still has ownership of his land and must simply change the use to which he puts it. But the farmer might have paid for farmland, not ranchland, and might be unable to use it profitably for ranching; and the rancher's land might not be fertile enough to farm. In this case a resolution of the dispute in favor of one party will make the other party's land worthless. There appears to be no way for a court in this case to uphold both parties' natural rights to the ownership (use) of the land.

Coase supposes that where there are social costs, it is necessary for the state to adjudicate the assignment of these costs. Hence, for Coase, we must allocate these costs by appeal to formal property or liability rules. He fails to recognize the role of custom in court decisions and the existence of cases in which the parties themselves settle disputes apart from the courts by custom and consent. In his *Order without Law*, Robert Ellickson points up this limitation of Coase's position.[7] Ellickson examines disputes between neighbors with regard to straying cattle in Shasta County,

[7] Robert Ellickson, *Order without Law* (Cambridge: Harvard University Press, 1991); see especially ch. 3.

California, and finds that the social costs that arise as a result of the straying cattle are often settled without reference to formal law. The neighboring landowners allocate these costs on customary principles of mutual cooperation and cost-sharing that tend, Ellickson finds, to maximize the welfare of all involved. The settlement of the disputes in these cases is a matter of being a good neighbor.

However, although one might admit that Coaseans claim more of a role for formal law and the state in the resolution of property disputes than is warranted, not all rights conflicts can be settled apart from the state. Informal resolution is more probable where the parties are neighbors and belong to a community in which they interact repeatedly with one another and find it in their interests to be on good terms. It is also more likely where the imposition of costs is more or less reciprocal, as in Shasta County, where few property owners devote their land solely to raising crops, to the exclusion of raising livestock. Moreover, informal resolution is more likely to occur when the damage tends to be relatively minor in any given instance; and it requires that the dispute be of a sort that arises with sufficient frequency to establish customary norms. On the other side, consensual resolution of disputes typically fails when the stakes are very large, where there is no settled precedent for the conflict, where there is no reciprocity in the magnitude of the costs imposed, and where those who impose the costs do not benefit from cooperation with those on whom they impose them.

When we can appeal to custom and informal consensual agreement to settle property disputes, we might be said to settle these in a manner consistent with the natural rights of the parties, so long as the position from which the parties make the agreements is itself consistent with natural rights. Moreover, even when we must appeal to the courts to settle disputes, it might still be possible to settle them in a manner that respects natural rights. For where courts can invoke customary rules of negligence to decide disputes, the courts in effect appeal to how a reasonable person in the community would assign liability, and in this sense they appeal to the consent of the reasonable agent. If this consent is itself an exercise of natural rights, as it might reasonably be construed to be, the courts might be said to base their decisions in these cases upon the natural rights of the parties.

But not all rights conflicts can be settled in terms of customary negligence rules. For, in some disputes, there is no relevant custom and no consensus as to what is reasonable. To see that this is so, consider the disputes that arise from the use of new technology for which there are no customary resolutions. Hence, for example, when one first builds airports that cause noise pollution or introduces satellite dishes that block the view of neighboring residents, there are no customary negligence rules to which to appeal, and the disputants might not be able to find a mutually acceptable settlement of the dispute. In these cases there exists a conflict in regard to the exercise of legitimate property rights that requires appeal to formal adjudication that cannot satisfy the claims of all of the parties to the disputes. The nuisance from the airport undermines the property values of the surrounding neighborhood, and satellite dishes may block views for which the residents paid a large premium. But airlines make the case that they are only exercising their right to use the land that they have purchased for the purpose of their business, and the satellite users make the case that they are simply exercising their rights to use their own property for a legitimate purpose.

Public goods raise a second set of problems for proponents of natural rights. A public good is an indivisible good from which each can benefit without reducing the benefit to others. These goods often cannot be provided at an acceptable level by the unanimous two-party transactions of market exchange. For in contrast to market goods, public goods require multiparty agreements that make it costly to obtain unanimity. Unanimity is costly in these cases not only because of the costs of negotiating with the many relevant parties but also because, in the case of public goods, a party might be able to obtain the good at no cost if a sufficient number of others agree to pay for the good. Each party therefore has a motive to be a free-rider who enjoys the good without contributing to pay for it. Moreover, no party finds it in his interest to contribute to the cost of a public good unless he can be assured that a sufficient number of others will also contribute. This assurance is often difficult to achieve. The cost of unanimous agreement with respect to public goods is increased further by the fact that all parties receive the same quality and quantity of the good but not all parties have the same preferences with respect to the quality and quantity of the good. In order to obtain agreement from all parties, no party must be charged more for a good than it is worth to him. In order to assure this in the absence of the ability to vary the quality and quantity of the good that an agent receives, it is necessary to vary the amount that each pays for the good. But this is made difficult by the fact that it is in each agent's interest to conceal his preferences in this regard and to claim that he prefers less of the good than he actually does prefer, in order to obtain the good more cheaply.

Unless we solve the unanimity problem, however, a collective decision might impose costs on an agent that he would not voluntarily consent to pay, and therefore might violate his initial set of natural property rights. In affirming majority rule as the decision-making procedure of the state, Locke fails to recognize the risk that non-unanimous decision-making rules pose to natural rights.[8] He fails to see that a non-unanimous collective procedure for making decisions on public goods might violate initial

[8] Locke. *Second Treatise.* ch. 8. section 96.

property rights by imposing costs on a minority that the minority is unwilling voluntarily to pay. On a non-unanimous decision procedure, it is the satisfaction of a requirement such as majority rule, not the voluntary exercise of rights independent of collective-decision procedures, that determines the validity of state action and resolves disputes over legal rights.

The argument that non-unanimous decision-making procedures might violate an initial set of natural rights and might, in this sense, be inconsistent with them does not imply that we must unanimously agree to these rights themselves. As I have noted, since natural rights define the appropriate initial status quo from which we make legitimate agreements, they cannot be a result of agreement. However, once we affirm natural rights, these define a sphere of action in which others cannot legitimately interfere without our consent. For this reason, natural rights theories require that any transactions that affect these rights be unanimous on the part of all parties to the transactions.

III. Neo-Lockeans on Rights Conflicts and Public Goods

A. Robert Nozick

For Robert Nozick, as for Locke, each person possesses property rights independent of and prior to the state. Nozick maintains, as does Locke, that each person is naturally free of the authority of others. However, Nozick puts more weight on a proviso on original acquisition than Locke does, and as a consequence, he permits a more limited scope for natural rights than Locke does. Nozick maintains that, "[w]hether or not Locke's particular theory of appropriation can be spelled out so as to handle various difficulties, I assume that any adequate theory of justice in acquisition will contain a proviso similar to the weaker of the ones we have attributed to Locke."[9] Nozick's proviso permits the appropriation of natural objects only if it does not make others worse off than they would be apart from the private appropriation of such objects.

In the same manner as Locke's proviso, Nozick's prohibits appropriation that deprives us of otherwise available natural resources that we need for our lives unless there remains enough for each. However, Locke's proviso applies prior to commerce and industry while Nozick's applies to all transactions. Hence, for Nozick, "[e]ach owner's title to his holding includes the historical shadow of the Lockean proviso on appropriation."[10] Unlike Locke, Nozick does not appeal to a presumptive consensual waiving of the proviso in market exchanges. Moreover, Locke's proviso

---

[9] Robert Nozick, *Anarchy, State, and Utopia* (New York: Basic Books, 1974), p. 178.
[10] *Ibid.*, p. 180.

does not require that appropriation not make anyone worse off than he or she would be apart from it. Instead, it prescribes that there be "enough and as good" natural resources left for other people so that they may preserve their lives without subordinating themselves to others. This is weaker than the demand that the appropriation not reduce others' welfare.

Nozick offers two formulations of his proviso. The first prohibits making a person worse off than he would be if he were free to "use" the appropriated object; the second forbids making "the situation of persons who are unable to appropriate (there being no more accessible and useful unowned objects)" worse off than they would be under "a system allowing appropriation and permanent property."[11] On the first formulation, the proviso prescribes that no one be made worse off by the appropriation of a particular appropriated object. On the second, the proviso prescribes that no one be made worse off by a system that allows private appropriation.[12]

The distinction between use and full ownership (appropriation) of property is explicit in the first formulation of Nozick's proviso; and it is implicit in the second. For how well off we would be in the absence of appropriation appears to be determined by how well off we would be if we were able to use but not appropriate natural resources. However, while one can make the distinction between use and other modalities of property rights in an advanced legal system in which there are legal conventions governing property rights, it is hard to see how this applies to a pre-legal situation. Apart from a formal legal system that introduces limitations on the exercise of natural property rights, these appear to bestow upon the owner the right to dispose of his property as he chooses so long as he does not violate the property rights of others. Moreover, if a natural right to a good were simply a right to use it, natural property rights would have limited significance in protecting our liberty against the state, and would have no significance at all in establishing the parameters of market exchange. For market exchange is not use in the relevant sense.

Nozick argues that his proviso forbids the owner of an island from ordering a castaway back to sea as a trespasser and forbids the owner of the only remaining water hole in a desert from charging travelers what he will for the water.[13] He supposes that, apart from the appropriation, the castaway and the desert travelers would be able to use these resources without cost. But requiring the island's owner to admit castaways might

---

[11] *Ibid.*, p. 177.

[12] In my article "Nozick's Proviso," *Journal of Value Inquiry*, vol. 20 (1986), pp. 51–56, I criticize Nozick's proviso for being incompatible with natural rights to property, on the ground that these rights can no more be limited by their impact on the welfare of others than our right to our bodies or our lives can be so limited. I do not deal with the issue raised in this essay of the conflict of rights that results when one person's exercise of rights imposes a social cost that infringes on another's exercise of rights.

[13] Nozick, *Anarchy, State, and Utopia*, p. 180.

interfere with his own use of the island. He might have acquired the
island to get away from others or to enjoy an unspoiled setting. Similarly,
the owner of the water hole might have acquired it to assure himself an
ample supply of water or to derive an income from the sale of water.
What precisely is the right of the castaway or the desert travelers to the
land or water already acquired by others?

Even if Nozick can make a case consistent with his theory for the rights
of those negatively impacted by others' appropriation of natural resources (and I do not see how he can), he must still make the further case
that the rights of those negatively impacted take priority over the rights
of the appropriators. The examples to which he appeals have the force
that they do because they raise the issue in life-and-death situations. The
shipwreck victim and the desert travelers need the resources in question
in order to survive. If those claiming the right to use others' property
made the claim simply on the ground that they are worse off than they
would be apart from the others' appropriation, their claim would be less
forceful than it would be in a life-and-death situation, since it is by no
means clear on Nozick's or any other position why no one should ever be
worse off as a result of another's appropriation of resources than he
would be apart from permitting the appropriation.

In the same manner as Nozick, Locke would forbid turning away shipwreck survivors or desert travelers who need water for their survival. But
for Locke we are forbidden to do this because of a duty to preserve the
lives of others when our own preservation is not in question, not because
of the "enough and as good" proviso. Since Nozick admits no duty to
preserve the lives of others, he relies on his proviso to protect those whose
lives are threatened by private ownership of the resources that they need
to preserve their lives. Nozick would have imposed less of a restriction
upon appropriation if he had simply accepted a duty to preserve the lives
of others rather than prescribing that appropriation must never make
others worse off than they would be in its absence.

Nozick holds that those who suffer "boundary crossings" from others'
actions must be compensated.[14] He therefore appears to affirm a principle
of liability which requires us to compensate for losses to others' property
that we cause by our actions even apart from any fault in our actions and
apart from our right to perform them. However, he fails to address the
problem posed by the fact that the payment of compensation, in cases
where the damage arises from the exercise of the offending agent's own
property rights, diminishes the value of that agent's property precisely as
his actions diminish the value of the property of others. Nozick is no more
successful than Locke in dealing with the reciprocity of the social costs of
incompatible exercises of property rights. The conflict over the allocation

---

[14] *Ibid.*, p. 63.

of these costs puts Nozick's theory of natural rights as much into question as Locke's.

Nozick recognizes that the non-unanimous provision of public goods by the coercive action of the state might force some parties to pay for benefits to others, and in this manner might violate an initial distribution of natural property rights. For this reason, he denies that a state has a right to engage in the non-unanimous provision of public goods. However, he still supports what he calls the minimal state. The minimal state is a monopoly on the enforcement of rights. The problem is, the minimal state might not be unanimously agreed to. There might be agents who do not voluntarily accept the authority of the minimal state as the sole protective agency and who choose instead to defend themselves. How is the imposition of a monopoly of protective services compatible with the natural rights of those who do not consent to it?

Nozick answers that the dominant protective agency can justly protect its members against the "unreliable procedures" that "independents" employ to enforce their (the independents') rights, so long as it compensates the independents for the loss that the prohibition of the self-enforcement of their rights imposes upon them. For Nozick, independents have a natural right to protect themselves in a manner that they themselves determine. However, the members of the dominant protective agency possess a natural right to do the same; and they decide to protect their rights through the dominant protective agency. The issue in this case is a conflict between legitimate exercises of rights on each side.

For Nozick, the minimal state is not redistributive and does not violate initial natural rights because it does not impose taxes to pay for benefits for others, but simply permits those who voluntarily join it to protect themselves against the enforcement procedures of the independents (while at the same time respecting the rights of the independents by paying them compensation for losses that result from forbidding them to protect themselves). The problem is that the payment of compensation is itself, as we have seen, redistributive, in the sense that it requires a party to pay to perform actions that he has an initial right to perform. Why should the members of the dominant protective agency suffer costs from their interaction with nonmembers so that the nonmembers will not suffer costs from their interaction with them? Why is it not acceptable for members of the dominant protective agency to impose the full cost of defending themselves against the unreliable enforcement procedures of the independents on the independents themselves?

On the other side, the independents might not voluntarily accept the enforcement procedures of the dominant agency even when they are offered compensation in the form of a discount on protective services. Why, they might object, should it be permissible to coerce them into accepting services that they have a right to perform for themselves? If the discount is sufficiently large and the service sufficiently appealing to obtain voluntary consent, why not use the market rather than coercion to obtain the independents' membership in the dominant protective agency?

Nozick fails to answer this. He could reply that apart from a prohibition on the independents' enforcement of their own rights, the independents would hold out for too large a subsidy, and therefore would undermine the dominant agency (an agency whose existence is to the advantage of all). But if Nozick makes this reply, how can he restrict his claim to the public good of a mutually beneficial monopoly on protective services? Why would the same argument not justify a non-unanimous procedure to decide on any mutually beneficial public good?[15] But if he admits this, he cannot rule out a more extensive state. The appeal to a non-unanimous decision-making procedure to establish the minimal night-watchman state raises the same challenge to natural rights theories as does the appeal to a non-unanimous procedure on behalf of other public goods that the state might provide. The appeal to non-unanimous collective decision-making procedures supersedes natural rights in either case. For non-unanimous decision-making procedures authorize takings of property or limitations of rights apart from an agent's consent, whereas natural rights prohibit nonconsensual infringements of rights.

B. David Gauthier

Unlike Locke and Nozick, David Gauthier starts with Hobbes's premise that prior to consensual agreements by which agents restrict their natural liberty, persons may permissibly do anything that they choose, regardless of the effects on others. For Gauthier, as for Hobbes, we originally have a right to use the minds and bodies of others without their voluntary consent. But this does not imply that natural rights are more problematic for Gauthier than for Locke or Nozick. Instead, it implies a different argument for such rights. For Locke, natural rights are a consequence of the natural absence of subordination of one man to another, that is, a consequence of men's equal natural freedom and independence; for Nozick, they follow from the intuitive priority of liberty over competing values. But for Gauthier, natural rights are necessary conditions of mutually beneficial cooperation among equally rational agents. For Gauthier, it is not rational to comply with cooperative agreements unless the parties to the agreements refrain from taking advantage of each other in

---

[15] Protective and judicial services are not themselves public goods. However, having a single agency to handle all disputes and avoid the costs of adjudicating the conflicts among diverse independent protective and judicial agencies is a public good. The monopoly of these services results in positive externalities that cannot be attained apart from the monopoly; and Nozick in effect appeals to these benefits when he argues for the monopoly of enforcement on the part of the minimal state.

the initial situation in which they make such agreements. This constraint against taking advantage defines our natural rights.

Gauthier puts himself in the Lockean natural-rights tradition by naming his constraint against taking advantage of others "the modified Lockean proviso." The modified Lockean proviso defines a domain of natural rights because it prescribes the conditions of legitimate agreements. Unlike Lockean rights, those proposed by Gauthier apply only to those who propose to cooperate; nevertheless, they apply to these agents independently of their consent.

For Gauthier, to take advantage of others means to better one's own position at the expense of others through coercion or in other ways.[16] This proviso takes as a baseline how well off a person would be "in the absence of (his) fellows."[17] However, while it does not allow a person to profit from the presence of the other at the other's expense, it does permit a person to make another worse off in order to avoid making himself worse off than he would be in the absence of the other person.

In contrast with those of Locke and Nozick, Gauthier's proviso is not concerned with the negative effects of original appropriation. Moreover, it does not exclude profiting from actions that interfere with the legitimate exercise of property rights on the part of our cooperative partners; it merely excludes our profiting *from their presence* by doing so.

But why is it rational for our cooperative partners to accept losses to their property so that we can avoid losses to our property? Why should others be free to make us worse off so that they will not be made worse off? Gauthier fails to address these questions because he unaccountably supposes that all social costs in cooperative contexts "are displaced costs, benefiting you by worsening my competitive position, and so, if uncompensated, constitute violations on the proviso."[18] He supposes that we never impose a social cost on those with whom we interact cooperatively without gaining a competitive advantage from doing so.

However, even Gauthier's own illustration of the operation of his proviso fails to support this supposition. To illustrate his position, Gauthier considers a case in which agents upstream trade with partners downstream, and the downstream partners suffer from pollution caused by those upstream. He holds that the proviso prescribes that the polluters compensate their downstream partners for the costs of the pollution as a condition of cooperation, presumably because they would otherwise derive a competitive advantage from the costs that they impose. But on Gauthier's own admission, the polluters are simply disposing of the wastes as they would if there was no one downstream. They benefit from trading

[16] David Gauthier, *Morals by Agreement* (Oxford: Clarendon Press, 1986), p. 203.
[17] *Ibid.*, p. 221.
[18] *Ibid.*, p. 213.

with those downstream, but it is not clear how they benefit from the costs they impose on those downstream.

If, as Gauthier supposes, the pollution indeed worsens the downstream partners' "competitive position" and therefore enables the upstream polluters to profit from making the others worse off, then, as Gauthier points out, the polluters can compensate their partners out of the gains from the competitive advantage without violating an equal proportional distribution of the gains from cooperation itself. But if the polluters do not profit sufficiently from the imposition of the costs to pay the compensation, the payment of compensation will give them proportionately less of a gain from the cooperation than their cooperative partners, unless they have already, for some other reason, negotiated an agreement that gives them the lion's share of the gains. For if the polluters do not profit sufficiently from the competitive advantage that they derive from the costs that they impose, they would have to pay compensation out of their otherwise equal proportional gains.

But Gauthier argues that if one party benefits proportionately less than another from cooperation, the former party will not find it rational to agree to cooperate on those terms. If Gauthier is correct in this regard, it follows that when compensation would result in less than an equal proportionate gain for the party that pays the compensation, it would not be rational for that party to agree to pay it. This means that if full compensation for all social costs were indeed a necessary condition of rational cooperation, then rational cooperation would not be possible when one party imposes social costs from which that party does not sufficiently profit to pay compensation to its cooperative partner without gaining proportionately less from cooperation than the partner does. In cases of this sort, there is simply no solution to the conflict posed by the conflicting uses of property on Gauthier's conception of natural rights.

For Gauthier, the point of cooperation is to remedy market failure. Market failure is a failure of rational equilibrium to produce an optimal outcome. Rational equilibrium is the equilibrium that results when multiple agents each act to maximize their own individual utility; optimality is an outcome that cannot be improved for any agent without making another worse off. For Gauthier, the operation of a perfect market leads to a coincidence of equilibrium and optimality. For in a perfectly competitive market, individual utility-maximization achieves an optimal outcome.

Gauthier takes the prisoner's dilemma as a paradigm of market failure. This dilemma arises in a situation in which each agent finds that his individual utility-maximizing action leads to a suboptimal outcome. In the classical example of the dilemma, two prisoners each confront two options. One option is to confess; the other is to refuse to confess. If one prisoner confesses and the other does not, the one who confesses is released; the one who does not confess receives a maximum term of ten years. If both prisoners confess, each receives five years. If neither confesses, each receives one year. The optimal outcome is a one-year sentence for each prisoner. But when each independently chooses the option that promises to maximize his own utility, each chooses to confess and each achieves a worse outcome for himself than he would if he chose the option that did not maximize his expected utility. When each chooses independently, each finds it utility-maximizing to confess, because each correctly reasons that whatever the other does, confessing leads to a more favorable outcome for himself. For if he confesses and the other does not, he goes free; and if he confesses and the other also confesses, he protects himself against the ten-year sentence that he would receive if he did not confess.

For Gauthier, cooperation is the agreement among agents to constrain their utility-maximizing activities to achieve an optimal outcome when they would otherwise fail to achieve an optimal outcome. In the case of the prisoners, this would be an agreement not to confess. If agents comply with their cooperative agreement, each can expect to do better than he otherwise would. For Gauthier, market failure of the sort illustrated in the prisoner's dilemma holds for the public goods that the market cannot provide at an optimal level. In order to obtain optimal public goods, each individual may have to constrain his individual utility-maximization. He constrains his utility-maximization in the case of public goods by refraining from attempting to obtain the good without agreeing to pay for it. Refusing to contribute to the cost of the public good would maximize his expected utility as an independent agent. For if he refuses to contribute, either a sufficient number of others would independently agree to provide the good without his paying the cost, or a sufficient number would not. If a sufficient number did agree to pay, he would obtain the good as a free-rider; if a sufficient number did not agree to pay for the good, he would not obtain it even if he did pay his share of the cost. Since all would reason in this same manner, all would refuse to pay, and none would obtain the good.

In spite of the fact that Gauthier sharply distinguishes cooperation from market interaction, he regards cooperation as a result of bargaining. Bargaining requires unanimous agreement in the same manner as market transactions do. However, as we have seen, unanimity is often prohibitively costly in the case of the multiparty decisions needed for public goods—goods which the market fails to provide and for which cooperation is needed. How does Gauthier propose to attain unanimity in multiparty agreements in the face of the high transaction costs of unanimity in the case of these agreements?

He proposes to do so by appealing to hypothetical rather than actual agreement.[19] The appeal to hypothetical bargains provides a solution to the problem posed by those who hold out for larger proportional shares

[19] *Ibid.*, p. 128.

of the benefits of agreement in actual bargaining. For in hypothetical bargains, we appeal to what is in each agent's rational interest to consent to; and it is not in a rational agent's interest to reject an agreement that gives him as large a gain as is consistent with the agreement of the others who make the gain possible. However, the appeal to a hypothetical bargain does not avoid the cost of calculating precisely what each agent's preference is with regard to the good to be attained by the cooperative agreement and charging him no more than the good is worth to him. The cost of this calculation in a hypothetical bargain may not be much less than it is in an actual bargain in the case of public goods where there are large numbers of agents.

If these costs make it prohibitively expensive to provide public goods that we prefer to have, we may find it rational to give up the unanimity condition. But once we do so, we cannot ensure that the agreement will not make one party better off at the expense of the otherwise legitimate claims of another; nor can we ensure that each party enjoys an equal proportional benefit. For a non-unanimous decision might worsen one party's legitimate initial situation while improving the situation of another. Hence, for example, a non-unanimous decision might provide services to one group at the expense of another by taxing the other group to pay for the lion's share of the costs. If a state imposes these costs on agents, it violates their natural rights by violating Gauthier's modified Lockean proviso.

Gauthier is no more successful than Locke or Nozick in reconciling the need for non-unanimous decisions to provide public goods with the requirements of natural rights. There can in fact be no reconciliation at the level of particular public-goods decisions. For non-unanimous decisions limit an agent's rights against his consent, and natural rights forbid non-consensual limitations of rights.

IV. RIGHTS WITHOUT NATURAL RIGHTS

In this final section, I consider whether we can protect individual liberty and property once we permit the state to decide rights conflicts and disputes over public goods independently of natural rights. If the state need not respect natural property rights in these cases, we face the danger of unlimited state intervention in our lives and the loss of secure property rights. Is it possible apart from natural rights to protect individuals from a state's discriminatory actions against them?

I believe it is possible. First of all, if the arguments in support of natural rights hold, nothing that I have said here puts them into question except in the cases where we cannot adjudicate rights conflicts by the consent of the parties or obtain an acceptable level of public goods by unanimous agreement. Secondly, it turns out to be possible (as we shall see) to establish procedures for making decisions where natural rights fail that are consensual and, in this sense, consistent with natural rights, even though each and every decision which results from these procedures is not consensual apart from the procedure.

For F. Y. Edgeworth and John Harsanyi, the goal of maximizing average utility can be used to establish a unanimously acceptable procedure for guiding state action.[20] For them, the state ought to act in such a manner as to maximize the average expected utility of the citizens affected by its actions. The average expected utility is the sum of the utility of all those affected by an action divided by the number of persons affected by it.

For Edgeworth and Harsanyi, the principle of average utility is unanimously acceptable because it maximizes the expected utility of each agent, and it is rational for agents to consent to what maximizes their expected utility. Edgeworth and Harsanyi attempt to argue for this in different ways. Edgeworth postulates that each individual over the course of his life has an equal chance of occupying each position in society; Harsanyi argues that, from an impartial position of radical uncertainty, each will find it rational to assume that he has an equal chance *ex ante* of occupying each position in society. Both authors rightly recognize that since the principle of average utility maximizes the utility of the average of all positions, and since an equal chance of occupying each position gives each agent the expectation of the utility of the average position in society, the principle of average utility maximizes the expected utility of those with an equal chance of occupying each position. Since it is rational for each agent to maximize his expected utility, it is therefore rational for agents with an equal probability of occupying each position to accept the principle of maximum average utility.

The problem with this, as John Rawls points out, is that actual agents do not have an equal chance *ex ante* of being rich or poor, laborers or landholders. The existing institutions of society, as Rawls recognizes, favor some starting places over others and affect men's initial chances in life.[21] For this reason, the principle of average utility is not in fact equally beneficial *ex ante* to each agent, and therefore fails to provide the *ex ante* justification for *ex post* losses that Edgeworth and Harsanyi claim it provides.

However, in spite of the fact that the *ex ante* prospect of maximal possible gain does not justify a principle of average utility, Edgeworth and Harsanyi are right to hold that a principle that promises *ex ante* the

[20] F. Y. Edgeworth, *Mathematical Psychics* (London, 1888), pp. 52–56; J. C. Harsanyi, "Cardinal Utility in Welfare Economics and in the Theory of Risk Taking," *Journal of Political Economy*, vol. 61 (1953).

For Edgeworth and Harsanyi, the principle of average utility is not a principle to adjudicate rights conflicts or decide on public goods but a principle to decide all rights. But it can be used in this more limited manner.

[21] See John Rawls, *A Theory of Justice* (Cambridge, MA: Harvard University Press, 1971).

prospect of maximum gain for each agent would be rationally acceptable to each agent. If it is rationally acceptable to an agent, then the use of it to resolve rights conflicts and disputes over the provision of public goods would respect his rights. For even though the particular outcomes that result from the application of the principle might not accord with natural rights and might not be unanimously acceptable in their own terms, the principle by which these are decided might itself accord with natural rights and be unanimously acceptable.

However, a principle that maximizes the prospects of one agent appears to do so at the expense of the prospects of others. There is no acceptable principle that maximizes the absolute prospects of any given agent. For a principle to be rationally acceptable to each party, it must offer each party an equal probability of maximum gain. No party would accept a lesser probability of gain than another, and therefore no principle that offered any party a lesser probability of gain would be acceptable as a means of settling disputes among the various parties. Nor would a principle be acceptable if it failed to maximize the prospects of each party subject to this constraint.

This principle of *ex ante* maximum equal gain is a procedural principle that can be used to resolve substantive rights conflicts and settle disputes over public goods. It is procedural in that it does not prescribe particular substantive rights or particular public goods; instead, it provides a method for deciding these disputed issues that is acceptable to all.[22] The principle does not promise a maximum *ex ante* equal gain in an absolute sense, since it is not, on the assumption of a framework of natural rights, a principle for the assignment of rights *de novo*; rather, it is a principle for deciding the assignment of rights when natural rights fail. Hence, it offers each party an equal chance *ex ante* of a settlement of a rights dispute in that party's favor, and an equal chance *ex ante* of a public-goods decision favorable to that party's interests.

The principle of equal maximum expected gain is impartial in that it does not favor any party to a dispute *ex ante* over any other. It is not possible to determine *a priori* whether a principle is in fact impartial. In order to decide this, it is necessary to test a principle by the actual outcomes of its application. If a principle repeatedly results in decisions favorable to one party over another, this counts against it, even if we find

[22] The principle of equal prospective gain must not be mistaken for the principle of fair equality of opportunity. The principle of fair equality of opportunity prescribes that those who are disadvantaged be subsidized by others so that they receive educational and employment opportunities equal to the opportunities of those with similar talents and abilities—so that their overall prospects are not diminished by their social and economic disadvantages. This might or might not be a policy that arises from an impartial procedure, but it is not in itself a procedure for settling conflicts, and it is not in actual fact impartial. For it subsidizes those who are talented but less advantaged economically at the expense of those who are more advantaged economically, and it does nothing for the less talented poor. For a further discussion of the bias of substantive principles and the need to appeal to procedural principles to settle rights disputes, see my article "Constitutional Contractarianism," *Constitutional Political Economy*, vol. 8, no. 3 (1997), pp. 179–88.

no bias apart from disproportionate outcomes. For although the equal promise of gain in particular cases is measured *ex ante*, not *ex post*, the cumulative results of the implementation of a principle must be assessed *ex post* as well. It is past performance that justifies claims about future prospects.

For example, libertarians argue that the history of U.S. Supreme Court decisions on issues of property rights and economic liberty reveals a bias against the protection of these rights in favor of other social goals. If these libertarians are correct, this puts into question the impartiality of the U.S. legal system with regard to these issues even though there might be no particular procedural principle that we can identify *a priori* as biased against property rights. Bias in the historical outcomes justifies constitutional reform in the domain of property rights.

However, the impartiality of the decision-making procedure is neither a sufficient nor a necessary condition of consensual resolution of disputes; it is no more than a supporting condition. A supporting condition is one that holds absent a countervailing condition. The countervailing condition in this case is that the outcome not impose a risk of so great a loss that a reasonable person would be unwilling to accept the risk for the sake of the *ex ante* expected gain. It is necessary to limit cost-benefit considerations when there is a significant risk of a loss that radically diminishes prospects of future gains for a particular agent. For, as Rawls rightly points out in his criticism of Harsanyi's argument for the principle of average utility, it is not rational to consent to a high risk of a catastrophic outcome simply because taking that risk maximizes one's expected utility. This constraint on a principle of the equal probability of gain is grounded in the same requirement of rational consent as is the principle itself.

Rawls deals with the challenge of unacceptable outcomes by prescribing that social institutions maximize the prospects of those least advantaged. However, this so-called "difference principle" not only appears to be biased against those more advantaged, and therefore unacceptable to them, but also is far more stringent than is needed to prevent unacceptable risks of losses. One can rule out unacceptable risks without an appeal to a principle that minimizes the risks of loss.

The inability of Locke, Nozick, and Gauthier to solve the problems posed to natural rights theories by rights conflicts and public goods arises from their failure to see that the solution to these problems is to be found in a procedural principle that it is in our *ex ante* interest to consent to, rather than in the supposed priority of the rights of one party over those of another or in a denial of all non-unanimous public-goods decisions.

V. CONCLUSION

The point of my argument is that natural property rights fail to provide a substantive standard of state action in two kinds of cases: when incompatible exercises of these rights lead to conflicts over social costs which the parties fail to resolve by agreement, and when respect for these rights unacceptably limits the state provision of goods that the market cannot efficiently provide. I have tried to show that this failure does not inevitably open freedom and property to unlimited infringement on the part of the state. For we might still appeal to a substrate of natural rights which puts the burden of proof on those who propose to override them. Where we must override these rights, we can protect freedom and property by constitutional procedures that each individual finds it rational to accept.

I have argued that each agent will find it rational to accept procedures that promise him a more or less equal chance of an affirmation of his rights, subject to the constraint that he be protected against losses so large that he cannot hope to recover from them. While the procedure might result in an infringement of otherwise justified rights, such an infringement arises from a procedure that even those who face a negative decision find it rational to accept. The losing party accepts the negative outcome by accepting the procedure that produces it. He finds it rational to accept the procedure because he otherwise faces an unacceptable irreconcilable conflict with others or the loss of a public good which he is unwilling to lose. Since the rights-holders find it rational to settle disputes by these procedures rather than by an appeal to rights apart from them, the outcomes of the procedures are compatible with natural rights. For we can presume that agents would consent to what is in their rational interest. If they consent to settle disputes by these procedures, they in effect consent to waive the use of natural rights as principles for settling the disputes in these cases.

These constitutional procedures admittedly do not assure individuals the fixed domain of liberty and property that natural rights theories endeavor to assure. However, these procedures limit the ability of any individual or group to use the power of the state against other individuals or groups. They provide the best protection of liberty and property possible in a world in which the exercise of rights on the part of one person may lead to rights conflicts that otherwise cannot be resolved in a consensual manner, and in which neither market exchanges nor unanimous collective decisions can in every case achieve acceptable outcomes.

Philosophy, Vanderbilt University

TOWARD A LIBERTARIAN THEORY OF CLASS

By Roderick T. Long

I. INTRODUCTION

Libertarianism needs a theory of class.

This claim may meet with resistance among some libertarians. A few will say: "The analysis of society in terms of classes and class struggles is a specifically Marxist approach, resting on assumptions that libertarians reject. Why should we care about class?" A greater number will say: "We recognize that class theory is important, but libertarianism doesn't *need* such a theory, because it already *has* a perfectly good one."

The first objection is simply mistaken. While the prominence of the Marxist theory of classes may have left rival approaches obscured in its shadow, class analysis is thousands of years older than Marx; and in Marx's own day the Marxist version of class analysis was only one of a number of competing and very different theories, including several far more congenial to libertarianism. The problem of class is one that faces any serious political theory, Marxist or otherwise.

The second objection is also mistaken, but not so simply. It is true that a libertarian theory of class already exists. More precisely, several different theories of class are current among today's libertarians, inherited from different strands within libertarianism's intellectual ancestry. But although each of these theories offers important insights, I propose to argue that none of them is adequate, and that the shortcomings of libertarian thinking about class have done serious harm to the libertarian cause.

I shall also be offering some suggestions as to the direction in which libertarian class analysis might best develop. But my aims in this regard are limited. It is from no false modesty that this essay is titled "Toward a Libertarian Theory of Class" rather than simply "A Libertarian Theory of Class." The development of libertarian class analysis is a project for the cooperative efforts of sociologists, economists, political scientists, historians, and philosophers. My principal hope is simply to call attention to the need for such a project.

II. LIBERTARIANISMS

What does it mean to speak of a libertarian theory of class? To answer that question, we must first have some conception of what libertarianism is, and then what a theory of class is.

For the purposes of this essay, I propose to define as *libertarian* any political position that advocates *a radical redistribution of power from the coercive state to voluntary associations of free individuals*. This definition draws the boundaries of libertarianism rather more expansively than is customary, and includes under the libertarian aegis a number of conflicting positions. For example, my definition does not specify whether this redistribution of power is to be total or merely substantial, and so allows both anarchists and nonanarchists to count as libertarians; it also does not specify whether the criteria for "voluntary association" can be met by communal cooperatives, or market exchanges, or both, and so grants the libertarian label indifferently to socialists (of the anti-statist variety) and capitalists (of the anti-statist variety).

These results may be taken, by some, as sufficient reason to reject my definition of libertarianism as excessively broad. But thinkers satisfying the definition have frequently described themselves as libertarians, whatever their views on the nature of voluntary association or the appropriate extent of redistribution; and it is my conviction that the different varieties of libertarians generally have more in common than they are accustomed to recognizing, and a great deal to learn from one another. As I have written elsewhere:

> Today, for the most part, libertarian capitalists begrudge socialists, and libertarian socialists likewise begrudge capitalists, the title "libertarian"; yet there seems to me sufficient commonality of ideological concern and intellectual heritage between the two camps to justify using the term in a broad but univocal sense to cover them both.[1]

Currently there are three quite disparate movements that qualify as libertarian by my definition. Two of them I have already mentioned: Libertarian Capitalism and Libertarian Socialism. A third I shall call Libertarian Populism. As these terms are a bit of a mouthful, I shall abbreviate them as "LibCap," "LibSoc," and "LibPop," respectively.[2]

Libertarian Capitalism (LibCap) is the position that has largely monopolized the term "libertarian" in contemporary academia, thanks largely to the influence of Robert Nozick's book *Anarchy, State, and Utopia*.[3] LibCaps

---

[1] Roderick T. Long, "Immanent Liberalism: The Politics of Mutual Consent," *Social Philosophy and Policy*, vol. 12, no. 2 (Summer 1995), p. 12, n. 26.

[2] An alternative possibility would be to abbreviate them as LC, LS, and LP, respectively. But "LP" is so commonly used within LibCap circles to designate the U.S. Libertarian Party that its use to designate some other aspect of libertarianism would be likely to generate confusion.

[3] Robert Nozick, *Anarchy, State, and Utopia* (New York: Basic Books, 1974). Indeed, for many academics *Anarchy, State, and Utopia* is the definitive statement of, indeed virtually interchangeable with, the Libertarian Capitalist position in general. Within the LibCap community itself, however, Nozick's work, while respected, is quite controversial and is the target of frequent criticism. "Nozick's book has come to enjoy canonical status among academics, who normally assign it to students as 'the' libertarian book, with little appreciation of the broader tradition of libertarian thinking and scholarship within which Nozick's

uphold (sometimes on the basis of imprescriptible natural rights, sometimes on the basis of beneficial social consequences, usually on the basis
of both) the right of individuals to do as they please with their own lives
and peacefully acquired private property, so long as they do not aggress
against the like liberty of anyone else. This leads LibCaps to oppose state
interference with *both* personal lifestyle choices and market transactions,
favoring spontaneous order over coercively imposed order equally in the
market for goods and services (hence their conflict with the left) and in
the market for ideas and experiments in living (hence their conflict with
the right). LibCaps who wish to restrict government to the basic function
of protecting libertarian rights—essentially the "night-watchman state" of
classical liberalism—are traditionally called "minarchists," while a minority who favor replacing the state entirely with private protection agencies and private courts competing on the free market are traditionally
called "anarcho-capitalists."

It still comes as a surprise to many LibCaps to learn that socialist critics
of centralized power have been using the term "libertarian" for at least as
long as their capitalist counterparts have. One recent LibCap writer offers
his readers a short history of the use of "libertarian" as a political term,
without ever mentioning that many opponents of capitalism have also
considered themselves libertarians.[4] (Libertarian Socialists often repay the
favor by writing as though "libertarian" has always designated a purely
socialist movement.) But there is a robust tradition of Libertarian Socialism (LibSoc), whose roots, like those of LibCap, run back to the radical
movements of the seventeenth, eighteenth, and nineteenth centuries. At
present the most prominent spokesman for this position is Noam Chomsky.

LibSocs share with LibCaps an aversion to any interference with freedom of thought, expression, or choice of lifestyle. But unlike LibCaps,
LibSocs do not see the right to engage in market transactions, or to maintain exclusive control over one's private property, as examples of freedom
in need of protection. Rather, LibSocs see capitalist property relations as
forms of domination, and thus as antagonistic to freedom. Yet, unlike
other socialists, they tend (to various differing degrees, depending on the
thinker) to be skeptical of centralized state intervention as the solution to
capitalist exploitation, preferring a system of popular self-governance via
networks of decentralized, local, voluntary, participatory, cooperative
associations—sometimes as a complement to and check on state power,
sometimes as a complete substitute for it. In this respect, LibSocs count as
libertarians for the same reason LibCaps do: they both seek to empower
individuals to govern their own lives through voluntary cooperation with

---

work took shape." Tom G. Palmer, "The Literature of Liberty," in David Boaz, ed., *The
Libertarian Reader: Classic and Contemporary Readings from Lao-tzu to Milton Friedman* (New
York: The Free Press, 1997), p. 417.

[4] David Boaz, *Libertarianism: A Primer* (New York: The Free Press, 1997), pp. 22–26. A
welcome exception to LibCap silence on the existence of LibSocs is Jerome Tuccille, *Radical
Libertarianism* (San Francisco: Cobden Press, 1985), p. 36ff.

one another, as opposed to top-down control of individuals by the state.[5] Where they disagree is on the question of whether economic *laissez-faire* and the unregulated market represent an *instance* of, or instead an *obstacle* to, the freedom and empowerment that libertarians seek. This disagreement is a deeply important and often intractable one, of course; nevertheless, I think it should be seen more as a conflict over the proper implementation of a common ideal than as a conflict of ideals themselves.

The LibSoc and LibCap perspectives can be seen not only as the socialist and capitalist wings of a broader libertarian tradition, but also as the libertarian wings of the broader traditions of socialism and capitalism in general, traditions that each possess an anti-libertarian, authoritarian wing also. We can gain a better understanding of both LibSoc and LibCap by contrasting them with their authoritarian counterparts.

The libertarian and authoritarian wings of socialism share a common hostility to capitalist property relations; but authoritarian socialists (also known as state socialists) offer, as an antidote to capitalism, a powerful centralized state exercising control over every aspect of economic life. The turn-of-the-century Russian anarcho-communist Pyotr Kropotkin (1842–1921) offers a typical LibSoc indictment of authoritarian socialism:

> The Anarchists consider the wage system and capitalist production altogether as an obstacle to progress. But they point out also that the State was, and continues to be, the chief instrument for permitting the few to monopolise the land, and the capitalists to appropriate for themselves a quite disproportionate share of the yearly accumulated surplus of production. Consequently, while combatting the present monopolisation of land, and capitalism altogether, the Anarchists combat with the same energy the State, as the main support of that

---

[5] Hence, a number of libertarians have hoped for a rapprochement between the LibCap and LibSoc approaches.

The issue of capitalism vs. socialism is irreconcilable if one views it in terms of political control. For whenever appeals are addressed to a central governing agency, an all-powerful, all-pervasive authority with the power to take away and dispense favors . . . the public will divide itself into two general camps and organize myriad lobby groups to pressure those in command for 'favorable' legislation. . . . [Both] capitalist and socialist schools of anarchy . . . are united on the most crucial question of all: the absolute necessity for people to take control over their own lives, and the dismantling and final elimination of state authority over the life of man. . . . Their major disagreement is one of personal attitudes concerning the makeup of human nature itself. . . . Who is right? Is there any way of reconciling these two opposing views of human nature without resorting to violence, pressure politics, or deceit? . . . The Left and Right can be harmonized only under anarchy. . . . Here is the broad spectrum of libertarianism, of voluntarism in the intellectual, economic, social, and spiritual life of society. . . . The main purpose here is to demonstrate the concept of radical decentralization as a viable alternative to our present centralized and chaotic system. It is to show how a bridge can be made between the individual and the collective, the socialist and the capitalist mentality, without resorting to force and coercion. (Tuccille, *Radical Libertarianism*, pp. 31–58; cf. also my "Immanent Liberalism," pp. 26–31)

system. . . . The State organisation, having always been . . . the instrument for establishing monopolies in favour of the ruling minorities, cannot be made to work for the destruction of these monopolies.
The Anarchists consider, therefore, that to hand over to the State all
the main sources of economical life—the land, the mines, the rail-
ways, banking, insurance, and so on—as also the management of all
the main branches of industry, in addition to all the functions already
accumulated in its hands (education, State-supported religions, defence of the territory, &c), would mean to create a new instrument of
tyranny. State capitalism[6] would only increase the powers of bureaucracy and capitalism. True progress lies in the direction of decentral-
isation, both *territorial* and *functional*, in the development of the spirit
of local and personal initiative, and of free federation from the simple
to the compound, in lieu of the present hierarchy from the centre to
the periphery.[7]

Within the capitalist tradition, on the other hand, both libertarians and
authoritarians agree in rejecting the monopolization of all economic power
in the hands of the state—but there the resemblance ends. While LibCaps
endorse unregulated competition, authoritarian capitalists favor government provision of subsidies, protections, and grants of monopoly privilege to big business to insulate it from competition both foreign and
domestic. Defenders of the business lobby argue that such "corporate
welfare" is beneficial to society as a whole, because companies on which
many workers and consumers depend (for jobs and products, respectively) deserve public assistance; in the United States, Lee Iacocca and the
government bailout of Chrysler Motors come to mind. But LibCaps argue
that such government favoritism creates a corporate elite with no incentive to cut costs, improve efficiency, or be responsive to the needs of its
employees and customers. As one LibCap author notes:

> The corporation had never been for markets, limited government,
> private property, or the other values associated with the business
> cause. . . . It had always tried to derive private advantage from public
> policy. . . . The corporation was created by people who thought the
> market generally inefficient, backward, a drag on progress, a diffi-
> culty to be gotten around. . . . From the dawn of the modern corpo-

---

[6] The term "state capitalism" has been common for some time among political radicals of
various ideological stripes, but it is frequently used in two different senses. In one sense,
"state capitalism" refers to state intervention in the marketplace to promote the interests of
the corporate elite; here it is synonymous with authoritarian capitalism. In the other sense,
"state capitalism" refers to a state's monopolizing all economic activity and resources under
its own control so that the nation as a whole may act as a single firm; here it is synonymous
with authoritarian socialism. Kropotkin is using the term in this second sense.

[7] Peter Kropotkin, *Anarchism and Anarchist Communism* (London: Freedom Press, 1993),
pp. 8–9.

ration . . . the business lobby continued its campaign for public policies
to keep prices high, provide subsidies and incentives, and control
new entrants.[8]

Part of the hostility of LibCaps and LibSocs to one another derives from
the fact that each libertarian camp tends to identify the other libertarian
camp with that other camp's authoritarian counterpart. While this identification is generally a mistake, it is not entirely ungrounded, for many
libertarians on both sides have failed to distance themselves sufficiently
from the authoritarian wings of their movements. For example, many
(though by no means all) LibSocs in this century have tended to downplay or apologize for the despotism and genocide practiced by Marxist
regimes,[9] while on the other side many (though again, by no means all)
LibCaps have readily served as willing intellectual foot-soldiers in the
corporatist-imperialist programs of Reaganism and Thatcherism.[10] It is
understandable that such conduct has led to some confusion.[11] But it is
also true that—for the most part, with a few notable exceptions—neither
libertarian camp has expressed much diligence in attempting to form an
accurate picture of the other libertarian camp's beliefs. (In general, Lib-
Caps and LibSocs have as distorted a view of each other as nonlibertarians have of both!)

These difficulties multiply when we turn to the third major libertarian
movement of the present time—namely, the libertarian wing of what I
shall call "conservative populism" (or "populism" for short). "Conservative populism" is my name for what in the United States generally goes
by the name of the "patriot movement," though analogous movements
without that label are to be found in other countries as well. The phenomenon of "citizens' militias" is currently the most visible, though not
necessarily the most representative, aspect of this movement.

---

[8] Paul H. Weaver, *The Suicidal Corporation* (New York: Simon and Schuster, 1988), pp. 99–
116.
[9] Among the notable exceptions: in the 1920s, the anarcho-socialist couple Emma Goldman and Alexander Berkman were among the earliest critics of the Soviet regime. See Emma
Goldman, *My Disillusionment in Russia* (New York: Crowell, 1970); and Alexander Berkman,
The Bolshevik Myth (London: Pluto Press, 1989).
[10] This is not to deny that there were genuinely LibCap elements to the programs of
Reagan and Thatcher, though I think those elements have been greatly exaggerated.
[11] There are still other sources of confusion. Libertarian and authoritarian versions of
capitalism have both called themselves "socialist" upon occasion (e.g., Benjamin Tucker's
"voluntary socialism" and Adolf Hitler's "National Socialism," respectively). Indeed, some
LibCaps claim to be the only true "socialists," since they favor social power over state
power. To add to the confusion, not only do LibCaps and LibSocs generally deny one
another's libertarian credentials, but also within each movement one finds *both* writers who
take anarchism as a prerequisite for being a libertarian, *and* writers who take the *rejection* of
anarchism as a prerequisite for being a libertarian. Then there is the ongoing dispute about
the relation between libertarianism and liberalism: Is either LibCap or LibSoc a version of
liberalism? Is LibCap identical with classical liberalism, or is it a subset of it, or does it
merely overlap with it? Do non-classical liberals count as genuine liberals? And so on!

Like LibCaps, populists endorse such ideals as private property, school choice, reduced taxes, and the right to bear arms. Like LibSocs, however, populists are suspicious of free trade, usury, and finance capitalism. And, unlike both groups, populists tend to be traditionalists, culturally and morally conservative, anti-abortion, with strong religious commitments and a concern to protect their preferred way of life from being undermined by secular and foreign values.[12] On this much, populists are generally agreed.

However, the populist movement can also be divided into libertarian and authoritarian wings. Unlike LibCaps and LibSocs, Libertarian Populists (LibPops) do not use the term "libertarian" to describe themselves, but they share with their capitalist and socialist counterparts a desire to effect a thoroughgoing redistribution of power from the state to freely associated individuals. By contrast, the authoritarian wing of populism opposes existing state power only because it seeks to replace such power with an oppressive regime of its own, in which populist values will be coercively imposed on the population. At its worst, authoritarian populism descends into the noxious morass of militant nativism, racism, and intolerance, calling for the subjugation of nonwhites, non-Christians, women, immigrants, and homosexuals, glorifying violence and bigotry, and making common cause with neo-Nazis. This side of the populist movement has received so much publicity that it is often taken as an accurate representation of the whole, and LibPops end up being tarred with the same brush, despite having no more in common with neo-Nazis than Chomsky's current political views have with Stalin's.[13] As in the previous cases, this is partly the LibPops' own fault for not making stronger efforts to dissociate themselves from their authoritarian counterparts[14]—but it is also the fault of critics of populism who have been remarkably careless in getting their facts straight about the people and views they criticize.[15]

[12] Of course, these are only generalizations, with many individual exceptions. For example, I have certainly met LibCaps and LibSocs who opposed abortion rights, and LibPops who supported them.
[13] Some examples may be helpful. Groups like the Aryan Nation and the Ku Klux Klan are obvious examples of authoritarian populism at its most racist extreme. The weekly populist newspaper *The Spotlight* is an unsettling mix of libertarian aspects with moderately authoritarian-racist aspects. The "militia movement," broadly defined, also appears to include groups from both camps. By contrast, the U.S. Taxpayers Party and the secessionist "Republic of Texas" movement—as near as I can tell—appear to be *predominantly* LibPop and anti-racist, though these movements might not be a LibCap's or LibSoc's cup of tea. (By the "Republic of Texas" movement I mean the main organization, not the splinter group—repudiated by the main group—that made the news in 1997 by seizing hostages!)
[14] In addition, canny politicians like Pat Buchanan have learned to pitch their message in such a way as to appeal to substantial numbers of populists in both the libertarian and authoritarian camps.
[15] In a number of instances, peaceful, tolerant anti-statists (in some cases not even populist in orientation) have been labeled "white supremacists" or members of "Aryan hate groups" by critics who never bothered to discover that the persons so labeled were in fact Jewish or black.

When I speak of "libertarianism," for the purposes of this essay I mean all three of these very different movements. It may be protested that LibCap, LibSoc, and LibPop are *too* different from one another to be treated as aspects of a single point of view. But they do share a common—or at least an overlapping—intellectual ancestry. LibSocs and LibCaps can both claim the seventeenth-century English Levellers and the eighteenth-century French Encyclopedists among their ideological forebears; and all three groups (LibSocs, LibCaps, and LibPops) usually share an admiration for Thomas Jefferson and Thomas Paine. In the nineteenth century it was fairly common for libertarians in different traditions to recognize a commonality of heritage and concern;[16] this mutual recognition has been largely lost sight of in the twentieth century, but is beginning to return.[17]

To be sure, we should not lose sight of the differences among LibSocs, LibCaps, and LibPops. But we also should not commit the much more common error of allowing the differences to overshadow the common liberatory, anti-authoritarian impulse. Moreover, as we shall see, the need for an adequate theory of class—a need common to all three libertarianisms—may lie at the root of some of those differences.

III. THEORIES OF CLASS

Class analysis in the Western tradition begins in ancient Greece and Rome, with an approach I shall call the *republican theory of class*. Ancient theorists thought of classes in economic terms: the wealthy minority versus the poor majority. The chief task of ancient constitutional thought was to balance the interests and influence of each of these classes against the other, in order to prevent the rich from running roughshod over the poor, or vice versa. This goal was adopted in part for reasons of justice; the ancient republic was supposed to represent the interests of the entire people, not just one faction of them. But the goal also had a pragmatic justification: each class was powerful, the one because of its wealth and

---

[16] For example, the contributors to *Liberty*, the leading American anarchist journal of the day, drew inspiration equally from Pierre-Joseph Proudhon and Herbert Spencer.

[17] A few examples: *Nation* columnists Christopher Hitchens and Alexander Cockburn, both broadly LibSoc in orientation, have expressed some sympathy for the LibCap and LibPop movements, respectively; LibSoc Noam Chomsky acknowledges an intellectual debt to LibCap idol Adam Smith; U.S. Congressman Ron Paul has attracted a following that includes both LibCaps and LibPops; "community technologist" Karl Hess is admired by both LibCaps and LibSocs; followers of Henry George engage in dialogue with LibCaps and LibSocs; and the International Society for Individual Liberty, a LibCap organization, addresses concerns important to both LibSocs and LibPops. One might also include the highly influential LibCap theorist Murray Rothbard, who in the 1960s and 1970s made common cause with LibSocs, and in his later years became associated instead with LibPops. Unfortunately, Rothbard's outreach to socialists and populists did not always confine itself to the libertarian aspects of those movements. During his socialist-friendly days, Rothbard cheered the Communist sack of Saigon (on the rather dubious grounds that the fall of any state is an event to celebrate, regardless of what replaces it), while in his later, populist-friendly days he (along with his associates at the Ludwig von Mises Institute) condoned the Los Angeles Police Department's beating of Rodney King.

the other because of its numbers, and therefore no political system could long remain stable unless it could attract the support of both classes.

Ancient theorists disagreed about how best to achieve this balance. Conservatives like Thucydides, Aristotle, and Polybius (as well as Plato in his later years)[18] favored the "mixed constitution," a combination of aristocracy and democracy; for their model they looked to Sparta, Rome, or the "ancestral constitution" of Athens under Solon. Ancient liberals like Demosthenes and Athenagoras, by contrast, thought that the mixed constitution undercompensated for the influence of the rich and over-compensated for the influence of the poor; they favored instead the democratic system of post-Kleisthenean Athens (508–338 B.C.E.), where laws were passed by popular referendum and subjected to judicial review in jury courts manned by lot, and public officials were likewise picked by lot to ensure proportional representation. (As these examples show, Athenian democracy, contrary to popular misconception, was never a system of unchecked majority rule.) For us, democracy is synonymous with elections, but in ancient times elections were regarded as antidemocratic; the worry was that wealthy candidates would be better able to influence the electoral process and thus would be disproportionately represented in the government, a problem that random selection by lot avoids.

But both Greek liberals and Greek conservatives, while differing about means,[19] agreed on the basic premise that constitutional design should aim at achieving a balance between the rich and poor classes so that neither class could achieve complete domination over the other. It was this ancient republican perspective on classes that was inherited by the modern liberal and republican traditions, as represented by such thinkers as Machiavelli, Montesquieu, and Madison.

But in the eighteenth century, two new, more radical ways of thinking about class began to emerge. These radical approaches differed from traditional republican class analysis in identifying a particular class as *inherently exploitative*; the internal dynamic of this class was such that, if allowed to exist, it would inevitably gain and maintain the upper hand. Such a class in its nature could not be *checked*; the only solution was to *eliminate* it—not by exterminating its members, of course, but by destroying the class *as a class*, by removing from it the characteristics that made it the class it was.

One of these theories originated with Rousseau and was later inherited by Marx; I shall call it the *Rousseauvian theory of class*. Like its republican counterpart, the Rousseauvian theory identified classes in economic terms;

---

[18] I am thinking in particular of the *Laws*, where Plato defends a version of the mixed constitution, as opposed to such earlier writings as the *Republic* (and, to a lesser extent, the *Statesman*), where Plato relies on virtuous rulers rather than on constitutional devices to safeguard the pubic interest.

[19] The ancient liberals arguably had the better case; for discussion, see my "The Athenian Constitution: Government by Jury and Referendum," *Formulations*, vol. 4, no. 1 (Autumn 1996), pp. 7–23, 35.

the defining characteristic of a class was its economic status (in Marxist terms, its control over the means of production, e.g., land and capital equipment). But the Rousseauvian theory is pessimistic about the possibility of providing any reliable constitutional safeguard against the tendency of superior wealth to translate itself into superior power. Socioeconomic inequality inherently leads to oppression, and so must be eliminated in order to establish freedom; and since the ruling class is defined by its superior socioeconomic position, in abolishing inequality we abolish the ruling class as well.

The other radical approach had its roots in the writings of Rousseau's contemporary Adam Smith, but received its full development only in the nineteenth century: in France, by the followers of the economist Jean-Baptiste Say;[20] in England, by James Mill and the Philosophical Radicals; and in the United States, first by Jeffersonian agrarians like John Taylor and John Calhoun, and later by individualist anarchists like Lysander Spooner and Benjamin Tucker. I shall call it the *Smithian theory of class*.

Smith is often thought of today, by admirers and detractors alike, as a defender of business interests; but Smith saw himself as a defender of laborers and consumers against the "mercantile interest."[21] Smith's defense of *capitalism* did not translate into a defense of *capitalists*; on the contrary, Smith maintained that businessmen never meet together without the conversation ending in a "conspiracy against the public." Smith's antagonism was not toward economic inequality as such; Smith had a positive-sum approach to economics, maintaining that the free market that allowed a few to amass vast fortunes also created dramatic improvements in the living conditions of the many. Rather, Smith's concern focused on the ability of the wealthy to use their wealth to influence the political process in their favor through governmental grants of subsidy and monopoly. The danger was not wealth per se, but the ability of

---

[20] The most important in this context were Charles Comte, Charles Dunoyer, Augustin Thierry, Frédéric Bastiat, and Gustave de Molinari. For a good introduction, see Leonard P. Liggio, "Charles Dunoyer and French Classical Liberalism," *Journal of Libertarian Studies*, vol. 1, no. 3 (Summer 1977), pp. 153–78; and David M. Hart, "Gustave de Molinari and the Anti-Statist Liberal Tradition: Part I," *Journal of Libertarian Studies*, vol. 5, no. 3 (Summer 1981), pp. 263–90; cf. also Ralph Raico, "Classical Liberal Exploitation Theory," *Journal of Libertarian Studies*, vol. 1, no. 3 (Summer 1977), pp. 179–83; Mark Weinburg, "The Social Analysis of Three Early Nineteenth Century French Liberals: Say, Comte, and Dunoyer," *Journal of Libertarian Studies*, vol. 2, no. 1 (1978), pp. 45–63; and Joseph T. Salerno, "Comment on the French Liberal School," *Journal of Libertarian Studies*, vol. 2, no. 1 (1978), pp. 65–68.

[21] See Adam Smith, *An Inquiry into the Nature and Causes of the Wealth of Nations* (William Benton Pub., 1952), p. 211:

> The capricious ambition of kings and ministers has not, during the preceding century, been more fatal to the repose of Europe than the impertinent jealousy of merchants and manufacturers....That it was the spirit of monopoly which originally both invented and propagated this [mercantilist] doctrine cannot be doubted; and they who first taught it were by no means such fools as they who believed it.... [T]he interested sophistry of merchants and manufacturers confounded the common sense of mankind. Their interest is, in this respect, directly opposed to that of the great body of the people.

wealth to sway the counsels of state. It was this concern that Smith's French, English, and American admirers developed into a full-fledged theory of class. For the Smithian liberal, the source of the ruling class's dominant position was not its economic status as such, but its differential access to state power; the ruling and ruled classes were defined not by their relative socioeconomic position, but by the extent to which they were beneficiaries or victims of state power. One contemporary LibCap proponent of the Smithian theory of class explains the difference this way:

> While Marxist class analysis uses the relationship to the mode of production as its point of reference, libertarian class analysis uses the relationship to the political means as its standard. Society is divided into two classes: those who use the political means, which is force, and those who use the economic means, which requires voluntary interaction. The former is the ruling class which lives off the labor and wealth of the latter.[22]

By its nature, the Smithian theorists thought, a powerful state attracts special interests who will try to direct its activities, and whichever achieves the most sway (presumably by being the wealthiest) will constitute a ruling class. So long as this class holds the reins of power, attempts to check its influence will prove ineffective. Since the Smithian theory defines the ruling class as an artifact of state power, the way to attack that class is to go after state power instead. The anarchist wing of Smithian liberalism favored eliminating the state altogether; more moderate liberals favored keeping the state but severely curbing its power through structural and constitutional safeguards (and here they drew once more, though in a different context, on the checks and balances of republican tradition). The idea common to both anarchists and moderates, however, was that the key to a ruling class's power is a powerful state, and that the ruling class must wither away if that power source is either eliminated or sufficiently curtailed. While Rousseauvian socialists saw a ruling class as an elite group that developed its power in the cutthroat capitalist marketplace and then used this power to gain political domination as well, the Smithian liberals saw the state as the crucial source of power for elites, arguing that the power of such "special interests" could not survive in a free marketplace but depended crucially on special privileges from government. A power must exist in order for it to be abused to benefit those with political pull; so every power we strip away from government is one more brick removed from the foundation that upholds the ruling class. Special interests cannot win favors from the state if it has no favors to give out.

---

[22] Wendy McElroy, "Introduction: The Roots of Individualist Feminism in Nineteenth-Century America," in McElroy, ed., *Freedom, Feminism, and the State: An Overview of Individualist Feminism*, 2d ed. (New York: Holmes and Meier, 1992), p. 23.

Rousseau and his intellectual heirs, by contrast, were far less sanguine about the ability of market competition to keep the power of the rich in check. Unlike the positive-sum Smithians, Rousseau viewed the market as a zero-sum or even negative-sum process, in which those who gain can do so only at the expense of others who lose. For Rousseau, the ability of the rich to oppress the poor does not presuppose state intervention, but arises naturally even in the absence of government. As Rousseau views the historical process, it is the introduction of private property and the division of labor that puts an end to primitive anarcho-communism and leads to socioeconomic stratification and the emergence of a wealthy ruling class; that class then creates the political state in order to solidify the power it has already achieved on the market, thus ending the class struggle by winning it:

> So long as men remained content with their rustic huts [and] adorned themselves only with feathers and shells . . . so long as they undertook only what a single person could accomplish, and confined themselves to such arts as did not require the joint labour of several hands, they lived free, healthy, honest, and happy lives. . . . But from the moment one man began to stand in need of the help of another; from the moment it appeared advantageous to any one man to have enough provisions for two, equality disappeared, property was introduced, work became indispensable, and vast forests became smiling fields, which man had to water with the sweat of his brow, and where slavery and misery were soon seen to germinate and grow up with the crops. . . . [I]t was iron and corn, which first civilized men, and ruined humanity. . . . No sooner were artificers wanted to smelt and forge iron, than others were required to maintain them . . . and as some required commodities in exchange for their iron, the rest at length discovered the method of making iron serve for the multiplication of commodities. . . . [T]he strongest did most work; the most skilful turned his labour to best account; the most ingenious devised methods of diminishing his labour. . . . Thus natural inequality unfolds itself [and] the difference between men, developed by their different circumstances, becomes more sensible and permanent in its effects. . . . [W]hen inheritances so increased in number and extent as to occupy the whole of the land, and to border on one another, one man could aggrandize himself only at the expense of another; at the same time the supernumeraries, who had been too weak or too indolent to make such acquisitions, and had grown poor . . . were obliged to receive their subsistence, or steal it, from the rich; and this soon bred, according to their different characters, dominion and slavery, or violence and rapine. The wealthy, on their part, had no sooner begun to taste the pleasure of command, than they disdained all others, and using their old slaves to acquire new, thought of nothing but subduing and enslaving their neighbours; like ravenous wolves,

which, having once tasted human flesh, despise every other food and thenceforth seek only men to devour. . . . The new-born state of society thus gave rise to a horrible state of war. . . . Destitute of valid reasons to justify and sufficient strength to defend himself . . . the rich man, thus urged by necessity, conceived at length the profoundest plan that ever entered the mind of man: this was to employ in his favour the forces of those who attacked him. . . . "Let us join," said he, "to [establish] a supreme power which may govern us by wise laws . . . and maintain eternal harmony among us." All ran headlong to their chains, in hopes of securing their liberty. . . . The most capable of foreseeing the dangers were the very persons who expected to benefit by them. . . . Such was, or may well have been, the origin of society and law, which bound new fetters on the poor, and gave new powers to the rich; which irretrievably destroyed natural liberty, eternally fixed the law of property and inequality, converted clever usurpation into unalterable right, and, for the advantage of a few ambitious individuals, subjected all mankind to perpetual labour, slavery, and wretchedness.[23]

The Marxist theory of the origin of classes essentially recapitulates that of Rousseau. As Friedrich Engels writes, in what seems almost a paraphrase of Rousseau's *Second Discourse*:

Civilization opens with a new advance in the division of labor. . . . Confronted by the new forces in whose growth it had had no share, the gentile constitution was helpless. . . . [H]ere was a society which by all its economic conditions of life had been forced to split itself into freemen and slaves, into the exploiting rich and the exploited poor. . . . Such a society could only exist either in the continuous open fight of these classes against one another or else under the rule of a third power, which, apparently standing above the warring classes, suppressed their open conflict and allowed the class struggle to be fought out at most in the economic field, in so-called legal form. The gentile constitution was finished. It had been shattered by the division of labor and its result, the cleavage of society into classes. It was replaced by the *state*. . . . As the state arose from the need to keep class antagonisms in check, but also arose in the thick of the fight between the classes, it is normally the state of the most powerful, economically dominant class, which by its means becomes also the politically dominant class and so acquires new means of holding down and exploiting the oppressed class.[24]

[23] Jean-Jacques Rousseau, *Discourse on the Origin of Inequality*, in Rousseau, *The Social Contract and Discourses*, trans. G. D. H. Cole et al. (London: J. M. Dent, 1982), pp. 83–89.

[24] Frederick Engels, *The Origin of the Family, Private Property, and the State*, trans. Alec West et al. (New York: International Publishers, 1985), pp. 224–31.

But Rousseau was not the only influence on Marx and Engels, who actually drew on the Smithian theory of class as well. Indeed, Marx always acknowledged (if somewhat ironically) his debt to the "bourgeois economists," but of course he transformed the details of their theories in order to bring them more in line with the Rousseauvian position. As LibCap theorist Murray Rothbard notes:

> Interestingly enough, the very Marxian phrase, the "replacement of government over *men* by the administration of *things*," can be traced, by a circuitous route, from the great French radical laissez-faire liberals of the early nineteenth century, Charles Comte (no relation to Auguste Comte) and Charles Dunoyer. And so, too, may the concept of the "class struggle"; except that for Dunoyer and Comte, the inherently antithetical classes were not businessmen versus workers, but the producers in society (including free businessmen, workers, peasants, etc.) versus the exploiting classes constituting, and privileged by, the State apparatus.[25]

> The French theorists [Comte, Dunoyer, and Thierry] developed the insight that Europe had originally been dominated by a ruling class of kings, or of feudal nobility. They believed that with the rise of capitalism and free markets, of *"industrielisme,"* there would be no ruling class, and the class-run State would wither away, resulting in a "classless," Stateless, free society. Saint-Simon was originally a Comte-Dunoyer libertarian, and then in later life he, and particularly his followers, changed the class analysis while keeping the original categories, to maintain that employers somehow rule or exploit the workers in a free-market wage relationship. Marx adopted the Saint-Simonian class analysis so that Marxism to this day maintains a totally inconsistent definition of class: On Asiatic despotism and feudalism, the old libertarian concept of ruling class as wielder-of-State-power is maintained; then, when capitalism is discussed, suddenly the definition shifts to the employers forming a "ruling class" over workers on the free market. The alleged capitalist class rule over the State is only extra icing on the cake, the "super-exploitation" by an "executive committee" of a ruling class previously constituted on the market.[26]

Since Rousseau and Marx saw the source of power for elites as the marketplace, they concluded that it was the marketplace that needed to be

---

[25] Murray N. Rothbard, *Left and Right: The Prospects for Liberty* (Washington, DC: Cato Institute, 1982), p. 7.

[26] Murray N. Rothbard, "Concepts of the Role of Intellectuals in Social Change Toward Laissez Faire," *Journal of Libertarian Studies*, vol. 9, no. 2 (Fall 1990), p. 66, n. 30; cf. Rothbard, "The Laissez-Faire Radical: A Quest for the Historical Mises," *Journal of Libertarian Studies*, vol. 5, no. 3 (Summer 1981), pp. 244–45.

restrained (Rousseau) or eliminated (Marx), and that big government could be trusted, once the marketplace could no longer corrupt it, to wield dictatorial powers in a benign fashion either indefinitely (Rousseau) or until it was no longer necessary, at which point it would politely wither away (Marx). The Smithian liberals, by contrast, since they saw the state as the source of the dominant elites' power, concluded that it was the state that needed to be restrained or eliminated, and that the free market could be trusted to coordinate human interaction once the state could no longer intervene on behalf of the economic aristocracy.

Today's LibCaps, when they think about class at all, tend to endorse some version of the Smithian theory, and to reject the Rousseauvian alternative as bad economics. By contrast, LibSocs and LibPops consider LibCap faith in the beneficence of the unregulated market to be naive, and tend to be much more attracted to some version of the Rousseauvian theory, though they are likely to temper it with elements of the Smithian theory as well. Therefore, the fundamental question of class theory is also one of the main issues at the root of the divisions among the various libertarian camps; as Walter Grinder succinctly puts it: "Which comes first—classes and then the State or the State and then classes?"[27]

IV. STATOCRATS AND PLUTOCRATS

We can gain a better understanding of the nature of a ruling class if we distinguish two possible subclasses within it: those who actually hold political office within the state, and those who influence the state from the private sector.

> If the State is a group of plunderers, *who* then constitutes the State? Clearly, the ruling elite consists at any time of (a) the full-time *apparatus*—the kings, politicians, and bureaucrats who man and operate the State; and (b) the groups who have maneuvered to gain privileges, subsidies, and benefices from the State. The remainder of society constitutes the ruled.[28]

I propose to call group (a) the *statocratic class*, or *statocracy*,[29] and group (b) the *plutocratic class*, or *plutocracy*. It is self-evident that a statocratic class must depend for its power on the existence of the state; the question at

---

[27] Walter E. Grinder, "Introduction," in Albert Jay Nock, *Our Enemy the State* (New York: Free Life Editions, 1973), p. xx.

[28] Murray N. Rothbard, *For a New Liberty: The Libertarian Manifesto*, rev. ed. (San Francisco: Fox and Wilkes, 1994), p. 52. Unfortunately, Rothbard does not go on to tell us much about the dynamic between these two components.

[29] I borrow these terms from Bertrand de Jouvenel, who defines "statocrat" as "a man who derives his authority only from the position which he holds and the office which he performs in the service of the state." See Bertrand de Jouvenel, *On Power: The Natural History of Its Growth*, trans. J. F. Huntington (Indianapolis: Liberty Fund, 1993), p. 174, n. 4.

issue between Smithians and Rousseauvians is whether the same is true of a plutocratic class as well.

For those who view society in terms of ruling classes, then, there are five salient possibilities.[30] One might accept the existence of a statocratic ruling class, but deny the existence of a plutocratic one; call this the *Statocracy-Only* position. Or one might accept the existence of a plutocratic ruling class, but deny the existence of a statocratic one; call this the *Plutocracy-Only* position. If instead one grants the existence of both statocratic and plutocratic classes, then three possibilities remain. First, one might think, with the Smithians, that the statocratic class is the basic source of oppression on which the power of the plutocratic class depends; call this the *Statocracy-Dominant* position. Second, one might think, with the Rousseauvians, that the plutocratic class is the basic source of oppression on which the power of the statocratic class depends; call this the *Plutocracy-Dominant* position. Finally, one might think that neither class is more fundamental than the other, that statocrats and plutocrats represent equal and coordinate threats to liberty; call this the *Neither-Dominant* position.

What might motivate these various positions? Consider first the Plutocracy-Only view. To take this position is to deny that the state represents a significant source of oppression at all; political institutions are beneficent (or at least neutral), but they have not yet succeeded in overcoming the power of private wealth, the only true ruling class. This view or something like it is held by some socialists, but generally not by libertarian ones; suspicion of the state is central to libertarianism in all its forms.

A more attractive position for libertarians is the view I call Plutocracy-Dominant. On this view (essentially the Rousseauvian approach), the state is oppressive, yet not because of its inherent nature, but rather because it has become a tool of the plutocratic class. One LibSoc theorist who seems to subscribe to this view is Noam Chomsky:

> [Y]ou can't get away from the fact that there are sharp differences in power which in fact are ultimately rooted in the economic system. . . . Objective power lies in various places: in patriarchy, in race. [But c]rucially, it lies in ownership. . . . The society [is] governed by those who own it. . . . That's at the core of things. Lots of other things can change and that can remain and we will have pretty much the same forms of domination.[31]

> The government is far from benign—that's true. On the other hand, it's at least partially accountable, and it can become as benign as we make it.

[30] These five are not the only possibilities, of course. Indeed, I shall be arguing that none of them gets it exactly right. But the sixth approach that I favor will not become salient until we see what is wrong with the initially salient five.

[31] Noam Chomsky, *Keeping the Rabble in Line* (Monroe: Common Courage Press, 1994), pp. 109–11.

What's not benign (what's extremely harmful, in fact) is . . . business power, which is highly concentrated and, by now, largely transnational. Business power is very far from benign and it's completely unaccountable. It's a totalitarian system that has an enormous effect on our lives. It's also the main reason why the government isn't benign.[32]

Although Chomsky is an anarchist, these remarks suggest that in his view the abolition of state power, while perhaps desirable, would be a matter of no great urgency in the absence of "business power."

This perspective is not confined to LibSocs. While LibPops are staunch defenders of inviolable private property at the level of homesteads and small businesses (and so would part company with the Rousseauvians when it comes to blaming oppression on private property as such), they see the power of big banks and corporations as a threat to liberty; and although they see "business power" as using the state for its ends, they seem to regard the former as the cause of the latter's malfeasance rather than vice versa. Consider, for example, LibPop criticisms of the U.S. Federal Reserve. Although in principle LibPops generally oppose central banking, one often gets the impression from their literature that it is the *private* character of the Federal Reserve that most attracts their ire, and that a central bank run directly by Congress would be far more acceptable to them. (By contrast, the typical LibCap objection to the Federal Reserve is that it is a government monopoly *rather* than a private bank.)

The Plutocracy-Only and Plutocracy-Dominant positions, whether in socialist or populist guise, rest on the assumption that while there is an internal dynamic within the capitalist market that leads to greater and greater centralization of power, there is no analogous internal dynamic within the state itself. This is a difficult claim to believe. Public-choice economics has shown that politicians and bureaucrats respond to incentives in the same way that private individuals on the market do, and that the state's insulation from market competition makes many of those incentives perverse.[33] Moreover, considerable evidence suggests that states have an inherent tendency to grow and aggrandize power.[34]

---

[32] Noam Chomsky, *Secrets, Lies, and Democracy* (Tucson: Odonian Press, 1994), p. 37. Yet Chomsky does distinguish, as many LibCaps would, between a free-market system and the kind of economic system favored by plutocrats: "Any form of concentrated power, whatever it is, is not going to want to be subjected to popular democratic control or, for that matter, to market discipline. Powerful sectors, including corporate wealth, are naturally opposed to functioning democracy, just as they're opposed to functioning markets, for themselves, at least" (*Keeping the Rabble in Line*, p. 242).

[33] See, for example, James M. Buchanan and Robert D. Tollison, eds., *The Theory of Public Choice: Political Applications of Economics* (Ann Arbor: University of Michigan Press, 1972); and Gordon Tullock, *The Economics of Special Privilege and Rent Seeking* (Boston: Kluwer, 1989).

[34] See, for example, Robert Higgs, *Crisis and Leviathan: Critical Episodes in the Growth of American Government* (Oxford: Oxford University Press, 1987).

Not all LibSocs would agree with Chomsky's suggestion that the state would be benign without the influence of the business interest. When Marx invoked the Plutocracy-Dominant approach in calling for a "dictatorship of the proletariat" during the transitional phase between capitalism and anarcho-communism (on the theory that once it was no longer a tool of the capitalist class, a dictatorial state could be trusted to wield vast powers in the short run and wither away in the long run), the Russian LibSoc anarchist Mikhail Bakunin took Marx to task for naïveté about the internal dynamic of political power:

> The question arises, if the proletariat is ruling, over whom will it rule? ... If there exists a state, there is inevitably domination [and] slavery. ... What does it mean for the proletariat to be "organized as the ruling class"? ... Can it really be that the entire proletariat will stand at the head of the administration? ... There are about forty million Germans. Will all forty millions really be members of the government? ... The entire nation will be governors and there will be no governed ones. ... Then there will be no government, no state, but if there is a state, there will be governors and slaves. ... So, in sum: government of the great majority of popular masses by a privileged minority. But this minority will be composed of workers, say the Marxists. ... Of former workers, perhaps, but just as soon as they become representatives or rulers of the people *they will cease to be workers.* ... And they'll start looking down on all ordinary workers from the heights of the state: they will now represent not the people but themselves and their claims to govern the people. He who doubts this simply doesn't know human nature. ... They say that such a state yoke, a dictatorship, is a necessary transitional means for attaining the most complete popular liberation. So, to liberate the masses of the people they first have to be enslaved. ... They maintain that only a dictatorship, their own naturally, can create the people's will; we answer: no dictatorship can have any other aim than to perpetuate itself, and it can only give rise to and instill slavery in the people that tolerates it. ...[35]

In effect, Bakunin was predicting the rise of what Milovan Djilas would later call the "New Class."[36] But Marx remained unpersuaded. To Baku-

[35] Bakunin, in "After the Revolution: Marx Debates Bakunin," in Robert C. Tucker, ed., *The Marx-Engels Reader*, 2d ed. (New York: W. W. Norton, 1978), pp. 542–48.

[36] Milovan Djilas, *The New Class: An Analysis of the Communist System* (New York: Frederick A. Praeger, 1957). Interestingly, Djilas seems to regard the Plutocracy-Dominant position as a viable explanation of most class systems, while treating the Soviet regime as an exception: "In earlier epochs the coming to power of some class, some part of a class, or some party, was the final event resulting from its formation and development. The reverse was true in the U.S.S.R." (p. 38).

nin's suggestion that workers in charge of the State would start to identify with statocratic rather than proletarian interests, and thus effectively cease to be members of the working class, Marx replied:

> No more than a factory-owner ceases to be a capitalist nowadays because he has become a member of the town council. . . . If Herr Bakunin knew even one thing about the situation of the manager of a workers' cooperative factory, all his hallucinations about domination would go to the devil.[37]

Marx was convinced that an oppressive statocracy presupposes an independent plutocracy pulling the strings: cut the state's ties to the capitalist class, and an authoritarian centralized dictatorship would no longer pose any danger. In light of the horrors perpetrated by socialist regimes in this century, Marxist insouciance in the face of criticisms like Bakunin's must strike us today as chillingly unconvincing. In their confidence that a socialist dictatorship would govern benignly once established, and then politely wither away when its job was done, it is Marx and Engels who are now seen to have been "utopian socialists," while the anarchist critics they dismissed as idle dreamers turn out to have been the genuine hard-headed realists. Marxism, with its call for dictatorship now and anarchy later, represents a confused attempt to unite opposite tendencies, to merge the authoritarian and libertarian wings of socialism. Janus-headed, Marxism turns its left face toward Proudhon, Bakunin, and Kropotkin—and its right face toward Stalin, Mao, and Pol Pot.

If the Plutocracy-Only and Plutocracy-Dominant positions lack credibility, what of Statocracy-Only? Some LibCaps do seem to hold this view, regarding corporate interests as purely benign, and the victims of socialistic government oppression. Ayn Rand[38] (1905-1982), for example, called

---

[37] Marx, quoted in *ibid.*, p. 546.

[38] Ayn Rand and her "Objectivist" followers (the orthodox ones, at least) would not accept the title "libertarian." Indeed, one prominent Randian, Peter Schwartz, has authored a thundering condemnation of the entire LibCap movement. (See Schwartz, *Libertarianism: The Perversion of Liberty* [New York: The Intellectual Activist, 1986]; a revised and condensed version appears in Ayn Rand et al., *The Voice of Reason: Essays in Objectivist Thought*, ed. Leonard Peikoff [New York: Penguin, 1989], pp. 311-33.) But I challenge anyone to construct criteria that are simultaneously broad enough to include the major thinkers and traditions of the LibCap movement yet narrow enough to exclude Rand. In my judgment, Rand and her followers should be considered Libertarian Capitalists whether they like the label or not, since the features of the LibCap position they reject are either (a) held by only *some* LibCaps and therefore not essential to the LibCap position, or (b) not held by *any* LibCaps at all and therefore based on misunderstandings (often fantastic ones). Randians try to distance themselves from LibCaps on the grounds that the LibCap movement tolerates a number of different philosophical approaches to grounding libertarianism, while Randians insist that Ayn Rand's Objectivist approach provides the only acceptable grounding. But this is a bit like denying the existence of God yet declining to be called an atheist on the grounds that there are many different kinds of atheists with grounds for disbelief different from one's own; disbelief in God makes one an atheist, regardless of how one feels about other atheists.

big business a "persecuted minority,"[39] and denied the very existence of the military-industrial complex.[40] To her credit, she did acknowledge that many businesses have historically looked to the state for political favors:

> The giants of American industry—such as James Jerome Hill or Commodore Vanderbilt or Andrew Carnegie or J. P. Morgan—were self-made men who earned their fortunes by personal ability, by free trade on a free market. But there existed another kind of businessmen, the products of a mixed economy, the men with political pull, who made fortunes by means of special privileges granted to them by the government, such men as the Big Four of the Central Pacific Railroad. It was the political power behind their activities—the power of forced, unearned, economically unjustified privileges—that caused dislocations in the country's economy, hardships, depressions, and mounting public protests. But it was the free market and the free businessmen who took the blame.[41]

> So long as a government holds the power of economic control, it will necessarily create a special "elite," an "aristocracy of pull," it will attract the corrupt type of politician into the legislature, it will work to the advantage of the dishonest businessman, and will penalize and, eventually, destroy the honest and the able. . . . The issue is not between pro-business controls and pro-labor controls, but between controls and freedom. It is not the Big Four against the welfare state, but the Big Four and the welfare state on one side—against J. J. Hill and every honest worker on the other.[42]

All this *sounds* like the Statocracy-Dominant position. However, Rand seriously downplayed the importance of the "political pull" variety of

---

[39] Ayn Rand, "America's Persecuted Minority: Big Business," in Rand et al., *Capitalism: The Unknown Ideal* (New York: New American Library, 1970), pp. 44–62.

[40] "Something called 'the military-industrial complex'—which is a myth or worse—is being blamed for all this country's troubles." Ayn Rand, "Philosophy: Who Needs It," in Rand, *Philosophy: Who Needs It* (Indianapolis: Bobbs-Merrill, 1982), p. 10. On the same page, Rand wrote, breathtakingly, that "the United States Army [is] the army of the last semi-free country left on earth, yet [it is] accused of being a tool of imperialism—and 'imperialism' is the name given to the foreign policy of this country, which has never engaged in military conquest. . . . Our defence budget is being attacked, denounced, and undercut [and] a similar kind of campaign is conducted against the police force." Despite Rand's fierce anti-statism, her equally fierce Vietnam-era pro-American patriotism had a tendency to lead her into what can only be described as astonishingly naive statements, not only about the plutocracy but about the statocracy itself. (Most LibCaps would have a far more skeptical assessment of U.S. foreign policy, for example.)

[41] Rand, "America's Persecuted Minority," pp. 48–49.

[42] Ayn Rand, "Notes on the History of American Free Enterprise," in Rand et al., *Capitalism*, pp. 108–9.

businessmen, by treating the business lobby's use of bribery and influence-peddling as generally benign, thus moving to the Statocracy-Only position instead:

> Yet what could the railroads do, except try to "own whole legislatures," if these legislatures held the power of life or death over them? What could the railroads do, except resort to bribery, if they wished to exist at all? Who was to blame and who was "corrupt"—the businessmen who had to pay "protection money" for the right to remain in business—or the politicians who held the power to sell that right? ... [The railroad owners] had to turn to the practice of bribing legislators only in self-protection. ... It was only when the legislatures began the blackmail of threatening to pass disastrous and impossible regulations that the railroad owners had to turn to bribery.[43]

This view of American economic history is challenged by a great deal of current scholarly research, which shows that the call for governmental regulation of the economy was largely orchestrated by big business in the first place, as a way of securing its hold on the market and strangling competition.[44] Moreover, Rand's list of "good" businessmen—what historian Burton Folsom would call "market entrepreneurs" as opposed to "political entrepreneurs"[45]—shows the extent to which Rand underestimated the extent of the problem. James J. Hill of the Great Northern Railroad is plausible enough as an example of an independent "market entrepreneur" who refused to seek governmental favors, but Vanderbilt and Carnegie hardly fall into that category, while J. P. Morgan is its antithesis; indeed, it would be difficult to name any turn-of-the-century American businessman who did more to help build

---

[43] *Ibid.*, pp. 107–8.

[44] For a LibSoc analysis, see Gabriel Kolko, *Railroads and Regulation* (Princeton: Princeton University Press, 1965); and Kolko, *The Triumph of Conservatism* (Chicago: Quadrangle Publishing, 1967). For a LibCap analysis, see Roy A. Childs, Jr., "Big Business and the Rise of American Statism," in Joan Kennedy Taylor, ed., *Liberty against Power: Essays by Roy A. Childs, Jr.* (San Francisco: Fox and Wilkes, 1994), pp. 15–47, as well as Weaver, *The Suicidal Corporation.*

[45] Burton W. Folsom, *The Myth of the Robber Barons* (Herndon: Young America's Foundation, 1991), pp. 1–2:

> Those [entrepreneurs] who tried to succeed ... primarily through federal aid ... we will classify as *political entrepreneurs*. Those who tried to succeed ... primarily by creating and marketing a superior product at a low cost we will classify as *market entrepreneurs*. No entrepreneur fits perfectly into one category or the other, but most fall generally into one category or the other. The political entrepreneurs often fit the classic Robber Baron mold; they stifled productivity (through monopolies and pools), corrupted business and politics, and dulled America's competitive edge. Market entrepreneurs, by contrast, often made decisive and unpredictable contributions to American economic development.

the regulatory pro-business regime than Morgan, the *consummate* "political entrepreneur."[46]

Rand saw figures like Vanderbilt, Carnegie, and Morgan as market entrepreneurs because they were *self-made men*. True, their initial *acquisition* of wealth depended primarily on their own ability and initiative, not on political favoritism. From this fact, however, Rand made the erroneous inference that these men did not use their vast fortunes, once they had acquired them, to gain political advantage:

> It is significant that the best of the railroad builders, those who started out with private funds, did not bribe legislatures to throttle competitors nor to obtain any kind of special legal advantage or privilege. They made their fortunes by their own personal ability—and if they resorted to bribery at all, like Commodore Vanderbilt, it was only to buy the removal of some artificial restriction, such as a permission to consolidate. They did not pay to *get* something from the legislature, but only to get the legislature out of their way. But the builders who started out with government help, such as the Big Four of the Central Pacific, were the ones who used the government for special advantages and owed their fortunes to legislation more than to personal ability. . . . It is only with the help of government regulations that a man of lesser ability can destroy his better competitors—and he is the only type of man who runs to government for economic help.[47]

But this claim will not withstand historical scrutiny. Businessmen cannot be divided into two classes, one rising by economic means and using economic means thenceforth, and another rising by political means and using political means thenceforth. On the contrary, many of those who

---

[46] In *Liberty against Power*, pp. 30, 38–39, 41–43, Roy Childs offers a LibCap analysis of Morgan less favorable than Rand's:

> [S]uch key figures in the Progressive Era as J. P. Morgan got their starts in alliances with the government. . . . J. P. Morgan & Co. . . . sponsored legislation to promote the formation of "public utilities," a special privilege monopoly granted by the state. . . . AT&T, controlled by J. P. Morgan as of 1907, also sought regulation. The company got what it wanted in 1910, when telephones were placed under the jurisdiction of the ICC, and rate wars became a thing of the past. . . . Morgan, because of his ownership or control of many major corporations, was in the fight for regulation from the earliest days onward. Morgan's financial power and reputation were largely the result of his operations with the American and European governments. . . . One crucial aspect of the banking system at the beginning of the 1900s was the relative decrease in New York's financial dominance and the rise of competitors. Morgan was fully aware of the diffusion of banking power that was taking place, and it disturbed him. . . . From very early days, Morgan had championed the cause of a central bank, of gaining control over the nation's credit through a board of leading bankers under government supervision. . . . J. P. Morgan, the key financial leader, was also a prime mover of American statism.

[47] Rand, "Notes," p. 108.

initially achieved their wealth simply through success on the free market, then used their new economic position to lobby the state for favors.[48] Such men were market entrepreneurs by necessity, until they had acquired enough money to play the political game, at which point many of them made the transition to political entrepreneurship with alacrity.[49] Because Rand denied this, she saw no danger in market-based wealth per se; she failed to see how wealth that arises peacefully on the market can then be translated into political power, and as a result she severely underestimated the extent of "political pull" on the part of business interests. Hence her position comes perilously close to the Statocracy-Only view. For Rand, the only ruling class worth worrying about is the state itself.[50]

Thanks in part to Rand's influence, this attitude toward big business is fairly common in the conservative wing of the LibCap movement.[51] For a conservative LibCap, the paradigmatic example of a special interest advancing its interests through government favoritism is that of impoverished welfare recipients—an unlikely candidate for a ruling class! If asked, a conservative LibCap will generally agree that corporate welfare exists and that it is bad, but conservative LibCaps nonetheless spend far more time and energy fulminating against subsidies to the poor than they do against subsidies to the affluent. Business interests are seen primarily as the "good guys," the victims of governmental regulation. Such LibCaps tend to find themselves in sympathy with the "right," as repre-

---

[48] In the same way, Folsom (in *The Myth of the Robber Barons*, p. 2), despite his caveat that "[n]o entrepreneur fits perfectly into one category or the other," divides historical business figures rather too neatly into market entrepreneurs and political entrepreneurs, with the implausible result that John D. Rockefeller, of all people, comes out as a benign market entrepreneur untainted by political favoritism. One would scarcely guess from Folsom's presentation that Rockefeller, like Morgan, was a vigorous lobbyist for federal regulation of industry; see, e.g., Kolko, *The Triumph of Conservatism*, pp. 63–64, 78.

[49] Of course, from the fact that they became political entrepreneurs, it does not follow that they necessarily ceased to act as market entrepreneurs; many businessmen pursued both strategies simultaneously. Rand's assumption that no one who was succeeding by his own economic efforts would be interested in becoming a political parasite at the same time is unwarranted; her mistake was to read her own Manichaean ethical stance into other people's motivations. Real people are messier and more complicated than the streamlined characters of an Ayn Rand novel.

[50] This is not to say that Rand herself would put it this way. Randians generally eschew the language of class; for example, when the Libertarian Party Radical Caucus issued a statement that "American society is divided into a government-oppressed class and a government-privileged class, and is ruled by a power elite," so that a distinction must be drawn "between those who hold state power and those who do not—between those who rule and those who are ruled . . . between two *opposing* classes with mutually exclusive relations to the state" (quoted in Schwartz, *Libertarianism*, p. 17), the response of Randian orthodoxy was to dismiss this clearly Smithian-liberal analysis as "blatantly Marxist" (*ibid.*, p. 17), with no apparent recognition of its pre-Marxist historical provenance.

[51] By the conservative wing of the LibCap movement I mean the wing that tends to soften libertarian principles in a direction congenial to mainstream conservatives. The conservative/radical distinction within the LibCap movement does not necessarily line up neatly with the division between minarchists and anarcho-capitalists.

sented by, for example, the Republican Party in the United States and the Conservative Party in Britain. By contrast, the radical wing of the LibCap movement is more likely to see business interests, and their political apologists, as the enemy:

> To a large degree it has been and remains big businessmen who are the fountainheads of American statism. If libertarians are seeking allies in the struggle for liberty, then I suggest that they look else- where . . . and begin to see big business as a destroyer, not as a unit, of the free market.[52]

It is important for libertarians, of whatever ideological stripe, to recog- nize the existence of both statocratic and plutocratic classes. The relation between them is something like that between church and state in the Mid- dle Ages: their interests overlap heavily but are not identical, so the two will commonly cooperate in holding down the people; but at the same time each wants to be the dominant partner, so they will frequently come into conflict as well. When the plutocracy gains the upper hand, the polity tends toward authoritarian capitalism (and sometimes a version of fascism); when the statocracy gains the upper hand, the polity tends toward authoritarian socialism. Left-wing and right-wing political parties (e.g., Labour versus Tory in Britain, Democratic versus Republican in the United States) may represent the interests of both factions, but not equally; left-wing parties can be seen as favoring a shift of power in the direction of the statocracy, while right-wing parties prefer to see the scales tip toward the plutocra- cy.[53] Hence it is that mainstream political dialogue is restricted to disputes

---

[52] Childs, *Liberty against Power*, p. 45.

[53] Charles Tilly has suggested an ingenious criterion to measure the degree to which one or the other of these classes is dominant. Drawing on categories developed by economic historian Frederic Lane, Tilly distinguishes between

> (a) the monopoly profit, or *tribute*, coming to owners of the means of producing [governmental] violence as a result of the difference between production costs and the price exacted from 'customers' and (b) the *protection rent* accruing to those customers— for example, merchants—who drew effective protection against outside competi- tors. . . . If citizens in general exercised effective ownership of the government—O distant ideal!—we might expect the managers to minimize protection costs and trib- ute, thus maximizing protection rent. . . . If [instead] the managers owned the govern- ment, they would tend to keep costs high by maximizing their own wages, to maximize tribute over and above those costs by exacting a high price from their subjects, and . . . to be indifferent to the level of protection rent. . . . [This scheme] yields interesting empirical criteria for evaluating claims that a given government was "relatively au- tonomous" or strictly subordinate to the interests of a dominant class. Presumably, a subordinate government would tend to maximize monopoly profits—returns to the dominant class resulting from the difference between the costs of protection and the price received from it—as well as tuning protection rents nicely to the economic interests of the dominant class. An autonomous government, in contrast, would tend to maximize managers' wages and its own size as well and would be indifferent to protection rents.

See Charles Tilly, "War Making and State Making as Organized Crime," in Peter Evans, Dietrich Rueschemeyer, and Theda Skocpol, eds., *Bringing the State Back In* (Cambridge:

within the reigning authoritarian paradigm, while genuine challenges to top-down control as such are marginalized.[54]

A plutocratic ruling class need not operate via conscious machinations, of course (though such machinations are not necessarily to be ruled out, either). A malign invisible-hand process may come into play instead. Suppose that a variety of governmental policies are proposed or adopted, perhaps at random. Those that adversely affect entrenched and concentrated interests will get noticed and become the object of attack. By contrast, those that injure the average person will meet with less opposition, since average people are too busy to keep track of what the government is doing, too poor to hire lawyers and lobbyists, and too dispersed to have an effective voice. Thus, legislation which is disadvantageous to the rich will tend to be filtered out, while legislation which is disadvantageous to the poor will not. Over time, this skews state action more and more in the direction of advancing the interests of the powerful at the expense of those of the weak.

Recognizing the existence of both plutocratic and statocratic classes helps to answer an objection brought by David Friedman[55] against the whole concept of a ruling class:

> Such a "ruling class" analysis fails to explain government activities, such as airline regulation, which consist mostly of destroying wealth, and the wealth of the rich at that.... It seems more reasonable to suppose that there is no ruling class, that we are ruled, rather, by a myriad of quarreling gangs, constantly engaged in stealing from each other to the great impoverishment of their own members as well as the rest of us.[56]

Friedman is correct in pointing out that the state often does act in ways injurious to big business. But there is room for a middle ground between the idea of a monolithic ruling class and Friedman's alternative of an amorphous collection of disparate pressure groups. A ruling class with

---

Cambridge University Press, 1985), pp. 175–76. While this criterion's validity can be no more than *ceteris paribus*, it does cast a most instructive light on the policy positions traditionally adopted by left-wing and right-wing political parties.

[54] Long, "Immanent Liberalism," p. 27 (text and note 61):

> Under [statocracy], vast quantities of resources and power are transferred to the bureaucratic state, on the theory that some of these benefits will trickle down to the common people—while under [plutocracy], the bureaucratic state follows a "supply-side" policy of granting special privileges and protections to favored corporations, once again on the theory that some of these benefits will trickle down to the common people.... For example, the current debate over health care in this country may be seen as a struggle over the precise balance of power between, on the one hand, the state bureaucracy, and, on the other hand, the quasi-private beneficiaries of state privilege....

[55] Milton Friedman's more radical, anarcho-capitalist son.

[56] David Friedman, *The Machinery of Freedom: Guide to a Radical Capitalism*, 2d ed. (La Salle: Open Court, 1989), pp. 154–55.

two cooperating but competitive factions, one statocratic and the other plutocratic, seems to have a great deal of explanatory power. (Nor is either faction completely unified internally; we are dealing with matters of degree.) If the business community controlled everything, we would not see such high capital gains taxes. On the other hand, if the business community were simply an exploited victim, we would not see such high levels of corporate welfare (i.e., subsidies, protections, and grants of monopoly privilege). Any position that focuses only on one class and ignores the other is unacceptably one-sided.

Yet this still leaves open the question: Is the power of the plutocratic class parasitic on the presence of a powerful state open to influence by the wealthy, or is political influence simply the consolidation of power already won on the market? In other words, once the Plutocracy-Dominant position is ruled out, which is closer to the truth: Statocracy-Dominant or Neither-Dominant?

Statocracy-Dominant is the orthodox position in the more radical wing of the LibCap movement. As against Chomsky's claim that government is more accountable than business, LibCaps argue that *in a genuinely free market*, business is more accountable than government, since businesses must be responsive to customer needs in order to avoid losing them to competitors, while government is a monopoly and thus is insulated from the incentives that competition provides. What makes business power unaccountable, radical LibCaps argue, is government intervention in the economy that hinders competition (either through direct protections and subsidies for big business, or else indirectly through regulatory hurdles that in theory apply equally to everyone, but in practice disproportionately affect the less affluent who are less able to afford the fees, licenses, and lawyers required to engage in business). The radical LibCap position is recognizable as a resurrection of the Smithian-liberal position:

As soon as institutionalized predatory force begins to encroach upon legitimate voluntary social and economic human intercourse, a class of the exploited and a class of the exploiters is born. These political-economic classes, in turn, tend to maintain and exacerbate the socio-economic distinctions (that is, the distinctions of wealth, income, and status) which otherwise would remain far less rigid in a totally free market society where one's mobility, both social and economic, would be far more dependent on one's own merits. . . . Different groups . . . vie for control of the State apparatus . . . and one group, over the course of time, always finishes considerably "more equal" than the others. It is to this more powerful group that the wealth, plundered by the political means, accrues. In time this group becomes entrenched both politically and economically through its plundered wealth. . . . In the United States, for example, the net gain continues to flow to the corporate-financial super-rich. The middle-classes are the net losers as tax payers and as consumers. The poor probably pay about as much as they receive in the more visible form of welfare. They pay, both directly and indirectly, through various forms of state-induced exploitation (such as exclusion from the work force by union restrictions, minimum wage rates, etc.). Thus, the poor are kept in their place through a kind of welfare colonialism, just as the State maintains the wealthy and relatively few in their favored class position.[57]

But LibCaps do not have a monopoly on the Statocracy-Dominant position. LibSoc Alexander Berkman (1876–1936) noted that his LibCap opponents accept the Statocracy-Dominant view,[58] but he also endorsed it himself: "It follows that when government is abolished, wage slavery and capitalism must also go with it, because they cannot exist without the support and protection of government."[59] Friedrich Engels also attributed the Statocracy-Dominant position to LibSoc Bakunin.[60]

---

[57] Grinder, "Introduction," pp. xviii–xix; cf. Hans-Hermann Hoppe, "Marxist and Austrian Class Analysis," *Journal of Libertarian Studies*, vol. 9, no. 2 (Fall 1990), pp. 86–87:

> The state is not exploitative because it protects the capitalists' property rights, but because it itself is exempt from the restriction of having to acquire property productively and contractually.... Marxists are ... correct in noticing the close association between the state and business, especially the banking elite—even though their explanation for it is faulty. The reason is not that the bourgeois establishment sees and supports the state as the guarantor of private property rights and contractualism. On the contrary, the establishment correctly perceives the state as the very antithesis to private property that it is and takes a close interest in it for this reason. The more successful a business, the larger the potential danger of governmental exploitation, but the larger also the potential gains that can be achieved if it can come under government's special protection and is exempt from the full weight of capitalist competition. This is why the business establishment is interested in the state and its infiltration.

Cf. also Walter E. Grinder and John Hagel III, "Toward a Theory of State Capitalism: Ultimate Decision-Making and Class Structure," *Journal of Libertarian Studies*, vol. 1, no. 1 (1977), pp. 59–79.

[58] Alexander Berkman, "The ABC of Anarchism," in Gene Fellner, ed., *Life of an Anarchist: The Alexander Berkman Reader* (New York: Four Walls Eight Windows, 1992), p. 300:

> Individualist anarchists and Mutualists believe in individual ownership as against the communist anarchists who see in the institution of private property one of the main sources of injustice and inequality, of poverty and misery.... But, as stated, Individualist anarchists and Mutualists disagree with the communist anarchist on this point. They assert that the source of economic inequality is monopoly, and they argue that monopoly will disappear with the abolition of government, because it is special privilege—given and protected by government—which makes monopoly possible. Free competition, they claim, would do away with monopoly and its evils.

[59] *Ibid.*, p. 285.
[60] Friedrich Engels, "Versus the Anarchists," in Tucker, ed., *The Marx-Engels Reader*, pp. 728–29:

> Bakunin ... has a peculiar theory of his own, a medley of Proudhonism and communism, the chief point of which is, in the first place, that he does not regard capital—and therefore the class antagonism between capitalists and wage-workers which has arisen through social development—but the *state* as the main evil to be abolished. While ... our view [is] that the state power is nothing more than the organisation with which the ruling classes—landlords and capitalists—have provided themselves in order to pro-

But while the LibSoc tradition has its Chomskyan defenders of the Plutocracy-Dominant position and its Berkmanite defenders of the Statocracy-Dominant position, it is probably fair to say that most Lib-Socs have taken the intermediate Neither-Dominant position, regarding concentrated economic power and concentrated political power as co-ordinate evils to be combated, neither more fundamental than the other.[61] Yet while LibSocs are more likely than LibCaps to adopt this view, it has had its LibCap adherents. For example, the individualist anarchist Benjamin Tucker (1854–1939)—essentially a LibCap, despite some Lib-Soc elements in his thought—seems to have moved from a Statocracy-Dominant to a Neither-Dominant position as his thought developed:

> The high water mark of [Tucker's] repute was his appearance as the spokesman for anarchism at the Conference of Trusts held by the Chicago Civic Federation late in the summer of 1899. . . . In an environment in which his fellow speakers shared the conviction that the remedy for the trust problem lay in the extension of gov-ernmental restriction and supervision, Tucker [argued] that the trusts of their time were not the result of competition, but due to the denial of competition through other than economic means. . . . Mo-nopolies were created by the state through patent, copyright, and tariff legislation, through the system of land grants and centraliza-tion of finance in the hands of a few. . . . He concluded by re-emphasizing his belief that the money monopoly was the most serious, and that "perfect freedom in finance would wipe out nearly all the trusts." . . . [But in later years] Tucker gradually lost enthu-siasm, and in a postscript to a 1911 London edition of his *State Socialism and Anarchism*, he admitted that the anarchist solution for monopoly and the centralization of economic power in the hands of a minority was no longer applicable. . . . Admitted Tucker, "The trust is now a monster which . . . even the freest competition, could it be instituted, would be unable to destroy," since upon the re-moval of all existing restrictions on competition, "concentrated cap-

---

tect their social privileges, Bakunin maintains that it is the *state* which has created capital, that the capitalist has his capital *only by the grace of the state*. As, therefore, the state is the chief evil, it is above all the state which must be done away with and then capitalism will go to blazes of itself. We, on the contrary, say: Do away with capital, the concentration of all means of production in the hands of the few, and the state will fall of itself.

[61] We can identify optimistic and pessimistic versions of this thesis. The optimistic version is that plutocracy and statocracy arise together and depend on each other, so that to vanquish one is to vanquish both. The pessimistic version is that each one is capable of exercising domination even in the absence of the other. The optimistic version seems to have greater affinity with the Statocracy-Dominant view than the pessimistic version has. Henceforth when I speak of the Neither-Dominant view I shall mean the pessimistic version.

ital" could set aside a sacrifice fund to remove any new competitors and continue the process of expansion of reserves.[62]

In other words, Tucker came to believe that a sufficient concentration of wealth could manage to stifle competition and retain its dominant position even in the absence of governmental assistance.[63] Most LibCaps, however, retain confidence in either the Statocracy-Only or Statocracy-Dominant positions.

The differing attitudes of LibCaps, LibPops, and LibSocs concerning the relation between statocracy and plutocracy help to explain the ways in which these movements can be tempted to compromise with their authoritarian counterparts. If Libertarian Socialists and Libertarian Populists have sometimes flirted with authoritarian statism (of the leftist and rightist varieties, respectively), the tendency to downplay the importance of the statocratic class is part of the reason. If Libertarian Capitalists have sometimes soft-pedaled the influence of corporate power, the tendency to downplay the importance of the plutocratic class is part of the reason. LibSocs have on occasion acted as apologists for Marxist regimes. Also, political activists with strong LibSoc leanings (I am thinking of American figures like Ralph Nader and Jerry Brown) frequently call for a larger and more powerful government, while even Noam Chomsky, the self-professed anarchist and foe of all concentrated power, advocates national health care and public control of the airwaves. These positions are motivated in large part by the perception that the power of the plutocracy is the real evil to be combated, and that the danger from statocracy is comparatively minor. This opens the door to authoritarian socialism.

LibPops largely share the LibSoc focus on the evils of plutocracy, but with a difference. LibSocs tend to think of business power as an *institutional* or *systemic* problem; but LibPops, in part because of their religious concerns, are more likely to see it in *personal* terms, as a matter of wickedness in high places. Hence, LibPops are more prone to conspiracy theories than are LibSocs.[64] But seeing social problems as deriving from

[62] James J. Martin, *Men against the State: The Expositors of Individualist Anarchism in America, 1827–1908* (Colorado Springs: Ralph Myles, 1970), pp. 271–73.

[63] Another LibCap who may endorse a version of the Neither-Dominant position is Herbert Spencer, who, despite his well-known conquest theory of state origination, traces the origin of class domination not to the organized violence of a state or proto-state, but rather to the division of labor—above all, to the division of labor between the sexes, which leads to the oppression of women by men. It is with the subjection of women, Spencer argues, that a distinction between ruling and ruled classes first emerges. (Spencer, *The Principles of Sociology*, vol. 2 [New York: D. Appleton, 1884], pp. 288–91, 643–46.) Spencer looks forward to an eventual end to class domination, but he puts his faith less in market forces than in the progressive moral development of the human race. (For other versions of the conquest theory of state origination, see Franz Oppenheimer, *The State*, trans. John Gitterman [Montreal: Black Rose, 1975]; and Alexander Rüstow, *Freedom and Domination: A Historical Critique of Civilization*, trans. Salvator Attanasio [Princeton: Princeton University Press, 1980].)

[64] Conspiracy theories as such should not necessarily be regarded as inherently suspect. After all, the greater the extent to which power is *concentrated* in a society, the easier it is to

the immorality of individuals rather than from system-wide incentives makes LibPops more amenable to the idea that the system might work if *good* people took it over; it also makes them more susceptible to the suggestion that perhaps it is the wrong *cultural* or *ethnic* groups that have gotten in power. This opens the door to authoritarian populism.

On the other side, LibCaps' tendency to deemphasize the power of plutocracy can lead them to severely underestimate the maleficent influence of big business in society, and to downplay the plight of the poor. LibCaps, especially conservative-leaning ones, can be too quick to see existing capitalism as an approximation to the free market they cherish, and to defend it accordingly. When LibCaps blame the government for harming the poor, they are all too likely to use the conservative argument that handouts create a welfare mentality and a culture of dependence, without the distinctively libertarian supplement that government regulations actually *prevent* the poor from rising out of poverty.

Insufficient sensitivity to the power of plutocracy can also lead LibCaps to be peculiarly blind to the reasons that free trade is opposed by many LibPops and LibSocs. LibCaps argue that when big corporations decide to cut costs by increasing their reliance on inexpensive foreign parts and labor, domestic laborers and producers of parts may indeed suffer an income loss as the price of their goods and services is pushed down by foreign competition, but that loss in income that they face in their role as laborers and producers will be offset by the lower prices they face in their role as consumers. But this argument assumes that the big corporations will pass their savings on to their customers. This is something they will indeed be compelled to do in a vigorously competitive market, to avoid being undersold by rival firms; but if government regulations tend to insulate the big corporations from competition, those corporations can pocket the savings with impunity. Citizens will receive lower incomes in their role as producers, without seeing any compensating drop in prices in their role as consumers. So when LibSocs and LibPops describe free trade as a redistribution from small manufacturers to giant corporations, they are often quite right. The answer LibCaps should be giving is that the fault lies not with free trade (the presence of foreign competition) but with regulation (the strangling of domestic competition); but instead Lib-Caps all too often dismiss protectionist arguments as motivated by an irrational anti-business bias.

An excessively rosy view of actually existing capitalism has also led LibCaps—who were once in the vanguard of the struggle for women's

---

form an effective conspiracy (because the number of people that need to be involved to pull off a major change is smaller); so we should predict that more conspiracies will indeed occur in societies with centralized power. However, it is also true that incentive structures can coordinate human activities in ways that involve no conscious cooperation. LibPops seem to see the visible hand everywhere; LibSocs are more aware of invisible-hand explanations, and thus tend to produce somewhat more sophisticated analyses.

equality—to be quite insensitive to the obstacles faced by women in the marketplace. This is true even among those LibCaps with the highest feminist consciousness. For example, Wendy McElroy, a self-described "individualist feminist," writes:

> The notion of women as a distinct class presents a difficult problem for Marxists. Orthodox Marxism distinguishes classes solely according to economic criteria (the ownership of the means of production), not according to sexual characteristics. By this theory, women belong either to the exploited working class or to the exploiting ruling class; individual women can be laborers or capitalists. There is no unity provided by sharing a common sex. It is therefore difficult for Marxists to define women as a sex.
>
> Marxist feminists have offered different solutions to this dilemma. The most popular of these seems to be the postulating of a dual system; capitalism and patriarchy are viewed as separate systems which coexist and support each other. Thus, women can be categorized not only according to their economic status as workers, but also according to sex.[65]

This solution seems plausible enough; but McElroy will have none of it:

> Feminism is based on the idea of women as a "class." ... The libertarian theory of justice applies to all human beings regardless of secondary characteristics such as sex or color. Every human being has moral jurisdiction over his or her own body. To the extent that laws infringe upon self-ownership, they are unjust. To the extent that such violation is based upon sex, there is room for a libertarian feminist movement. Women become a political class not due to their sexual characteristics but because the government directs laws against them as a group. As a political class, feminism is a response to the legal discrimination women have suffered from the state. ... Although discrimination may always occur on an individual level, it is only through the political means that such discrimination can be institutionalized and maintained by force.[66]

McElroy seems unwilling to consider the possibility of institutionalized discrimination not supported by state action. In general, because of their focus on combating statocracy, LibCaps often have trouble recognizing entrenched power except when it comes attached to some governmental office. This may also explain why in recent years some writers associated with the LibCap movement have been attracted to theories of innate

[65] McElroy, *Freedom, Feminism, and the State*, pp. 21–22.
[66] *Ibid.*, pp. 22–23.

sexual and racial superiority.[67] If women and minorities systematically lose out on the market, despite the absence of explicitly discriminatory laws aimed at impeding their success, then this failure cannot be the fault of the beloved market—so perhaps it indicates inherent inferiority!

In my judgment, each of the three libertarianisms needs to do two things. First, clean house—that is, free itself from the tendency toward its authoritarian counterpart. Second, enter into dialogue with the other two libertarianisms, to gain a better understanding of its rivals' positions[68] and to correct some of the one-sidedness in its own.

V. Two Cheers for Smith, One Cheer for Rousseau

As we have seen, on the issue of what a ruling class is and how it achieves and maintains power, there is a spectrum of possible positions from Plutocracy-Only at one end to Statocracy-Only at the other. Plutocracy-Only is rejected by almost all libertarians. As for the remaining views, the portion of the spectrum ranging from Plutocracy-Dominant through Neither-Dominant to Statocracy-Dominant is largely the domain of Lib-Socs and LibPops, while the remainder of the spectrum from Statocracy-Dominant to Statocracy-Only is occupied primarily by LibCaps. Plutocracy-Only, Plutocracy-Dominant, and Statocracy-Only have been seen to rest on highly unrealistic assumptions about human nature. This leaves the field to be disputed between the Statocracy-Dominant and Neither-Dominant positions. Which should libertarians favor?

I suggest that neither contestant is adequate. The Statocracy-Dominant position underestimates, while the Neither-Dominant position overestimates, the ability of wealthy elites to maintain dominance in the absence of government favoritism. The truth, I hope to show, lies in a position intermediate between the two, which I shall accordingly call the Statocracy-Mostly-Dominant view.

The fatal flaw in the Statocracy-Dominant view is its limited historical applicability. The political communities of the classical world—the city-states of Greece, as well as the Roman Republic—had surprisingly weak and decentralized governments, with nothing we would recognize as a police force.[69] Yet, notoriously, these city-states were class societies, in which powerful elites managed to maintain dominance. The same is true of medieval Iceland, whose political institutions were so decentralized

---

[67] I am thinking in particular of Michael Levin and Charles Murray. See Michael E. Levin, *Feminism and Freedom* (New Brunswick: Transaction Books, 1987); Richard J. Herrnstein and Charles Murray, *The Bell Curve: Intelligence and Class Structure in American Life* (New York: Free Press, 1994).

[68] Currently each tends to accept a distorted stereotype of the other two. More specifically, each libertarian group tends to be seen, by the other two, through the lens of its authoritarian counterpart: LibSocs are seen as Stalinists, LibCaps as fascists, LibPops as neo-Nazis.

[69] A regular police force was not introduced in Rome until the Empire, during the reign of Augustus.

that they hardly count as a government at all. Where did the power of the ruling class come from, if not from a powerful state?

The most plausible answer has been offered by the historian Moses Finley: ruling classes maintained their power through the device of *patronage:*

> The ancient city-state had no police other than a relatively small number of publicly owned slaves at the disposal of the different magistrates [and] the army was not available for large-scale police duties until the city-state was replaced by a monarchy. . . . The ancient city-state was a citizen militia, in existence as an army only when called up for action against the external world. [Yet] a Greek city-state or Rome was normally able to enforce governmental decisions. . . . If Greek and Roman aristocrats were neither tribal chieftains nor feudal war lords, then their power must have rested on something else . . . [namely,] their wealth and the ways in which they could disburse it.[70]

In effect, the wealthy classes kept control not through organized violence but by buying off the poor. Each wealthy family would have a large following of commoners who served their patrons' interests (e.g., supporting aristocratic policies in the public assembly) in exchange for the family's largesse.

Finley offers an example from Athens:

> [Solon established] the right given to a third party to intervene in a lawsuit on behalf of someone who had been wronged. . . . No classical state ever established a sufficient governmental machinery by which to secure the appearance of a defendant in court or the execution of a judgment in private suits. Reliance on self-help was therefore compulsory and it is obvious that such a situation created unfair advantages whenever the opponents were unequal in the resources they could command. The Solonic measure and [similar] Roman institutions . . . were designed to reduce the grosser disparities, characteristically by a patronage device rather than by state machinery.[71]

This aristocratic device of offering to defend the suits of the poor and weak has been used in more recent societies too as a means of consolidating power; consider the case of Anglo-Saxon England. As Tom Bell writes:

---

[70] M. I. Finley, *Politics in the Ancient World* (Cambridge: Cambridge University Press, 1994), pp. 18–24, 45.
[71] *Ibid.,* p. 107.

Two factors prepared the stage [for political centralization]. First, the constant threat of foreign invasion, particularly the Danes, had concentrated power in the hands of England's defenders. Second, the influence of Christianity imbued the throne with a godly quality, allowing kings to claim a divine mandate. Onto this stage strode Alfred, king of Wessex, during the last quarter of the ninth century. [Alfred] volunteered to champion the cause of the weak—for a fee. Weak victims sometimes found it difficult to convince their much stronger offenders to appear before the court. Kings balanced the scales by backing the claims of such plaintiffs. This forced brazen defendants to face the court, where they faced the usual fines *plus* a surcharge that went to the king for his services. [This] made enforcing the law a profitable business. King Alfred, strengthened by threat of invasion and emboldened by his holy title, assumed the duty of preventing all fighting within his kingdom. He did this by extending the special jurisdiction which the king had always exercised over his own household to cover the old Roman highways and eventually the entire kingdom.[72]

By beginning the process of political centralization in England, King Aelfred (or Alfred) paved the way for the loss of English liberty; for when the Norman invaders conquered England two centuries later, they found an embryonic centralized structure already in place for them to take over—a skeleton to which they quickly added flesh.

Note Bell's reference to the threat of Viking invasions from Denmark as a factor contributing to Aelfred's power. The threat of war played a similar role in early Republican Rome. Whenever the plebeians seemed on the verge of winning too many political concessions, the patricians would endeavor to involve Rome in a war. This gave the patricians an excuse to put off the plebeians' demands in the name of national unity. The Roman historian Livy describes a typical instance:

[The tribunes advanced] a bill by which the people should be empowered to elect to the consulship such men as they thought fit. . . . The senatorial party felt that if such a bill were to become law, it would mean not only that the highest office of state would have to be shared with the dregs of society but that it would, in effect, be lost to the nobility and transferred to the commons. It was with great satisfaction, therefore, that the Senate received a report . . . that troops from Veii had raided the Roman frontier. . . . [T]he Senate ordered an immediate raising of troops and a general mobilization on the largest possible scale . . . in the hope that the revolutionary proposals which the tribunes were bringing forward might be forgotten. . . . Canuleius

---

[72] Tom Bell, "Polycentric Law," *Humane Studies Review*, vol. 7, no. 1 (1991/92), p. 5.

[the tribune] replied . . . that it was useless for the consuls to try to scare the commons from taking an interest in the new proposals, and [declared] that they should never, while he lived, hold a levy [for military service] until the commons had voted on the reforms. . . .[73]

As Livy indicates, involving Rome in a war also gave the plebeians some leverage; for they could refuse to march to war until their demands were satisfied. Such situations often deteriorated into games of chicken between the patricians and the plebeians: the patricians would refuse to yield, and the plebeians would refuse to arm, while the enemy marched closer and closer. Eventually one or the other would lose nerve first; the patricians would give in and accept the tribunes' reforms, or else the plebeians would agree to fight off the enemy without having gained the desired concessions. But the patricians must presumably have won these games more often than they lost them—because it was almost always the patricians who initiated them. (And even the patricians' losses were seldom serious. For example, the plebeians eventually won the concession to which Livy refers—the right to elect plebeians to the consulship—but thanks to an effective patronage system, the plebeians almost always elected patricians to the office anyway.)[74]

States fight wars because those who make the decision to go to war (or create the climate that makes other nations likely to go to war against them) are distinct from those who bear the primary costs of the war. (The internal class structure of states thus makes it a mistake to treat potentially adversarial states as if they faced incentives to cooperate analogous to those faced by potentially adversarial individuals.) We have seen in the Roman case that a ruling class can use war to advance its agenda even in the absence of strong centralized power.

Even in the modern nation-state, which does *not* suffer from a lack of centralized power, the influence of statocracy and plutocracy alike depends at least as much on old-style patronage as on the direct use of force. As the sixteenth-century political theorist Étienne de la Boétie pointed out in his classic *Discourse of Voluntary Servitude*, no government can wield enough coercive force to subdue an unwilling populace; thus, even the absolutist monarchy of Renaissance France rested in the end on patronage:

> It is not the troops on horseback, it is not the companies afoot, it is not arms that defend the tyrant. This does not seem credible on first thought, but it is nevertheless true that there are only four or five who maintain the dictator, four or five who keep the country in

[73] Livy, *The Early History of Rome*, trans. Aubrey de Sélincourt (London: Penguin, 1988), p. 269.

[74] That is why in classical times aristocratic political parties in Greece and Rome always preferred elections over the Athenian practice of choosing officials by lot.

bondage to him. Five or six have always had access to his ear, and have either gone to him of their own accord, or else have been summoned by him, to be accomplices in his cruelties, companions in his pleasures, panders to his lusts, and sharers in his plunders. . . . The six have six hundred who profit under them. . . . The six hundred maintain under them six thousand, whom they promote in rank, upon whom they confer the government of provinces or the direction of finances. . . . And whoever is pleased to unwind the skein will observe that not the six thousand but a hundred thousand, and even millions, cling to the tyrant by this cord to which they are tied.[75]

The problem for the Statocracy-Dominant view, then, is this: since patronage appears to be an effective tool for maintaining class privilege even in the absence of a powerful state, then even if the power of the statocracy were broken, so long as economic inequalities were not abolished at the same time, would not the rich be able to maintain the status of a plutocratic ruling class by buying off the poor (and perhaps use this power to reestablish a statocracy as well)?

Yet we should not be too quick to rush to the Neither-Dominant view instead. There is an important kernel of truth in the Statocracy-Dominant view that the Neither-Dominant view ignores. Consider all the ways in which the statocracy holds down the poor and prevents them from rising through their own abilities: minimum-wage laws increase the cost to businesses of hiring unskilled workers, and thus decrease the supply of such jobs, causing unemployment; rent-control laws increase the cost to landlords of providing housing, and thus decrease the supply of such housing, causing homelessness; licensure laws, zoning restrictions, and other regulations make it nearly impossible for the poor to start their own businesses.[76] All these laws conspire, whether by intention or otherwise, to entrench the more affluent in their current positions by keeping the poor poor and unable to compete.[77] Similar principles apply higher up the economic ladder, as tax laws and economic regulations entrench the power of big corporations by insulating them from competition by smaller businesses (and incidentally helping to ossify the favored corporations into sluggish, hierarchical, inefficient, irresponsible monoliths). Having rendered the poor unable to help themselves effectively, government then

---

[75] Étienne de la Boétie, *The Politics of Obedience: The Discourse of Voluntary Servitude*, trans. Harry Kurz (New York: Free Life Editions, 1975), pp. 77–78.

[76] Two examples: urban black teenagers have been prosecuted for offering hair-braiding services without benefit of expensive beauticians' degrees; and in many cities, a taxi license costs as much as $100,000. Such low-capital enterprises as hair-braiding and taxi service are natural avenues for people of modest means to start earning money and achieving independence; but the coercive power of the state closes such avenues off.

[77] I do not mean to imply that these results were consciously aimed at by the wealthy. Rather, plutocratic interests frequently shape public policy unintentionally, via the "malign invisible hand" mechanism described earlier (in Section IV).

makes itself seem indispensable to them by giving them handouts via welfare;[78] but at the same time, the state is vigorously redistributing money *up* the economic ladder via corporate welfare and the like.[79]

Moreover, in addition to crippling the poor, government *magnifies* the power of the wealthy. Suppose Daddy Warbucks wants to achieve some goal that costs one million dollars. Under a free-market system, Warbucks has to cough up one million of his own dollars in order to achieve this goal. If a powerful state is present, however, Warbucks has the option of (directly or indirectly) bribing some politicians or bureaucrats to the tune of a few *thousand* dollars to persuade them to divert a million dollars of taxpayers' money to Warbucks's favored project. Since the politicians are spending other people's money rather than their own, they lose nothing by the deal.

Centralized state power—in its *effects*, regardless of its intentions—is Robin Hood in reverse: it robs from the poor and gives to the rich.[80] Government regulation has the same effect on the economy that molasses has on an engine: it slows everything down. The more hoops one has to jump through in order to start a new venture—permits, licenses, taxes, fees, mandates, building codes, zoning restrictions, etc.—the fewer new ventures will be started. And the least affluent will be hurt the most. The richest corporations can afford to jump through the hoops; they have money to pay the fees and lawyers to figure out the regulations. Small businesses have a tougher time, and so are at a comparative disadvantage. For the poor, starting a business is close to impossible. Thus, the

[78] This leads conservatives, and some conservative-leaning LibCaps, to see the poor as beneficiaries of statism—parasites feeding at the public trough. A more realistic assessment would see the poor as net losers, since the benefits received through welfare are rarely large enough to compensate for the harms inflicted through regulation.

[79] For example, the recent debate over farm policy in the United States has largely ignored the fact that most agricultural subsidies go to giant agribusiness conglomerates rather than to family farms. Another example is government support for higher education—a benefit received disproportionately by members of the middle class, yet funded through taxes by lower-class workers who cannot afford to postpone their earnings for four years. But one of the worst instances of upward redistribution is inflation, caused by government manipulation of the currency. An increase in the money supply results in an increase in prices and wages—but not immediately. There is some lag time as the effects of the expansion radiate outward through the economy. Under central banking, the rich—i.e., banks, and those to whom banks lend—get the new money *first*, before prices have risen. They systematically benefit, because they get to spend their new money before prices have risen to reflect the expansion. The poor systematically lose out, since they get the new money *last*, and thus have to face higher prices *before* they have higher salaries. (Moreover, the asymmetrical effects of monetary expansion create artificial booms and busts, as different sectors of the economy are *temporarily* stimulated by early receipt of the new money, encouraging over-investment that goes bust when the boom proves illusory. The unemployment caused by this misdirection hurts the poor most of all.)

[80] "The high cost of aggression makes it a tool of the rich. Only the well-to-do can afford to lobby, bribe, or threaten our elected representatives effectively." Mary Ruwart, *Healing Our World: The Other Piece of the Puzzle*, rev. ed. (Kalamazoo: SunStar, 1993), p. 154. Ruwart's book is a rich source of examples of how big government tends to help the wealthy and hurt the poor.

system favors the rich over the middle class, and the middle class over the poor.

When one considers the enormous extent to which the wealthy owe to state intervention their position of dominance over the poor and middle class, it is hard to believe there isn't *some* truth to the Statocracy-Dominant view. Surely the elimination of statocratic rule would *have* to shift the balance of power between rich and poor much farther in the poor's favor than is the case today. These arguments suggest the Smithians were on to something. On the other hand, history shows us that the power of patronage gives the rich substantial clout even in the absence of governmental favoritism; so the Statocracy-Dominant view cannot be the whole story. Classes should not be defined in solely economic terms *or* in solely political terms.[81] There are groups in society who depend heavily on the power of the state for their dominant position, but who would still pose a serious threat to liberty even in the absence of state favoritism. Libertarians need to think seriously about ways of checking their power.

For LibSocs and LibPops, this might involve using compulsory means to eliminate certain socioeconomic inequalities; but, ethical worries aside, the question is whether this can be practically achieved without a centralized state apparatus of the sort that we have seen tends to become inherently exploitative itself. For LibCaps, coercive expropriation of the wealthy is not an option, but in that case LibCaps need to consider what capitalistically permissible resources may be available to them to combat the problem.[82] This is a problem that libertarians of all schools need to explore in light of the fact that plutocratic power is *largely* but *not solely* dependent on statocratic power. (As I've noted, I call this the Statocracy-Mostly-Dominant view.)

---

[81] An adequate theory of class would also have to distinguish more groups than just "rulers" and "ruled." As Chomsky writes: "[T]o do a really serious class analysis, you can't just talk about the ruling class. Are the professors at Harvard part of the ruling class? Are the editors of the *New York Times* part of the ruling class? Are the bureaucrats in the State Department? There are differentiations, a lot of different categories of people" (*Keeping the Rabble in Line*, p. 109). Dividing the ruling class into statocratic and plutocratic factions is valuable as a start, but only as a start.

Libertarian sociologist Phil Jacobson, whose work draws on both the LibCap and LibSoc traditions, is making some valuable developments in this area. Jacobson distinguishes three main groups: the Idea, Force, and Wealth classes. These basically correspond to the priests, warriors, and merchants of traditional class theory: Plato's philosopher-kings, auxiliaries, and craftsmen; India's brahmins, kshatriyas, and vaishyas. In turn, each of these three groups is subdivided into two factions with somewhat divergent interests. The Wealth class is divided into a symbol-manipulation component (e.g., banking and finance) and a physical-reality component (e.g., actual manufacturing). The Force class is likewise divided into a symbol-manipulation component (e.g., politicians) and a physical-reality component (e.g., police and the military). The Idea class is all symbol-manipulation, but can be divided into elite-culture and popular-culture groups (i.e., intellectuals versus entertainers). Jacobson analyzes social change in terms of the interaction and shifting alliances among these six groups.

[82] Perhaps the ancient republican theorists—particularly the Athenian democrats (as opposed to the more oligarchy-friendly proponents of the "mixed constitution")—deserve a second look.

There may be grounds for optimism, though. Patronage might pose less of a threat in a modern, industrialized, commercial society than in ancient Rome or medieval Europe. Perhaps such earlier societies, despite their nearly stateless character, failed to develop in a libertarian direction because they came closer to having only a fixed pie of resources to fight over. Conceivably, the release of creative energy made possible by the Industrial Revolution, together with the rapid increase in the standard of living which resulted for the working classes, and the accompanying social mobility that upset traditional hierarchies, has made a ruling class impossible without the aid of a centralized state.

The increasing pluralization of society may be a positive factor as well. In the passage on King Aelfred quoted earlier, Bell noted that religious ideas about royal authority helped the English kings to centralize their power. Religion was a similar factor in Rome, where the patricians were also the priestly class, being the only ones permitted to "take the auspices" (an official ceremony of divination required at most public occasions). We find a similar development in stateless Iceland, where the *godhar* (chieftains) who ruled via patronage were also priests—first pagan and later Christian.[83] In a society characterized by religious uniformity, it is much easier for a single group to claim a religious (or other traditional) sanction for its authority. By contrast, in modern society, with its religious, ethnic, and cultural diversity, it would be much harder for any single group to succeed in demanding allegiance.[84]

VI. COLLECTIVE ACTION: A PUZZLE FOR LIBERTARIAN CAPITALISTS

The whole question of class is intimately related to the issue of collective action, for it is by collective action that a ruling class maintains power—and likewise by collective action, sometimes, that a ruling class is overthrown. How easy, or difficult, would collective action be in a libertarian society? LibCaps, in particular, seem to be committed to giving inconsistent answers to this question. When the collective action in question is something good or desirable, LibCaps are confident that market incentives and natural human sympathies will unite to bring the collective action about without the need for coercive coordination from government. But when it comes to harmful or unpleasant collective action (including the formation of a plutocratic ruling class), this, LibCaps are sure, can flourish only with the help of state intervention, and will quickly

[83] And when they were not Christian priests, they at least maintained exclusive control over Church lands—and their associated tithe revenues.

[84] The role of ideology in supporting a ruling class is considerable. "An exploiter creates victims, and victims are potential enemies. It is possible that this resistance can be lastingly broken down by force, as, for example, in the case of a group of men exploiting another group of roughly the same size. However, more than force is needed to expand exploitation over a population many times [the exploiter's] own size. For this to happen, a firm must also have public support. A majority of the population must accept the exploitative actions as legitimate" (Hoppe, "Marxist and Austrian Class Analysis" [*supra* note 57], pp. 84–85).

wither and die when exposed to the light of freedom and economic rationality.

Consider the problem of racial and sexual discrimination. Discriminatory hiring practices represent a form of collective action, in that a pattern of discrimination against the same groups occurs in society.[85] Discrimination is a problem that LibCaps like to think would be solved by the free market. Firms that choose their employees on the basis of race and gender, instead of on the basis of merit, will end up with a less capable workforce, and the firm's overall performance will suffer, thus exposing it to the risk of being edged aside by its competitors. Thus, rational firms, in their pursuit of the economic bottom line, will have to abandon their discriminatory practices on pain of losing out to the competition. In this way, *Homo economicus* comes to the LibCaps' rescue: racism and sexism are simply too expensive. They represent costly luxuries in which a competitive firm cannot afford to indulge—unless governmental favoritism shields it from competition, thus subsidizing bigotry by lowering its cost.

This argument assumes that economic self-interest is likely to be a more powerful motive than such purely emotional motives as racial and sexual prejudice. LibCaps do not always make this assumption, however. When it comes to the provision of public goods, then LibCaps suddenly start to heap scorn on the narrow *Homo economicus* conception of human motivation that had served them in such good stead in the prejudice case. Now LibCaps want to insist that economic self-interest is not the only human motive, that incentives such as conscience and solidarity can override the quest for profit. The relentless concern for the bottom line that turned up so conveniently to impede harmful collective action, now just as conveniently drops out so as not to impede beneficial collective action. What entitles LibCaps to this double standard?

All human motivations can be divided into three categories, which I shall label, rather simplistically, *love, hate,* and *greed*. Under *love* I rank all those motives that have as their end the satisfaction of the legitimate interests of other people. Under *hate* I rank all those motives that have as their end the frustration of those interests. And under *greed* I rank all those motives whose ends make no essential reference to the interests of others one way or the other.[86] (A person acting from greed may harm or benefit others, but only insofar as doing so happens, under the circum-

---

[85] If discrimination did not follow a common pattern, it would be far less problematic. That is, if it were a purely *random* matter which groups were discriminated against by any one employer, then those who experienced discrimination from a given employer could be sure of finding plenty of other employers who lacked that particular prejudice. The prejudice might still be a vice, to be sure, but it would at least be a harmless vice. It is only when there is a consistent and widespread prejudice throughout society against certain groups that members of those groups find themselves *systematically* disadvantaged across the board. This result is what makes discrimination so especially objectionable.

[86] As defined, the three categories are meant to be exhaustive: one either aims to help, or aims to harm, or does not aim at either helping or harming. (The term "greed" is not meant to be pejorative; it is simply a useful shorthand for any motive that does not involve the welfare of others, whether or not that motive is "self-interested" in any strong sense.)

stances, to advance her ends. Greed *as such* is indifferent to the interests of others.)

The first thing we should recognize is that motives of all three varieties are available in plentiful supply. Any account of human nature that emphasizes just one of these motives at the expense of the other two can safely be dismissed as unrealistic.

Now we can see that the standard LibCap responses to the public-goods and prejudice problems seem to assume that greed is stronger than hate but weaker than love. When the racist employer hires the minorities he despises because it is good for business, greed is conquering hate. When the public-spirited citizen contributes to a public good out of a sense of moral duty or community solidarity, love is conquering greed.

It would be delightful, of course, if greed could be counted on to be strong in its conflicts with hate and weak in its conflicts with love. But we know, all too well, that motives of hate can often conquer motives of love; so there is no guarantee that love is always strong and hate is always weak. Thus, it is not implausible that hate should often be strong enough to conquer beneficent greed, or that love should often be too weak to prevail against harmful greed.

A similar tension can be found in LibCap discussions of conflicts between different kinds of greed. Consider the many cases in which it is in my long-term interest to acquire a reputation as a cooperator, while it is in my short-term interest to renege on cooperation just this once. In the absence of statocratic interference, which are people more likely to do?

When the cooperation is a beneficial one, LibCaps rush to say that long-term greed will win out. Citing such works as Robert Axelrod's *The Evolution of Cooperation*, they point out that cooperators, by developing a reliable reputation, will attract a cluster of like-minded cooperators to them, whereas habitual defectors will be shunned and excluded from the benefits of cooperation, so that both market competition and natural selection will tend to make cooperation prevail as a strategy. Actors in the market will realize that the benefits of keeping to a consistent policy of cooperation outweigh the meretricious short-term gains of opportunistic defection.

Sometimes cooperation is not so nice, however, and then LibCaps tend to have a different attitude. Consider the standard LibCap response to the problem of cartels. In an unregulated free market, what would prevent profit-minded firms from joining together and agreeing to keep prices high, or wages low? LibCaps usually answer that once the cartel is in place, it is in the interest of any individual member to break the agreement by selling at a slightly lower price or hiring at a slightly higher wage, so as to win all the other members' business for oneself. Soon, LibCaps like to predict, all the members will be tempted into trying the same strategy, and the cartel will collapse. (For similar reasons, a plutocratic ruling class is supposed to be impotent in the absence of government support.)

But what has now become of the idea that rational individuals will choose to maintain a system of cooperation rather than defect for the sake of immediate gain? Axelrod has been thrown to the winds: short-term greed, so fragile a hindrance to beneficial cooperation, now proves itself a powerful bulwark against harmful cooperation, while long-term greed, on the other hand, has dwindled from its former glory as guardian angel of cooperation, and now is nowhere to be seen.[87] The balance of motivational power between long-term and short-term greed keeps swinging back and forth as needed. This is cause for LibCaps to worry.

The problem I have been describing should make LibCaps uncomfortable, but it should not necessarily drive them to despair. After all, the mechanisms that LibCaps like to trumpet have actually proven successful in the real world in a great many cases.

Consider first the case of prejudice. It is no coincidence that there were Jim Crow *laws* in the pre-civil-rights South. White racists were unwilling to rely on voluntary compliance alone to keep blacks "in their place," and this reluctance on their part was a shrewd one. The famous segregated buses in Montgomery, Alabama, were segregated *by law*, not by the choice of the bus company. In fact, the bus company had petitioned, unsuccessfully, to get the law repealed—not out of love (i.e., concern for the equal rights of blacks) but out of greed (i.e., the policy was costing it customers). So LibCaps are quite right in thinking that racism *can* be undermined by a concern for the bottom line (though it would be naive to assume that it must *always* be so undermined; people do care about things other than money, and some of those things are pretty repugnant).

It is also true, of course, that people voluntarily contribute to good causes all the time. The amount of money given to charity every year (over and above taxes) is staggering. So love frequently does defeat harmful greed, while beneficial greed likewise defeats hate.

Similar remarks apply to the issue of long-term versus short-term greed. On the one hand, beneficial collective action occurs all the time without coordination by government; our cooperative impulses are the product of evolution, and are further reinforced by our social environment. To pick just one example mentioned by Axelrod, soldiers on opposite sides of World War I trench warfare found it in their mutual interest to coordinate their firing patterns in such a way that each side would know when and where the other was going to fire and so could avoid injury. Score one for Axelrod, it seems. On the the other hand, history is full of cartels collaps-

---

[87] This now-you-see-it-now-you-don't phenomenon proves particularly embarrassing for LibCap defenders of free-market anarchism. What ensures that, in the absence of government, private protection agencies will choose to resolve their differences through arbitration rather than violent conflict? The typical answer is: Long-term greed, which recognizes that the value of maintaining a system of cooperation outweighs the value lost by submitting to arbitration. But what ensures that these protection agencies won't merge into a giant cartel, thus, in effect, bringing back government and a new ruling class? The typical answer is: Short-term greed, which undermines cartel agreements in the usual way.

ing because of members' breaking the agreement in order to reap the benefits of underselling; one such defection (by Kuwait against its oil partner Iraq) triggered the Gulf War. Score one against Axelrod, it seems.

These examples may serve to reassure LibCaps that their analyses of collective action problems are not simply drawn from some fantasy world unconnected to reality. But can anything more than this be said for the LibCap position? I think perhaps it can.

We would have stronger reasons for confidence in the prospects for a successful LibCap society if we had some reason to think that the motives for harmful cooperation had some weakness, some fatal flaw, which the motives for beneficial cooperation did not share. I think there is at least one such weakness.

Notice that the motives for harmful cooperation are motives for *selective* cooperation. The white racist who cooperates with other white racists in discriminating against blacks is not taking a cooperative attitude toward the blacks themselves; likewise, those who cooperate to form a cartel are colluding to engage in decidedly noncooperative behavior toward their customers. In both cases, the cooperation in question is cooperation for mutual advantage *within* a select group, and is directed *against* the advantage of those excluded from the group. Such cooperative ventures are easier to undermine *when there is free competition*, because they create a large group of excluded people who have an interest in seeing that cooperation fail, and this group constitutes an attractive market for any entrepreneur interested in defying the cooperative venture.

To be sure, pressure *within* a selectively cooperative venture of the kind I have described may be strong enough to discourage defections. The racist, tempted by profit to hire the qualified black over the unqualified white, may think again when he realizes he will be subject to severe social sanctions from his fellow racists within the community. The pull of the bottom line can be quite limited in the face of social ostracism by one's peers.

But that is precisely why I stress the importance of free competition. The beneficent power of greed in overcoming harmful cooperative ventures lies not so much in its ability to undermine the venture from within, as in its ability to attract rival cooperative ventures to outcompete the bad ones. The white racist who has lived all his life in Kluxville may prefer social conformity to profit, but if the resulting low wages for blacks in the Kluxville area serve as a cheap-labor magnet motivating Amalgamated Widgets to open a new plant in Kluxville, the folks who run Amalgamated Widgets may not care that much if the whites in Kluxville shun them; they already have their own peer group, after all.

The ease with which the greed of outsiders can defeat the hate of the exclusive group (or, switching to the cartel situation, the ease with which the short-term greed of outsiders can defeat the long-term greed of the exclusive group) depends on the degree of competition. If regulations make it extremely difficult to start new ventures or expand old ones, then there will be a smaller number of long-established players, insulated from competition and therefore free to try their hand at harmful cooperation. (It is in this sense that governmental regulation may be described as *subsidizing* racism and cartelization.)[88] The easier it is for a new venture to start up, the easier it is for harmful cooperative ventures to be undermined from without. Assuming free competition is present, it is the *selectivity* of harmful cooperation that sounds its death knell.

Beneficial cooperation is not selective in the same way. That is not to say that a virtuous cooperator cooperates with everyone equally. Any cooperative venture—be it a family, a business, or a political movement—is focusing *more* on the advantage of its participants than on the advantage of outsiders. But that kind of preferential or even competitive concern is not the same thing as a concerted *opposition* to the welfare of outsiders. What creates trouble for the bad cooperative ventures is that they create an aggrieved, excluded class which forms the natural market for a competitor to enter the field. Mere preferential concern alone does not do that.

It might be objected that at least one beneficial cooperative venture, the libertarian legal system itself, creates at least one excluded class: criminals. Doesn't this create an incentive for a competitor to enter the field and offer criminals the wherewithal to fight back against law enforcement?

It surely does. Hence organized crime might exist in a libertarian society. After all, LibCaps are fond of pointing out that governments in effect subsidize organized crime by prohibiting, and thus creating an attractive black market for, such victimless crimes as prostitution and drugs. But a LibCap legal system, whether minarchic or anarchic, would at least prohibit *victimful* crimes (i.e., crimes that *do* have victims) such as murder, theft, assault, rape, arson, fraud, and the like, and thus, by the same reasoning, would create a black market for these crimes.

Still, cooperative ventures against victimful crimes are likely to be more successful than ones against victimless crimes, precisely because the former have a crucial source of support that the latter lack: namely, the *victims* (and potential victims).

A similar point applies to boycotts: some are self-enforcing while others are not.[89] For example, if I have a policy of refusing to do business with anyone who does not belong to my religion, this policy will clash with my financial incentives. The financial incentives may still lose out, of course; but then again they may not. On the other hand, if I have a policy of refusing to do business with people who cheat their customers, my financial incentives are likely to *reinforce* this policy. Choosing criminals as one's target market is risky precisely because people who make a profes-

---

[88] That is why large corporations in America during the "Progressive Era," and racists in South Africa at the beginning of apartheid, were such enthusiastic fans of government regulation.

[89] The distinction was first brought to my attention by Bryan Caplan.

sion out of noncooperative behavior cannot be relied on to cooperate with you either.[90]

It should also be pointed out that the need for beneficial collective action may be overstated. After all, collective action (whether on the basis of love or of long-term greed) is only one way to provide public goods. Another way is to privatize the public good, either absolutely (i.e., by figuring out some way to exclude noncontributors) or else by packaging it with a private good, and using the revenue from the private good to fund the public good (e.g., using advertising to pay for radio and TV broadcasts, or using harbor fees to fund lighthouses). So the fact that beneficial collective action is not 100 percent reliable is no reason for despair, given that the same ends can often be achieved through noncollective means.

Cultural factors can also influence the success or failure of collective action. In general, there are two reasons that collective action can fail. One reason, the reason we have been considering so far, is *motivational*. Collective action can fail because not enough people want to participate in it. But the other reason is *informational*. Suppose everyone in Shangri-la wants to go on a general strike to protest the actions of the government. There is no motivational problem here; everyone wants the same thing. But there is an informational problem: *when* should the strike begin? If only a few people start on their own, they will simply be punished and nothing will be achieved. As in many cases, the acts of resistance must be simultaneous in order to be effective.

This is a coordination problem; and the key to solving such a problem is known as *salience*. The classic illustration of the role of salience is as follows. Suppose you and a friend intend to meet in New York City on a specific date. Unfortunately, neither of you will be able to contact the other ahead of time to arrange a time and place to meet. So you have to try to find your friend (and your friend has to try to find you) with no more specific information than the city and the day.

What should you do? Well, you should go wherever you think your friend would go; but your friend is trying to figure out where *you* would go, so you have to predict what your friend would predict about what you would predict—and so on. The answer most people give—which in effect makes it the right answer—is that you should go to Grand Central Station at noon. In New York, Grand Central Station is an "obvious" meeting place, and noon an "obvious" meeting time. That place and that time *stand out* from their competitors; they have *salience*.

Salience is likewise what the Shangri-la strikers need. If there is a tradition in their culture of going on strike on a certain date, that is the

---

[90] That is one reason that the most successful criminal organizations have been ones whose members shared some ethnic, religious, political, or family connections, making them less likely to defect vis-à-vis each other than vis-à-vis outsiders. That is also why the monarchies of different countries have sought to join their families by marriage.

date to pick. In the absence of any such tradition, something else is needed to provide the salience. That is one function of a *leader*; if there is some one person whom the strikers all respect, that person can *make* a particular date salient by saying, "Let's strike then!"

One might also see salience as a way for people to get themselves from an unproductive cooperative venture into a productive one. After all, resistance to an oppressive regime is an instance of collective action, but so is the existence of that oppressive regime itself. I do not just mean that the rulers in the regime are cooperating with one another; in some sense, the ruled have to be cooperating too in order for the regime to be effective. Rulers have power only so long as people obey them. And why do people obey them? Partly because they think it is their duty to do so, or else because they think they can benefit from government power; to that extent, overthrowing a tyrannical government runs up against a motivation problem. But people also obey partly because everyone is afraid to be the *only* person resisting the government. Even if everyone hates the existing regime, there is still the problem of knowing when and how to resist. In that case, salience can help people escape from a trap of their own making. To switch from obedience to resistance is to switch from one mode of collective action to another; and, as in switching from driving on the right to driving on the left, people are going to get run over unless the switch is made *en masse* rather than one person at a time.

To the extent that prospective cooperators share a common cultural background, it will be easier for them to overcome both the motivational and the informational obstacles to cooperation. Motivationally, people from the same culture are more likely to have similar values and a feeling of solidarity, and thus will be more willing to cooperate with one another. Informationally, it will be easier for people from the same culture to find salient points to build coordination on, since they share either a common tradition or a common set of leaders or both.

Consider a medieval case of collective action. In the Middle Ages, the Catholic Church promulgated the Peace of God (forbidding warfare during certain months of the year) and the Truce of God (forbidding warfare during certain days of the week). These restrictions on warfare were fairly widely observed, with extremely beneficial results to all parties concerned, since adherence to these rules prevented warfare from becoming all-consuming, and allowed the usual business of life—commerce, agriculture, etc.—to continue relatively undisturbed. But this beneficial collective action was possible only because the warring parties shared a common allegiance to the Catholic Church. Their religious faith gave them a motivation to obey the Church, and the Church's authority made the particular provisions of the Peace and the Truce salient. By contrast, when Christians fought Muslims there were no such constraints, because the combatants lacked a shared cultural basis to support anything like a Peace of God or a Truce of God.

Having a common culture makes bad collective action easier too, however. As noted above, adherence to a common religion on the part of the ruled was a large part of what held the ruling classes of ancient and medieval societies in power, since such religions generally taught that those in power ruled by divine right. In a more pluralistic society, it would be much harder for any one group to claim a divine mandate, and so such ruling cliques should be easier to oust.

What, then, are the cultural prospects for collective action, good and bad, in a libertarian society? That depends on whether the world is moving toward or away from cultural unity, and that is not an easy thing to tell. *Within* each society, we see a great deal of pluralization and splintering going on; but we also see a great deal of homogenization going on *between* and *among* societies. So it is difficult to say whether collective action *in general* is going to become easier or more difficult. But at least the arguments I have given do offer us some reason to expect that in the absence of a powerful state, beneficial collective action is easier to maintain than harmful collective action.

This does not mean that libertarians should be complacent about the risks of concentrated power in a free society. The Smithian, Statocracy-Dominant position is false. But there is at least reason to hope that, in the absence of statocracy, a sufficiently alert and vigilant populace may be able to prevent the rise of plutocracy.

VII. Conclusion

Libertarianism is a many-sided movement, comprising capitalist, socialist, and conservative-populist elements, with very little mutual understanding among the separate camps. For those who share the basic libertarian conviction that a radical redistribution of power is needed from the state to freely associated individuals, this lack of mutual dialogue should be seen as unfortunate; and one of the purposes of the present discussion has been to help open a door to such dialogue. The three libertarianisms' differing views on class are at the heart of what divides them from one another, and each camp needs to avoid the distortions of a one-sided vision, and take much more seriously the insights of its rivals. In particular, I have argued that LibCaps need to be more concerned than they traditionally have been with the danger posed by plutocracy, while at the same time, LibPops and LibSocs have much to learn from LibCaps about the ways in which market mechanisms, in the absence of statocratic interference, can undermine plutocracy by fostering good collective action over bad. But more research needs to be done. Libertarianism still needs a theory of class; and its best hope of getting one is to exploit the conceptual and theoretical resources of all three of its main traditions.

Philosophy, University of North Carolina at Chapel Hill

LIBERTARIANISM AS IF (THE OTHER 99 PERCENT OF) PEOPLE MATTERED*

By Loren E. Lomasky

I. Introduction

In this essay I wish to consider the implications for theory and practice of the following two propositions, either or both of which may be controversial, but which will here be assumed for the sake of argument:

(L) Libertarianism is the correct framework for political morality.

(M) The vast majority of our fellow citizens disbelieve (L).[1]

The question I will address is how we as libertarians ought to respond to this pairing. I say *we libertarians* because, as I am using the term here, someone who subscribes to (L) is, definitionally, a libertarian. Of course, one who rejects (L)—or (M)—may, as an exercise in the logic of political theory, scrutinize the relationship between these two propositions. But for those who find themselves members of a political minority that unsteadily oscillates between the minuscule and the merely negligible, the implications are of more than academic interest. They concern nothing less than how one ought to live one's life among others, where the others are substantially more numerous than oneself. This is, then, an investigation not only of libertarian theory but also of libertarian praxis in the actual political world and those possible worlds that are its near neighbors.

It may be useful to say a few words concerning what I do not intend to pursue in this essay. First, I do not intend to argue for the truth of either proposition. In other contexts I have had my say on matters of political justification and on why an order of basic rights that are predominantly rights to noninterference meets the justificatory challenge better than any

* This essay originated in an informal talk presented at *Liberty* magazine's August 1996 conference for editors and readers. Although subsequent discussion revealed considerable disagreement among those assembled with the thesis being advanced, it also suggested that these issues are central to the practical concerns of libertarians both inside and outside the academy. I am grateful to Bill Bradford for affording me the opportunity to launch these ideas in that forum. I am also grateful to my friend, tennis bête noire, and sometimes editor, Ellen Frankel Paul, for freeing this essay from numerous syntactic infelicities and for conceding, albeit grudgingly, that the argument of this essay does not entirely disqualify its author from the title *libertarian*.

[1] The labels are mnemonic, indicating, respectively, the truth of the *L*ibertarian credo and the rejection of this credo by the *M*ajority of the citizenry.

alternative political order.[2] It is difficult to find an academic libertarian who has not done something similar. That this project is meritorious is not disputed, but it is not the project of this essay. Nor is the project to offer a definition, or necessary conditions, or even a rough-and-ready characterization of the essence of libertarianism. I well understand that libertarians tend to argue furiously among themselves concerning which is the most pristine expression of that theory. I will have some things to say about the symptoms of that debate, but I will not attempt to resolve who are the real libertarians and who the imposters. Rather, for purposes of the argument that follows it will suffice to lend maximum latitude to the term "libertarian." Some libertarians insist that only under anarchy can respect for basic rights and nonaggression be realized. Others countenance a state that scrupulously refrains from any undertakings other than those of the night watchman. Still other libertarians are willing to add to the legitimate scope of the political entity provision of some public goods (beyond those that the minimum state includes in its protective package) and perhaps also relief of extremes of exigency. This, I believe, brings us to the far boundaries of moderate libertarianism.[3] But there is no need to erect the bar here, at least not for the purposes of this discussion. For the sake of argument, let us stipulate that a *much more expansive* state, one that commandeers a level of resources up to half of that claimed by America in the 1990s (say, 20 percent of gross domestic product), squeezes into the big libertarian tent. Let it additionally be stipulated that a state proscribing a few marginal capitalistic acts between consenting adults[4] will count as libertarian under this expansive definition. For example, if the polity refuses to enforce contracts by means of which one sells oneself into slavery, or if its criminal statutes prohibit the practice of blackmail for pecuniary remuneration, it is not thereby excluded as a matter of definition from the libertarian ranks. If the perimeter of libertarianism is stretched in this way, well beyond what virtually every self-described libertarian advocates as the limits of state action, we remain within the comfort zone of the application of (M). It may be that such a profligately expansive conception will raise the level of support for libertarian policies among the general population to 2 or even 3 percent. But that is still low enough to ground a tension between (L) and (M).

Just what is meant by describing libertarianism as the correct theory of politics also merits philosophical investigation, but that too will be skirted here. Is it to maintain that the libertarian credo (in its optimal statement, whatever that might be) is *true* in the sense that the sentence "Snow is

---

[2] See especially my *Persons, Rights, and the Moral Community* (New York: Oxford University Press, 1987).

[3] In the interest of full disclosure, I announce that my own view falls within such moderate libertarianism.

[4] Robert Nozick's wonderful coinage; see his *Anarchy, State, and Utopia* (New York: Basic Books, 1974).

white" is true if and only if snow is white? Or is it to say something about the *justifiability* of libertarianism in terms of the actual or hypothetical assent of all agents, or all maximally rational agents, or all maximally rational and reasonable agents? Concerning these issues, too, I wish to be as noncommittal as it is possible to be while nonetheless saying something interesting about the relationship between (L) and (M). That means that I will not be able to adopt a stance of complete neutrality concerning what moral propositions are *about*, what they are *for*. I do believe, though, that most of the genuinely vexing issues that separate, say, moral realists from nonrealists can be set aside.

Some will dispute the truth of (M). The perpetual location in electoral tabulations of the Libertarian Party somewhere between Ross Perot and Mickey Mouse,[5] decidedly closer to the latter than the former, will be dismissed by some as quite epiphenomenal, not really indicative of underlying sentiment. I have heard this view espoused both by ardent libertarian activists and by the viscerally anti-libertarian. The former are wont to bring to state fairs diagrams with the four corners assigned political labels, one representing the libertarian dispensation and the others combinations of economic and/or civil-liberties authoritarianism. When unwary visitors wander away from displays of apple pies and champion hogs and come within arm's reach of the libertarian booth, they are found to reject at cheeringly high levels these various authoritarianisms. Voilà! They discover that not only have they been speakers of prose all along, they also have been libertarians. Similarly, those who fear the capture and subsequent dismantling of the state by cutlass-wielding libertarian buccaneers also find libertarians everywhere.[6] Here, as elsewhere, pleasant daydreams converge with chilling nightmares. The methodologies that generate these counterintuitive results are, I must confess, beyond my ken. If they should nonetheless prove to have been accurate, I shall be delighted to concede that the thesis of this essay has been rendered moot. Those who deny or doubt the truth of (M) are invited to transpose the investigation that follows into a conditional mode: What *would be implied* if both (L) and (M) obtained?

II. THE TENSION BETWEEN (L) AND (M)

So much by way of preliminaries. I now proceed to considering what may be elicited from the pairing of propositions (L) and (M). One moral

---

[5] It is, admittedly, a disputable question of metaphysics whether these "two" candidates are in fact numerically distinct.

[6] I am serving, for reasons that are not entirely clear to me, on a scholar's panel of the Commission on Civic Renewal co-chaired by William Bennett and Sam Nunn. At our initial meeting, one of the paper authors opined without a millimeter of tongue in cheek: "Most of the nation's political and opinion leaders seem bent upon a revival of old-fashioned laissez-faire at the national level." This drew not a single demurral from my fellow panelists. As Dave Barry would say, I am not making this up.

that may suggest itself is that of *fallibilism*. Even if one is abundantly certain in one's heart of hearts that libertarianism is the correct political stance, one may simultaneously reflect that intense subjective feelings of certainty are sometimes accompanied by profound error. Further, if those subjective feelings are matched by equal and opposed feelings held by others—and especially if those opposed feelings are held by *many* others— then, as a prudent individual, one may find oneself constrained to lend serious consideration to the possibility that one's belief that p is true may be best explained by something other than p's being the case. Fallibilism has a lot going for it. That, though, is not the moral of the pairing. Recall that for the sake of the present argument (L) is presumed to be true. The question is: Given the truth of (L), what is the libertarian to say about those who persistently deny (L)?

One possible response is: So much the worse for the benighted masses! Their ignorance does not at all diminish the warrant or force of that which they disbelieve. It is easy, after all, to display many rock-solid propositions that are denied by a majority. Most people believe that there are more natural numbers than there are even natural numbers. Most people believe that if the four previous tosses of a fair coin have yielded heads, then there is a better than even chance that the next toss will be tails.[7] That they are mistaken is demonstrable. Majorities do not count in matters of demonstration. But neither do they count in ascertainable matters of empirical fact. Suppose, as some surveys indicate, that most of our compatriots believe that early man coexisted with dinosaurs: what are the implications for the theory and practice of paleontology? Plausibly: none whatsoever. If in these areas there is a fact of the matter that is not constituted by counting noses, then why should morality, including its political component, be different?

Some people indeed do believe that morality is not different. This judgment is not independent of the moral theory to which one subscribes. If, for example, one holds to a divine-command theory, such that a Supreme Being issues ascertainable edicts which then become binding on all those to whom they are delivered, then there is a fact of the matter concerning what ought and ought not be done. If the majority disregards or disdains those edicts, then that is simply a sign of their wickedness. It is the righteous remnant, no matter how small or besieged, that is in possession of the truth.

Few libertarians are divine-command theorists.[8] Many, however, suppose that the rights individuals possess can be derived in rigorous,

---

[7] My empirical data here about people's beliefs comes from trials I have conducted with my students. I admit that a population of Bowling Green State University undergraduates may not accurately represent the prevailing overall level of ignorance.

[8] Locke might be so described, but on his account the divine will, insofar as it establishes the basic rights of persons, is not expressed in positive commands, but rather is read off the structure of the natural order.

unequivocal fashion from facts about human nature coupled with uncontroversial propositions such as "a = a." Even more significant, perhaps, than beliefs about what is needed to carry out such derivations are concomitant views concerning what is *not needed*. Among the unnecessary items are references to particular localized conventions and popular sentiments. Rather, libertarian natural law/natural rights are logically prior to convention and ought properly to regulate those conventional forms. They are properly the conditions of moral belief rather than conditioned by them. Without too much violence to history or language, we may call this family of theories *Aristotelian libertarianism*. A variation on this theme is the purported derivation of libertarian axioms via some transcendental conditions bearing on the possibility of action or assertion. This we may call *Kantian libertarianism*.[9] On the former account, libertarian precepts are to be read off from nature—our nature—on the latter account, they are strict consequences of the logic of practical reason. The differences between these conceptions is considerable from the perspective of moral foundational theory, but they pose equivalent issues concerning the interplay between (L) and (M).

If libertarian civil association is the law of nature, then it is a law observed mostly in the breach. We must wonder: Why? If libertarian precepts were extraordinarily recondite truths, comparable in their complexity and subtlety to, say, the principles of quantum mechanics or the geometry of seventeen-dimensional space, then the failure of most people to espouse libertarianism would be abundantly explicable and excusable. I am not aware, however, of any libertarian theorist who so conceives these precepts. To be sure, many of us believe that a fully rigorous and elegant presentation of the theory of libertarianism in all its ramifications is not easy to come by, and if no identification of the person who has to date best accomplished that task is proffered, the omission is to be understood as an expression of commendable modesty. Nonetheless, the accounts that I have seen do not depict libertarianism, at least in its rudiments, as dauntingly inaccessible lore. Rather, virtually without exception these accounts maintain that a relatively straightforward application of basic logical reasoning to evident facts about the human condition generates familiar libertarian principles of basic rights and nonaggression. It is well within the capacity of ordinary men and women to follow these demonstrations, if not independently to generate them. Yet for some reason only a very few people arrive at the libertarian summit—or even ascend to one of its foothills. As (M) asserts, the vast majority of individ-

---

[9] As I understand their arguments, Ayn Rand and Murray Rothbard fall within Aristotelian libertarianism. For Kantian libertarianism, see Hans-Hermann Hoppe, *A Theory of Socialism and Capitalism* (Boston: Kluwer Academic Publishers, 1989), in which it is argued that acknowledgment of the liberty rights of one's interlocutors is a necessary presupposition of discourse.

uals find libertarianism eminently resistible. The question that suggests itself with no little urgency is: Why?

Two answers leap to the fore. One possibility is that the vast majority of people are wicked; the other is that they are invincibly ignorant. In the former case they are our moral inferiors, in the latter our intellectual inferiors. Or perhaps they are *both* knaves and ignoramuses. Whichever branch of the explanatory tree is mounted, the inescapable conclusion is that there exists a vast, even unbridgeably vast, gulf between the libertarian few and the nonlibertarian many. This is the secular equivalent of Isaiah's depiction of the Saving Remnant. Not surprisingly, although libertarians who fit this description typically display a virulently antitheistic orientation, their language and behavior is reminiscent of familiar sectarianisms. They recognize the authority of charismatic, inspired teachers. They take easily to denunciatory rhetorical tropes in which those outside the fold are held up for scorn and obloquy—not so much scorn or obloquy, though, as those who had formerly occupied a position within the favored group, but who subsequently were seen to waver or defect from the pristine creed. Nonbelievers hover in limbo, but heretics are consigned to the deepest circle of libertarian hell. Schism, purges, and ostracism are regular episodes in the libertarian drama. That this reduces the population of the saved from, say, 1 percent to 0.1 percent is of no consequence when insistence on doctrinal purity is at issue. Nor is the fact that these mini-convulsions appear thoroughly ludicrous to outside observers a deterrent. Libertarians are not, of course, the only denomination that affords this spectacle; American Trotskyites regularly put themselves through similar cathartic purges, and fringes of the contemporary paleo-right seem intent on choreographing equally arcane dances.[10] Given the assumption of readily accessible but overwhelmingly neglected truths of fundamental importance, such practical consequences are almost unavoidable.

This sort of creedal wrangling is unlovely. But how is it to be avoided by those who are convinced that (L) is true, indeed a truth of the utmost practical significance? Heroic self-restraint in the face of invincible human obduracy is one path of egress, but heroism is an exceedingly scarce moral commodity. So the more likely route is via abandoning the presuppositions that generate the contretemps. One can, for example, give up the claim that moral principles are grounded in nature, and instead swing to the opposite pole, holding that they are purely conventional understandings rooted in local social mores. Perhaps these conventions will display considerable regularity across cultures, or perhaps they will be expansively diverse. In either event, the meta-ethical pigeonhole into which they fall is moral relativism. If moral relativism is true, however,

---

[10] See, for example, the symposium on "The End of Democracy?" in the November 1996 issue of the Christian conservative journal *First Things*.

then (L) is false. Libertarianism could be at most *a* correct moral framework, not *the* correct one. Therefore, whatever the merits of pure conventionalism, it is not relevant to the topic under consideration.[11]

A. Locating morality

I understand morality, including libertarianism, to be neither the law of nature nor purely conventional. Rather, I believe it to be convention grounded in nature. That is, there are certain fundamental facts about the makeup of human beings and their circumstances that are, if not constitutive of what it is to be a human person, then so pervasive and characteristic of the world in which we act that they might just as well, for all practical purposes, be necessary conditions. (The old, not quite yet defunct term for this halfway house between metaphysics and sociology is *philosophical anthropology*.) It is in virtue of these facts that we are a species that cannot dispense with morality. Least of all can we dispense with *justice*, the precinct of morality that houses libertarianism. However, only insofar as these needs stimulate the development within actual human communities of a technology of moral norms and practices will there come to exist an effective structure of rights and duties, oughts and obligations.[12]

The fundamental facts I have in mind are thoroughly familiar, even banal. They can conveniently be put into three groupings. First, human beings are *vulnerable*. When we are cut, we bleed. More specifically, we are vulnerable to incursions by others. As Hobbes noted, even the mightiest can be laid low by the humble while sleeping or unobservant. Second, individuals' *interests conflict*—not always and everywhere, but enough so that my exercise of prudence does not carry any guarantee of your well-being. If nature had strapped us together like mountaineers at opposite ends of a rope, morality might be dispensable. Instead, nature has given us ropes that can easily be adapted to function as nooses around others' necks. Therefore, what we each need from all others is, if I may be allowed to put it that way, a little slack. Third, should we manage to mesh our actions, a *cooperative surplus* is available. However, to use the game theorists' term, the cooperative strategy is not dominant. In the absence of conventional forms, individuals will often be able to improve outcomes for themselves by following a beggar-thy-neighbor strategy. Thus dissolves the potential cooperative surplus.

---

[11] I discuss moral relativism at greater length in "Harman's Moral Relativism," *Journal of Libertarian Studies*, vol. 3 (Fall 1979), pp. 279–91.

[12] I say *technology* to underscore the fact that these norms and practices must be *created* through skilled artifice rather than simply *discovered* as preexisting components of the natural order. Whether virtues are similarly dependent on conventional undertakings is a separate question. I am inclined to believe that some virtues can be genuinely natural to an extent that so-called natural law or natural rights cannot be.

Framed within this context, morality is seen to have a *point*, one embedded in concern for human interests. It is not a set of abstract propositions read off the book of nature or distilled *a priori* from pure practical reason. Like money, mattresses, and marriage, morality is artifactual. It represents a creative response to perceived needs and, as such, has the capacity to make life go better. (Though not necessarily so: consider avarice, back ache, and messy divorces.) As some narratives, for example that of Hobbes, tell the story, morality is constructed from whole cloth as a deliberately engineered violence-avoidance mechanism. In other versions, those of Hume and F. A. Hayek for example, moral structures are almost entirely the product of human action but not human design. They are born, mutate, evolve, die out, or thrive in almost Darwinian fashion. I find the second way of relating the story more credible, but there is no need to take sides here. A helpful analogy is to language. Particular phonemes are entirely conventional, at least within the constraints set by the human vocal mechanism. That we have language, though, and use it to describe, to ask questions, to give commands, to berate and praise, are not random bits of happenstance. Rather, they are grounded in deep facts about the human condition and the significance to us of communication. And, if Noam Chomsky is correct in ascribing to all human language a common deep structure, then all conventional manifestations of the linguistic capacity have a natural basis.

Along with the three fundamental facts from which morality (and again, I note, most especially justice) takes its point, we can identify three conditions that bear on how successful it is liable to be in meliorating the human condition. Taking a cue from Hume and John Rawls, I refer to these as the *circumstances of morality*, though no identity between my formulation and theirs is claimed.

1. *Moderate goodwill.* Most people most of the time are capable of being motivated in an appropriate direction by the weal or woe of others. A somewhat different dimension of moderate goodwill is that people are willing to bind themselves in schemes of cooperation with other willing cooperators. This is not to demand a general willingness to live by the terms of the Golden Rule or utilitarian impartiality; that would render morality utopian in the most literal sense of that word. It is, though, to invoke more than the calculative rationality that Hobbes and David Gauthier[13] believe to be sufficient for bootstrapping one's way out of the war of all against all and into morality. The classic expression of the rationality-alone construal is Kant's bold announcement that "[a]s hard as it may sound, the problem of setting up a state can be solved even by a nation of devils (so long as they possess understanding)."[14] But even if it can be

---

[13] David Gauthier, *Morals by Agreement* (Oxford: Clarendon Press, 1986).
[14] Immanuel Kant, "Perpetual Peace," in *Kant's Political Writings*, ed. Hans Reiss (Cambridge: Cambridge University Press, 1970), p. 112.

solved, it is also susceptible to being dissolved. Fresh outbreaks of dev-
iltry will disrupt the delicate equilibrium. (Think of cease-fires in Bosnia.)
For the sake of stability, if nothing more, we had better hope to have a
population with greater moral aptitude than that possessed by devils.

2. *Moderate intelligence.* Most people most of the time are capable of
learning at least the most central moral rules, recognizing situations calling for the application of those rules, and figuring out which actions on
their part will constitute compliance with the rules. Beyond this, it will be
useful if individuals are able to sensibly adjust their conduct when exceptional circumstances suggest that the usual considerations might not
apply, to adjudicate conflicts among rules, to act in concert with others to
meet new circumstances, and to assimilate new information by modifying the system of rules to which they declare allegiance. For the most part,
though, it suffices that morality be the province of proles, not archangels.[15]

3. *Moderate demandingness.* From saints and heroes anything can be
asked and they will provide it—and more. This is a proposition of striking irrelevance to the quotidian practice of morality. The vast majority of
individuals are neither saints nor heroes, and therefore the magnitude of
the restraints they may be expected regularly and reliably to place on
their own conduct is small. Morality can hold up ideals to which people
are *invited* to aspire or admire, but what it can *demand* as a matter of strict
obligation is sharply limited.

If, then, communities of human beings bring to the circumstances of
nature (including their own nature) moderate goodwill and moderate
intelligence regulated by principles under which ordinary men and women
can comfortably live, then they will do better at shielding their vulnera-
bilities, brokering conflicting interests, and availing themselves of the
potential surplus from cooperation. The point of morality will have been
realized.

B. *Morality and libertarianism*

Where do the precepts of libertarianism fit into this model? By hypothesis, (L) is true: libertarianism is the correct framework for political morality. Minor qualifications aside, that is to say that libertarian precepts
are not onerously demanding for moderately intelligent persons of moderate goodwill, and that if such persons manage to arrive at libertarian
precepts as the regulative principles under which they commit themselves to live, then they will tend, under a wide, if not infinitely wide,
range of conditions, to do better with regard to confronting the three
natural facts. General respect for libertarian rights will render them less
vulnerable to breaches of the integrity of their persons, especially those
breaches initiated by other individuals. Acknowledgment of a moral space

[15] The contrast is from R. M. Hare, *Moral Thinking* (Oxford: Clarendon Press, 1981).

within which each individual is sovereign will afford them epistemically accessible bases for peacefully resolving conflicts of interest. And robust rights over one's person and property make possible exchange relations that tap for mutual benefit the potential cooperative surplus. This is the condensed version of the story that I (as well as many other libertarians) have spun at greater length. To it I add a pair of follow-up points. First, although libertarianism represents the optimal solution to problems of human interaction, nothing said here is meant to deny that other, less good but nonetheless creditable solutions can be crafted. A fine red Burgundy is the optimal beverage to consume with filet mignon, but a cold lager or, in extremis, water is better than nothing. Second, libertarianism serves as the optimal solution only insofar as it is embodied within some actual community as its regulative political framework. A libertarianism that is the esoteric doctrine of a coterie of moral savants does not fulfill this function.[16]

At present, libertarianism does not regulate our interactions with each other; that, alas, is the unavoidable upshot of (M). What does this hard fact imply for libertarian belief and practice? One thing that it does not imply is that one should reject libertarian precepts; (L) is, after all, true. One might instead conclude that because libertarianism fails to obtain, one lives in a morally bankrupt society. Let us call this *rejectionist libertarianism*. Concomitant with adherence to rejectionist libertarianism is denial of legitimacy to all social institutions that are incompatible with pristine libertarianism. As much as possible the embrace of such institutions will be avoided. If it should prove feasible, one may choose to emulate the disaffected Essenes who withdrew from wicked Jerusalem to the Qumran caves, where they could establish their enclave of the godly and deposit their sacred texts. It has often been a fantasy of rejectionist libertarians to be able to retreat from the wider society to some offshore libertarian paradise. But if geographical isolation is too costly, then one can attempt to effect a spiritual retreat, avoiding as far as one is able the touch of any appurtenances of the state. What one cannot withdraw from, one will defend against. Swiss bank accounts, multiple passports, a well-stocked bunker, a copious supply of armaments, the collected writings of Ayn Rand: these are the instruments of choice.

Without in any way denying the right of individuals to detach themselves from the greater society, I believe that this response to the conjunction of (L) and (M) is overreaction that borders on hysteria. It expresses the conviction that no moral technology other than full-blown libertari-

---

[16] That is not to say that a libertarianism that is not realized is impotent. It can serve as a beacon for seeing one's way through the moral mists with sufficient clarity to realize that we could lead better lives with our fellows under a regime of expansive liberty. As such, libertarianism can be a valuable object of study, advocacy, and inspiration. It also, as I argue below, yields significant implications concerning how one ought to act in venues at considerable distance from the libertarian desideratum.

anism merits one's respect or allegiance. I suspect that this judgment is belied by the conduct of many of its adherents insofar as they implicitly rely on others, even agents of the government, to exercise moral self-restraint so as not to rape, assault, murder, and even not to snatch too much of one's property. It also represents, I believe, a serious misestimation of what sorts of lives are rewarding and how inimical the presence of an overly large state is to prospects of individual flourishing. Hysteria, though, is not something that people can easily be talked out of, and in any event I shall not attempt to practice such therapy here. Rather, the remainder of the discussion is directed to those who share the belief that the depressingly nonlibertarian character of the United States is not *too* depressing, that productive and morally respectful interchange with the unconverted is both feasible and desirable.

III. Cooperative Libertarianism

For those who believe that libertarian precepts can be read off the book of nature by all those who enjoy the moral equivalent of something like a tenth-grade reading level, it is virtually unavoidable that those who fail to subscribe to libertarianism will be regarded as dunces or as wicked. The alternative libertarianism, what I shall refer to as *cooperative libertarianism*, is more generous. It is willing to concede that the nonlibertarians among whom one lives are mostly well-meaning, honorable people with whom one may cooperate without thereby dishonoring oneself. (Of course, just as the fact that one is paranoid does not mean that one has no real enemies, so too are there nonlibertarians—and libertarians!—who genuinely *are* evil and stupid.) Nonlibertarians are, to be sure, importantly mistaken concerning a momentous matter, but that mistake discredits neither their intellect nor their character. Possession of moderate goodwill and moderate intelligence do not immunize people from statist persuasions. Indeed, neither does an abundance of goodwill and intelligence. That is because the moral terrain that must be traversed in order to arrive at the libertarian destination is steep, rocky, and dotted with mirages. Nongeneralizable items within one's personal experience heavily influence the likelihood that one will achieve that happy consummation. Rawls refers to these epistemic obstacles as the "burdens of judgment."[17] Let me offer some examples that specifically relate to acceptance of (L).

Libertarians know that market relations are the superior institution for distribution of property. Nonlibertarians typically hold that there is an important role for the market but that distribution via democratic determinations is also indicated. Why might a reasonable person adopt this stance? Several reasons suggest themselves. First, one might believe that

[17] See John Rawls, *Political Liberalism* (New York: Columbia University Press, 1993), pp. 54–58.

although free markets promote efficiency, their justice remains question-able until and unless it can be established that individuals' initial endow-ments are fairly determined; and one might believe that we do not possess a satisfactory account of how original acquisition of property is supposed to work. In fact, many libertarians share this unease. Second, even if we possess an adequate theory of original acquisition and justice in sub-sequent transfer, it is transparently clear that actual property holdings do not derive from this straight and true path. Therefore, it may seem plau-sible to maintain that intervening in markets by way of compensation or rectification is called for. Again, even some libertarians share this appre-hension. Third, one may suspect that voluntary market arrangements will not suffice to produce an adequate quantity of public goods and, there-fore, that provision by the state is called for. This may be an economic misconception, but even Adam Smith, not usually identified as a notori-ous statist, was taken in by it. Fourth, someone who has been treated to photos of thalidomide babies, or followed ValuJet Airlines stories on tele-vision, or knows someone who fell into the clutches of a medical quack, may be persuaded that some measure of regulatory oversight and occu-pational licensure are needed. This view may be false, but it is not obvi-ously false. Fifth, one may observe that the quality of life enjoyed by people who live in proactive democracies such as the United States and Germany tends to be considerably higher than that experienced by those who live in places like Zaire or Yemen where democracy is conspicuously less present. Therefore, it may seem reasonable to allow large scope for democratic determinations, including oversight and correction of the mar-ket. To reiterate, I do not hereby endorse these conclusions, but I do maintain that they are not ludicrous.

It would not be difficult to supply similar considerations in other spheres where libertarians diverge from nonlibertarians. It is a mistake to hold that the government ought to fund and run school systems, but it is not an egregious mistake. People who believe this are not to be lumped with those who think that Jews have horns or that Elvis is pumping gas at the corner Texaco station. Ditto for those who believe that zoning enhances the livability of neighborhoods, that commercial establishments ought to be legally required not to exclude black customers, that Yosemite ought not be auctioned off to the highest bidder. These are people with whom we literally and figuratively can do business.

Consider an analogous area in which toleration and blanket rejection are options. Perhaps no more vexing issue than abortion roils the Amer-ican polity. Some hold that abortion is nothing other than the slaughter of innocents; others retort that opposition to abortion is opposition to wom-en's sovereignty over their own bodies. It is news to no one that between these parties arises contention aplenty. At least equally noteworthy, al-though much less often remarked on, is the extent of accommodation achieved between them. Many abortion-is-murder believers work or live next to abortion-is-a-woman's-right exponents. They may even be friends who have learned to agree to disagree. They can do so despite the gravity of the issue if they perceive that the burdens of judgment are especially heavy in this domain and that one who sees matters differently may nonetheless be one's moral and intellectual peer.[18] Of course the rhetoric pedaled on both sides of the dispute is intended to disrupt such accommodation, and every so often someone is gunned down outside an abortion clinic. What is remarkable, though, is how few shootings there are. On any given day, such an abortion-related eruption is less probable than a California freeway fracas in which one enraged motorist pulls out his shotgun to blow holes in another motorist who has committed the sin of tailgating.

The moral of the abortion analogy is not merely vapid praise of toleration, but rather a more capacious understanding of what is genuinely tolerable. Still, the implications drawn so far may strike the reader as not especially venturesome. Wasn't it Mom who said on the first day of kindergarten, "Play nicely with the other little boys and girls"? Perhaps it seems that the foregoing discussion is little more than an updated version of her wisdom. Accordingly, I now move to argue for implications that will be more controversial.

Libertarians are wont to intone, "Taxation is theft!" It is our clever variation on Proudhon's "Property is theft!"[19] Cleverness is to be applauded, but not when it leads to outsmarting oneself. It is one thing to *say* that taxation is theft, another to *believe* it. Causal relations run between assertion and belief in both directions, and many libertarians who say it also believe it. They are mistaken. Moreover, they are mistaken in a way very difficult to achieve unless one is in the grip of an ideology. Taxation is *not* theft. It may resemble theft in important respects; it may be the case that some of the reasons that lead us to condemn theft will, if properly considered, lead us to condemn taxation; it may even be the case that taxation is as morally reprehensible as theft; nonetheless, and with apologies for the repetition, it is not theft.

The point is not semantic but rather phenomenological. The perceived reality of theft is notably distinct from that of taxation. When I return home from a libertarian scholars' conference to find the lock on my door broken and my television set gone I am outraged. That which I expected

---

[18] Unaccountably, Rawls denies this. See *ibid.*, p. 243, n. 32.

[19] See Pierre-Joseph Proudhon, *What Is Property: An Enquiry into the Principle of Right and of Government* (New York: Howard Fertig, 1966), p. 11. I have been unable to discover who originated "Taxation is theft." In *Libertarianism* (Los Angeles: Nash Publishing, 1971), John Hospers refers to a pamphlet entitled "Taxation is Theft," issued by the Society for Individual Liberty, Silver Springs, Maryland, but no publication date is indicated. Lysander Spooner is the spiritual ancestor of the locution, but he identifies taxation with *robbery* rather than *theft* in *No Treason, No. VI: The Constitution of No Authority* (1870; reprint, Larkspur, CO: Pine Tree Press, 1966), p. 17. It is mysterious why the equation with theft has won out in contemporary libertarian circles; Spooner's phrasing makes the point more effectively.

to be secure from encroachment has been violated. The perpetrator of the theft has transgressed rules that both he and I recognize to be the *de facto* as well as *de jure* principles of cooperation that undergird a framework of civility from which all citizens can expect to derive benefit. The moral ire I feel is, then, not some amorphous feeling that things are other than they ought to be. Rather, that animus is precisely localized: it is focused on *this* act by *this* individual. Moreover, I possess a justifiable confidence that my animus will be seconded by those among whom I live. What is primarily a violation of my rights is understood by them to be more than a private conflict of interest between me and the individual who coveted my television.[20] Accordingly, I am able to avail myself of the formal apparatus of the legal system and the informal vindication afforded by a consensus among the members of the moral community that I have been violated and ought to be made whole. And if I am exceptionally lucky, this solidarity may even help me to recover the TV set.

In nearly all relevant respects the perceived context of taxation is significantly different. I look at my pay stub and observe that a large slab of my salary has been excised before I ever had the opportunity to fondle it. This is an annoyance, perhaps an intense one. But it is not focused on the particular extraction. Rather, its object is some or all of the tens of thousands of pages of the tax code, the political order within which the power to tax is lodged, and the constitutional foundations on which that political order is erected. I wish some or all of it were otherwise; that, though, is the inverse of a highly specific grievance. Moreover, I cannot count on the solidarity of my fellow citizens. That is both a descriptive and a normative statement. If I have adopted the cooperationist rather than rejectionist attitude toward the society in which I live, then I am thereby committed to acknowledging that although my fellow citizens' views concerning the ethics of taxation are, as I see it, mistaken, the perspective from which they adopt those views is not so unreasonable or uncivil as to disqualify them from moral respect. I am entitled, perhaps even obligated, to attempt to persuade them to think otherwise. However, prior to the dawning of that bright day in which the veils are lifted and freedom reigns, I shall, if I am not a fanatic, concede the legitimacy (not, of course, the optimality) of the overall moral framework within which taxation takes place. It is, therefore, not only misleading but also an exercise in borderline incivility to equate taxation with theft, for if it is taken in its straightforward sense, that pronouncement denies the legitimacy of the social order and announces that I regard myself as authorized unilaterally to override its dictates as I would the depredations of the thief. It says to my neighbors that I regard them as, if not themselves thieves, then confederates or willing accomplices to thievery. Is it pusillanimous to suggest

---

[20] Thus the characterization of crime as a wrong done not only to the individual victim but to *the people*.

that declaring war, even cold war, against the other 99 percent of the population is imprudent? I would therefore caution libertarians to shelve the "Taxation is theft!" slogan despite its sonorous ring, and if they cannot bring themselves to do that, then at least to cultivate a twinkle in the eye when they haul it forth.[21]

Another example: Libertarians decry the Social Security system's enforced transfers from the young to the old. I share that antipathy. I do, however, part company from those who, when asked to contemplate a transitional regime, snarl that the geezers have been enjoying the fruits of illegitimate plunder lo these many years and that justice would best be served by cutting them off forthwith. To these hard-liners it is entirely immaterial that for more than fifty years Social Security has enjoyed a level of popular support unmatched by any other welfare-state program, that it has garnered the electoral support not only of the old who are its recipients but also of the young who fund it.[22] The hard line bears softening. The Social Security administration is a blot on the body politic, but it does not render that body too putrid to merit preservation. This means that although it was an error to create these claims of the old on the young, now that they exist and have been repeatedly validated in a political arena that is far from ideal but not so defective as to merit wholesale rejection, those claims carry moral weight that libertarians disregard at their peril.

IV. LIBERTARIANISM AND PERSONAL CONDUCT

I turn now to a different family of implications that flows from the conjunction of (L) and (M), implications concerning the personal conduct of libertarians as they warily confront the state and its various bastard progeny. Some libertarians are uneasy about driving on state-funded roads or utilizing the state's postal services. That degree of scrupulousness seems extreme because there does not exist an alternate network of purely

---

[21] Compare with Susan Brownmiller's claim that "from prehistoric times to the present ... rape has played a critical function. It is nothing more or less than a conscious process of intimidation by which *all men* keep *all women* in a state of fear." Brownmiller, *Against Our Will: Men, Women, and Rape* (New York: Simon and Schuster, 1975), p. 15 (emphasis in the original). She does not say that many/most men are beneficiaries, direct or otherwise, from violent sexual impositions on women. Nor does she maintain that all heterosexual intercourse *resembles* rape in relevant respects, nor even that all heterosexual intercourse is morally defective for *reasons that correspond* to those rendering rape morally defective. These latter claims are merely far-fetched and eminently disputable. But what she actually maintains is dumbfoundingly preposterous—moreover, preposterous in a way that announces a relation of hostility to all men and, perhaps, to all women whose coital practices she disapproves. This is not, I believe, an example that ought to commend itself to libertarians.

[22] Polls have revealed that a majority of those in their thirties and younger believe that Social Security will not be there for them when they retire. Nonetheless, they have not shown themselves to be politically mobilizable in opposition to the system. I explore why that might be so in "Is Social Security Politically Untouchable?" *Cato Journal*, vol. 5 (1985), pp. 157–75.

private roads or other providers of first-class mail delivery of which one can avail oneself. Becoming a libertarian is not—or ought not be—a commitment to don a hair shirt. The freeway isn't free; it is funded from coercively extracted imposts. But to regard it as off-limits on the basis of moral scruples is a further, self-imposed restriction of one's freedom. So most libertarians will feel few compunctions about driving on an interstate highway or mailing back their sweepstakes entry to Publishers Clearing House.

Somewhat more troubling are activities like vacationing at a national park or attending a concert in a tax-subsidized auditorium. For these there are reasonably satisfactory private alternatives. Is one morally obliged, then, to vacation at Disney World rather than at Yellowstone? An affirmative answer still evinces a high degree of scrupulousness. Donald Duck is not all that close a substitute for Old Faithful. Libertarians ought not be required by their principles to lead geyserless lives.

Here is an example that strikes closer to home. Although I believe that there should be no such thing as a state university, I am employed at one. In the United States there exist hundreds of private colleges and universities; perhaps I could get a job at one of these if I tried. Or failing that, I certainly could secure some job in the private sector that would afford me a middle-class mode of life. (I have, for example, some cooking talents from which I probably could derive a flow of income.) Nonetheless, I have not attempted to do so. The position I currently occupy is, to the best of my knowledge, the most desirable one available to me. Securing alternate employment would involve bearing a non-negligible opportunity cost, not one so great as eschewing highway use, but nonetheless substantial. Should I, as a libertarian, accept that cost? Similarly, my children have been educated mostly in the public school system. There existed plausible private alternatives, though none that I judged worth the cost. Should libertarian scruples have led me to reconsider this decision?

Formerly I regarded these questions as indeed posing a thorny dilemma for me and, by extension, for other libertarians whose involvement with the state is similarly deep. The response I gave when the questions were put to me, either by some mischievous interlocutor or by myself, was to haul out the "hair shirt" argument, although I had to admit that these particular garments were not insufferably scratchy. And I conceded that if one had the option of taking only slightly inferior employment in the private sector, then it would be an act of bad faith for a libertarian not to do so. In part as a result of thinking my way through the preceding argument of this essay, however, I have convinced myself that this view was mistaken. Teaching philosophy in a state university is not morally inferior to teaching philosophy in a private institution. Some readers may take that as a reductio ad absurdum confirming the corrupting tenor of this essay's argument. In response I note that even self-serving arguments can happen to be valid.

Consider the following analogy. The American League has adopted the designated-hitter rule, and the National League has rejected it. Baseball fans often feel strongly concerning which is the better arrangement.[23] Those who oppose the designated-hitter rule tend to despise its effect on the great American pastime. Suppose that you are among their company. If you are offered a job managing a National League team and a slightly better job managing an American League team, do your principles oblige you to accept the former? I do not believe that they do. If you take the American League managerial job, would it then be morally better of you to decline to avail yourself of the option to designate a specialized hitter and instead have the pitcher bat in his spot in the lineup? I do not believe that it would be.

Some will reject the analogy on the grounds that baseball is merely a game and thus is not a serious affair for serious-minded adults. That is to betray an egregious misunderstanding of the nature of baseball. I shall not, however, take up that particular cudgel in this essay. Rather, I note that reasonable people can differ concerning the rules under which baseball ought to be played, and reasonable people can likewise differ concerning the rules under which educational services ought to be provided. A disestablishment of education is desirable, but, to my personal and professional regret, the vast majority of Americans reject that proposition. They believe that the common good is better served by systems of tax-supported schools. Their endorsement of public education is, apparently, genuine, as opposed to a thinly disguised cover for plundering one segment of the society for the sake of another. ("Public education is theft!" is, therefore, another no-go.) One who is committed to cooperating with others on terms that all can reasonably—if not joyously—accept may, then, unapologetically act as a consumer or producer of tax-funded educational services. My previous reluctance to accept this conclusion was, I now believe, the result of confusing considerations bearing on how one may permissibly act under a system of rules with considerations bearing on how one may permissibly act with regard to selecting and maintaining those rules. If a libertarian who enjoys a comfortable living within the public sector declines, because she cherishes that comfort, to oppose its extension and advocate its abolition, if she prudently decides to focus her political activities on areas the freeing-up of which will not affect her own welfare, if she refrains from suggesting to her students that she and they are the beneficiaries of an unjustifiable practice of transfers from the less well-off to the more well-off, then she has indeed been corrupted. One need not be so pessimistic as to suppose, however, that such corruption is the inevitable consequence of entente with the overinflated state. Nor,

---

[23] George Will writes on this issue with an eloquence and passion rarely matched in his oeuvre.

for that matter, need one be so pessimistic as to maintain that the preceding sentence itself necessarily manifests that corruption.

It can be objected that complicity with statist undertakings willy-nilly expresses support for those undertakings. That objection deserves to be taken seriously. To the extent that action under the rules implies or may seem to imply endorsement of those rules, libertarians are obliged to be wary. Conscientious objection and conscientious abstention are, therefore, honorable stances that acknowledge the force of one's expressive obligations.[24] There are, however, other ways in which one can articulately convey one's attitude toward prevailing norms. The concept of a "loyal opposition" has application outside the legislative arena. It may be as difficult for a libertarian who is employed by a public body effectively to display his convictions as it is for a socialist bringing home millions on Wall Street (although, for the latter, the example of Engels is instructive). Difficult does not, however, mean impossible. Indeed, it can be argued that if libertarians impose on themselves a social apartheid, then they will be less able to make their voices heard in precisely the domain where they are most needed. Nothing is more banal than a farmer plumping for higher agricultural subsidies, steel manufacturers lobbying for quotas on steel imports, educators advocating more dollars for education; but when representatives of these industries urge withdrawal of the governmental teat, that is striking. Libertarians may, I conclude, honorably avail themselves of governmentally provided benefits. It is also, I hasten to add, possible for them thereby to dishonor themselves. It all depends on how the game is played—and on how the game of choosing the rules of the game is played.

The critic may complain that this is far too undemanding a prescription. Just so long as one footnotes in nine-point type one's demurral from the coercive practices of the prevailing regime, anything goes. Are there no limits, it may be asked, on the extent to which one may involve oneself in illiberal practices? Is the vox populi utterly determinative of the vox libertarii?

To the contrary, there are limits, and these limits are implicit in the model of cooperative libertarianism itself. These limits are not algorithmic; their application requires discernment and sophistication. But, contra those who wish to reduce ethics to an automated decision procedure, the need for discernment is endemic to moral life. Living well isn't easy; so what else is new? For the cooperative libertarian, the task of discernment is to distinguish between, on the one hand, those measures that can reasonably (if mistakenly) be construed as responsive to the interests of

---

[24] For a discussion of expressive ethics, see Geoffrey Brennan and Loren Lomasky, *Democracy and Decision: The Pure Theory of Electoral Preference* (New York: Cambridge University Press, 1993), esp. ch. 10, "Toward a Democratic Morality."

all citizens acting within a framework of reciprocity and mutual advantage, and, on the other hand, those policies that are designed to plunder some for the sake of serving the interests or prejudices of others. Because legislative packages do not come neatly labeled as to which of these categories they fall under—or rather, because those that ought to carry the second description are invariably packaged under the first—judgment must be exercised. It is, therefore, neither feasible nor desirable to offer a comprehensive demarcation of clean and unclean here. The following examples are presented as indicative rather than clear-cut, and they are intended as a stimulus for further discussion among libertarians rather than as the blueprint for a new libertarian paradigm.

One class of governmental enterprises that libertarians need not reject as inherently unacceptable are those that supply public goods. Insofar as their provision serves the interests of all individuals rather than treating some people as mere means for the ends of others, public goods can reasonably be taken to be fit objects of concern for a polity founded on terms of mutual advantage. National defense is the stock example of a good which, once provided to some citizens, cannot feasibly be withheld from others, and for which the consumption by some does not diminish the amount available to others. Publicness in this sense is an economist's term of art, and within that context there is ample debate concerning the fine points of the concept, including debate over the extent to which it admits of more and less and over how the public/private ratio is to be ascertained. Although these discussions bear significantly on efficiency and equity questions surrounding political provision of items that more or less closely fulfill the criteria of being public goods, they need not detain us here. Arguably public in the relevant sense are police and fire-fighting services, roads, basic (as opposed to applied) research, environmental protection, and the like.

A second class of activities that may pass the test are social insurance programs. Medicaid for the indigent, unemployment insurance, and food stamps are examples. The argument for governmental provision taps into familiar equity considerations concerning the desirability of a social safety net, but also into somewhat more recherché arguments that attempt to establish that because of moral hazard and adverse selection phenomena, these insurance functions cannot satisfactorily be carried out via market arrangements. Taken together these may fail to make a case for government involvement. The failure is not so palpable, however, that a conscientious libertarian must not allow them to soil her hands. So, for example, a libertarian physician may treat Medicaid patients; a libertarian grocer may accept food stamps.

A third class of activities that may qualify as acceptable are measures that incorporate the practice of moderate paternalism. Some examples are a Food and Drug Administration that rules on the safety of the pharmaceuticals we consume, seat belt and motorcycle helmet laws, and forced savings for retirement. At the risk of becoming tiresome, I repeat that I am not hereby announcing myself in favor of such policies. Were I the philosopher-king who ruled America, I would shut down the FDA tomorrow and delegislate mandatory seat belts and helmets the day after tomorrow. But I am not the philosopher-king, and it is a very good thing that no one else is either. Our political order, though far from perfectly liberal, incorporates a much higher degree of consent among moral equals than does that of Plato's *Republic*. For better or worse, the citizenry accepts the propriety of making people do some things for their own good whether they want to or not. These paternalistic practices do not constitute a summary abandonment of civility, but rather the adoption of a somewhat inferior version of it. A word about the qualifier *moderate* paternalism: By that is meant measures that impinge on individuals in areas closer to the fringes than to the centers of their lives. If I am forced to buckle up when I drive, that only slightly affects my ability to devote myself to personal projects; if because I have had the temerity to don saffron robes and chant "Hare Krishna" I am kidnapped and subjected to the tender ministrations of the deprogrammer, that impales my pursuit of the good at its heart. No libertarian can conscientiously accord any legitimacy to the latter sort of paternalism.

That brings us to the question of that which is beyond the pale of toleration by cooperative libertarians. I do not have any neat schematism for the display of these breaches. Rather, I can offer nothing more exact than this rule of thumb: All those measures that deliberately or foreseeably trample on the rights-respecting activity of some to advance the interests or designs of others merit all the disdain and noncooperation libertarians can muster. If slavery were still around and enjoyed the support of millions of one's compatriots, it would be the paradigm of an institution with which no accommodation is possible. But it is not exactly bold and provocative theorizing to send one's moral principles into battle against Simon Legree. Since slavery is blessedly dormant, the War on Drugs is perhaps the best example of a contemporary practice enjoying wide popularity with which libertarians must conscientiously refuse any degree of accommodation. Hundreds of thousands of individuals have been jailed for illicit chemical consumption; civil rights have been obliterated by glinty-eyed G-Men; vast swatches of our cities have been rendered unlivable by fallout from the battles. To be sure, drug crusaders have offered rationales for these policies, rationales that invoke time-honored moral concepts. Some drug warriors profess that by threatening to lock up drug users and then carrying out those threats, they are acting for the sake of the users' good. It is a wondrous if not entirely benign feature of human lips that they can be employed to say virtually anything. This is one of those cases where discernment is needed to distinguish between the plausible and the pathetic. The level of discernment which is needed to see through the various drug czars' rhetoric does not, I confess, seem to me to be great. Whether great or small, though, I do not see that a conscientious libertarian can have any truck with this crusade. One may not relieve oneself of the burden of one's unpleasant neighbor by informing the authorities where he keeps his stash, and one may not become one of those authorities. Period.[25]

Similarly, a libertarian cannot tolerate practices of punishing individuals for "victimless crimes." Nor can censorship from the religious right or the feminist left be accepted. Insofar as these are attempts to impose on individuals one's own conception of what is good and proper by making it too costly for them to hold on to their own conceptions, these practices cannot with any credibility be understood as passing the test of cooperating for mutual benefit with one's moral peers. Rather, these are the acts of would-be moral superiors imposing on their inferiors. Enforced monopolies, coercively extracted rents, and restraint of competition are other clear-cut instances of plunder and, as such, are to be afforded no credibility. In a world distinctly suboptimal from a libertarian perspective, it may be impossible entirely to avoid their embrace without simultaneously donning the hair shirt (recall the example of the monopoly post office), but what libertarians may not do is endorse these, through word or conduct, as even plausible simulacra of policies reasonably conceived as respecting the interests of all citizens.

Could it not be objected that all of these measures are widely approved by the general public, the same general public toward whom cooperative respect has been urged? The short answer is: Yes. How can one continue to display moral respect for those who have been gulled by the Drug Warriors, the vice-squad gendarmes, and the import restricters? The short answer is: With considerable difficulty. The somewhat longer answer is to respond to the question with another question: What is the alternative? If it is tacitly or openly to enter into a state of war vis-à-vis those majorities, then the choice of alternatives is truly momentous. One must not only realistically consider one's own prospects, to cite a 1996 sub–1 percent libertarian candidate, of finding freedom in an unfree world,[26] but one must also attempt accurately to reckon the costs of forgoing cooperative

[25] Or almost period. May I, as a cooperative libertarian, camouflage my views and take a job as a Drug Enforcement Agency employee so as to be able to sabotage its efforts from within? To do so is extremely dangerous, not only in the personal sense that if one were detected the consequences for one's well-being would be severe, but also in the sense that it puts one perilously close to abandoning the cooperative camp for the rejectionist one. Perhaps, though, it is possible to be a rejectionist in one limited sphere while otherwise being a cooperator. These are difficult and important issues that deserve more consideration than I can lend them here.

[26] The candidate was Harry Browne, author of a book entitled *How I Found Freedom in an Unfree World* (New York: Macmillan, 1973).

activity with the exasperatingly nonlibertarian many. That, in turn, involves considering whether they suffer from localized and remediable patches of unreasonability or whether these are global and terminal. Someone who stodgily and unreflectively takes the president at his word that it is a good thing to continue to imprison pot smokers (presumably only those who inhale) is not automatically to be lumped in with the fervent Nazi who willingly bore great hardships so as to be able, even as Allied boots could be heard in the distance, to continue with his mission of gassing Jews. To be a libertarian is a doleful fate indeed if it entails despair on each occasion when the vast multitude fails to be persuaded by one's own lucidly compelling arguments. It can, however, be a matter of some joy if one conceives one's station as being a participating member of a society of mostly reasonable and mostly civil individuals, and enjoying in virtue of one's libertarianism a perch of honor in its 99th percentile.

Philosophy, Bowling Green State University

ON THE FAILURE OF LIBERTARIANISM TO CAPTURE THE POPULAR IMAGINATION*

By Jonathan R. Macey

I. Introduction

In this essay, I identify the reasons that libertarian principles have failed to capture the popular imagination as an acceptable form of civil society. By the term "libertarian" I mean a belief in and commitment to a set of methods and policies that have as their common aim greater freedom under law for individuals. The term "freedom" in this context means not only a commitment to civil liberties, such as freedom of expression, but also to economic liberties, including a commitment to a laissez-faire policy of free enterprise and free trade between countries.[1] Libertarians, therefore, are committed to the absolute minimum state intervention in the economy as well as in people's private lives. In a world constrained by these libertarian principles, people should be permitted to do as they please, constrained only by rules that prevent them from encroaching on the liberty of others.

The goal of this essay is to explain why libertarian ideas do not exert a greater hold on the popular imagination. Early libertarian (or "classical liberal") thought was identified not only with a set of ideas and theoretical concepts, but also with particular political parties and specific social programs.[2] Today, while political parties that bear the name "liberal" (which, in this context, is typically used to connote left-wing political theory) are still to be found, "in contemporary usage the term 'liberalism'

* I thank Enrico Colombatto, John Lott, Fred D. Miller, Jr., Jeffrey Paul, and participants at a seminar on welfare at the International Centre for Economic Research in Turin, Italy, and at workshops at the Bowling Green State University Department of Philosophy and the Cornell Law School, for useful comments. Matthew F. Gorra, Cornell Law School class of 1999, and Donald J. Kochan, Cornell Law School class of 1998, provided valuable research assistance.

[1] The definition of libertarianism that I adopt in the text is consistent with the definition used by David Boaz in a recent work directed at a popular audience, in which he defines libertarianism as the view that "each person has the right to live his life in any way he chooses so long as he respects the equal rights of others." David Boaz, *Libertarianism: A Primer* (New York: Free Press, 1997), p. 2; see also John Hospers, "What Libertarianism Is," in *Liberty for the Twenty-First Century: Contemporary Libertarian Thought*, ed. Tibor R. Machan and Douglas B. Rasmussen (Lanham, MD: Rowman and Littlefield, 1995), pp. 5–17; and Charles Murray, *What It Means to Be a Libertarian: A Personal Interpretation* (New York: Broadway Books, 1997).

[2] David Smith, "Liberalism," *The International Encyclopedia of the Social Sciences* (New York: Macmillan, 1991), p. 276.

refers to a system of thought and practice that is less specific than a philosophical doctrine and more inclusive than party principle."[3] This essay explores why this is the case and suggests some possible remedies.

I begin with the assumption that there is great merit to the theoretical concept of liberty and to the practical notion of libertarianism as a guiding principle for organizing civil society. If one accepts that assumption, then the fact that libertarian ideas are almost completely absent from modern political discourse in modern democracies is something of a mystery. After all, if ideas have force, and libertarianism has merit, then why hasn't the libertarian concept of public ordering captured the popular imagination?

We live in a time of unparalleled opportunity. The Cold War is over. Outside of university settings, no one seriously debates the relative merits of private markets for allocating resources within society. Instead, debate in public-policy circles has shifted to arguments about the level of resources that should be allocated to the welfare state—that is, to social security programs which, broadly construed, include publicly administered health insurance, publicly administered retirement funds, and publicly administered unemployment insurance schemes. The pervasiveness of these programs presents a very difficult problem for those who support the libertarian principle of limited government. After all, even if one could demonstrate unequivocally that a shift to a libertarian world would improve aggregate wealth or gross domestic product, the effect of such a shift on individuals is by no means clear. And risk-averse people, even if they are only modestly well off, might prefer the certainty of the existing order to the risk and uncertainty associated with a sudden change to a society organized under libertarian principles. By contrast, those who are subjected to the vagaries of the market are likely to be far less hostile to the idea of adding more layers of welfare-state protections than to the idea of reducing restrictions on free markets. This is because the welfare state provides protections for those who fare poorly under free-market conditions. This is part of the reason why libertarianism often has been opposed more vigorously than socialism, not only by statists and other collectivists, but also by those conservatives (a group I identify as generally opposed to change) who have pondered the relative merits of libertarianism and socialism.

Besides general opposition to change, another reason that conservatives traditionally have opposed libertarianism is because libertarian ideas often are associated exclusively with the promotion of market capitalism. Conservatives (and socialists for that matter) make serious arguments that something more than free markets is required for human flourishing. Libertarians must address these concerns. The appeal of libertarianism must be based on claims of ethics and morality, not simply on the ability

[3] *Ibid.*

of a libertarian state to deliver superior material goods. And, perhaps most importantly, libertarians must be able to identify the concrete things that people want (that are currently being offered by government) and explain how these things still will be available (in the market) under a libertarian system of social and economic ordering.

Put differently, voters in democratic regimes are unwilling to give up the protections offered by the welfare state, even when those protections are produced inefficiently, and at very high cost. Libertarians are not going to succeed politically by telling voters that they should give up welfare-state protections. Rather, libertarians need to show how free-market programs will produce social security at levels comparable to those provided by welfare-state systems.[4]

The basic thing that people want from government is protection, that is, insurance. Rather than ignoring the fact that people want this protection, libertarians should argue more publicly and forcefully that the government does a poorer job than free markets at providing this good. Libertarian policy perspectives would gain popular currency if it could be shown that the types of insurance protection that liberals or conservatives might want would be available in a libertarian society. What libertarians need to do is show how private *insurance* markets can deliver this protection better (and not just at lower cost) than government. In other words, libertarianism has failed to understand the primordial nature of the demand for insurance. More fundamentally, libertarians have not heeded the notion that "it is impossible to reflect on evolutionary processes without recognizing the intrinsic role of insurance. Any species that relied on nature's harmony and regularity and ignored its stochastic whims was soon extinct."[5] The demand for bigger government is inexorably linked to the demand for insurance from nature's uncertainties. Libertarians must explain how markets can do a better job than governments at handling insurable risk. They then must convince people that the costs associated with risks that cannot be insured against ought not be spread to other parties—including the government.

---

[4] This approach is very similar to the approach taken by Daniel Shapiro in his essay "Why Even Egalitarians Should Favor Market Health Insurance," elsewhere in this volume. Shapiro argues that libertarians should promote market health insurance by using what he calls an "internal strategy," i.e., one that accepts the goals of those who defend the welfare state, but then shows that a libertarian approach will do a better job of achieving those goals than a statist approach.

[5] "Insurance," in *The New Palgrave: A Dictionary of Economics*, vol. 2, ed. John Eatwell, Murray Milgate, and Peter Newman (London: Macmillan Press, 1987), p. 868. See also Kenneth J. Arrow, *Essays in the Theory of Risk-Bearing* (Chicago: Markham, 1971); Irving Ehrlich and Gary S. Becker, "Market Insurance, Self-Insurance, and Self-Protection," *Journal of Political Economy*, vol. 80, no. 4 (July–August 1972), p. 623; S. A. Lippman, "Optimal Reinsurance," *Journal of Financial and Quantitative Analysis*, vol. 7, no. 5 (December 1972), pp. 2151–55; M. Rothschild and J. E. Stiglitz, "Equilibrium in Competitive Insurance Markets: An Essay on the Economics of Imperfect Information," *Quarterly Journal of Economics*, vol. 90, no. 4 (November 1975), p. 629.

Any risk that is "independent" of other insured risks can be insured. Risks that are not independent are said to be noninsurable. An independent risk is one that is not affected by the occurrence of another event. Thus, for example, the risks of a house fire in two houses in different parts of the world are independent risks, while the risk of fire in one apartment is not independent of the risk of a fire starting in the adjoining apartment.

The demand for insurance comes from the fact that individuals are "unable to predict the timing and the magnitude of events that profoundly affect their well-being."[6] Insurance is simply the generic name for the contractual devices that mitigate the influence of uncertainty that characterizes any economic system. Risks that have been mitigated through the use of insurance contracts include "not only fire, theft, sickness and death but also fluctuating prices, equipment malfunctions, zero inventory levels causing unsatisfied demands, and failure of basic research."[7] Securities markets exist to shift the risks of business from entrepreneurs to those purchasing securities, and futures contracts permit farmers and food processors to shift the risks of future price fluctuations in order to specialize in production.[8]

Comparing what government does with what insurance markets do brings into sharp focus the fact that the welfare state is simply socializing the provision of insurance, and makes it easier to show that people would be helped by a shift to a regime guided by libertarian principles. Unfortunately, as the discussion of the minimum wage presented below (in Section III) demonstrates, the people that would benefit most from such a shift are those without power and influence. Consequently, economic arguments alone[9] are unlikely to succeed in public policy debates over the desirability of a shift to libertarianism. In order to succeed, libertarianism must be supported by credible appeals to people's higher conceptions of themselves, both as individuals and as citizens in a broader society characterized by mutual respect for individual liberty.[10]

---

[6] "Insurance," p. 868.

[7] Ibid., p. 869.

[8] Ibid.

[9] See, e.g., F. A. Hayek, Law, Legislation, and Liberty (Chicago: University of Chicago Press, 1979); Milton Friedman, Capitalism and Freedom (Chicago: Chicago University Press, 1973); and Adam Smith, The Wealth of Nations [1776] (New York: Random House, 1991).

[10] The idea that communitarian ideals must be embraced in order for the libertarian paradigm to survive is not new: see Stephen Macedo, "Community, Diversity, and Civic Education: Toward a Liberal Political Science of Group Life," Social Philosophy and Policy, vol. 13, no. 1 (Winter 1996), pp. 240–68. Libertarians have not ignored the communitarian vision in their scholarly writings: see, e.g., Stephen Holmes, The Anatomy of Antiliberalism (Cambridge: Harvard University Press, 1993), chs. 7 and 11; Chandran Kukathas, "Liberalism, Communitarianism, and Political Community," Social Philosophy and Policy, vol. 13, no. 1 (Winter 1996), pp. 80–104; Neera K. Badhwar, "Moral Agency, Commitment, and Impartiality," Social Philosophy and Policy, vol. 13, no. 1 (Winter 1996), pp. 1–26; and Douglas B. Rasmussen, "Community versus Liberty?" in Machan and Rasmussen, eds., Liberty for the Twenty-First Century, pp. 259–87. Unfortunately, libertarianism's lack of success as a political movement suggests that libertarians have failed in their efforts to convince people that they

Recognizing others' efforts to defend against communitarian attacks,[11] this essay attempts to provide further evidence that the libertarian model is consistent with communitarian principles. By describing how the ideal libertarian state can provide a person with an increased sense of security, I will show why the libertarian regime is well-suited for a modern society that puts so much emphasis on community.

In Section II of this essay, I explain the intellectual attraction of the libertarian ideal. In Section III, I use an example from the current debate about the minimum wage to illustrate my assertion that the libertarian idea is largely missing from modern discourse about public policy. In Sections IV, V, and VI, I explain why this is the case.

While it is possible to explain how a society might be wealthier if libertarian values were respected, for many it is difficult to conceptualize what life itself would be like in a libertarian world. In particular, I will argue that libertarians need to develop their conception of security more fully if libertarian ideas are going to reemerge as viable concepts in the social philosophy and public policy of the nation. The arguments that follow all are based on the assumption that libertarians have not adequately addressed people's innate need to cope with nature's stochastic quirks.

First, libertarians need a convincing response to the question of how to deal with the uncertainty caused by the phenomenon of rent-seeking in a libertarian world. The term "rent-seeking" defines the process of expending resources in order to obtain favors from government.[12] In the real world, people make predictions about how they will fare in society if certain policy changes are instituted.[13] And, of course, people make predictions about how they will fare under various alternative legal regimes, and they formulate policy positions based on these predictions. Thus, those who expect to fare relatively well under conditions of unfettered rent-seeking can be expected to be strong opponents of libertarian efforts to create a "night watchman state" in which profit-seeking activities are pushed from the public sphere to the private sphere and the possibilities for rent-seeking consequently are reduced dramatically.

---

will lead more meaningful—and more secure—lives under a legal regime controlled by libertarian principles.

[11] Most notable of these efforts is Holmes's *The Anatomy of Antiliberalism*. Although Holmes does recognize that notions of community are not altogether absent from libertarian thought, he does not address the central issue of this essay, which is the need for people to feel a sense of security in a libertarian world.

[12] James Buchanan, Robert Tollison, and Gordon Tullock, eds., *Toward a Theory of the Rent-Seeking Society* (College Station, TX: Texas A&M University Press, 1980). Somewhat more formally, rent-seeking refers to the process by which market participants seek to obtain higher prices for goods and services than would be obtainable under competitive market conditions. Thus, for example, when an automobile manufacturer lobbies the government for tariffs on the import of foreign cars, that lobbying process is "rent-seeking." If the lobbying effort succeeds, the higher prices that the manufacturer can charge are called "economic rents."

[13] Cf. John Rawls, *A Theory of Justice* (Cambridge: Harvard University Press, 1971).

Those who are considering abandoning rent-seeking inevitably will be concerned about the behavior of others within the civic community. This is because it would be ruinous for a single person or group to abandon rent-seeking unless many, if not most, others within the community simultaneously abandoned the practice as well, since abandoning rent-seeking (including "defensive" rent-seeking, in which people expend resources to oppose wealth transfers and other burdensome rules that reduce wealth) without a simultaneous commitment from others to do the same would have disastrous consequences.

Next, libertarians need to tie their arguments about how to deal with uncertainty with libertarian theories about community. The ineluctable reality is that people all over the world exhibit a strong redistributive impulse. Libertarians would do well to recognize that this emotional impulse exists. Libertarians are also wrong in thinking that they can win supporters merely by demonstrating that the state does a poor job in helping the neediest. That is beside the point. What matters is that the state allows private citizens to have an excuse to avoid charity. The all-powerful state substitutes for the principle of personal responsibility. People have the state, and the state allows them to think that something is being done for the neediest. The state provides a convenient, albeit costly, outlet for the redistributive impulse. And, more importantly, the state provides the assurance that something will be done for them if they become needy.

Finally, and most importantly, libertarians must render more accessible their conception of civic life in a libertarian world. In particular, libertarians must render accessible their notions of such things as public spirit, civic participation, and valor—including military valor—in the life of a citizen living in a libertarian state.[14] While it is probably true, as David Boaz asserts, that people feel increasingly alienated from government,[15] there is a need, perhaps more in some countries than in others, for national identity, for cultural and political identity, and for grandeur in what has been described as "some reconciliation of poetry and politics."[16]

II. The Intellectual Attraction of Libertarianism

As I noted at the outset, I define libertarianism as the philosophy of liberty under law. Consistent with this definition, a society ordered by libertarian principles will be designed to give individuals the maximum possible amount of personal liberty and individual freedom, subject only

---

[14] After all, as Holmes points out (in *The Anatomy of Antiliberalism*, p. 200): "[C]ommon goods [such as justice] are enjoyed by individuals, to be sure, but *jointly, not atomistically*" (emphasis added).

[15] Boaz, *Libertarianism: A Primer*, p. 11.

[16] Roger Cohen, "For France, Sagging Self-Image and Esprit," *New York Times*, February 11, 1997.

to simple, well-known legal constraints (laws) designed to prevent people from encroaching on the liberty of others. Following John Locke (among others), civic society can be thought of as based on a contractual agreement among people to protect themselves from others' aggression.[17]

The libertarian philosophy is supported by two foundational ideas. The first is that individuals can only flourish and realize their full potential as human beings if they are allowed to control their own lives free of outside coercion. John Stuart Mill captured this notion in his essay "On Liberty":

> He who lets the world or his own portion of it, choose his plan of life for him, has no need of any other faculty than the ape-like one of imitation. He who chooses to plan for himself, employs all of his faculties. He must use observation to see, reasoning and judgment to foresee, activity to gain materials for decision, discrimination to decide and, when he has decided, firmness and self-control to hold to his deliberate decision. . . . It is possible that he might be guided on some good path and kept out of harm's way, without any of these things. But what will be his comparative worth as a human being? It really is of importance, not only what men do, but also what manner of men they are that do it.[18]

The implication of Mill's idea is that liberty is critical to individual flourishing. Consequently, only third-party effects (externalities) can justify constraints on individual freedom.

The second, broader foundational claim of libertarianism is that individual freedom of action produces positive externalities. This claim, which is consistent with the writing of Adam Smith rather than with that of Mill, starts with the idea that economic freedom allows people to strive to better their individual conditions. This, in turn, leads to the spontaneous development of markets which provide the fora in which people can engage in transactions that produce mutual gains from trade. The development of markets then leads to economic growth, development, and prosperity. Smith made this point in his *Wealth of Nations*:

> Every individual is continually exerting himself to find out the most advantageous employment for whatever capital he can command. It is his own advantage, indeed, and not that of the society, which he has in view. But the study of his own advantage naturally, or rather necessarily leads him to prefer that employment which is most advantageous to the society. . . . [H]e intends only his gain, and he is in this, as in many other cases, led by an invisible hand to promote an

[17] John Locke, *Second Treatise of Government* [1690], ed. T. P. Peardon (New York: Liberal Arts Press, 1952).
[18] John Stuart Mill, *On Liberty* [1859] (Oxford: Oxford University Press, 1942), Book III.

end which was no part of his intention. Nor is it always the worse for the society that it was no part of it. By pursuing his own interest he frequently promotes that of the society more effectually than when he really intends to promote it.[19]

In other words, individual liberty is not only necessary for human flourishing, it also is necessary for economic growth, and for the adjustment of economies "to the changing preference structures of [their] members."[20] As F. A. Hayek observed, the market is the only discovery process capable of processing and reflecting in a meaningful way constantly changing information about human preferences.[21] Consequently, the state ought not interfere with the private exchanges that constitute the market, but rather should adopt the laissez-faire policies consistent with libertarian principles: free enterprise for firms and free trade between countries.

Thus, the libertarian position endorsed here does not reject the idea that there is a role for government, or at least for some well-defined mechanism for enforcing property rights. Government is necessary in order to protect contractual rights and property rights, without which there would be no incentive to invest the resources necessary to acquire the specialized knowledge and specialized assets necessary for economic growth.[22]

The point here is that libertarianism can be powerfully explained and defended, but perhaps only at a very high level of intellectual abstraction. When there is rank poverty or tremendous oppression, freedom seems to have a very powerful appeal. After all, the English Revolutions of the seventeenth century and the American and French Revolutions of the eighteenth century reflected strong libertarian ideals. But these revolutions were in response to strong systematic oppression and needlessly poor economic conditions. Now, in the shadow of the dawn of the twenty-first century, libertarianism seems dead.

In other words, libertarianism as an idea appears to have strong appeal to people in dire straits; but once a society reaches a certain level of

---

[19] Adam Smith, *An Inquiry into the Nature and Causes of the Wealth of Nations*, ed. R. H. Campbell, A. S. Skinner, and W. B. Todd (New York: Oxford University Press, 1976), Book IV, ch. 2, pp. 454, 456.

[20] Alan Peacock, "Economic Freedom," in *The New Palgrave: A Dictionary of Economics* (*supra* note 5), vol. 2, p. 34.

[21] Hayek, *Law, Legislation, and Liberty*, vol. 3.

[22] There are, of course, two wings of libertarian thought, one anarchist, the other minimalist. The central debate among libertarians over the past twenty-five years has been between these two strains of thought. Compare Murray Rothbard, *For a New Liberty: The Libertarian Manifesto* (New York: Collier, 1978); and Herbert Spencer, *Social Statics* (London: John Chapman, 1851); with Richard Epstein, *Simple Rules for a Complex World* (Cambridge: Harvard University Press, 1995); Ayn Rand, "Man's Rights," in *Capitalism: The Unknown Ideal* (New York: New American Library, 1967); Robert Nozick, *Anarchy, State, and Utopia* (New York: Basic Books, 1974). Here I follow Adam Smith's notion in advocating the absolute minimum amount of state intervention in the economy necessary to enforce the contracts made in private markets.

wealth, the appeal of libertarianism seems to dwindle in the popular imagination. Once an economy appears to be functioning with success, concerns about redistribution, alienation, citizenship, and fairness encroach on the libertarian idea of the night watchman state. Often libertarian writers characterize this situation as a problem of raw power: How do we create a state powerful enough to protect property rights without making it so powerful that it threatens the very liberties and contractual freedoms that it was supposed to nurture and protect?[23]

This characterization of the libertarian dilemma is incomplete. While it is clearly true that the state systematically has grown at the expense of individual liberty, it is important to recognize that this growth has reflected popular preferences. Moreover, it is by no means clear that a nation can long survive if it does not redistribute income to those who exist outside of the market. Of course, this is an empirical question and the data is by no means clear. What matters, however, is not whether a society actually will collapse in the absence of systematic wealth redistribution by the state. What matters is that (1) powerful groups can make credible threats that it will, and (2) these groups clearly can organize into effective political coalitions to effectuate such wealth transfers.

To put the matter differently, despite the intellectual appeal of libertarian arguments, such arguments have not been able successfully to compete with redistributivist ideas in the political sphere. As I have argued elsewhere, this is largely due to a prisoner's dilemma that forces individuals and firms in a free-market economy to turn to the government for special favors, or for regulatory forbearance.[24]

The prisoner's dilemma results from the fact that, once a civil society is formed, rational members of the society will recognize that it is in their best interests to form into political coalitions in order to be more successful at rent-seeking. These political coalitions employ a wide variety of methods to obtain favors—ranging from outright bribes to simple endorsements and campaign contributions of time and money. The legislative wealth transfers these coalitions obtain range from outright government grants, to protectionist legislation, to regulations that erect barriers to entry, cartelize an industry, or impose differentially high costs on one's competitors. While everyone would be better off if they could make a credible, binding commitment to refrain from playing this rent-seeking game, there is no way to make such a commitment. Consequently, the

[23] Murray, *What It Means to Be a Libertarian*, ch. 1; Machan and Rasmussen, eds., *Liberty for the Twenty-First Century*, p. 99; John Locke, "Understanding Can Not Be Compelled," in *A Letter Concerning Toleration* (Buffalo, NY: Prometheus, 1990), pp. 18–65; and Richard A. Epstein, "Self-Interest and the Constitution," *Journal of Legal Education*, vol. 37, no. 2 (June 1987), p. 155.

[24] Jonathan R. Macey, "Property Rights, Innovation, and Constitutional Structure," *Social Philosophy and Policy*, vol. 11, no. 2 (Summer 1994), p. 192.

optimal strategy for each rational individual and group is to engage in rent-seeking.

In other words, in a civil society with a government holding the power to coerce wealth transfers, it simply is not possible to avoid the rent-seeking game. At a minimum, economic actors must expend resources in order to resist efforts by others to regulate the markets in which they do business.[25] The prisoner's dilemma described here has two implications. The obvious implication is that rent-seeking is difficult to avoid absent very strong structural constitutional impediments to the rent-seeking game. The more subtle implication of the prisoner's dilemma analysis is that people have very strong incentives to engage in public rhetoric and discourse that disparages rent-seeking by others in order to decrease the competition for wealth transfers.

It would seem desirable to construct a set of civic norms and values that abhors rent-seeking and ostracizes those who engage in it. Oddly enough, however, this has not happened. Those who engage in rent-seeking do not characterize their activities as such. Quite to the contrary, they characterize what they are doing as simple civic participation. And political participation and citizenship are considered virtues. It is very difficult to distinguish political participation designed to improve the public good from political participation designed to procure private benefits. The essence of citizenship involves the responsibility to be actively engaged in civic life. Far from shunning those who participate actively in the rent-seeking game, the current *zeitgeist* appears to favor them; and civic participation—whatever the consequences—is seen as the means to a satisfying social and spiritual life.

The following discussion illustrates this phenomenon with reference to the recurring policy debate over the minimum wage. As will be seen, despite the seemingly obvious applicability of libertarian perspectives to the minimum-wage debate, libertarian principles did not play a prominent role in the policy debates over the minimum wage. The latter part of this essay identifies the deficiencies in the libertarian perspective that have led to this state of affairs.

III. The Influence of Libertarian Thought on Policymaking

Libertarianism has little, if any, effect whatsoever on policymaking. Perhaps the best example of this point may be seen in the debate that took place in the early 1990s over the minimum wage. On April 1, 1992, a law in New Jersey took effect which raised the minimum wage in that state from $4.25 to $5.05 per hour. The bill, which was strongly opposed by

---

[25] Fred S. McChesney, "Rent Extraction and Rent Creation in the Economic Theory of Regulation," *Journal of Legal Studies*, vol. 16, no. 1 (January 1987), p. 103.

business leaders in the state, made New Jersey the state with the highest minimum wage in the country.[26]

Most mainstream economists believe that raising the minimum wage will increase unemployment, and that an increase of 10 percent will lead to a cut in low-wage employment of 1 to 2 percent.[27] Nevertheless, the Clinton administration proposed and obtained legislation raising the federal minimum wage from $4.25 per hour to $5.15 per hour.[28] The Clinton administration defended its proposal against economic critics based on recent empirical studies claiming that a moderate rise in the minimum wage would not harm employment very much. Of particular interest to the Clinton administration was a study by David Card and Alan Krueger claiming that employment in New Jersey's fast-food restaurants (leading employers of low-wage workers) actually rose relative to employment levels in neighboring Pennsylvania.[29]

Card and Krueger's explanation for the wage increase for workers in New Jersey's fast-food establishments is unconvincing. They argue that after the minimum-wage increase fast-food restaurants could substitute high-quality workers for low-quality workers and pass the savings on to consumers. This explanation is unconvincing because restaurants could have hired high-quality workers (at the higher wage levels mandated by the new statute) before the law required that they do so. But if consumers really do not want to pay more for higher-quality workers in fast-food restaurants, then, over time, consumers will reveal those preferences by eating fewer meals at fast-food restaurants and more meals in other types of restaurants or at home.

Moreover, Card and Krueger's methodology was flawed. Their study was based on telephone surveys of what fast-food restaurants *said* they were going to do, rather than on what such restaurants actually *did*. There is no reason to doubt the standard textbook account of the effects of an increase in the minimum wage. Such an increase reflects an increase in the price of labor. When the price of labor rises, some workers will be better off because they will be paid more. Others will be worse off because they will lose their jobs—or never be hired in the first place. Moreover, those

---

[26] The New Jersey law, enacted in 1990, imposed increases in the minimum wage for 1990 and 1991 with a final increase to $5.05 effective April 1, 1992; see Bureau of National Affairs, *Daily Labor Report*, May 5, 1990.

[27] "American Survey," *The Economist*, April 27, 1996, pp. 25–26.

[28] Minimum Wage Increase Act of 1996, 29 U.S.C. § 206(a) (1994). The act, which implemented a gradual increase in the hourly minimum wage from the 1991 level of $4.25 to $5.15 by September 1, 1997, was embedded in the Small Business Job Protection Act of 1996 (SBJA). The SBJA's main objective is "to provide tax relief for small businesses, to protect jobs, to create opportunities, [and to] increase the take home pay of workers . . ." (Publ. L. No. 104-188 [H.R. 3448]).

[29] David Card and Alan Krueger, "Minimum Wage and Employment: A Case Study of the Fast Food Industry in New Jersey and Pennsylvania," *American Economic Review*, vol. 84, no. 4 (1994), pp. 772–93.

who lose their jobs are likely to be disproportionately young, black, and female.[30]

The narrow point here is not simply to illustrate the way that flawed economic findings are used for political gain. Leaving aside the economic studies, approximately 85 percent of the American public supported the Clinton administration's plan to raise the minimum wage.[31] Nonetheless, the administration felt compelled to support its policy position with something more than opinion polls; and the administration was able to find the intellectual support it needed for its position in the Card and Krueger study.

The broader point about the minimum-wage debate is that the terms of the debate were purely consequentialist: opponents of increasing the minimum wage argued only that such an increase would raise unemployment levels.[32] Libertarian principles of freedom of contract and individual rights were not taken seriously. To someone committed to libertarian principles, the lack of a serious, sustained discussion of the implications for the poor of raising the minimum wage is strange.

The argument against the minimum wage that could succeed politically begins with the proposition that the weakest in society are likely to be harmed most when the minimum wage is raised. This is true for two reasons. First, the worst off among those who are lucky enough to be employed will be the first to be let go when the minimum wage is raised, because the wage will rise above their marginal productivity—in other words, above their incremental value to the firm.[33]

It is straightforward to see how increasing the minimum wage will lower employment. Firms will hire workers as long as the revenue produced by the last worker hired equals or exceeds the costs imposed by that worker on the firm. When the minimum wage is imposed, the firm will find that the additional costs to the firm of the last workers hired before the minimum wage was increased exceed the additional revenue

---

[30] "American Survey," pp. 25–26.

[31] Ibid.

[32] John Joudis, "TRB: Bare Minimum (Questionable Amendments in the 1996 Minimum Wage Law)," New Republic, October 28, 1996; Paul Richter and James Gerstenzang, "Clinton Signs Minimum Wage Hike," Los Angeles Times, August 21, 1996; Glen Johnson, "Weld/Kerry Minimum Wage Positions Encapsule Government Views," Associated Press, July 8, 1996.

[33] The marginal productivity of a worker is the amount of revenue that the last worker hired by a firm will add to the total revenues of the firm. Neoclassical economic theory holds that firms will continue to add workers until the revenue produced by the last worker hired falls below the costs associated with hiring that last (marginal) worker. The reasoning behind marginal productivity theory is simple: if an extra worker adds more to a firm's revenues than to its costs, then that worker should be hired. As more and more workers are hired, the amounts that the additional workers add to a firm's productivity begin to decline; i.e., the marginal productivity of additional workers declines. To calculate the marginal productivity of labor, one subtracts the cost of hiring an additional worker from the revenue to be produced by that worker. See John Sloman, Economics (London: Harvester Wheatsheaf-Prentice Hall, 1991), p. 276.

contributed by those workers. Thus, while some low-paid workers—those lucky enough to keep their jobs—will be made better off when the minimum wage rises, the most vulnerable of the working poor will be worse off, because they will lose their jobs.

Second, it is a fact that most people earning the minimum wage are not poor.[34] Only 11 percent of people earning the minimum wage are the sole breadwinners for a family with children, and 35 percent of those earning the minimum wage still live with their parents.[35] The truly poor in America are not earning the minimum wage: the truly poor are not employed at all. And there will be more of these after the minimum wage is raised, because that raises the cost of hiring additional workers. There is no question that if politicians really wished to help the poor, there are things they could do that would be more effective than raising the minimum wage. For example, they could amend the tax code to reduce taxes for poor wage-earners, or give tax advantages to firms that hire additional workers. Unlike increasing the minimum wage, these strategies, which involve lowering taxes, would increase employment. Lowering taxes for poor wage-earners would increase employment by giving workers incentives to work for lower wages (since the lower taxes would allow them to keep a higher percentage of what they earned). Lowering taxes for employers would increase employment by lowering the costs to firms of hiring workers. These strategies, however, would reduce the government's tax receipts for the benefit of a group with precious little political clout.

The point of this discussion of the minimum wage is to show that although a very strong libertarian argument against the minimum wage could be made, that argument was not made in any prominent way when the issue was debated. Consequently, the libertarian perspective had no chance to capture the public imagination. Clearly, libertarians need a new strategy if their ideas are to gain currency.

In the following three sections of this essay, I sketch my strategies for libertarians to advance their ideas in a way that will be more likely to capture the popular imagination. I also counter possible objections to the libertarian perspective.

IV. NATIONAL SECURITY: ANOTHER PRISONER'S DILEMMA

Perhaps the easiest conceptual problem for libertarian thinkers to deal with is the problem of national security. The basic problem can be put in the prisoner's dilemma framework. While it might be optimal for all governments to invoke a minimalist state framework, if there are any

---

[34] Ibid., p. 26.
[35] Ibid.

holdout nations, these will be able to mount an offensive against weaker, albeit more libertarian, states. This is a well-known problem in libertarian thought, that need not be rehashed here at length.[36]

Libertarians seeking to counter the argument that libertarian, night watchman states will not have strong survival possibilities against stronger, more aggressive neighbors point out that being a libertarian is not the same thing as being suicidal. Consequently, it is perfectly consistent with libertarian thought to organize defensive forces sufficient to defend against aggression.

Of course, reasonable people can always argue about precisely how much defense is required, but this will always be the case. The harder problem will be to control the state once it has a military powerful enough to control outside aggression. In other words, the problem of national security is, at bottom, simply a special variant of the general problem of creating a night watchman state. The trick is to create a government that is strong enough to protect property rights—even against outside aggression—without it transforming into a Leviathan that threatens individual liberty.[37]

Unfortunately, libertarians' strong distaste for the state has caused them to miss compelling arguments about the compatibility of a strong military with a libertarian framework. The traditions of a professional military in the United States and elsewhere in the West prove conclusively that a highly professional military force can be successfully separated from politics. Several U.S. presidents, most notably Bill Clinton, have been extremely unpopular with the military. Yet the professional traditions of the military, and the strongly held value that the military must remain under civilian control, have prevented a crisis. Constitutional law is a required course in all of the U.S. service academies. In these courses, future officer corps are taught the importance of respecting the rule of law within the civil society, despite the important differences between the system of justice within the military and the system of justice in civilian life. This modern experience illustrates conclusively that, in fact, national security

---

[36] See David Friedman, *The Machinery of Freedom* (La Salle, IL: Open Court, 1989); and Eric Mack, "Rights, Just War, and National Defense," in Machan and Rasmussen, eds., *Liberty for the Twenty-First Century*, pp. 101–20. For a description of the prisoner's dilemma created by concerns for national security, see Morton Davis, *Game Theory: A Nontechnical Introduction* (New York: Basic Books, 1983); and Edwin M. Smith, "Understanding Dynamic Obligations: Arms Control Agreements," *Southern California Law Review*, vol. 64 (September 1991), p. 1551.

[37] James Madison captured this sentiment in one of the most quoted passages of *The Federalist Papers*: "If men were angels, no government would be necessary. If angels were to govern men, neither external nor internal controls on government would be necessary. In framing a government which is to be administered by men over men, the great difficulty lies in this: You must first enable the government to control the governed; and in the next place, oblige it to control itself." James Madison, "Federalist No. 51," in *The Federalist Papers* [1788], ed. Jacob E. Cooke (Hanover, NH: Wesleyan University Press, 1961), p. 349.

concerns do not pose a real obstacle to the creation of a libertarian state. The incidence of military coups in developed countries is virtually non-existent. In fact, military regimes are far more likely to fall to military coups led by rival military factions than civilian regimes are. Indeed, the restraint shown by the professional military in developed countries is one of the great success stories of the libertarian paradigm.[38]

V. Credibility and Risk-Aversion

A closely related, but deeper, problem for libertarians than the problem of military coups is the problem of bureaucratic drift. Even the most committed libertarian must recognize that it will be far easier to establish a minimalist state governed by a rule of law designed to protect property rights than to *maintain* such a system against the relentless onslaught of rent-seekers. History has shown that bureaucracies, not armies, are the real enemy of the minimalist state. And while history gives cause for hope about the prospects for designing a constitution that will protect its citizens against foreign aggression, the historical evidence provides grounds for pessimism about the prospects for designing a constitution that will succeed in combating the growth of bureaucracy.[39]

In earlier work, I have modeled the process of successful constitution-building as involving a multi-period game, in which the crucial first period is characterized by a brief, one-shot effort to control the rent-seeking that is sure to take place in the subsequent periods.[40] In this earlier work, I asserted that, so long as citizens realize that future states of the world will involve rent-seeking, which is a negative-sum game,

---

[38] Of course, the problem of military coups, which is discussed in the text, is wholly distinct from another problem posed by the military: namely, how to prevent a country with a large standing army from using force in adventuristic ways. Thus, for example, the experiences of the United States in Granada, Korea, Kuwait, Panama, Somalia, and Vietnam might be described as extremely costly and wasteful adventures that would not have occurred except for the fact that the U.S. had a large standing army. This criticism of the military has significant force. However, it is a criticism from within the libertarian perspective. There is no reason to think that the military forces associated with a government committed to libertarian principles would be more likely to act in adventuristic ways than the military forces associated with other forms of government.

Indeed, since libertarian organizations like the Cato Institute consistently have opposed military intervention by U.S. forces, there is reason to believe the opposite to be true. Thus, the problem discussed in the text, namely, that a libertarian state might be subject to coups by more-interventionist forms of government, must be addressed by those seeking to advance the libertarian cause. However, the problem discussed in this note, namely, that governments may use the military in inappropriate, adventuristic ways, is not a problem peculiar to libertarianism.

[39] See William Niskanen, *Bureaucracy and Representative Government* (Chicago: Aldine-Atherton, 1971), which argues that bureaucrats seek to maximize their budgets. See also Ludwig von Mises, *Bureaucracy* (New Haven: Yale University Press, 1944); George C. Roche, *America by the Throat: The Stranglehold of Federal Bureaucracy* (Old Greenwich, CN: Devin-Adair, 1983).

[40] Macey, "Property Rights, Innovation, and Constitutional Structure," p. 192.

"each citizen has a strong interest in agreeing *ex ante* (i.e., at the time of constitutional creation) to protect property rights and to constrain rent-seeking."[41] However, I believe there was a flaw in my previous analysis, which I wish to address now. The flaw is that while it is true that rent-seeking is a negative-sum game, it still may not be in the best interests of *all* citizens to prevent rent-seeking, because some citizens will be better at effectuating wealth transfers in a rent-seeking world than at creating wealth in private-market endeavors.

Thus, while it is *possible* for the citizens of a polity to come together during a "constitutional moment"[42] in which they simultaneously agree to create a system of rules that constrain rent-seeking, it is by no means clear that bargaining over the contents of a new constitution necessarily will lead to this result. Those with a comparative advantage at rent-seeking, who have disproportionate influence over the structure of legal rules during times of normal politics, are likely also to have disproportionate influence during times of constitutional creation. In order to achieve a libertarian constitutional structure that impedes rent-seeking, the rent-seekers must be disarmed. Of course, it might be possible simply to exclude from the process of constitutional formation those people or groups that will be net winners in the rent-seeking game during the post-constitutional period. Perhaps this could be done by force, or perhaps it could be done by constructing a legal argument about why such people *ex ante* should be excluded from the bargaining table. It is likely, however, that excluding these groups would undermine the legitimacy of the new constitution, particularly if discrete ethnic groups or other identifiable minorities were represented disproportionately among the membership of the rent-seeking class. Moreover, whatever legitimacy the constitution might have in the eyes of those responsible for crafting it, those excluded would be unlikely to recognize its legitimacy.

A more likely possibility would be for the wealth creators to "buy off" the rent-seekers, by agreeing to share with them the overall gains in productivity—and hence wealth—that would result from a reduction in rent-seeking. Here the intuition is simple. Rent-seeking is a game that is both unproductive and negative-sum. To obtain $100 in wealth transfers, a party will be willing to spend up to $100; and others will be willing to pay up to $100 to block the transfer. In other words, far more than $100 will be spent to obtain each $100 in wealth transfers. Thus, while any expenditures to obtain wealth transfers from the state represent waste, because the money used to obtain such transfers would otherwise be put to productive use, the degree of waste is exacerbated by the fact that so much money and energy must be expended to avoid rent-seeking by others.

---

[41] *Ibid.*

[42] See Bruce Ackerman, "The Storrs Lectures: Discovering the Constitution," *Yale Law Journal*, vol. 93, no. 6 (May 1984), p. 1015.

To illustrate this point more precisely, suppose that a particular society is divided into two groups, group R and group P. Group R is composed of rent seekers and group P is composed of productive people. Suppose that the society's aggregate wealth, where wealth is defined as the sum of the current capital stock of the two groups, plus the sum of the present values of the expected future earnings of the two groups, is 100 prior to the debates that characterize a constitutional moment. This sum equals the wealth of R, which is 40, plus the wealth of P, which is 60. Suppose further that a super-majority is needed to approve a new, libertarian constitutional framework, so that either group could block a change in the rules of the game that would make rent-seeking more difficult.

Suppose further that if the constitutional structure were changed so as to impede rent-seeking and implement a libertarian, night watchman state, overall societal wealth would increase from 100 to 140. Overall wealth would increase to 140 because group P would have incentives to work harder and produce more, knowing that group R would not be able to obtain as much in the way of wealth transfers under the new regime. But if the change to the new constitutional structure were made without any side payments, group R would have much less wealth, due to the decrease in their ability to engage in rent-seeking, while group P would have more wealth due to the greater incentives associated with their enhanced ability to keep what they produce. For purposes of this illustration, suppose that the wealth of group R decreases from 40 to 10 after the constitutional change, while the wealth of group P increases from 60 to 130.

Under this set of stylized assumptions, members of group R would obviously block all efforts to enact a libertarian constitutional scheme, since their wealth would decrease from 40 to 10 if such a scheme were enacted. But, if group P could pay group R some amount greater than the 30 they would be losing under the changing conditions, but less than the entire 70 that group P would gain from such a change, both groups would be better off. Suppose, for example, that group P agreed to pay group R 40 in order to cause group R to assent to the new constitutional structure. Under this scenario, group R would be better off because of the change. Its aggregate wealth would improve from 40 to 50 (R would have a wealth of 10 under the new rules of the game, plus the 40 received in the form of transfers from P). Group P would improve its wealth from the 60 that it had before the constitutional change to 90 (P would have a wealth of 130 under the new libertarian structure, minus the 40 paid to the members of group R for the purpose of buying their cooperation).[43]

---

[43] Of course, the payment from P to R would diminish P's incentives to produce, and thus the total level of production might decrease from 140 under a new constitutional regime in which P had to make wealth transfers to R. If P's productivity fell below the level at which its aggregate wealth fell to 60 or below, the constitutional reform effort would fail, because P has the power to block the reform and P would be worse off under the new regime than under the old regime in which P's aggregate wealth was 60.

In previous work, I have argued that those in group R, that is, those who expect to be net winners in the political process, can be bought off easily because of the threat of exclusion from the new civil society.[44] I think this argument is wrong for two reasons. First, as discussed above, I think that I overstated the ease with which other groups (those in category P) can exclude those in category R from the bargaining process. It is more likely that those in group R, who (by hypothesis) have a comparative advantage at rent-seeking, will be able to exclude group P from the bargaining process. And those in group R will be able to raise significant moral objections to being discriminated against if their "voices" are excluded from the bargaining process.

Moreover, it must be stressed that a severe contracting problem will plague the efforts to reach a new constitutional consensus among the various factions within a society. This problem arises because R and P will not be performing their obligations to one another simultaneously. Those in group R must agree to rules that restrict the rent-seeking game during the initial period of constitutional formation—before group P is in a position to pay them the sum necessary to buy their cooperation. Group P is unable to pay because the sums necessary for payment must come out of future gains in productivity that will be realized only if rent-seeking is restricted now. The trap is that it is by no means clear that the members of group P can make a credible promise to the members of group R that they will make future payments in exchange for R's current promise to submit to a constitutional structure that impedes rent-seeking. Indeed, it is this very trap that is impeding efforts to achieve meaningful reform in Russia and the former Soviet republics. Where it is not possible for those who seek genuine reform to make a credible commitment to exchange future payments for current libertarian reforms, bureaucrats remain in power and prevent meaningful change.[45]

To summarize, various groups do not live behind a veil of ignorance in which it is not possible to tell how one will fare under various alternative

---

[44] Macey, "Property Rights, Innovation, and Constitutional Structure," p. 193, n. 31.

[45] Of course, it is important to distinguish those countries that are still run by (un-reformed) communists from those countries that are being run either by noncommunists or by reformed communists. But this distinction fits within the model presented in the text: those countries that have enjoyed relative success in making the transition to market-driven economies are those in which the bureaucrats have been co-opted into the privatization process. See, e.g., economist Thomas W. Hazlett's description of state managers' involvement in privatization in the Czech Republic: Hazlett, "The Czech Miracle: Why Privatization Went Right in the Czech Republic," *Reason*, April 1995; and Hazlett, "Bottom-Up Privatization: The Czech Experience," in *The Privatization Process: A Worldwide Perspective*, ed. Terry Anderson and P. J. Hill (Lanham, MD: Rowman and Littlefield, 1996). This co-option has involved keeping large numbers of bureaucrats in leadership positions, either within the bureaucracy or within the newly privatized enterprises. It is precisely in this way that reformers have been able to pay the price for reform by "buying off" the politicians and bureaucrats capable of blocking such reform. See Enrico Colombatto and Jonathan R. Macey, "Path Dependence, Public Choice, and Transition in Russia: A Bargaining Approach," *Cornell Journal of Law and Public Policy*, vol. 4, no. 2 (Spring 1995), pp. 379–413.

possible legal regimes and states of society. In fact, people can make accurate predictions about how they will fare under various alternative states of society, and people will formulate policy positions based on these predictions. Those who expect to fare relatively well under conditions of unfettered rent-seeking are likely to be strong opponents of libertarian efforts to create a night watchman state in which profit-seeking activities are pushed from the public sphere to the private sphere, consequently decreasing dramatically the possibilities for rent-seeking.

At bottom, consistent with the notion that economic analysis can be applied to constitutional theory, the problem of establishing a libertarian constitutional structure is a bargaining problem. Unfortunately, the fact that the relevant groups are not performing their obligations simultaneously makes the puzzle far easier to describe than to solve. This problem arises because those who expect to be winners in the rent-seeking game must agree immediately to refrain from such rent-seeking activities, while those who expect to be losers from rent-seeking but winners in the realm of market exchanges must make payments to the rent-seekers out of future wealth. Of course, there is nothing unusual about a contract in which one side is called upon to perform before the other. In fact, most contracts exhibit this feature of non-simultaneity of performance, because it is very rare for both parties to any contract to perform their obligations under the contract simultaneously.[46] The law of contract is, in large part, designed to deal with the core problem of non-simultaneity of performance by one of the parties to the contract. Contract law does this by providing relief, in the form of damages, when parties breach their obligation of performance under a contract after full or partial performance by the other side. The problem in the political context is that there is no obvious enforcement mechanism for insuring that one group or the other will not change the rules of the game *ex post*. For example, suppose that R agrees to refrain from rent-seeking by acceding to the placement of restrictions on rent-seeking in the constitution. It is not clear how one could credibly enforce P's promise to make future payments to R. And, of course, people in group P would have incentives to claim to be members of group R in order to receive payments. The core of the problem is that in ordinary, garden-variety contracts, the counter-parties are clearly specified, and the respective rights and obligations of each side also are generally clear. By contrast, in the context of the constitutional contracting being described here, the parties are not identified by name, and their rights and obligations are contingent upon how well they fare in the post-constitutional marketplace.

Moreover, even those who might be willing to give up rent-seeking would be willing to do so only on the condition that others similarly

---

[46] Richard A. Posner, *Economic Analysis of Law*, 3d ed. (Boston: Little, Brown, and Company, 1986), p. 79.

agree. This is because most citizens are in a prisoner's dilemma game with respect to rent-seeking. Citizens in a civic community will be made better off by abandoning rent-seeking only if other citizens also abandon rent-seeking. This is a straightforward application of the point that much "rent-seeking" is actually defensive: in a rent-seeking society rational individuals must spend resources to prevent others from effectuating wealth transfers from the state at their expense. Thus, before accepting life in a libertarian society, people will demand to know what constraints will exist to prevent others from rent-seeking.

One implication of the above analysis is that some level of coerced wealth transfers is not inconsistent with a practical libertarian model.[47] The intuition is that such transfers are the price that must be paid to buy freedom. Thus, for example, Hayek argued that a minimum uniform income should be provided by the state to all those who, for whatever reason, are unable to earn an adequate income within the confines of the market.[48] Similarly, Mill argued that sustained concentrations of wealth should be avoided because they lead to political and social instability that can endanger both political and economic freedom.[49]

Clearly, Hayek's minimum-income proposal would not be likely to attract sophisticated rent-seeking coalitions like environmental groups or big business. On the other hand, his proposal would appeal to the very large numbers of risk-averse individuals who would oppose any shift to a libertarian regime on the grounds that, for them, even the small possibility of a lower quality of life under such a regime is enough to outweigh a high probability of improvement. In addition, Hayek's proposal would also appeal to those interest groups who purport to represent the poor and needy by lobbying for government transfer programs on their behalf. Such programs often benefit the lobbyists more than they benefit the recipients of the transfers.

But the point of this essay is to articulate ways that libertarian ideas can be made to appeal to the popular imagination. The reason libertarian ideas are not taken seriously is because these ideas have not taken into account the fact that people are risk-averse and thus have a high demand for the kinds of protections described by Hayek.

By focusing on the bargaining problem described here, framers of new constitutional orders can derive rules that ameliorate the non-simultaneity of performance issue that impedes true reform. To be successful, a constitutional regime that wishes to succeed in enshrining freedom from government coercion must not only restrict the rent-seeking game that

---

[47] Cf. Jan Narveson, "Contracting for Liberty," in Machan and Rasmussen, eds., *Liberty for the Twenty-First Century*, pp. 19–39. Narveson argues that constitutional creation should focus on rights alone.

[48] Hayek, *Law, Legislation, and Liberty*, vol. 3.

[49] Mill, *On Liberty*; see also John Stuart Mill, *Principles of Political Economy* (New York: D. Appleton, 1864), Book IV, ch. 7.

leads to big government, but must also neutralize the rent-seeking establishment that constitutes the natural enemy of freedom. Consistent with this argument, buying off rent-seekers might both account for and justify the fact that the *nomenklatura* of the former Soviet Union and Eastern Europe have succeeded in many countries in seizing so many state assets as their own newly privatized property.[50] Libertarians in former communist countries would do well to adopt a general strategy of buying off the *nomenklatura* in exchange for the adoption of a constitution that enshrines economic freedom by protecting private property and freedom of contract.

Any rule that impedes rent-seeking will necessarily impede the ability of rent-seekers to acquire wealth. The solution must be to erect a system that promises everybody, including rent-seekers, substantial wealth in the future, on the condition that they refrain from rent-seeking. This may account for the fact that many of the new constitutions of the so-called emerging democracies in Eastern Europe may contain provisions that include incredible promises to their citizens purporting to give them the right to happiness and prosperity.[51] In other words, Hayek's guaranteed minimum income can be justified, despite the fact that it is likely to involve a substantial level of immoral wealth transfers, on the grounds that such a program can be administered without a large bureaucracy, and therefore does not do as much violence to the concept of a night watchman state as the complex regulatory apparatus needed to support the welfare state. In other words, the idea of a guaranteed minimum income may create a stable environment in which market processes can flourish because rent-seeking is reduced.[52]

Building on Hayek's idea, the above discussion envisions a system of fixed, finite, automatic cash transfers that eliminate the need for a welfare state. A skeleton crew of administrators could administer this program, which would enable people to qualify for such transfers solely on the basis of their income levels. It is worth stressing that this scheme has not been advanced on any moral grounds. Rather, it can be argued that the scheme is actually immoral in that it appropriates property (wealth) from rightful owners to those with no legitimate claim to it. In other words, economics and morality would seem to be united in the notion that an individual's claim to the wealth created in an economy should be in direct proportion to the amount of wealth that the person has created. The economists' valuable contribution is to observe that the prices—including

---

[50] See, e.g., Colombatto and Macey, "Path Dependence, Public Choice, and Transition in Russia."

[51] On the other hand, these provisions may simply be holdovers from the thought process instilled in people for fifty to seventy-five years under communism.

[52] It is true that wealth transfers may be another type of buy-off, but since money is transferred overtly, widely dispersed factions can mount political pressure against such payments, reducing the total amount of rent-seeking that actually occurs.

wages—generated by spontaneous, unbiased market processes are the best gauge of any individual's marginal contribution.

In the absence of a moral justification, the defense of the wealth transfers described above is purely pragmatic. Despite the immorality of governmentally coerced wealth transfers, such transfers can be defended on the grounds that they are necessary to attract popular support for reform. But the poorest groups in countries are not adroit enough to accomplish change by themselves: at best they can block reform. To achieve real change, it will be necessary to buy the cooperation of bureaucrats and interest groups that are in a position to accomplish the reforms necessary for prosperity. This generally will involve buying off the cooperation of bureaucrats and interest groups in order to co-opt them into supporting reform.[53]

Another justification for the system of wealth transfers described here is that they satisfy, in the least destructive way possible, man's ineluctable taste for charity and wealth redistribution. Economics is concerned primarily with wealth creation. The distribution of wealth is of secondary importance. Indeed, it is often said that economics is the science concerned with maximizing wealth subject to constraints, including limited resources and uncertainty. Economists are accustomed to taking initial distributions of resources as given. It is for moral philosophers to worry about the legitimacy of such initial distributions.

Leftists who oppose libertarian reforms argue that economic liberty will result in two classes, one fabulously wealthy, and the other impoverished. This is probably not the case, but the question is ultimately an empirical one, and opponents of the libertarian position seem unwilling to move to a night watchman state in order to provide the necessary conditions for the natural experiment necessary to test the issue. Moreover, whatever the distribution of wealth in a libertarian state happens to be, it seems likely that there will be at least *some* very poor people. And, whether this number is large or small, libertarians remove themselves from serious public policy debate by relying on vague promises that private charity can replace the welfare state in providing a safety net for these desperate individuals. In fact, private charity, in all likelihood, could provide such a safety net.[54] But that is not the point.

The problem is that people don't trust private charity. In other words, people are willing to accept the well-known inefficiencies in the public sector in order to achieve the certainty of welfare.

Moreover, even if a system with great inequality between the richest and the poorest could be maintained, it is not clear that it would be

[53] See Hazlett, "The Czech Miracle"; Hazlett, "Bottom-Up Privatization"; and Colombatto and Macey, "Path Dependence, Public Choice, and Transition in Russia."

[54] Michael Tanner, *The End of Welfare: Fighting Poverty in Civil Society* (Washington, DC: Cato Institute, 1997), pp. 131–49.

tolerated in a democracy. The fact is that people have a strong taste for redistribution. We observe people voluntarily giving great sums to charity, and the act of charity is widely believed to have moral value. Of course, there are economic explanations for charity. Suppose that person A cares about person B—or, more generally, suppose that A has a taste for reducing poverty generally. Assume that person A is quite wealthy, and person B is quite poor. Suppose further that, due to the diminishing marginal utility of wealth, person A would not consider a $100,000 gift to person B to involve a particularly large sacrifice. On the other hand, person B would value this $100,000 gift enormously. Not only B, but A as well, might benefit from a gift from A to B, if the transfer increased B's utility enough—assuming, of course, that A cares about B's utility. Richard Posner states the point very precisely:

> [S]ubtracting a dollar from A's income may . . . reduce A's utility by vastly less than adding a dollar to B's income would increase B's utility: Let us assume 100 times less. Then A would derive a net benefit from giving a dollar to B as long as he valued B's welfare, at the margin . . . any more than one-hundredth as much as he valued his own.[55]

Under this analysis, of course, no government intervention would be needed to satisfy individuals' taste for charity, since charity would make both donors and recipients better off. Posner argues that free-rider problems create a justification for government intervention.[56] According to Posner, person A can free-ride on the charitable inclinations of others. A is even better off if he relies on C to make a charitable donation to B, because he gets the utility of having B better off, and he also gets to keep his money.[57]

The free-rider problem is offset by the fact that A may derive some independent utility from the act of charity. And even if there is a free-rider problem, there is no argument here for giving the government a role in *operating* charitable systems that transfer wealth. Indeed, there are strong

---

[55] See Posner, *Economic Analysis of Law*, p. 439.
[56] *Ibid.*, p. 440.
[57] As Posner describes the problem (in *ibid.*, p. 440):

The altruist faces a free-rider problem. A in our example will derive welfare from the increase in B's income whether or not A is the source of the increase. Naturally A would like to buy this increase in his welfare at the lowest possible price, so he will have an incentive to hang back in giving to charity in the hope that others will give. It might seem that regardless of what others give his contributions will add to the total amount of resources devoted to the end he values. But this is not certain. His contributions may lead others to cut back their contributions, since now a smaller contribution on their part will buy the same reduction in poverty. So A will get less than a dollar benefit for every dollar he contributes, and this will lead to a lower contribution.

efficiency arguments against it. Nevertheless, the government could participate in the collection of the money from voluntary contributors, and then in a program of matching grants to charity.[58]

People view public charity as a good. Many productive people will lobby hard for government transfer programs even when the probability that they personally will be on the receiving end of such charity is fleetingly small. Any successful transition to a state of minimalist government must be able to constrain these well-meaning people. A program of lump-sum transfers, such as that envisioned by Hayek, could achieve this goal.

Advocates of coerced wealth transfers sometimes offer another efficiency-based justification: in a free-market economy, risk-averse wealthy people may wish to purchase insurance policies that guard against their becoming poor in the future. Libertarian thought must address concerns about uncertainty and risk-aversion if it is to be a successful rival to statist conceptions of public and private ordering. The failure to recognize that risk-aversion is systematic is one of the foremost shortcomings of the libertarian model. In particular, the failure to convince risk-averse people that they would be better off in a libertarian society governed by a minimalist state is the largest single reason why the minimalist state has failed to capture the popular imagination.

The behavioral model that predicts that people are risk-averse is based on the simple assumption that the marginal utility of wealth diminishes as one becomes more wealthy. The diminishing marginal utility of wealth is a robust assumption in economics. The utility of wealth diminishes marginally because people buy the things they really want (necessities) when they initially acquire wealth. After those necessities are acquired, they buy things they value less ("comfort goods"), and ultimately people purchase luxury goods. Thus, by hypothesis, the things that people buy with their one-billionth dollar matter less to them than the things they bought with their one-hundredth dollar. Thus, the utility of wealth diminishes marginally.

The conclusion that people are risk-averse follows inexorably from the principle of diminishing marginal utility. Because the marginal utility of wealth is diminishing, for most people (most of the time) the pleasure (utility) of gaining $100,000 is greatly outweighed by the pain (disutility) of losing $100,000. To illustrate the point in a manner appropriate to a debate about the general desirability of social welfare programs (such as government-subsidized or government-managed health insurance, retirement pensions, or unemployment insurance), imagine an even bet such as a coin toss between two people of equal wealth. Under the rules of the

---

[58] Matching grants are suggested because such grants would mitigate the free-rider problem associated with making charitable gifts that is discussed in the text. See *ibid.*, section 19.3, pp. 496–99.

game, the winner's wealth would double, while the loser's wealth would fall to zero. Economists doubt that rational, utility-maximizing people would take this sort of bet, because the disutility associated with losing outweighs by a wide margin the utility associated with winning. The "risk-premiums" that people raising capital must pay to attract investors provides additional support for the idea that the diminishing marginal utility of wealth leads to risk-aversion.[59]

The effort to provide a libertarian conception of a civil society must confront the fact of risk-aversion. If people are risk-averse, they will demand social welfare, that is, some form of insurance scheme that will protect them in the event that they are unsuccessful in marketplace competition. As Posner has observed, "[a]n affluent person who is risk averse will want to insure against the possibility of becoming poor sometime in the future, because of business reverses, poor health, changes in the labor market, or other misfortunes."[60]

Trying to convince people to embrace a love of risk-taking romantically linked with the entrepreneurial spirit or the pioneer spirit will not be a winning strategy for people who push for free-market solutions to social and economic problems.[61] The success of private markets for insurance proves that people do not want to live with risk. What libertarians must do instead is to convince people that private insurance markets can provide them with protection against unforeseen misfortune in a way that is qualitatively superior to the protections provided by state-sponsored insurance schemes. And this must be done not only in terms of the payoffs on the upside, but also in terms of the risks on the downside.

Because the government has co-opted many of the private insurance industries, broad-based private insurance schemes do not exist, and their absence adds to the public's apprehension about their potential. For example, in the United States, as in other countries, the government's Social Security system has greatly curtailed the public's demand for private retirement insurance. And government-sponsored welfare programs have reduced the public's demand for private insurance against loss of employment.[62] Similarly, the provision of government-sponsored insurance for bank deposits through the Federal Deposit Insurance Corporation (FDIC) has driven out market-based alternatives in this area.

An analysis of FDIC insurance on bank deposits illustrates that this government system has crowded out private solutions to the risks of deposit. Before the FDIC, bank shareholders provided insurance for de-

---

[59] Burton Malkiel, *A Random Walk Down Wall Street* (New York: W. W. Norton, 1985), pp. 305-6.

[60] Posner, *Economic Analysis of Law*, p. 441.

[61] See Milton Friedman, *Free to Choose: A Personal Statement* [1979] (New York: Harcourt Brace Jovanovich, 1990), pp. 18–19, 137–38.

[62] Historically, the majority of insurance against loss of employment was provided by family members, or by private charity. The government has, to a considerable extent, succeeded in crowding out support by these institutions.

positors. Shareholders provided insurance in the form of double and sometimes triple liability for losses to depositors, established in order to encourage people to deposit money in their banks.[63] Under these systems, shareholders were liable to depositors for losses suffered by such depositors in amounts equal to, double, or triple the amount of their initial capital investments. Today, the liability of shareholders in banks is limited to the amount of the shareholder's initial investment and no more, because government-subsidized insurance decreases consumer demand for private deposit insurance and causes consumers and bank shareholders to undervalue risks. Should the FDIC be eliminated, both banks and consumers would have incentives to encourage the reemergence of this form of private insurance market to spread the risks of potential loss. There is every reason to believe that a system similar to that existing prior to the FDIC would quickly reemerge. And, contrary to popular belief, depositors did not lose money in the Depression from the bank failures or as a result of being inadequately insured.[64] Rather, although a large number of banks failed, these were generally smaller banks, and depositors did not lose money because the system of private insurance worked. Ninety-nine percent of the losses were absorbed by the shareholders.[65] And even if insurance markets would not emerge to protect people from every harm, private charity could fill the gap to protect against extreme or unforeseen risks.[66]

Comprehensive health insurance with a disability feature addresses, to some extent, the problem of loss of income due to extreme or unforeseen risks. However, Posner takes a contrary view with respect to social welfare insurance: he argues that moral hazard problems prevent people from obtaining complete insurance against poverty. "Moral hazard" describes the phenomenon that someone with insurance is less likely to take precautions against the event covered by the insurance.[67] In the context of social welfare insurance, Posner has observed: "If it were really possible to insure against being poor, anyone who bought such insurance would have an incentive to engage in extremely risky economic behavior."[68] Because of these moral hazard problems, Posner reasons that private insurance programs that would provide benefits to contributors who became poor would inevitably fail, and that government programs are superior at resolving problems of moral hazard.[69]

---

[63] Jonathan R. Macey and Geoffrey P. Miller, "Double Liability of Bank Shareholders: History and Implications," *Wake Forest Law Review*, vol. 27, no. 1 (1992), p. 31.

[64] *Ibid.*, p. 61.

[65] *Ibid.*, p. 56.

[66] Tanner, *The End of Welfare*, pp. 131–50.

[67] For example, someone with automobile theft insurance is less likely to buy an alarm system, or even to lock his car, than someone without such insurance.

[68] Posner, *Economic Analysis of Law*, p. 441.

[69] *Ibid.*

Posner's analysis is unpersuasive. First, Posner does not explain why government programs are better than private firms at minimizing the moral hazard problem that hinders the provision of poverty insurance. Indeed, there is substantial evidence that the government is less capable than the private sector in dealing with moral hazard. The government is unable to deal with moral hazard in banking, where the moral hazard problem manifests itself in the form of bank shareholders who try to increase the risk taken by their firms when government insurance programs are in place. Similarly, the government has been unable to deal with moral hazard problems in employment insurance, or in health care, or in any other area of economic life.

Second, administering a government program that deals with moral hazard necessarily involves a complex bureaucratic determination as to whether a person claiming benefits could have avoided poverty. The depth and breadth of the government involvement required to administer such a scheme necessarily requires legions of government bureaucrats with significant discretionary powers. This, in turn, leads to the very bureaucratic drift and rent-seeking that a libertarian constitution would seek to prevent.

In sum, Posner may be right to argue that there are serious moral hazard problems associated with the provision of a comprehensive insurance scheme against poverty. However, there is no reason to believe that the government is better at dealing with this moral hazard problem than private firms are. This is an extremely important point because fear surrounding the lack of social welfare is one of the major obstacles to efforts aimed at making a libertarian manifesto attractive to large numbers of people. If, as Posner suggests, the state could do a better job of providing social welfare programs than the private sector, libertarianism could not realistically hope to succeed. But he is wrong.

The reality is that government does not deal well with moral hazard. The private sector, which has a great deal more flexibility (not to mention stronger incentives) than the public sector, routinely handles the problem of moral hazard in insurance markets through such incentive-oriented means as requiring deductibles or increasing premiums in relation to claims filed, and should be allowed to expand its efforts to replace the government's social welfare programs.

Libertarianism cannot succeed if people believe that problems of social welfare must be handled by the state. And libertarians must concede the point that their efforts to promote a world without pervasive, government-sponsored social welfare programs have failed. In rivalrous competition among politicians, those politicians who promise to save the welfare state have triumphed over those who promise to dismantle it. Social welfare programs are a sacred cow for both Republicans and Democrats, and risk-aversion explains why this is so.

It must be stressed that people support these programs despite a general mistrust of big government, and despite knowing that big government is necessary to maintain such programs if they are to be government-sponsored. Indeed, this is precisely the point. A bureaucracy big enough and powerful enough to administer the battery of programs that comprise a modern welfare state could not possibly be constrained from expanding its power. It inevitably would succumb to bureaucratic drift and turf grabbing, and the regulatory state eventually would emerge.[70] By "regulatory state," I mean a state which extensively regulates all aspects of society, from social welfare to industrial management and economic policy.

To succeed politically, libertarians must demonstrate that the private sector can do a better job than the public sector in dealing with risk and uncertainty. Clearly, the best thing ever to happen for the cause of collectivism was the Great Depression. Somehow, despite the facts, the free market was blamed for the hardships of the Depression, and the high unemployment and general uncertainty that dominated this era enabled the federal government to solidify its power and bring to an end America's noble experiment with economic liberty and strong protection of private property rights. And once the welfare state was in place, it has proven impossible to dislodge.

If libertarians are to compete with statists and socialists for public support, they must mount convincing arguments that a libertarian social order would be superior to the welfare state, not only as the way to organize private exchange, but also as the way for people to achieve personal security. If a society can offer its citizens only the chance of wealth, without the hope of security, it is unlikely that it will be successful in capturing popular support.

The argument, then, should not be about whether society should provide the safety net of social welfare programs (including, of course, low-cost, generally available, comprehensive health insurance). Libertarians would do well to shift the debate to the issue of whether social welfare programs should be provided by the public sector or by the private sector.

VI. LIBERTY AND COMMUNITY: POLICY, TECHNOLOGY, AND CITIZENSHIP

One problem with the analysis up to this point—and a fundamental issue for libertarians more broadly—involves the rights of people as citizens to participate fully in the political life of a nation. A fundamental

---

[70] Anthony Downs, in his classic work *Inside Bureaucracy* (Boston: Little, Brown, 1967), observed that, over time, all bureaucracies will substitute private, bureaucratic objectives for the public objectives that characterized their origination.

conflict between libertarians, on the one hand, and statists and conserva-tives, on the other, involves differences of opinion on the moral value of participating in public life.[71]

The point can be succinctly illustrated in the context of the bargaining model presented in the previous section. In that model, I posited that the salutary forces of the free market could be unleashed—and the destruc-tiveness of rent-seeking and welfare-reducing bureaucracies eliminated—if capitalists and bureaucrats could find a constitutional solution to the bargaining problem that prevents capitalists from making the side pay-ments necessary to buy off the bureaucrats and the rent-seekers. This bargaining problem, which is, in essence, a non-simultaneity of perfor-mance problem, was presented as the only obstacle to the attainment of a libertarian state.

Three objections may be raised to this analysis: a policy objection, a technological objection, and an objection about the way that people would live their lives as citizens in a society organized according to libertarian principles. The policy objection reflects the position of those who reject free-market solutions as the best organizing principle for society. The technological objection addresses the issue of whether it is *possible* to create a constitutional regime that can effectively prevent the growth of rent-seeking and bureaucracy. In other words, even if the non-simultaneity of performance problem could be eliminated, and consensus could be reached about the desirability of drafting a constitution that impeded rent-seeking, one must wonder, particularly in light of U.S. constitutional history, whether it is technologically feasible to create a constitution that succeeds in preventing post-contractual opportunistic behavior which manifests itself in the form of rent-seeking and bureaucracy building. The final issue addressed in this section is a form of moral objection and concerns conceptions of citizenship and involvement in civic life in a libertarian state.

A. Policy

There is not much to the policy argument against the libertarian posi-tion. In Bill Clinton's State of the Union speech in 1996, he declared that "the era of big government is over." Of course, those who are wise to the ways of Bill Clinton were well aware that the era of big government was not over. But the age in which big government could be praised certainly was. As MIT economist Rudiger Dornbusch has observed, "[t]he world has seen a broad intellectual swing away from emphasizing the beneficial role of the state in the 1980s, and protection[ism] is seen as one of the

---

[71] See Rasmussen, "Community versus Liberty?" (*supra* note 10).

manifestations of an overly intrusive state."[72] People are demanding prosperity, and economic freedom is seen as the only way to prosperity.

As the leaders in the Soviet Union discovered, once poor economic performance could no longer be blamed on the ravages of the Second World War, even a highly repressive state could not block the march toward liberalization. However, as the world has discovered in the wake of the breakup of the Soviet Union, bureaucracies can do far more than armies to block the march to freedom. The problem is fascinating. Citizens worldwide are exposed to information about the opportunities available in other countries:

> It is no longer possible to conceal that goods in a country cost three or four times the world price or that they are not available. The elite want their BMWs, almost as a civil right, and the poor want cheap food and low cost consumer durables that are available in world markets, firms know what technologies and inputs their competitors abroad can use and insist on the same access.[73]

In an important and highly influential book, social scientist Francis Fukuyama has argued that libertarian democracy, and to a somewhat lesser extent, capitalism, have emerged as the only means for creating the conditions necessary for human flourishing.[74] For a generation now, economic thought has been dominated by free-market economics "associated with names like Milton Friedman, Gary Becker and George Stigler."[75]

However, a number of economists associated with the Clinton administration have argued that free-market economics is wrong and that government has an important role to play in development.[76] These critics point out that in Asian countries, particularly Japan and Korea, bureaucracies such as Japan's Ministry of International Trade and Industry (MITI), rather than the markets, have guided the economy to extraordinarily high growth. The so-called neo-mercantilists argue that the way to improve economic performance is by protecting chosen domestic industries through high tariffs, restrictions on foreign investment, licensing to favored com-

---

[72] Rudiger Dornbusch, "The Case for Trade Liberalization in Developing Countries," *Journal of Economic Perspectives*, vol. 6, no. 1 (Winter 1992), p. 69.

[73] *Ibid.*, p. 70.

[74] Francis Fukuyama, *The End of History and the Last Man* (New York: Free Press, 1992).

[75] Francis Fukuyama, *Trust: The Social Virtues and the Creation of Prosperity* (New York: Free Press, 1995), p. 13.

[76] Berkeley economist Laura D'Andrea Tyson, former chairman of President Clinton's council of economic advisors, has been the most outspoken of these critics of free markets. See, e.g., Chalmers Johnson, Laura D'Andrea Tyson, and John Zysman, eds., *Politics and Productivity* (Cambridge, MA: Ballinger Books, 1989). Perhaps the most important book in this genre is James Fallows, *Looking at the Sun: The Rise of the New East Asian Economic and Political System* (New York: Pantheon Books, 1994).

panies, outright subsidies, promotion of cartels, government-sponsored research and development, and the allocation of market shares to particular industries.

Nobody seriously believes that this analysis can be successful at doing much more than promoting the political careers of its proponents. In particular, there is no theory or evidence whatsoever to support the contention that the government can pick winners and losers in an economy. In fact, as technology and markets develop at ever-increasing rates of speed, the ability of government to pick which industries, much less which firms within industries, are likely to succeed is dwindling rapidly. If there are people within an economy who are good at picking future winners and losers, it is far more likely that these people will gravitate toward employment in the private sector as venture capitalists or investment bankers, where they can be rewarded for their skills, than toward the bureaucracy, where they must compete along vectors (such as skill at bureaucratic in-fighting and ability to make strategic alliances with politicians) in which they have no comparative advantage.

Industrial policy everywhere has failed in the absence of competitive forces. The Japanese automobile industry has thrived because of vigorous international competition, not because of protection provided by all-knowing bureaucrats. As Fukuyama has observed, political factors usually intervene to skew government policy in the wrong direction.[77] This point is best illustrated in the context of likely government policy toward so-called sunrise and sunset industries. Sunrise industries are the industries of the future. Sunset industries are the industries that dominated the economy in the past:

> By definition, sunrise industries do not yet exist and therefore have no interest groups promoting them. Sunset industries, on the other hand, are often big employers, and usually have vocal and politically powerful proponents.[78]

Thus, at best, industrial policy and neo-mercantilism can work for a time. When the world changes, however, the bureaucracy cannot be trusted to abandon the industries that it has helped for decades. For this reason, the economies tied to industrial policy and neo-mercantilism are bound to atrophy over time. The problems in the French, Italian, and Japanese airline, automobile, and banking industries all are directly attributable to the failure of industrial policy. These industries were protected from outside competition, and thus are now suffering because they are unprepared for the era of global competition. The bureaucracies linked to these

[77] Fukuyama, *Trust*, p. 15.
[78] *Ibid.*, pp. 15–16.

industries have exacerbated the problems facing these industries by making consistently bad, and often politically motivated, decisions about capital allocation.

Consistent with this analysis, as Fukuyama has pointed out, the only industrial policy that has ever actually worked is industrial policy aimed at dismantling older, noncompetitive industries in a systematic way. In Japan, industrial policy led to massive reductions in employment in the shipbuilding, coal, and steel industries. The same holds true for Taiwan and South Korea, where industrial policy generally has meant government intervention to assist in the orderly winding up of certain firms and industries.[79] This should not be read as an endorsement of government intervention to accomplish restructuring of outmoded industries. Countries with adequate bankruptcy laws, and an adequate market for corporate control, have no need for government intervention to accomplish restructuring. In countries with market-based bankruptcy laws and a free market for corporate control, outmoded and poorly run firms will be efficiently dismantled, restructured, or reorganized under new management teams.[80]

The point here is that the latter third of the twentieth century has seen the emergence of capitalism as the clear winner among competing systems of organizing exchange. Moreover, public-choice analysis has shown that politicians, like other economic actors, compete in a market in which they obtain payments (honoraria, campaign contributions, political support, and bribes) from interest groups in exchange for regulation. Legal rules are supplied to those groups that bid the most for them. The bids are made in the form of promised political support. The precise contours of the laws that we observe will reflect a political equilibrium representing the preferences of many groups.[81] Thus, even putting aside the failures of governments to effectively manage economies with the goal of maximizing efficiency and wealth, we should not even expect the motives or goals of government managers to remain focused on pure economic concerns, efficiency, or societal wealth maximization.

Finally, of course, industrial policy and neo-mercantilism inevitably lead to the corruption of public officials, as union and industry officials press to make sure that their firms rank as high as possible on the list of companies singled out for special protection. The problem of corruption is not simply a problem of welfare loss due to the inefficient allocation of government contracts and other benefits. Rather, the phenomenon of cor-

[79] *Ibid.*, p. 16.

[80] This point is now well-known in the literature of corporate finance. It was originally made in Henry Manne, "Mergers and the Market for Corporate Control," *Journal of Political Economy*, vol. 73 (1965), pp. 141–66.

[81] Sam Peltzman, "Toward a More General Theory of Regulation," *Journal of Law and Economics*, vol. 19, no. 2 (August 1976), pp. 211–40.

ruption has very broad effects. As corruption grows, citizens lose the incentive to make investments in their own human capital, since merit is not the mechanism by which people advance in a society riddled by corruption. Similarly, as corruption, rather than merit, becomes the basis for allocating wealth, resentment of those who have succeeded naturally goes up, and the subtle bonds of citizenship necessary to keep a society together begin to fray. The persistent problems in the south of Italy, a region long favored by government wealth transfers, are an excellent example of this phenomenon. The recent scandals that have plagued the Japanese government also illustrate this point.

B. Technology

A second, extremely practical criticism of the libertarian ideal is whether it is *possible* to draft a constitution that credibly protects property rights. The problem considered here presupposes that there is a general consensus to promulgate a set of foundational rules that prevents, or at least impedes, rent-seeking. The problem, of course, is that once the agreement has been made, and society has left the special environment that characterizes the process of constitutional bargaining and has returned to the world of ordinary politics, both sides have incentives to defect. As noted above, those with a comparative advantage in creating wealth within society have an incentive to defect by reneging on their promises to pay off bureaucrats in exchange for the bureaucrats' promise not to engage in rent-seeking. Likewise, those with a comparative advantage in rent-seeking have an incentive to defect by lobbying for increases in the level of transfers, as well as for the creation of new bureaucracies which will allow them to augment their wealth in the future.

The technological question is whether the contracting parties can credibly commit to one another during the time of constitutional formation. The technology problem is usually formulated as the problem of creating a government structure that is sufficiently powerful to protect citizens' property rights, and to provide for public goods such as national defense, without creating a government structure that encourages rent-seeking. Constitutional economics and public choice teach that it is possible to solve the technology problem by making the restrictions embodied in a constitution self-enforcing.[82]

---

[82] See Geoffrey Brennan and James M. Buchanan, *The Power to Tax: Analytical Foundations of the Fiscal Constitution* (Cambridge: Cambridge University Press, 1980); G. Brennan and J. M. Buchanan, *The Reason of Rules: Constitutional Political Economy* (Cambridge: Cambridge University Press, 1985); James M. Buchanan and Gordon Tullock, *The Calculus of Consent: Logical Foundations of Constitutional Democracy* (Ann Arbor: University of Michigan Press, 1962); Hayek, *Law, Legislation, and Liberty*; R. McKenzie, *Constitutional Economics* (Lexington, MA: Lexington Books, 1984); and Jonathan R. Macey, "Promoting Public-Regarding Legislation through Statutory Interpretation: An Interest Group Model," *Columbia Law Review*, vol. 86, no. 2 (March 1986), pp. 223–68.

Even strong language that appears clear becomes, over time, precatory at best. Thus, even seemingly clear constitutional language—such as the statement that "private property [shall not] be taken for public use, without just compensation,"[83] or that a citizen's "right . . . to keep and bear Arms, shall not be infringed"[84]—is unlikely to be effective. The problem with these sorts of language-based protections is that they are not self-enforcing.[85] However, constitutional provisions that organize the very *structure* of government so as to prevent or impede rent-seeking can be effective. For example, once a consensus is reached about the allocation of rights and benefits within a society, a unanimity rule can be invoked, which would require that everyone agree to a change in the agreed-upon allocation. As Nobel laureate economist James Buchanan and public-choice theoretician Gordon Tullock have observed, the U.S. Constitution, by requiring a bicameral legislature and making a provision for presidential vetoes of legislative acts, moves the structure of government in the U.S. in the direction of requiring unanimity.[86] However, over time the U.S. Congress has been able to organize its own internal rules, particularly with respect to the committee system, in such a way as to undermine the near-unanimity requirement.[87] These changes were clearly introduced to benefit incumbent congressmen and senators by lowering the costs of rent-seeking.[88]

Perhaps more importantly, a constitution could prohibit the formation of a bureaucracy, and limit the number of people employed by the government in civil service jobs to a very small number, by requiring that government services either be contracted out, or, preferably, transferred wholly to the market.[89]

Finally, federalism, or competition among governmental units, can be used to permit citizens to exit regulatory structures they dislike in search of superior regulatory regimes. Unfortunately, the U.S. attempt at constructing a federalist system has failed because local governments lack both autonomy and primacy in promulgating economic legislation. In the U.S., the federal government can require local governments to regulate in particular ways, and can overrule any legislation that such local governments promulgate by preempting it with legislation of its own. Thus, the U.S. lacks a federalist system in the true sense of the word.

As Stanford political scientist Barry Weingast has observed in an important article, a constitution can preserve markets and restrict rent-

---

[83] U.S. Constitution, Amendment V.
[84] U.S. Constitution, Amendment II.
[85] See Macey, "Property Rights, Innovation, and Constitutional Structure," pp. 194–95.
[86] Buchanan and Tullock, *The Calculus of Consent*, pp. 233–48.
[87] Jonathan R. Macey, "The Theory of the Firm and the Theory of Market Exchange," *Cornell Law Review*, vol. 74 (1989), p. 56.
[88] *Ibid.*, p. 53.
[89] Gordon Tullock, "Public Choice," in *The New Palgrave: A Dictionary of Economics* (*supra* note 5), p. 1044.

seeking by creating a federalist system of local governments in which the autonomy of each government is institutionalized in a manner that makes federalism's restrictions self-enforcing.[90] A properly functioning federalist system will have three characteristics. First, a federalist system must employ a common market free of trade barriers. Second, consistent with this absence of trade barriers, the system must give the sub-national governments primary regulatory responsibility over the economy. Finally, the federalist system must require local governments to face a hard budget constraint by depriving such local governments of the ability to print money or have access to unlimited credit from another source. Unfortunately, all of these features are important components of a successful federalist system, and, in the U.S., sub-national governments lack primary regulatory responsibility over the economy. Consequently, the U.S. lacks a truly federalist system, since local governments lack meaningful regulatory power, particularly in the area of economic legislation.

The three features of a federalist system identified by Weingast can be stable components of a constitutional structure because, once they are in place, an equilibrium can be produced in which proposed state actions that undermine the status quo inevitably will be blocked by coalitions that will be harmed by such actions.[91] Thus, it is at least technologically possible to secure the political foundations for markets, provided that the rules of the game can be agreed upon in advance.

C. Citizenship

A final goal for libertarians is to craft an attractive vision of what public life would be like in a world governed by libertarian principles. For example, in Aristotelian thought, man is viewed as a political creature. For Aristotle, "[t]he city-state is prior in nature to the household and to each of us individually."[92] Similarly,

> Confucianism emphasizes duties because its basic image of man is one in which individuals are embedded in a web of existing social relationships. By nature, human beings have obligations to one another. A human being cannot perfect himself in isolation; the highest human virtues, like filial piety and benevolence, must be practiced in relation to another human being. Sociability is not a means to a private end, it constitutes an end of life in itself.[93]

[90] Barry R. Weingast, "The Economic Role of Political Institutions: Market-Preserving Federalism and Economic Development," *Journal of Law, Economics, and Organization*, vol. 11, no. 1 (January 1995), p. 2.
[91] *Ibid.*, p. 15.
[92] Aristotle, *Politics*, Book II, chs. 11–12.
[93] Fukuyama, *Trust*, p. 285.

Libertarians must create a credible portrait of life in a libertarian world where participation in markets is encouraged, and participation in politics is viewed with suspicion. In neoclassical economic theory, man is portrayed as isolated, self-sufficient, and happy in this condition. This portrayal conflicts dramatically with Aristotelian and Confucian views of man, which see not only human interaction, but *political interaction*, as necessary preconditions for human flourishing.

In a recent effort to make libertarian ideas accessible to a popular audience, an effort which demonstrates the self-defeating nature of libertarian attempts to capture the popular imagination, noted libertarian Charles Murray argues that an increasing "demand to be left alone" will help make libertarianism achievable.[94] Murray's argument does not address the inherent desire of man to be involved in political interaction. Furthermore, even if we accept that man will become more alienated, there is no reason to believe that this will make him embrace libertarianism. First, alienation will detach the individual from the social institutions from which he gains comfort and trust. People's isolation and fear will lead them to become even more risk-averse and thus all the more likely to embrace and rely upon the government. These fears may lead individuals to believe that change is necessary, but may also lead them to believe that the government can be made more efficient in order to bring that change without gambling on a dramatic shift in the political landscape.

The key to overcoming the citizenship objection to libertarianism lies in an examination of the relationship between religion and the state. Unlike many European countries, there is no established church in the United States. However, religion is an extremely important component of life in the U.S., much more important than in those European countries with established churches, as measured by church attendance, the percentage of people who affirm that they believe in God, and the level of private charitable donations to religious organizations.[95] Where the state co-opts and undermines competition among religions, religion tends to wither. And religious organizations serve as a superior substitute for the efforts of the state to provide an outlet for people's desire to participate in public life. The Mormon Church is a particularly good example of the opportunities for participation provided by religions, because it is a relatively new entry into the global market for souls.[96] Mormons are expected to support the poor within their own community.[97] And the Mormons' Welfare Services Program—which is far more extensive, and intrusive, than

---

[94] Murray, *What It Means to Be a Libertarian*, p. 149.

[95] *Ibid.*, p. 188; Seymour Martin Lipset and Jeff Hayes, "Individualism: A Double-Edged Sword," *The Responsive Community*, vol. 4 (1993–1994), pp. 69–81.

[96] The origins of the Church of Jesus Christ of Latter-Day Saints, as the Mormon Church is called, can be traced to the revelation of the Angel Moroni to Joseph Smith in 1823.

[97] Albert L. Fisher, "Mormon Welfare Programs: Past and Present," *Social Science Journal*, vol. 15 (1978), pp. 75–99.

the federal government's Aid to Families with Dependent Children—supports those within the community who are unable to support themselves.[98] Unlike U.S. government programs, not only must the beneficiaries of the Welfare Services Program work, but they must become self-sufficient as soon as possible.[99]

The extent of participation in civic life among Mormons vastly exceeds the national average: Mormons devote, on average, over fourteen hours a week to church-related activities, and have established what has been described as "an astonishing variety of enduring social institutions."[100]

The Jewish experience in America, characterized by systematic assimilation, illustrates the difficulties that religious groups can have when they try to compete with the state. Like the Mormons, Jews have had a rich tradition of civic involvement. The charitable activities of Jewish groups were so extensive at the turn of the century that in 1900 the German-Jewish United Hebrew Charities could claim to have cared for every impoverished Jew in its community.[101] Unfortunately, as government grew and began to assume the tasks that had traditionally been the responsibility of private charities, involvement in the charitable aspects of religious life began to decline.

More importantly, if one compares the economic fates of Jews, Mormons, Irish, and Italians, one can readily see that those groups that have had the least to do with the government have had the most significant economic success. The Irish, and later the Italians, dominated the political machines in big cities like New York, Boston, Chicago, Buffalo, and Milwaukee. But this involvement did not lead to superior economic advancement; on the contrary, Jews and Mormons, who relied much more on the private sector and the growth and nurturing of small business, have fared better economically than the Irish or the Italians.[102]

The point here is that those groups that have tended to devote themselves to wealth creation have flourished, while those that have devoted themselves to wealth transfers have stagnated. Nowhere is this contrast more evident than in a comparison of black Americans and Asian Americans. Asian Americans have flourished by organizing small businesses, something that black Americans have not succeeded in doing.[103] There are undoubtedly historical explanations for this phenomenon. Perhaps the most convincing explanation is the one offered by UCLA sociologist Ivan Light, who theorizes that the traditions and patterns of repeated game-cooperative behavior that existed among blacks in Africa were de-

---

[98] Fukuyama, *Trust*, p. 291.
[99] *Ibid.*
[100] *Ibid.*, p. 293.
[101] *Ibid.*, p. 304.
[102] *Ibid.*, pp. 292, 304–5.
[103] Ivan H. Light, *Ethnic Enterprise in America: Business and Welfare among Chinese, Japanese, and Blacks* (Berkeley: University of California Press, 1972), pp. 15–18.

stroyed when the slaves were transported to the New World.[104] This claim seems particularly convincing when one compares the success of blacks from the West Indies with blacks from the U.S. The slave system in the West Indies preserved much more of blacks' native culture, and as a consequence community structures have flourished to a much greater extent among West Indian blacks than among American blacks.[105] Therefore, it is not surprising that West Indian blacks in the U.S. have fared far better economically than American blacks, despite the fact that American blacks have been here longer. American blacks have been relatively more successful in the political sphere than in the economic sphere, and this has not contributed to their long-run benefit.

The point is that the appeal of involvement in public life should be at the forefront of libertarian thought.[106] Not only is involvement in civic community valuable to individual human flourishing, but, as Harvard political scientist Robert Putnam has observed, it also is important to economic success.[107] It seems clear that Americans' propensity to join voluntary associations has been a key factor in the economic success of the nation. As Alexis de Tocqueville observed:

> Americans of all ages, all stations in life, and all types of disposition are forever forming associations. There are not only commercial and industrial associations in which all take part, but others of a thousand different types—religious, moral, serious, futile, very general, and very limited, immensely large and very minute. . . . Thus the most democratic country in the world now is that in which men have in our time carried to the highest perfection the art of pursuing in common the objects of common desires and have applied this new technique to the greatest number of purposes.[108]

The winning argument for libertarians is that civic virtue and responsibility need not take place under the umbrella of government. Indeed, civic virtue thrives when government is weak and withers when it is strong. Public life within the confines of government is inevitably corrupting, while public life within the orbit of other public organizations,

---

[104] Ibid., pp. 30–44.

[105] Ibid.

[106] Admittedly, some modern authors have recognized the need to defend libertarian arguments against communitarian criticism. See Rasmussen, "Community versus Liberty?"; Macedo, "Community, Diversity, and Civic Education"; Kukathas, "Liberalism, Communitarianism, and Political Community"; and Badhwar, "Moral Agency, Commitment, and Impartiality." However, these authors represent a minority of those writing in the libertarian camp.

[107] Robert Putnam, Making Democracy Work: Civic Traditions in Modern Italy (Princeton: Princeton University Press, 1993).

[108] Alexis de Tocqueville, Democracy in America, ed. J. P. Mayer, trans. George Lawrence (Garden City, NY: Anchor Books, 1969), pp. 513–14.

such as religious groups or civic leagues, is uplifting and leads to a more spiritual, more fulfilling life.

Libertarians must expose and discredit the myth that the results of democratic processes somehow are inherently legitimate even when these processes undermine people's property rights. Public-choice theory teaches that majority rule often serves the narrow interests of discrete interest groups that can overcome the free-rider and rational ignorance[109] problems that reduce the incentives of ordinary citizens to become involved in the political process. Moreover, in contrast with voluntary associations in the private sphere, the promulgation of legal rules by the state ensures that people who are wholly uninterested in becoming involved in politics will be forced to enter the political sphere in order to protect their interests against the political activists who would impose their will upon them. In this sense, even democratic regimes are coercive, particularly when compared to voluntary associations, because such regimes force people to become involved in the political realm.

VII. CONCLUSION

I have argued that libertarian thought has not succeeded in becoming a broadly popular movement because it has not succeeded in responding to people's systematic risk-aversion and to people's concomitant demand for insurance. To the extent that libertarianism is linked in people's minds to the embrace of free-market economics and individualism, people who favor extensive social welfare programs have not felt comfortable within the libertarian orbit, because they believe that a libertarian world would lack such social welfare programs.

In this essay, I have contended that libertarians should argue that goals of economic security and low-cost health care are more consistent with libertarian ideals than with statist ideals. Libertarians must make their ideas popular in a world in which true individualism is rare and risk-aversion is a near-universal human characteristic. Risk-aversion calls for people to place economic security above prosperity in a wide range of circumstances. Libertarians must convince people that the best way to provide the social services that people need, including education, health care, disability benefits, old-age pensions, and other forms of social welfare programs, is through the private sector. In other words, at the very least, libertarians must convince people that the government should not have a role in operating social programs, but that such programs should and would exist, and indeed flourish, in private markets in a society that conformed to libertarian principles.

---

[109] "Rational ignorance" refers to the fact that sometimes the costs of discovering something are greater than the benefits that come from the discovery. For example, it is not worthwhile for a taxpayer to spend $100 to discover that a government program is wasteful when the government program being investigated only costs that particular taxpayer $25. In this case, the taxpayer is "rationally ignorant" of this wasteful program.

Despite the fact that people gravely mistrust government, libertarianism has failed to capture the popular imagination as the ideal form of civil society. The basic reason for this, in my view, is that libertarians fail to understand people as they really are—insecure, risk-averse, and willing to sacrifice personal freedom and wealth to pay for social insurance delivered by inefficient, low-quality, government providers. Libertarians should stop trying to change people's preferences. Rather, libertarians should adopt arguments showing people that a system in which the state protects property rights and freedom of contract offers the best operating principle for society and the best way to satisfy their existing preferences.

Similarly, even those libertarians who are most attracted to the ideal of free markets should embrace a conception of man as a social animal with strong needs to participate actively in civil society. This conception is not inconsistent with the idea that, over a wide range of human interaction, people pursue their own self-interest. Indeed, constructing a society in which people both participate actively in civic life and, at the same time, bear the costs (and benefits) of their own decisions, is a worthy goal. It seems clear that both individuals and society as a whole are better off to the extent that people embrace these goals.

Libertarians must recognize two things, however. First, we live in a world of great uncertainty. Systematic risk-aversion causes people—even honest, hard-working people—to fear the outcomes of unconstrained market processes. Consequently, libertarians must further explain not only how private markets will create more wealth, but also how private markets can do a better job of delivering the social insurance that large segments of the population demand.

Second, libertarians need to deal in a systematic way with the school of thought, dating back to Aristotle and Confucius, that maintains that man is a highly social being who needs to participate in public life in order to flourish. Libertarians have a very strong response to this conception of the world. They can argue persuasively that private and consensual civic, social, and religious organizations offer much greater opportunities for meaningful self-expression than the coercive organs of the state. Libertarians can also show that the state systematically squashes nongovernmental outlets for civic virtue and civic expression.

It might be said that what I have argued for in this essay is simply a "kinder, gentler" libertarianism. To some extent that is a correct characterization of the arguments I have presented. But more than this, it also seems clear that libertarian thought needs to alter its basic conception of human interests. The concepts of security and risk-aversion must be given primacy of place if libertarianism is to become something more than the exotic fringe movement that it is now.

Law, Cornell University

IMITATIONS OF LIBERTARIAN THOUGHT*

By Richard A. Epstein

I. Imitation or Confusion?

Imitation is said to be the sincerest form of flattery. Socially, the proposition may well be true. But in the world of ideas it is false: to the extent that two incompatible traditions use the same words or symbols to articulate different visions of legal or social organization, imitation begets confusion, not enlightenment. The effects of that confusion, moreover, are not confined to the world of ideas, but spill over into the world of politics and public affairs. Words are more than tools of description: they work also as tools of persuasion and transformation. Let a term have a favorable connotation in one context, and its imitative use can mislead people into thinking that a major departure from established practice is merely the extension or updating of an old principle to deal with new circumstances.

The risk of confusion born of imitation is familiar within the law. It is precisely to combat the dangers of confusion between rival firms and rival products that the law of trademarks and trade names grants exclusive rights in perpetuity to the creator of the name or the mark.[1] The losses from confusion, moreover, are not confined to the holder of the name or the mark. Some losses are also borne by consumers, present and future, who now find it more costly to distinguish the real article from its substitutes. Even if these rival goods are not inferior—and imitative goods often are—the inability to distinguish goods by source allows the new entrant to free-ride on the name, mark, reputation, and advertising of the established firm. The net effect would be to stop innovation in brand names and in the products they shepherd to the marketplace. Our system of intellectual property rights authorizes injunctions to prevent repetition of the improper use of name or mark, and damages to compensate, at least roughly, for losses already incurred.[2]

* I should like to thank Elizabeth Garrett, Daniel Klerman, Martha Nussbaum, and Richard Ross for their comments on an earlier draft of this essay. I also profited from comments on the essay at a workshop at the University of Chicago. Rex Sears of the class of 1999 provided valuable research assistance.

[1] Lanham Act, 15 U.S.C. §§ 1051 et seq. For an instance of its application, see *Warner Bros. Inc. v. Gay Toys, Inc.*, 658 F.2d 76 (2d Cir. 1981).

[2] For a compact statement of the relevant principles, see American Law Institute, *Restatement of the Law Third: Unfair Competition* (St. Paul, MN: American Law Institute Publishers, 1995). Chapter 3 covers the law of trademarks. For a discussion of remedies, see ch. 3, Topic 6, § 35 (injunctions); § 36 (damages); and § 37 (accounting for defendant's profits).

This legal protection, moreover, does not block new entry into product markets, provided this entry takes place under new names or marks. In the long run, the rule facilitates entry by protecting from imitation the new entrant who creates his own name or mark. The protection of names and marks blocks the unwanted transformation of competition into expropriation. A competitor is not allowed to make his own widgets in the factory of his rival, without consent; likewise, he may not market those products under a rival's name or mark, without consent. Allow the imitation, and the creator cannot obtain a full return to labor or capital. Prevent it, and multiple marks can compete in every product niche from soft-drinks to perfumes. No wonder that brand names and brand marks, from Coca-Cola to the Chicago Bulls, rank among the most valuable assets of the modern firm.

Intellectual discourse lacks the same definitive structure of property rights as trademarks and trade names. Even in this rarefied context, however, an informal network of trademarks, names, and associations helps separate out the extraordinary scholar from the pack. Just mention phrases like "transaction costs," "human capital," "veil of ignorance," "the war of all against all," and everyone can name the scholar associated with the idea—which is why no footnote will be added. Legal doctrines undergo the same kind of information compression: terms like "strict scrutiny,"[3] "clear and present danger,"[4] "the police power,"[5] and "regulatory takings"[6] all bring forth relatively distinct pictures of critical legal doctrines. Complex and rich thoughts can be captured in a single sentence, or, better, in a single phrase. Abbreviated expressions that use accurate shorthand to communicate strong positions are as important in scholarship as they are in advertising. It is thus not simple praise for an admired figure that allows people to sort themselves out as Hobbesians, Lockeans, Humeans, Kantians, Marxists, Freudians, Rawlsians, and Coaseans. (It also helps to have last names with single syllables, a sore point to some Hayekians.)

In this market, to be sure, no court sits in judgment on what names evoke what theories. Proper attribution depends on order of publication, as buttressed by local lore, academic convention, and common practice. But many ideas are so pervasive that they are no longer associated with authors, but with causes and principles. The principle of human freedom, the vital role for individual security, and the fear of individual harm all resonate far and wide in popular and professional discourse. These conceptions cry out for a clear pedigree and a common meaning. But they receive neither. The purpose of this essay is to explain how libertarian language is first imitated and then captured by collectivist programs that

---

[3] *Skinner v. Oklahoma*, 316 U.S. 535 (1942).

[4] *Schenck v. United States*, 249 U.S. 47, 52 (1919).

[5] *Mugler v. Kansas*, 123 U.S. 623 (1887).

[6] *Pennsylvania Coal v. Mahon*, 260 U.S. 393 (1922); *Lucas v. South Carolina Coastal Council*, 505 U.S. 1003 (1992).

envision a relationship between the individual and the state which is fundamentally different from that envisioned by classical libertarianism.

Several steps are necessary to implement this program. The first task is to establish the temporal priority for the libertarian version of these terms relative to libertarianism's collectivist rivals. The second task is to explain why the earlier conception is superior to its modern rival. The third task is to examine why the shift took place. The first inquiry is necessarily historical: Which set of usages was established first? That question cannot be answered with categorical certainty, especially if one is prepared to include the full range of philosophical literature that addresses the matter. But it can be said with great confidence that the traditional legal materials have, virtually without deviation, until quite modern times gravitated toward libertarian accounts of the law's key conceptions—the two I shall stress here are security and coercion. For example, the Roman law contrasted the position of a free man with that of a slave, and treated their legal status, not their economic wealth, as the hallmarks of their positions.[7] Similar conceptions of legal rights and duties worked their way through all the major treatises and cases in the common-law tradition: the duties correlated with basic rights were obligations of noninterference toward (not support of) others.

One reliable indicator of this phenomenon is Blackstone's basic formulation of natural liberty:

> This natural liberty [of mankind] consists properly in a power of acting as one thinks fit, without restraint or control, unless by the law of nature; being a right inherent in us by birth, one of the gifts of God to man at his creation, when he embued him with the faculty of free-will.[8]

But what are the limitations of this freedom of action? These begin and end with the need to respect the security of other persons: "The right of personal security consists in a person's legal and uninterrupted enjoyment of his life, his limbs, his body, his health, and his reputation."[9] The articulation of correlative duties is therefore decisive. In speaking of "limbs" Blackstone refers to those "members that enable man to protect himself

---

[7] See, e.g., *The Institutes of Justinian*, 5th ed., trans. J. B. Moyle (Oxford: Clarendon Press, 1913), Book I, Title 2, paragraph 3:

> But the law of nations is common to the whole human race; for nations have settled certain things for themselves as occasion and the necessities of human life required. For instance, wars arose, and then followed captivity and slavery, which are contrary to the law of nature; for by the law of nature all men from the beginning were born free.

[8] See William Blackstone, *Commentaries on the Law of England* (1765; Chicago and London: University of Chicago Press, 1979), vol. 1, p. 121.

[9] *Ibid.*, p. 125.

from external injuries in a state of nature."[10] Shortly thereafter he makes his meaning still clearer: "Besides those limbs and members that may be necessary to man, in order to defend himself or annoy his enemy, the rest of his person or body is also entitled by the same natural right to security from the corporal insults of menaces, assaults, beating and wounding; though such insults amount not to destruction of life or member."[11] Thereafter, the right to health takes the same defensive posture: freedom from control by others, not the right to control them—so that the right embraces "[t]he preservation of a man's health from such practices as may prejudice or annoy it."[12]

The rest of Blackstone's general program is consistent with his views on the right to security and its correlative duties:

> Next to personal security, the law of England regards, asserts, and preserves the personal liberty of individuals. This personal liberty consists in the power of loco-motion, of changing situation, or removing one's person to whatsoever place one's own inclination may direct; without imprisonment or restraint, unless by due course of law.[13]

The correlative wrongs are false imprisonment and blocking individuals' rights of way on public roads. The next conception Blackstone describes is broader still: "The third absolute right, inherent in every Englishman, is that of property; which consists in the free use, enjoyment and disposal of all his acquisitions, without any control or diminution, save only by the laws of the land."[14] Here the basic relationship posits the preferred position of the owner in matters relating to his land. The right also extends beyond the mere possession of land (which is all that receives categorical protection under current U.S. takings law)[15] to cover the right to use, enjoy, and dispose of land, the latter by voluntary contract. These rights are not absolute because they are limited by the correlative duties that exist between neighbors, and the requirement that property must be surrendered, in some cases, to satisfy the debts of its owner. However, the phrase "save by the law of the land" surely requires only that property be surrendered pursuant to judgment made in a recognized court of law. The phrase does not mean, at least in its original context, that all claims to private property could be extinguished by simple legislative command.

---

[10] *Ibid.*, p. 126.
[11] *Ibid.*, p. 130.
[12] *Ibid.*
[13] *Ibid.*
[14] *Ibid.*, p. 134.
[15] Compare *Kaiser Aetna v. United States*, 444 U.S. 164 (1979) (right to exclude protected under takings clause), with *Penn Central Transportation Co. v. City of New York*, 438 U.S. 104 (1978) (limited protection against land-use restrictions).

Blackstone's picture is relatively complete, and the modern transformation in the conception of civil rights brings the point home.[16] The early definition of individual civil rights is associated with capacity: the rights to contract, to make wills, to own property, to give testimony, and the like, are consistent with Blackstone's basic system. It is only with the rise of modern civil rights legislation in the twentieth century that the emphasis moves away from civil capacity. Today, the law transforms the correlative duties associated with civil rights, and thereby transforms these rights themselves. Indeed, the inversion is so complete that today the list of civil rights *excludes* the rights it originally included and addresses instead the role-specific rights, for example, of employees or tenants to be free from certain forms of discrimination at the hands of a present or prospective employer or landlord. The original ideal of freedom, as in freedom of association, becomes the target of the law.

The full task here requires more, however, than identification of the relevant differences between these two legal conceptions (that is, the traditional common-law conception and the modern one). It also requires some analysis of why the older versions should be preferred to their upstart impostors. On some occasions, it is said that the decline of traditional libertarian thought—or its parallel manifestation in legal circles, the decline of common-law conceptions of rights and duties—should be not only expected, but welcomed. The traditional rules themselves often appealed, as Blackstone freely did, to the intuitive conception of natural rights, but that principle cannot carry the weight heaped on its frail shoulders. To those who believe in such rights, their claim to truth by self-evidence is, to borrow their phrase, self-evident; but to those who harbor genuine skepticism as to the common-law conceptions, the classical formulations beg every major substantive question about the structure of legal rights and duties. To defend the libertarian conception against its imitators, therefore, requires more than a simple showing of how modern writers have stood traditional usages on their head. It also requires, so to speak, proof that those usages were properly on their feet to begin with.

To achieve this goal, it is necessary to abandon the language of self-evidence and to meet and vanquish the skeptic on neutral turf—a task that requires showing how the older meanings not only generate understandings that are more consistent with ordinary understandings and language, but also generate outcomes that are socially more desirable. Both parts of this assignment invite a certain level of murkiness. History is never univocal, and any discussion of anticipated social consequences, on which this empirical contest eventually turns, contains a large dose of unpleasant philosophical messiness. But just because the arguments for the older position do not attain the status of a categorical imperative does

---

[16] For discussion, see Richard A. Epstein, "Two Conceptions of Civil Rights," *Social Philosophy and Policy*, vol. 8, no. 2 (Spring 1991), pp. 38–59.

not mean that the differences between rival forms of social arrangements are unimportant. The levels of economic growth among those nations that have respected libertarian traditions are far higher than among those that have denied them: just compare North and South Korea today; East and West Germany before unification; Hong Kong (before July 1997) with China. The same can be said of firms and economic sectors within the United States: compare the track record of the United States Postal Service with that of Federal Express, or the satisfaction of consumers in the reg- ulated health-care area with that of consumers in the relatively unregu- lated computer business.

The plan of this essay, therefore, is to examine the transformation of classical-liberal (or libertarian) conceptions over time. Section II deals with the conceptual transformation. In choosing security and coercion for special consideration, I will follow Blackstone's progression of interests. The basic concern is with security, and its kindred conception of stability, or security over time. The next portion of the analysis (in Section III) looks at the set of terms—coercion, force, duress, and harm—which denote the kinds of conduct that the law prohibits in order to protect that basic interest in security. Woven throughout this discussion is consideration of the impact that the intellectual transformation of these concepts has on the grander conception of individual liberty or personal freedom, which finds its own meaning in tandem with both security and coercion. The progression begins with the narrow core, security, and then imperceptibly branches out to the most general concept, liberty. Yet this order does have a certain institutional and historical logic. Liberty may be the broader concept, but security is surely the less contested concept. It is for just this reason that the expansion of state power has taken place through redef- inition of the idea of security and its correlative notion of coercion (that is, the threats against which security is provided). But all these ideas are part of a unified tapestry; the modern expansions of security necessarily lead to a contraction of the classical conception of liberty that lies at the heart of the traditional system.

II. Security: The Universal Virtue

It takes little argument to show that a simple conception of security lies at the root of the classical conception of the good society. The word itself comes from the Latin "*se cura*," which means to be "without care."[17] From Roman times forward, the preservation of security has been one of the major objects of social arrangements, both large and small. The main fear of Hobbesian political philosophy is the "war of all against all," a world that degenerates into chaos and disorder through the unbridled use of

---

[17] *Merriam-Webster's Collegiate Dictionary*, 10th ed. (Springfield, MA: Merriam-Webster, Inc., 1995), p. 1056.

force and fraud. "And therefore, as long as this natural right of every man to every thing endureth, there can be no security to any man, how strong or wise soever he be, of living out the time, which nature ordinarily alloweth men to live."[18] The Humean vision lists the stability of possession (a virtue closely affiliated with security) as the first of the virtues of any sound social order.[19] Modern-day international law stresses the security of territorial boundaries against aggression. The Fourth Amendment to the United States Constitution affirms "[t]he right of the people to be secure in their persons, houses, papers, and effects, against unreasonable searches and seizures. . . ." Any sound commercial order depends on the security of exchange, so that one party to an exchange can perform first, secure in the knowledge that, when the appointed time comes, courts will, if necessary, intervene to compel performance from the other party. The law of secured transactions goes one better by structuring in advance the creditor's claims against particular assets of the debtor, claims which ripen into full title when and if the debt is not repaid. From political philosophy to international affairs, from constitutional law to commercial practice, security is a gilt-edged virtue that none dare to deny.

Universal appeal is what makes security a political virtue worthy of imitation. People crave security against the vicissitudes of life. The farmer who plants his crops wants to secure his profit from their sale. Individual retirees seek to be secure financially against the ravages of old age. All of us seek security against the downsides of bad health. Hence, in short order we see the emergence of crop-support programs, the Social Security Act of 1935, and the well-named (if ill-conceived) Health Security Act of 1993 (which went down in flames a year later). The choice of names is not an accident, for all these programs consciously seek to make use of a strong word with few, if any, negative connotations in public life or political theory. Security is everyone's ultimate defensive virtue.

It is this virtue that is exploited to account for the modern transition in belief structures. Here it is useful to make the point by looking at a pair of strange bedfellows, both of whom were writing toward the end of World War II, with a conscious eye toward the future: I speak of Franklin Roosevelt and F. A. Hayek. In particular, it is instructive to look at two texts: Roosevelt's 1944 Annual Message to Congress, which contained the text of "An Economic Bill of Rights";[20] and chapter 9 of Hayek's famous *Road to Serfdom*, fittingly entitled "Security and Freedom."

Roosevelt's Economic Bill of Rights offers a textbook imitation of the traditional libertarian position on rights. Its key passages set the tone for the modern debate on this issue. In his address, Roosevelt notes the

[18] Thomas Hobbes, *Leviathan*, ed. Michael Oakeshott (New York: Collier Books, 1962), p. 103.
[19] David Hume, *A Treatise of Human Nature*, ed. L. A. Selby-Bigge (Oxford: Clarendon Press, 1888), Book III, section III.
[20] Franklin D. Roosevelt, *Nothing to Fear* (Freeport, NY: Books for Libraries Press, 1946), p. 387.

steady progress of the war effort, and, anticipating victory, gives his word that the Allies made "no secret treaties or political or financial commitments"[21] like those that marred the aftermath of World War I. Without breaking stride, Roosevelt then sets out his own vision for the postwar era:

> The one supreme objective for the future, which we [i.e., Roosevelt and the leaders of other Allied nations] discussed for each nation individually, and for all the United Nations, can be summed up in one word: Security.
>
> And that means not only physical security which provides safety from attacks by aggressors. It means also economic security, social security, moral security—in a family of nations.[22]

Lest the message be misunderstood, Roosevelt hammers his theme home:

> We have come to a clear realization of the fact that true individual freedom cannot exist without economic security and independence. "Necessitous men are not free men." People who are hungry and out of a job are the stuff of which dictatorships are made.
>
> In our day these economic truths have become accepted as self-evident. We have accepted, so to speak, a second Bill of Rights under which a new basis of security and prosperity can be established for all—regardless of station, race or creed.
>
> Among these are:
>
> The right to a useful and remunerative job in the industries or shops or farms or mines of the nation;
>
> The right to earn enough to provide adequate food and clothing and recreation;
>
> The right of every farmer to raise and sell his products at a return which will give him and his family a decent living;
>
> The right of every business man, large and small, to trade in an atmosphere of freedom from unfair competition and domination by monopolies at home or abroad;
>
> The right of every family to a decent home;
>
> The right to adequate medical care and the opportunity to achieve and enjoy good health;
>
> The right to adequate protection from the economic fears of old age, sickness, accident and unemployment;
>
> The right to a good education.[23]

[21] *Ibid.*, p. 389.
[22] *Ibid.*
[23] *Ibid.*, p. 396.

Roosevelt's new bill of rights rests on a conscious, powerful, and complete imitation of the old. Roosevelt makes an unmistakable reference to the 1776 Declaration of Independence: "We hold these truths to be self-evident, that all men are created equal, that they are endowed by their Creator with certain unalienable Rights, that among these are Life, Liberty and the pursuit of Happiness." By 1944, he could insist that certain "economic truths have become accepted as self-evident." The verb between "truths" and "self-evident" has changed ("have become accepted") to reflect the emergence of the new understandings. Roosevelt's implicit conclusion is that the incorporation of these new truths into the legal pantheon will not displace the older truths on which they build. But the older definition of freedom is nonetheless implicitly modified by the insertion of the word "true" before "individual freedom," so as to state Roosevelt's view that opportunities and capacities (without results) do not suffice for freedom. Last in Roosevelt's address comes the long list of positive rights from government, and a concluding attack on special interests coupled with a statement that his proposed program responds to the needs of our fighting men abroad: "It is to their demands that this Government should pay heed, rather than to the whining demands of selfish pressure groups, who seek to feather their nests while young Americans are dying."[24] Roosevelt's address ends without a single mention of either the correlative duties imposed, for example, on employers or landlords, or the taxes needed to fund his ambitious new account of economic security.

Coincidentally, Hayek's *Road to Serfdom* was first published in 1944. It echoes some of the same themes as Roosevelt's address, but with far more analytical detachment. Hayek begins chapter 9 by noting that the word "security" is used in two senses, one "limited" and attainable, the other "absolute" and unattainable:

> first, security against severe physical privation, the certainty of a given minimum of sustenance for all; and second, the security of a given standard of life, or of the relative position which one person or group enjoys compared with others; or, as we may put it briefly, the security of minimum income and the security of the particular income a person is thought to deserve.[25]

What is striking about the Hayekian position is that *neither* form of security under discussion refers to the protection that the state supplies against external aggression, independent of the wealth of its citizens. Rather, both conceptions involve some level of support that the state grants to all of its citizens. The choice is between universal minimum

[24] *Ibid.*, p. 397.
[25] F. A. Hayek, *The Road to Serfdom* (Chicago: University of Chicago Press, 1994), pp. 132–33.

security and some higher level of personal security that depends on past earnings instead of basic needs.

Putting aside delicate questions at the margin, Hayek opts for the former: "There is no reason why in a society which has reached the general level of wealth which ours has attained the first kind of security should not be guaranteed to all without endangering general freedom."[26] On matters of "sickness and accident," he concludes, reminiscent of Roosevelt, that "the case for the state's helping to organize a comprehensive system of social insurance is very strong."[27] He therefore reserves his wrath for the second kind of security, the one that preserves for each group in society its relative position of wealth notwithstanding changes in demand and technology. Thus, blacksmiths as a group are not entitled, after the rise of the automobile, to the same income they had fifty years before. In Hayek's view, the effort to preserve the absolute position of any group against economic changes introduces price and wage rigidities that undermine the possibility of rational individual behavior in a competitive economy. But so long as the system of entry and exit is left open, fortunes should be allowed to rise and fall, as long as they remain above the social minimum. Because Hayek does not think that attempts to ensure minimum security will cause overall social performance to diminish, he regards such limited security as a proper object of government effort. Hayek departs from Roosevelt on minimum prices for farm support. Nonetheless, he in effect adopts a definition of security that is far broader than the one found, for example, in Hobbes or Blackstone. The upshot is a powerful consensus: both left and right endorse some ideal mix between a competitive economy and a system of minimum welfare rights.

That consensus—albeit in a form more congenial to Roosevelt than to Hayek—has worked itself forward in time. The International Covenant on Economic, Social, and Cultural Rights (ICESCR) borrows copiously from the list of rights that Roosevelt articulated.[28] Even within the United

---

[26] Ibid., p. 133.

[27] Ibid., p. 134.

[28] For example, Article 6 of the ICESCR provides:

> 1. The States Parties to the present Covenant recognize the right to work, which includes the right of everyone to gain his living by work which he freely chooses or accepts, and will take appropriate steps to safeguard this right.
>
> 2. The steps to be taken by a State Party to the present Covenant to achieve the full realization of this right shall include technical and vocational guidance and training programmes, policies and techniques to achieve steady economic, social and cultural development and full and productive employment under conditions safeguarding fundamental political and economic freedoms to the individual.

Article 11(1) provides as follows:

> The States Parties to the present Covenant recognize the right of everyone to an adequate standard of living for himself and his family, including adequate food, clothing and housing, and to the continuous improvement of living conditions. The States Parties will take appropriate steps to ensure the realization of this right, recognizing to this effect the essential importance of international co-operation based on free consent.

States and other Western democracies, much modern scholarship has sought to redefine the scope of constitutional and administrative law to incorporate this broader account of security for all.[29] Yet the political and intellectual success of the new vision of security invites a comparison with the older view. Let me begin with the classical notions of security of the person, security of possession, and security of exchange, and then work forward to our more modern conception.

A. Security and freedom

The first item of business of any legal order is to define for each person the sphere of self-control. Try as one may, it is very difficult to think of a conception of the person, for example, that allows him to be killed, injured, or enslaved at the will of another.[30] It is for this reason that Roosevelt adds his new economic rights to an already existing right to "physical security which provides safety from attacks by aggressors." Yet for our purposes, security of the person is a more restricted, less controversial, and (pun intended) more defensible ideal than freedom of the person.

Freedom guarantees to each person the right to pursue a wide range of choices. Even so, the line between freedom and license must be carefully drawn.[31] Aggression is clearly ruled out. Nonetheless, in the eyes of many, the protected sphere of individual conduct need not allow people to do just what they like so long as they refrain from committing acts of aggression against strangers. The broad class of offenses against morals goes beyond the classical-liberal prohibitions against force and fraud. Prohibitions against incest, prostitution, gambling, blasphemy, assisted suicide, sodomy, polygamy, homosexuality, drug use, and even usury (damned by Aristotle as a peculiarly vile form of human behavior, even worse than the retail trade)[32] fall within this category; and state regulation of these activities was, for better or worse, accepted at the time of the Founding of the United States.[33] Many of these prohibitions are defended

---

[29] See, e.g., Cass R. Sunstein, *After the Rights Revolution: Reconceiving the Regulatory State* (Cambridge: Harvard University Press, 1990).

[30] "For, the very idea that one man may be compelled to hold his life, or the means of living, or any material right essential to the enjoyment of life, at the mere will of another, seems to be intolerable in any country where freedom prevails, as being the essence of slavery itself." *Yick Wo v. Hopkins*, 118 U.S. 356, 370 (1886). The connection with Locke's *Second Treatise* should be evident. See, e.g., John Locke, *Second Treatise* [1690], ch. 2, in Locke, *Two Treatises of Government* (Cambridge: Cambridge University Press, 1960).

[31] Locke, *Second Treatise*, section 6: "But though this [a world of free, equal, and independent individuals] be a *State of Liberty*, yet it is *not a State of Licence*. . . ."

[32] See Aristotle, *Politics*, trans. Benjamin Jowett (New York: Random House, 1943), 1256b40–1258b8.

[33] For discussion and examples, see *Bowers v. Hardwick*, 478 U.S. 186 (1986); Forrest McDonald, *Novus Ordo Seclorum: The Intellectual Origins of the Constitution* (Lawrence: University Press of Kansas, 1985). For the continuation of economic and morals regulation in the nineteenth century, see William J. Novak, *The People's Welfare: Law and Regulation in Nineteenth-Century America* (Chapel Hill: University of North Carolina Press, 1996).

with great passion and agility. The modern debates over the legalization of gambling, physician-assisted suicide, and same-sex marriages show that claims for the proper exertion of state power do not easily stop at the prevention of force and fraud.

I freely confess my inability to sort out the relative merits of these various prohibitions. My views on these questions are far more cautious than my strong conviction that government should not interfere with wages and prices in competitive markets—period. For my purposes, however, the critical point is that all these restrictions on individual *liberty* pass political and constitutional muster in large measure because, wise or foolish, they pose no threat to individual *security*. These rules are directed against certain kinds of conduct: consensual practices between adults done in private, or violations of religious and cultural norms. Individuals subject to these restrictions are properly aggrieved. But none of these prohibitions attack or limit bodily integrity or tolerate murder, trespass, assault, rape, or theft. The individual right to exclude others from his or her own person remains sacrosanct even as freedom of action is curtailed. Everyone retains the unquestioned right to resist forced associations with others, even if he or she is denied the right to form certain intimate associations. This model contains concessions to state power that should, and do, cause deep intellectual discomfort to the committed libertarian. Nonetheless, this classical demarcation between private autonomy and social power reflects an undeniable pattern throughout our history. The "keep off" sign carries more clout than the unbridled right to use what others may not take or touch. Security forms the indisputable core of any conception of personal autonomy. Security becomes the dominant social trope because no intellectual or political movement rises up against it.

What is true of the person also applies to external things. The security of possession is a far more modest conception than a full-blown scheme of private property. As traditionally understood, private property carries with it the rights to possession, use, and disposition. This system of property rights can be justified by a theory of natural rights, or by utilitarian concerns, or by some combination of the above. But, however justified and however acquired, the right to exclusive possession receives a far greater measure of legal protection than either of the other two attributes of use or disposition. In each and every case, the title to a piece of property, however established, is made secure against physical invasion by other individuals. *Dispossession* by force is the cardinal sin in all legal systems ancient or modern. Roman law rejects the displacement of sitting owners by force,[34] and medieval real actions (those used to recover land) at common law were designed for that same end.[35] The preferred status of continuous possession continues strongly into the present day:

[34] For a discussion, see Barry Nicholas, *An Introduction to Roman Law* (Oxford: Clarendon Press, 1962), pp. 153–57.
[35] Frederic W. Maitland, *The Forms of Action at Common Law*, ed. A. H. Chaytor and W. J. Whittaker (Cambridge: Cambridge University Press, 1936), Lecture III.

in the U.S., when the government takes permanent physical possession of any part of an owner's land, however small, compensation is typically required.[36] In contrast, the freedom of an individual to use or dispose of property is often sharply circumscribed.[37] Why the difference? Because the protection of possession offers security against aggression.

Exchange relationships are subject to a parallel analysis. *Freedom of contract* receives far less protection than the more limited idea of *security of exchange*. Often the legal system restricts the types of contracts that individuals may enter into to dispose of either property or labor. Freedom of contract is often circumscribed—by wage or price constraints, by required warranties, terms, and conditions, or by limitations on the choice of trading partners, such as those imposed by an antidiscrimination law. But even though freedom of contract is commonly limited, the security of exchange under the class of contracts allowed in the legal system receives robust legal protection. One party to a contract may perform first, secure in the knowledge that (if necessary) the law will assist him in gaining the performance that has been promised in return. Viewed from the *ex post* perspective, this rule looks as though it favors one side over the other; but viewed from the *ex ante* perspective, the rule benefits both parties simultaneously by preserving the joint gains from trade. Stated in this narrow fashion, security of exchange gains universal acceptance. Defenders of a minimum-wage law could ban labor contracts paying less than $X per hour, and still insist on strict enforcement of all contracts that pay a wage equal to or more than the minimum. Whether we deal with liberty, property, or exchange, the protection of individual security is so closely aligned with the advancement of social welfare that it is easy to see why Roosevelt treats security as the *summum bonum* in his Economic Bill of Rights.

B. Economic security

The same set of desirable social consequences are not, however, preserved when the idea of security is expanded beyond its initial account. To see the dangers in any broader conception of security, be it Roosevelt's or Hayek's, it is critical to attend to the duties that are made correlative to the newly created right. As mentioned earlier, Roosevelt was peculiarly silent on these correlative duties: exposing an Achilles heel of one's position is not the way to win political converts. But the need to articulate the correlative duties cannot be ignored or papered over for very long. Security of possession and exchange has positive consequences for the legal system writ large, not merely for particular groups within it. Originally, the duties correlated with these rights to security were (1) a duty to refrain from using force to interfere with others, and (2) a duty to

---

[36] *Loretto v. Teleprompter*, 458 U.S. 419 (1982).
[37] See, e.g., *Lucas v. South Carolina Coastal Council*, 505 U.S. 1003 (1992).

comply with promises made pursuant to voluntary exchanges. These duties require some public enforcement, funded by a system of taxation whose benefits, broadly speaking, exceed its costs. This legal arrangement should prove stable politically and attractive economically. It is stable politically because no person may opt out of paying taxes while still receiving the benefits those taxes supply. It is attractive economically because everyone prospers from the public enforcement of these two duties. Once law and order are recognized as public goods, all members of society are in or all are out. In a pinch, no one chooses the latter. Security thus starts life as an individual virtue, but it ends up as a social virtue whose benefits are diffused throughout the group.

Not so with the security that is created under the newer system of positive rights, as conceived by either Roosevelt or Hayek. The simple economic truth is that it is not possible to subsidize all activities simultaneously: some activities have to be relatively overtaxed if others are to receive extra support. What is true of activities is true as well of individuals. Hayek clearly saw this basic point when he directed his attention to the need for preserving flexible wages and freedom of entry into the marketplace:

> [T]he politics which are now followed everywhere, which hand out the privilege of security, now to this group and now to that, are nevertheless rapidly creating conditions in which the striving for security tends to become stronger than the love of freedom. The reason for this is that with every grant of complete security to one group the insecurity of the rest necessarily increases. If you guarantee to some a fixed part of a variable cake, the share left to the rest is bound to fluctuate proportionally more than the size of the whole. And the essential element of security which the competitive system offers, the great variety of opportunities, is more and more reduced.[38]

Hayek's point here shows the close connection between political theory and financial analysis. To see why the argument is so strong, it is instructive to conceive of a system in which the dollars held by individuals are thought of as shares in a corporation. Each dollar therefore represents some fractional claim against the corporation's assets. In the simplest capital structure, all the shares are common stock, so there is no need to sort out the relative claims of common stock, preferred stock, unsecured debt, and secured debt in the corporation. The public equivalent is that no one person holds some superior claim against the nation's assets above and beyond those represented by his fractional share.

---

[38] Hayek, *The Road to Serfdom*, p. 141. For a similar recognition of the risks of political guarantees, see David Schmidtz, "Guarantees," *Social Philosophy and Policy*, vol. 14, no. 2 (Summer 1997), pp. 1-19.

In a world with this simple capital structure, leverage is not an issue.[39] But when debt is introduced, leverage becomes critical. Thus, suppose that a corporation has $1,000 worth of assets and 100 shares of common stock, so that each share is worth $10. Now give a creditor a lien (that is, a secured first claim) on the assets of the corporation for $200. Since the value of the business remains unchanged, the net value of the shares drops, as a first approximation, by $200 in aggregate to $800, or $8 per share. This analysis is incomplete, however, because it ignores the standard financial proposition that the introduction of debt increases the riskiness of the firm equity. Some shareholders could well value their leveraged shares at less than $8.

To see why, note what happens to shares when the value of the firm shifts by $700, up or down. In the unleveraged firm, a decrease in value of $700 still leaves the shareholders above water, with shares worth $3 each (a 70 percent decrease). By the same token, an increase in value of $700 will result in an increase in share value to $17 (a 70 percent increase). But in a leveraged firm, the firm's $200 debt implies that the $700 shift in value now generates a larger percentage change in share value. Now, the up or down movement equals 87.5 percent of share value (that is, $700/$800). Let the decrease in firm value go to 80 percent ($800), and the leveraged shareholders are wiped out, even though the creditors are paid in full. Only when losses exceed 80 percent do the creditors suffer financial loss, but until the firm loses all its value, creditor losses are always less than shareholder losses. It is for that reason that Hayek speaks of fluctuations that are "proportionately more" for some when guarantees are extended to others.

Yet it would be a mistake to assume that this static analysis captures the full extent of the changes brought about by the introduction of corporate debt, and by analogy, political guarantees. The shift in priority not only increases the riskiness of the stock interest, it also alters the behavior of the firm shareholders during the period when they retain effective control of the enterprise.[40] Leverage routinely induces the shareholders to engage in riskier business practices. The debt holders receive no portion of the upside gains, for they obtain their cash priority by surrendering their fractional interests in the gain. As risk increases, however, debt holders share an ever-larger portion of the losses, even though their priority partly insulates them from the shock of shareholder miscalculation.

[39] In finance theory, the meaning of the term "leverage" is analogous to its physical meaning. The use of borrowed money allows an owner to leverage (i.e., extend) his investment beyond what it would otherwise be. A highly leveraged firm is, therefore, one which has a high debt-to-equity ratio. The risk of using a long pole to leverage the force of a large rock is that the pole may break. The financial analogue is bankruptcy.

[40] For one among many demonstrations of this point, see Lucian Arye Bebchuk and Jesse M. Fried, "The Uneasy Case for the Priority of Secured Claims in Bankruptcy," *Yale Law Journal*, vol. 105, no. 4 (January 1996), pp. 873-75.

To see the conflict of interest, simply envision one scenario that promises investors equal chances of double or nothing on the money they invest. Shareholders will be more willing to take that gamble if they keep all the gains but export 20 percent of the losses to their creditors. Most investment choices are not that stark, but the incentives are still somewhat skewed even when the anticipated payouts are bunched more tightly about the median. Lenders therefore must protect themselves by requiring a substantial cushion of assets to deter shareholder boldness, or by including some specific bond covenants that limit the kinds of ventures that the borrower firm may undertake. When the dust settles, however, these risks are often worth taking because they increase the value of assets under the business control of skilled entrepreneurs. Indeed, if these shareholder-creditor conflicts of interest created insurmountable difficulties, we would observe few, if any, voluntary loan transactions at all, for knowledgeable parties would not repeat familiar mistakes to their own financial detriment. These conflicts of interest are best understood as generating costs: the lower the costs, the greater the velocity of transactions.

This brief discussion of lending (including secured lending) carries over to the public sphere. Recall that Roosevelt was constantly preoccupied with protecting farmers from the vagaries of the market, domestic and international. A rule that fixes the prices farmers receive for produce is, as Hayek noted, an explicit priority of access to public money. Its precise nature is unimportant to the basic analysis, so for exposition consider the rule of "parity," long United States policy, whereby federal statute guaranteed farmers a price for their crops equal in real terms to world market prices during the period from 1910 to 1914.[41] That guarantee obviously reduced farmers' uncertainty and eased their decisions on investment and planting relative to a world beset by sharp fluctuations in agricultural prices.

Parity gave the farmer a first lien on national assets, but it did not require farmers to forfeit any part of their share of the general social gain. It is as though they had been made creditors of the corporation without having been asked to surrender any fraction of their equity. The upshot was the classic lock against the future: heads-I-win and tails-you-lose. Now nonfarmers held leveraged shares that made their own activities riskier than before, not by virtue of their own activities, but by virtue of their having been forced to become involuntary guarantors of market fluctuations. This one-way protection was secured through legislation. This arrangement therefore lacked the key ingredient for ensuring that this risk-shifting enterprise produced social gains. The winners had dictated the result without any obvious consent from, or compensation to, the losers.

[41] Agricultural Adjustment Act of 1938, Pub. L. No. 75-430, 52 Stat. 31 (1938).

In this legal environment, the winners only had to compare their costs of securing passage of the required legislation with their private gains from its passage. They did not register the losses imposed on others—a clear financial externality. As Hayek said, government subsidies *increase* on net the economic insecurity of the general population in the hope of softening it for some special-interest group. The greater the number of state subsidies, the larger the aggregate distortions, for these errors do not cancel out; they only accumulate. This overall result stands in stark contrast with the outcomes from the classical system, which respects, universally, security of possession and exchange. Strong rules of property and contract reduce insecurity across the board. The new accounts of economic security are not an extension of an old system: they are its repudiation.

Thus far, the analysis only makes more explicit what Hayek had said in a few cryptic sentences. But what remains quite astonishing about Hayek's synthesis was his failure to perceive that the same dangers lurked in his own preferred programs to provide "limited" forms of security to all. If forced to choose between a regime that barred entry into certain occupations or markets and fixed wages and prices, and one that guaranteed minimum levels of certain preferred goods and services, our choice would be clear: over the full range of feasible political alternatives, we should prefer the latter alternative, as Hayek recommends. But why be put in the position to choose at all? The moment that society commits itself collectively to the minimum protection of individual citizens' standards of living, we have but another variation on the old problem: certain groups receive first dibs on resources, and this, in turn, necessarily increases the residual risks to others.

Unfortunately, Hayek's own formulation of the problem did not build in an explicit public-choice component. To be sure, in some abstract sense, he was well aware of the problem of setting minimum standards too high. Nevertheless, he failed to see that the field for political manipulation is coextensive with the areas of permissible regulation. Political trends may cycle, so that it becomes difficult for any one interest group to obtain entry restrictions or wage and price controls. Now the way is clear for new coalitions to form around the very set of minimum welfare rights that found favor with Hayek, which is why (for example) the American Association of Retired Persons (many of whose members still work) has become a juggernaut for redistribution based on age, capable of sweeping aside everything before it.

The American Social Security system is one illustration of the process. The decision to protect the real income of Social Security benefit recipients gives them fiscal protection which is denied to younger workers who have yet to make it into the promised land. A downturn in real wages is thus magnified for younger workers. And their risks are magnified. To see why, assume that 20 percent of the population receives Social Security, and that real income levels have declined by 4 percent. To insulate retired workers from the downturn in income requires 80 percent of the population to absorb a 5 percent wage loss. Thereafter, the increased tax burdens (needed to offset the loss of payroll-tax revenues due to lower wages) reduce overall production, so as to make further declines in the standard of living of younger workers more likely. Matters are made worse when the Social Security benefits index overstates the level of inflation, and thus allows nonworkers to have real increases in living standards while the rest of the population sees its living standard go down. The short-term dislocations that result from this system do not even out over time: they accumulate.

Hayek was also moderately sanguine about state provision of medical care. The Medicare system in the U.S. offers a cautionary story. A 1973 technical congressional amendment capped the increase in Medicare premiums to the general rate of inflation.[42] However, medical inflation subsequently advanced at a more rapid clip; the technical adjustments thus gave Medicare recipients a first lien on health-care dollars, which reduced the funds available to other individuals. The (improved) security of one portion of the population thus ushered in an increased risk for the remainder of the population. The logic of displaced risk works as well in the domain of minimum rights as it does in the domain of entry restrictions, and often on a far grander scale.

Nor are the dangers restricted to cash transfers: other forms of regulation also impose displaced risks. Today in the U.S. the Age Discrimination in Employment Act removes all mandatory retirement restrictions for workers over forty.[43] Workers may be dismissed only for cause (that is, only for some reason which is deemed legitimate, not at the mere will of the employer);[44] thus, incumbent jobholders (who tend to be older than new entrants into the job market) receive a substantial insulation from market pressures. The fluctuations in demand in the employment market are now concentrated on younger workers. In academic markets, senior faculty have *de facto* tenure for life; they receive high wages (including additional employer contributions to their pension accounts after the traditional retirement age) and payouts from their pension funds. Young entrants into the profession take up a set of post-doctoral fellowships or compete to fill short-term non-tenure-track positions. The overall graying of universities augers ill for their continued intellectual vitality. Yet considerations of income or wealth distribution offer scant justification for the practice: government gives its greatest guarantees of security to those with the most wealth and political influence.

---

[42] For a general account, see Steven Hayward and Erik Peterson, "The Medicare Monster: A Cautionary Tale," *Reason*, vol. 24, no. 8 (January 1993), pp. 18–25.

[43] Age Discrimination in Employment Act, 29 U.S.C. §623(a), first passed in 1967.

[44] *Ibid.*, § 623(f)(1).

Nor does the social position get any better when dynamic issues are added to the mix. As Hayek stressed, markets constantly supply everyone with wage and price signals regarding those areas that promise the greatest return on labor and capital. Productive assets migrate in the direction of the strongest signals. But once farm prices, for example, are insulated from falling demand, this signal is dulled. As a result, labor and capital exit an overstocked field at too slow a rate; why leave if you are cushioned against price drops? This market imbalance increases the real costs of a counteracting subsidy. In the long run, these dislocations impact other product and labor markets. From any perspective, then, Roosevelt's (and, within limits, Hayek's) version of economic security ignores the offsetting disadvantages. But that is exactly the consequence that we should expect when correlative duties are not built into the ground floor of the analysis, as they were in the traditional accounts of security of the person, of possession, and of exchange.

III. COERCION AND DURESS

The same mistakes that mar the conceptual analysis of security also generate similar confusion with respect to the concept of coercion. Indeed, the two arguments are flip sides of one another. Security is what we want; and its scope expands without discernible limit. Coercion is what we fear; and its definition is also expanded in ways inconsistent with the original conceptions of freedom and security. Given the strength of these parallels, it is possible to retrace the unwarranted transformation in the definition of coercion with greater rapidity.

The stakes in this enterprise are high. The most noteworthy prohibition within the libertarian worldview is directed at coercion—that is, the use or threat of force. The broader the definition of coercion, the larger the role for the use of state power. On every account, the use of force encompasses the use of fists, knives, guns, explosives, and traps. Similarly, the mere threat of force can be used to generate compliance on the part of those who fear its sting. Making a threat allows the threat's target an element of choice, but it is the choice between one's money and one's life, both of which a person enjoys as a matter of right.[45]

Legal protection against the threat of force in ordinary transactions is easy to justify on consequentialist grounds. An ordinary contract requires a person to compare what he owns with what another owns; a voluntary exchange takes place in anticipation that it will leave both sides better off.

---

[45] The point was made by Justice Oliver Wendell Holmes in one of his famous aphorisms (in *Union Pacific Railway Co. v. Public Service Commission of Missouri*, 248 U.S. 67, 70 [1918]):

> It is always in the interest of a party under duress to choose the lesser of two evils. But the fact that a choice was made according to interest does not exclude duress. It is the characteristic of duress properly so called.

In contrast, transfers by force typically produce negative-sum games.[46] The coerced individual will surrender his car to the thief even if it is worth more to him than to his attacker.

The distinction between voluntary and coerced transactions has consequences. To illustrate: In a beneficial transaction, I value your car at $120 and you value your car at $80. An exchange at $100 (or, indeed, at any price between $81 and $119) leaves both of us better off.[47] But suppose that you value your car at $120 and I value it at $80. No voluntary transaction will take place. But if I threaten to break your leg (at a cost of, say, $150 to you), you will surrender your car in order to avoid the greater loss. The use of coercion makes your choice turn on your relative valuation of car and leg. In principle, however, the correct social calculation turns on the relative (subjective) value of the car to the two of us. In any case, where coercion happens to move a resource to a higher-valued use, a voluntary transaction could achieve that same result; but only coercion moves resources to lower-valued uses. The personal abuse involved in coercion correlates with the social loss. In order to prevent the undesired outcome, physical force (without threats) and coercion (through threats) must be proscribed in any legal system worthy of its name.

The theme of imitation arises when various other forms of economic activity are condemned as forms of coercion. Verbally, the allure is great: economic duress is thus likened to physical duress. To be sure, the concept of economic duress makes sense when it covers those cases where one party threatens to breach a contract in order to obtain some collateral advantage from its trading partner.[48] One stock example of the so-called "duress of goods" involves a cleaner who agrees to return his customer's clothes, but only if the customer pays twice the agreed-upon price for the cleaning. The protection of rights is sensibly extended to rights under ongoing contracts, on the same terms that it applies to threats between strangers. But the political power of the coercion image is quickly taken beyond its common-law contours to cover any disappointment in commerce. It is just this larger conception of coercion that becomes the focal point of the attack on the larger system of laissez-faire economics.

---

[46] Note that these same arguments apply to the risks of special-interest legislation set out above (in Section IIB).

[47] In this analysis I ignore the role of transaction costs. Speaking generally, these must be smaller than the potential for gain in order for the transaction to go forward. In the example in the text, the voluntary exchange will not take place if the transaction costs exceed $40. And if they are less than $40, they will still reduce the overall extent of the gain. Either way, we should work to reduce them. For the obligatory discussion, see Ronald H. Coase, "The Problem of Social Cost," *Journal of Law and Economics*, vol. 3 (1960), pp. 1–44.

[48] For my earlier analysis of this issue, see Richard A. Epstein, "Unconscionability: A Critical Reappraisal," *Journal of Law and Economics*, vol. 18 (1975), pp. 293–315, criticizing John Dalzell, "Duress by Economic Pressure I," *North Carolina Law Review*, vol. 20 (1942), pp. 237–77, and John P. Dawson, "Economic Duress—An Essay in Perspective," *Michigan Law Review*, vol. 45 (1947), pp. 253–90.

One influential early effort to extend the concept of coercion beyond its traditional common-law contours is found in Robert L. Hale's famous essay "Coercion and Distribution in a Supposedly Non-Coercive State,"[49] written as a review of Thomas Nixon Carver's *Principles of National Economy*.[50] Carver's book took the sensible position that government

> should exercise sufficient constraint to prevent destruction and deception, to standardize measures, qualities and coins, to enforce contracts, to conduct certain enterprises (like light houses) which cannot well be carried on otherwise, to regulate monopoly prices and to control the feeble-minded and otherwise incompetent in their own interest.[51]

For Hale, however, Carver's effort to minimize the level of state coercion is doomed to failure, because coercion permeates all public and private activities. Let the state decide to protect private property from aggression by others, and, on Hale's account, it has used coercion just as if it had ripped that property down or allowed some nonowner to destroy the property or take it for his own use. In effect, no assignment of rights is able to avoid the use of force or the threat of coercive action. Laissez-faire thus comes apart at the seams not because of its empirical shortcomings, but because of its conceptual incoherence.[52] Its own chosen criterion of evaluation requires the minimization of coercion—an impossible task. To make matters worse, mutual agreements are powerless to reduce legal coercion, because these agreements themselves are tainted by coercion. The worker who does not accept an employer's terms is forced to do without the wages the employer would pay.[53] Coercion is so embedded in all human arrangements that the only question worth asking is what form of coercion we prefer, and why. Hale explains his views as follows:

> If the non-owner works for anyone, it is for the purpose of warding off the threat of at least one owner of money to withhold that money

---

[49] Robert L. Hale, "Coercion and Distribution in a Supposedly Non-Coercive State," *Political Science Quarterly*, vol. 38 (1923), pp. 470-94. Hale himself was a distinguished professor of law at Columbia University whose writing frequently dealt with the scope of coercion in constitutional-law and private-law frameworks. See, e.g., Robert L. Hale, "Unconstitutional Conditions and Constitutional Rights," *Columbia Law Review*, vol. 35 (1935), pp. 321-59. For my critique of this position, see Richard A. Epstein, *Bargaining with the State* (Princeton: Princeton University Press, 1993), pp. 39-49.

[50] Thomas Nixon Carver, *Principles of National Economy* (New York: Ginn and Co., 1921).

[51] Hale, "Coercion and Distribution," p. 471.

[52] This theme also arises in contract literature. See Grant Gilmore, *The Death of Contract* (Columbus: Ohio State University Press, 1974); Lawrence Friedman, *Contract Law in America* (Madison: University of Wisconsin Press, 1965); and Patrick S. Atiyah, *The Rise and Fall of Freedom of Contract* (Oxford: Oxford University Press, 1979). For my response, see Richard A. Epstein, "Contract Large and Contracts Small: Contract Law Through the Lens of Laissez-Faire," University of Chicago Law and Economics Working Paper Series.

[53] Hale, "Coercion and Distribution," pp. 472-73.

from him (with the help of the law). Suppose, now, the worker were to refuse to yield to the coercion of any employer, but were to choose instead to remain under the legal duty to abstain from the use of any of the money which anyone owns. He must eat. While there is no law against eating in the abstract, there is a law which forbids him to eat any of the food which actually exists in the community—and that law is the law of property. It can be lifted as to any specific food at the discretion of its owner, but if the owners unanimously refuse to lift the prohibition, the non-owner will starve unless he can himself produce food. And there is every likelihood that the owners will be unanimous in refusing, if he has no money. There is no law to compel them to part with their food for nothing. Unless, then, the non-owner can produce his own food, the law compels him to starve if he has no wages, and compels him to go without wages unless he obeys the behest of some employer. It is the law that coerces him into wage-work under penalty of starvation—unless he can produce food.[54]

So there we have it. Coercion between private persons is an unavoidable necessity, so the only issue left on the table concerns who gets coerced for what reason. Hale himself acknowledges that the social position is not quite so bleak as it appears: for the worker, of course, can coerce the employer by refusing to accept work unless the wages that are offered gain his consent.[55] But that concession gives away the game. Coercion becomes a fact of life practiced by all those who decide to take their business elsewhere. The condemnation once reserved for robbers and ruffians can now be applied to every decision that market actors make under the constraint of scarcity, which is to say, to any decision at all.

What, then, does Hale gain from this particular maneuver? It is surely not some improved understanding of the operation of labor, product, or service markets. Quite the opposite, Hale uses language that tends to blur the distinction important to folks like Carver and other defenders of laissez-faire, by writing as though the "unanimous consent" of the owners has been reached by collective decision (which surely hints at the monopoly practices that Carver, on Hale's own admission, thought it proper to restrain). In effect, Hale is saying that competitive markets are necessarily coercive arrangements. But is that ostensible coercion equivalent to that which was found on the collective farms of Stalin or Mao?

One way to see the error of Hale's argument is to ask who is coercing whom in any particular negotiation. When a worker does not get a job, he either has received no offer that he finds satisfactory or has been turned down by all the firms to which he has applied. To which firm do we attach our strong sense of disapprobation, and why? When a manufacturer is unable to sell any of its wares, which of the millions of consumers

[54] *Ibid.*, p. 474.
[55] *Ibid.*

is guilty of coercion, and why? Surely a firm is not coercive because it does not hire every applicant for a given position. Nor are consumers coercive when they do not purchase every different brand of breakfast cereal. So long as scarcity is a constraint on human behavior, it is just wrong for Hale, or indeed anyone else, to treat ordinary refusals to deal (that is, refusals to engage in particular transactions) as tantamount to the use of force. Hale's all-encompassing definition of coercion saps the term of both its analytical use and its moral opprobrium.

Nor is there anything inexorable about the outcomes Hale posits. It may be inevitable that people have to make choices as to what to buy and sell, where to work, and whom to hire; but it is not inevitable for people to rob and steal. Only confusion is sowed when the term "coercion" is applied to the two situations indiscriminately. Indeed, to treat market transactions as coercive deprives that term of its necessary and proper sting in cases of aggression and force. The two situations—force and the refusal to deal—only tend to converge when a *single* supplier controls a given good or service, as with public utilities or common carriers. But then we are back into the world of monopoly, over which regulation cannot be ruled out-of-bounds as a matter of course, and for which it has long been the common-law rule that the monopolist must supply his goods or services at reasonable prices.[56]

This reference to monopoly shows how disciplined analysis is only possible when we shun imitative labels, and look at the overall social consequences of any particular set of social arrangements. That kind of overall analysis makes it quite clear that competitive arrangements do best in the long run precisely because everyone can decide when to enter markets and with whom to deal. Since that is the case, we are all better off ignoring the inconveniences and frustrations in individual transactions rather than turning them into legal grievances to be remedied by the coercive power of the state (by which we mean far more than its refusal to deal). The danger here is one of equivocation: the government regulator places the moral power of the narrow definition of coercion in service of a far broader account that elevates to a legal grievance any keenly felt economic loss.

The simplest illustration of the potential risk here is the so-called "competitive harm" that leads, for example, to the creation of protective tariffs against foreign competition. The imitation of libertarian thought is evident in the metaphorical extension of "protection" in speaking of protective tariffs, but the content of that term wholly changes in the context of

---

[56] *Allnut v. Inglis*, 12 East 525, 104 Eng. Rep. 206 (K.B. 1810). The common law's concern with monopoly most obviously extended to cases of state-created monopolies. But it also carried over to the less frequent cases of natural monopolies that were stable, not because they were propped up by state power, but because they were the initial entrant in a field that was characterized by uniform declining marginal costs of production over the relevant range of output. That low marginal cost of production would block the second entrant into the field unless he could capture all of the market.

a tariff policy. Far from the protection of life, liberty, or property, economic protectionism gives one person first dibs on certain resources, while exposing other customers and competitors to far greater risks. The broad definition of "coercion" dovetails perfectly with the broad definition of "security." Only when protection receives its narrower, libertarian interpretation do the intellectual confusion and social dislocation vanish, for that narrower definition permits each person, domestic or foreign, to sell his goods at prices lower than his rivals. All are protected in their right of entry, but none receives the power to exclude rivals.

The conceptual disputes are not confined to these economic issues. Any form of decision could be said to be made under coercion because of the undefined levels of social pressure from family members and friends that lead to it. In discrete contexts, it is often possible to say that people are coerced by these social forces into smoking cigarettes, disregarding the environment, or engaging in various forms of discrimination. In this transfigured environment, regulation is now said to liberate people from coercion. But this argument assumes that we can tie coercion to a particular point of view or form of conduct that some wise portion of the community regards as unfashionable or incorrect. Once again, the broader account of coercion differs from the narrower common-law definition, which posits that the use of force is illegitimate *regardless* of the substantive positions that its user seeks to advance. The newer view of coercion is therefore content-bound, while the older view was content-neutral.

It is, however, a mistake to treat these looser definitions of coercion as though they are tantamount to a threat of force used to induce someone else to conform to a particular end. Social coercion comes from all directions simultaneously. It is equally easy to think of cases where people who want to smoke refuse to do so because of the social pressures directed against them; or where people engage in affirmative-action programs for fear that they will meet social stigma or disapproval if they make decisions on a color-blind basis; or where people decline to speak out against environmental excesses for fear of retaliation from the politically correct. What determines which forms of coercion legal regulation must combat? Clearly it is nothing about the process whereby views are formed and decisions are made. Rather, the selection of examples does all the heavy lifting, so that regulation is simply directed at those forms of conduct that a particular writer, or a majority of the population, dislikes at any given time. The upshot is that because coercion, broadly conceived, lurks everywhere, it is nowhere. Only if we return to the narrower account of coercion as the threat or use of force, and distinguish it sharply from the undifferentiated cross-currents of social opinion, will we be able to break the circle in which all actions, and their opposites, are simultaneously coercive.

What is true of the definition of "coercion" carries over to the definition of "harm" and "duress." These terms are also capable of expansion so that, for example, they work against the original purpose of John Stuart

Mill's "harm principle," which was to find a limited sphere of operation for government.[57] Under the modern view, when we focus on the harm or duress suffered by a single actor, the systematic approach to defining harm is lost. The scope of government action is thus increased as various forms of disappointment are singled out for special protection, without sufficient attention to the correlative duties placed on others. And, like the expanded definitions of "harm" and "duress," these expanded duties presage a huge increase in the number of occasions on which government coercion, old-style, is exercised against persons who are themselves guilty of no old-style coercive action. All the mischief that is caused by rate regulation in competitive industries, or by protective tariffs and anti-dumping laws (which require that goods not be "dumped" into the host country at below their "cost" of production in the country of origin), stems from this mind-set.

The conclusion by now should be clear. Scarcity always places constraints on what human beings can have; scarcity always makes it impossible for all legitimate human wants to be satisfied simultaneously; scarcity makes it necessary to figure out which forms of human action should be prohibited as antisocial and which should not. On this view, people who offer to sell goods and hire workers should not be seen as coercers, but as liberators. They expand the range of opportunities; they do not constrict it. The bottom line is that scarcity is not the same as coercion, just as security is not the same as protectionism.

Libertarian principles usher in huge advances in social organization by picking out those human actions that should be proscribed and those that should be protected. These principles do so by setting their presumption in favor of liberty of action, which is limited only in cases of force or (a matter not fully discussed here) misrepresentation. The modern uses of the concepts of economic security and economic duress undo the good that the libertarian system has been able to achieve. By the constant overuse of hard-edged terms like "security" and "coercion," the modern view weakens the level of social disapproval for acts of force and coercion that do deserve full-throated moral and legal condemnation. The use of state control against force and fraud advances security of the person, security of possession, and security of exchange. The state protection of economic and social rights only undercuts these strong achievements and creates the very kind of insecurity and public coercion that any sound legal order should seek to forestall. Bad imitations exact a high social toll.

Law, The University of Chicago

[57] John Stuart Mill, *On Liberty* (1859; Oxford: Oxford University Press, 1991).

INDEX

Printed in the United States
By Bookmasters